The Rise of Modern Egypt

The Rise of Modern Egypt

A Century and a Half of Egyptian History
1798 – 1957

by

George Annesley

The Pentland Press Limited
Edinburgh • Cambridge • Durham

© George Annesley 1994

First published in 1994 by
The Pentland Press Ltd.
1 Hutton Close
South Church
Bishop Auckland
Durham

ISBN 1 85821 174 3

Typeset by CBS, Felixstowe, Suffolk
Printed and bound by Antony Rowe Ltd., Chippenham

CONTENTS

CHAPTER 1

The French Invasion of Egypt

'Egypt,' said Napoleon at St. Helena, 'is the most important country in the world.' Such an assertion might well appear somewhat bold or unwarranted, considering that at the time it was made, Egypt was little more than a mediaeval backwater of the Mediterranean. Yet it was not entirely without justification. Insignificant though Egypt was in point of wealth, commerce, culture and civilisation two centuries ago, her key position on the bridge of east and west gave her a strategic importance in an expanding and aggressive world which Napoleon was one of the first to detect, an importance which has secured ample recognition in world politics ever since. The strategic position of Egypt, in fact, dominated British policy in the Near East for nearly a century.

At the close of the eighteenth century, the period which marks the beginning of Egypt's emergence from mediaevalism, she lay approximately halfway, as the crow flies, between western Europe and the struggling powers of England and France, and England's empire in India and the lands of the Far East whose trade was the subject of such bitter rivalry among the mercantile countries of Europe. But the eastern end of the Mediterranean was a cul-de-sac, blocked off by the narrow isthmus of Suez; only an occasional caravan plied across the deserts from archaic Alexandria to primitive Suez. The great sea-lanes from Europe to the east lay round the Cape of Good Hope over 12,000 miles of ocean, a long and tedious voyage. Long it was, but safe for England. No country in the world was in a position to challenge her naval supremacy in the oceans or to threaten her Indian and far eastern trade. The lands of the eastern Mediterranean thus had no commercial or political significance for the energetic and enterprising Englishman. It suited him rather that they should sleep on in the lethargy and stagnation which had enveloped them for centuries and remain untouched

1

by the hand of modern civilisation and progress. Egypt is probably the oldest country in the world. Thousands of years ago when the majority of mankind were still savages, the Egyptians built up a wonderful civilisation even now so well remembered by her temples and monuments. But like all others her civilisation softened her people and she decayed. During the course of the centuries Egypt became overrun by a succession of foreign invaders, Greek, Roman, Arab, Mameluke and Turk. From being once the leader of the world she sank into a state of subservience to the alien overlord.

In 1517 Egypt was invaded by the Ottoman Turks of Selim I, subdued and incorporated into the rising Turkish Empire. From that time onwards until close on four centuries later Egypt remained theoretically a province of the great empire in the Near East and vassal to the Sultan and Khalif, 'Shadow of God on Earth'. Yet Turkish sovereignty was rarely more than nominal. A Turkish *pasha* was appointed by the Sublime Porte, the Sultan's government at Constantinople, to govern the province, but the executive power lay in the hands of a body or corps of foreigners, the Mamelukes. Egypt has frequently been called 'the land of paradox'. In no case is this description better illustrated than by the peculiar system of government which prevailed during the time of the Mamelukes. The word 'Mameluke' in Arabic signifies 'slave' but this definition, though accurate in origin, would hardly describe the corps of tyrants who for centuries held Egypt in their grip.

The following extract from Cameron's *Egypt in the Nineteenth Century* gives a useful summary of the origins of these Mamelukes and their place in Egyptian society:

The system of slave-recruiting appears to have begun during the decline of Baghdad, and to have spread through Syria to Egypt; but whatever its origin it first attracts notice under the rule of Saladin, who thoroughly organised his Mameluke corps into an army of occupation . . . Moreover, when once the system had been developed, it had to be continued as a measure of self-preservation, for without constant recruits the foreign Mameluke garrison would have naturally dwindled away, and been extinguished.

Sold by his parents, or stolen from his village in the Caucasus and brought to Cairo by the dealer, who sold him again to a Mameluke chieftain, the young recruit thenceforth lost his country and his home; he had become a member of a military caste which despised the *fellahin*, or peasants, and abhorred the idea of marriage, or of family, as fatal to his profession of a soldier. On the other hand, the highest career was open to his talents. Saladin himself, and his generals, and most of the Sultans and their generals, had been slaves in their youth. The crown was seized by the strongest bey, and though a son and grandson might succeed to the throne, a dynasty rarely continued beyond the third generation without being broken by a fresh usurper. Slavery was merely a name, a form of honourable military service for life; the Mameluke was bound apprentice to a warlike and aristocratic guild, he took the vows as an adopted child of his master's household regiment. War was incessant and troops were ever on the march between the Nile and Euphrates, between Aleppo and Mecca. The Mamelukes may be likened to the ancient warrior caste of India, and the real slaves were the Egyptian peasantry and working classes.[1]

Thus from the middle of the thirteenth century the government of Egypt lay in the hands of this military sect, whose numbers were maintained by yearly influxes of new recruits brought from Circassia, the land between the sea of Azov and the Caucasus mountains. For the reasons outlined above they neither became absorbed into the indigenous population, nor did they establish families and dynasties. They did, however, maintain their power and continued to hold their own, even after Egypt became subject to the Ottoman Sultan.

At the time our story opens in 1798 the situation had resolved itself as follows: the central government of Egypt, based on the *pashalik* of Cairo, was in the hands of the Turkish governor appointed from Constantinople, while each of the twenty-four provinces, or *mudirliks*, was ruled by a Mameluke and his personal regiment or household corps of Mameluke troops. These provincial governors, or *mudirs*, were given the rank of *bey*, and it became part of the established tradition that no Mameluke could be promoted to *bey* unless he had actually been a slave, bought and sold. It is not surprising that under such an unusual system the land which was theoretically governed by the Sultan's appointed officer became in reality increasingly the domain of a number of foreign slaves and ex-slaves who, united together, were powerful enough to enforce their will on the Turkish *pasha*.

Of the heterogeneous agglomeration of nationalities that dwelt in the valley of the Nile there were three principal groups: the Turks consisting of the Pasha, his entourage and officials; the Mameluke *beys* and their compatriot slaves and soldiers, the rulers of the provinces; and the native Egyptian *fellahin*, the peasants who tilled the fields, performed the menial tasks and were considered no more than beasts of toil and burden, down-trodden and oppressed, dirt beneath the feet of their foreign masters.

In Europe covetous eyes were being cast on this bright jewel in the Sultan's imperial crown. Napoleon Bonaparte, France's ambitious young general, was urging upon the Directors the desirability of seizing Egypt and adding her to France's domains. At this time France was endeavouring to make herself master of Europe and the foremost military power in the world. The greatest obstacle to her programme of aggrandisement was her traditional enemy and rival, the compact islands of Britain, master of the seas and impregnable to Bonaparte's land armies. He himself was the exponent of total warfare against England: 'Our government,' he wrote in 1797, 'must destroy the English monarchy, or it must expect itself to be destroyed by these active islanders. Let us concentrate our energies on the navy and annihilate England. That done, Europe is at our feet.'[2]

The prosecution of the proposed assault was entrusted to the brilliant young commander, but when he went himself to examine the coastline and the obstacles to be overcome, he abandoned the idea of a trial of strength with the British fleet and an assault on the forbidding cliffs of Dover. It appeared to him that England was more vulnerable elsewhere, especially in the long lines of communication to her new empire in far-off India. The main routes to India lay round the Cape of Good Hope and across the Indian Ocean, although the shorter land and sea route through the Persian Gulf, Syria and the Mediterranean was also occasionally used for fast despatches and the carrying of small packages. Bonaparte fixed his eyes on the land of Egypt. A French expedition sent to conquer and occupy the ancient land of the Nile would be sitting astride the shortest route of all; French navies operating in the Red Sea and the Arabian Sea, based on Suez, would be able to harass and perhaps cut Britain's sea lines to India. Opportunity might also offer itself for an incursion into Syria and a frontal attack on the declining empire of the Sultan, from which rich rewards could well be expected. There were many reasons which made the venture into the East so tempting.

Bonaparte had no difficulty in persuading the Directors to approve his plan, especially as, in addition to the advantages it promised, it afforded them an excellent opportunity of sending their popular general abroad, where he could not meddle in the politics of the capital. With the blessing of the Directors Bonaparte accordingly fitted out his expedition and sailed from Toulon on 19 May 1798 with a well-equipped army of 38,000 men and four hundred ships and troop-carriers. Included in the contingent were a number of scientists and *savants* who were to make a complete survey of the country and carry out research on the monuments and relics of ancient Egyptian culture.

It is perhaps strange that Bonaparte, who had recognised the dangers of a sea-borne operation across the English Channel, a distance of barely thirty miles, in face of the British Navy, should have willingly committed a large French army to a sea voyage of 1,400 miles through the Mediterranean. It can only be supposed that he believed that England could not spare a naval force of sufficient strength to interfere with his convoy to any considerable extent. He was in fact singularly fortunate in that he suffered no molestation on this lengthy voyage. The transformation of the Mediterranean into an entirely French lake being an integral part of his plan, he paused at Malta to subdue and garrison the island which might prove a useful base or staging point in his extended line of communications.

So far the objectives and the destination of the expedition had been kept a closely-guarded secret, known only to Bonaparte and the Directors, and it was not until the convoy approached the coast of Egypt that the objective was disclosed to the troops. On 1 July the convoy came in sight of land at a point some four miles west of Alexandria. Here Bonaparte received news from the French consul that a British naval force was in the area hunting the convoy. It therefore became a matter of great urgency that a force should be landed and the port occupied with a minimum of delay, so that the transports could be sheltered in the harbour under the protection of the shore batteries. This factor decided Bonaparte to land his army immediately on the open beach and to march on Alexandria and occupy it. By midnight of the same day only 4,300 troops had been put ashore, but Bonaparte deemed this a sufficient number for his immediate purposes. A forced march along the sandy shore through the remaining hours of darkness brought the French under the crumbling walls of the town and, upon the governor curtly rejecting Bonaparte's ultimatum to surrender, the port was stormed with ease shortly after dawn on 2 July.

The unexpected arrival of a French army created consternation among the ruling factions of Egypt; even the unfortunate *fellahin* of the fields and merchants of the towns, long inured to the hazards of war, rapine and extortion, were perplexed. Bonaparte, however, had no immediate intention of disclosing the true aims of his expedition; he clothed his actions in high-sounding fictions and soothing words. His proclamation, printed in Arabic at Alexandria, was as follows:

In the name of God the Merciful and Indulgent. There is no God but God. He has no son and reigns without a partner. On the part of the French Republic, established on the principles of liberty, and on the part of the General-in-Chief,

Bonaparte the Great the Emir of the French armies, we make known to all the inhabitants of Egypt, that for a long time back the Beys who govern this country overwhelm the French nation with contempt and opprobrium, and cause their merchants to experience weary exactions and injustice. But the hour of their chastisement is come.

For a long time back this troop of Mamelukes, drawn from Circassia and Georgia, tyrannises over the fairest spot of the globe; but the Lord of the Worlds, whose power extends everywhere, has ordained the termination of their power. Egyptians! you will be told that I come here with the design to overthrow your religion, but this is a gross falsehood. Do not believe it. Answer the imposters that I have come to restore your rights, which have been invaded by usurpers – that I adore God more than the Mamelukes and that I respect the Prophet Mohammed and the Noble Koran. Tell them that all men are equal before God – that intelligence, virtue and science, are the only distinctions between them. What intelligence – what virtues – what science – distinguish them from other men, and render them worthy of possessing all that constitutes the happiness of life!

Wherever there is a fertile land, it belongs to the Mamelukes; the most costly dresses, the handsomest slaves, the most agreeable houses, belong to them. If Egypt is their farm, let them show the lease that God has given them for it. But God is merciful and just, and henceforth all will be able to arrive at the most elevated functions; henceforth the most intelligent, virtuous and learned will direct public affairs, and in this way the people will be happy.

Cadis, Sheikhs, Imams, Tchorbajis, tell the people we are the friends of the true Mussulmans. Have we not destroyed the Pope, who says that war ought to be made upon the Mussulmans? Have we not discharged the Knights of Malta, because those bigots believed that God required them to raise their swords against the Mussulmans?

Happy those, therefore, who will promptly unite with us, for they shall be exalted. Happy those who remain neutral in their dwellings, without troubling themselves about the two parties that dispute possession of the country. When they come to know us better they will proffer us a cordial union. But woe to those who join the Mamelukes. Every vestige of them shall disappear from the face of the earth.[3]

But no matter how honeyed his words it was impossible to eradicate the suspicion and prejudice of the Mussulman for the invader. The Egyptian might, and did, respect and fear his power, might admire his courage and his administrative achievements, might indeed pay lip-service to the new master, but never did he cease to hate and despise him as an infidel.

Immediately following the occupation of Alexandria, Brueys, the French admiral, sailed his fleet of transports into the port, and the unloading of the rest of the contingent and its stores took place. Not wishing to risk his warships through the unknown entrance, he conducted them to the bay of Abu Qir, a few miles east of Alexandria, where they were deployed in a defensive position across the bay. Time was a most pressing factor to Bonaparte. For one thing, it was necessary to reach and occupy the capital and subdue the Delta before the annual 'cutting of the dyke' took place by which the rising waters of the Nile were released to flood the fields. The normal route from Cairo to Alexandria lay by boat along the western arm of the Nile, over the bar at Rosetta and by sea to the port. The shortage, or rather the complete lack, of shallow-draft barges precluded this method of approach, and Bonaparte was compelled to resort to the only alternative – a march under the pitiless sun across the sandy wastes to Damanhur and Shubra Khit, and thence along the banks of the western Nile to Cairo. Even this route could only bring him to a point in the region of Giza which was separated from the capital by the full width of the great river.

In Cairo deliberations were going on between the two leading Mamelukes, Murad and Ibrahim, the Turkish Pasha, Said Abu Bekir, and the principal religious dignitaries, as to what course should be pursued in face of the new threat. The counsels of Murad Bey prevailed over the cautious Ibrahim, and it was resolved that the infidel French should be met in battle and put to the sword. One half of the Mameluke horse and *fellahin* troops were deployed along the western bank of the Nile between Embaba and Giza under Murad, while Ibrahim garrisoned the capital with the remainder.

On 21 July after a few skirmishes with the enemy the French army, almost exhausted by the heat, the long march and the lack of provisions, came in sight of the Victorious City glittering in its splendour on the far side of the Nile, while before them lay the Mameluke cavalry thirsting for the blood of the infidel. That day within sight of the ancient Pyramids took place a battle the result of which was a foregone conclusion. The archaic charges of the Mameluke cavalry, reminiscent of the days of the Crusades, crumbled and disintegrated before the wall of fire and steel and the blast of cannon in the hands of the hardened, disciplined French soldier. The battle of the Pyramids cost Bonaparte 10 killed and 30 wounded; the Mameluke losses were estimated at 2,000 men, 400 camels and 50 guns. Murad, aghast at the fate of his army, took to flight up the valley of the Nile, while at the same time Ibrahim Bey and Said Abu Bekir Pasha, commanding the garrison in Cairo, fled in the direction of Syria leaving the capital to be entered at will by the French.

It is not clear why the leaders deserted Cairo at such an early opportunity. In spite of their victory the French were still separated from their objective by the full expanse of the river, and were without means of transporting their army across. But with the flight of the commanders all resistance to the French collapsed, and a delegation of *ulema*, the religious leaders, came out to treat with Bonaparte and offer their submission. On 27 July, less than four weeks after his disembarkation at Alexandria, he made a triumphal entry into Cairo and became master of Lower Egypt. The pursuit of Murad Bey and his Mamelukes was prosecuted with unabated vigour by Desaix, one of Bonaparte's divisional generals, but although the chase extended into the wastes of Nubia Murad managed to evade his pursuers.

The French entry into Cairo occasioned considerable trepidation among the Cairenes who undoubtedly expected to receive the same sort of treatment as would have been meted out to an infidel city fallen to the arms of the faithful. But Bonaparte was anxious to conciliate the Egyptians and, more particularly, the Turks, for an understanding had been reached between Bonaparte and the Directors that while the former was occupying Egypt, the latter would be negotiating with the Porte and assuring them that the Republic was not meditating the conquest of Egypt, but merely the punishment of the Mamelukes and the restoration of the Sultan's proper authority. But Talleyrand, who held the portfolio for foreign affairs, had no intention of carrying out his part of the agreement, and nothing was done to allay the fears of Constantinople or to secure Turkish acquiescence. Ignorant of this breach of faith, Bonaparte endeavoured to maintain the fiction by appearing not as the conqueror, but as the liberator of Egypt. He even went so far as to send a messenger after the retreating Pasha of Cairo entreating him to return and resume the reins of government, but that official turned a deaf ear to his pleas and continued his flight.

It was Bonaparte's intention to occupy Egypt as peacefully as possible, for seizure of the country was only the first phase in the great conception, the cutting of the isthmus of Suez and the extension of French arms in the direction of British India. To win the sympathy of the Egyptians he endeavoured to enlist their services in the local government of their own country, but most of the experiments failed. Accustomed to foreign domination for hundreds of years, the native Egyptians either could not or would not participate in the government or assume individual responsibility. The task therefore fell to a great extent upon the shoulders of the Commander-in-Chief and his own appointed French governors. A visit was paid by Bonaparte and a number of engineers to the Isthmus to investigate the possibilities of launching a fleet of ships on the Red Sea and of linking up the two seas with a maritime canal. Bonaparte himself favoured the idea of rebuilding the ancient canal of Necho from Suez to the Nile, but he also commissioned one of his engineers, Lepère, to make a survey of the Isthmus itself to examine the possibility of linking the two seas by a direct canal. Lepère arrived at the erroneous conclusion that there was a difference of 29 feet in the levels of the two seas, a belief which prevailed for many years until a subsequent survey showed that there was substantially no difference at all.

Shortly after his occupation of Cairo Bonaparte ran into difficulties. His treasury ran dry and his paymasters were at their wits' ends to find funds to meet current expenses and even to pay the troops. Torn between his desire both to appear as the benefactor of Egypt by avoiding taxation and to keep his troops happy, the general found himself in a dilemma. But economic necessity asserted itself, and Poussielgue, the financial adviser, was obliged to levy heavy taxes upon the people. The Minister, indeed, proved himself singularly fertile in devising new methods of extracting piastres from the unfortunate merchants and *fellahin* and in later years these methods were closely imitated by the founder of Egypt's dynasty, Mohammed Ali.[4]

Within two weeks of his entry into Cairo Bonaparte received news which shattered all his carefully laid plans. Even before the French convoy had sailed from Toulon rumours of a projected French expedition had reached British ears, and a British naval squadron, the first independent command of Nelson, hurriedly assembled, had slipped into the Mediterranean in search of the convoy. Misfortune had dogged the British admiral persistently, for on two occasions he had narrowly missed the armada on its voyage from Toulon to Alexandria. Strong in the belief that the French were making for Egypt, Nelson had in fact put in to Alexandria a few days before the French arrived and, not finding them there, had hastened to scour the waters of the Levant. It was not until nearly a month later that Nelson received definite news that the convoy had landed at Alexandria. Making full sail for Egypt he discovered the French naval contingent of Admiral Brueys moored across the bay of Abu Qir. On 1 August 1798 Nelson drove his ships in to engage the French. Part of the British squadron swept in between the French line and the shore, while the remainder engaged the enemy to seaward. Caught between the broadsides of the British ships on both sides, the French fleet was almost completely annihilated; only two ships managed to escape. This engagement, the battle of the Nile, set the seal on Nelson's reputation and doomed Bonaparte's expedition to failure.

Back in Cairo, Bonaparte tasted for the first time the bitterness of defeat. In short he discovered himself in an inextricable position, isolated from his bases by hundreds of miles of sea with neither the means of receiving news, supplies and reinforcements nor of making a retreat except across vast stretches of desert whichever way he turned. These doleful events were to have their repercussions within the two ensuing months. The Egyptians were not slow to realise that the French had suffered a serious disaster at Abu Qir, and that they were not so invincible as they had first appeared. To their unceasing prejudice against the Christian infidel were added the mounting irritations of heavy taxation and the regimentations of French bureaucracy. Discontent with existing conditions combined with religious fanaticism to make the population of Cairo restless and seething with revolt.

Insurrection burst out suddenly on 21 October in Cairo. General Depuy, military governor of the city, rushed to the scene of action and was promptly assassinated. Like a flame the revolt spread to all districts of the city, while a committee of the insurgents was formed in the mosque of El Azhar. Up to this time Bonaparte had made a point, as far as possible, of sparing the Egyptians the horrors of war, and once again he offered terms to the rebels. But they, mistaking clemency for weakness, contemptuously rejected them. His patience exhausted, Bonaparte determined to teach the Cairenes a sharp lesson. His artillery was deployed on the Mokattam Hills overlooking the city, and a barrage of shot rained down on El Azhar. Within a few hours the rebellion was over. The gates of El Azhar were opened and the rebels marched out in submission while the mosque was given over to plunder.

Loss of the fleet was a serious embarrassment to Bonaparte, for without some means of reinforcement he could not hope to maintain his grip on Egypt indefinitely. The campaign had not been unduly arduous, but the casualties normal to any army in the field were sapping his strength, and his troops were beginning to pine for their homes. The best that Bonaparte could hope for was that the Directory would equip and despatch him another fleet and restore his mobility. But the affairs of the Republic had deteriorated in his absence and France found herself surrounded by enemies; she could not spare ships to help Bonaparte in his empire-building. In truth there was little sympathy between the General and the Directors, and the latter, no doubt congratulating themselves on having got rid of him, were not anxious to have him back. Talleyrand had failed to honour his promises to reassure Constantinople; he had even treated the Porte with studied indifference by not refilling the post of French Ambassador to the Porte when it fell vacant.

The result was that the Porte, already alarmed at the French descent on Ottoman territory, listened willingly to the overtures of Spencer Smith, the British minister at Constantinople, who urged them to take up arms and drive the French out of Egypt. Russia, anxious to curtail any French expansion towards the east, also joined the councils of the Porte. On 9 September war was declared by the Porte against the French and mobilisation of a military force was begun.

The first threat to Bonaparte came from the *pashaliks* of Syria which were ordered by the Sultan to prepare for an invasion of Egypt, while another army was mustering at Rhodes to be convoyed to Egypt by Sir Sidney Smith, commander of a small naval force left to patrol the Levant after Nelson's departure. Bonaparte was aware of the preparations taking place in Syria and even wrote to the Bosnian governor of St Jean d'Acre, Ahmed El Jezzar, asking his intentions. On receiving no answer Bonaparte judged that it was time to take action. If he waited in Egypt for the arrival of the Sultan's armies, it was certain they would be joined by the Egyptians themselves. The best plan was to take the offensive and carry the war into the enemy's camp. Indeed, the possibility of occupying the Holy Land and marching through Syria, and perhaps on to Constantinople had been in Bonaparte's mind even before he left France. Now that ample justification was provided, he lost no time in putting the plan into operation.

In February 1799 with a force of only 13,000 troops he advanced into Sinai on the coast route to Syria. The frontier town of El Arish had already been occupied by Turkish forces, and offered unexpected opposition; it had to be taken by storm. Gaza, taking note of the fate of El Arish, opened its gates to the French army and provided supplies and provisions. Indeed, although marching distances in this campaign were relatively short, the going was exceedingly hard. The coast route to Palestine lay through barren desert, and every item of provision and fodder had to be carried; even more important was the question of water. Wells, where such existed, were few and far between, and the water they yielded was so salty that it was barely drinkable. Well may the French soldiers have likened themselves to the children of Israel, and equally relieved were they when they finally passed into the fertile plains of Palestine.

On reaching the town of Jaffa Bonaparte, following his usual practice, offered terms to the garrison and his protection in exchange for capitulation. Characteristically the Turks replied by hoisting the head of the French messenger on the ramparts for all to behold. A howl of rage rose from the French army at this atrocity and, surging forward, they breached the fortifications in a flood and gave the town up to massacre. It is said that over four thousand Turks and many of the inhabitants lost their lives in the blood-bath on that day, 7 March 1799; two thousand prisoners were marched out and shot down in cold blood.

After a short interval of rest and provisioning he continued his advance northward, and on 20 March arrived under the walls of the ancient and historic fortress of St Jean d'Acre, the garrison and headquarters of El Jezzar Pasha the governor. Acre had been the scene of many battles dating back to the days of the Crusades and had earned a reputation for invincibility. Sited on a promontory, bordered on two sides by the sea and surrounded by massive walls, it presented a formidable obstacle to any attacker. However, there is no doubt that alone and unaided the fortress would have succumbed to Bonaparte's siege and assault operations in course of time, but once again he found himself contending not only with the Turks, but with the exasperating naval power of England and the energy and astuteness of an English naval officer. Sir Sidney Smith with his two ships *Tigre* and *Theseus* and a few captured vessels had been active in the Levant during Bonaparte's advance. On the latter's arrival under the walls of Acre, Sir Sidney hove to offshore and proceeded to embarrass the French. Enfilading the trenches with his broadsides, he poured death and destruction among the enemy. Phélippeaux, his friend, was landed in the fortress to assist El Jezzar in strengthening the fortifications and organising the defence. Supplies and munitions were smuggled in, while the heavy siege guns, which were being brought from Egypt by sea to enable Bonaparte to breach the walls, were prevented from landing by the constant watchfulness of the English. Encouraged by his allies, El Jezzar grimly held on, and the siege dragged on from week to week.

In the French camp the operations of 'these active islanders' were having disconcerting results. Every assault on the fortifications was thrown back, and on each occasion the cost in men to Bonaparte's dwindling army was heavy. Already the plague and other diseases had taken a heavy toll of his strength and there were no reinforcements to be had. For weeks the siege dragged on, and each succeeding day witnessed a further aggravation of the Frenchman's plight. This was further complicated by news received that Abdallah, Pasha of Damascus, was advancing at the head of a Turkish army, and Bonaparte was obliged to detach a part of his besieging force to meet them. At Mount Tabor on 15 April, a tiny French force inflicted a crushing defeat on a Turkish army of overwhelming numbers, a tribute indeed to the courage and tenacity of the weary French soldier.

But still the fortress of Acre held out. In the middle of May Bonaparte was forced to the conclusion that he must either take the fort at once or retire. One further assault was made but it failed. On 20 May he raised the siege and began to withdraw from Syria back to Palestine. For the second time the French commander experienced the humiliation of defeat at the hands of the British navy, for undoubtedly all honours went to Sir Sidney Smith and his company.

The French retreat was attended with great hardship. Short of horses, the entire army was compelled to traverse the desert on foot. It had lost a third of its effective strength and many of the sick and wounded had to be left at the wayside, abandoned to the terrible vengeance of the Turks. They arrived back in Cairo on 14 June 1799, a weary, weakened and despondent army. Bonaparte endeavoured to give his Syrian campaign the appearance of success, but it was manifest that no useful result had been achieved, except perhaps that the Turkish descent on Egypt had been delayed.

Bonaparte had already decided to quit Egypt. Whether his reasons were altruistic and patriotic, or dictated by personal interest, is debatable. It may be that reports of the deteriorating situation in France prompted him to believe that his services would be more valuable at home than in Egypt. On the other hand, he may have felt that no more personal glory was likely to accrue from a continued stay in Egypt; that Europe offered more scope to his ambition. He intended to slip away and leave his army to his deputies. There was of course no suggestion of abandoning Egypt or terminating the French occupation. He himself had won Egypt for the Republic, but he had no intention of wasting his own time supervising the maintenance of the occupation. That could be done by lesser men.

But new developments prevented him from carrying out his design immediately. The ponderous machinery of the Sublime Porte was at last grinding into action. It is symptomatic of Turkish supineness that Bonaparte had been in occupation of Egypt for more than a year before there appeared any concerted effort on the part of the Porte to act against him. Once again it was left to the Englishman, Sir Sidney Smith, to prod the Turkish armies into activity.

During the past nine months the Turks had been mustering in the island of Rhodes preparatory to a sea-borne invasion of Egypt, but even up to July 1799 there had been no indications of any forward movement. Upon Bonaparte's retreat from Acre, Smith had hurried to Rhodes to urge upon the Turkish commander, Mustapha Pasha, the desirability of an immediate landing in Egypt while the French defences were still disorganised, and accordingly the Turkish forces at last moved. Escorted by the British squadron, the army arrived in the bay of Abu Qir on 11 July and proceeded to land. The French garrison there, numbering only three hundred men, did their utmost to prevent disembarkation, but the attempt was hopeless. News of the landing reached Bonaparte a few days later and, summoning every available soldier, he marched on Abu Qir arriving there on 25 July.

The Turks, entrenched on a narrow peninsula protected in front by earthworks, occupied a strong position, but it had one fatal defect. In the event of a repulse there was no means of retreat except into the sea. Recognising this, Bonaparte attacked frontally. Outnumbered two to one he depended entirely on the superior courage and discipline of his own troops against the unorganised horde of Turkish *bashi-bazouks*. At one time the French faltered in the face of unexpected opposition, but so intent were the Turks on cutting off the heads of the enemy slain (a reward was given for each head brought in), that the French were afforded a slight respite, and a fresh charge decided the issue. The Turks were completely routed and many of them were driven into the sea. Among these, it is related, was a junior officer, one Mohammed Ali from Kavalla. He was however saved from death by drowning when he was pulled out of the sea by a boat of Sir Sidney Smith's squadron. Thus was rescued a man who was later to found a dynasty.

The victory of Abu Qir gave Bonaparte the opportunity he required. No longer need he slip away from Egypt as if running from defeat; he could leave now in an aura of glory, the victor in the field. He could arrive back in France as a conqueror returned home to put the affairs of state in order. Nevertheless he kept his intention secret from the troops; only the few senior officers he wished to take with him were aware of it. On 22 August he went on board the *Muiron* at Alexandria and sailed away, leaving Egypt and the army of occupation under the command of General Kléber.

It may be well to review the situation in Egypt as it existed at the time of Bonaparte's departure. The French still controlled the country and, undisturbed by external interference, could have continued to do so for some considerable time. On the other hand, no reinforcements had arrived to replace the sick and fallen, and the strength of the army was in consequence a diminishing quantity. The Turks and their English allies had for the moment been repulsed, but further attempts to drive out the French could be expected at any time. Unless some considerable reinforcement arrived, the

French would eventually be compelled to retire or capitulate. The former rulers of Egypt, the Mamelukes, had been scattered at the battle of the Pyramids, but their strength and influence in Egypt largely remained. Ibrahim Bey and his faction had disappeared into Syria to join the Turkish forces, while Murad Bey had sought refuge in Upper Egypt. It is hardly necessary to point out that the Egyptian of the Delta still held the French invader in the same hostility as of yore and was willing, at the slightest opportunity, to revolt and wreak his vengeance upon the hated infidel.

Undeterred by the reverses suffered by his army in Syria and again at Abu Qir, the Sultan was preparing a new expedition under the command of Yusuf Pasha, the Grand Vizir. This army, numbering some 40,000 troops, was beginning to advance along the coast road of Sinai towards Egypt. Sir Sidney Smith, who probably sympathised with the unfortunate French, approached General Kléber with a view to securing an evacuation of the French troops from Egypt. Kléber, realising the hopelessness of the situation and echoing in his heart the longing of all his troops to see their homeland again, agreed. On 26 January 1800 the Convention of El Arish was signed between Kléber, Smith and Yusuf Pasha under the terms of which France agreed to evacuate Egypt, the British ships to conduct the troops back to France. Such an agreement was calculated to satisfy honour on all sides.

But the British Government refused to ratify the agreement. Kléber was notified that the French troops were to be treated as prisoners of war and that they must hand over all their arms and stores. On receipt of this ultimatum Kléber immediately dropped all his evacuation plans and proceeded to dig himself in. The position, in fact, reverted to the *status quo ante* the Convention, and the Turks continued their advance into Egypt. To meet them Kléber mobilised all his available forces and took up his position at Heliopolis, a few miles north of Cairo. Once more the magnificent French soldier, outnumbered six to one, inflicted a crushing defeat on the Grand Vizir's armies. The Turks were completely routed. Victorious at Heliopolis, Kléber returned to find that again Cairo had revolted in his rear. Throwing his troops round the city, he starved it into submission. The city capitulated on 18 April 1800 and the French once more resumed the administration of the land they had conquered. But Kléber's rule was of short duration; two months later on 14 June he was assassinated and command devolved upon General Menou.

The course of Egyptian history might well have been different, had Kléber lived. He was a vigorous and courageous soldier, popular with his troops, and a good administrator when the spirit moved him. His successor

Menou was, from all reports, a mediocre general who inspired little confidence with his men. He had already adopted the Mussulman religion and married an Egyptian wife, but even these measures induced little sympathy on the part of the native population, while his troops naturally looked at him askance. Menou was more a politician than a field commander, and his lack of military ability led to the final withdrawal of the French and the loss of Egypt to the Republic. Even his own compatriots, writing of this period, speak of him disparagingly.[5]

It has already been observed that the Convention of El Arish drawn up between Smith, Kléber and the Grand Vizir, had not been ratified by the British Government and that in consequence, instead of peacefully evacuating Egypt, the French had dug in and determined to maintain their grip on the country. In this instance, the British Government had failed to heed the advice of their own commander on the spot, and had been guided more by Kléber's despatches to France, the contents of which were known to the British Government. Kléber shared the feelings of all his troops in longing to return home. These sentiments prompted him to paint a dismal picture of the condition of the French army, and he urged the Directory to recall it as soon as possible. It is not therefore surprising that the British Government concluded that the French were in a desperate plight and were doomed to surrender in the near future. When the arrangements suggested by the El Arish Convention were presented to them, it seemed that Smith was proposing that a seasoned French army which was due to capitulate and lay down its arms, if pressed a little more, should be allowed freely to sail away under British safe conduct to reinforce the strength of the Republic. Not unnaturally the Government declined to concur in such proposals. But the British Government, as events subsequently proved, were wrong and Smith was right. The French army had indeed suffered considerable casualties and loss of fighting power since its arrival in Egypt in 1798; nevertheless, when fully mobilised for war under a determined and courageous commander such as Kléber, it was still a fighting machine of no mean order. The outcome of the battle of Heliopolis amply confirmed this contention and demonstrated that the French army in Egypt was still more than a match for any force the Sultan could muster. In short, one opportunity had been offered of getting the French out of Egypt by peaceful negotiation, but had been rejected in ignorance of the situation. Now that the true position was realised, it was recognised that in order to achieve the desired result, England herself must put forth her military strength.

The operation was planned with some detail. Sir Ralph Abercromby was gazetted to command the force which was to be transported to Egypt by Admiral Keith. The British army was to be joined by a new Turkish force arriving overland from Syria, whilst General Baird with six thousand sepoys from India would disembark from a Red Sea port and march on Cairo. The defect of the plan was obvious and would have been turned to advantage by a Bonaparte or a Kléber; the allied forces were arriving at different times in different places. A resolute commander would have mustered every available soldier and marched against each enemy group and routed it, before it could effect a union with its allies. But Menou refused to recognise the threat until it was too late.

Abercromby, with a force of about 15,000, arrived in the bay of Abu Qir on 1 March 1801, but was delayed from disembarking by adverse weather until 7 March. This delay gave Friant, the French garrison commander at Alexandria, an opportunity of warning Menou in Cairo. Friant with his small force of 1,500 troops advanced on Abu Qir to contest the British disembarkation but, as Mengin the French historian relates, courage had to yield to superior numbers, and Friant's little force was obliged to retreat to Alexandria. Even in his retreat he had the wisdom to plant his artillery across the peninsula of Abu Qir and thus prevent the British from marching straight on Alexandria, and this gave the British a check sufficient to allow Menou to realise the situation, and concentrate a portion of his troops at Alexandria. His mistake was in not concentrating them all, for he left a large force to garrison the capital.

At Kanub (Canopus) the opposing forces met, the French taking the offensive. But Abercromby's men stood firm and the French were beaten off and compelled to retire within the walls of Alexandria. In the assault Abercromby himself received a wound from which he died a few days later, and command of the British forces devolved upon General Hutchinson. Leaving part of his army to invest Alexandria, Hutchinson pushed on up the Nile towards Cairo. *En route* he received news that the Turkish army was advancing on Cairo from the east; 1,200 Mamelukes also arrived to join him.

The French were now split in two, Menou besieged in Alexandria, and the garrison in Cairo under General Belliard in imminent danger from the converging allies. After a preliminary profitless skirmish with the Turks, Belliard asked for an armistice, and on 18 June another convention was drawn up between him and Hutchinson, under the terms of which the French agreed to evacuate Egypt, the transport to be provided by the allies. In Alexandria Menou refused to concur in the agreement and decided to hold out. But his position was hopeless. The dyke separating Lake Madieh from Lake Mareotis had already been breached, and the waters poured in, thus isolating Alexandria from the rest of Egypt. Hutchinson had only to wait until the city was starved into submission and Menou was compelled to capitulate in September 1801. The last of the French army were forthwith packed on board, and carried away from the land they had occupied for three years. The French adventure was over.

It is profitless to speculate on what might have been, had France continued to hold Egypt; we can only consider the actual results. It was a melancholy and ignominious end to such a great enterprise, and although later French writers pride themselves on the belief that France in her brief occupation implanted the seeds of French culture, civilisation and science, such was not the case. Far more than three years would have been necessary to overcome the prejudice and obstruction of the medieval Mussulman code. The infiltration of French thought and French methods which later became prevalent in Egypt were the result of many years of commerce and intercourse with France during the succeeding century. Bonaparte brought nothing of it.

We cannot, however, pass from this episode of Egyptian history without a word of praise for the *Institut de l'Egypte*, the product of Monge and his learned colleagues who accompanied Bonaparte on his venture. This body of scientists and philosophers cared little for the wars of the Republic; they were devoted only to the cause of learning. Their researches and studies of this ancient and historic land resulted in the publication of the monumental *Description de l'Egypte*, the only permanent and valuable result of the French invasion.[6]

CHAPTER 2

The Struggle for Power

The next four years were among the most wretched in Egypt's history. They were torn with faction, intrigue, strife and civil war, and do not make particularly interesting reading. Yet they are important because out of chaos arose a brilliant new star who was destined to dominate the Egyptian scene for nearly half a century, to found a new dynasty and awaken the country from its mediaeval somnolence. These years and their principal events therefore merit a brief mention.

Abortive though the French adventure had been, it produced momentous repercussions in the land of the Nile. It shattered the ancient order and overthrew its rulers who, in spite of incessant efforts during the following years to re-establish themselves, were destined to succumb to the new order. With the advent and departure of Bonaparte an old age died and a new era commenced. A further result was the awakening of interest in Egypt on the part of the European Powers, particularly of England. It was at this juncture that what subsequently became known as the Egyptian Question was born. Prior to the French invasion Egypt had been regarded only as a backwater of the Mediterranean, a mere province of the Sultan's great empire, of no particular interest or significance. But this view now had to be changed. Bonaparte had demonstrated the strategic importance of Egypt astride the isthmus of Suez which might prove to be a vital link in communications between East and West. England at any rate could not afford to be indifferent to the fate of Egypt, or to a predominance of French influence in the country.

A guiding principle of British diplomacy at the time was the maintenance of the Ottoman Empire in its integrity, and it agreed well with that principle that Egypt should remain firmly welded to the Empire, so that no hostile European Power could sit astride the possible short route to the east. The policy of the British, now temporarily in occupation of Egypt with their

Turkish allies, dictated that she should be restored to the *status quo*. But the old order had been toppled over, and there was little possibility of re-establishing it. A political vacuum existed which a number of opposing elements were eager to fill. The Mamelukes, ancient rulers of the provinces, were relying on the British to take their part against the Turks and restore them to their former offices, and then retire. The Sultan on the other hand, who had long yearned to take out this *imperium in imperio*, saw in the disorganised situation an opportunity of so doing. Having at last put a military expedition into Egypt, he had no intention of letting the country slip from his grasp into the hands of the Mameluke *beys*. This time it was to be brought back into the Turkish fold as a province governed solely by Turkish officials. In an attempt to cut at the roots of the Mameluke hierarchy, he decreed that no further Circassian slave boys were to be imported and sold in Egypt.

The future of Egypt depended to a great extent upon the British Commander-in-Chief, General Hutchinson, by whose reports and recommendations his Government would probably be guided. Certainly the dashing air, martial appearance and relatively disciplined ranks of the Mamelukes made a more favourable impression on the British than the rabble of irregulars and mercenaries which comprised the bulk of the Turkish armies, and Hutchinson was lured by the honeyed words of the *beys* into promising to uphold their rights, and so notified the Turkish Admiral. But both the latter and the Grand Vizir at Cairo had received secret instructions from Constantinople to neglect no opportunity of destroying the Mamelukes, and an attempt was shortly made to carry out this policy.

General Hutchinson was ordered to hand over his command and report back to England. In honour of his departure a ceremony was to be held at Alexandria which would be attended by all the leading dignitaries. That morning the Turkish Admiral invited the Mameluke *beys* to dine with him prior to attending the ceremony. After the feast the *beys* were embarked in boats and sailed out into the bay of Abu Qir, where they were suddenly fired on by the warships of the Turkish fleet. Many of the *beys* were massacred and the remainder made captive. At the same time in Cairo Yusuf Pasha, the Grand Vizir, arrested all the *beys* within his reach. Hutchinson was furious with this attack on the Mamelukes whom he had taken under his protection, and by threat of military action secured their release. The Turks in thus acting prematurely had ineffectually exposed their intentions and put the Mamelukes on their guard.

The positions of England and France in respect of Egypt were now reversed, and it was France who was angrily and jealously watching her enemy in the land of the Nile. However, under the Treaty of Amiens, concluded on 25 March 1802, it was agreed that England should withdraw from Egypt by the following July, and control of the country should be restored to the Sultan. A new Governor, Mohammed Pasha Khusrev, was designated by the Porte and arrived in his *pashalik* early in the year. The Turkish army and fleet retired, but a few Turkish troops and a corps of Albanian mercenaries were left as garrison troops at the disposal of the Pasha. The Albanians were commanded by Tahir Pasha and his lieutenant Mohammed Ali who, as has been noted, had been saved from drowning at the battle of Abu Qir and had since been much advanced in rank.

The month of July, the time fixed for the British withdrawal, passed, but General Stuart, now commanding the British force, showed no disposition to move. Indeed, he regarded the presence of the British forces in the Mediterranean ports as a safeguard against a further French invasion, and was lingering in the hope that some arrangement might be made for the retention of these troops. But Sebastiani, the French minister at Constantinople, demanded compliance with the terms of the Treaty, while the Porte too were growing nervous at the unexplained prolongation of the occupation, and perforce the British were compelled to withdraw. On 14 March 1803 Stuart handed over the government of Alexandria to Khurshid Pasha, a deputy of the Governor, and sailed away, taking with him one of the leading Mameluke *beys*, Mohammed el Alfy. The latter's object in visiting England is not entirely clear, but it is reasonable to assume that he was already aware of the British tendency to lean towards the Mamelukes and was hoping to strengthen this attitude by going in person to argue the Mameluke cause with the British Government. Thus one by one the foreign contingents abandoned Egypt, but all the elements of discord and faction remained: the Mamelukes divided in strength but united in their resolve to re-establish themselves; the Turkish Government intent on the extermination of their ancient rivals; and finally an imponderable factor, the Albanian corps. These were splendid ruthless soldiers, typical sons of the wild and lawless hills of their homeland, but dedicated only to gain and ever at the disposal of the highest bidder. As garrison troops they battened on the wretched inhabitants with their savagery and mania for plunder and Khusrev Pasha wisely sent them into the provinces in pursuit of the Mamelukes.

After a short period however Khusrev decided that these Albanians were more of a nuisance to him than an asset, and planned to return them to their Balkan homes. But in recalling them to Cairo for this purpose, he committed a blunder. Tired of campaigning and eager for the pleasures of the city they approached the Defterdar, or Finance Minister, for their arrears of pay. Upon the refusal of the Minister to meet their claims disorder ensued and Khusrev ordered his own troops to fire on the demonstrators whereupon Tahir Pasha forced his way into the Citadel which dominated the city and bombarded the palace of the Viceroy. Khusrev was forced to flee the city, leaving Tahir and his Albanian following in command.

Tahir was now master of Cairo, but he knew that he could not maintain himself in power without an alliance. There were three main factions in Egypt, none of which was powerful enough to prevail over a union of the others. This situation permitted a number of possible combinations, one of which had already occurred, i.e. an alliance of Turk and Albanian. This was now ruptured, and Tahir arranged a further combination by inviting the Mamelukes to return to Cairo and associate themselves with him in the Government. Delighted at this offer the *beys* hurried back to Cairo.

But Tahir was soon to founder on the same rock as his predecessor. The Turkish troops, who had remained in Cairo but had taken no part in the Albanian revolt, now reminded the new master of their own arrears of pay. Tahir, because the treasury was empty, replied that he could not be responsible for this for the period previous to his assumption of control. A heated altercation ensued between the Turkish officers and Tahir, and the latter was struck down; his head, it is reported, was cut off and thrown out of the window. The fate of Tahir Pasha, who had lasted in power only twenty-two days, was symptomatic of the chaos and anarchy which reigned in Egypt following the British withdrawal; events were happening too quickly for the Porte to keep pace with them; power fell to him who could seize and hold it. As deputy to Tahir, Mohammed Ali assumed control in collaboration with the Mameluke chieftain, Osman Bey el Bardissy. But there could be no security for them as long as the legitimate Viceroy, Khusrev Pasha, who had fled to Damietta, remained at large in the country, and their first concern therefore was to neutralise him. In July 1803 a combined force of Albanians and Mamelukes invested Damietta and after a stiff resistance stormed and plundered the town. Khusrev was taken prisoner, and lodged in the Citadel of Cairo.

News of Khusrev's flight from Cairo and the various alarums and excursions had already filtered through to Constantinople. What disturbed the Porte most was the news that the Mamelukes were once more back in power and, even before Khusrev was captured at Damietta, a new Viceroy, one Ali Jezairly, a former Circassian slave who had during the course of a varied career and by dubious means risen to high rank in the service of the Sultan, was appointed to restore order. The methods and intrigues of Jezairly well illustrate the type of official frequently designated by the Porte to rule the provinces of the Empire, and his brief appearance on the Egyptian stage is not therefore without interest. He arrived at Alexandria on 8 July 1803, and immediately sent out messages demanding the submission of the Mameluke *beys*. At the same time he aroused the resentment and indignation of the European community of Alexandria by allowing his troops to insult their consuls, and at one point the latter threatened to leave the country altogether. Khurshid Pasha, the Governor of the town, had to use all his tact and patience to soothe their ruffled feelings and induce them to stay.

When his attempts to intimidate the Mamelukes into submission failed, Jezairly approached them with honeyed words. He procured from the Sultan a *hatti-sherif*, or imperial decree, pardoning the *beys*, granting them permission to remain in Egypt and making them an allowance. But the Mameluke chieftains rightly regarded these promises with suspicion, and while ostensibly expressing gratitude for the promised concessions and inviting the new Pasha to come to Cairo to take over his *pashalik*, they added certain reservations regarding the number of his retinue and the route he should take. It appears that Jezairly set out for Cairo with the intention of exterminating the Mamelukes at the first opportunity, and by secret correspondence attempted to seduce the Albanians from their new allegiance. But his letters fell into the hands of the *beys*, and when he approached Cairo he found the Mameluke corps paraded in full strength, ostensibly to welcome him, but in fact to effect his capture. His own troops refused to fight the Mamelukes and he was taken prisoner. Even then he did not cease to intrigue against his captors by writing letters to the Arab chiefs inciting them to revolt against the Mamelukes. Again his letters were intercepted, and the discovery of his intrigues sealed his doom. He was taken under escort out on the road to Syria and on 31 January 1804 was put to death.

For the moment it seemed as if a period of tranquillity might follow. The Turkish power was broken and the two remaining forces in Egypt, Mameluke and Albanian, were in alliance. But the Mameluke chieftains, Bardissy and Ibrahim, had seized most of the power and were enjoying the fruits of office, while the Albanians were relegated to subordinate positions and were doing most of the fighting. They were dissatisfied with their lot but, guided by the patient and astute Mohammed Ali, they held their hands and waited on events. Nor had they long to wait. A few days after the murder of Jezairly, news arrived in Cairo that el Alfy, the Mameluke chief who had accompanied

General Stuart to England, had arrived back in Egypt. Alfy's fortunes in England had waxed and waned according as the situation in Egypt had developed for or against his party. While the Turks and Albanians had been in power he had been neglected and forgotten, but with the recent accession of the Mamelukes, he had been dug out of relative obscurity, fêted and loaded with presents and sent back to Egypt to resume his former position of influence with friendship and gratitude for England in his heart.

During his absence however he had lost much of his following to his rival Bardissy, who was unwilling now to share his power and who hoped to dispose of Alfy before he could rally his following. The Albanians saw in the new situation possibilities which they were quick to exploit. With the connivance of their leader, Mohammed Ali, they demanded eight months' back pay from Bardissy. He had not got the money, but he recognised that failure to make good the demand would be tantamount to inviting the Albanians to go over and reinforce Alfy's camp. A heavy tax was levied on the townsfolk of Cairo from which not even the Europeans were exempted, in spite of the protests of their consuls at this infringement of the capitulations. For the moment the Albanians were satisfied and good accord continued to reign between the allies, and the Albanians, ever avid for loot, willingly went forth at Bardissy's behest to attack and plunder el Alfy who was making his way towards the capital.

By this time Mohammed Ali had determined to destroy the other parties and take possession of Egypt for himself, but his military strength was insufficient to win him his ambition on the battlefield against the combined forces of the Turks and Mamelukes. The strategy was to keep them at each other's throats until they were both destroyed. Mohammed Ali realised that in the long run whoever ruled Egypt would have to obtain at least the acquiescence of the Sultan, if not his full support, and he himself was not likely to obtain this as long as the already appointed Viceroy remained. The time was not yet ripe for him to make a decisive bid for power; but an excellent opportunity arose of striking a blow in the furtherance of his aims. The petty wars between the Mameluke factions had led to a substantial weakening of Bardissy's power and influence and, as the author of much of their misery, he was hated by the people. Striking suddenly, Mohammed Ali attacked the house of Bardissy who was forced to cut his way out and flee the town. Bardissy had only his own lust for power to thank for his eclipse, for had he welcomed his *confrère*, Alfy, back and formed an alliance with him, his position as ruler of Cairo would have been almost unassailable, and Mohammed Ali unable to effect his coup.

Although this latest development left Mohammed Ali in control of the city, it was still not time to make his bid. Khusrev Pasha, the legitimate Viceroy, was still a prisoner in the Citadel, and Mohammed Ali now released him and proclaimed him Pasha of Egypt. But two days later this unfortunate man was again out of power and on his way to Constantinople. It is reported that a powerful group of Albanian captains, relations of the late Tahir Pasha, fearing the consequences to themselves of Khusrev's restoration, forcibly deposed him. But there is no doubt that this was part of Mohammed Ali's plan to clear the way for his own accession without being forced to open defiance of Constantinople. He had gained some credit with the Porte for expelling the Mamelukes and restoring Khusrev. Ostensibly he had no part in removing him, and his credit was thus little diminished.

The senior Turkish official in Egypt was now Khurshid Pasha, Governor of Alexandria, and the chiefs and notables of Cairo formally invited him to come to Cairo and take over the reins of government. Khurshid arrived on 3 April 1804 and was confirmed in the *pashalik* a month later by an imperial firman.

Khurshid's reign as Pasha of Egypt was short and stormy. He was no match for the cunning and able Mohammed Ali who was now actively intriguing his way to power. Moreover, the problems that beset him on his accession were well-nigh insoluble, for although he could count for the present on the support of Mohammed Ali who ostensibly recognised him as the legitimate Governor, he was still faced with the struggle for power. The immediate problem was the Mamelukes who, having been driven out of Cairo, proceeded to blockade it. The siege lasted for some months and produced a further aggravation in the plight of the wretched townsfolk. Not only did prices of commodities boom, but Khurshid, deprived of the revenues of the provinces, was compelled to levy heavy taxes on the Cairenes to pay the troops, a measure which cancelled all the goodwill which had greeted his first arrival. He early began to look with suspicion on his able lieutenant, Mohammed Ali, who was busy building up on his own account a store of goodwill with the notables and *ulema* of the capital. Khurshid was undoubtedly responsible for the arrival of a firman from Constantinople, addressed to the Albanians and forgiving them all their past sins and disloyalties, provided they now quitted Egypt and returned to their homes. Many had amassed considerable fortunes and were weary of the struggle; these, including some of Mohammed Ali's closest colleagues, availed themselves of the offer and took their *congé*, leaving Mohammed Ali leader of the remainder.

25

In an attempt to acquire a force of his own which would at least counterbalance the power of the Albanian corps, Khurshid sent for and received a contingent of Kurdish irregulars, known as the Dehlis or madmen, but in the end these proved his own undoing. Of the utmost primitiveness, cruelty and savagery, they battened like a terrible scourge upon the inhabitants, and Khurshid was helpless to stop the trail of desolation which attended their progress. As responsible for their presence, Khurshid was held in hatred and contempt by the people whose loyalties now rapidly switched to Mohammed Ali in whom they saw their only hope of release from terror. On 14 May 1805 the sheiks and *ulema*, unable to endure the excesses any longer, went with the Qadi (the head of the judiciary) to Mohammed Ali and, declaring they would no longer tolerate Khurshid as Governor, formally requested him to take over office. After some apparent hesitation Mohammed Ali consented, but Khurshid Pasha not unnaturally refused to be deposed by the people, particularly in favour of his own subordinate. Taking possession of the Citadel, he prepared to hold it until he received instructions from Constantinople. Again Cairo became the scene of a blockade, for Mohammed Ali proceeded to throw his troops around the Citadel and lay siege to it, and desultory skirmishing and sniping enlivened the city from 19 May to 9 July, when an imperial firman arrived confirming the decision of the sheiks in appointing Mohammed Ali as Governor and directing Khurshid to proceed to Alexandria, there to await further instructions. Even then the unlucky prince refused to move, declaring that he had been appointed by a *hatti-sherif* which took precedence over a firman, but a further instruction from the Porte reaffirmed the first and required him to hand over to Mohammed Ali. On 6 August he descended from the Citadel and departed, leaving Mohammed Ali in sole command.

When Mohammed Ali became Pasha and Viceroy of Egypt, it seemed beyond the bounds of possibility that this rough Albanian soldier of fortune could hold his office until the day of his death forty-four years later. Before therefore proceeding with this narrative, a thumb-nail sketch of this remarkable man's background and antecedents may not be out of place. The story of Mohammed Ali's life has often been told, with considerable embellishment at times, and in consequence much fable and legend has grown up around his name. It is, however, possible to sever some of the fact from the fiction.

He was born in 1769 – a year of destiny, it seems, which also saw the birth of Napoleon and Wellington – at Kavalla in Rumelia. His origins are little known, but it appears that his father was one Ibrahim Agha who, according to Sir Charles Murray,[1] 'was a peasant who supported himself partly by such negligent and imperfect cultivation of a small piece of land as was then understood in Turkey . . . and partly by fishing'. It is also said that he was the commander of the guard responsible for the safety of the roads. Howbeit, Ibrahim Agha died while his son was a child, and the young Mohammed Ali was placed in the care of the local governor in whose household he was brought up.

> He was a bright-eyed eager boy, full of humour and good spirits, and soon became a favourite with the cavasses and pipe-bearers who loitered about the ante-chambers and porticos of the rustic potentate. He showed himself especially adroit in settling such disputes as arose over their *nargillys* . . . He learnt to read a little, to write less and to repeat by rote the first chapter of the Koran . . .[2]

He seems to have grown to manhood in an atmosphere of horses, the stirrup and the sword, and legend has it that he brought himself to the Governor's notice by daring and cunning exploits in collecting taxes from recalcitrant subjects. At any rate he earned his master's gratitude and was given the rank of subaltern in the town guard, and later took his captain's post and his widow on the death of that officer. While still retaining his military appointment, he became a trader in tobacco, one of the most important products of the country, but it is not known how successful he was in this business. He thus had no special education, and little military training in the accepted sense of the term, to fit him for the role of general, statesman and administrator. These qualities were born in him and developed by experience and the hard school of war and intrigue. His opportunity came with the French invasion of Egypt in 1798, when the Sultan mobilised his armies to drive the invaders out. Levies were raised in the Ottoman domains, and Kavalla was called upon to furnish its contingent. The Governor of the town sent three hundred men under the command of his son, Ali Agha, with Mohammed Ali as his lieutenant, who soon took over command when his superior retired from the contest and returned home.

He took part in the disastrous battle of Abu Qir in July 1799 when Bonaparte drove the Turkish armies into the sea. Mohammed Ali himself might well have met his fate on this occasion had he not been pulled out of the water by a boat from the English squadron. His numerous activities in the war against the French brought him the recognition of Hussein, the Capitan Pasha, or Turkish Admiral, and he was promoted to high rank. The

Admiral, before leaving Egypt, recommended him to the new Viceroy, Khusrev Pasha, who gave him the position of second-in-command to Tahir Pasha, the commander of the Albanian contingent. Whatever criticism may be levied against the Turkish régime, it had one redeeming feature: there was no snobbery or class distinction, and many were the instances when slaves and the most humbly born and bred reached high rank in the service of the Osmanlis. Mohammed Ali had his opportunity and took it. With his Albanian troops he was a great success.

> His rough manners, his ready jests, his daring courage had succeeded in winning their entire devotion. They looked upon him as the defender of their rights against the generals who embezzled their pay, and the commissaries who sold their rations. He was the chosen spokesman on all occasions – the sole mediator between them and authority. He took care always to display an ostentatious anxiety for their welfare. By these means he had acquired great personal influence. His mind, singularly shrewd and alive to everything that could promote his interests, perceived at a glance the immense advantage that might be derived from the affection of the army in troublous and unsettled times.[3]

It may seem strange that the Porte should have agreed to the appointment of Mohammed Ali as Viceroy of Egypt, considering that he had himself deposed their own appointed officers, Khusrev and Khurshid. This attitude merits a word of comment. It was Turkish policy to have in the seat of power one who could fulfil a number of understood conditions, i.e., to maintain peace and establish orderly government, to keep the province (and himself) loyal and dutiful to His Majesty the Sultan, and to ensure the regular payment of the tribute. It mattered little to the Porte who was the actual Governor of a province of the Empire, as long as he was efficient at his post and obedient to his sovereign. If one man showed himself to be stronger and more able than another, the Porte were prepared to accept him on this valuation. There was, of course, the point that even had the Porte preferred to support their own nominees, they often had not the necessary means to do so; the acceptance of a *fait accompli* was often more expedient.

Although Khurshid Pasha had departed, and the Porte now recognised him as Viceroy, Mohammed Ali was not yet out of difficulty. For the first time, he was standing alone, without allies, while the Mamelukes were all around him anxious to get back into the capital and also to wipe off old scores with the new Pasha. The ever-insistent question of raising money to pay his troops also pressed him, a problem which had baffled his predecessors and encompassed their ruin. But Mohammed Ali had a more fertile mind. He arrested Gohary, the Copt intendant-general, required him to present his accounts for the past five years, and compelled him to disgorge 4,800 purses.[4] Thus in one stroke he obtained the funds he required promptly, probably very justly, and without incurring any ill-will from the population. Having temporarily replenished his coffers, he turned his attention to the next problem, the Mamelukes who were sitting round Cairo awaiting events. These had been substantially reinforced by Khurshid's Turkish troops and also by a number of Albanians who had deserted the Pasha. It is probable that the same petty jealousies and animosities existed in the Albanian corps as in any oriental army. When Mohammed Ali became Pasha of Egypt, he found himself alone in face of the combined force of Mamelukes and Turks, and since, generally speaking, the Albanians knew no loyalty and were only motivated by greed, many of them probably believed that Mohammed Ali would soon be overwhelmed and preferred themselves to be on the winning side.

Characteristically, Mohammed Ali decided that what he could not accomplish by force, he would by strategem. He arranged with a number of his principal officers and the sheiks and notables that they should secretly get in touch with the Mamelukes and offer to open the gates of the city to them and allow them to take possession, all this while Mohammed Ali was absent presiding over the annual ceremony of cutting the dyke. The Mamelukes readily swallowed the bait. On 18 August 1805 they marched into the trap. Arriving in the neighbourhood of Husseinieh, they advanced on the Bab el Futuh (Gate of Victories), where the column split up, some proceeding towards the Mosque of el Azhar, while others approached the Bab Zuweila. While riding through the narrow streets of the city, they were suddenly attacked by a murderous fire from the Pasha's soldiers who were concealed in the houses. Barricades were thrown up behind the *beys* and their retreat cut off. Many of the Mamelukes were massacred on the spot; others sought sanctuary in the Mosque of Barkukyeh. These surrendered and were taken prisoner before Mohammed Ali. Only a few of those who entered the city escaped. The next day the prisoners were butchered one after another in the presence of their comrades. It is said that their heads were skinned and stuffed with straw before the very eyes of their fellows, and were later sent to Constantinople as trophies of victory. Only three of the Mameluke chiefs who entered the trap survived this ghastly fate; they bought their freedom with a huge ransom.

The massacre was promptly followed up by an attack on the remaining *beys* at Giza under Ibrahim Bey. But the latter charged the oncoming Albanians and cut them to pieces and retired, the victors of the field, feeling no doubt that they had to some extent avenged their fallen comrades. Mohammed Ali now felt that he could dispense with the Kurdish Dehlis, the scourge of Egypt who unhindered had continued their trail of pillage and destruction. He sent his lieutenant Hussain Pasha with an army of two thousand against them and forced them to retire to Syria. Although they carried an immense amount of plunder with them, including women and children, at least Egypt and Mohammed Ali were rid of a loathsome plague. The rest of the year was occupied in sending out expeditions against the remaining Mamelukes who were moving about from province to province pillaging and levying contributions from the *fellahin*. To secure a respite Mohammed Ali was disposed to treat with el Alfy who was camped in the area of Damanhur, but the Bey always demanded more than the Pasha was prepared to grant, and no agreement was reached. The Capitan Pasha paid a visit to Alexandria to examine the situation in Egypt and report to Constantinople, but his visit was of short duration. Ever-pressing financial necessities required Mohammed Ali to levy contributions, but these he wisely inflicted on those who had by intrigue and plunder waxed fat during the preceding years. Many were obliged to disgorge their ill-gotten gains; the Jewish and Christian minorities in the country were the especial victims, nor did he hesitate to seize merchandise imported into Egypt and sell it back to its rightful owners.

During these years of faction and civil war Britain had been closely watching the fortunes of her protegé Mohammed Bey el Alfy, who had visited England in 1803 to enlist British support. The final arrival of the Albanian Mohammed Ali to power was an unexpected and disconcerting event, since the British Government were hoping to see in power one who would be willing to further British interests in Egypt to the detriment of France. All the events had been duly reported to the Government by the consular officials at Alexandria and Cairo. These prompted the Foreign Office to instruct the British Ambassador at Constantinople to bring pressure on the Sultan to favour el Alfy and depose the Albanian. In these failing days of the Empire, the Sultan was much dependent upon British support and could not afford to ignore the British suggestion. In fact, however, the whole idea was ill-conceived, for el Alfy did not even have the support of the majority of the Mamelukes in Egypt. Since his return from England, he had not played any conspicuous part on behalf of his compatriots. All honours in

30

that respect had gone to Bardissy and Ibrahim Bey, and it is unlikely that he would have been able to maintain himself even if he had been hoisted into power. Flattered by the attentions of the great Western Power, el Alfy addressed letters to the sheiks and notables of Cairo declaring that the Porte had appointed him Governor, that the Capitan Pasha was on his way to reinstate him, and requiring them to give their submission. These letters were merely passed to Mohammed Ali who, forewarned and forearmed as to the turn which events had taken, laid his plans accordingly.

On 1 July 1806 the Turkish Admiral arrived at Alexandria with a force of about three thousand troops to enforce the Sultan's orders and remove Mohammed Ali from his post. A few days later he sent instructions to Mohammed Ali to quit his post and proceed to Alexandria whence he would be conveyed to Salonica of which he was to be governor. Mohammed Ali glibly replied that he was only too glad to leave this land of anarchy and had already prepared to go, but he was virtually held prisoner by his own troops to whom he owed 20,000 purses in back pay. At the same time he persuaded his army chiefs to swear on the Koran that they would never desert him, and proceeded to make ready for war. The sheiks and *ulema,* who gave him their full support, wrote to the Sultan declaring that it was the Mamelukes who were responsible for all the misery and anarchy in Egypt, that they were without honour, and in consequence they (the sheiks) could not support them. The Capitan Pasha countered Mohammed Ali's evasive reply with a stern warning that he was come to execute the orders of the Porte and reminded him of what could be expected from a refusal to obey instructions. These warnings were ignored by Mohammed Ali.

El Alfy had not been able to secure the Sultan's support without some monetary consideration; he had pledged himself to pay 1,500 purses to the Capitan Pasha. When the latter sent his representatives to el Alfy to collect the money, the Bey explained that the Mamelukes were divided into three main groups, those of Bardissy, Ibrahim and himself. He therefore instructed the envoy, Soliman Agha, to collect two-thirds of the sum stipulated from the other chiefs, and he would pay the other third himself. Bardissy and Ibrahim of course refused to pay, and Soliman Agha was led a pretty dance from one chief to another, carrying their messages and trying to collect the money. In the end, nothing was paid and the Admiral was much incensed, as he had been instructed to collect the money and was unwilling to return to Constantinople without it. This was precisely the sort of situation which Mohammed Ali knew so well how to turn to his advantage. He had already taken the precaution of sending some of his officers to intrigue with the members of the Admiral's entourage, while the French consul who was anxious to see Mohammed Ali retained in power did much to sway the Capitan Pasha in his favour. The opportune moment arrived when a despatch was received from Constantinople authorising the Capitan Pasha to make such dispositions as he thought fit for the settlement of the country. This promptly decided him to come to terms with Mohammed Ali who agreed to pay a sum of 4,000 purses in consideration of his being confirmed as Pasha and Viceroy of Egypt. Thus adroitly he won his battle by bribery and persuasion. This time he took the money from the wives of the Mameluke *beys*, the Copts and some Christians from Damascus, promising that it would be repaid from the taxes. In all these financial operations he was careful to avoid levying his exactions on the native population, the *fellahin* or the Moslems. It was his policy to milk those who could offer no effective protest or resistance.

Shortly afterwards the imperial firman arrived from Constantinople confirming the arrangements of the Capitan Pasha on condition that Mohammed Ali provided all possible assistance for the pilgrims to Mecca, that he paid over the revenues of the ports of Alexandria and Rosetta, and that he made peace with the Mamelukes. The latter had by this time lost all prospect of regaining their former power or driving out the Albanian who daily was consolidating and strengthening his position. They were no match against his powers of persuasion, his machinations and intrigues. United in a solid bloc, they might have fought their way back to power but, divided by their petty jealousies and private ambitions, they accomplished their own ruin. This was accelerated in November 1806 by the disappearance of the most powerful chieftain, Osman Bey el Bardissy who died at the age of forty-eight. Ibrahim Bey, his principal colleague, now much advanced in years and weary of the incessant struggle and endless wanderings of the past few years, wished to desist and live out the remainder of his days in peace. After the departure of his former ally, the Turkish Admiral, el Alfy besieged the town of Damanhur whose inhabitants were reduced to great hardship and misery. He now received an invitation from the Mameluke groups of Ibrahim and Osman Bey Hassan to join them in Upper Egypt, but he was still hoping that the English would honour their promises and send an expedition to establish him in power. But his own followers, who were wearied beyond measure by hardship and starved of provisions, compelled him to raise the siege of Damanhur, now more than four months old. During his retreat to Upper Egypt, el Alfy fell ill and on 30 January 1807 followed his rival, Bardissy, into the grave. It seemed that Mohammed Ali's adversaries were disappearing at close and regular intervals. On hearing the news of his enemy's death, Mohammed Ali set himself to seduce the deceased's followers from the party. Many quietly left, returned to Cairo and enrolled in the service of the Pasha. The remainder stayed with Shahin Bey who succeeded el Alfy as chieftain of the group.

Mohammed Ali decided that the time was ripe to conclude once and for all the struggle between himself and the remains of the Mamelukes. A large force was prepared to seek out the enemy in Upper Egypt and subdue them. He set off from Cairo on 12 February 1807 and marched upstream to Beni Suef. But at that moment, a new situation developed in Europe which was to have repercussions in Egypt. Hostilities broke out between England and Russia on the one hand, and Turkey on the other. This news was immediately sent from Constantinople to Cairo with urgent instructions to the Pasha to be on the alert for possible British landings on the Egyptian coast. Nor were these warnings unwarranted, for on 17 March a British fleet appeared off Alexandria, ordering the Governor to open the gates of the city and allow the British to enter. General Mackenzie Fraser, the British Commander, despatched a brigade under General Wauchope to take possession of the port of Rosetta, and the town was entered on 27 March. News of the landing of the British expedition inspired terror in the hearts of the Turks and Albanians in the Delta, and the Rosetta garrison in their fear had allowed the British an unopposed entry into the town. But the Governor, Ali Bey, saw that the British troops were in disorder, oppressed by heat and weariness, and had taken no defensive precautions. Rallying his own men around him, Ali Bey counter-attacked the invaders and drove them with some loss from the town. Twenty prisoners were taken and ninety killed, and the heads of the latter were struck off and sent in triumph to Cairo where they were mounted on poles along the main streets of the city.

News of the arrival of the British reached Mohammed Ali at Assiut where he had just gained a useful victory over the Mamelukes. He now made them an offer promising to satisfy all their demands, provided they joined him now in driving the British out of Egypt. This offer was accepted and both parties executed an about-turn and set off down the Nile. Arrived at Cairo, Mohammed Ali rallied his forces, put the city in a state of defence and concentrated his forces at Minuf. General Fraser had meanwhile sent the bulk of his army, about four thousand, to avenge Wauchope's defeat at Rosetta and lay siege to the town. Thus it was that on 22 April 1807 the Pasha's forces under the command of Hussan Pasha met the British army at Rosetta under General Stewart. A bloody struggle ensued round the town in which the slaughter was heavy on both sides, but the Turks emerged victorious, and the British were obliged to fight their way back to Alexandria.

This was the most significant of Mohammed Ali's victories to date, for no Turkish army was expected in normal circumstances to prevail over the discipline and superior equipment of a trained British or French army. But this particular British expedition was composed largely of inexperienced and poorly disciplined troops, and the officers, although lacking nothing in personal courage, were poor tacticians. The heads of four hundred British dead were sent to Cairo to join those of their comrades on sticks in the public streets, while the unfortunate prisoners were bundled off in barges and taken to Cairo to adorn the Pasha's triumph, after which they were thrown into dungeons. The officers, however, were well treated and entertained by the European residents of the city.

The Mamelukes, in spite of their promises, had taken no part in the battle of Rosetta. They had intentionally procrastinated in the hope that the English would defeat Mohammed Ali and restore them to power. But the English had been beaten, and the Mamelukes thought them poor troops, 'For how,' they said, 'could Europeans allow themselves to be defeated by Turks?' For the moment the Mameluke chiefs were undecided which policy to pursue: reconciliation and union with Mohammed Ali, or an alliance with General Fraser at Alexandria. As ever, a division of opinion reigned and no decision was taken.

But Mohammed Ali knew his own mind, and resolved to press the campaign against the English. But before he could take the field again, he received an invitation from General Fraser to come to an amicable agreement. The General had received orders to quit Egypt but not to leave any prisoners behind. He therefore offered to evacuate Alexandria in exchange for the release of the prisoners in the hands of the Turks. Mohammed Ali eagerly embraced this offer and returned the prisoners. On 14 September 1807 General Fraser packed his troops on board, handed over Alexandria to Mohammed Ali and sailed away. Again the Pasha had emerged triumphant.

But there were still troubles awaiting him at home. Firstly there was the problem of the Mamelukes to be settled. Then, too, there was the eternal question of paying his troops, and much disaffection arose when he was tardy in this important matter. He was shot at by his own troops on one occasion and on another his palace was attacked. Although he turned his attention to some much needed public building and repair, the state of the country generally was desperate. Taxes were levied heavily and arbitrarily while the pillage and destruction of years had reduced the country to a pitiable condition. The *fellahin* in their wretchedness had left their lands and stolen away into Syria or out into the deserts and settled in the oases. Mohammed Ali tried to prevent these mass desertions or to counteract them by putting townsmen on the land – a futile measure. The revenues were thus much diminished, and the Pasha was continually on the alert for new sources of income. On one occasion he ordered a contribution from the Wakfs, or religious foundations, and when the sheiks protested at this demand, he warned them that he was well aware that they had secured exemption from taxation on their own lands and yet were forcing contributions from their *fellahin*, and threatened to confiscate any property where he found this practice in evidence.

Since the deaths of el Alfy and Bardissy, the open enmity between the rival Mameluke groups had somewhat subsided; in fact, they recognised that there was need for unity, if they were to survive as a power at all. It was Mohammed Ali's policy now to allay their fears and suspicions until such time as he could deal them a knock-out blow. His first overture was to Shahin Bey whom he invited to return to Cairo and make peace. The chieftain, forgetting the warnings of his late leader, accepted and returned and was given the province of Fayum and a number of other villages. The Pasha next sent out feelers to the aged Ibrahim Bey offering him peace on advantageous terms. A spate of negotiation ensued which finally came to nothing, and Ibrahim and his followers remained in Upper Egypt, and for the next three years an uneasy peace reigned in the valley of the Nile.

On numerous occasions during this latter period, Mohammed Ali had received from the Porte first exhortations, then requests, and finally positive instructions to put an expedition in the field against the heretic Wahabis in Arabia. He had delayed obeying these instructions as long as he dared, offering various specious reasons and excuses for non-compliance, but the time had come when he could no longer ignore his sovereign's explicit orders without danger to himself. Any further delay would only mean his replacement as Pasha of Egypt by one more amenable to the Sultan's demands. Yet the moment he dispatched his armies from Egypt he could expect a fresh outburst of hostility from the Mamelukes of Upper Egypt which would have very good prospects of success. He was on the horns of a dilemma, and he decided to resolve the problem by treachery.

He announced that the expedition to Arabia would be commanded by his favourite son, Tussun, who was now promoted to the rank of Pasha. A grand ceremony was to be held in the citadel for the investiture of the youth with his command, to be followed by a ceremonial procession through the city. All the sheiks, notables and Mamelukes were invited to be present in full dress. There are many versions of this historic occasion, all varying slightly in detail but agreeing on the main points. The following is the account of Sir Charles Murray:

> It was on the morning of March 1st 1811 . . . that the Mameluke Beys rode for the last time along the streets of Cairo . . . Chahyn Bey was the first who appeared at the head of his household. The other Beys followed and the Viceroy received them with great pomp and courtesy in his great hall of audience. Coffee and the conversation of the East beguiled the time during the ceremony. When it was over the signal for departure was given, and the Beys took horse to form part of a magnificent procession to the camp. A punctilious etiquette was enforced, and everyone was compelled to take place according to his rank. A corps of the famous Dehlis whose reckless courage was the pride of Egypt [*sic*!] opened the march, commanded by Ouzoun Aly. In the centre rode the Mamelukes led by Solyman Bey el Baouab . . . The main body of the infantry, the cavalry and the civil authorities followed. So the column moved towards the gate of El Azab opening on the square of Roumeleh. The road leading thither is now so changed that were a Mameluke to return to life he would not recognise the spot where he was trapped. But a credible witness who was present on that dreadful day relates that it was a winding narrow pathway cut in the rock and flanked by high houses and fortifications. Sharp turns and angles made it impossible for two horsemen to ride abreast. The ground was broken and rugged.
>
> No sooner had the Dehlis and Janissaries passed the gate of El Azab than Saleh Koch ordered it to be closed and communicated to his men the Viceroy's orders for the massacre of the Mamelukes. The Albanians immediately faced about and their light active figures were seen ascending the rock with the agility of goats. A suspicion of treachery immediately flashed across the minds of the Beys, but escape or resistance were alike impossible. A volley of musketry from above revealed the horror of their position. On this preconcerted signal the troops in the rear, posting themselves in the neighbouring houses and behind walls, opened a murderous fire. Men and horses fell under a shower of balls; no courage could avail against an invisible enemy. In vain the Beys turned to fly, hoping at least to regain the Citadel and sell their lives dearly; they could neither advance nor retire. Wherever they moved they were picked off by the sharp-sighted Albanians. Their horses, maddened by the shouts and firing, became unmanageable, slipping and falling at every plunge. Some of the Beys rolled themselves to the ground and endeavoured to disentangle

themselves from the mass of clothes in which they were enveloped; but the unseen enemy shot them as they lay tumbling about on the ground. Chahyn Bey fell, pierced with balls, before the gates of Saladin's palace. His body was dragged through the streets with a cord round its neck. Solyman Bey El Baouab found his way bleeding and half-naked to the Viceroy's palace. There, gaining the harem, he implored the immemorial right of sanctuary, in words dear to many generations of fugitives and captives – *Fy ard el harem!* – under the protection of the women. But he was dragged away by the Prince's order and beheaded with a ruthless ferocity such as only fear could inspire. Emin Bey who leapt his horse over a gap in the wall was the only one who escaped. [This statement is disputed; other accounts state that Emin Bey was delayed from attending the ceremony in the Citadel.] It is said that hardly had the cortège begun to defile when Mohammed Ali became unquiet. His uneasy movements betrayed his emotion. When he heard the first discharge of musketry his agitation increased to a degree quite uncontrollable. He grew pale and trembled; perhaps he felt that his orders would be executed by faltering hands, and that a bloody struggle might end in his own ruin and murder. Perhaps he repented. The sight of wounded prisoners and trunkless heads soon dispelled all apprehension for his own safety, but could not restore composure to his face nor to his mind. At length the Genoese, Medrici, one of his physicians entered the apartments where he sat, and approaching him said with a gay air . . . 'The affair is over; this is a happy day for your Highness.' The Viceroy replied nothing, but his silence was expressive, and opening his parched lips, he gasped out a call for water.

The narrative is continued with a free translation from Mengin:[5]

In the meantime the people were awaiting the passing of the cortège; all the inhabitants were assembled in the streets to take part in the solemnity of the occasion; the crowds were lining the streets in front of the shops. After a long wait they saw the Dehlis and the Aghas and their escorts appear. The passage of this troop was succeeded by a dismal silence, an omen of sinister events soon to be known. A moment later frightened grooms rushed past without saying a word. Thus sudden flight brought forth a thousand conjectures, when suddenly a dull clamour was heard. 'Shahin Bey has been killed,' cried a voice. Immediately all the shops put up their shutters, and everyone rushed home. Soon the streets were deserted. All that remained were bands of soldiers rushing pell-mell into the houses of the proscribed in search of plunder. These madmen committed all sorts of horrors; they raped the women, tore the very clothes from their backs; one soldier in trying to tear off the bracelets from a woman's arm, struck off her hand.

On that day the ferocity and lusts of the soldiers knew no bounds; every Mameluke house was stripped; the loot taken on that and the following day was enormous, and the atrocities committed indescribable. Mohammed Ali was finally obliged to go down personally and put a stop to the carnage that was converting Cairo into a charnel house, and even executed some of the looters. Orders had already gone out to his men that all Mamelukes remaining in the city, its environs and the provinces were to be sought out and put to the sword. In all more than a thousand Mamelukes lost their lives during these fearful days. Some few managed to escape the Viceroy's net and fled to the Sudan and Ethiopia. At any rate the Mamelukes, as a caste or corps, had ceased to exist in Egypt. Mohammed Ali was now complete and undisputed master of Egypt.

CHAPTER 3

The Holy Places

During the first half of the eighteenth century Islam was disturbed by the appearance of a new reformer, one Mohammed ibn Abdul Wahab. As happens with many religions the original doctrines and tenets of Islam had during the centuries been variously interpreted to suit the expedients of the times until wide divergences existed between religious practice and the original precepts of the Prophet. The new reformer set himself to bring his fellows back to rigid observance of the doctrines recorded in the Koran. But the teacher's puritan creed found no following in his native land, and he was driven forth, and finally found asylum at Derayeh in the fastnesses of the Arabian mountains, the domain of Mohammed ibn Saud. Here the teacher attracted large numbers of adherents, and the Amir reckoned to use him and his teachings as instruments for his personal aggrandisement. From this point the Wahabis, as they came to be called, began to extend their domains under the Amir and his descendants; they collected a large following of militant Arabs and carried their wars from Iraq to the Red Sea. Saud (the grandson) captured the cities of Medina and Mecca and sacked and plundered the holy shrines.

The operations of these heretics were viewed at first with alarm and finally with horror by the Turkish Government. The Sultan as Khalif derived much of his prestige in the world of Islam from his role of protector of the holy places, and it was his duty to keep the routes and the towns open for the pilgrimages which came annually from all parts of the Moslem world. The occupation of the Hejaz by the Wahabis who regarded Mecca and Medina as centres of the tainted idolatry had brought the pilgrimages to an end, and it became a matter of urgency to the Porte that the heretics be annihilated and the holy cities reopened to the pilgrims. On several occasions the Sultan had exhorted the Pashas of Damascus and Baghdad to expel the intruders, but these princes, feeling safe in their *pashaliks*, had turned deaf ears to their sovereign's orders and it thus fell to Mohammed Ali, now firmly entrenched in the *pashalik* of Egypt, to undertake this important task. In many ways this proved a welcome diversion to the Pasha of Egypt. Now that he had eliminated all his rivals for power in Egypt, he was anxious to divest himself of the motley and undisciplined rabble of Turks, Albanians and other mercenaries who comprised the bulk of his following, on whom he felt he could place little reliance in crucial times. They had served their purpose in the past, but with their plunder mania and lack of restraint they could be reckoned to prove more a liability than an asset in the plans which were already forming in his mind of raising himself and his country to a position of power in the Levant. He could moreover expect to derive substantial prestige in the Moslem world as liberator and defender of the Holy Places and even earn the goodwill of the Sultan. The Mamelukes had now been finally broken and the way was open for further adventures.

After the massacres of 1 March Mohammed Ali threw all his energies into the preparation of the Arabian expedition. Every detail of supply and organisation was personally supervised by himself. Unlike most officials of the Turkish Empire, he was not content to issue orders and accept the reports of his subordinates that they had been carried out; he went to see for himself that nothing was neglected or overlooked. Although his rivals for power were gone, there remained much in the way of consolidation and administration to be done in Egypt, and Mohammed Ali therefore deemed it inadvisable to leave the country and lead the expedition himself. He therefore entrusted the command to his sixteen-year-old second son Tussun, who was apparently his favourite. It is probable that he intended Tussun to succeed him and was therefore anxious that he should have some experience of the art of war and the exercise of command. Tussun was invested ceremonially with his command a month after the massacre of the Mamelukes and departed with his troops on 6 October 1811. His army numbered some six thousand foot and two thousand cavalry, the former being shipped from Suez to Yenbo, the nearest port to Medina, the latter proceeding overland. Mohammed Ali took care to ensure that the expeditionary force included a number of the most turbulent Albanians who might otherwise have proved a source of trouble to him. The launching of the expedition had involved him in a considerable outlay of expenditure which he recouped by selling corn to the British Navy in the Mediterranean, by exacting heavy contributions from the merchants, and by forcing a tribute from the nomadic Bedouin tribe of Awlad Ali.

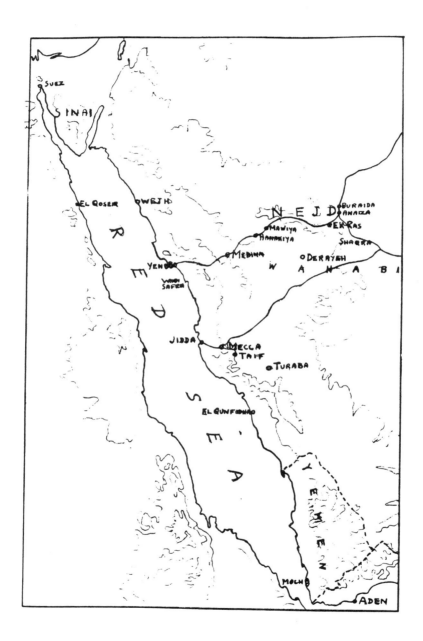

In its early days the campaign proceeded smoothly. The Sharif Ghaleb, who was ostensibly a supporter of the Wahabis, opened the port of Yenbo to the invading Turks, and the cavalry safely effected a union with the infantry. But shortly afterwards disaster overtook Tussun Pasha when his forces fell into an ambush at Wadi Safra and lost half their effectives. Disgusted with the lack of plunder and the hardships of campaigning in the torrid and barren Arabian peninsula, many deserted and slipped back to Egypt, and a further batch of reinforcements had to be sent by Mohammed Ali to his son. With these Tussun Pasha advanced on Medina and after a siege lasting two months took it by storm. This action was followed closely by the capture of Mecca and Jidda, and the holy cities were once more restored to the Turkish fold.

The good news was received with great rejoicings in Cairo and messages were sent to inform the Sultan. But this was by no means the end of the campaign; indeed, the fanatical Wahabis had not yet even been brought to any serious engagement, and there was need for a more vigorous prosecution of the war, so Mohammed Ali decided to go and supervise operations himself. He arrived at Jidda, the port of Mecca, on 28 August 1813, and after a short stay made the pilgrimage to Mecca in October and took up his residence there as guest of the Sharif Ghaleb who had opened the Port of Yenbo to Tussun. Mohammed Ali formed the opinion – undoubtedly a right one – that Ghaleb was only trying to further his own interests and was not to be trusted. In consequence, the Sharif one day found himself placed under arrest and bundled off to Egypt. His fortune which was considerable fell into the hands of Mohammed Ali.

Although he had come to supervise operations, Mohammed Ali did not divest his son of command of the armies, but confined himself rather to questions of supply and reinforcement and to local politics. But Tussun was not particularly successful as a general. In an expedition to the village of Turaba, he found himself unable to execute the capture of the place owing to lack of supplies and was obliged to turn back. The Wahabis who were watching these operations swooped on the retreating Turks and captured much of their equipment. A second misfortune ensued shortly afterwards when Mohammed Ali sent the Governor of Jidda, Zaim Oglu, to take possession of the Yemen. The force successfully occupied the port of el Qunfidha, but foolishly neglected to seize the wells outside the town which supplied it with water. The Wahabis promptly took advantage of this omission by occupying the wells themselves, and the Turks were deprived of this vital commodity. Zaim Oglu gave orders for the re-embarkation of the force which somehow deteriorated into a rout. Again the Wahabis attacked and possessed themselves of large quantities of material.

Mohammed Ali was disturbed but not unduly disheartened by this lack of success. Master of the art of persuasion, he seduced the local Bedouin tribes to his standard, a process much facilitated by the news that the able and courageous Wahabi leader, the Amir Ibn Saud, had died leaving his eldest son Abdullah in command.

More reinforcements arrived from Egypt and various expeditions were sent out against the enemy, while Mohammed Ali remained at Jidda to supervise the supply arrangements and conduct his correspondence with the various sheiks and notables of the district. The expeditions met with indifferent success. An insuperable difficulty was the problem of maintaining supplies for more than a few days at a time, and it was impossible to follow up any local successes that might be achieved. Mohammed Ali, however, himself won a success which is worthy of record. He left Jidda in June 1814 and betook himself to Mecca. During the following months a new Wahabi army assembled in the neighbourhood of Turaba of between twenty and thirty thousand men under Faisal, another son of the late Ibn Saud. Hassan Pasha, the Pasha's old comrade in arms and principal lieutenant, brought up a force of four thousand Albanians, and together they advanced on the enemy. On 15 January 1815 a signal victory was achieved over the Wahabis, who were compelled to retire leaving much of their equipment behind – some compensation no doubt for what had previously been lost. This success was followed up by a march on el Qunfidha which was successfully occupied.

In the meantime Tussun Pasha had set out on the north-easterly road into Nejd and, passing through the mountains, reached the fortified town of er-Ras. Here he awaited reinforcements from his father, but at this juncture Mohammed Ali was obliged to hurry back to Egypt to subdue an incipient revolt. Tussun Pasha was in a precarious position, for the supply problem was pressing heavily on him, yet strangely the timid Abdullah, instead of pressing his advantage, decided to ask for a truce. Although Tussun preferred to press on with the campaign his troops, exhausted by the heat and hardship, refused to go on and demanded that the truce offer be accepted. In face of this and other considerations Tussun decided to come to terms and, as representative of the Sultan, duly received the submission of Abdullah ibn Saud who promised to pray for the Khalif in the mosques and pledged himself no more to rebel against the Sultan's authority. Superficially it looked as if the Arabian war was over, but it was clear that the armistice would be broken by the Wahabis as soon as the time became propitious.

Abdullah had no intention of presenting himself at Constantinople to explain his conduct, which was one of the conditions of the truce. Such an action would inevitably be the prelude to a painful and lingering death in the torture chambers of the Sultan's capital. Nor did he intend to yield to Mohammed Ali all the territory which he and his forefathers had acquired without a fight.

Tussun Pasha had now been campaigning in Arabia for nearly four years and he decided to return home. Although a truce reigned and Abdullah had given his submission, the campaign had not been entirely successful, for the Wahabis still remained in power in Arabia, and it was almost certain that they would resist the authority of the Sultan. For this lack of success Tussun Pasha cannot be blamed; he was still only a youth with little experience of men and affairs, and the difficulties of the campaign were great. At any rate the campaign was temporarily suspended and in November 1815 Tussun returned to Egypt.

No sooner had the Turks quitted Arabia when it became evident that Abdullah was putting his towns into a state of defence, collecting new forces and sowing disaffection among the Arab tribes which had allied themselves with the Turks. In letters to Mohammed Ali, Abdullah attempted to disguise his plans with the usual honeyed words which come so readily to oriental lips, but the Pasha of Egypt was undeceived and replied that he was sending another expedition under his eldest son Ibrahim Pasha to take him, Abdullah, dead or alive to Constantinople and to leave no stone of Derayeh, Abdullah's mountain fortress, on top of another. Once more the forces were mustering for battle.

Ibrahim Pasha, the eldest son of Mohammed Ali, was destined to play a momentous part in the fortunes of his country. It has often been suggested that he was not the son of Mohammed Ali, but of his wife's former husband. There is, however, no evidence that supports this allegation especially as he possessed so many characteristics of Mohammed Ali.

He had been born at Kavalla in 1789 and was now twenty-six. Of low stature, but powerfully built, he enjoyed abundant energy and could resist alike the fatigues of pleasure and of war. He had clear blue eyes, a high forehead, a fair beard. He was very active in both mind and body. Uneducated, like his father, he possessed, like his father, a rare combination of courage and prudence. He lacked his father's charm of manner and his insight into men and situations. He was austere and would overawe where his father charmed. He would never have raised himself so high out of obscurity as Mohammed Ali had done, but in any event he would have been a soldier of mark, and he became his father's right hand, regarding him with filial awe and obedience, and carrying out his orders with scrupulous fidelity. He possessed too his father's love of looking into matters for himself, instead of implicitly trusting the reports which were made to him.[1]

It is not clear why Ibrahim was selected to command the Pasha's armies in this new campaign in preference to Tussun. Dodwell[2] suggests that Ibrahim was appointed because Tussun had died, but this cannot have been the case since Ibrahim had already been appointed to his command and had actually departed from Egypt before Tussun's death. Perhaps Mohammed Ali considered that Tussun was not a suitable commander for such an arduous task or that he had already done his tour of duty. At any rate he could not have made a wiser choice than Ibrahim.

In his thorough and orderly fashion Mohammed Ali spent several months on the preparation for this new operation, and it was not until 3 September 1816 that Ibrahim received his final instructions from his father. He left Egypt three weeks later from the Red Sea port of el Qoseir and made for Yenbo. Every aspect of Ibrahim's operations was marked with forethought and meticulous attention to detail. He appreciated that much greater advantages could be gained from treating the inhabitants courteously than from browbeating and pillaging them. Every ounce of food, forage and other supplies was therefore paid for promptly in cash, and no mercy was shown to any of his troops found guilty of stealing or plundering. This was a new kind of warfare, quite unknown to the Turks who bitterly resented the loss of their right to plunder. On one occasion Ibrahim was nearly killed by a shot fired by one of his own men. He was a stern disciplinarian and forced his men to undergo severe hardships, but he won their respect by cheerfully sharing these himself.

Ibrahim's first act was to go to Medina, offer prayers at the Prophet's tomb and make his vows. These included promises to refrain from wine and to emancipate all his slaves who served during the campaign. During the following weeks he moved his camp to Hanakiya on the north-easterly road that Tussun had taken. His advance had the appearance of leisureliness but in fact his time was well spent in reducing turbulent Arabs and seducing them from their allegiance to the Wahabis; he was determined to leave no enemies in his rear. His most effective weapon in these negotiations was the money with which he was well supplied and which he used to pay for services rendered. To the avaricious Arabs this was an irresistible lure. But he was beset with other problems. The climate was the most difficult for an army to endure; in daytime the heat was almost intolerable, while at night an intense cold settled on the desert. These variations of temperature together with the bad weather wrought havoc among the troops who were racked with fevers and dysentery.

In February 1817 Ibrahim attempted to advance from Hanakiya to er-Ras, the mountain fortress which Abdullah had strongly garrisoned. But the rains compelled him to abandon the advance and to retire to his base where he was obliged to pass the summer months. In April he sent a small force under Ouzoun Aly to take possession of el Mawiya on the mountain road to er-Ras. Abdullah, who was hovering in the area, attacked but was beaten off with heavy losses of camels, food and equipment and obliged to retire into the mountains. This was the first substantial encounter between the Turks and the Wahabis, and his lieutenant's success prompted Ibrahim to move his main body up to the newly occupied village of el Mawiya. The advance had commenced. In July he pressed on through the mountains to er-Ras which had been strongly fortified and garrisoned by Abdullah, and here he was reinforced by a party of Arabs led by Faisal el Darwish who, hating Abdullah, had come to the assistance of Ibrahim in the hope and expectation that he would be given Derayeh when Abdullah was finally defeated. He and his men were warmly welcomed by Ibrahim who promised to grant his wishes at the end of the campaign.

The fortress of er-Ras turned out to be the most stubborn obstacle of the whole campaign. Time and time again Ibrahim threw his troops at its walls and fortifications but in vain; every attack was driven off with heavy loss of men and material. The climate and elements came to the aid of the defenders; the Turkish wounded died like flies, while the remainder suffered heavily from storms and shortage of provisions. But Ibrahim refused to retreat or raise the siege; he was prepared to sit round the town until his last round and his last provisions were exhausted. Even after three months of investment the fort was not taken by assault; it capitulated only on definite terms, viz., that Ibrahim should not garrison the town or demand supplies, and that the inhabitants should be free to depart. In the siege Ibrahim lost 3,400 troops.

The way to Derayeh now lay open, while Abdullah hastened to this last stronghold deep in the mountains to put it in a state of defence. After taking possession of Anaiza, Buraida and Shaqra, Ibrahim pressed on to Derayeh which he reached during the first week of April 1818 with about five thousand fighting troops and the usual camp followers. His siege of the stronghold was methodical and systematic, but after two months a disaster befell him. Accidentally his powder magazine caught fire and disintegrated in a series of gigantic explosions. Many of the troops were killed and wounded and the loss of equipment was considerable, but even more disastrous was the loss of the powder without which Ibrahim was in a dangerous position. The Wahabis, taking advantage of the situation, made a sortie and were only driven off with difficulty. But Ibrahim held on until new supplies and reinforcements reached him a month later. He then heard that his father was sending Khalil Pasha with a further three thousand men to assist in the assault. Feeling his honour touched by the suggestion that he could not complete the campaign alone, Ibrahim pressed his attacks with increasing vigour and frequency. In the first week of September he stormed part of the town and on the 9th Abdullah capitulated and presented himself at the Pasha's tent. Derayeh, the last fortress of the Wahabis, had fallen.

For the uncultured son of an uncultured father Ibrahim exhibited unexpected qualities of courtesy and respect towards a defeated enemy. The terms of the capitulation were discussed between them almost in a spirit of sympathy. Ibrahim explained that he was only acting on instructions and could not therefore give any guarantees regarding the fate of Abdullah, his followers or the town, but he believed that Abdullah, who would be required to present himself at Cairo and Constantinople, would be spared his life. The unhappy Amir, fearful for his family and friends, agreed to go. Escorted by four thousand Turks, he departed for Egypt.

Abdullah ibn Saud had only one great virtue – courage; but this did not save him from his fate. His severity and miserliness estranged from him those on whom he might have counted for support, while his lack of imagination and his ignorance of strategy encompassed his defeat. Had the Wahabis possessed an able leader, they might have defeated any number of armies that Mohammed Ali could send against them. The wildness of the terrain, the desert and mountains, the intense heat and cold, lack of water, forage and food would have favoured the defender and defeated the invader every time, if the defenders had retained their mobility and used it effectively. Lightly armed, fast moving bodies scattered in the enemy's rear could have easily cut the line of communication and compelled the Turks to retreat or starve in the desert. But Abdullah placed all his faith in the walls and defences of the towns, and this was his undoing. One after another the fortresses fell to Ibrahim until nothing was left.

Abdullah had voluntarily placed himself in Ibrahim's hands, trusting in his assurance that his life would be spared. It is true that Ibrahim had given no guarantees, but he had led the hapless prince to believe that he would be treated generously by the Sultan. Abdullah arrived in Cairo carrying Ibrahim's despatches in November 1818 and was graciously received by Mohammed Ali who entertained him and even asked his opinion of Ibrahim. 'He has done his duty,' said Abdullah, 'and we have done ours. It is the will of God.' At the same time Abdullah offered the Pasha the relics and treasures which his father had pillaged from the holy shrines, but Mohammed Ali sealed the box containing them and instructed Abdullah to take them with him to Constantinople. A few days later Abdullah set sail for the Sultan's capital where, in spite of a plea for mercy by Mohammed Ali, he and his retinue were put to death. Ibrahim and Mohammed Ali had kept their pledges, but the Sultan, not having given any undertaking in this respect, did not feel himself bound to the promises of his subordinates. With the death of Abdullah the Wahabi revolt came to an end.

In Arabia Ibrahim sent out small forces to subdue the remaining rebels in the district and the country was eventually partially pacified. The war had brought in its train the usual famine and destruction, and Ibrahim had difficulty in finding food for his troops, a situation which nearly occasioned a mutiny and threatened Ibrahim's life. Orders were received from Cairo to destroy all the fortifications of Derayeh, to send Abdullah's brothers to Egypt, and to return to Mecca and Medina. But in the meantime news of Abdullah's fate had reached the town, and the Arabs were in such a ferment of terror that they might meet the same fate that Ibrahim was at times compelled to fight his way back to his bases. Derayeh he left in ruins and almost depopulated, the inhabitants having gone forth to seek new homes and new lives. After arriving at Medina, Ibrahim paid another visit to the Prophet's tomb and then took ship for Egypt. He arrived in Cairo on 9 December 1819, having been absent for over three years.

The war against the Wahabis had lasted in all over eight years, had necessitated two separate expeditions and had cost thousands of lives and much treasure. What then had resulted from all this outlay? It cannot be said that in 1819 Mohammed Ali exercised much more control over the deserts of western Arabia than in 1811 when his troops first set their feet on Arabian soil. It was not a country which could be ruled effectively from outside its borders. To garrison the villages and towns over this vast region would have entailed far more expense and trouble than the benefits of occupation would have warranted. But Mohammed Ali had achieved the principal objects of the campaign: to overthrow the power of the Wahabis, to bring their leaders in chains to Constantinople to answer for their sins, and to reopen the routes to the Holy Cities so that the pilgrimages could be resumed. Furthermore, he had considerably enhanced his reputation in the Moslem world, and many turbulent spirits in the army who might have been a source of embarrassment to him had left their bones to whiten in the sands of the Arabian desert. All things considered Mohammed Ali had good reason to be content with the results of the Arabian war.

CHAPTER 4

Mohammed Ali, Pasha of Egypt

Mohammed Ali was one of the most remarkable men of his age. He was of humble, even obscure, origin; he had been born and brought up in the stagnant and circumscribed atmosphere of an unfrequented by-way of the declining Turkish Empire; he had had no formal education and was even illiterate. Such knowledge as he possessed of the world, men and affairs, he had gained in the hard school of experience. But he was endowed with that rare combination of qualities in his character which would have pushed him to the front at any time or in any part of the world, a lively imagination, an innate shrewdness of judgment, an amazing grasp of psychology and an instinctive perception of the hidden motives which direct human action; a magnetic personality which enabled him to bend others to his will and that rare, indefinable quality of leadership which made men look up to him and follow him. To these characteristics were added a restless energy, boundless ambition and political dexterity. In spite of his narrow upbringing and background, he was totally uninhibited and believed nothing to be beyond his powers.

By his own efforts he had hoisted himself to the exalted position of Pasha and Viceroy of Egypt, but this was the beginning, not the end of his ambition. It is not clear precisely when his thoughts began to turn to further aggrandisement but it was probably early in his career. In common with other provincial governors of the Empire he had little or no loyalty to Constantinople, and it was not long before he began to think of ways and means of breaking away, of establishing his and Egypt's independence and even of building a new eastern empire for himself. A combination of fortune and his own abilities had brought him his first reward, the *pashalik* of Egypt; almost immediately he had won another prize, the Holy Places. From this point his restlessness and insatiable ambition drove him ever onward for greater prizes.

But first he must prepare the way and provide himself with the weapons he needed. His province Egypt was a poor, dejected and wretched place, broken down and neglected for centuries. But Mohammed Ali recognised its immense possibilities. Its land, though limited in extent, was the most fertile in the world, its people patient and docile but hardy and industrious. All the elements of wealth and power lay to his hand if he could seize and organise them. The first necessity was a single, strong and stable government; this had already been achieved by the annihilation of the Mameluke chieftains and by the sweeping away of all rivals for power. The next step was to be the acquisition of wealth and military strength, without which there could be no hope of fulfilling his ambitions. This involved the development of the country to its maximum productive capacity and the reorganisation of the fiscal system. In the Egypt of Mohammed Ali the system of financial and commercial credit was hardly known, the lending of money on interest being contrary to the precepts of Islam., Everything therefore had to be paid for cash down, so the raising of ready money for his schemes was the Pasha's first consideration, and he gave the closest attention to this important problem.

Over the course of the years a system of farming out the taxes had come into use which had the ultimate result of enabling the tax gatherers to collect much more than was their due, to the detriment of the Treasury. This was a situation which Mohammed Ali refused to tolerate. The basis of all revenue in Egypt had been for centuries the land tax or *myry* which was in theory destined as tribute to the Porte, while other revenues were at the disposal of the Viceroy. Under the Mamelukes there had rarely been any regular or fixed taxation schedule; demands were made and collection enforced whenever the need arose. In consequence of this vicious and haphazard practice the *fellahin* never knew what sum they would be required to pay during the year, but they could be sure that before the year was out they would be compelled to disburse their last piastre. Taxes were normally assessed and levied by villages according to their theoretical capacity to pay, and this was calculated from the number of cultivable *feddans* in the possession of the village. The revenues of the village were generally divided into twenty-four *qyratts* which could be purchased from the Government by individuals who thereafter received the revenues of the their purchases. It is not therefore surprising that in many of these manipulations the proprietors or *multezim* became possessors of more revenues than they had paid for. A survey was carried out by order of Mohammed Ali which showed that in many cases the *multezim* were receiving revenue from twice as much land as their title deeds showed them to be entitled to or for which they had paid the *myry*. Again the interests of the *multezim* were heritable and passed from father to son. Mohammed Ali struck a single blow at this system. He had already possessed himself of the lands and revenues of the Mamelukes; he now followed this up by expropriating all the *multezim* of their holdings and taking the revenues to himself. The dispossessed proprietors were compensated by an annuity paid by the Government according to the number of *feddans* shown in their title deeds. In many cases it had happened that the *multezim* had lost these documents but their rights were well known and had long been recognised. These were dispossessed without compensation – a harsh but necessary measure, since recognition of rights unsupported by proof would have involved the Government in endless, and for the most part false, claims for compensation. A further clause in the decree stipulated that the annuity payable to the former proprietor terminated with his death after which the Government was under no obligation to make further payments, and many families which had been wealthy under the old system found themselves destitute on the death of the pensioner. The measure, though harsh and arbitrary, enabled a vicious and well established system to be finally broken. The *multezim* were however allowed to retain in their possession their own personal land which also included the *ussieh*, or land which had been left ownerless and which the *multezim* had acquired for a small payment.

There were also in Egypt certain lands and properties which had been bequeathed to or become the property of the religious and charitable foundations, the *rizaqs* and *wakfs*. The income from these lands was intended for the maintenance of the mosques, schools and cisterns, for paying the sheiks and providing for the families of the poor *ulema*. Frequently a large proportion of these funds found its way into other pockets. In like manner the Pasha expropriated all these lands amounting to more than 660,000 *feddans* and undertook to fulfil all the obligations of the foundations at the expense of the Treasury. This measure was much resented by the greedy sheiks who had for years been lining their pockets with the revenues of these properties, but their protests were unavailing.

Hitherto, it had been left to the landowner whether the land was cultivated or not, and as the long succession of civil wars had driven many of the native cultivators off the land, much of it remained neglected. The tax on land had previously been assessed on its productive capacity, and the tax ranged from about 6 pataks, or 15 piastres, to about 20 pataks, or 50 piastres per *feddan*. It appears that no tax at all was paid on uncultivated land. Mohammed Ali now put a flat tax on all cultivable land with a few exceptions while in addition a cadastral survey was carried out under his orders by which the measurements of the *feddan* were somewhat diminished, with the result that the owner of a hundred *feddans* now found himself the possessor of 105, all of them taxable at the authorised rate. Under the new system it made no difference whether the land was cultivated or not. The idea was not only to increase the revenue but also to stimulate the *fellahin* into cultivating the maximum area, but it frequently happened that the *fellahin* paid the taxes but left the land fallow, calculating that the cost of cultivation would exceed the value of the harvest.[1]

Much of this reorganisation took place during the first few years of Mohammed Ali's rule, between 1805 and 1814, when he was driven to desperate expedients by the demands of the Arabian war. Encouraged by the lack of opposition to his appropriations by the *fellahin* and landlords, he resolved to execute the final act of his design to make himself the owner of every *feddan* of the land of Egypt. But he shrank from executing the order himself and availed himself of his absence in Arabia in February 1814 to instruct his chief executive officer, the Kiaya Bey, to issue a decree that all the lands of Egypt were henceforth the property of the Pasha. 'The sheiks in the utmost terror and consternation immediately waited on him, remonstrating against the injustice of the measure, which deprived so many families of their estates, but the Kiaya replied that such were the orders of his master, which he dared not recall.'[2] These murmurs and grumblings were apparently the only resistance offered to the Viceroy's coup, and the whole country thus passed into his hands.

Having taken possession of the whole country, he carried his ideology to the next logical stage, a monopoly of almost every activity, trade and enterprise. All the products of the soil became in practice the property of the Government. At any rate the Government became the only dealer in all commodities, buying from the *fellahin* at one price and selling to consumers at a large profit. The following passage, quoted from St John's *Egypt and Mohammed Ali*, illustrates the extent of his operations:

. . . He now proceeded to monopolise every production of the soil, every article forming the ordinary food of the inhabitants, so that an artificial scarcity is maintained, by which the expenditure of every individual in the country has been augmented three or four fold. Wheat is purchased by the government, in Upper Egypt, at twenty-five piastres per *ardeb*, and resold at Cairo at one hundred and twenty. Beans, one of the principal articles of food among the poor, are bought up, and doled out to the people at the same enormous rate of profit. The prices of beef, mutton, fish, etc. have been increased in proportion. A novel property tax called *furdé* has likewise been imposed, by which every man in Egypt is compelled to contribute according to his supposed capacity of bearing the burden. The amount of the sum thus produced it would be difficult to ascertain; but it must be very considerable, since every menial servant, every person living on fixed annual wages; every artizan, whether European or native, in the service of the government; every public officer or employé, pays annually the amount of one month's stipend. Precisely the same rule is observed in the house tax called *salyan*, by which the proprietor is compelled to pay annually one month's rent, whether the house be occupied or not. At the time of the general spoliation of 1814, the lands in the vicinity of the large towns were left in the possession of their proprietors, but the taxes have been at length increased to such an amount that they now exceed the value of the produce.

To outside observers it seemed impossible that even the docile inhabitants of Egypt would tolerate indefinitely the burdens thrust on them by their master or that they could find the money to pay the inflated taxes. Yet with uncanny instinct the Pasha maintained his dominance and succeeded in increasing his revenues substantially year by year. For example, in the ten years 1821 to 1830 inclusive the revenue rose from 240,141 purses or £2 millions, to over 498,000 purses or £5,118,000.

Yet in spite of the hardships undergone by the people there were substantial compensations. Public security reached a stage hitherto unknown. The Bedouin Arabs living in the desert or on the fringes of the Nile valley who had always earned their livelihood by raiding the settled areas and carrying off crops, livestock, women and children, were pursued with such relentless vigour by the Pasha's troops that they found it more profitable to come to terms with the Pasha and abide by his decrees. As far as possible for an oriental country where bribery and corruption were the usual accompaniments of litigation, justice was administered swiftly and impartially. Every inhabitant had the right to appeal or carry any complaint direct to Mohammed Ali. Rank or position carried no weight with him in deciding an issue. He was scrupulous and attentive in all his dealings with Europeans and ensured them the full protection of the capitulations. A journey through Egypt was as safe as a stroll in Hyde Park.

Many of Mohammed Ali's schemes to increase the revenue were unhappy and fruitless because they were ill-conceived and took no account of human nature. In his monopolies of agricultural produce, especially the cotton crop, the government was the dealer and the cultivator merely the servant. In consequence it mattered nothing to the *fellah* what condition his crop was in; all he had to do was collect it from the fields and transport it to the local government warehouse.

> Under such a system, no person in the country can, in fact, have any interest in protecting the property amassed by the government; and in the event of an invasion, the inhabitants, instead of preserving or defending his Highness's stores, would undoubtedly be the first to pillage and destroy them . . . The peasant has little inducement to bring his produce to market in the best marketable state; he will therefore bestow no trouble in picking, cleaning and assorting his cotton; consequently this article rarely sells in Europe at more than half or two thirds of what it is intrinsically worth. The care and attention bestowed by a trader on the preservation of his commodities, are not to be expected from the public officer, who is only solicitous that the article shall not be deficient in weight or measure.[3]

A similar loss attended the Pasha's monopolistic operations with coffee imported from the Yemen. He took over the whole business from import to retail in the shops, and raised the selling price from 15 dollars a *kantar* to 22. Not only did he lose the normal customs duty and transit revenue levied on the merchants who used to import the coffee on their own account, but the increased price led to a sharp falling off in the demand with the result that on the final balance sheet of his operation in this commodity, he was well out of pocket.

An amusing instance of the Pasha's faulty plans and the action he took to overcome its defects is given by St John[4]:

> Another of the Pasha's unpopular measures is the monopoly of salt of which the Egyptians generally consume a great quantity. On the imposition of a very heavy tax, however, many villages partly perhaps through poverty, partly through a spirit of resistance, entirely dropped the use of it, thereby causing a great deficiency in the revenue. For some time His Highness, notwithstanding his peculiar genius for finance, was considerably embarrassed by this novel kind of opposition; but the fertility of his invention is truly extraordinary; while the sagacious *fellahs*, charmed with this strategem, were congratulating themselves on what they regarded as a masterpiece of policy, a number of government boats, laden with salt, were observed mooring under the villages.

Presently the merchandise was disembarked, and piled in pyramidal heaps upon the plain. This done, an officer waited on the Sheik el Beled, informing him that His Highness, having ascertained the quantity of salt formerly consumed in his village, had forwarded the necessary supply, for the value of which he would be held responsible to government, whether the article were consumed or not.

However, it should not be thought that the whole of Mohammed Ali's administration was confined to wringing every possible piastre from his subjects. This was only a means to an end, the development of the land, for which capital on a large scale was necessary. His crowning achievement, which has been of lasting benefit ever since, was his introduction of the cultivation of cotton. So successful was this that cotton has become the most important and lucrative of all the crops grown in Egypt. Hearing of the value of cotton and the possible advantages to be derived from its cultivation, he experimented and sowed some two thousand acres in the Delta with the plant. The success which attended this experiment was beyond all expectation; the plant flourished in the fertile mud of the Nile and produced a fibre of exceptional quality and long staple. Further experiments showed that it flourished even better along the Nile valley of Upper Egypt where climatic conditions were ideal. Cotton became a valuable commodity for export to Europe and especially to England, and this together with the corn which Mohammed Ali had long been selling to the British navy, provided him with the foreign exchange to buy the machinery, weapons and manufactured goods he required for the equipping of his armed forces and the development of the country. The cultivation of cotton spread through the land of Egypt and became one of the most important sources of revenue. The income from the cultivation of the soil rose from 21,000 purses in 1821 to 65,000 purses in 1830, and much of this increase can be ascribed to the increased production of cotton.

It occurred to Mohammed Ali that this cotton which he was selling abroad was returning to Egypt in the form of manufactured cloth. It smacked of waste and folly that this should be so, that his country was unable to convert the raw material into finished goods. Surely, he thought, what the British labourer could do in the cotton mills of Lancashire could also be done by Egyptians if supplied with the mills, looms and machinery. In this case, the Pasha's lack of education and understanding of technical problems led him into error. In 1819 he initiated his plans to make Egypt a partially industrial country by setting up textile factories in Cairo, Mehalla el Kubra and Mansurah. During the years following the number of mills was much increased and they were spread all over the land.

From the beginning these cotton mills were a failure and continued to be so throughout Mohammed Ali's reign. Most of the power supply for the machines was derived from oxen employed in the traditional manner. Such an uneven source of power was detrimental to the machines which were designed for water or steam. The *fellahin* whom the Pasha pressed into the mills had no industrial tradition or training; they were underpaid, badly fed and clothed, and overworked; accustomed as they were to life in the fields, the factory was only a hell on earth, and they took every conceivable opportunity of escaping from this particular form of bondage. Punishments in the mills were of exceptional severity, five hundred lashes being not unknown as against fifty lashes which was the normal punishment in the Pasha's navy. Lack of technical skill and maintenance resulted in the machines wearing out or breaking down with monotonous regularity, and often attempts by ignorant hands to repair defects only resulted in greater damage. Nearly every mill at one time or another was burnt down, no doubt at the hands of the labourers who saw in the destruction of the mill the only escape from intolerable drudgery. The physical conditions of the country were unfavourable to the good maintenance of mechanical equipment. The strong winds that blow across Egypt every year carried clouds of sand which permeated every nook and cranny. This combined with the lubricating oils formed a paste guaranteed to grind away the moving parts and wreck the machines in a short time. The operatives themselves had no interest in the work they were forced to do, and in consequence took no care to minimise loss or waste or to produce good quality work. The overseers were mostly Turks who 'though in the receipt of handsome salaries, sordidly availed themselves of the mal-organisation of the establishments to commit dishonesty, and plunder their master and inferiors . . . Thus it is that commissioners from the treasury are perpetually engaged in examining accounts and detecting imposition.'[5] Some of the mills were supervised by English spinners imported for the purpose, and although they did good work and made improvements, they were faced with obstacles to success which no talent or ingenuity could overcome.

The result of this misplaced enterprise and ill-conceived planning was that much of the cotton crop, already very inferior owing to methods of picking, cleansing and transporting, was completely wasted, while the remainder furnished a cloth of very poor quality unfit for export, and the losses of money to the Government must have been substantial. For this state of affairs it would be unjust to hold Mohammed Ali entirely to blame, for he had had no education and no opportunity for studying industrial problems at first hand. His only source of information on these points was the colony of European merchants who were only too eager to unfold before the Pasha's eyes a vista of abundance and prosperity, if he would buy their machines and tools. It was not an error to make the experiment, but he would have done better if he had abandoned it as soon as it became clear that it was not bearing fruit. Instead, however, he kept on pouring more and more money into these ventures, hoping that experience would bring more skill and better results. In 1833 St John wrote the following summary of the Pasha's cotton industry:

> It is now nearly fourteen years since the first attempt was made to introduce the cotton manufacture into Egypt, and the wisdom of the Pasha's policy may be estimated with tolerable accuracy by the result. At present most of the mills are in ruins, and immense heaps of machinery, no longer employed, are covered with rust and mouldering to decay. Nevertheless, Egypt is haunted by a class of foreign mechanics and adventurers, who adduce the example of England to prove to the misled Pasha that a change of machinery and management will quickly convert his mills into a lucrative source of revenue; indeed I believe they have even gone so far as to allude to the possibility of successfully competing with Manchester and Glasgow. The Pasha, in all doubtful matters, generally embraces the most flattering side; for in his manufacturing schemes he appears to think nothing beyond his powers of creation. His Highness having been informed that coal is to be found in great quantities in Syria, has, in consequence, adopted the determination of making his own steam engines, to drive an immense number of cotton mills. But these are not to be set up in Egypt which, he has at length discovered, can never be converted into a manufacturing country . . . There is only one man in Egypt interested in the success of the manufacture. The Europeans engaged in the mills are, for the most part, unprincipled adventurers, who find their advantage in the ignorance and dilatoriness of the Turks.[6]

Cotton manufacture was not by any means the only industrial adventure of the Pasha. In every way possible he attempted to make his country self-supporting and independent of foreign manufactured goods. The growth of sugar cane in Upper Egypt was strongly encouraged and excellent crops were produced. The best syrups were exported for refining into first grade sugar, while a certain amount of refining was carried out in Government factories in Egypt. Armaments were an important item in Mohammed Ali's economy and an arsenal was established in the Citadel of Cairo. Here cannon were cast and ammunition manufactured, while at the same time nitre, or saltpetre, an important constituent of gunpowder, was made in large quantities. Among the industries set up and developed may be mentioned copper mills, iron foundries, dyeing works, tanneries, corn-mills, glass factories, forges, paper mills and printing works. There is a long term result from these operations of Mohammed Ali which have only been felt during the last century. Many of the industries were so new to Egypt that failure in some cases was inevitable; yet not all have become defunct. Mehalla el Kubra houses a giant textile industry, and others have survived and substantially developed and are now flourishing businesses. It is probable that without the beginnings marked out by Mohammed Ali many small industries which now flourish in Egypt would never have been started.

If he was deceived into thinking that he could transform *fellahin* into factory workers, he was not slow to realise that the general state of education was as low as it possibly could be. 'When I came to Egypt,' he said, 'it was really barbarous, utterly barbarous. Barbarous it remains to this day. Still, I hope that my labours have rendered its condition somewhat better than it was . . . '[7] He recognised that the development and welfare of Egypt lay in pulling it out of the ignorance and prejudice which engulfed the native population, and infusing some elements of education and technical ability. To this end numbers of young Turks and Egyptians were sent to France and England to be educated in the Western ways of administration and commerce. Schools were founded, and those whom he had sent abroad were expected to teach their fellows what they had learnt, on their return. No doubt consciousness of his own lack of education weighed heavily on Mohammed Ali. His efforts in the field of education were truly remarkable and afford evidence of his interest in the welfare of the people. Any despot intent only on his own personal power and aggrandisement would have made sure that education was not encouraged among his subjects; such was not the case with Mohammed Ali. Under his auspices a college was opened at Kasserlyne which accommodated twelve hundred students who were fed, clothed, and provided with pocket money at the Pasha's expense. The boys who entered the college were intended to serve in the army or navy, and they became virtually the Pasha's property as soon as they entered the college. Nearly all branches of education were taught here, especially mathematics and the art of war. The college was, in fact, organised on a military basis. In addition a school of artillery for training officer cadets was established at Toura and commanded by a Spanish ex-officer, Colonel Seguera, which drew most of its recruits from the college, and another school for cadets, reckoned to be the best in Egypt, was set up at Giza. High standards of education were achieved in these establishments, and the study of French was added to that of the Turkish, Persian and Arabic languages.[8] A well educated and efficient corps of officers was the result of these institutions. So anxious was Mohammed Ali for the development of the country that he tended to withdraw the students from their colleges before they had completed their studies, so that sometimes they were only half-trained.

'The school of medicine at Abou Zabel is without doubt one of the most extraordinary of the Pasha's establishments.'[9] This was equipped with a hospital, theatre, laboratory and dispensary, and a large school room. It also contained a printing press which was installed to print Arabic translations of European medical works. The school itself contained sufficient accommodation for six hundred students.

It has been said that Mohammed Ali spent large sums on the higher education of the few rather than on the primary education of the masses. This was undoubtedly true, but it was in line with his principal objective, the development of the country and the creation of a military machine. He was prepared to leave the *fellah* to till his fields where he was doing the most useful work; he had no need of books to tell him how to plant and reap his crops. Mohammed Ali aimed to create new industries in Egypt, and for this he required men who could read and write and think intelligently; he required an army which could at least match that of the Sultan. Primary education was too slow and too costly for Mohammed Ali to consider. Everything, he felt, that he wanted to be done must be done in his lifetime, otherwise it would never be done.

Irrigation and water communications, the mainsprings of Egypt's existence, received much attention from Mohammed Ali. Before 1819 the route from Cairo to Alexandria lay down the Rosetta branch of the Nile and thence by sea, a lengthy and often dangerous voyage in which the barges and *feluccas* sometimes came to grief. A project was suggested to Mohammed Ali by a Mr Briggs, an Englishman, that a canal should be dug linking the Nile direct with the great seaport. With his customary vigour and enthusiasm the Pasha seized on the idea and commissioned a Turkish engineer, Ismail Pasha, to execute the task with all haste. The *corvée*, the system of forced labour employed on works of public utility, was used to provide the labour, and it is reported that 313,000 *fellahin*, men and women, were collected along the line of the intended canal. It appears, however, that the director of the operations had either neglected or forgotten to provide any digging tools. Characteristically undeterred by such a small omission, he ordered the *fellahin* to dig with their bare hands, and the work was enforced by the presence of the Pasha's troops who compelled the wretched *fellahin* to labour from morn till night. This intolerable treatment, combined with lack of food and water, wrought havoc among the labour corps, and 23,000 of them are reported to have died within ten months. This new canal, to which he gave the name Mahmudiya in honour of the reigning Sultan, was some eighty kilometres long, but was not a very satisfactory feat of engineering since it had to have sluices fitted at both ends to prevent the escape of water when the Nile was low, but in addition to providing a short water route between the two principal cities, it also provided a water supply for the irrigation of adjacent land. Towards the end of his reign, Mohammed Ali ordered the construction of the great Nile Barrage below Cairo which was intended to store up a head of water for irrigating the whole of the Delta, if the annual inundation failed, as it frequently did, and also to bring under cultivation between two and three hundred thousand acres above the Barrage.[10] The work was carried out by Linant Bey, a French engineer and, although somewhat defective in construction, the project was a great success, the forerunner of the many irrigation developments of later years. It is reported that the Pasha was only with difficulty dissuaded from using the stone of the Pyramids for the work. To a man who looked only to the future and showed little interest in the past, the giant blocks of stone already cut to size must have been very tempting material.

Every effort was made, and every inducement offered to the *fellahin*, to reclaim waste or abandoned land and bring it under cultivation. Thousands of new water-wheels were installed to pump up the precious water and mud from the river, and Mohammed Ali even relaxed the land monopoly by granting land outright to those who would cultivate it.

Besides developing the land he ruled, Mohammed Ali had dreams of enlarging his domains and carving a new Egyptian empire out of the neighbouring territories of the Near East. Already his successes in Arabia and the firm grip in which he held the province of Egypt had aroused the suspicions and envy of the Sultan, and in the Pasha's mind there was no doubt that a day would come when he would cross swords with his imperial master. An army, then, capable of overcoming all possible adversaries, was a prime necessity, and no expense was spared to create it. During his early career in Egypt he had had occasion to observe the organisation and discipline of Bonaparte's army and the advantages which these qualities brought.

61

Here, he saw, was no rabble of men such as were the usual Turkish armies, but a disciplined, well-armed and efficient fighting machine which could cut its way through an adversary ten times its number. To possess such an army was one of the most cherished ambitions of Mohammed Ali's life. The mixed bag of Albanians, Turks and Dehli's which he had under his command at the time of his accession to power, were not to be counted on in an emergency, nor could any degree of loyalty be expected from them. As has already been remarked, many of these were packed off overseas to leave their bones in the deserts of Arabia. Mohammed Ali intended to replace them with new material, the untapped sources of manpower in the Sudan. He had early decided that he would create a completely new army, organised, trained and equipped on European lines, and it was this project which prompted him to send expeditions to conquer the Sudan and bring back slaves to man his new army. Some account will be given of these campaigns in a later chapter.

The reorganisation of the army was entrusted to a French officer, one Colonel Sève who, having retired from the French Army after the battle of Waterloo, had come to Egypt in 1819 and offered his services to the Pasha of Egypt, who had cordially welcomed him. He adopted the faith of Islam, was made a *pasha* and took the name of Soliman. One of the principal streets of modern Cairo is named after him. A vast barracks was erected at Aswan where the Sudanese conscript-slaves were to be trained as soldiers. By 1824 20,000 of these had been recruited and organised into regiments on European lines. But this great innovation was destined to miscarry. It turned out that the Sudanese, wrenched from their native lands and taken into bondage into Egypt, could not or would not stay alive. In spite of the utmost attention of the army doctors, the majority lost heart and strength, and died. It may have been because they were thrust into a different climate and way of life, or because they had been brought into slavery. At all events the Pasha was compelled to abandon this plan and seek his manpower elsewhere.

It is strange that he should have looked abroad for material for his army when there existed in his own land a body of men long inured to hardship, toughened by heavy manual labour almost from birth to death, and docile in character. But for centuries the *fellahin* had been regarded with contempt as a servile and spineless race, fit only to scratch the earth and do menial work. But it was now suggested to Mohammed Ali that he should seek his soldiery from among this element of the population, a proposal he vigorously adopted.

Recruiting parties sent out to enforce the conscription of the *fellahin* displayed callous disregard for the ordinary humanities. The unfortunate wretches were seized and dragged away from their homes at a moment's notice. To the *fellah* whose only happiness lay with his fields, his family and his village, this ruthless press-gang method of recruitment was the Pasha's most hateful infamy. Such was the terror which conscription into the army inspired in the *fellahin* that they went to every length to escape from it, even to the extent of self-mutilation. It is recorded that they cut off their own fingers, especially the 'trigger finger', extracted their teeth and even blinded themselves, deeming these shocking disfigurements preferable to the misery of service in the Pasha's army. St John, in the record of his travels in Egypt at the time, mentions that of a party of thirteen *fellahin* who performed some work for him, all except the old sheik had their right-hand forefinger missing.[11] Conscription into the army meant virtually the loss of everything to the *fellah*. His wife and family were frequently left destitute of all subsistence with the result that many of the women were compelled to resort to a life of prostitution to avoid starvation, so that even if a soldier was fortunate enough to return to his home, he found his family broken up and his wife lost. The methods of conscription were simple and conformed to the usual administrative system. Orders were sent down to the *mudirs* of the provinces to supply a quota of men for the army. These divided the number up among the villages in the province, and the sheik of each was responsible for finding the stipulated number of men. 'The sheiks seized as many as they could, released those who offered the largest bribes, and sent the remainder chained two and two like felons.'[12] There was, however, this to be said for service in the army. The *fellahin* had no military tradition and feared the army above all else. As Dodwell justly points out, nothing could have done so much to raise the spirit of men who had been serfs from time immemorial. The Pasha made them play a man's part in spite of themselves and from this time onwards they could hold up their heads and look their traditional masters, the Turks, in the face.

Under the direction of Colonel Sève or Soliman Pasha a fighting machine was born out of this new and untried material, in spite of a motley collection of low class Europeans who were enlisted to help him and who were described as 'void of truth, faith or honour; in short the worst set of rascals to be found anywhere in the world'.[13] The creation of this army was indeed a masterpiece of enterprise on the part of Colonel Sève. On many occasions he barely escaped with his life; it is reported that on one occasion the troops he was training deliberately fired on him, but missed, whereupon he roundly upbraided them for their poor marksmanship. Even in the ranks, Mohammed Ali encouraged education. 'The rude *fellah* from the wilds of Gournou,

63

taken away from the fields at the age of thirty, is now daily seen bending over his slate. No solder unable to read and write can be promoted to the rank of corporal.'[14] The importance which Mohammed Ali attached to his army is witnessed by the fact that of his total annual expenditure of 240,000 purses in 1821, one half went to pay his troops, and although ten years later this proportion was reduced to rather less than a third, the net figure was even greater; every year the expenditure on the army was the principal item in his accounts.

Other demonstrations of the methods of modern warfare witnessed in the past were not lost on Mohammed Ali. Strong in his mind were the lessons which Nelson and the British fleet had taught when Bonaparte, victorious in the field, found himself stale-mated by sea-power. If he were ever to take up arms successfully with the Sultan, he would need a naval force of his own to combat the Turkish squadrons. He had not forgotten either that on two occasions British troops had landed in Egypt without difficulty solely owing to their command of the sea. He managed to purchase a few vessels at Venice and Genoa, but his applications to Britain and France to purchase warships in those countries were rejected, and he therefore resolved to build his own fleet. But although a land of abundant fertility, Egypt was particularly barren of timber forests, while to the north on the wooded slopes of Lebanon and Syria lay the forests which would afford him an ample supply of the necessary material. This was one of the principal considerations which later prompted him to undertake the invasion of those countries. But in the meantime he scoured the shipyards and ports of the Mediterranean, and secured enough ships to form the nucleus of a navy. For his technicians and commanders he tried to enlist into his service retired British naval officers, but the British Government was slow to approve this proposal, and the Pasha in consequence obtained most of them from France. Sparing no expense he established a great naval arsenal at Alexandria and considerably expanded the facilities of the port. The arsenal included ship-building yards and a naval school where all branches of the science were taught to the cadets and officers. A good start was made to make Egypt an important and powerful maritime nation, and the navy did good work during the Pasha's reign. But for a navy to be effective the sea-faring tradition must be ingrained in the ship hands, and such was never the case in Egypt. The Egyptians hated the Pasha's navy even more than his army, and no skill or ability on the part of his European commanders could compensate for this inherent dislike of the service on the part of the ratings. Only the enthusiasm of Mohammed Ali and his constant attention enabled the navy to be built up at all, and on his death the vessels were sold off to the Porte.[15]

In spite of his many reforms and innovations Mohammed Ali made little change in the long-established and well tried system of civil government and administration, except that where formerly there had been twenty-four provinces, each administered by a Mameluke *bey*, these were amalgamated into seven provinces, each under a Turkish *mudir* directly responsible to the Pasha. Under the *mudirs* the hierarchy was continued, the provinces being divided into a number of districts, each in the charge of a *mamur*, and the districts into villages of which the headman, or Sheik el Balad, was the executive officer answerable to his superiors for the conduct of the villagers, the collection of taxes and the enforcement of the Pasha's decrees. It seems unlikely that any more efficient system of government could have been devised for Egypt, but clearly it gave considerable opportunity for dishonest officers to indulge in bribery and corruption and to line their pockets at the expense of both the government and the native. Mohammed Ali was thus obliged to occupy himself incessantly in touring the provinces, enquiring personally into the state of affairs, checking the accounts and hearing the complaints of the *fellahin*. Only his ceaseless industry in looking into everything personally and inflicting severe punishment on defalcators prevented unlimited peculation.

In addition to the provincial administration there were seven Government departments – war, navy, agriculture, finance, commerce, education and police.[16] These appear to have come directly under Mohammed Ali who retained all effective control in his own hands. The principal executive officer, or chief secretary, of the Pasha was the Kiaya Bey who was responsible for the issue and execution of all his orders and decrees, and who acted as intermediary between him and his officials. In the larger towns a special administrative system was established.

In matters of justice Mohammed Ali was cautious in his reforms since civil law came within the province of the religious authorities and conformed to the *Sheria*. The law was administered by a *Qadi* who was appointed every year by the Porte and had under him a body of sheiks and *ulema*, who seem to have been paid by the *Qadi*, while he in turn received a percentage of the damages awarded in civil actions. But justice was by no means impartial in the courts. 'If a poor man is contesting against a rich, rarely can he hope to see his cause prevail; the law is evaded in favour of the powerful.'[17] Much no doubt as he desired to improve the judicial system, the Pasha felt that any interference on his part with the system which operated according to the precepts of the Koran would bring down a hornet's nest upon his head and stern rebukes from Constantinople. But he was able to effect some improvements in commercial matters by instituting Tribunals of Commerce at Cairo and Alexandria whose function was to decide on all disputes arising from trade and business. The Tribunals were composed of members of different nationalities, Arabs, French, Jews and Greeks, and these together formed a court which decided an issue on the merits of the case rather than according to an archaic religious code. Such an institution was of value in encouraging foreign merchants to trade with Egypt.

Under the capitulations which protected the nationals of the capitulatory powers in their dealings with the Ottoman Empire, the Europeans received certain privileges, chief among which was exemption from taxation and freedom from the jurisdiction of the Islamic courts. Where a European was charged with an offence or felony, he had the right to be tried in the court of his own consul who himself judged the case, sometimes with the assistance of assessors, and who meted out the appropriate punishment, which might include imprisonment or exile. It followed from this that many a scoundrel of the Levant sought by any means to get his name on the register of one of the European consuls and thus obtain his protection from the local courts.

More could be said of Mohammed Ali's methods and achievements during his reign, but enough has been outlined to illustrate the fact that here indeed was someone of an entirely different calibre from the traditional Turkish *pasha*. Hitherto the Governor of Egypt had been a Turkish officer appointed by the Sultan at Constantinople. Such officials generally had no special interests in the countries or provinces they governed; they were time-servers whose principal work was the collection and forwarding of the tribute to the Porte, and keeping their territories in the Empire. None of them had any intention of settling in the countries they ruled, and in consequence it mattered little whether the people were contented and prosperous or not. Most governors considered that for a period they were exiled from their homes, that service abroad was something to be endured rather than enjoyed. Compensation for these hardships was only to be found in the rapid accumulation of wealth at the expense of their subjects. But Mohammed Ali was entirely different. When he seized the reins of power in Egypt he intended to remain there for the rest of his life. Egypt was to be his land of adoption, his home and his child. He had no ambitions to enrich himself in a short time so that he could live the remainder of his days in luxury at Constantinople. His dreams were not only to hold Egypt in his hands, but to make it his own, to raise it to a condition of wealth and power, to cut his country and himself adrift from the Ottoman Empire and build up his own empire.

The execution of these plans required a determination and ability of no mean order. That Mohammed Ali possessed the necessary qualities is proved by the fact that, as will later be shown, he succeeded in winning large areas of the Near East, that his military victories against his imperial master nearly toppled over the ageing Ottoman Empire, and brought two great powers of Europe, France and England, to the brink of war. In Egypt itself a completely new order of things began under his guidance. True it is that his subjects were often driven to great hardship by the demands made on them, but at the same time they were completely protected from all outside interference and oppression. On balance the native Egyptian was probably richer, happier and more secure than at any time within his living memory. At least he knew where he stood provided the Government was strong and firm, no matter how autocratic; the Egyptian understood, respected and even liked it, for it was the system to which he had been accustomed for centuries. Mohammed Ali was conscious that every development, every reform and improvement, that came to Egypt depended entirely on himself. No doubt he was filled with foreboding that as soon as he died, progress would cease. He was thus fighting a battle or running a race against time, the span of his own life, and everything which had to be done, must be done within that period. Thus it was, of course, that he had no time for experiment, no time to build upon firm foundations, to allow progress and development to proceed on their normal slow course. Everything had to be done quickly or not at all, and his subjects had to be driven mercilessly. If his successors had been men of equal capacity, the subsequent story of Egypt would have been vastly different. But as it turned out, much of the structure which he had built up so carefully and laboriously over the years tumbled like a pack of cards to the ground, and Egypt slipped back into the old ways, with disastrous consequences.

CHAPTER 5

Incursion into Europe

Some mention has already been made in the previous chapter of Mohammed Ali's resolution to invade the virgin and unexplored lands of the Upper Nile, *the Bilad es Sudan*, land of the black men, to acquire a source of supply for the new armies he proposed to raise. This invasion took place during the years 1820 to 1824, but, as has already been remarked, the results of these incursions were disappointing. Over half a century later the Sudan was destined to loom large in Egyptian affairs, and for this reason some departure is here made from the strictly chronological order of events, and the account of the Egyptian conquest of the Sudan is deferred to a later chapter in which the threads of Sudanese affairs will be picked up and fitted into their place in Egyptian history. For the moment it is only noted that the northern areas of that vast territory were subdued and incorporated into the Pasha's domain.

So far Mohammed Ali had confined himself to the internal affairs of his *pashalik* and to external operations which were outside the limit of European interest, i.e. Arabia and the Sudan. But it was not long before the rising tide of events involved him in Europe itself and focused on him the attention of the great Powers. The rapid regeneration of Egypt and her increasingly healthy economy combined to excite the envy of the Sultan, while at the same time the Pasha's growing access of military and naval strength was a cause for some concern with the Porte who were conscious of the dangers of permitting provincial governors to become over-powerful. These had a tendency to flout the authority of their imperial overlord and to assert their own independence. Policy at the Porte therefore ruled that provincial governors should be curbed in one way or another and prevented from amassing sufficient power to threaten the Sultan's position. '*Divide et impera*' could well have been the imperial motto. A popular method of securing this desirable result was to encourage the *pashas* to undertake

68

enterprises well calculated to sap their strength and deplete their coffers without offering any commensurate awards. Already the rising Pasha of Egypt had been invited to undertake the prosecution of the Arabian War, but the results of this, from the Sultan's point of view, had not been altogether satisfactory. Although the long drawn out contest had cost the Pasha large sums of money and thousands of lives, his resources seemed to be inexhaustible, and the end of the war had apparently left him as strong as at the beginning, and considerably more experienced in the art of war.

The origins of the Greek rebellion which broke out in 1821 and the diplomatic wranglings which occupied Europe during ensuing years are not relevant to this narrative except in so far as they affect the course of Egyptian history. A short prefatory note of the situation may therefore suffice.

For many years the Ottoman Empire had been in the process of gentle decline, growing weaker in proportion as the Christian powers of Europe became stronger and more civilised. To ensure the stability of Europe and the maintenance of the balance of power, it was recognised by the Powers that the Empire must be kept alive, propped up if necessary from without and prevented from disintegrating. No one could foresee the results which might accrue from its dissolution, but certain it was that such an occurrence would be followed by a struggle among the powers to pick up the pieces; a European war would have been very probable. The Turkish Empire contained a large number of Christian subjects, *rayahs*, living for the most part in the European provinces of the Empire, i.e. in the Balkan peninsula. Although the *rayahs* were allowed considerable privileges and even more freedom in the pursuit and practice of their religion than Christians in certain other parts of Europe, at the same time they were ever conscious that they had no rights as such and that they existed only on the sufferance of the Sultan. In ever-turbulent Greece there had been disaffection for some time, a longing for release from the Moslem yoke and a half-expressed movement for national liberation, but circumstances had prevented these hopes from coming to fruition.

At the same time as Mohammed Ali was building his sub-empire in Egypt, a compatriot of his, Ali Pasha of Yannina, was pursuing a similar course in the Greek Epirus and Albania. He had reached the stage of openly defying the Sultan by putting his fortune to the test of arms against the imperial forces. But the story of Ali Pasha is only significant here in that his revolt drew off from the garrison towns of the Epirus and Morea the bulk of the Turkish forces. The restless Greeks, taking advantage of such opportune circumstances, likewise revolted against the Sultan. The Greek revolt does not appear to have been the outcome of any concerted plan or to have been organised by any central authority. It was a sporadic yet spontaneous affair, which erupted almost simultaneously throughout the Greek towns and villages. The leaders of the rebels were the numerous bandits and brigands who infested the country, and such was the character of the revolt that it was virtually impossible to distinguish between combatants and peaceful civilians; the one became the other and vice versa whenever it suited.

The revolt was signalled in April 1821 by a general uprising of the Christian Greeks against the Moslem Turkish inhabitants of the Morea. Atrocities were committed on the hapless Moslems, many thousands of whom were butchered outright. Those who could escaped into the fortified garrison towns of the Morea, and these were closely invested by the attackers. Like a flame the revolt flashed through the Morea across the Gulf of Patras into the Epirus and throughout the Greek islands of the Aegean and Mediterranean. The islanders, who were skilled and daring sailors, regarded the revolt as an excellent pretext for extending their piratical practices to the ships of all nations.

The romantic legends which have sprung up regarding the Greek rebellion, and such episodes as Byron's death at Missolonghi, have tended to glamorise the Greeks and portray them as the noble and valiant descendants of the ancient heroes, struggling to throw off the Moslem yoke and attain their liberty. But the truth is far from this: humanity and honour formed little part of the Greek conduct of the war. The slaughter of helpless and innocent victims, whose only crime was their devotion to the Crescent instead of the Cross, was appalling and treachery rife. The news of the massacres of the Moslems in the Morea were greeted in Constantinople by an outburst of blood-lust and a thirst for revenge. Reprisals were taken on the Christian elements in the capital, and Gregorias, the Patriarch of the Greek Church, and two of his bishops were seized and hanged and their bodies thrown in the Bosporus.

During the first two years of the revolt no substantial victory was achieved by either side. On balance fortune appeared to be favouring the Greek rebels who were receiving the moral, and also material, support of their co-religionists in the Christian countries of Europe. Had it not been for the liberal out-pourings of gold from foreign sympathisers to nourish the revolution, there seems little doubt that it would have collapsed at an early date. As it was, this encouragement enabled it to survive the initial assaults of the imperial forces. Sultan Mahmud for his part was not slow to realise that the situation was beginning to get out of hand, that the forces at his disposal were insufficient to subdue the rising, and that the solution to the problem lay in the employment of trained and disciplined forces and the mastery of the sea. In only one part of his empire could he find such instruments, in Egypt. Pocketing his pride he applied to Mohammed Ali for assistance. The reward offered was the island of Crete to himself, and the *pashalik* of the Morea to his son, Ibrahim, if he would come and take it.

Here indeed was precisely the type of situation which Mohammed Ali reckoned he could turn to good account, and undoubtedly he had been sitting back waiting for the invitation. Here also was a golden opportunity of testing his new army and even more important his newly formed navy against some of the most skilled sailors of Europe. Preparations were immediately put in hand for the new enterprise, and Hussein Bey Jeritli, the Pasha's son-in-law, was placed in command of the expedition to Crete. In June 1823 a well-equipped Egyptian force landed in Suda Bay on the northern coast of the island.

The subjugation of the island was systematic and barbarous. Thousands of Greeks were put to the sword, while women and children were seized and bundled on board the transports to be ferried across to Alexandria, there to adorn the Pasha's slave markets. Throughout the island the rebels were sought out and slaughtered so that by April 1824 barely an atom of resistance remained, and the Viceroy was able to report to the Sultan that the island was free of rebels. The cruelty and barbarity employed in the initial strategy of Mohammed Ali seem to have been quite deliberate. It was good policy, he believed, to show the weight of his arm in the opening stages to terrify the enemy into early submission. At the same time he probably felt little sympathy for the slaughterers of the thousands of Moslems who had perished at their hands. The subjugation of Crete was followed by attacks on the pirates' haunts in the islands of Kasos and Scarpanto; the first was stormed and its inhabitants almost annihilated, the second submitted and was treated with unexpected leniency.

While Hussein Bey was making himself master of Crete and the neighbouring islands, vast preparations had been going on at Alexandria for the invasion of the mainland. Already in January 1824 the imperial firman had arrived bestowing on Ibrahim the *pashalik* of the Morea and he was impatient to get under way. Finally in June all was ready, a fleet of about a hundred transports carrying an army of 17,000 troops, and sixty warships stood out from Alexandria, and sailed for the island of Rhodes where it was to join the Turkish fleet under Khusrev Pasha. But Khusrev was already busy capturing and punishing the pirates of the Greek islands, and it was not until September that a union was effected between the Egyptian and Turkish fleets off Budrun on the coast of Asia Minor. It was intended that the combined fleets should escort the transports to Crete, but the recent successes of Khusrev and Hussein in the islands had aroused the Greeks to a new sense of danger. Thus a number of sea-fights and skirmishes took place with varying degrees of success on both sides, and it was not until December that Ibrahim got his army as far as Crete. Two months later the final voyage was made, and the Egyptian army was landed on the continent of Europe, at Modon on the south-western tip of the Peloponnese.

The events of the year 1824 demonstrated the folly and lack of cohesion of the Greek rebels. Had they had the wisdom to overcome their own petty jealousies and personal vendettas, to unite and form a solid national movement, they would have had plentiful opportunities of sending the Egyptian fleet to the bottom during its voyages from Egypt to Greece. But such Greek leaders as there were thought only of their own aggrandisement and were so passionately devoted to intrigue against their fellows that they were totally oblivious to external threats. Moreover the Greek sailors and sea-captains who, united by a common purpose, could have inflicted untold damage on the Egyptian fleet, were interested only in their pay and flatly refused to stay at sea without it. The result was that many opportunities were lost and the full power of the Egyptian army was allowed to land in their fatherland almost unmolested.

From that day onward the fortunes of war turned completely against the rebels. Without delay Ibrahim advanced on the fortress of Navarino and invested it closely. A hastily mustered force of Greeks advanced to its relief, but when faced with the ordered legions of Ibrahim Pasha, even though only half their own number, they turned and fled like rabbits. With the dispersal of the Greeks in this encounter Ibrahim pressed the siege of Navarino. On the advice of Hussein Bey, who pointed out that the key to Navarino was possession of the island of Sphacteria, a naval force was sent to occupy the island which the improvident Greeks had neglected to garrison. This was followed by the capitulation of the neighbouring town of Pylus whose garrison was allowed to march out unmolested. The example of this unexpected act of clemency persuaded the inhabitants of Navarino likewise to surrender albeit hesitantly, for the Greeks, never having honoured their own pledges to the Moslems who had surrendered to them, hardly expected the Egyptians to do likewise. But Ibrahim kept his word and the garrison of Navarino was escorted to the harbour and allowed to sail away.

With his bases thus secured Ibrahim lost no time in taking possession of the *pashalik*, and immediately marched on Tripolitza in the heart of Morea which he captured with little opposition. In truth this bright new sword of Sultan Mahmud was something totally unexpected and formidable to the Greeks, and before its sharp edge they fell like corn to the scythe. The Greeks in fact refused to face Ibrahim's legions in open combat; the most they were able to do was to harass his advance and swoop on his rear, but such efforts produced no effect. Backwards and forwards across the Morea marched the victorious Egyptians, leaving a trail of death and destruction. Only at Nauplia and on the eastern coast of the peninsula were the Greeks able to retain a tenuous hold. The fortunes of the rebels had indeed reached their lowest ebb.

There was however one gleam of light in the darkness. In the Epirus north of the Gulf of Corinth the rebellion had for the most part succumbed to the power of the Sultan's armies. Almost the only stronghold remaining to the Greeks was the small seaport of Missolonghi which for years had defied the Turks. Every assault had been hurled back with such loss that it became almost a mania with the Sultan that it must be taken. In April 1825 a new Turkish army, commanded by the Sultan's ablest general, Rashid Pasha, passed down the peninsula in a final attempt to take the recalcitrant fortress. To ensure that his orders were carried out the Sultan deemed it expedient to remind Rashid Pasha that either Missolonghi or his own head must fall.[1]

The defence of Missolonghi is perhaps the only memorable chapter in the whole history of the Greek war of independence. The spirit, courage and idealism of their forefathers of Marathon and Salamis seem to have entered the hearts of the small company of defenders. In face of the combined artillery barrages and assaults of the Turks, the Missolonghiots gave not an inch. As the months went by, the little port became a crumbling mass of shell-scarred ruins, and the defenders grew gaunt and weak with hunger, but no quarter was asked or given on either side. Every device of siege and assault known to the Turks was employed but without success, and as the weary months passed the condition of the Turks became almost as pitiable as that of the wretched Greeks cooped up in the town. Both sides depended for their supplies upon their own fleets, neither of which were very dependable instruments.

In November, eight months after the commencement of the siege, Ibrahim, who was busy depopulating his *pashalik*, received an urgent instruction from his father to go to the assistance of Rashid Pasha at Missolonghi. Pleased to have the opportunity of demonstrating the prowess of his armies,

Ibrahim dropped everything and set off by forced marches to join his colleague. He crossed the Gulf and landed near Missolonghi on 27 November 1825.

From this moment the defence of Missolonghi becomes an unforgettable epic of history. Assault after assault was hurled at the ruins which once had been a town, but all to no avail. The Greeks had taken their decision long before and never once did they falter; there was no surrender. For another four months the operations continued, while all Europe held its breath. In desperation the Greeks decided to cut their way out, as they could hold on no longer. But the plan was betrayed to Ibrahim by a Bulgarian deserter, and when the moment came the Egyptians were ready. On the night of 22 April 1826, the Greeks sprang from their entrenchments and hurled themselves on the waiting enemy. A wall of fire and steel met the heroic defenders who were mown down in their hundreds, and the Moslems poured into the town. 'Then began a slaughter grim and great. From a cloudless sky the moon gazed calmly down on the awful scene of carnage. It seemed as though hell had suddenly been let loose on earth.'[2] Thousands fell on that terrible night, while only a few hundreds managed to make their escape from the death-trap. The siege of Missolonghi was over and the fortress finally taken, but at what a price! A whole year had been spent in this one operation, and the bodies of thousands of Turks and Egyptians lying in the ditches and approaches bore mute testimony to the grimness of the contest and the valour of the defenders.

In view of the uneasy condition of the European Concert in which the Ottoman Empire was an important factor, no event, however trivial, which took place in the Sultan's dominions, failed to arouse the interest of the Powers. In particular, anything which tended towards a diminution of the Empire's ability to survive had varying repercussions in the capitals of Europe. When, therefore, the Greek rebellion flared up, it was viewed in various ways. Rebellion in any quarter and from any cause, whether just or otherwise, was anathema to imperial Austria, and Metternich felt, no doubt with justification, that a successful rebellion in the Turkish Empire might germinate similar seeds in Austria's dominions.

True to her traditional policy England viewed with grave misgivings any outbreak which tended to weaken the Osmanlis and so disturb the equilibrium of Europe. Ambitious Russia on the other hand deemed the rebellion an excellent occasion for intruding in Turkish affairs. Not only did she consider herself protector and patron of the Orthodox Church, but she was ever searching for some pretext for planting her feet on the banks of the narrows separating the Black Sea from the Aegean. It was only the persuasions of England and Austria which prevented active Russian intervention in the rebellion during its first years.

For once, however, the fate of nations was not resolved by politicians and statesmen alone. The efforts of the Greeks to throw off the centuries-old domination of the Moslem Turk caught the imagination of Europe. The atrocities perpetrated by the Greeks on thousands of Moslems were either glossed over or forgotten; reports received and beliefs held in Europe regarding the nature and conduct of the rebellion were often so distorted and exaggerated that they bore little relation to the truth. The fact remained that strong sympathies were entertained on all sides for the struggling Greeks and their cause. During the first years, although no decisive result was achieved, there was a strong belief in Europe that the Greeks would eventually prevail, and that a settlement would be reached according the Greeks a measure of freedom and independence perhaps on the lines of the Danubian Principalities. Proposals to this effect had at one time been suggested to the Porte, but were indignantly rejected. At any rate Europe was prepared to wait and watch as long as the struggle promised a fair prospect of success for the rebels.

The situation was, of course, completely changed by the arrival of Ibrahim Pasha and his armies in the Morea. The Egyptian hammer-blows, the continuous succession of reverses suffered by the Greeks, culminating in the storming of Missolonghi and the capture of Athens by Rashid Pasha, the reports of the mass-exterminations of the native population of the Morea by Ibrahim, and the shipping of thousands of slaves to Alexandria; all these factors combined to arouse the indignation and sympathy of Europe. Even Canning was obliged to bow to public opinion by recognising the rebellion. The British Ambassador at Constantinople was authorised to enter into relations with the Greek Government. To prevent the utter annihilation of a Christian nation became an urgent necessity requiring prompt and vigorous action.

The fate of the Greeks lay not so much in the hands of the Sultan and the Porte as in those of his powerful vassal, Mohammed Ali. It was the ordered legions of his son Ibrahim which were crushing the spirit and strength of the Greeks, and it was not therefore unnatural that a certain amount of pressure and persuasion was exercised on him by the European consuls. It is clear that Mohammed Ali's ultimate ambitions had by this time taken shape in his mind, although he took pains not to voice them too openly. The severance of Egypt from the body of the Empire, the recognition by the world of the independence of Egypt with himself as sovereign and creator of a new empire in the Near East, powerful and progressive – these were the dreams that haunted him. Every twist and turn in the political labyrinth of the Near East he was ready to exploit in the pursuit of this cherished aim. Had it not been for external factors, there is little doubt that he could have achieved his objectives without difficulty, for the Porte alone could never have found sufficient strength to dispute successfully a unilateral declaration of independence on the part of Mohammed Ali. But dominating the relations of Egypt with the Porte was the power of England whose policy was to tolerate no action which would result in a weakening of the Ottoman Empire. A trial of strength with the Porte necessarily implied a trial of strength with England's naval power, and from this Mohammed Ali wisely shrank.

The situation created by the Greek rebellion and Ibrahim's successes disposed Mohammed Ali to bargain in the furtherance of his own ends. In 1826 the British Ambassador at Constantinople, seeking a peaceful solution to the impasse, suggested to Salt, the British Consul General in Egypt, that a share of the tribute from the Greeks and a *pashalik* for Ibrahim in Syria might be more advantageous to Mohammed Ali than wasting his strength in the Morea.[3] But the Pasha was not to be side-tracked. One word from England that she was prepared to acknowledge Egyptian independence was all he required to induce him to withdraw his armies from Greece, but this was not forthcoming.

Entreaties were urged before the Pasha by an Austrian emissary, Prokesch-Osten, to pursue with even more vigour the prosecution of the war against the Greeks, and so resolve the question once and for all. The Sultan too, haunted by this rebellion which seemed to have no end and which threatened such profound repercussions, sent a special emissary to Egypt to spur Mohammed Ali to further efforts and to bring new firmans entrusting him with sole conduct of the war.

New preparations were already in hand in the dockyards of Alexandria, but the Pasha was unwilling to launch them while there remained a hope that a favourable proposal might emanate from England. Thus the first half of 1827 was occupied with fruitless and inconclusive negotiation, and the Sultan's urgent demands upon his vassal could no longer be legitimately ignored. In August the Egyptian fleet once more put to sea for the Morea. Had it waited until two days later when a British envoy arrived, a calamity might have been averted. The new arrival, Major Cradock, was sent to advise the Viceroy that the Powers were decided to intervene and bring the strife in Greece to an end, and that the Turks might expect no support from Europe. In the discussions that ensued, Cradock expressed his private opinion that England might be prepared to recognise Egyptian independence if Mohammed Ali could establish it, provided that he offered no resistance to the solution of the Greek question.[4] But the discussions came too late; the Egyptian fleet was already on its way to its doom.

In Europe the Powers were endeavouring to grapple with the Greek problem. For some years Metternich had succeeded in preventing any Russian intervention in Greece, but the death of Tsar Alexander in December 1825 and the succession of Nicholas I had altered the situation. In March 1826 Canning sent the Duke of Wellington to St Petersburg to effect a rapprochement with Russia with a view to joint action in settling the affairs of Greece. British policy was complicated and difficult of execution. On the one hand wishing to maintain amicable relations with the Porte, at the same time she desired to see the Greeks established in some form of independence under the nominal suzerainty of the Sultan. The results of these discussions, which became known as the Protocol of St Petersburg, and in which France was induced to associate herself, were presented to the Porte in April 1827. The Grand Vizir indignantly rejected the terms which would give the European Powers the right to interfere in what the Porte held to be an internal affair of the Empire. Thereupon the Powers in July 1827 converted the Protocol into the Treaty of London which 'bound themselves to secure the autonomy of Greece under the suzerainty of the Sultan, but without breaking off friendly relations with the Porte.'[5]

The method of operation which commended itself to the contracting parties was the despatch of a joint naval task force to the Morea with the object of blockading Ibrahim Pasha and starving him into voluntary withdrawal. It was hoped that these ends would be accomplished without the employment of actual force, but that the demonstration would be sufficient evidence of what was intended. Unfortunately such hopes were destined not to be fulfilled.

It is unnecessary to dwell in detail upon the events which led up to the final crisis. Admiral Codrington, commanding the British squadron, was able to inform the Turkish Admiral of the contents of the Treaty of London and the decision of the Powers in September 1827. On the 25th a conference was held at Navarino between Codrington, de Rigny the French naval commander, and Ibrahim Pasha. The latter refused to submit to the terms offered without the authority of the Sublime Porte, but agreed to a form of truce until instructions arrived. As it turned out, this agreement was not honoured, for the Greeks, considering that the Turks had not bound themselves to a cessation of hostilities, deemed themselves free to continue the struggle. In consequence a number of minor actions took place on land and sea during the ensuing month. In October Ibrahim received instructions from Constantinople to continue the war, whereupon the Allied admirals decided to put more pressure on him.

On 20 October Codrington led the combined squadrons of England, France and Russia into the harbour of Navarino where the Turkish and Egyptian fleets were moored. This manoeuvre was intended to be merely a demonstration of Allied strength and determination to enforce the terms imposed upon the Porte. It was too much perhaps to expect that peace could be maintained between the opposing forces in such close proximity. Accounts vary as to the sequence of incidents which led to the clash, but undoubtedly mutual distrust of each other's intentions produced a tense situation, and an action became almost inevitable. Musketry fire led to cannon and an unpremeditated sea-battle flared up. The Turkish and Egyptian gunners were no match for their British and Allied counterparts and by midnight both the Turkish and the Egyptian fleets had disintegrated into masses of floating wreckage on the placid waters of Navarino harbour. Ibrahim Pasha, on shore with the Egyptian army, was compelled to witness the total annihilation of the navy which his father had built up at the cost of so much labour and treasure.

The battle of Navarino as a naval action had no significance; but in international politics its repercussions were far-reaching and resulted in the end of the long-drawn-out struggle. The news of the action was greeted at Constantinople with an outburst of bitter resentment and violent denunciation against the Powers for a wanton act of aggression. An apology and compensation for the death of six thousand Ottoman subjects was demanded. Both were refused by the Powers who thereupon withdrew their ambassadors from Constantinople. The vacillating British cabinet of Lord Goderich who had succeeded Canning on his death in August 1827 were much embarrassed by the action at Navarino, since their policy had ever been to interpose only peaceful and friendly intervention between the Sultan and his subjects and at all costs to maintain amicable relations with the Porte. Codrington's action had completely shattered the fabric of Anglo-Turkish relations, and England retired huffily for the present from the Eastern Question, leaving Russia, and her greatest rival, to resolve the affair finally, In its denunciations the Porte had likewise accused Russia of aggression and had denounced the recently signed Treaty of Akkerman as null and void. This was avidly seized upon by the Tsar as a pretext for declaring war on Turkey; the waiting Russian armies were launched into the Danubian Principalities, and did not halt until they were in sight of the Sultan's capital. The Treaty of Adrianople forced upon the humiliated Sultan finally brought the Greek war of independence to an end in 1828.

The battle of Navarino, though it left Ibrahim, as it were, high and dry without means of support or reinforcement from Alexandria, did not disconcert him overmuch. There is even reason for believing that the destruction of the fleets came as a slight measure of relief to him, as it left him free to follow his own inclinations on land. He still had his army which was strong enough to keep his *pashalik* in subjection and for the present at any rate the Allies were powerless to touch him. Left to himself Ibrahim would undoubtedly have carried on the war with his customary vigour. But Mohammed Ali realised that as far as he was concerned the game was played out. The loss of his fleet at Navarino must have come as a bitter blow to him, but he bore it with fortitude and composure. He merely drew from the disaster the conclusion that it was useless to continue the struggle in Greece in face of the combined might of England, France and Russia and as evidence of his intention to withdraw he reassured the British Consul that British subjects in Egypt should suffer no hurt.[6] He ordered Ibrahim to stay his hand in the Morea and await further instructions.

In the middle of 1828 Russia, not unwilling to create a favourable diversion on Turkey's southern flank, agreed to a French expedition into the Morea with the intention of forcing Ibrahim to evacuate entirely. But before a collision could take place, Admiral Codrington hastened to Alexandria, and there on 9 August 1828 persuaded Mohammed Ali to sign a convention by which he agreed to withdraw his armies from Greece. On 3 October Ibrahim packed the remains of his forces on board ship and sailed home. As far as he and Egypt were concerned the war of Greek independence was over.

Mohammed Ali's incursion into Europe was an untoward step in his career, yet it is difficult to see how he could have avoided it. He was not yet ready to defy the Sultan and he could not therefore fail to heed the pressing demands made upon him. In any case he had no reason to anticipate the turn that events would take. Up to the time of Ibrahim's arrival in Greece Europe had taken no active interest in the Greek rebellion, and the affair might reasonably have turned out well for the Turks and the Egyptians. It was, in fact, impossible to foresee and take into account all the factors. It only remained to accept the consequences with as much grace and fortitude as possible. His expenditure and his losses had been great; his fleet lay in the harbour of Navarino, a mass of wreckage; thousands of his soldiers lay dead in the ditches of Missolonghi and other parts of the peninsula; those who returned home are reported to have been in the most pitiable condition. But so far his greatest loss was the fact that his intervention in Greece had deprived him of any possibility of a rapprochement with England without whose support or acquiescence he could not hope to fulfil his ultimate ambition – independence from the Porte.

CHAPTER 6

Syria Won

Mohammed Ali welcomed the enforced withdrawal of Ibrahim and his armies from Greece. Nothing had been gained from the campaign; on the contrary, he had poured out vast sums to finance it, many of his soldiers had been killed, and he had lost the major part of his fleet at Navarino. As a reward for his assistance in the Greek affair the Sultan had promised him the Pashalik of Crete which was bestowed in 1822, that of the Morea which was now of course lost, and those of Syria and Damascus which were the prizes he most coveted. But Sultan Mahmud had lost nothing of his hatred for his powerful vassal, envying him his great wealth and influence and fearing him as a threat to himself. The Sultan also considered that Mohammed Ali had betrayed him by withdrawing his troops from Greece at the critical moment and had thus assisted in a partial dismemberment of the Empire.

In Alexandria Mohammed Ali was fully conscious of his sovereign's attitude towards him and not a little apprehensive, especially as his old enemy Khusrev Pasha whom he had ousted from Egypt in earlier years was now Grand Vizir and was urging His Majesty to have done once and for all with the rebel in Egypt. It did not require much foresight to realise that the Sultan would take the first opportunity of driving him out of Egypt. Nor was Mohammed Ali the type of man to wait idly for events to shape their course; if there was to be a struggle between the Sultan and himself, he was resolved that it should take place on his own terms and in circumstances favourable to himself. For some time he had vainly awaited the arrival of the firmans investing him with the promised *pashaliks* of Syria, and it was clear that these were not likely to materialise unless pressure was exerted on the Sultan. In short he decided that what the Sultan would not voluntarily bestow he would take by force.

Without further delay he invaded Syria in November 1831. He had

81

already, once again, been requested by the Sultan to supply forces to assist in subduing a rebellion in Rumelia, and this provided him with a cloak for his military preparations. But when he was informed that this assistance was no longer required, he announced that he had some scores to settle with Abdullah, Pasha of Acre, and that unless the Porte was prepared to intervene on his behalf he would himself send a punitive expedition. It appears that during his reorganisation of Egypt and the establishment of his monopolies, his land expropriations and military conscriptions, many of the *fellahin* had stolen away and sought asylum in Syria; they had begged the protection of Abdullah and had been welcomed. Mohammed Ali made repeated demands for the return of these fugitives and for the settlement of other differences, and had even at various times approached the Sultan for his intervention. Whatever attitude the Sultan held in regard to the dispute, he was not in any case likely to intervene on behalf of his most formidable vassal and potential enemy.

The preparations for the offensive were somewhat delayed by an epidemic of cholera which broke out in Egypt during 1831, but in October all was complete. A force of about eleven thousand marched across the Sinai Peninsula, while Ibrahim Pasha, again in command, sailed from Alexandria, effecting a junction with the land forces at Jaffa, and the investment of Acre was begun. This ancient stronghold had been the scene of many a struggle and many a siege, and was one of the most strongly fortified garrisons of the Empire. It will be recalled that it had baffled Napoleon Bonaparte who had invested it for months without success. To Ibrahim, though assisted by his fleet and supported by short lines of supply, it presented no less an obstacle and held up his advance for several months.

News of the offensive into Syria created much stir at Constantinople. The Sultan's envoy at Alexandria brushed aside Mohammed Ali's innocent pleas that he was merely chastising Abdullah and asked him what were his real intentions.

'To keep what I have,' he replied; 'and let me explain to you my policy and my views, in a few words. In a few days Acre will be mine. If the Sultan consents that I should keep it, I will stop there; if not I will take Damascus. There again, if Damascus be granted to me, I will stop; but if not I will take Aleppo; and if the Sultan will not then consent - who knows? Allah Kerim! - God is merciful.'[1]

Here indeed was an unvarnished declaration of rebellion and a challenge to the Sultan. At the Porte there were some who counselled His Majesty to bury the hatchet and come to terms with Mohammed Ali - who was only demanding what he had been previously promised - so that the Empire could present a united front to the encroachment of Europe. But in face of Mohammed Ali's insolent declaration, the Sultan brushed these arguments aside. The struggle which had been fermenting for many years broke into flame.

Hampered by insurrections and troubles in Albania and Bosnia, the Sultan was, during the early months of the invasion, unable to pose any effective resistance to Ibrahim's advance into Syria, and it was not until April 1832 that a force was mustered and set off from Constantinople. This was followed immediately by a proclamation denouncing Mohammed Ali and dismissing him from his offices. The names of Mohammed Ali and Ibrahim were both omitted from the list of Pashas of the Empire published annually at the feast of Bairam.[2] If Mohammed Ali were to maintain himself in power, he must rely on his own strength in face of the combined power of the Ottoman Empire. These proclamations indeed made their mark in Egypt itself which, tyrannised as it was by the relentless Pasha, would have done much to throw off his yoke. But he held his domain in an iron grip, and a few well-chosen and publicised executions were sufficient to quell incipient revolt at home.

Abroad Mohammed Ali was not without allies or sympathisers. Syria had always been a favourite field for extortion by the Turkish *pashas*, and the inhabitants saw in Egypt an apparently powerful and prosperous state and in its Pasha an enlightened and tolerant ruler. Certainly the religious freedom and toleration afforded to Christians in Egypt by Mohammed Ali produced a very favourable impression on large numbers of powerful and wealthy Christians in Syria, and the possible transfer of their land to him was not an altogether unattractive proposition. The result was that much of the resistance which might have met the arrival of a foreign invader was not forthcoming.

In the meantime Ibrahim was meeting with great difficulties in his efforts to capture the fortress of Acre. Whatever may have been the faults of Abdullah, he was a resolute and vigorous commander and every attempt on the part of the Egyptians to carry the fort was beaten off with heavy loss. Ibrahim finally left part of his force to press the siege, while he himself with the remainder proceeded north to face a Turkish army of some twelve thousand troops under Osman Pasha which was on its way. For some reason unknown, news of Ibrahim's approach filled Osman with panic. Deserting his army, his baggage and guns, he took to flight while his army scattered throughout the country - all this without a shot being fired. 'So extraordinary a circumstance unverified by weighty testimony, would unquestionably appear incredible; but the Sultan, with lamentable imprudence, confirmed the charge of cowardice against his general by depriving him of his rank, and ordering him to retire to Amasia . . .'[3] This precipitate flight filled the Egyptians with elation and confidence in their invincibility. It must be said, however, that the Turks, feeling their honour touched, rallied at Homs and turned to give battle but without success. Ibrahim easily put them to flight.

As long as Acre remained untaken in his rear Ibrahim dared to make no further advances. The fortress must be taken as a prelude to further operations. Accordingly he turned southwards once more to press the siege. In Constantinople where Ibrahim's recent achievements had caused consternation, this retrograde movement was hailed as a defeat and retreat, and even in Egypt the continued resistance of Acre had caused a certain amount of misgiving and unrest which Mohammed Ali was obliged to put down with customary vigour. The time had now come to take the fortress.

Ibrahim personally made the plan and supervised the operations, and on 27 May 1832 a combined attack of all his forces culminated in the storming of the stronghold, but not without the bitterest resistance and exceptional gallantry of its defenders. Ibrahim is said to have cut down some of his own officers who had fallen to the rear of the attacking columns.[4]

Abdullah proudly declared, 'I had walls, men and money, with which to defend Acre. When Ibrahim took it the walls had been destroyed; of my 6000 men, 5600 were dead, and of my treasure nothing remained but a few jewels.' He laid with good reason the blame of his defeat upon the Sultan who had done nothing to relieve him. 'The Porte', he said bitterly, 'has the honour of a dancing girl.'[5]

Abdullah was sent to Egypt where he was received with the honour and courtesy due to his rank and conspicuous courage.

On 13 June 1832 Ibrahim followed up his victory by marching on Damascus which, having no means of resistance, sent a deputation to meet him and offered him the city unopposed.

After the capture of Acre the progress of Ibrahim and his armies was that of the invincible conqueror brushing aside all resistance. Leaving Damascus behind, he advanced northwards towards Homs to meet the advance guard of the Turkish forces which had mustered at Hama, a short distance north of Homs, under Mohammed, Pasha of Aleppo. Again Ibrahim inflicted a crushing defeat upon the Turks; his own report of the battle states:

The enemy had 7000 regulars engaged; of these 2000 were killed and as many taken prisoners. Our loss amounts to 102 killed and 162 wounded. Never have I seen such a rout, and I do not hesitate to say that even two or three thousand of such troops would cause me no anxiety. We will beat them, please God, wherever we may find them.[6]

So sudden and complete were the collapse and flight of the Sultan's army that Ibrahim suspected an ambush and refrained from pursuing the fugitives. Had he done so, it is likely that barely any of the Turkish forces would have escaped. This battle took place on 8 July 1932, barely three weeks after the capture of Damascus.

In the meantime the main Turkish forces which, it will be recalled, had left Constantinople under the Commander-in-Chief, Hussein Pasha, had arrived in the neighbourhood of Aleppo. But the townsfolk had manifested such hostility to the Sultan during the war that Hussein considered it dangerous to trust his troops within its walls. The result was that Ibrahim, taking the initiative, hurried his armies to Aleppo by forced marches and entered the town unopposed on 17 July amid the acclamations and rejoicings of the inhabitants. St John, who was in Egypt at the time, reports that 'the Turkish general . . . fearing with his dispirited forces, to encounter the victorious Arabs, fled precipitately, abandoning his camp and artillery, which accordingly became the spoil of the enemy.' Indeed, during his great advance Ibrahim must have been little worried by the problems of supply; the quantity of enemy stores which were abandoned to his possession must have been enormous, while at the same time he was greeted everywhere as liberator from Turkish tyranny and showered with presents. 'The news of the Sultan's army's defeat flew along the coast, and the towns vied with one another in sending deputations to welcome the conqueror.'[7]

Unceasing in his pursuit of the demoralised enemy, Ibrahim set forth immediately from Aleppo and caught up with Hussein Pasha who with the remnants of his forces had occupied the heights above the pass of Beilan near the sea, the gateway into Anatolia and Turkey proper. In the encounter which took place on 27 July the Turks put up a vigorous resistance, but all their efforts failed to stem the charges of the triumphant Egyptians, and in the evening the Turks gave way and fled towards Adana.

Thus, in a phenomenal 'Blitzkrieg' of only eight months' duration, six of which had been occupied in reducing the stubborn fortress of Acre, Ibrahim succeeded in driving the last soldier of the Sultan from Syrian territory and making himself undisputed master of the country. He was undoubtedly assisted to victory by the unsparing efforts of his father who had built up the highly organised and well disciplined fighting machine, to his chief of staff, Soliman Pasha (Colonel Sève) who had shaped the Pasha's armies, and in a certain degree to the past tyrannies in Syria of the Turkish Pashas who were detested by the people. Some mention must also be made of Mohammed Ali's fleet which, although not playing a prominent part in the campaign, gave useful service. The fleet, manned largely by *fellahin* forced into service by the usual press-gang methods, were not sailors by instinct or tradition, and their naval skill was consequently of mediocre quality and no match for the Turkish squadrons. Although proud of his fleet Mohammed Ali was under no delusions about its capabilities, and accordingly instructed its admiral, Osman Pasha, not to seek any decisive engagement with the Turks, but to confine himself to defensive operations and to observing and reporting to Ibrahim enemy troop movements along the Syrian coast.

So long as Mohammed Ali confined his attentions to Syria, his activities were not likely to attract the attentions of the European Powers. All the world knew that he had been promised the *pashaliks* of Syria as a reward for his services in Greece, and none of the powers viewed with concern his efforts to compel His Majesty to fulfil his promises. All the time the campaign had been going on Mohammed Ali had continued to protest his loyalty to the Sultan, affirming that he was merely liberating the Syrian towns from the tyranny of the Pashas, a fiction which deceived no one. For it was generally believed that he was seeking independence for Egypt and himself. He instituted certain measures in Egypt, such as the prohibition of the use of Turkish coinage, to test the reaction of public opinion in Egypt to the idea of regarding him not merely as Viceroy but as monarch. At all events, as far as the Powers of Europe were concerned there had been in Mohammed Ali's Syrian campaign nothing to suggest anything more than an internal dispute in the Ottoman Empire - and such disputes were common - or that the integrity of the Empire itself was threatened. The Turkish Empire was only of interest to Europe in relation to the balance of power, and the policy generally pursued was to maintain the integrity of the Empire so that the balance should not be disturbed. Any incident calculated to upset the status quo would thus have powerful repercussions in the chancelleries of Europe. The policy of the Powers was adequately summed up by M. Guizot, French Foreign Minister in the following words:

L'Angleterre et L'Autriche avaient une idée simple et fixe; elles ne s'inquiétaient que de maintenir l'empire ottoman et de le défendre contres ses ennemis. La

Russie aussi n'avait qu'une idée, moins simple, mais également exclusive et constante; elle voulait maintenir l'empire ottoman sans l'affermir et le dominer en le protégeant . . . Le politique de la France était compliquée et alternative; elle voulait servir à la fois le Sultan et le Pacha, maintenir l'empire ottoman et grandir l'Egypte. La Porte se trouvait en presence de deux alliés veritables d'un protecteur hypocrite et d'un ami dont le coeur était partagé . . .[8]

The result was that the Ottoman Empire became, in effect, a sort of neutral zone which was jealously watched and guarded by the Powers.

The Sultan himself had at first welcomed the opportunity for coming to grips with his powerful vassal in Egypt and expected to effect his complete overthrow. But the wily Pasha had chosen a time when the Sultan's available forces were already engaged in troubles in Albania and Bosnia, so that he had been slow in getting off the mark. Ibrahim's remarkable series of victories over the Turks and the unceasing disasters suffered by the latter threw an altogether different complexion on the situation. Ibrahim had proved that Turkish arms were powerless against Mohammed Ali's military machine. In a sequence of brilliant battles he had overrun Syria and driven the Turkish armies beyond its frontiers. Flushed with victory the Egyptian general stood on the passes of Beilan looking into the heart of the Empire; a few more steps and he would be inside the land of the Osmanlis. Following the instructions of his father to keep on advancing wherever he found himself Ibrahim did not pause to consider unduly the political aspects. As soon as the Turks had been driven off the heights of Beilan, Ibrahim despatched the young Abbas, son of his deceased brother Tussun, to Adana in Turkey itself. Ibrahim descended upon the seaport of Alexandretta and possessed himself of vast quantities of stores which had been landed by the Sultan's fleet for the provisioning of Turkish forces.

It is probable that had Mohammed Ali been directing operations in the field himself, he would have fortified the frontier passes and halted his advance, consolidating what he had already gained, and awaited a permanent settlement with the Porte. For he would have realised that any direct attack on the heart of the Empire and the Sultan himself would bring swift retribution on himself by one or other of the European Powers. But Ibrahim apparently had other views. He believed in acting first and talking afterwards, in presenting the world with a *fait accompli.* Although not lacking in political foresight he did not fully appreciate the results of an invasion of Turkey itself. Moreover he was first a general at the head of an army flushed with success looking across the mountains at a scattering and demoralised enemy.

To him it seemed that with a few more judicious thrusts at the enemy, the Sultan would be overthrown and his father the master of Constantinople and head of the ancient empire of the Osmanlis.

Hussein Pasha, commander of the defeated Turkish army and viceroy designate of Egypt – if he could ever fight his way into that country – abandoned his army and fled after the battle of the Beilan pass, and passes here from our story. Attributing this latest disaster to him Sultan Mahmud dismissed him from his command and replaced him with the Grand Vizir, Mohammed Rashid, Khusrev having now been moved to the Ministry of War. Khusrev was the power behind the throne in all imperial machinations. He it was who controlled the Turkish armies from Constantinople, and he who sacrificed the interests of his master to his own personal ambition. For Khusrev coveted above all else the *pashalik* of Egypt for himself; to overthrow Mohammed Ali who had so bitterly humiliated him thirty years before at Cairo; and to avenge himself by replacing him in the seat of power: these were the secret yearnings of his heart. But the Sultan refused to let him go; he relied too much on the experience and political dexterity of this veteran to let him leave the capital. Khusrev, therefore, in his efforts to obtain command of the army in the field, withheld the reinforcements collected to assist Rashid Pasha to drive Ibrahim out of Turkey.

News of the Egyptian victory at Beilan awoke fresh apprehensions at Constantinople. The Sultan, realising that even his own person was threatened, that his empire was likely to tumble about his ears unless Ibrahim could be stopped, humbled himself to seek outside assistance. His first approach was to the empire's traditional friend and supporter, Great Britain. The British Ambassador at Constantinople, Stratford Canning, reported on 7 August 1832 that he had received overtures from the Porte with a view to a formal alliance. Canning with much foresight approved the proposal since it would prevent any closer relations between the Porte and ambitious Russia, and suggested to Lord Palmerston that a British squadron should be sent to help the Sultan. But Palmerston, not realising the situation in the Levant and considerably underestimating the Egyptian power, rejected the suggestion on the ground that an Anglo-Turkish pact would be regarded by the other Powers as trespass on that carefully guarded neutral zone. As a result of Palmerston's inadequate appreciation of the situation, the Porte was driven into that very alliance which was most abhorrent to England and France. Mahmud was for various reasons loth to seek aid from France, Austria or Russia, but the daily increasing threat of Egyptian arms forced him to grasp at any straw. Now his only hope was Russia from whom he had suffered such humiliation in 1829 at Adrianople and who was moreover only too anxious to set both her feet astride the strategic waterway linking the Black Sea to the Mediterranean. From this last extremity Mahmud recoiled for as long as possible, for the moment putting his trust in his own arms in a final attempt to crush the insurgent Egyptians.

Soon after his victory at Beilan Ibrahim moved on to Adana and there awaited further instructions from his father; the commission he had received was now fulfilled. In the interval he occupied himself with the administration of the vicinity and in inspecting the timber forests which abound in that part of Asia Minor, for here indeed was the very material so much needed by Mohammed Ali for the building of his fleet. But with the news that a Turkish army was mustering and making preparations to advance, Ibrahim deemed it advisable to advance likewise. The road from Adana into the great plains of Antolia lay through the Cicilian Gate, the pass through the mountains which was manned by Turkish troops and fortified with batteries. In October 1832 Ibrahim left Adana and fought his way through the mountains into the great plain. From here to Konia – the ancient Iconium – which lies astride the highway to the Bosporus, his advance was unopposed and he occupied the town without resistance. Indeed, his arrival was heralded by deputations of welcome from the villages around who, bitterly resenting Sultan Mahmud's attempts to introduce European methods into his territories, saw in the victorious Ibrahim, not an invader or despoiler, but a liberator from the despotism of an infidel Khalif.

Contact was first made by advance guards at Akshehr, but Ibrahim, having thoroughly reconnoitred the ground round Konia and exercised his troops there, decided to fight the forthcoming battle on this ground. Rashid Pasha had first received orders to hold his forces in readiness to defend the capital against the Egyptian advance, but later counsels at Constantinople decided the Sultan to take the initiative and attack. Rashid was therefore ordered to advance. But the treachery of Khusrev Pasha, the War Minister, here intervened. Forty-five thousand Bosnian veteran troops had been mustered at Constantinople to reinforce Rashid, but at the last moment Khusrev withheld these and left Rashid to face Ibrahim with the ten thousand regulars and forty thousand irregulars which he had with him, persuading the Sultan that these would be ample for the purpose.[9] Nor did Rashid receive the supplies and rations he had been promised, and his forces were in a pitiable state even before they took the field.

Rashid and Ibrahim were old comrades in arms, having fought side by side at Missolonghi in the Greek War, and it was this which prompted the

Turkish commander to address a letter to Ibrahim recalling their former association, stating that he was only advancing at the express order of the Sultan and begging him to withdraw and thus avoid the effusion of Moslem blood. Ibrahim courteously replied regretting the situation and pointing out that he too was acting under orders from his father, and that neither could therefore be held responsible for bloodshed.[10] On 21 December 1832 battle was given before the town of Konia. The struggle was bitter while it lasted and the Turks, valiantly commanded by the Grand Vizir, bore themselves well, but the issue was not long in doubt. Before the close of the day Rashid Pasha was himself a prisoner and his forces broken and put to flight. The last Turkish resistance barring Ibrahim's advance on Constantinople had disappeared. The road was open and the victors lost no time in taking it. Following the highway across the plains of Asia Minor, Ibrahim made straight for Constantinople, hoping to capture it and depose the Sultan before the European Powers could take action. But at Kutaya, less than a week's march from the capital, a letter reached Ibrahim from his father instructing him imperatively, wherever he might be, to halt his advance. Almost within a stone's throw of his objective Ibrahim was cast down on the rock of international diplomacy.

For soon after the battle of Konia, rumours had filtered through to Alexandria that negotiations were proceeding between the Sublime Porte and Russia on the basis of Russian military aid in case Turkey was unable to stem the invader's advance. General Muravief, the Russian representative, was at Constantinople urging the Sultan to accept the assistance which Russia was eagerly offering. This news cast a profound gloom on Mohammed Ali who well foresaw that the intervention of a European Power spelt disaster to his great hopes. Sultan Muhmud also found himself on the horns of a dilemma and for some time was unable to make up his mind which course to take. Acceptance of Russian assistance would be an open admission to the world of his inability to control his subordinates and maintain his authority. At the same time he would incur the odium of his subjects by admitting the hated Christian and foreigner to the shores of the Bosporus. Thereafter he might never be able to free himself from the Russian clutches. On the other hand every unchecked advance by Ibrahim spelt his own ruin and the fall of the ancient house of Osman. Fear of Russian influence and blind hate of Mohammed Ali were powerful and conflicting emotions in the Sultan's breast.

After various discussions had taken place at Constantinople General Muravief himself went to Alexandria to urge Mohammed Ali to call off the

Egyptian advance and make peace with the Sultan. He arrived on 13 January 1833. In his conversations with the Pasha he intimated that Russia could not view with indifference the fall of the Ottoman Empire and that if such were threatened, Russia would be moved to prevent it. Whether or not the Pasha took these warnings seriously to heart, he was no less unremitting in calling up fresh conscripts for his army and collecting in the taxes. Barely a week after Muravief's arrival, Halil Pasha, envoy of the Porte, came to see Mohammed Ali on a similar mission. An amusing description of the ceremony which attended the arrival of the Turkish envoy is given by Barker.

> On reaching the palace at the foot of the flight of stairs, Haleel Pasha was assisted by two officers of the Viceroy . . . each supporting an arm, as he advanced to ascend the steps. The Viceroy descended at the same time, and they met nearly in the middle, Haleel Pasha continually entreating His Highness not to descend. On meeting Haleel Pasha attempted to seize the Viceroy's hand with the intention of carrying it to his lips, but the Viceroy prevented him by embracing him and kissing him on the cheek, but Haleel Pasha succeeded in imprinting a kiss on the hand of His Highness. They then made their way . . . to the Hall of Audience, the Viceroy's right hand being locked in the right hand of Haleel Pasha who had his other arm around the waist of His Highness.

Mohammed Ali was thus still putting up every outward appearance of loyalty and submission. As nothing tangible resulted from these various missions to Egypt, and all the time the distance between Ibrahim and Constantinople was decreasing, the Sultan was finally forced to a decision. Early in February a formal application was made by the Porte to Russia for assistance. Thus the contingency which Britain had been so anxious to avoid came to pass: Russian forces were on their way to Constantinople.

This latest political alliance produced startling effects in London and Paris, both Governments frantically endeavouring to undo the damage to their position *vis-à-vis* the Porte which their own remissness had brought about. In justice to the Sultan it must be admitted that the fault for this shift in alliance was not his. Some time previously he had approached the British Government for assistance and Palmerston had refused. In face of imminent danger from Ibrahim's armies, all that Britain and France had offered was words of advice. No British ships had appeared in the Mediterranean to scatter Mohammed Ali's fleet, no British or French soldier had landed in Syria or Asia Minor to inspire terror in the Pasha's heart, and all the time the Egyptians were advancing. Mahmud had only one other source of support, and if he clung to a serpent, he could not be blamed for it. However, from the British and French point of view the damage was done; the Russians were on their way and a squadron of their ships entered the Bosporus on 20 February, only a few days after the application for assistance was made.

But the arrival of these reinforcements did not inspire terror in the wily Pasha of Egypt. While he recognised that the presence of Russian troops at Constantinople meant the end of his hopes of overthrowing the dynasty of the Osmanlis, at the same time he foresaw that not only would the Russians create an international situation which the other Powers would give much to save, but also that his son Ibrahim was firmly entrenched in Anatolia rallying the inhabitants to his cause, and that it would take considerably more than a few Russian ships and troops to dislodge him and drive him back. Thus Mohammed Ali, though checked, was still in a strong position and he felt he could afford not to be intimidated by Russian threats. His foresight was well rewarded. On the representation of General Muravief he had sent instructions to Ibrahim to pause in his advance, and await developments. The French Ambassador, Admiral Roussain, recently arrived in Constantinople, in concert with the British Ambassador, made representations to the Porte requesting the withdrawal of the application for Russian aid, and engaged himself, if the Porte would agree to this course, to bring Mohammed Ali to terms. The Porte, with a turn of political dexterity, took advantage of Roussain's relative ignorance of the position by agreeing to this proposal, provided that Mohammed Ali would accept the districts of Acre, Nablus, Jerusalem and Tripoli, which for the purposes of this negotiation were magnified into *pashaliks*.

The terms of this proposal were embodied in a letter dated 22 February 1833, addressed by Admiral Roussain to Mohammed Ali, pointing out the danger to peace occasioned by the presence of Russian troops both to the empire and to Europe, and advised the Pasha to accept the terms to which France had pledged herself, i.e. acceptance of the above-named districts. A similar missive and warning was sent to Ibrahim camped in the vicinity of Kutuya. Mohammed Ali's reply was admirable and characteristic. In it he poured forth his bitterness at this apparent betrayal by France who had always called herself his friend; he recounted the injustice of being asked to give up everything he had fought for and won, and ended on a note of defiance:

But I feel confident that France and England will not deny me justice. They will acknowledge my rights. Their honour is opposed to this step. But if I am unhappily deceived in this expectation, I will submit myself, under such circumstances, to the will of God; and preferring an honourable death to ignominy, joyfully devote myself to the cause of my nation, happy to consecrate to it the last breath of my life . . .

This letter was followed up by further representations to Britain and France that their aims were, in fact, identical, the maintenance of the Ottoman Empire and the expulsion of the Russians, but that the Ottoman Government was effete and exhausted, and that Sultan Mahmud had proved himself unfit to rule. These arguments, however, carried little weight in London and Paris. The Empire must be maintained in the status quo.

The Pasha rejected the French demands and insisted on his being granted the *pashaliks* of Syria and Adana, and backed up his demands with the threat that unless they were granted immediately, Ibrahim would be ordered to continue his advance. Under pressure of this threat Britain and France pressed the Sultan to accede to Mohammed Ali and grant his requests. In April the Sultan capitulated and news arrived on 16 April in Alexandria that on condition of the withdrawal of Ibrahim's troops from Turkish territory, the *pashaliks* of Syria, Aleppo and Damascus would be ceded; Adana, however, was excluded. Before this news reached Alexandria, certain developments had taken place to modify the Sultan's views; a further contingent of Russian ships and troops arrived in the Bosporus and the presence of these encouraged Mahmud in the view that the Egyptian threat was substantially diminished. He therefore proposed to the Powers that the offer of Aleppo and Damascus should be withdrawn. But Britain and France, who had been urging Mahmud to make adequate concessions so that the whole problem could be settled and thus deny Russia any excuse for remaining in Turkish territory, refused to re-open the negotiations. On 8 April the Convention of Kutaya was therefore concluded under the terms of which the *pashaliks* of Syria and Adana were handed over to Mohammed Ali, and Ibrahim had perforce to be content with these. Immediately the retreat of the Egyptian army commenced.

True to Ottoman practice the Sultan took this opportunity of revoking his promises by reserving Adana to himself, and when Ibrahim heard of this, he halted his retreat. Finally, on 3 May, the Sultan once more gave way and compromised by investing Ibrahim with the appointment of *Muhassil* or collector of revenue for the province of Adana.[11] This was accepted and the war was over.

These three years were indeed an unhappy period in Ottoman history, for they constituted irrefutable proof of His Majesty's inability to control the affairs of his empire. He suffered the deepest humiliation at the hands of his vassal, lost control of one of the most important areas of his domains, and allowed the Russian infidel a footing on the jealously guarded straits. Mohammed Ali had by his own exertions and those of his son increased his dominions substantially and made himself a power to be reckoned with, not merely by the empire but by the great Powers of Europe. Yet his secret ambitions were still unfulfilled and he was advancing in age. In his heart remained the deep yearning to establish his independence, to make himself a King, with hereditary rights for his descendants over Egypt. No doubt at one time he had hopes of marching on Constantinople and deposing the Sultan, possibly in his own favour, but these ambitions he was forced to swallow. The Powers of Europe had made it clear that they would not tolerate any alteration in the existing political situation. One of Mohammed Ali's most cherished desires was an alliance with, or at least a friendly disposition from, England. However much he was courted by France, he never forgot that in the long run it was the British fleets patrolling the seas which were the ultimate arbiters of the fate of the lands of the eastern Mediterranean. With England as his friend, he felt convinced that he could achieve the independence of Egypt from Constantinople. But Ibrahim in invading Turkey itself had committed a blunder which militated against his father's designs. For his invasion had brought Russian troops to Constantinople, had upset the balance of power and caused endless embarrassment to England. Palmerston never forgave Mohammed Ali for this and thereafter regarded him as a mischievous upstart and source of potential trouble.

A further development arose out of the war which, though not directly relevant to Egypt, is of some interest. As a reward for Russian services in stemming the Egyptian tide, the Porte was obliged to conclude with Russia the Treaty of Unkiar Skelessi in July 1833. Outwardly the Treaty contained no more than agreement between the two countries to render mutual assistance in case of need, but a secret clause pledged the Porte to close the straits to the warships of all nations '*en faveur de la cour impériale de Russie*' in place of rendering other material assistance. This treaty and the secret clause which was allowed to slip out resulted in the alienation of Britain from Russia for some considerable time. Mohammed Ali had indeed cast a dark shadow over the Concert of Europe.

CHAPTER 7

. . . and Lost

It may perhaps be trite to put forward the proposition that he who gives unwillingly gives not at all, but it has a particular application to the relations between the Pasha of Egypt and his imperial overlord. In face of the overwhelming might of Ibrahim and the inexorable pressure of the Western Powers, Sultan Mahmud had been driven to the humiliation of passing into the hands of his worst enemy one of the gems of the Empire, the provinces and *pashaliks* of Syria. His own power was reduced in proportion as that of Mohammed Ali was increased. It cannot therefore be any cause for wonder that the relations between the two potentates were even more embittered than before the Syrian affair, or that the Sultan could be expected to take the first opportunity that offered of depriving his powerful vassal of his newly acquired domains. Mohammed Ali too, in spite of his great new accessions, had little cause for satisfaction from the present arrangements. For one thing, the concessions granted fell far short of his original ambitions. The Powers had confirmed his subordination to the Porte, had reaffirmed in no uncertain terms the inviolability and integrity of the Ottoman Empire with Egypt a mere province, while the new *pashaliks* were granted only on an annual tenure subject to renewal, and could be withdrawn, in theory, by the Sultan at any time he felt himself in a position to enforce his commands. There was no doubt in the Pasha's mind that Sultan Mahmud was nursing these designs and would execute them at the earliest opportunity. The situation may perhaps be best described as a temporary armistice, enforced willy-nilly on both sides by external agencies. The Sultan's breast was filled with hate and the Pasha's with distrust.

Under these circumstances the administration of Syria which fell to Ibrahim Pasha was beset with problems which vitiated its success. Barker, who was succeeded as Consul-General at Alexandria in 1833, returned to his former home in Syria, and as an eye witness gives an insight into the events in that territory. The fundamental policy on which the actions of both Ibrahim and Mohammed Ali were based was the certainty that war between themselves and the Porte would sooner or later flare up again. Syria therefore, not only a fertile and valuable territory but also a buffer between Turkey and Egypt, warranted the most active measures of defence. Guns were to take considerable precedence over butter. The Syrian population, though inured from time immemorial to exactions and oppression from the Turkish *pashas*, yet had still been left to enjoy more butter than Ihrahim was to allow them. Military defence was the Pasha's principal preoccupation and he allowed nothing to divert him from his purpose.

Within a short time Syria became a land of barracks and military training establishments; the principal towns became garrison areas and defended localities. 'Indeed there were no towns in Syria or Adana of any importance where he did not build barracks or military hospitals.'[1] The military occupation of their territory was not a cause of overwhelming concern to the native Syrians. Like other provinces of the Empire they were accustomed to the presence of Turkish troops, and they accepted the concomitant levy of contributions as inevitable. But they were filled with horror and consternation when it became known that Ibrahim had decided to swell his ranks with Syrians themselves. Not only was Syria to be defended against the Turk, but Syrians were to be forced to defend it themselves under the Egyptian banner. To the Syrian, military service was a fate worse than death.

The methods of conscription in Syria resembled closely those employed in Egypt of which some mention has already been made:

> Youths were seized in the middle of the night and drafted into the regiments; some sent to Egypt or to the Hedjaz to supply the constant waste of men carried off by war and disease . . . When a youth entered the ranks, his relations looked upon him as dead, for entering the hospital was fearful odds. As the value of exemption was great, the price paid for it was also great, and many of the men in office received large sums for the favouring of exemption or invaliding of recruits.[2]

The heavy drain on manpower from what was essentially an agricultural country had inevitable repercussions on its economic condition. Large tracts of land formerly productive of great wealth fell into disuse from a shortage of labour. To this evil was added the aggravation of excessive taxation, the penalty for the maintenance of a large standing army. The prosperous and indolent Syrians who but a short time before had welcomed Ibrahim as their liberator from the heavy hands of the Turk, now began to groan under their new master.

In Syria there existed a larger proportion of Christians than elsewhere east of the Bosporus. Although the Moslems were dominant in power and number, the disparity was not so great that the followers of the Crescent could ignore those of the Cross. Fanaticism was far more rife than in any other part of the Empire, and the Moslems had always relied upon their *pashas* to ensure the dominance of the Faithful over the Christian *rayahs*, and the latter had been kept in subservience. But Ibrahim Pasha, following in his father's footsteps, insisted on religious toleration and freedom from persecution in his *pashalik*, a boon much appreciated by the *rayahs* but bitterly criticised by every staunch Moslem who cursed Ibrahim for a heretic an eater of pork and drinker of wine.

In all the years of his governorship Ibrahim never completely succeeded in pacifying his territories. In the hinterland the Druses and Beduin continued their raids on the settled communities of the fertile agricultural areas, and campaigns and punitive expeditions were incessant. It has been suggested, and there is little reason to doubt, that these revolts and the unrest which subsequently pervaded Syria were instigated by the Sultan and his emissaries who were only too happy to witness any embarrassments which attended Mohammed Ali and his followers.

By 1834 the unrest which had steadily been increasing through the various causes enumerated above produced widespread revolts against Ibrahim's military rule. All the principal towns of Syria in turn defied him, and so hard pressed was he that Mohammed Ali was himself obliged to come to his son's assistance.[3] Although his authority was restored, the revolts were symptomatic of the condition of the country. Sultan Mahmud was only with difficulty restrained from openly coming to the aid of his rebellious subjects in Syria.

Ibrahim was never the same able and subtle administrator as his father. He lacked the finesse, the understanding of the motives which direct human action; he had only one answer to all problems, the mailed fist. However, it must be said in justice to him that he was the victim of circumstance. The security of his *pashalik* was tenuous. Across the border in Turkey proper it was common knowledge that Sultan Mahmud was making all preparations to re-open the war and win back the prizes he had lost at the Convention of Kutaya; all Ibrahim could do was make like preparations in Syria.

That the Sultan and his mentor, Khusrev Pasha, would resume hostilities as soon as the time was propitious was daily becoming only too clear, and Mahmud made no secret of his hatred for Mohammed Ali. Khusrev too had never forgiven or forgotten the humiliation of 1803 or the abject surrender of the Porte in 1832 to the arms of Ibrahim and his victorious Egyptians. At the door of Mohammed Ali the Sultan could with reason lay much of his unpopularity with his own subjects, for the Pasha had literally forced the Porte into the waiting arms of Russia and had brought the hated infidel to the shores of the Bosporus. For this and other reasons the Sultan found himself much disliked and distrusted by his own people, nominal head of a vast empire, but in reality a puppet in the hands of the Empire's traditional enemy. Every event during the ensuing years tended to aggravate the strain between the two opponents. When Mohammed Ali perceived the active preparations taking place in Anatolia which could only be directed against himself, he refused to pay the tribute, deeming it folly to pour out money which would only be used against him. This question was temporarily patched up in 1834 but no arrears were paid.

Abroad, the situation *vis-à-vis* Egypt and Turkey was viewed with increasing concern. Russia, by her *coup de main* in 1833, had secured her predominance over all the other Powers at Constantinople and the Tsar's Ambassador was the only foreign dignitary to attend the Sultan's councils. The Tsar, anxious to profit from his position to the best advantage, was unwilling to see a resurgence of hostilities between Turkey and Egypt which would undoubtedly produce strong reactions from France and England, the outcome of which was uncertain. In October 1833 a convention was signed at Munchengratz between Russia, Austria and Prussia by which all three Powers agreed to the maintenance of the integrity of the Ottoman Empire. Had the terms of this convention been published and communicated to London and Paris, much distrust and suspicion would have been eliminated, but for reasons of his own the Tsar preferred to shroud the agreement in secrecy, and the contents remained unknown to the Foreign Office in London. Palmerston was in consequence left with the suspicion that Russia was still bent on the dissolution of the Ottoman Empire with consequent gains to herself.

The events of the first Syrian war and its outcome, the convention of Kutaya and the hateful Treaty of Unkiar Skelessi had come as a shock to Palmerston. At one blow a barbaric Egyptian *pasha* had shattered the whole edifice of his laboriously built diplomacy. He had brought about the very circumstance that Palmerston had done his utmost to circumvent, the planting of Russian boots on the shores of the Bosporus. Mohammed Ali in fact had become a most disturbing factor in the harmony of European relationships. To him could fairly be attributed the rupture in the European Concert, the humiliation of the Sultan and above all the predominance of Russian influence at Constantinople. Palmerston thus had no cause to look on Mohammed Ali with favour. These sentiments were nourished by reports received from the various consular officials stationed in the Levant. For these, in addition to their consular status, were generally merchants and traders on their own account, and sometimes were not unduly scrupulous in using their official positions to serve their own interests, and it was quite the norm to sell the protection afforded by the capitulations to any native or Levantine who had the means to pay, by granting them European status and thus defrauding the Egyptian and Syrian authorities of their revenues. In like manner it was not unknown for the consuls to cover their friends' merchandise from taxation by issuing certificates declaring it to be for their own personal use and therefore exempt from duty. The system of government monopolies which was introduced by Ibrahim in Syria on the same pattern as that existing in Egypt smote the merchants in their tenderest spot – their pockets. All the lucrative enterprises and commissions in which they had been indulging were swept away. The official consular reports from the Levant which poured into the Foreign Office were all coloured with grievance or hostility towards Ibrahim and Mohammed Ali. Pictures were frequently painted of shocking conditions existing in Egypt and Syria, the results of tyranny and extortion, much of which had little foundation in fact. Every report which predisposed Palmerston to believe that Mohammed Ali was a barbarian tyrant and his innovations and reconstructions a sham were welcomed, for they accorded with his own sentiments.

From the British point of view much damage had resulted from the outcome of the Syrian war, and Palmerston felt it his duty at all costs to nullify if possible or at least minimise the Treaty of Unkiar Skelessi. Resumption of the war between Egypt and Turkey would be unpleasant for Britain, for there could be little doubt about the outcome of such a clash. In spite of the Sultan's militant preparations and the reorganisation of his armies under Prussian Officers, Ibrahim Pasha could be expected to scatter the Turks and march once more on Constantinople. The Russians would come hurrying back to the Bosporus and preside over the dissolution of the empire. Such was Palmerston's summing up of the situation. Thus the maintenance of peace in the Levant and the curbing of the Pasha of Egypt and of the Sultan assumed paramount importance at the Foreign Office.

In France however the situation was viewed in a different light. She had no special interest in the maintenance of the Ottoman Empire in the status quo and had even detached Algiers from it. Even after the expulsion of Bonaparte's army from Egypt in 1801 she had not ceased to interest herself in that country and even hoped to acquire an ascendant influence in the Pasha's divan, especially over England. France in fact arrogated to herself the role of benign protector of Mohammed Ali and mediator between him and the Porte.

> L'Egypte . . . est devenue l'une des fantaisies populaires de la France; nous avons eu à coeur ses destinées; et le nouveau maître [Mohammed Ali] . . . qui la gouvernait alors avec éclat en se tournant vers nous, a été pour nous, un allié natural que nous avons soutenu par penchant et entraînement bien plus que par reflexion et intérêt.[4]

Resentment and humiliation burned deep in Sultan Mahmud's heart. *'"Que m'importe l'empire," s'écriait-il un jour, 'que m'importe Constantinople? Je donnerais Constantinople et l'empire à celui qui m'apporterait la tête de Mehemit Ali."'* The Turkish fleet was re-equipped and the army reorganised by Moltke and other Prussian officers. Preparations for war were going on so openly that the Powers were moved to dissuade the Sultan from disturbing the peace. Russia warned him that he could expect no assistance if he were the aggressor in a new war, while France and England jointly stated that they would take no steps to save him from his own folly.[5] For a few uneasy years the peace was maintained. Even so, affairs nearly came to a head in 1835 when the Turkish fleet made for Rhodes and the Syrian revolts were flaring up. Only an insurrection in Albania – which may well have been fanned into flame by Mohammed Ali's intrigues – prevented Sultan Mahmud from committing his forces to another war with his vassal.

The cold war continued up to the year 1838, each party in his own fashion manoeuvring for position, while the rising pressure of events tended to precipitate a crisis. As has already been noted, the system of monopolies enforced by Mohammed Ali had been the cause of much bitterness and querulousness on the part of the foreign traders. The Powers, with Britain taking the lead, were pressing the Sultan to agree to a commercial treaty which would abolish all monopolies in the empire. Such a treaty was actually signed in August 1838. Again, the troubles of Syria were fully occupying Ibrahim, and the tide of fortune was slowly turning against the Pasha of Egypt. Under the circumstances he thought it time to bring the differences to a head while he was still in a position to master the situation.

In May 1838 he therefore assembled the principal consuls-general and announced his intention of declaring his independence of the Porte. As reasons for this proposal, he adduced the peril in which his family would stand after his death and the fact that the country would revert once again to Turkish pashadom with all its concomitant evils, and that all his labours, developments and reforms in Egypt would be swept away once he was gone. No fair critic could quarrel with the justice of these views. The object of this announcement was clear. Before any decisive action could be taken, it was necessary to ascertain the attitude of the Powers. Of England's attitude there could be little doubt, but France, the self-appointed mentor and protector of Mohammed Ali, might be a counter-balancing weight. But such hopes as the Pasha had of this were disappointed; both consuls were instructed to press him to desist from such a course. France however let it be known that she would not oppose any amicable arrangement that Mohammed Ali and the Sultan might make for the future.

But Sultan Mahmud was in no frame of mind to make any bargains or compromises. For years he had suffered humiliation and defeat at the hands of his own viceroy; he was suffering from a fatal disease and he was resolved to put all to the test of fortune in a final attempt to annihilate his enemy before he threw off his earthly fetters. He had already in 1838 ordered the Viceroy to dismantle his fleet and reduce his army as being a threat to the empire. Mohammed Ali had of course refused and had stated that he would no longer pay the tribute.

In April 1839 the Sultan ordered his forces to advance into Syria. The army, supposedly well disciplined and equipped to the number of some seventy thousand under the command of Hafiz Pasha, crossed the River Euphrates at Bir into enemy territory. This aggression came as a relief to Mohammed Ali. Throughout the long years of tension he had conducted himself with scrupulous regard so that none could say he had provoked the conflict. The Sultan had committed himself against the advice of the Powers, and none could blame the Viceroy if he defended himself. Even so he enjoined Ibrahim Pasha to be on the alert, but to make no offensive move against the Turks. Ibrahim therefore concentrated his forces at Aleppo and awaited events.

These developments created much stir in the capitals of Europe where it seemed that a new Eastern crisis was boiling up. The diplomats were active on all sides according to the policies of their respective governments, but all together urged a withdrawal on both sides so that an actual clash of arms might be averted. Two months thus passed with both armies stationary, but poised for battle. During this interval Hafiz Pasha did not hesitate to attempt to stir up insurrection in Ibrahim's rear, while the latter was intriguing with the enemy officers. On 25 June 1839 Ibrahim Pasha, feeling himself in danger, attacked the Turks at Nezib. The result was Ibrahim's last and greatest victory.

> The Sultan's forces were completely routed, losing 10,000 prisoners, 15,000 muskets, 104 cannon, besides stores and provisions. Hafiz Pasha made no attempt to rally his forces; the confusion and scamper was disgraceful, justifying the reports of corruption . . . The Turks in this case were more numerous, better equipped and better provisioned than the Egyptians who were very short in this latter respect, some of the soldiers not having eaten anything for twenty-four hours. The quantity of rich silver furniture, gilt trappings, and articles of luxury brought into Aleppo after the battle showed that the Sultan's troops had been well provided with everything.[6]

For the second time in a decade the road to Constantinople lay open and undefended to the victorious Egyptians, but beyond manning the passes Ibrahim paused and awaited his father's instructions.

The luckless Mahmud was happily destined never to learn of the disaster which had befallen him. On 30 June, cursing Mohammed Ali and Ibrahim, cursing his counsellors who had so ill served him, he died leaving the throne of the Empire to the sixteen-year-old Abdul Mejid. Hotfoot on these events befell an even greater disaster. On 13 July Ahmet Fevzy Pasha, commanding the Turkish fleet, sailed off to Alexandria and delivered it complete into the hands of Mohammed Ali. Stripped of almost every means of defence the Empire seemed to lie at the mercy of the Pasha of Egypt.

Under the circumstances the Porte, now no longer dominated by the ungovernable passion of Mahmud, decided to send peace feelers to Mohammed Ali. Khusrev Pasha, again Grand Vizir, was authorised to communicate with him that the new Sultan was willing to forgive him all his sins, to bestow new honours and confer the hereditary *pashalik* of Egypt upon him and his heirs, and furthermore to grant the *pashalik* of Syria to Ibrahim until Mohammed Ali's death. Altogether it was a very handsome offer and one which Mohammed Ali was at least disposed to regard as a basis for negotiation. He hoped however to secure Syria as a hereditary *pashalik* as well as Egypt. But direct discussions between Suzerain and Viceroy were destined never to take place. The settlement of the fate of Syria, Egypt and the Empire was taken from the hands of the principals and transferred to the capitals of Europe.

The diplomacy which culminated in the final settlement was intricate and tortuous, but without going into elaborate detail, we may briefly follow it. Russia, wishing to maintain her predominant influence at Constantinople without being obliged to send troops into Turkish territory which would probably precipitate a European war, was willing to let negotiations between Sultan and Viceroy go forward without interference. France and England however took an entirely different view. The recent conflict was a signal to Palmerston that the Eastern Question must be finally settled, and France felt similarly disposed. The only difference between the two Powers – a difference which did not become apparent until later – was how the settlement was to be made. Marshal Soult wrote to the Sultan that whilst the Powers, i.e. France, England, Austria and Prussia, approved of his temperate attitude towards Mohammed Ali, they must require him not to negotiate except through the medium of the Powers.

Thus so far the principal Powers of Europe, Russia excepted, had agreed that the Eastern Question must be settled among themselves, but no actual proposals had been put forward. The Tsar, not wishing, as it were, to be left out in the cold, sent Baron Brunnow to London with an offer to Palmerston which struck him with surprise and admiration.[7] Russia was willing to drop all pretensions at Constantinople, to abandon the Treaty of Unkiar Skelessi and to concert with England and the Powers in the settlement of the Egyptian Question.

As a result of this apparent general agreement a joint note was presented to the Porte by the ambassadors of all the Powers in the following terms:

> Les soussignés ont reçu ce matin de leurs gouvernements respectifs des instructions en vertu desquelles ils ont l'honneur d'informer La Sublime Porte que l'accord sur la question d'Orient est assurée entre les cinq grandes puissances, et de l'engager à suspendre toute détermination définitive sans leurs concours, en attendant l'effet de l'intérêt qu'elles lui portent.[8]

In other words, the Porte should leave all negotiations to the Powers who would resolve the question favourably for the Porte. Russia reported that she would accept any settlement fixed by England; Austria and Prussia did likewise. The matter was thus virtually to be settled by England and France. At this juncture a rift appeared in the lute.

France in fact had views quite at variance with those of Palmerston as to how the dispute should be settled. She had however placed herself in a difficult position by agreeing to concert with all the Powers in the settlement. At a conference she would have been outvoted four to one. In brief, it was Palmerston's policy to sweep Mohammed Ali right out of Syria, allowing him only to retain the *pashalik* of Acre and confine him to the land of Egypt, thus putting the desert between him and Turkey and removing all possibility of further clashes. ' . . . Que Méhémet Ali reste maître de son Egypte; qu'il y obtienne l'hérédité, qui a fait le but constant de ses efforts; mais qu'il n'y ait plus de voisinage et par conséquent plus de collision possible entre les deux puissances rivales.'[9]

But to the French Government carried forward by the overwhelming weight of public opinion which saw in Mohammed Ali a friend, ally and champion, the mere suggestion of depriving him of the territories which were his by right of conquest, was utterly repulsive. For France to agree to this would have been an affront to her national honour. Above all the final settlement must confirm Mohammed Ali, not only in the hereditary possession of Egypt, but of Syria as well. The respective attitudes of France and England were thus diametrically opposed, but the latter had with her the concurrence and weight of the other three Powers. France, having in the first place agreed to act conjointly, could, not legitimately withdraw without placing herself in an invidious position and in opposition to all the other Powers. During the latter part of the year 1839 Soult's Ambassador at London, General Sebastiani, had long discussions with Palmerston in an attempt to persuade him to modify his stand. The outcome was a grudging concession by Palmerston that in addition to the hereditary *pashalik* of Egypt, Mohammed Ali should also enjoy that of the province of Acre except for the fortress itself which should revert to the Porte. This was the limit of concession to which Palmerston was prepared to go.

Unsatisfied with the outcome Soult replaced Sebastiani with Guizot who, he considered, would be more acceptable to London. But scarcely had Guizot arrived when the Government of Soult was defeated and resigned. The new French Premier, M. Thiers, was an even greater supporter of Mohammed Ali and was moreover labouring under the delusion that the Pasha possessed sufficient military power to defy all Europe, if encouraged to do so by France. Guizot, who sensed the political atmosphere in London, had to pursue his mission warily, to steer between the intransigence of both his own superior, Thiers, and of the British Foreign Minister. By some diplomatic lobbying he managed to persuade the Austrian Ambassador, Baron Newman, to support a modification of Palmerston's 'limit of concession' to the extent of granting to Mohammed Ali Acre as well and the greater part of the province as far as the frontiers of the *pashaliks* of Tripoli and Damascus.

The proposal to leave Mohammed Ali still in possession of the great fortress of Acre was most distasteful to Palmerston, but as an earnest of his desire to concert with all the Powers and to carry France with him he was prepared to accept. Guizot had in fact achieved a considerable diplomatic victory, and had the matter stopped at this juncture Mohammed Ali would have had good reason to bless France for her good offices. He would probably have seen the warning light and embraced this offer with gratitude. But Thiers, either believing that having extracted so much France could extract more or that Palmerston would not presume to ignore the weight of France, refused to countenance the partition of Syria. Mohammed Ali, he said, would never consider it. It must be added that he never gave the Pasha the opportunity of considering it or even of acquainting him with the terms of the proposed settlement.

While all this diplomatic wrangling was taking place in London and Paris, Mohammed Ali was concerting on his own account. The downfall of his ancient and inveterate enemy, Khusrev, came as a signal to negotiate direct with Constantinople. He confided to Cochelet, the French Consul-General, his intention of approaching the Porte with a view to making a peaceful settlement, and as evidence of his good intentions he offered to return the renegade Ottoman fleet. Sami Bey, his secretary, was despatched to Constantinople to carry through the negotiations. Thiers to whom all this was reported saw therein a way out of his predicament. If he could present to the Powers a solution worked out between the Pasha and the Porte agreeable to both, it would be difficult for Palmerston to offer any valid objections, and French honour and French interests would thus be saved. But it was an underhand scheme which Palmerston immediately detected and which moved him to wrath; for France had clearly engaged herself to act in concert with the Powers. Here she was manifestly co-operating in a private settlement which took no cognisance of the interests of the remainder of Europe.

The tedious negotiations and *pourparlers* briefly outlined above had dragged on over a period of a year and still no solution had been found. To these latest developments Palmerston's reactions were swift and characteristic. On 17 July 1840 he summoned Guizot to his presence, read him a sermon which hinted at French duplicity and announced that since the four Powers, Russia, Austria, Prussia and Britain had been unable in spite of their greatest efforts to carry France with them, they had now decided to settle the matter without French co-operation. A convention, he said, had now been made by the Powers and the Sultan 'destinée à resoudre d'une manière satisfaisante les complications actuellement existantes dans le Levant.'[10] If Mohammed Ali was not willing to comply with the terms of the convention, the necessary pressure would be exerted by the Powers to enforce his acceptance.

The terms of the Convention signed by the four Powers on 15 July 1840 are important. The preliminaries contained a guarantee by the Powers to come to the aid of the Sultan in the defence of Constantinople and the Straits, and to assist in forcing the Viceroy to comply with the terms. Under the Convention the Sultan offered the *pashalik* of Egypt to Mohammed Ali and his heirs by direct succession, the *pashalik* of Acre and command of the fortress and southern part of Syria for his lifetime. The offer would only valid provided that it was accepted by Mohammed Ali within ten days of receiving it and on condition that instructions were immediately given for the withdrawal of all naval and military forces from Arabia and the Holy Cities, from the island of Crete, Adana and all other parts of the Empire not comprised within the limits of Egypt and Acre. If, on the other hand, Mohammed Ali did not accept these terms within a period of ten days, the offer of Acre was to be withdrawn, but Egypt would still remain to him on a hereditary basis, provided that this offer was accepted within a further ten days. The Turkish fleet was to be handed over complete to authorised agents of the Sultan, and no deduction was to be made from the tribute payable to the Porte on account of expenses incurred in maintaining the fleet while it had been in Egyptian ports. If at the expiry of the twenty days stipulated no acceptance had been received, the Sultan would hold himself entirely free to act in his own interest.

The hand of Palmerston can be clearly detected in the framing of these terms. The game of procrastination was played out. The longer Mohammed Ali dallied, the more he would lose. To France the Convention came as a national insult. For a while the populace clamoured for war and Thiers ordered all military and naval preparations. But a little sober reflection decided Louis Philippe that the stake was not worth the risks, and France was content to let the furore die a natural death. The most she could do was to advise Mohammed Ali to hold out and make no acceptance. Believing in the sincerity of France and that her national honour would be touched to render material assistance in case of need the Viceroy followed this advice. But he was leaning on a broken reed and the last act of the drama in the Levant was being rapidly played out. The first ten days slipped by with no response from the Viceroy; the second ten had nearly lapsed when he announced acceptance of the first proposal, but he did not return the Ottoman fleet.[11] On the expiry of the period the Sultan announced the deposition of Mohammed Ali from all his offices, and the consuls left Alexandria. The Pasha received notice of his dismissal with his customary calm, but undoubtedly the development of events was pressing heavily on him. France showed no active sign of support and the intentions of the Allies were becoming more obvious.

On 16 September 1840 Sir Charles Napier, commanding the British squadron in the Levant, appeared before Beirut and demanded its evacuation by the Egyptians; the port was attacked and taken. Immediately all Syria flamed into revolt against Ibrahim and his tyranny. A few days later Saida fell to the Allies, followed by Tripoli and Latakia. Of the coastal towns only Acre itself remained in the possession of Ibrahim; here the valiant and loyal Soliman Pasha was in command. On 3 November Admiral Stopford and Napier appeared before the ancient fortress and opened fire. The action was of short duration. In the late afternoon a shot exploded the powder magazine and almost blew the place to pieces; two thousand defenders are said to have perished, and by the following morning the remnants had evacuated the fort.

In the interior Ibrahim Pasha, surrounded by hordes of fanatical rebels, had to cut his way back towards Egypt. Death and desertion reduced his forces from sixty thousand to twenty thousand. The retreat of the Egyptian army from Syria in 1840 is strongly reminiscent of Napoleon's in 1799. Hardship, thirst and starvation dogged their every step, but special mention must be made of the gallant Soliman Pasha who, like a true gunner, brought his artillery safely back to Cairo.

By December 1840 Syria was lost. The power of Mohammed Ali, the Great Pasha, which for years had dominated nearly every part of the Levant, had crumbled before the combined might of the Allied Powers of Europe and of the Sultan. France, who during all these months had encouraged his resistance and had virtually pledged herself to stand by him through all vicissitudes, had scuttled at the first sign of Allied concerted action. Paradoxically, when all seemed lost, Mohammed Ali found a friend among his enemies, when Sir Charles Napier, an old admirer of his, appeared before Alexandria on 25 November. No doubt exceeding his authority, Napier cajoled the old Pasha to sign a convention by which he promised to return the Ottoman fleet as soon as the Powers should guarantee him the hereditary *pashalik* of Egypt. At the same time he sent a message ordering Ibrahim to evacuate Syria entirely.

Now that the object of his long-drawn out policy was achieved, the formidable Palmerston relaxed his severity. Like a good sportsman he ratified Napier's convention and recommended to the Porte that Mohammed Ali should be confirmed in the hereditary possession of his *pashalik*. In this he was supported by the other three Powers. Characteristically, now that they held the winning hand the Porte demurred, anxious if possible to secure the complete demise of the Pasha who had for so long been so formidable. But the steady pressure of the Powers, now reversed in direction, persuaded the Sultan to withdraw his notice of dismissal and confirm the Pasha and his descendants in their rights to Egypt. A memorandum, signed by the four Powers on 30 January, was presented to the Porte in the following terms:

> The Powers invite the Sultan to show himself generous towards Mohammed Ali, not only by revoking the act of dismissal, but also by promising that his descendants in the direct line will be appointed Pashas of Egypt . . . The four Powers in advising the Porte to accede to this favour, far from expressing any fresh proposition, are only recalling to the Sultan the intentions which he himself had expressed at the beginning of the Eastern crisis . . .[12]

As a consequence of the recommendations embodied in this memorandum, an imperial firman was promulgated on 13 February 1841 the terms of which, slightly modified by those of a later firman, were to regulate the relations of Turkey and Egypt for the future. The following is a summary of its principal clauses:

1. Mohammed Ali to be reinstated in the government of Egypt.

2. The vacancy on his death to be filled from among his sons, the person to be chosen by the Sultan.

3. The governors of Egypt to receive equal distinction and precedence with other vizirs of the Empire.

4. All laws enacted and treaties concluded by the Porte to be applicable to Egypt.

5. All taxes to be levied in the name of the Sultan and to be applied in conformity with the provisions in force in other parts of the Empire.

6. One quarter of the gross revenue of Egypt to be paid as tribute to Constantinople.

7. A control to be established to enable the exact revenue to be ascertained by the Porte.

8. All currency struck in Egypt to be the same as that struck at Constantinople.

9. The army necessary for the internal security of Egypt not to exceed eighteen thousand troops.

10. Egyptian flags, officers' and soldiers' uniforms to be the same as those of the imperial army.

11. The Governor to have power to promote up to the rank of Kol Aghassi (major) only; all superior officers to be appointed by the Sultan.

12. The building of warships by the Governors of Egypt to be forbidden except with the consent of the Sultan.

13. Failure to comply with these instructions would result in the revocation of the hereditary privileges.

Mohammed Ali accepted the new firman, but in subsequent negotiations he secured modifications of three of the clauses. These were embodied in a further firman dated 1 June 1841:

1. The principle of hereditary succession should conform to the system of seniority customarily in use in the Empire. The *pashalik* would thus fall to the eldest male of the family instead of a member selected by the Sultan.

2. The annual tribute was fixed at 18,000 purses (9 million francs) instead of a percentage of the revenue.

3. The Viceroy had authority to promote officers up to the rank of colonel.

These firmans of investiture were publicly proclaimed at Alexandria on 10 June 1841, and the Eastern Question was at last considered to be closed.

The results of this last episode came as a shattering blow to the old Pasha. He was now seventy-two years of age, and grief and disappointment were already having their effect on his mind. He became subject to intense fits of depression. The great sub-empire which he had carved out during the past thirty years had all but crumbled in the dust. Arabia and the Holy Cities, Crete and Syria were gone; all that was left to him was Egypt and the vast but useless Sudan. Had he been at liberty to make his own settlement with the Porte in 1839 and 1840, no doubt he would have retained nearly all of what he had won by prodigious enterprise, labour and expense. His evil genius was the arrogant Government of France who, in demanding too much, lost him almost everything. What was left to him was in fact the result of a generous gesture on the part of Palmerston and the Powers. In spite of all his years of incessant activity, he had failed to realise his most cherished ambition: the separation and independence of Egypt from the Porte. Yet he had not laboured entirely in vain. Despite the fact that he was still in 1841, as he had been in 1805, simply the Pasha and Viceroy of Egypt, a vassal and tributary to His Imperial Majesty, yet there was a substantial difference. He and his family now held Egypt by right of succession. For the first time for centuries there was a settled dynasty in the land of Egypt. With the exception of certain relatively unimportant details the administration of Egypt was a separate entity supported and guaranteed by the united Powers of Europe and ratified by the imperial firmans. No alterations in the relationship between Sultan and Pasha could be effected without the consent of the Powers. There could be a bright future in store for Egypt, if the same degree of determination and energy as had been employed in previous years in building up an empire, could now be turned to the development and welfare of Egypt. But such was not to be. The aged Pasha had shot his bolt; from the promulgations of the 1841 firmans until his death, he ceased almost entirely to be a figure in history.

There can be no doubt that in the long run the severance of Egypt from all her territorial appendages proved a blessing in disguise. There had never been true peace in Syria since the day the Convention of Kutuya was signed, and the unrest had led to a general deterioration of the country. The maintenance of a large standing army is a luxury which no country can support for long and prosper at the same time. Likewise the barren wastes of Arabia proved more of a liability than an asset. The only value to be derived from the possession of this desert peninsula lay in the prestige which accrued in the Moslem world to the governor and protector of the Holy Places. Crete too was a typical example of the impoverishment which accompanies continual rebellion and disorder. It had only value as a naval base in time of war, and it had indeed served this purpose more than once during the period of Mohammed Ali's reign. But in peacetime Crete was of little value.

In any case the governmental system which prevailed in the Levant at the time was quite inadequate to deal with the complexities of an empire of any size. In this particular case the Government of Egypt was one man, the Pasha, and it was unusual for him to delegate any of his authority; every measure, great or small, was decided by him. He had no ministers in the accepted sense of the word, only servants to carry out his behests. As long as he was a man of the calibre of Mohammed Ali with his boundless energy, resource and sagacity, it might have been possible to hold the sub-empire together, but a lesser man would have failed. Since the old Pasha was destined shortly to be succeeded by lesser men, it was perhaps as well that the boundaries of his domains were shortened.

It is perhaps as well also that the final settlement came at the time it did instead of a decade earlier; for had it done so the ambition and restless energy of Mohammed Ali in his prime would probably have created new situations later. It came, however, in his old age, when he was on the point of becoming a spent force. The incessant activity of a lifetime now began to take its toll. The disaster of 1841 completed the collapse of a great old man, and his mind began to give way. Early in 1844 Barker paid a visit to Alexandria and had an interview with him. '*Heu mihi*; how altered from that Hector. He had become quite childish. The great mind which had inaugurated such reforms in Egypt and had accomplished such great things, had collapsed! The man "who never had a master" was now like a child!'[13]

In 1846, for the first time in his life he paid a visit to Constantinople, where it is reported, he was received with great distinction, and even made peace with his lifelong enemy Khusrev Pasha now also considerably advanced in age. He also visited Kavalla, the place of his birth. During these latter years the administration fell more and more into the hands of Ibrahim, who continued along the path mapped out by his father. In 1848 the mental powers of the old Pasha had become so feeble that, by virtue of a *hatti-sherif* from the Sultan, Ibrahim Pasha formally took over the government as Viceroy and Pasha of Egypt. His tenure of office was short, seventy days to be precise. He died a few weeks later, whereupon his aged father once more resumed the reins of office and held them until his death the following year.

On 2 August 1849 the founder of the last dynasty of Egypt died at

Alexandria, the place he most loved. His body was taken to Cairo where it lies interred in a corner of the great mosque which he had built on the Citadel of Cairo. From many points in the city and for miles around one can behold the slender minarets of this edifice which dominates the heart of Egypt and which encloses the mortal remains of the man who made Egypt a nation. The following letter is moving testimony of the veneration in which he was held by the people:

My Lord,

I have the honour to inform Your Lordship that the grave has just closed over the mortal remains of the Old Pasha Mohammed Ali. He died about midday on the 2nd instant at Alexandria, aged eighty.

His funeral at Alexandria was followed by all the chief Egyptian officers, the consular body, and all principal merchants and inhabitants.

At Bulak it was met by all the surviving members of the family, with the exception of Abbas, and they walked in funeral procession to the tomb chosen by the late Pasha for his place of rest in the new mosque which he built in the Citadel.

The attachment and veneration of all classes for the name of Mohammed Ali are prouder obsequies than any which it was in the power of his successor to confer.

Very rarely would it be that Your Lordship would hear in any part of the Turkish Empire such a phrase as the following:

'If Allah would permit me, gladly would I give ten years of my life to add them to that of our old pasha.' Yet this I have known to fall from the lips of more than one during the last illness of Mohammed Ali.

The British Agent to his Government.

Half a century had elapsed since the old Pasha had first set foot in the land of Egypt, for forty-four years of which he had been Governor and Viceroy. It will be of interest therefore briefly to compare the condition of Egypt at the beginning of this period with that of the end. Only thus is it possible to assess Mohammed Ali as a power for good or evil. Harking back over nearly half a century, it will be recalled that the condition of Egypt and its people following the withdrawal of the French and British troops was as pitiable as it could be. The land was scourged with the incessant wars of the Mamelukes, Turks and Albanians. There was no stable government; no vestige of respect was shown towards life, property and the human decencies. Harried and pillaged

112

on all sides, the docile and industrious native *fellahin* were slipping away, grateful if only they could save their lives, and leaving their fertile lands to run to waste. Trade and commerce were at a standstill. It would in fact be no exaggeration to claim that for the humble, ignorant people Egypt in those days must have been a close approach to hell on earth.

Looking forward now to Egypt on the day Mohammed Ali was finally laid to rest, what a difference can be discerned. Here was a prosperous well-governed land, marching forward steadily, if somewhat reluctantly, on the road to civilisation. Life and property were as safe as anywhere in the world. Justice was rough but swift. Economically the country was richer than ever before, and the land was producing crops at a rate hitherto unknown. New industries and new trades were practised; schools, hitherto unthought of, abounded. The sloth, ignorance and darkness of centuries had at last been thrown off, and Egypt had emerged as a new country; there were even indications of the birth of a new nation. Mohammed Ali's greatest gift to Egypt was his ridding the country for all time of the Mamelukes and their incessant wars, and of the Turkish Pasha who came for a few months or years to squeeze her dry and return whence he came. Henceforth the land was to owe loyalty to one only, the hereditary Viceroy, the blood of Mohammed Ali. At least there was a prospect of steady progress under the guidance of a Pasha whose heart and home were in the land he ruled.

CHAPTER 8

Abbas and Said

With the death of the grand old Pasha and his warrior son Ibrahim, the renaissance of Egypt received a considerable shock. For reasons which will unfold, relatively little is known of Abbas Pasha, the next Viceroy, and his reign. This period in fact may be said to represent the doldrums of modern Egypt's history. To glean such little harvest of information as there is about this period, reference must be made to the writings of various contemporary travellers and visitors to Egypt; for with the closing of the Eastern Question in 1841 Egypt faded almost entirely from world affairs. In the foreign offices of Europe Egypt had to all intents and purposes reverted to its pristine condition, that of a backwater of the Ottoman Empire; the files were closed.

As evidence of the singular lack of accurate information may be cited the fact that even the origin and parentage of Abbas Pasha himself seems to have been the subject of some misapprehension. Edward Dicey[1] states that Abbas was the son of Mohammed Ali, while De Leon[2] reports that Abbas' father was burnt alive at Shendy in the Sudan. This can only refer to the death of Mohammed Ali's son, Ismail, whom he had sent to subdue the Sudan in 1820. Senior[3] on the other hand, writes, quoting Hekekyan Bey, a prominent official in Egypt, 'Abbas Pasha, as eldest son of Ibrahim, had the misfortune of enjoying a long prospective of power.' All these contemporary commentators were in error regarding the descent of Abbas. He was in fact the child of that well beloved second son of Mohammed Ali, Tussun who, it will be recalled, conducted the first campaign of the Arabian War in the years 1811 to 1815 and who died a few months after his return to Egypt. Abbas was thus Mohammed Ali's grandson, and his accession to the Viceregal throne well illustrates the principle of hereditary succession customary in the Ottoman Empire. The imperial firman of 1 June 1841 had laid down that succession should pass to the eldest male of the blood of

Mohammed Ali. Abbas, though the issue of the Pasha's second son, had been born in 1813 and took precedence over the remaining sons of Mohammed Ali, all of whom were born later.

Despite the variations in the accounts of the new Viceroy's parentage, nearly all historians and commentators are unanimous in their summing up of his character. At the time of his accession in August 1849 he was about thirty-six years of age.

> His complexion was much darker than that of the majority of his family, most of whom are fair, with reddish beards. Abbas was swarthy, with a scant beard, short and stout of figure, with a bloated sensual face, and dull, cruel eyes. Yet there was both energy and intelligence manifested in this repulsive countenance, when warmed into interest or animation on any matter that touched him dearly.[4]

His early years had been spent, in accordance with Turkish custom, in the harem and it does not appear that any steps were taken to equip him with the liberal education necessary to fit him for the station and duties of a ruler. He had however, taken part in Ibrahim's Syrian campaign and had served with distinction. Thus it was that on reaching maturity he became a Turk of the Turks, a fanatical Moslem and a hater in all respects of things European and of Western civilisation. In this he was in marked contrast with his grandfather Mohammed Ali who, though not a slavish imitator of Western veneer, had seen in Western methods the answer to many of his problems, and also to both his successors, Said and Ismail, who went to extremes in introducing the new civilisation into oriental Egypt.

Already the tranquillity and security which Mohammed Ali had brought to Egypt were beginning to attract the motley swarm of low class and unprincipled Europeans to batten on her potential wealth. Mohammed Ali in his day had encouraged a certain amount of immigration, taking the view that Turks and Egyptians were not possessed of the necessary ability to develop the commerce and resources of the country. He had been ever ready to lend an ear to the blandishments of the foreigners and, as has already been remarked, he had been induced by the honeyed words that dripped from the lips of these needy adventurers to embark on many expensive and impossible schemes of development. Abbas Pasha had had sufficient opportunity to watch the antics of the European community, had seen many of their schemes come to grief and had noted also the benefits that they enjoyed from the immunity conferred on them by the capitulations. From the time of his succession to the day of his death he shut himself off from all social contact with the Europeans and, it must be added, for the most part from his own people as well. It was only with the greatest difficulty that any European consul or official could obtain an interview with the Viceroy, and even then he could be sure that he would be treated with suspicion and his addresses ignored. It must not however be inferred from this that he was rude or boorish with his visitors. 'His manners, like those of all high Turks, were bland and polished; for in all that constitutes perfect good breeding the Eastern surpasses the Western man.'[5]

For these reasons it is to be supposed that the Europeans viewed Abbas with a particularly jaundiced eye and that their accounts of him and his actions may well have been coloured by their own prejudices. It does not appear, however, that his subjects had any love for him either. He was endowed with certain unenviable traits: insatiable avarice, ignorance and superstition, cruelty and hatred of all things new and everything that even hinted of Europeanism. Thus the establishments on which his grandfather had lavished so much love and labour and which had been intended to promote the welfare and prosperity of Egypt were closed down and suppressed.

> ... the fleet is gone, the army which in Mehemet Ali's time exceeded 150,000 men, was reduced by Abbas to 60,000 and does not now amount to 40,000. All the expensive schools which Mehemet Ali founded have been suppressed. Few of his great manufacturing establishments remain, and those which exist have been much reduced. Much land, formerly irrigated, is now dry and waste ... [6]

Abbas' mania appears to have been the construction of vast and expensive, but useless, palaces in inaccessible and inhospitable places. Their design and architecture adequately reflected his twisted and suspicious nature, for each room had several doors and access to them lay through tortuous corridors and staircases. All his reign he lived in fear of assassination and this untimely end he ultimately met.

Holding himself aloof from the public eye he was the subject of much malicious comment and gossip. It was whispered that he was of a depravity which shocked even the morals of Egypt. It is impossible to state with any degree of certainty how much truth lies in these allegations.

The ambition of nearly all rulers to pass their heritage to their own offspring was as powerful in Abbas as it had been in his grandfather. According to the existing law, succession to the *pashalik* of Egypt was to devolve on the eldest male of the blood of Mohammed Ali, and although the operation of this principle had been the instrument of his own succession, he was loath to see its continued application in the case of his successor, whereby his own son Il Hami would be excluded from inheritance. By the outlay of vast sums of *bakshish* at Constantinople Abbas hoped to secure from the Sultan a revision of the hereditary principle and retain the viceregal throne in his own line. While the Sultan did not despise the gifts so lavishly bestowed by his vassal, he made no move to satisfy the yearnings of his heart, and the established order of succession was destined to endure for some years to come.

Much that is ignoble has been ascribed to Abbas Pasha and in all probability much of the criticism was well founded, yet there were indeed some redeeming features in his character. His total rejection of Europeanism with all its devices was the proper course to pursue according to his own lights, and his attitude in this respect undoubtedly staved off the disasters which were to befall Egypt for at least the span of his reign. In addition Abbas appears to have shown sympathy for that patient, downtrodden and unvocal section of the population, the *fellahin*. Their rights and privileges, which had been usurped by Mohammed Ali, were revived and secured by Abbas, especially those relating to land tenure. '. . . The Egyptian fellah really has . . . cause today to bless the memory of the gloomy and cruel Abbas . . . in so far as this land question is concerned.'[7] At the other extreme, the possession of riches was virtually the passport to Fazougli, the Egyptian Siberia, an outpost in the remotest corner of the Sudan. The Viceroy had little compunction about trumping up spurious charges against the wealthy and sending them into exile in order to seize and expropriate their possessions. It is understandable that the notables avoided the attentions of the Viceroy as much as he avoided the society of all but his own entourage of slaves and menials.

Many stories are told of his sadism and cruelty. One writer recounts that when he was honoured with an interview with Abbas, the latter had just come from sewing up with his own hands the mouth of a woman of his household who had been discovered smoking. It is suggested that the exaggerated cruelty of his nature was ultimately responsible for his own death. This, like nearly all the other events of his life, was shrouded in mystery, but although the official verdict put out by the Government announced that his death was due to apoplexy – and physicians were found to sign a certificate to this effect – it soon became current gossip that he was murdered in his palace at Benha on 12 July 1854 by two of his slaves who strangled him in his bed. Some attempt was made by the Governor of Cairo, an adherent of Abbas, to put his son Il Hami on the vice-regal throne of Egypt, but the young prince was absent from Cairo at the time, and before he could be recalled the consuls had prevailed upon the Governor to desist from this unlawful course, and the rightful heir, Prince Mohammed Said, assumed the Government of Egypt.

The reign of Abbas was a short one, from August 1849 to 1854. It may be added that it was also singularly barren of achievement. The only development of importance which occurred during this period was the launching of a railway between Alexandria and Cairo. Even this, however, cannot be ascribed to the benevolence of the Viceroy, who opposed the project as much as lay in his power. The railway owed its inception and establishment to the British Government who, in fulfilment of Kinglake's prophecy, were already 'straining far over to hold their loved India'.

The question of communication between England and India was already beginning to loom large in British foreign policy. Up to the reign of Mohammed Ali the traditional sea route round the Cape had provided a secure and simple, if rather protracted, means of communication. On this route Britain's Government was averse to any change. But the French invasion of Egypt had directed attention to the potential threat to the overseas empire – across the isthmus of Suez, the cutting of which by a maritime canal would bring France, the traditional rival, some thousands of miles nearer to India than England herself. As a possible counterpoise to this new line of approach, the British Government instituted an investigation into the possibilities of developing the alternative short route via Syria, the Euphrates and Persian Gulf, but without satisfactory result. On the other hand, during the 1830s the activities of Lieutenant Waghorn, RN, in the service of the East India Company, proved that the overland route between Alexandria and Suez provided an expedient and rapid means of transmitting mail and parcels between England and India. The work of this pioneer awoke Britain to the possibilities of this route which would be vastly improved by the laying down of a railway between the Mediterranean port of Alexandria and the Red Sea port of Suez. Even during the reign of Mohammed Ali overtures had been made to him to support the construction of this link, but French opposition had effectively persuaded him to refuse sanction.

A word of explanation on this point may not be out of place. The events of 1840 and 1841 had resulted, for the second time in the half century, in the humiliation of France in Egypt at the hands of England. Mohammed Ali, it will be recalled, had staked his existence on French promises to back him and his claims, only to be left in the lurch at the eleventh hour. Conscious of her disgrace in the Pasha's eyes, France had exerted herself by every means to re-establish her influence in Egypt. The weapons employed by her agents were hints and innuendoes that England had aggressive intentions against Egypt as the halfway house to India. Thus, when Mohammed Ali was approached by England on the question of a railway from Alexandria to Suez, the suspicions fostered by France sprang to his mind and caused him to reject the proposal.

During this time Abbas had protested at the undue influence of France, and on his accession to the throne one of his first acts was to rid his administration of the many Frenchmen whom the diplomacy of their fatherland had managed to introduce into the service of Egypt. For the nonce France was again eclipsed, and England came to the fore sufficiently at any rate to procure sanction for the railway. As in all things European, Abbas disliked the railway and took no active steps to expedite its construction. The line in fact had not reached Cairo by the time of his death in 1854. Writing of his visit to Egypt in November 1855 Senior says he travelled from Alexandria to Cairo by boat. 'We are among the last who will make that voyage, for in a fortnight the railroad will be open to Cairo.'[8]

It is remarkable how much the attitude of Egypt to the rival European powers, France and England, varied according to the Viceroys who sat on the throne. Mohammed Ali had always wooed England, only to have his suit rejected. France for her part had assiduously courted the Pasha almost to the point of declaring war. Abbas had shunned them both as far as possible, but had recognised that it was England with her seapower who dominated the Mediterranean and the countries of its eastern littoral. As will be later shown, the next Viceroy, Said Pasha, with his Gallic education naturally inclined towards France.

The attempt to foist Abbas' son, Il Hami, having failed, the rightful successor, Mohammed Said, was proclaimed Pasha and Viceroy of Egypt. He was the fourth son of Mohammed Ali and had been born in 1822. The accession of Said Pasha was like a ray of sunshine after a long and dreary winter. It will already have been inferred that the history of Egypt was synonymous with the biography of her Pasha, so much did he direct the destiny of his country. In almost every respect Said was the antithesis of his predecessor. As a favourite son of Mohammed Ali he had been carefully nurtured in his youth and reared to fit him for the pre-eminent position of ruler of Egypt.

Carefully educated by an accomplished French tutor (Koenig Bey) who took good charge of the morals as well as the mind and manners of his pupil, Said Pasha was a gentleman in our acceptation of that term, a good French scholar, with some knowledge of English, a man of large and liberal views, and extremely fond of association with Europeans, whose manners and habits he had adopted in his private life; with the exception of course of his harem arrangements.[9]

In this last respect, however, he had only one wife and was thus a model of virtue to his subjects.

The new Viceroy was in the unfortunate position of having been vouchsafed a glimpse of Western civilisation with all its achievements and potentialities, while the somewhat seamy side had been hidden from him. He was by nature open-hearted and generous and tended to see only the better side of human nature. In the hope and anticipation of raising his inheritance to the same standards of culture and civilisation as the countries of Western Europe, he cordially welcomed foreign visitors to his court and surrounded himself with them. These he hoped would take a prominent part in the development and commerce of Egypt. Needless restrictions were thrown off and the benevolence of the Pasha towards the foreign communities ensured for them freedom and protection in their various occupations. Unfortunately the well-intentioned and honourable members of these communities were outnumbered by a host of disreputable profit-seekers who swarmed to Egypt in the hope of making quick and easy fortunes at the expense of Said and his people. The attractive but insidious system of easy money on credit was for the first time introduced into the valley of the Nile and the Viceroy, seeing in this a means of raising funds for the development of his country, and without realising fully the implications of pledging the future for the benefit of the present, eagerly availed himself of it. During his reign Egypt was saddled with its first public debt wherein lay the seeds of the financial disasters which were to encompass his successor.

Seeing in himself a follower of his father's footsteps, Said interested himself particularly in the army. But these were years of peace and the forces on which he lavished much time and money were not called upon to render any active service in the field, except occasionally against the Beduin. It will be recalled that the firman of 1841 had stipulated that the army was to be limited to eighteen thousand troops. This restriction does not appear to have weighed heavily upon either Abbas or Said, for it has already been noted that during the reign of the former, the army, although drastically reduced, still numbered some fifty thousand men. Said too maintained his forces at about this figure, but they were more of a plaything with him than an active serviceable force. It amused him to deck out his troops in gorgeous uniforms and to direct drills and manoeuvres in the desert in which he took an active part himself.

A number of developments took place in the short span of his reign. The railway was completed to Cairo and several other lines were pushed out into the Delta. In common with all other projects of public utility the *corvée* was employed to supply the necessary labour.

The institution of the *corvée* was centuries old, and owed its existence to the necessity of clearing the canals and irrigation ditches of the mud which the Nile yearly deposited. The very existence of Egypt depended upon the adequate irrigation of the Delta, and the maintenance of the canals in good order was therefore a work of high importance. Every year large numbers of men, at times numbering as much as one fifth or one sixth of the total working population, were called out to scrape away the accumulations of mud and silt which threatened to choke the waterways. There was justification for this particular form of national conscription, since such vital work could not be left to the discretion or initiative of the Egyptian *fellah*, who was perhaps the most improvident soul in the world. The *corvée* was thus a system of spreading a national task over the bulk of the population, but it often bore very hardly on the native cultivator who was generally wrenched from his fields and marched away, sometimes over great distances, to work in the ditches. For his labours, he received no pay, food or accommodation of any type. Such means of subsistence as he had acquired during his absence he had to provide himself and take with him. His wife and children were generally left to fend for themselves. Such a system was feudal and even barbaric, but it was to a great extent justified by the urgencies of the situation. A more civilised country would probably have raised funds for such work by additional taxation to pay the labour force, but if such a system had been applied in Egypt, it would have been the *fellahin* who would have borne the extra burden, so that in effect the result would have been much the same. Whether rightly or wrongly, the construction of the railway was regarded as a work of public utility, and the *corvée* was employed to provide the necessary labour force.

The reign of Said Pasha coincided with the American Civil War which temporarily resulted in the stoppage of American cotton exports to Europe. Demand for the fine long staple Egyptian product boomed and prices soared; prosperity to a degree hitherto unknown flowed into Egypt. Said

Pasha had the welfare and improvement of his people very much at heart, and many of his acts were designed to alleviate their burdens. In one instance he tried the experiment of building a model village in the Delta of clean and comfortable houses in place of the appalling filth and squalor of the traditional mud hovels of the *fellahin*. But he had counted without his people. In no other country in the world is diehard conservatism and resistance to change, even for the better, more deeply ingrained than in Egypt. De Leon, who reports this incident[10] writes that he 'found that the model houses had been deserted, and were rapidly falling to ruin, while, like sugar loaf ant-hills, on the outer circle were again grouped the mud huts, in all their primitive dirt and discomfort, with their fowls and filth and prowling dogs, into which the villagers with their swarming families had squatted down.' Half a century later Sir Thomas Russell Pasha, writing of his forty-two years' experience in Egypt, bears out the same story:

> . . . what is still more fatal to reform is the obstinacy of the *fellah* and his inability to understand what is being done for him; he continues to go his own way, insists on drinking from the canals even when clean water is provided, prefers to sleep with his cattle in his mud hut instead of in a modern cottage and refuses to take the most elementary of sanitary advice.[11]

In the higher spheres progress was substantial. The extension of the telegraph system not only throughout the Delta but also into Upper Egypt, may be cited as an example. At the instigation of the British Government and the societies established for the purpose, Said Pasha dealt a blow, if rather ineffectual, at the classic institution of slavery, by promulgating a decree limiting the buying and selling of slaves in Egypt and requiring an owner to manumit his slaves at their request.

A brief word of explanation is here required to bring the institution of slavery into its correct perspective. The picture of slavery which exists in the average European mind is very much coloured by the terrible conditions which prevailed in the American cotton and tobacco plantations of the last century. Such a picture bears no resemblance to slavery in the Ottoman Empire where by tradition and law slaves were endowed with certain inalienable rights. A master having once purchased a slave assumed an obligation which he could not throw off. It was in his own interest to see to the welfare of his property; he was moreover bound to feed and maintain his slaves in their old age until the day of their death. He could neither discharge them nor throw them into the street. A slave could apply to the Qadi and require him to take him from his master and sell him. The slave was thus not entirely subject to the tyranny of his master. Under the decrees of Said Pasha slaves could now demand to be set free, but this right was not exercised to any great extent. The slave in effect felt no degradation in his position; on the contrary he considered himself to be a part of the family. Senior relates[12] the case of a Nubian slave, the property of Sabbatier, the French Consul who 'looked down on the hired servants. "You are paid," he says "moi, je suis de la maison; you may be turned away – I cannot be."' This was the attitude of the majority of slaves. It is worthy of recall too that the Mameluke Beys who had dominated Egypt for centuries before Mohammed Ali had all been slaves originally, bought and sold. A further illustration of the condition of slavery may be mentioned. During the Greek War Ibrahim Pasha had captured thousands of Greeks and sent them in slavery to Egypt, most of them women and children. At the conclusion of the war, Lord Palmerston had insisted that all slaves who so desired should be released and returned immediately to their own country. Very few of this large number availed themselves of the opportunity, the majority preferring to stay in slavery with their Arab husbands and masters rather than return in liberty to the harsh rigours of Greece and its climate.

Thus slavery as it existed in Egypt at the time was by no means as rigorous or inhuman as popular clamour supposes. Normally the desires of the Viceroy were as good as law and no subject, however exalted, dreamed of questioning his orders or authority save only in one respect. Stronger even than the despotism of the Pasha were the traditions and customs of the people preserved over the centuries; even Mohammed Ali had rarely ventured to trespass on these or to issue decrees which conflicted with established tradition or religious custom. It is not therefore to be wondered at if little heed was paid to the new decrees on the subject of slavery. Buying and selling openly may have diminished somewhat, but it continued nevertheless secretly. Most of the slaves were girls and were hidden behind the locks and bars of the harem, the sanctity of which was inviolable even by the Viceroy's soldiers, and the passage of slave from one household to another thus continued unabated.

In spite of his good intentions, Said Pasha did not escape criticism, especially from his own people, but the hostility of many prominent Egyptians was undoubtedly occasioned by his marked proclivities for European society and manners. An action which drew upon him the enmity of a powerful section of the population was his conscriptions for military service. Hitherto only the Faithful, the followers of the Prophet, had been pressed into service, but Said saw no reason why the army, a national institution, should not be recruited from all elements of the population. The Christian Copts who had thus hitherto evaded service were required to supply their quota, an occasion for much grief and outraged feeling among that community. Similarly, another section which felt the heavy hand of the Viceroy's conscription was the Sheikhs el Belad, the village mayors whose families had long been exempt from service in the army. Said called up the sons of the sheikhs and formed them into special guard battalions.

> The Sheikhs and their families . . . were the most ignorant, ragged and useless aristocracy that were ever seen. They would not work, they could not read; they passed their lives in smoking and contriving how to oppress the Fellahs, and to defraud the Government. They owe forty years' arrears of conscription; I take from them the arrears of only twenty years, and I shall return their sons in a year or two educated and civilised, with more knowledge of men and things than they would have acquired in ten years squatting before the gates of their villages in the sun in winter and in the shade in summer.[13]

In a similar attempt to spread military duty over more of the population, Said attempted to invade the privileges of those wild, nomadic dwellers of the desert, the Beduin. For centuries these warlike tribes had lived on the fringe of the cultivated valley of the Nile with their tents and camels, making occasional incursions into the settled areas, raiding for cattle, crops and women. From time to time they would visit the markets and trade their camels for clothes, beads and ammunition and then disappear into the wildernesses. No traveller's life or property was safe from the assaults of these lawless kings of the desert until Mohammed Ali pursued and harried them with such vigour that they decided it was more to their interest to make a settlement with the Pasha of Egypt than to pillage his subjects. In token of their submission they were encouraged to abandon their nomadic form of life and settle on the fringes of the Nile valley and cultivate the land. They were exempted from taxation and also from any formal conscription into the armed forces. In recompense the Beduin agreed to keep the peace and supply the Pasha at need with a force of irregular cavalry. Such an arrangement admirably suited Mohammed Ali and he was well content to leave the position thus.

But Said Pasha saw them as his subjects as much as the *fellahin*, and considered that they should bear the same burdens and responsibilities of citizenship by paying taxes and submitting to conscription. The idea may have been noble, but was ill-adapted to the circumstances. The Beduin naturally refused to comply with these demands and a sporadic form of warfare between them and the Pasha developed. The Beduin left the land they had settled on and resumed their former mode of life in the desert, and according to their practice plundered the *fellahin* villages in their neighbourhood. Although Said sent his troops against them and dealt severely with those he captured, the war was never successfully concluded, for the Beduin had the vast expanses of the Sahara for a sanctuary whenever they were threatened. It was a foolish step to take, for Egypt lost the protectors of her frontiers, the *fellahin* were once again at their mercy, and travellers in Egypt lost the security which Mohammed Ali had firmly established in his domains. Even as late as the end of the nineteenth century the Beduin remained untamed. Lord Cromer records that the Beduin were still exempt from military service and that their ancient privileges had been largely preserved to them.[14]

Relations between Said and his suzerain, the Sultan, appear to have been fairly tranquil although Cairo gossip attempted to put it forward that they both hated and distrusted each other. It does not appear that Said attempted to secure any alteration in the law of succession to the advantage of his own line which consisted of one son, still a child. In 1858 a tragedy occurred which was to have repercussions on the succession. The next senior member of the family and heir apparent was Ahmed Pasha, elder son of the famous Ibrahim. In that year Said invited all the members of the family to a great ceremony and entertainment at Cairo. As most of them were resident at Alexandria a special train was provided to convey the party of princes and Pashas to Cairo. On approaching the Nile crossing at Kafr ez-Zayat the engine driver saw to his terror that the swing bridge across the river was open, and the train being unable to pull up in time plunged headlong into the river. Only one passenger, Halim Pasha, survived the disaster by leaping clear as the train plunged. The heir apparent, Ahmed Pasha, thus perished. By a peculiar coincidence his younger brother Ismail had excused himself from attending the ceremony, otherwise he would have shared a similar fate. He thus became heir and next in line to the viceregal throne of Egypt.

During his reign Said fell into the hands of the money lenders. For this misfortune he was not entirely responsible himself; it arose to some extent from the peculiar system of inheritance in regard to the throne of Egypt. There was never any clear distinction between the public revenues and the private purse of the Pasha in power. As absolute head of State he could, and did, raise whatever taxes were necessary and these he utilised for whatever purpose pleased his fancy. Some he spent on the expenses of government or on public works; the remainder he could spend on his own private interests. In fact, in spite of the passage of half a century, no substantial change had been made from the age-old institution of Turkish pashadom, under which the Pashas from Constantinople gave their closest attention to accumulating their own wealth, and left their successors to do the same.

During his short span Abbas had spent large sums on his palaces and on the estates of his son Il Hami, and on *bakshish* to Constantinople. Thus on his death an accumulation of debt was left to his successor, for he had neglected to pay his bills and debts. 'Abbas reigned for only four years and a half . . . and I had 360,000 purses (£1,800,000) of his debts to pay – debts for arrears of salaries, for supplies, for work and materials on the railway, and above all for wages due to the people who worked on his palaces, not one of which is mine.'[15] It thus appears that this peculiar system enabled a ruler to assign his properties to his family and his debts and encumbrances to his successor. Said could presumably have either rejected responsibility for the bulk of this load of debt bequeathed to him, or have seized and sold Abbas' properties. He chose however what seems to have been an honourable course and did neither. He allowed Il Hami to remain in possession of his father's estates and made every effort to pay off outstanding debts. This burden rendered him permanently poor and left him with insufficient funds to carry out his own plans. In 1862 he started the Egyptian Public Debt by borrowing £3,293,000 from the bankers Fruhling & Goschen at seven per cent. It is illustrative of the wizardry of the financiers who negotiated this loan that the Viceroy only received about £2,640,000; £653,000 therefore fell by the wayside, presumably in the form of fees, commissions, brokerages and other incidental expenses.

He had commenced his reign a generous open-hearted fellow with a high opinion of Europeans. During the ensuing years their dubious schemes, sharp practices and petty swindles modified his views considerably, and towards the end he was soured and distrustful of everybody. He appears to have suffered throughout his reign from a gnawing disease which sapped his health, strength and vitality and which finally produced his death at the early age of forty-one.

De Leon, who was American Consul during his reign, speaks well of him.

Of Said Pasha . . . it may be said that, as he was human, he sinned and suffered, both as a public and private man. His faith was that of Islam; many of his ways were not as our ways; his civilisation was blended with barbarism; but he was a brave, true-hearted man, a staunch friend, a forgiving enemy, a just, humane, and judicious ruler over the country which Providence had confided in his care.[16]

CHAPTER 9

The Suez Canal

The reign of Said Pasha would not have been particularly memorable had it not been for the fact that it was during this period that the first steps were taken in the construction of that great feat of engineering, the Suez Canal. Looking back over the history of world trade and communications since the opening of the Canal in 1869, it would be difficult to make a full assessment of the importance of this undertaking and the benefits it subsequently conferred on mankind, and it is equally hard to realise how few have been these benefits to the land of Egypt in whose territory it lies and who, as will be shown, contributed in one form or another the major share of its cost of construction. There was nothing original in the idea of a Suez Canal. There is in fact sufficient evidence to show that an artificial channel had been dug in early times linking the Red Sea with the Nile and thus the Mediterranean. With the passing of the centuries however the shifting sands of the desert had filled in these earlier works and nothing save an occasional shallow ditch remained to indicate their former existence.

The scheme for the present canal had its origins in Bonaparte's invasion of Egypt in 1798. His grand strategy included the cutting of a canal across the isthmus of Suez to enable French warships to pass into the Red Sea and Indian Ocean and attack England's lines of communication with her empire. There does not appear to be any evidence that Bonaparte intended the proposed channel to be used for normal commercial purposes or the plying of world trade; its operational value was to be purely military. But the French occupation of Egypt was too short-lived to allow the work to be carried out. With the compulsory evacuation in 1801 the idea was shelved, but not before a certain amount of exploratory work had been done. During the occupation Bonaparte had instructed his engineers to make a survey of the isthmus and prepare a scheme for the cutting of the canal. This survey was carried out by Lepère who issued a report in 1803 – long after it could have been of any practical value to Bonaparte – the most notable feature of which was the opinion expressed that a difference of about thirty feet existed between the levels of the Red and Mediterranean Seas, and that a direct canal from the one to the other would require a system of locks. Lepère appeared to favour the ancient scheme of joining the Nile to the Red Sea, thus making a continuous, if somewhat tortuous, waterway between the seas. Such a plan would not have encountered any great difficulty of construction, and would probably have been adequate for the military purposes for which it was intended.

However the French departed and the project was perforce abandoned. Yet the preliminary enquiries had not been entirely barren of result. The publication of Lepère's report tended during ensuing years to draw the attention of the Powers and the commercial world to this narrow neck of land which obstructed what was clearly the shortest shipping route of all between East and West, and to the possibilities of digging a canal across it. The question became a subject for discussion at regular intervals during the reign of Mohammed Ali, and an important milestone was reached in 1830 when Captain F.R. Chesney, acting on instructions from the British Government, made a new survey of the isthmus and established the fact that virtually no difference existed between the levels of the two seas. A further factor which focused attention on the project was the invention of steam power and the possibilities of its application to marine transport. The peculiarities of wind and climate rendered the Red Sea difficult for sailing ships; it had taken some months to transport Baird and his Sepoys from India to Kosseir during the French invasion. The use of steam power for ships would materially reduce the difficulties of navigation in the Red Sea.

The possibilities of the Suez route were allowed to lie dormant, if not neglected, until the 1830s when it was pioneered by Lieutenant Waghorn, for the fast transmission of mails, passengers and small parcels. Credit must go to Waghorn for proving that the key to rapid communications between East and West lay between Alexandria and Suez. New interest was taken in the possibility of cutting a Suez Canal by a French society, the Saint-Simoniens, and their leader, Prosper Enfantin, who came to Egypt in 1833 intent on the regeneration and development of the country. They included in their programme the cutting of the Suez Canal and the construction of a Nile barrage. But Mohammed Ali was not interested in maritime canals. He was far too astute not to recognise that such a waterway across Egyptian territory would renew the attention of the Powers upon Egypt and open up a new

Egyptian Question. He had no intention of allowing himself and his country to be internationalised. Also, he was clear sighted enough to see that such a project would operate to his own disadvantage financially. Such traffic as then plied between the two seas had to go overland across Egypt, and no small revenue in customs and porterage accrued from this traffic. This revenue would be cut off at source by the opening of a canal which allowed passage to merchandise without even touching the shores of Egypt. But the need for some regular means of transport between the seas was being increasingly felt with the expansion of world trade, and one has only to glance at a map of the world to realise that sooner or later a Suez Canal was inevitable. It was only a question of the time and the means.

Among those who had at various times given thought to this particular question was the Frenchman Ferdinand de Lesseps, whose father had at one time held the post of French political agent in Egypt during the reign of Mohammed Ali. In his youth, Ferdinand had become acquainted with the Pasha's son, Prince Mohammed Said and, it is said, formed a close friendship with him. Following his father's footsteps, de Lesseps entered the French consular service and did a tour as Consul at Cairo. He thus became well versed in the diplomatic arts and formed many useful contacts in Egypt which were destined to prove of considerable value in his later undertakings. He had read Lepère's original report and had kept himself fully conversant with all the various investigations and developments which followed it. It appears that this project interested him almost to the point of fascination, but the circumstances of Egypt and of his own career precluded him from promoting any action until he had retired from service and had gone to live in relative seclusion in France. He then addressed a memorandum on the subject to Abbas Pasha, but without result. Of all the schemes placed before Abbas this was probably the most hateful.

In September 1854 de Lesseps received news of Abbas's death and the accession of his former friend, Mohammed Said. To de Lesseps it seemed that the occasion afforded a golden opportunity of bringing to reality the great scheme which had been maturing in his mind for years. A letter of congratulation to the new Viceroy was rewarded with a cordial invitation to return to Egypt. A few weeks later on 7 November 1854 de Lesseps disembarked at Alexandria and was warmly welcomed by the Viceroy. De Lesseps had already worked out carefully the terms of the concessions he required to construct a Suez Canal, and within a few days of his arrival he submitted them to Said Pasha who accepted them and granted the concession. On 25 November Said publicly announced the fact to a formal meeting of the consuls and signed the concession on the 30th. This date is worthy of particular note. Let it be recorded as the Black Day of modern Egypt's history; let it be known as the day on which an open-hearted and generous patron unwittingly bestowed a concession which was shortly to become a merciless bond by which a full pound of flesh and more was exacted from a surprised and hapless Egypt. Let it be recorded as the day on which were born all the miseries, humiliations and bondage which were to encompass the land and its rulers for years to come.

It is said that Said Pasha did not even trouble to submit the proposals to his legal and financial advisers. Had he shown them to any unbiased expert he might have saved his country from a cruel fate. The terms of the concession therefore merit careful inspection. The full text may be found in the appendices of Sir Arnold Wilson's book *The Suez Canal*, but an admirable short synopsis from Cameron's *Egypt in the Nineteenth Century* will suffice for the present purpose.

A lease was granted for ninety-nine years, to count from the opening of the Canal. De Lesseps was to make also a freshwater canal from Cairo to Ismailia, with branches north and south to Port Said and Suez. For this purpose he was given the lands necessary for building and works gratis and free from taxation for ten years; the right to charge land-owners for fresh water which he was bound to supply; all mines found on the company's lands and the right to work State mines and quarries free of cost or tax; exemption from customs duties on imports for the service of the company; the whole enterprise to be completed, save for unavoidable delays, within six years. Native labour was to be employed to the extent of four-fifths, a special convention settling the terms on which the pasha was to supply relays of thousands of *fellahin* diggers every three months . . . The Company was to be Egyptian and subject to local jurisdiction. The profits were to be thus divided, after payment of five per cent interest to shareholders and five to reserve fund; namely fifteen per cent to the Egyptian Government, ten per cent to founders, and seventy-five per cent to shareholders. At the end of the lease the canal and its appurtenances were to revert to the Egyptian Government, the company retaining its materials and stores.[1]

Even at first glance the terms asked and granted were outrageous, and the Viceroy deserves a measure of censure for casting away so much of his heritage for virtually no reward. Yet it must be borne in mind that this was his first venture into European commercial propositions, and he had at the time implicit faith in the honour and good intentions of the Europeans he

131

entertained at his court. If he had received the proposals a few years later, he would undoubtedly have studied the implications more carefully, but de Lesseps was an old friend and a master of diplomacy. He must undoubtedly have exercised all his powers of persuasion on the young Prince to have exacted such a lavish concession, and the latter must have placed much faith in his friendship with de Lesseps and been dazzled by the glowing promises set before him. De Lesseps in fact promised him that it would render him master of the situation against England and the Porte, and it would cost him nothing, for it would be made with French capital.[2]

Certain features of the concession merit a word of comment. Firstly, the Canal was to be constructed by a private company. It would normally be inferred from this that sufficient capital would be subscribed to purchase the land, hire and pay the necessary labour force and provide for their needs, and purchase whatever material was needed for the work. But no such plans or arrangements figured in de Lesseps' scheme. He had persuaded the Viceroy to grant him outright not only the land for the Canal, but also about a mile on either side of it for its whole length, some two hundred square miles of Egyptian territory. Not only this, but Egypt would also supply the labour absolutely free and gratis to the company. Again the company was to have the right to take materials from the State mines and quarries free of charge. For all other materials brought from abroad, no customs or taxes would be charged. Perhaps even more insidious was the clause relating to the fresh water canal. Thousands of labourers would be required on the site where there was not a drop of fresh water to be found. The first necessity therefore was the digging of a canal from the Nile to the isthmus to supply the labour force with this precious commodity. The fact that this canal might in addition be utilised to irrigate bordering lands hardly seems sufficient justification for granting to the company all such lands outright, and free of tax for ten years. An examination of the terms of the concession brings out the startling fact that Egypt herself was actually providing nearly all the capital necessary to carry out the work, land, labour and materials. But what interest and what holding was Egypt to receive in recognition of all these manifold concessions and services? For all this she was not even to receive a single share, and her only recompense was to be a paltry fifteen per cent of the profits, but this only after ten per cent had been paid to shareholders and reserve fund. The presumption therefore is that if the profits did not exceed ten per cent per annum, Egypt would not receive a single piastre.

Enough has been said to show that de Lesseps played upon the generosity, faith and goodwill of a new and inexperienced Viceroy, unaccustomed to

European finance, to seduce him into granting a concession which was unfair and iniquitous in all respects. De Lesseps may justly be honoured for his great part in bringing this prodigious feat of engineering to fruition, but the means he employed to do it can scarcely be commended.

Said Pasha made one important stipulation, that the concession must be ratified by the Sultan at Constantinople. Herein proved a stumbling block. For when he went to Constantinople, de Lesseps found the Sultan, Abdul Mejid, courteous and affable but subject to the heavy hand of British diplomacy. In a matter of this nature he dared not act without the approval of the British Government, and Lord Stratford de Redcliffe, the British Ambassador, was not slow to make his Government's attitude crystal clear to the concessionaire. Britain would have absolutely nothing to do with the Canal and would strongly oppose its construction.

Looking back over the years since the opening of the Canal, Lord Palmerston's policy of opposition may seem unreasonable, callous to the interests of the world, and even prejudicial to British trade and imperial policy. At the time, however, it did not seem so. Lord Palmerston was the servant of the British people, and according to his code it was his duty to protect the interests of the people he served. In his opinion a Suez Canal could be nothing but prejudicial to British interests, and there was in fact a solid core of commonsense in his reasoning. In 1840 and 1841 he had laboured incessantly for a final and permanent settlement of the Egyptian Question so that no European power exercised a predominant influence or power in the valley of the Nile to the detriment of England, ever apprehensive for her lines of communication with the Empire. As long as this condition prevailed Palmerston was content, even anxious, to leave Egypt to her own devices. The proposal now to form a virtually French company to occupy a large and vital area of Egypt and construct a French canal to link the two seas would in effect constitute a complete reversal of the status quo which Palmerston so ardently desired to maintain. The Canal would become in practice, if not in theory, a part of France and subject to French political opinion and French ambition. Furthermore, there was the question of British mercantile and imperial interests. The British shipping routes to the East round the Cape of Good Hope, slow and lengthy though they were, were at least safe and free from all foreign influence. No European power of consequence was nearer to India and the Far East than Britain. But the cutting of the isthmus of Suez would entirely alter this fortunate situation. France, Italy and even Russia would henceforth be some thousands of miles nearer to India than England herself. New threats and new complications would immediately arise for which there might be only one solution, even though distasteful. 'Because if the Canal is made, England will have to annex Egypt; and I, for one, have no wish to see Egypt added to the British Empire.'[3] These words, attributed to Lord Palmerston, were destined to be substantially fulfilled at no distant date.

> Lord Palmerston persisted that the scheme was the greatest bubble that was ever imposed upon the credulity and simplicity of the people of this country; the public meetings on its behalf were got up by a pack of foreign projectors; traffic by the railway would always beat traffic by steamer through the canal; it would be a step towards the dismemberment of the Turkish Empire; it would tend to dismember our own Empire by opening a passage between the Mediterranean and the Indian Ocean, which would be at the command of other nations and not always ours. Away then with such a sacrifice of the interests of Great Britain to philanthropic schemes and philosophical reveries.[4]

Having thus taken up his stand Lord Palmerston was uncompromising in maintaining it right to the bitter end. It was not until the Canal was finally opened in 1869 that British opposition succumbed and the achievements of de Lesseps were adequately recognised in England.

In face of the British attitude to this particular question, the Sultan hesitated to ratify de Lesseps' concession, and the concessionaire, after much fruitless travelling round the capitals of Europe, was compelled to return to Egypt empty-handed. Time was passing and there was danger of interest in the project flagging through delay. De Lesseps therefore took a calculated risk when he decided to push on with the construction of the Canal without the necessary firman of ratification, trusting in the support of France and the public opinion of Europe to uphold him in case of further trouble. In November 1858 he formed in Paris the Compagnie Universelle du Canal Maritime de Suez. Invitations were issued for the subscription of 400,000 shares of 500 francs each, a total of 200 millions of francs or £8 million. It is said that de Lesseps refused Rothschild's offer to float the issue and did the work himself, thus saving the company some ten million francs. A proportion of the shares were offered to the leading countries of the world, with the object of making the company an international concern. It is of interest, however, that 207,000 of the 400,000 shares were offered to and subscribed by France, thus giving that country a controlling interest. 96,000 shares went to the Ottoman Empire, i.e. in this case Egypt, and a further 85,000 were offered to Britain, the United States, Austria and Russia but as these were not taken up, the Viceroy himself guaranteed them, in addition to his own investment.[5] France and Egypt between them thus held approximately ninety-seven per cent of the shares.

It was not until April 1859, nearly four and a half years after the grant of the concession, that work actually commenced on the site of the future Port Said. Thanks to the abundant supply of Egyptian labour provided by the Viceroy the work proceeded uninterrupted until November 1862 when the first half was completed and the waters of the Mediterranean flowed into Lake Timsah at Ismailia. Even so, the Canal was the occasion of much political activity in London, Paris and Constantinople during these years. Palmerston was unremitting in his protests, but Said Pasha, fortified by assurances of full support from the French Emperor, was able to permit continuance of the work. In spite of all difficulties it is probable that the works would have proceeded smoothly until the task was accomplished, if an unfortunate occurrence had not taken place. In 1863 Said Pasha, patron of the Canal and friend of de Lesseps, died leaving the throne to Ismail Pasha. Everything now depended on the new Viceroy. Ismail declared himself to be as much a '*canaliste*' as his predecessor, but he wanted the Canal to belong to Egypt, not Egypt to the Canal. These somewhat chilling words were followed very shortly by activity calculated to nip the scheme in the bud. The truth was that, while Ismail Pasha was eager to see the great feat successfully achieved to the glory of Egypt and her ruler, he was much perturbed at the terms of the concession which gave France, under guise of the company, so much untrammelled power in his domains. The company had acquired a great tract of Egyptian land and extensive rights and privileges which the Viceroy considered were prejudicial to his sovereignty. Although the company was nominally Egyptian and subject to local jurisdiction, Ismail had little doubt that in case of dispute the company would claim the protection of the capitulations and would be upheld by France. The Viceroy's feelings in effect marched with the attitude of the British Government. The latter had never ceased to protest against the use of the *corvée* for the benefit of the company, and even Said Pasha had eventually deemed it expedient to reduce the number of labourers supplied.

France bitterly inveighed against these protests asserting that the *corvée* had been utilised for the building of the British sponsored railway. Why therefore should it not be used for de Lesseps' canal? But there was a distinction between these two operations. As has already been pointed out, the *corvée* theoretically was only employed for work of public necessity or utility. The Alexandria-Suez Railway was an Egyptian enterprise, state owned.

Though built at the insistence of Britain it was clearly of considerable value and utility to the people of the Delta and could therefore be considered a work of national importance. The Canal on the other hand was the property of a private company in which Egypt was a shareholder only to the extent of the number of shares she bought and paid for. No matter how this question was viewed, it could not truthfully be asserted that the Canal would be advantageous to the people of Egypt. If anything it would be prejudicial, in that it would tend to draw off freight and passengers from the railway. Under the circumstances Palmerston's protests against the use of the *corvée* were justified. Ismail Pasha shared these views and was eager to bring about a revision of the original concession and put it on terms more favourable to himself.

At the instigation of the British Government and of Nubar Pasha, the Viceroy's Foreign Minister, the Porte delivered an ultimatum to the company requiring it to suspend all operations, and the Viceroy was ordered to give effect to these instructions on pain of dismissal. The labour was accordingly withdrawn and the work came to a halt. By this time the company had expended millions of francs on this vast enterprise, all of which would be lost unless some way could be found to overcome the new impasse. In any case, the struggle was no longer a question affecting the company only, it was more a contest of the powers, England and France. French honour and *amour-propre* were touched; even more to the point her pocket was threatened.

De Lesseps who had some distant family connection with Empress Eugénie sought the intervention of the Emperor Napoleon III and urged Ismail Pasha to agree to the submission of the dispute to his arbitration. Trusting to the fairness and impartiality of European justice, the Viceroy agreed and thereby unwittingly took Egypt one stage further on the road to ruin.

The award of the Emperor, which was delivered on 6 July 1864, was as follows. The right of the company to draw free labour from Egypt was withdrawn; 60,000 hectares of land bordering the Canal which had been granted to the company under the original concession were to be returned to Egypt, as was also the fresh water canal, still uncompleted. As compensation for the loss of the above properties and rights, the company was to receive an indemnity from the Egyptian Government of 84 million francs, or £3,360,000.

The unwitting sin of Said was now being visited upon his successor. The concession which had been generously bestowed upon de Lesseps in a spirit of philanthropy and good faith was thus turned into a bond which was to cost Egypt over £3,360,000. Let us consider for a moment the justice of the Emperor's award. It is granted that Said Pasha made the concession on the lines set out above, that he bound himself to supply a certain number of labourers, lands and other rights; he was indeed rash enough to give away so much. Accordingly the company was promoted and constituted on the expectation that Said would honour his pledges and provide these necessities. Yet Said made one reservation, that the concession must be ratified by the Sultan. This was neither valid nor binding upon the Viceroy until this ratification had been secured. Up to the time of the award the concession had not been ratified. In floating the company and commencing operations without the Sultan's authority de Lesseps had taken a calculated risk and he should have been prepared to face the consequences. De Lesseps had not fulfilled his side of the contract and it is certain that no unbiased court in the world would have made such an iniquitous judgement against the Egyptian Government as did Napoleon III. In this case, it would appear that financial interest and avarice affected the course of justice.

Of the 200 million francs subscribed, little was left even at this early date. How all this money came to be squandered in such a short time must remain a mystery, especially as the principal requirements of the work had so far been provided by Egypt free of charge. Much of it can be ascribed to the extravagance of de Lesseps himself. By 1864, when the Canal was only half completed, the company was already in low water and in any case would probably have been unable to complete the work with the funds available – at least at the present rate of expenditure. The award of Napoleon III thus came as a godsend to the company and increased its actual, but not nominal, capital by over three million pounds. It must be questioned whether the financial condition of the company influenced the award. Egypt's contribution to the Canal up to that time can thus be summarised: the land necessary for the Canal – for 200 metres on each side still remained to the Company; the labour necessary to dig the first half from Port Said to Ismailia; an indemnity of £3,360,000. For all this outlay she had no return.

At any rate Ismail Pasha had no option but to accept the award, and on the representations of the French Ambassador at Constantinople the imperial firman of ratification was finally issued on 19 March 1866, and the work was resumed, the recent access of funds enabling it to proceed smoothly to its completion which was effected in August 1869. In spite of the difficulties which had dogged its progress, the much-discussed Suez Canal was at last a reality. The opening ceremony, the expenses of which were paid by Ismail, took place on 17 November 1869 and was one of the most lavish of the age.

The guest of honour was the Empress Eugénie, while the Emperor of Austria and representatives of the royal families and Governments of Europe also attended. On that historic day a procession of ships, headed by *L'Aigle* bearing Her Imperial Majesty, passed from Port Said to Ismailia and proceeded later to Suez. The Canal was at last open.

That day the map of the world was substantially altered. The Mediterranean, which had hitherto been little more than a cul de sac, overnight became potentially the greatest maritime highway of the world, while Egypt, whose territory was bisected by the new canal, emerged from the background and took an important place among the nations. In the foreign offices of Europe the Egyptian files which had been closed in 1841 were now to be reopened for a new dossier.

The magnificent opening set the seal on French rejoicing. Not only had this event dispelled any doubt about the supremacy of French influence in Egypt, but her ancient rival, England, had been deeply humiliated. Henceforth it could safely be anticipated that the Viceroy would look to and lean for support on France who would assume the gratifying role of benevolent protector and mentor. No better causes for satisfaction could have been vouchsafed. Unfortunately these delightful expectations were destined to be short lived, for within a year France likewise experienced the pangs of humiliation from her defeat in the Franco-Prussian War. She was then in no position to flaunt her supremacy in Egypt.

The operation of the Canal was moreover particularly disappointing during its first few years. Naturally enough there had been little Far-Eastern shipping proceeding from the Mediterranean ports, and such a trade cannot be built up in a day. The principal trader with the East was Britain with her established sea route round the Cape, and she displayed no haste to divert her shipping through the shorter and faster Suez Canal route. The rate of transit was in fact modest, howbeit progressive. Thus the Suez Canal did not prosper at first and was operated at a considerable loss. In 1871-2 the shares slumped heavily and the ordinary 500 franc (or £20) share fell to a figure in the region of £7, and de Lesseps was driven to every expedient to save his creation from financial disaster.

But from this time forward the tide began to turn and the fortunes of the Canal improved. The diehard exponent of the anti-canal policy, Lord Palmerston, had died in 1865 and with his decease British opposition had shown signs of easing. Gladstone, though cautious and averse to foreign entanglements, at least displayed no hostility. It had taken a few years to convince the British shipowners of the tremendous advantages afforded by the Canal, and more and more shipping began to pass through it. By the year 1874 income began to overhaul expenditure and the company could show a modest profit, which increased perceptibly year by year. It is almost comical that Britain, who had so fiercely and consistently opposed the construction of the Canal, now contributed four-fifths of all the shipping using it, but such was the case.

In order to assemble the main facts relating to the construction of the Suez Canal, it has been thought desirable to depart somewhat from the strictly chronological order of events and to trace its progress from a dream to reality. A further important incident is also worthy of record here. In 1875 the Viceroy Ismail Pasha found himself in extreme financial straits. His credit which had been liberally pledged for twelve years was completely exhausted, and his only remaining readily negotiable asset was his holding in the Suez Canal, a block of 176,602 shares. His immediate necessity was a sum of £4 million to meet his most pressing obligations. A simple calculation would show his holding to be worth over 88 million francs or £3½ million if valued at par. But the steady increase in the fortunes of the Canal which heralded a much greater prosperity in future years would set the stock at a higher figure, and a hundred million francs (£4 million) was not an unreasonable price to ask, even though the dividend on these shares had already been mortgaged for some years to come.

The French and English versions of the transactions which culminated in the purchase of these shares by the British Government vary slightly. De Freycinet relates that Ismail Pasha first offered the shares to France through the agency of the Société Générale. In the meantime Lord Derby got wind of the affair and pointed out to Gavard, the French Chargé d'Affaires in London, that Britain would be much embarrassed by having her principal line of communication with the Empire completely in the hands of one power and could not in consequence view with favour the proposed transaction. Less than a week later the British Government entered the market and bought the shares. This account, however, undoubtedly does not tell the whole story. The purchase of the shares was unprecedented in two respects. On the one hand it was effected on the instructions of Disraeli the Prime Minister without prior sanction by Parliament, and on the other the British Government did not normally indulge in commercial speculations. Obviously there was a sense of urgency about the whole matter, and this would tally with the suggestion that French financiers, knowing the financial plight of Ismail, hoped to beat down his price by waiting. In the interval Disraeli, hearing of the proposed transaction, stepped in and bought the shares under the noses of the French for a little under £4 million. This account would explain why Disraeli did not wait for the authority of Parliament before spending four millions of British money. Had he done so French financiers would undoubtedly have stepped in and effected the purchase themselves.

Britain owes Disraeli much gratitude for using his Jewish instinct on her behalf, for England never made a better investment in all her history, while France felt bitterly that she had been forestalled by her rival. For her modest investment of £4 million Britain thereafter recouped herself many times over in dividends alone, but even more important: she became the largest single stockholder and secured representation in the management of the Canal's affairs.

It has already been stressed that the day on which Said Pasha granted the concession to de Lesseps was the Black Day in Egypt's history. Financially the Canal was disastrous to Egypt. De Leon quotes the following estimate of what the Canal cost Egypt including interest and incidental expenses connected with the enterprise:[6]

Shares taken in the company by H.H. Said Pasha	£3,544,120
Award of Emperor Napoleon to compromise concession of forced labour	2,960,000
Paid to Canal Company for land and buildings near Cairo, called Cheflik-el-Wady	400,000
Paid to Canal Company to cancel concession of land on two sides of canal, as per contract 23 April 1869	1,200,000
Paid to Canal Company for works executed on Sweet-Water Canal and as compensation for relinquishing company's claim to that canal	400,000
Cost of Works executed by Government in cutting Sweet-Water Canal	428,927
Paid to French contractors for completion of Sweet-Water Canal	815,833
Expenses of various missions to Europe and Constantinople in connection with canal and expenses in opening the canal	1,011,193
	10,760,073
Interest paid on above sums from respective dates to September 1873	6,663,105
	17,423,178

There is no warrant that these figures are strictly correct, but they are sufficiently so to indicate the general nature of Egypt's contribution to the whole enterprise. Even if the sum of £4 million, the price received for the sale of the shares to the British Government, is deducted, it will be seen that over £13 million were poured out by the Egyptian Treasury, for which all she received in the end was the Sweet Water Canal and the land irrigated by it. The financial embarrassments which were shortly to encompass the Viceroy and bring his country to bankruptcy undoubtedly had their origins in the tremendous outlay of expenditure occasioned by the concession.

As will be related later, Mohammed Ali's forebodings and Palmerston's prophecies were destined to be fulfilled. The creation of the canal led inevitably to a procession of political events which culminated in a military occupation of Egypt by Britain. If the Suez Canal did not exist, this occupation would have been unnecessary. Can it be said that any substantial advantage accrued to Egypt through the creation of the Canal? If the swarm of Levantine and low-class European vultures who descended on the country whenever a new project promised a dubious reward may be called an asset, Egypt certainly derived that from it. To offset these, however, there were un-doubtedly a number of honest and well-intentioned merchants and businessmen who settled near the Canal whose efforts over the years bestowed considerable benefits on the country. They contributed in no small measure to the development of Egypt's resources and her commercial education. It may also be added that the Canal afforded steady and lucrative employment to thousands of middle-class Egyptians.

In 1854 when the concession was first granted, the sites on which the prosperous and teeming ports of Ismailia and Port Said now stand were barren stretches of desert, uninhabited save perhaps for the occasional wandering Beduin, while Suez itself was a wretched poverty-stricken collection of mud huts. These are now three of the most populated and prosperous towns in Egypt. On the mole at Port Said was erected a statue of Ferdinand de Lesseps, a monument to the 'Great Frenchman', founder of the Suez Canal. His outstretched hand pointed the way to the Canal. It also pointed to these three new towns of Egypt, also his creation. The statue was demolished after the Suez Crisis in November 1956.

CHAPTER 10

Ismail Pasha

'The evil that men do lives after them, the good is oft interred with their bones.' The quotation, though spoken of Caesar, would indeed be equally applicable to Ismail Pasha, the successor of Said and first Khedive of Egypt. Ismail has passed down through the pages of history as the classic example of wastrel, spendthrift and bankrupt, who sold his country and heritage to the foreign bondholders and brought about the British occupation of Egypt. It is singular to observe that the world is able to forgive a man practically every sin except bankruptcy.

In the multitudes of accounts which have been written by historians, statesmen and journalists on this particular period of Egypt's history, the majority have vied with each other in the abuse and vilification they have cast upon Ismail Pasha. Their indictments have been stressed with all the insistent clamour of the Shylock who sees himself in danger of being deprived of the last morsel of his pound of flesh. The case for the defence has been ignored or at most dismissed in a few words. After this long interval of time it is possible to piece together the story of Ismail Pasha, to examine the circumstances and causes of his ultimate downfall and to arrive at an impartial verdict.

When Said Pasha died in January 1863 the viceregal throne of Egypt, in accordance with Mohammedan law and by virtue of the firmans of 1841, devolved upon the eldest male of the family of Mohammed Ali. Had it not been for the railway disaster at Kafr ez-Zayet, Ahmed, eldest son of Ibrahim Pasha, would have succeeded Said, but his death opened the way to his younger brother, Ismail.

During his uncle's tenure Ismail had kept himself much out of the public eye, 'devoting himself to agricultural pursuits, shunning publicity through fear of inspiring Said's jealousy, and acquiring real estates – one

142

of his passions – until he became perhaps the largest landed proprietor in Egypt.'[1] In the management of his own affairs he is reported to have displayed 'indefatigable energy, sound judgment and administrative ability.'[2] During his youth he had been sent to France to acquire some measure of Western education and culture, and he succeeded in learning to speak fluent, if not entirely accurate, French. Certainly he acquired a liking for Western ways and an appreciation of their values, for during his reign Egypt advanced more on the road to Europeanisation than it had ever done before.

Following the traditions of his predecessors, Ismail Pasha embodied his political testament in the one short sentence, 'I am the State.' He proposed to assume the direction of the administration of Egypt down to the last detail. 'From the negotiation of a treaty or loan to the approval of a contract for coals or machinery, he is cognisant of every detail of public business, and nothing above the importance of mere departmental routine is done without having first passed under his eye . . . In a word from Alexandria to Wady Halfa . . . His Highness not only reigns, but governs.'[3] The assumption of such a task necessitated tremendous determination and energy, and the work kept the Pasha at his desk from twelve to fourteen hours daily nearly every day of the year throughout the whole period of his reign.

It is questionable whether this system of personal government, of dictatorship, was the most beneficial method of administering Egypt at this period. It had many advantages, and was, moreover, the traditional form of government practised in Egypt from time immemorial and well understood by all from the Turkish Pasha down to the humblest *fellah* at the plough. But since the days of Turkish and Mameluke supremacy Egypt had made substantial advances. The sleep and apathy of centuries had been thrown off and Egypt had begun to blossom forth as a new country with new ideas, new industries and a general expansion of commercial activity. The civilisation and progress of the West had begun to seep into this oriental satrapy bringing with them not only their benefits, but also their attendant administrative problems. What had fifty years previously been a comparatively easy country to administer by any industrious and intelligent Turkish Pasha, was now developing into a complex organism with ramifications and tentacles stretching out in many directions. It is therefore problematical whether it was within the capacities of even the most gifted and resolute administrator to control every activity which fell within the orbit of government. Yet this was what Ismail Pasha proposed to undertake. To aid him in the work he employed a number of officials who were honoured with the appellation of Minister, but these exercised no powers by virtue of their offices or on their own judgment. They were merely senior officials of the Government whose sole task lay in executing the demands of their Viceroy. Ismail formulated all matters of policy; his officials carried them into effect.

It was during these early years that Ismail gave evidence of the boundless ambition which possessed him and which during the reign of his predecessor he had concealed. Ismail possessed this quality in abundance, and in 1863 found himself in a position to give full rein to it. Its first manifestation was his attempt to make himself undisputed master of the land of Egypt. Having, as it were, cleared the ground by removing the several claims of privileges of the canal company, he set himself to the problem of liberating as far as possible his country and himself from the suzerainty of the Sultan and the Ottoman Empire.

Before him lay the example of his grandfather Mohammed Ali. For well over a quarter of a century he had struggled by all the means at his disposal to remove Egypt from subservience to Constantinople. Although his efforts had not been entirely barren of result, they had failed in their principal objective, since they had culminated in the settlements of 1840 and 1841 which had welded Egypt even more firmly to Constantinople. For while the Powers had guaranteed the *pashalik* of Egypt to Mohammed Ali and his descendants, they had also confirmed Egypt as part of the Empire. Such a situation bit deep into Ismail's soul, for there was a considerable difference between the status of Egypt and her rulers, and the other provinces of the Empire. The vice-regal throne was hereditary in one family, and Egypt herself was the most important, powerful and wealthy of all the provinces.

Mohammed Ali had tried force of arms to wrest his independence from the Sultan. Not only had he failed but he had run the risk of losing everything. His grandson Ismail, though imbued with the same ambitions, lacked his martial qualities; he was no man of war. He saw that in any case resort to arms would have been equally unavailing. He chose another weapon of attack, more efficacious in its results and less likely to cause offence to the Powers of Europe: the traditional oriental system of bribery commonly known as *bakshish*. The prerequisite to the success of his design was to put himself in close touch with the imperial court at Constantinople. De Freycinet[4] mentions that Ismail visited the Ottoman capital no fewer than seven times during his reign; it is also recorded that Sultan Abdul Aziz paid a visit to Egypt early in Ismail's reign.[5] It can safely be assumed that these journeys

144

were not merely to render homage to the mighty; on each occasion no doubt some substantial advantage or privilege changed hands for due consideration. The Sultan had little interest in Egypt since the relations between sovereign and viceroy had been laid down years before and guaranteed by the Powers. Practically the only claim of Constantinople on Cairo was the annual tribute which had likewise been fixed, but which could no doubt be increased in consideration of some extra privilege which did not conflict with the terms of the settlement.

Mohammed Ali had at least succeeded in one of his greatest ambitions, making the *pashalik* of Egypt hereditary in his own line. Abbas Pasha endeavoured to do the same but his contributions were not apparently sufficiently lavish to procure the desired result. Said had, as far as is known, been content to let the traditional Islamic law of succession stand, but Ismail was determined to secure the *pashalik* for his own line, to the exclusion of the other descendants of Mohammed Ali. This project was naturally unpopular with the other members of the family, especially Halim Pasha, the next in line, a younger son of Mohammed Ali who was powerful in Constantinople where he spent the greater part of his life. Nor was the proposal to alter the laws of succession in the case of Egypt received favourably by the Porte, and it must therefore be assumed that the *bakshish* which Ismail poured into the imperial coffers and into the palms of the numerous palace officials whose support was so necessary, must have been on a lavish scale. As far as is known no official record was kept of the financial aspect of these negotiations, and it is therefore impossible even to hazard a guess as to the total outlay made by Ismail. As Dicey wrote in his *Story of the Khedivate*, 'Money passed hands, and as soon as the consideration for its transfer was forthcoming, the less said, and still less written, the better for both seller and buyer.'[6]

The result of these negotiations was that on 27 March 1866 an imperial firman was promulgated changing the order of succession in favour of the descendants of Ismail Pasha in order of primogeniture, i.e. from father to son. The old order of succession has been much criticised on the ground that it occasions intrigue and rivalry within the family where polygamy prevails.

It is obvious that this state of things creates a serious objection to the principle laid down by the law of Mahomet, that a man's heir is not his eldest son, as in the West, but his oldest surviving male relative. This objection tells especially in the case of royal personages . . . The temptation to expedite the termination

145

of a reigning prince's life is apt to overcome all scruples of conscience or considerations of blood relationships.[7]

It is therefore suggested that the alteration of the law of succession by Ismail was beneficial in that it would tend to remove a cause of family strife and minimise fear of assassination. On closer examination, however, this proposition is difficult to maintain, for it must be remembered that polygamy still continued and the likelihood was that the sons of the sovereign would be the children of different mothers, and thus still subject to intrigue and jealousy in the harem. In fact, a case could well be made out that jealousy would be heightened by the new form of succession. Had the law not been changed, the heir would have been Halim Pasha, and the possibilities of succession by any of the children of Ismail Pasha would have been remote, at any rate for some considerable time. The new law, however, would tend to focus attention on the Viceroy's children, and it would not be difficult to imagine with what fear each of the Pasha's wives would regard the others' children.

It is reasonable therefore to dismiss the suggestion that the change in the law of succession was intended to reduce family feud. Ismail Pasha was merely obeying the normal instincts of a father to hand on his heritage to his own children, instead of to some cousin, uncle or nephew. In this there was at least one tangible advantage. The urge to milk his heritage to the last drop so that he could leave his children well-endowed had disappeared, since it would be one of them who would automatically enter into possession.

As a result of further liberal sums of *bakshish* a new firman was issued on 8 June 1867, conferring the title of Khedive upon Ismail. This was the outcome of his negotiations to have his title and rank so modified as to give him some clear distinction and precedence over the other Pashas and provincial governors of the Empire who were still nominated to their posts by the Porte. It is reported that considerable difficulty was experienced in finding a title which was both appropriate and caused no complications. The title most favoured by Ismail was 'Aziz', a Turkish word signifying 'esteemed' or 'holy', one of the attributes of Allah. But the Sultan's own name was Abdul Aziz, meaning literally 'Servant of Aziz', and as Dicey points out, 'the conferring of the title of El Aziz upon the Viceroy might create some confusion among the followers of Islam as to the relative positions of the Suzerain and his vassal.'[8] However, after some diligent searchings, agreement was reached on the title 'Khedive', a word of Persian origin signifying 'a great prince, a man of high power and authority'.[9] This apparently satisfied

Ismail; of Pashas there were many both in the empire and in Egypt itself, but there was only one Khedive.

These two important concessions not only cost Ismail vast sums for which no account can be made, but further, they were made conditional upon the annual tribute being increased from £400,000 to £750,000. The tribute was derived by public taxation from the pockets of the native *fellahin*. Thus, in acquiring the two concessions outlined above, the Khedive saddled his country with additional taxation of £350,000 a year. It was a matter of indifference to the average *fellah* whether Effendina[10] was the son, uncle or brother of his predecessor, nor did it profit him that Effendina was now entitled to be called His Highness the Khedive instead of His Highness the Viceroy. Yet it was he who was to foot the bill. On the other hand, a certain indefinable advantage accrued from these innovations. The world began to take notice of Egypt and its ruler, and Egypt became one of the popular countries of the world for commercial and investment purposes.

During the course of his reign the Khedive extracted numerous other concessions from Constantinople, which were confirmed and embodied in the firman of 8 June 1873, of which the following is a summary:

We have wished to combine in one single firman all the firmans and *khats humayouns* which have been granted to the Khedives of Egypt since the firman which bestowed the inheritance of Egypt to your ancestor Mehemet Ali.

The order of succession to the government of Egypt has been modified such that the Khedivate of Egypt should pass to the eldest son of the Khedive and after him to his eldest son, and so on, that is, that the succession is by order of primogeniture. (This order applies to the dependencies of Egypt and to Suakin and Massawa.)

We set forth all the privileges which my imperial firmans, both formerly and recently, have granted to the Egyptian Government to be held in perpetuity by the Khedives to follow.

The civil and financial administration of the country and all the material and other interests of the country are within the province of the Egyptian Government and are confided to them; and inasmuch as the administration, the good order of every country, the development and the wealth and the prosperity of the people spring from the harmony established between the deeds, general relations, the conditions and nature of the country, as well as the characters and customs of the people, the Khedive of Egypt is authorised to make internal arrangements and laws whenever necessary.

He is also authorised to contract and renew, without prejudice to the political treaties of my Sublime Porte, agreements with the agents of foreign powers in respect of customs and commerce, and of all relations which affect foreign nationals, and all the internal and other affairs of the country, with the object of developing the commerce and industry and of regulating policy with foreigners, their situation and relations with the government and the people.

The Khedive has complete control of the finances of the country; he is authorised entirely to provide means and establishments of defence and protection according to the necessities of time and place, and to increase or reduce according to need the number of my imperial troops in Egypt without limit.

The Khedive will retain the right of promotion up to the rank of colonel in the army, and to the rank of *rutbé sanieh* in the civil grades. Coinage struck in Egypt must be struck in my imperial name; the flags of military and naval forces will be the same as those of my other troops; ironclads may not be built without my permission.

You will address your closest attention to remitting every year without delay and in its entirety to my imperial Treasury the 150,000 purses of the agreed tribute.

All these concessions were obtained in the same way, by the judicious employment of *bakshish*. Mr P. Crabitès, in his book *Ismail the Maligned*, gives a fascinating account of the machinery set up by Ismail to secure these concessions, based on documents, letters and telegrams found in the Royal Egyptian Archives. The Khedive employed an agent, one Abraham Bey, an Armenian, almost permanently at Constantinople. His duties included buying the services and support of the various ministers and palace officials, disbursing *bakshish* among them and intriguing on behalf of the Khedive his employer. Through this medium hundreds of thousands of pounds passed from the Khedive's purse into the palms of corrupt palace officials. The employment of *bakshish* in the Near East was not the exception but the norm, an established and recognised institution. Nothing could be done without it; a decision on any particular case rarely rested on its merits; the amount of *bakshish* either party was prepared to pay was usually the deciding factor. Even the most important and beneficial reform ever to be introduced into nineteenth-century Egypt, the creation of the Mixed Tribunals, of which some mention is now made, was only effected by the use of *bakshish*.

Throughout the Ottoman domains there existed a series of ancient treaties, better known as the Capitulations, which conferred substantial privileges upon the nationals of the European countries resident within the Ottoman empire. Among these privileges was one granting exemption from the jurisdiction of the native courts in which justice was administered, theoretically at least, in accordance with the sacred law of Islam.

> Hence arose the doctrine of extraterritoriality, which simply signified the absence of local jurisdiction over the foreigner throughout the Ottoman dominions, and legal authority of their own diplomatic or consular agents over them, in all civil or criminal cases in which they might be defendants.[11]

In brief, it meant that no European could be prosecuted for any criminal offence, or be a party in any civil action, in the native courts. Such cases were heard in the courts of his own consul. In earlier years, when but a bare handful of Europeans were resident in the empire, this system worked well enough, but during the latter half of the nineteenth century, when the commerce and industry of Egypt underwent tremendous expansion, the European colony increased substantially; in the time of Ismail it exceeded a hundred thousand. The amount of litigation, especially civil and commercial, involving European nationals, in consequence underwent a corresponding expansion, and these cases were heard in the consular courts. As long as these merely involved Europeans the Egyptian administration was little concerned, but when it was a crime or an action between European and Egyptian, it was a different matter. For in many cases, the justice administered by the consular courts was frequently not so impartial as might have been wished, and a decision was as likely to be influenced by the nationality of the parties as by the merits of the case. It thus happened that an Egyptian suing a European in his consular court had as little hope of getting satisfaction as the European would suing an Egyptian in the native courts. Since each consular court administered justice in accordance with the law of its own country, the legal system operating in Egypt was little short of chaotic.

In 1856 an attempt had been made to induce the consuls to cede their judicial powers in favour of a proposed international tribunal, so that some uniformity of code and procedure might be achieved. But the time was not yet ripe; the consuls were loath to cede their rights in favour of an institution which was not even in existence. Although this earlier proposal was allowed to lapse, the idea had at any rate been born. The revival of this proposal and the carrying of it through to ultimate reality was the achievement of the greatest of Egypt's statesmen in the nineteenth century, Nubar Pasha.

Nubar Pasha was one of the most honourable and able men of his time.

> Educated to diplomacy by his famous kinsman Boghos Bey, himself one of the ablest counsellors of Mehemet Ali, his life has been spent in this pursuit. Speaking and writing almost all the languages of Europe with equal facility, and conversant with European affairs and their directors, he has steered Egypt free from the breakers that surround her, under two successive reigns . . .[12]

All writers and commentators who were acquainted with him bore testimony to his high character and culture. No greater testimony to his character could be given than that he, an Armenian and a Christian, held high office in a Moslem country over long and difficult periods.

Early in the reign of Ismail Pasha, Nubar put forward new proposals for an international tribunal which would assume the powers and functions of the existing consular courts. In order to achieve this result it was necessary to secure the agreement and support of fourteen different consuls and the governments they represented, as well as of the Khedive and the Sultan. The Khedive Ismail, seeing the advantages that would accrue to Egypt from the establishment of tribunals administering one set of laws instead of fourteen courts using fourteen different codes, readily concurred in Nubar's scheme, and himself went to immense trouble and expense to further it.

This question affords a typical example of the difficulties facing the Egyptian Government of effecting reform and the venality of those who had the power to obstruct. Mr Crabitès[13] quotes evidence of the fact that, in order to secure the adherence of the Porte to the proposals for the new tribunals, the shadowy Abraham Bey was obliged to pour out vast sums of *bakshish* at Constantinople; the figure actually mentioned is £289,421, which included a payment of £150,000 to the Sultan himself. Not only this, but a further 'bribe' of £20,000 had to be paid to General Ignatiev, the Tsar's Ambassador at Constantinople, to ensure that Russia offered no opposition. It is clear therefore that without Ismail's moral and financial support, Nubar's tribunals would never have been established. Nubar himself was unremitting in his efforts to persuade the powers to accede to these proposals, both in Egypt and in the capitals of Europe, and his work was finally crowned with success. In February 1876 the first International Tribunals, more commonly known as the Mixed Courts, came into being in Egypt. Three courts of first instance were established at Cairo, Alexandria and Mansurah respectively, with jurisdiction over all civil cases between Europeans and Egyptians, and between Europeans of different nationalities.[14]

The legal system adopted was the Code Napoléon which, though not entirely suited to an oriental country, at least had the merit of being well-known and standardised. Not all the Powers concurred initially in the establishment of the new courts, France characteristically being the dissident.

France's attitude in this matter affords further evidence that her general policy towards Egypt was ever tinged with no small element of hypocrisy. It has already been shown how France continually posed as the champion, guide, protector and friend of Egypt, yet whenever these pretensions were put to the test, either by the need for action or, as in this case, by the sacrifice of a privilege, they were proved hollow. The Mixed Courts were finally established in spite of the protests of France, who once again found herself in a minority and forced to accept the situation with as good a grace as she could muster. Mr de Freycinet wrote feelingly on this point: 'C'est un avertissement de ne pas trop compter sur notre supériorité traditionelle.'[15]

The Powers agreed that the Mixed Tribunals should be tried as an experiment for five years. So well did they succeed that they remained in existence until after the Second World War. They were finally closed in 1948.

In 1869 the great feat of engineering across the isthmus of Suez was finally brought to completion and the waters of the Mediterranean and the Red Seas were fused together. The official opening of the Canal was used by the Khedive as an occasion for the display of munificence and hospitality on a scale almost undreamed of. The Khedive could rightly and reasonably have left the celebrations of the occasion to be organised and, even more important, to be paid for by the Canal Company. On the contrary he assumed the direction and responsibility for everything, much, it can be safely assumed, to the satisfaction of de Lesseps and his company. The Khedive, however, had particular reason for following this course, although it must be doubted in the light of subsequent events whether these reasons were fully justified. In some respects Ismail was the most progressive ruler Egypt had known for centuries. Like his grandfather he was fired with the ambition to bring his country to the same level of culture, civilisation and development as were enjoyed by the most progressive countries of Europe. For this purpose a vast influx of foreign capital was required to develop the potential resources of the country. Already Ismail had had recourse to the bankers and money-lenders of Europe, but the loans he had contracted were trifling compared with those he was contemplating for the future. An astute man and thoroughly conversant with human nature, he readily appreciated the axiom that nothing succeeds like success. All the world would be coming to Egypt for the opening of the Suez Canal, and to Ismail it was of importance that visitors should receive the impression that Egypt was enjoying unparalleled prosperity and could therefore be regarded as a safe investment for capital. It may be added that these hopes were amply fulfilled when the bankers of Europe gladly poured their gold into Egyptian securities.

The following extract from the account of Mr E. Dicey, who was one of the guests at the ceremony, will provide some idea of the lavishness of the celebrations, all of which were borne by the Egyptian Treasury:

> . . . there were some thousands of more or less well known visitors who arrived in Egypt, bearers of cards of invitation . . . Nothing could be more generous than the arrangements made for the entertainment of the visitors. The recipient of an invitation was entitled to a gratuitous passage from Europe to Alexandria or Port Said and back, to board and lodging during his sojourn in Egypt, to free passes on the railroads, and to admission to all the functions connected with the opening of the Canal. The Egyptian officials had instructions to show every attention to the visitors. Carriages, donkeys and dragomen were provided without charge for any guest who took the trouble to apply to the Master of the ceremonies. No bills were presented, no vouchers were required, and it is not too much to say that any one of the Khedive's visitors might have spent two months in Egypt without ever needing to put his hand in his pocket for anything except personal expenses such as baths, and washing, and even these expenses were refunded with alacrity if, as often happened, any visitor applied for their repayment.[16]

A road was built out to the Pyramids at Giza in case guests should wish to visit these ancient wonders, the opera *Aida* was specially composed by Verdi for the occasion, and a fine new opera house was built in the Ezbekia Gardens in Cairo in which to present it. These were only a few of the innovations and projects designed by the Khedive to mark the occasion. No record was kept of the total outlay on these magnificent ceremonies, nor is it possible to formulate any approximation. It is, however, safe to assert that it must have run into millions.

During these years the institution of slavery and the slave trade were very much in the public eye of the civilised world, especially after the conclusion of the American Civil War and the liberation of the slaves. More than ever was the attention of those agitating for the suppression of slavery directed to the source of the trouble, the interior of Africa and the countries surrounding it through whose territory the slave trade plied. While British men of war were patrolling the east coast of Africa, intercepting the dhows and relieving them of their human cargoes, yet another transit was still open to the slavers, down the River Nile through the Sudan and into Egypt where the slaves were sold and disappeared into the households and harems of wealthy Egyptians, Turks and Europeans. Said Pasha had during his reign paid a visit to the Sudan and issued a proclamation limiting the buying and selling of slaves, but little heed was paid to this by those engaged in this lucrative commerce. Khartoum, on the junction of the Blue and White Niles, became the centre and market for the trade whose outlet lay along the Nile, and the Egyptian officials of the Government not only gave open countenance to it, but took a hand in it themselves.

The Khedive recognised the existence of this canker in the lands under his rule and warmly espoused the cause of the Anti-Slavery Movement. This was a courageous stand to take, inasmuch as the institution of slavery had existed in Egypt since time immemorial, and the economy and mode of life of the country depended to a large extent on it. An outright attack on slavery might well have excited considerable discontent and even opposition, yet relying on his prestige as ruler and despot Ismail resolved to strike an effective blow at the slave trade by despatching an expedition into the heart of the Sudan to root out the nests of the slavers and to open the interior to commerce and civilising influences. In taking this step Ismail realised that his objectives might well be misconstrued by a suspicious Europe which could with difficulty believe that the Pasha of Egypt would of his own volition attack an institution of such standing and antiquity in his country. Might it not be said that Ismail, instead of fighting the slave trade, was sending troops to organise it more effectively? That there might be no shadow of suspicion regarding his intentions, he selected as commanders men of the highest reputation and character, first Sir Samuel Baker, and later Colonel Charles Gordon. Some mention of these expeditions is made in a later chapter on the Sudan. At the same time the prospect of enlarging the Egyptian empire was a source of satisfaction to a man of Ismail's ambitious character.

During his period of unfettered rule which lasted from his accession to 1877, the Khedive was free to indulge his unlimited ambitions for real estate. Ismail had a mania for land and buildings and he freely admitted it. Already the owner of extensive estates of about 30,000 *feddans* on his accession, he set himself during his reign to become the proprietor of as much land as possible. Whenever land came up for sale Ismail bought, and even when land was not offered for sale, it somehow came into his possession.

Thus over a period of thirteen years nearly a million *feddans*, one fifth of the total cultivable area of Egypt, passed into his possession. It may well be questioned how Ismail Pasha, even though undisputed master of the country, became the proprietor of such a vast area. There has been little suggestion that he went to the extremes of expropriating outright the original owners, but there is no doubt that he used the public revenues for this purpose, and even loaded his country with a large foreign debt contracted expressly for the purpose of acquiring land for himself and his family.

This was a retrograde step in every respect. Egypt is essentially a land of small-holders and the love of the land and the longing to possess even a few square yards are innate in every *fellah*. The immense acquisition of land by the Khedive entailed a corresponding loss of land ownership among the natural proprietors, the *fellahin*. Furthermore, the basis of all public revenue was the land-tax, and as long as the land remained predominantly in the possession of small-holders who would till it with loving care, the best yields of produce could be expected and the more revenue collected. The *fellahin* who lost their holdings to the Khedive, instead of being landed proprietors in their own right, became but hired labourers. It was likewise inconceivable that the Khedive and his family who held these vast estates between them should pay any taxes, and the public revenues to that extent suffered. A further point may be mentioned in this connection. Prior to his accession, Ismail had devoted his full attention to the administration of his relatively small holdings of 30,000 *feddans*. On his accession, he inherited the whole administration of Egypt, and he attempted himself to supervise every detail. It can thus be readily imagined how much time and care he was able to devote to the supervision of his immense new estates. In the working of these he did not hesitate to employ the *corvée* to which he had so strongly objected in the case of the Suez Canal, but he failed to appreciate that this only operated to the detriment of the State. Since the Khedive and the State were virtually synonymous, these factors not only cancelled each other out, but actually resulted in a net loss. A man of immense vision and ability in many respects with an amazing insight into human nature, Ismail nevertheless had no practical grasp of simple economics.

Building was another of the Khedive's obsessions, and it was during his reign that Cairo put on its modern face. Edwin de Leon, who had been American Consul in Cairo during the times of Abbas and Said, paid a visit to Egypt in 1877. In his book, *The Khedive's Egypt*, he records the vast improvements and alterations made in the capital by His Highness. The old mud huts and hovels, the wilderness of the Ezbekia, had been swept away and replaced by imposing new buildings of European architecture and stately gardens; filthy narrow alleys had given place to wide new carriageways, the streets of modern Cairo. Unable to carry out all the building plans himself, Ismail offered plots of valuable land in the city to anyone who would erect buildings to a certain value, and thus improve the capital value and amenities of the city. Many took advantage of these offers and erected palaces and blocks of shops and offices. Significant of the immense changes which took place in the space of a few years is the fact that the Muski, which is commonly considered by the modern traveller in Egypt to be the native bazaar, was in fact, in the days before Ismail Pasha, the district of European shops. Though travellers were wont to lament the passing of the picturesque squalor of the old Cairo, there can be no doubt of the benefits resulting to the population from the Khedive's remarkable mania for bricks and mortar. It is singular that he displayed little or no interest in the second great metropolis of Egypt, Alexandria, with the exception of its harbour works and marine facilities. There is a legend that it had been foretold that Ismail would die in Alexandria; in consequence, being a superstitious man, he avoided the city as much as possible. On the development of the harbour, however, he spent enormous sums and succeeded in making it one of the most modern and best equipped ports in the Mediterranean.

The Khedive initiated extensive schemes for the irrigation of the land and the improvement of the communications system of the country. Up to this time roads in the accepted sense of the term barely existed in Egypt, the only means of communication between population centres being the Nile and the system of canals, while the railway was as yet in its infancy, and only extended from Alexandria, via Cairo, to Suez. The subsequent commercial and agricultural development of Egypt was largely due to Ismail's improvements and extensions of the road and railway systems. Nine hundred miles of railway line were laid, and no fewer than 430 bridges of one sort or another, including a span of over four hundred metres over the Nile at Cairo, were built during his reign.

A hundred and twelve new canals were also dug, bringing the Nile waters to new lands for cultivation. 'By means of these canals, the people succeeded in reclaiming from the desert no less than 1,373,000 acres, representing a gross annual product of crops worth £11,000,000, or a rental value of £1,400,000 per annum.'[17] The total length of canals constructed during this period is estimated at 8,400 miles. The following brief table of schemes and their costs gives a fair picture of some of the principal developments of the time:

Work	Cost	Observations
The Suez Canal	£ 6,770,000	After deducting value of shares sold.
Nile Canals	£12,600,000	8400 miles @ £1,500 a mile.
Bridges	£ 2,150,000	430 @ £5,000 a bridge.
Sugar Mills	£ 6,100,000	Built 64 with machinery.
Harbour, Alexandria	£ 2,542,000	
Suez Docks	£ 1,400,000	
Alexandria water works	£ 300,000	
Railways	£13,361,000	Length 910 miles (new).
Telegraphs	£ 853,000	Built 5,200 miles (new).
Lighthouses	£ 188,000	15 on Red Sea and Mediterranean.
	£46,264,000[18]	

The full scope of the Khedive's work in this direction would merit a volume in itself, but sufficient has been said to indicate the progress achieved in the space of a few years. Not surprisingly, the nature and extent of all these schemes led Egypt and her ruler into great financial embarrassment which ultimately led to Ismail's downfall and deposition, but this will form the subject of the next chapters. Ismail Pasha is today principally remembered as the man who overwhelmed his country with a vast load of debt which took many years of stringent economy and careful administration to pay off. He has gone down in history as a spendthrift and profligate, terms which are generally understood to imply one who has squandered his wealth and has nothing to show for it. Indisputably his expenditure was prodigious and far beyond the capacity of the country to pay, but was it all squandered? Was there no return, nothing to show for it? Lord Cromer, who was destined to play an important part in the affairs of Egypt, wrote: 'Roughly speaking, it may be said that Ismail Pasha added, on average, about £7,000,000 a year for thirteen years to the debt of Egypt. For all practical purposes, it may be said that the whole of the money borrowed, except for £16,000,000 spent on the Suez Canal, was squandered.'[19] On page 1 of his great work, *Modern Egypt*, Lord Cromer propounds the theory that 'accuracy of statement is a great merit', yet it must be questioned whether his own statement, quoted above, that all the money borrowed was squandered, is not open to a charge of inaccuracy. The evidence, a small portion of which this chapter has attempted to produce, points to a contrary conclusion. No attempt is here made to justify the vast expenditure and loans which the Khedive incurred;

but merely to show that the money was spent largely on developments and public works, the majority of which have been of substantial and lasting benefit to Egypt and her people.

Ismail possessed the normal attributes of a man in his character, a measure of good and a measure of evil. It is questionable whether the *bakshish* paid to the Porte and the increase in tribute were worth the privileges granted. He deserved no praise for acquiring one-fifth of the land of Egypt as his own or his family's property. On the other hand, he does not appear to deserve the censure cast upon him by world opinion that he was a profligate. Much that he did was good and of lasting value, some however was bad, for which he was later to pay dearly.

However much may be said against him, one thing is beyond dispute. Egypt, during the sixteen years of his reign, has advanced more in all that pertains to modern civilisation than in the hundred, or perhaps five hundred years next preceding and more than it will be likely to advance for a long time to come; for this advancement the country is almost wholly indebted to him.

CHAPTER 11

Financial Difficulties

Limitations of space have precluded more than a brief mention of the programmes of development inaugurated by Ismail Pasha in Egypt. Much more could be said of his plans for the education of both sexes, scientific researches, exploratory expeditions and other activities, all of which were intended to further the welfare of the country. It will be evident that these schemes required a considerable outlay of capital and that they could only bear fruit after the passage of several years. Where then did all the money come from?

Various attempts have been made to assess the precise figure of the public revenue during the period that Ismail Pasha held unfettered power in Egypt; the estimated figures have varied somewhat, and this is not surprising. For one thing there must have been a great disparity between the amounts extracted from the tax-payers and that actually paid into the Egyptian Treasury. Again, sometimes the taxes were taken in kind, i.e. crops and produce, instead of money and it is unlikely that any accurate valuation was ever placed on these. Under the despotic system of government that prevailed it was likewise equally impossible to distinguish between the public revenues proper and the personal income of the Khedive. Inasmuch as the latter disposed of both, any such distinction would have been fictitious.

Receipts and expenses were transferred and retransferred from one account to another, according as it suited the policy of the Government to increase or diminish the respective liabilities of the Sovereign and the State. The accounts, in as far as they were kept at all, were kept entirely by Coptic clerks, who possess an unrivalled reputation in the East for manipulating accounts in any way which may be acceptable to their employers.[1]

Mr Stephen Cave, who made a report on Egyptian finances early in 1876, puts the revenue for the period 1864 to 1875 at £94,281,401, which would work out at about £8 million a year. This figure may possibly have been an overestimate since even as late as 1880, when some of the Khedive's development plans such as the increase in irrigation, would have begun to bear fruit, the revenue was only estimated at £8½ million. Be that as it may, the expenses of administration were reckoned to amount to a little more than half the revenue, so that a comfortable surplus of something in the region of £3 million or more remained for improvements and new developments.

But the demands made on Ismail early in his reign, notably the harsh arbitration award of Napoleon III and other expenses connected with the Suez Canal, wiped out this surplus and little, if any, remained to launch the Khedive's grandiose projects. Had not that insidious facility for easy credit been introduced to Ismail on apparently attractive terms, he would have been compelled to limit his expenditure to such amounts as were provided by the revenues. Social and economic progress would have been much retarded or postponed, but at least Egypt would have been saved from the burden of debt which encompassed her ruin and overthrew her ruler.

As it was, the wonderful prosperity enjoyed by Egypt at the commencement of Ismail's reign, due largely to the inflated cotton prices that prevailed at the time and her seemingly inexhaustible agricultural wealth, were too great a bait for the financiers of Europe to resist. Speculators and capitalists looking for large and easy returns for the investment of their capital were only too willing to invest it in Egyptian bonds, secured on the word of His Highness the Khedive. The latter, delighted at the prospect of glorifying his reign with a programme of development that would mark him out as the most enlightened monarch of Egypt since the days of the Pharaohs, made possible only by the eagerness of the financiers to invest in him, took the plunge and plunged deeply.

It does not appear that Ismail considered the full implications of the loans he so carelessly contracted nor that he gave much thought to the future ability of Egypt to repay them, principal and interest, the latter never at a rate less than seven per cent. It may well be that he expected his schemes to mature quickly so that a greater revenue would be forthcoming to meet the extra commitments. Possibly he anticipated that the investors would have no power to enforce repayment except on his own terms. Alternatively it may be that like a true Oriental he trusted in Allah and hoped for the best.

As the years passed and loan succeeded loan the Khedive found himself increasingly in debt and even much embarrassed to pay the coupons on the existing loans as they fell due. Too late, he found himself in the grip of the money-lenders. In common with all such victims, what he sought most was time and yet more time. Year after year he resorted to desperate expedients to stave off the disaster which grew more and more imminent. The climax of this struggle against the inevitable came with his deposition in 1879, his humiliation before the world and the financial enslavement of his country to the bondholders for decades to come.

While it is not intended to detract from the censure which must be attributed to Ismail Pasha for having recklessly disposed of his country's resources, it is important at the same time to insist that this measure of censure should not be exaggerated. There were many extenuating circumstances. Among these was Ismail's evil genius, his Minister of Finance, Ismail Sadiq Pasha. This remarkable character, who ruled the finances of Egypt for about eight years, was commonly known to the Egyptians as the Mufettish or Chief Steward.

> The Mufettish was a fellah by birth, of humble origin, a man of little education, who, by force of a certain perverted ability, had recommended himself to the favour of the Khedive. He, being a peasant, and knowing the ways of his fellow peasants, understood far better than the Turks . . . how to get money out of the fellahin. To Ismail, in his urgent financial straits, such knowledge was invaluable . . . It was on him, therefore, that Ismail chiefly relied to raise money from the fellahin, whenever money had to be provided at all costs and all hazards.[2]

In the course of his tax-gatherings and the involved financial transactions undertaken on behalf of his master the Khedive, the Mufettish amassed for himself a personal fortune reputed to have exceeded two millions sterling. Although the Khedive attempted to supervise every detail of the Government, he could not have been conversant with every aspect of the Mufettish's transactions on his account and, such is the custom of the Oriental to report no unwelcome news to the potentate, it is more than probable that the Mufettish painted the financial condition of Egypt to his master in much rosier colours than it justified. It was the task of the Mufettish to supply his master with money whenever he required it, which was constantly. The means adopted to satisfy his master's wishes were such as to leave the native *fellah* not only without a piastre to his name, but almost left to destitution with his lands or crops mortgaged at usurious rates to the money-lenders who invariably accompanied the tax-collector on his rounds. Thus, in spite of the apparent progress and prosperity of Egypt, the peasant cultivator was usually living on the brink of starvation.

Lord Cromer[3] gives an illuminating example of the methods adopted to raise funds:

> The Egyptian Government, being in want of ready money, sold to some Levantine firm a quantity of grain which they did not possess, and which, for the most part, they were never likely to possess. The purchase money was paid at once; the grain had to be delivered to the purchasers a few months later. When the time for its delivery arrived, a certain amount was in some cases delivered, as it was then the practice of the Egyptian Government to collect a portion of the taxes in kind. The remainder was bought back by the Government at a price of 25 per cent above that which had been paid by the original purchasers. In other cases, the Government never delivered any grain, neither was any money repaid at the time. The Government, however, still went through the form of repurchase, and the original purchasers received Treasury bills, bearing interest at the rate of 18 or 20 per cent, not for the amount which they had in the first instance advanced, but for the larger sum for which the Government eventually effected the nominal repurchase of the grain. It is impossible to say what rate of interest the Egyptian Government really paid in the end for money advanced under this system. It must have been something enormous.

The following table gives a summary of the foreign loans contracted by Ismail Pasha during his reign or by the Mufettish on his behalf.

Date	Bank	Nominal	Net Product
1864	Goschen	£5,704,000	£4,864,000
1865	Anglo-Egyptian	3,387,000	2,750,000
1866	Goschen	3,000,000	2,640,000
1867	Imperial Ottoman	2,080,000	1,700,000
1868	Oppenheim	11,890,000	7,193,000
1870	Bischoffsheim	7,143,000	5,810,000
1873	Oppenheim	32,000,000	17,810,000
		65,204,000	41,957,000

Some of these loans were secured on certain revenues of Egypt such as the Railways, the Daira Sanieh or State Domains, but all of them carried interest at the rate of seven per cent, except that of 1865 which was contracted at

161

nine per cent. Even the lower rate was excessive, especially as the loans were secured on the Egyptian government. It appears, however, that the bankers had no difficulty in persuading the Khedive to accept these onerous terms and it is certain that he did not appreciate their full significance. Ismail appears to have been as much a puppet in the hands of the suave and crafty bankers as his predecessor, Said, had been in the hands of the wily de Lesseps. The most odious feature of all these loans, however, is the enormous disparity between the nominal sum of the loans and the amounts which the Egyptian government actually received. For example, the nominal amount of the Oppenheim loan of 1868 is shown at £11,890,000, which was the figure of indebtedness contracted by the Egyptian government, on which interest at seven per cent was payable annually. The actual amount received by the government, however, was only £7,193,000. Thus, of the total loan contracted, £4,697,000 fell by the wayside. It can only be assumed that this staggering figure disappeared into the hands of the bankers, brokers and commission agents who did the Khedive the favour of negotiating the loan. In this case, which is typical of all the others, the Egyptian government had bound themselves to repay £11,890,000 where they had only received £7,193,000, and to pay an actual interest of 11½ per cent instead of the nominal seven per cent. When de Lesseps floated his Canal company, he rejected with scorn the offer of Rothschilds to float the subscription for a five per cent commission. When Oppenheims subscribed the 1868 loan to Egypt, the total commissions one way and another amounted to no less than 39½ per cent. Taking the grand total of the loans it will be seen that of the £65,204,000 nominal, only £41,957,000 was actually received by the Egyptian government. More than one-third thus fell in commissions and brokerages. No wonder that the bankers of Europe were so anxious to float loans for Ismail Pasha. At any time they could without difficulty have ascertained the state of Egyptian solvency and decided whether a new loan was a safe investment for the public, but it may well be questioned whether it was in their interests to do so, since such magnificent pickings were to be made from every transaction which passed through their hands.

Let us consider for a moment the crowning achievement of Oppenheims who negotiated the 1873 loan for £32,000,000. It is incontestable that this bank knew the approximate amount of the Egyptian revenue and that loans amounting to £33,204,000 had already been contracted by the Egyptian Government. They must also have known that Ismail Pasha had contracted a floating debt which at the time probably amounted to something in the region of £15,000,000. Let it be assumed that the Egyptian revenues amounted to about £8,000,000 a year. The expenses of administration, plus the tribute to Constantinople, may be modestly assessed at £4,500,000, although this is probably an understatement. This would leave about £3½ million for repayment of sinking funds and interest on loans already contracted. A simple calculation shows that seven per cent of £48 million (i.e. £33 million of loans already contracted plus £15 million of floating debt) amounts to £3,360,000, and this was the least figure that had to be paid out of the £3½ million and does not include any sinking fund. Can it be said that Oppenheims, in floating a further loan of £32,000,000, truthfully considered this a safe investment for the public? Yet the loan was floated and the reason not far to seek. Of this £32 million only £17,810,000 found its way into the Egyptian Treasury. It is not difficult to imagine what happened to the remaining £14,190,000.

During the same period as the foreign loans were being contracted, the Khedive was building up a large floating debt in Egypt, this in general at a far more ruinous rate of interest than the foreign loans. One such operation, typical of many, has already been quoted. Two more are worthy of mention as illustrative of the desperate expedients to which the Khedive was driven to stave off disaster for a little.

Lord Cromer reports that:

in 1874, a forced loan, entitled the 'Emprunt Rouznameh' had been raised in the provinces. Subscriptions had been invited for a loan of £5,000,000 bearing interest at the rate of 9 per cent. About £1,800,000 was actually paid into the Treasury. We obtained from some of the villages a list of the subscribers to the loan; each list was accompanied by a declaration signed by the Notables of the village stating that the subscriptions were 'perfectly voluntary'. They were, of course, in no sense voluntary. No bonds were ever delivered to the subscribers and, up to the date of our enquiry, one instalment of interest only had been paid to a few favoured individuals.[4]

In 1871 was evolved an operation known as the law of the Mukabala. Under this law any land-owner could reduce his land-tax by one half by the payment of six years' tax 'either in one sum, or in instalments spread over twelve years.'[5]

The whole system of taxation in Egypt was founded on the land-tax. But here was enacted a law entitling a land-owner to halve his taxes by the payment of a lump sum. It is obvious of course that this would have been the classic example of killing the goose that lays the golden egg, had it not been for the fact that there was clearly no intention of adhering to the engagements towards the land-owners. It could not possibly have been otherwise. Means would have easily been found to circumvent these engagements, if only by doubling the rate of taxation. In theory both the law of the Mukabala and the Rouznameh loan were only invitations to the public to subscribe money, but it was readily understood by all that such an invitation from the Khedive was tantamount to a command, and between 1872 and 1879 a sum of £16,000,000 was collected on account of the Mukabala.

Debts were 'paid' and new loans contracted by the issue of Treasury bills which had no solid backing, but were, as Dicey says, 'mere promissory notes guaranteed by the Egyptian Government, or, in other words, by Ismail.' So numerous did these Treasury bills become and so rarely were they actually paid in cash that they naturally lost much of their face value, and were hawked about Egypt at tremendous discounts. Their only real value lay in the fact that they could be used to pay debts to the Egyptian Government.

One of the last efforts of Ismail Pasha to raise money took place in 1875 when he sold his holding in the Suez Canal to the British Government. It appears to be current opinion that Ismail Pasha in selling his holding deprived Egypt of all her rights and interests in this vast enterprise to which she had given so much blood and treasure. Dicey states: 'With the sale of these shares Egypt forfeited her one chance of obtaining any return whatever for the vast sums she had contributed to the construction of the canal.'[6] This is a mis-statement. 'When in 1869 the Canal was nearing completion de Lesseps was so badly in need of funds that he appealed to Ismail to come to his rescue. Certain agreements were then made between the Khedive and the Canal Company. To obtain the necessary cash, which he put into the project to save it from bankruptcy, Ismail pledged any and all dividends which might be earned by his common stock until 1894.'[7] It thus appears that when he sold these shares to the British Government in 1875, the coupons had already been detached for nearly twenty years to come. This meant that the British Government had bought a large block of the shares which would not bring in any dividend until 1894. The fact that the Khedive sold them at rather more than their face value seems to indicate that he did rather a good stroke of business.

In spite of this sale the Khedive still had a substantial interest in the company, that fifteen per cent of the profits granted to the Egyptian Government in the original concession of 1854. This interest Ismail had preserved intact and never disposed of. 'This 15 per cent interest of

164

the Egyptian Government was sold in March 1880 to the *Crédit Foncier de France* which at once ceded its rights to la Société des Produits de la Compagnie Universelle du Canal Maritime de Suez Attribués au Gouvernement Egyptien.'[8] In March 1880 Ismail Pasha was in exile, having been deposed, and Lord Cromer, the Khedive's chief critic, was in the saddle of Egyptian finances yet, strange to say, no mention of this transaction figures anywhere in Cromer's *apologia pro sua vita, Modern Egypt.* Perhaps however there is no cause for wonder about this singular omission, for the sale of this fifteen per cent interest was effected for only 22 million francs or £880,000, the product of which returned tremendous dividends during all the years of Cromer's tenure of office in Egypt, a perpetual reminder of one of the poorest business deals ever effected by a son of a great banking house.

To return to the sale of the shares, the £4 million realised effected only a temporary respite to the Khedive in his race against time. The money was immediately swallowed up in the payment of interest and sinking fund upon existing loans. A few weeks before the sale of the Canal shares the first crack had appeared in the tottering edifice of Egyptian finance, and this from an entirely unexpected quarter. In October 1875 the Imperial Ottoman Government committed an act of bankruptcy by declaring that for the following five years the interest and sinking fund of the Public Debt would be paid half in cash and half in bonds bearing five per cent interest.[9] There was a panic on the London Stock Exchange, and Ottoman securities slumped heavily taking Egyptian securities with them. Although right up to this time the Khedive had made no default in his payments and the financial structure of Egypt had so far appeared reasonably firm, the two countries were so closely associated in the public mind that a fluctuation in one had immediate repercussions on the other. Almost immediately Egyptian stock fell to a quotation in the region of 57 and thus killed once and for all any hope the Khedive may have entertained of raising any further loans. The attentions of the financial world immediately centred upon Egypt; was she going to default as well? Confidence in Egyptian financial stability was further weakened by the sale of the canal shares, for it was well realised that the Khedive would only have disposed of this holding with some reluctance and must therefore be in a difficult position himself.

This delicate position prompted Ismail Pasha to make an unexpected move. Through General Stanton, the British Consul-General at Cairo, he communicated to the British Government a desire to secure 'the services of some competent Government Official, thoroughly acquainted with the system followed in Her Majesty's Treasury, to assist his Minister of Finance in remedying the confusion which His Highness admitted existed in that department of administration.'[10] The reasons which prompted the Khedive to make this unusual request are the subject of some conjecture. He probably hoped to induce the British Government to nominate someone to carry out the above task, and in so doing to associate themselves with the Egyptian Government in the administration of Egypt's finances. This might go far towards allaying the fears and suspicions of the public and the bondholders. Whether or not this was the true reason behind the Khedive's request, the British Government displayed commendable caution in acting upon it. After a delay of some three weeks they announced that they were sending a mission to enquire into the general state of Egypt's finances with a view to ascertaining the desirability of acceding to the Khedive's request.

A mission of enquiry was not what the Khedive had asked for nor indeed what he wanted. Indeed it may reasonably be asserted that it was the last thing he wanted. Yet in this case the caution of the British Government was fully justified. In spite of the many assertions that have been made to the contrary, Britain had no desire whatever to become involved in Egyptian affairs, and was determined as far as possible to steer clear of them. If the Government had nominated one of her Treasury officials to take a hand in Egyptian finances, the world would automatically have supposed that Britain was assuming some responsibility in the matter. The British Government had no intention of giving the world ground for such a supposition, nor of rescuing Egypt from any financial entanglements, supposing her to be in such a predicament. Obviously, the Government thought, before we let ourselves in for anything we must find out what it is. In December 1875, therefore, Mr Stephen Cave, Her Majesty's Paymaster General, was nominated to lead a mission to Egypt to enquire into the Khedive's finances.

Although the Cave Mission was treated with the utmost courtesy and hospitality on its arrival in Cairo, the very nature of the visit made it most unwelcome. On learning the purpose of the visit, Nubar Pasha is reported to have said to Mr Cave, 'Under the circumstances I think you would have done better not to have come at all.'[11] The Khedive professed complete ignorance about the finances of the country and referred all enquiries to the Mufettish.[12] Mr Cave was therefore confronted with a task of exceptional difficulty. Not only did he have to contend with the difficulty of examining accounts in Arabic, a language which he did not know, which were moreover kept according to some complicated and secret system, but he also had to extract information from officials who, if not actually hostile, were at any rate far from co-operative. Undaunted by these obstacles he pressed on with his enquiry and produced, if not an entirely accurate picture of Egyptian finances, at least a reasonably fair one.

Much criticism has been levelled against the Cave Report, notably that many of the figures in it are inaccurate. This is undoubtedly true, yet on the other hand, Mr Cave was not sent to do a complete audit of the Khedive's accounts for the past twelve years; that would have taken months or even years instead of the few weeks he spent at Cairo. The purpose of his visit was to present a general picture of the financial situation obtaining in Egypt which would guide the British Government in deciding whether to accede to the Khedive's request for an official. Whatever the shortcomings of the Cave Report, it was sufficiently accurate to furnish the required information. The accuracy of the figures is of minor importance compared with the general conclusions expressed.

The Cave Report contained a mass of figures and an attempt was made to draw a balance of the receipts and expenditure of the Egyptian Government over the period of the Khedive's reign. Both sides of the balance sheet appear to have omitted several items, and this is undoubtedly attributable to the fact that the Mission was unable to extract the information from the Egyptian account books, but was obliged to rely on information provided by the Mufettish and his staff. However the Report was valuable in that it set forth certain important conclusions, among which may be cited the following:

> . . . The country has made progress in every way under its present ruler, but notwithstanding that progress, its present financial position is . . . very critical. Still, the expenditure, though heavy, would not of itself have produced the present crisis, which may be attributable almost entirely to the ruinous conditions of loans raised for pressing requirements, due in some cases to causes over which the Khedive had little control.

The Report amplifies this conclusion in the following paragraph.

> This unfortunate position is due in great measure to the onerous conditions of the loan of 1873, which was contracted for the express purpose of clearing off the floating debt amounting at that time to £28,000,000. By these conditions the nominal amount of £32,000,000 was reduced to an apparent effective of £20,740,000 of which £9,000,000 were paid in the bonds of the floating debt. These bonds, purchased by the contractors at a heavy discount, and sometimes at a price as low as 65 per cent, were paid into the Treasury at 93 per cent, an

operation which materially enhanced the profits accruing to the negotiators of the loan.

It was pointed out that the financial embarrassment of the Egyptian Treasury was to some extent due to the fact that the

Khedive has evidently attempted to carry out with a limited revenue, in the course of a few years, works which ought to be spread over a far longer period and which would tax the resources of much richer exchequers.

In spite of the critical situation, however, the mission considered that Egypt was

well able to bear the charge of the whole of her present indebtedness at a reasonable rate of interest; but she cannot go on renewing floating debts at 25 per cent, and raising fresh loans at 12 or 13 per cent interest to meet this addition to her debt, which do not bring in a single piastre to her Exchequer.

From the above it was not possible in the opinion of the Cave Mission for Egypt to meet her commitments unless they were modified to the extent of adjusting the interest to a 'reasonable rate'. What was considered to be a 'reasonable rate' is not mentioned; it is to be supposed that debtor and creditor might have had difficulty in agreeing on the interpretation of this term.

The Cave Mission ceased its labours and returned to England in February 1876. The Report, being considered a confidential document as between the Egyptian and British Governments, was not immediately published. But the financiers knew full well that Mr Cave had been to Cairo and they wanted to know what he had found out. Questions were asked in the House, but Disraeli refused to divulge the contents of the Report without the Khedive's consent. This statement was interpreted as meaning that the Khedive feared to publish it and Egyptian securities thus slumped even lower. This unfortunate incident placed Ismail in a difficult position. To refuse to publish the Report would only be construed to the effect that the financial situation in Egypt was too parlous to be made known to the public. Likewise, to publish it would be to disclose the true state of affairs. He finally chose the latter course and on 3 April 1876 the Report was duly published. Although it was by no means as bad as the investors had anticipated, the damage was already done and Egyptian credit had taken a further plunge. Furthermore, it was obvious to Ismail that his scheme to induce the British Government to associate themselves in some form or another in the management of his finances had failed. Not only this but it had accelerated the crisis he most feared. Five days after publication of the Cave Report, on 8 April, Ismail suspended payment on his Treasury bills.[13]

CHAPTER 12

The Fall of Ismail Pasha

The financial crisis which had been growing more and more imminent since the Oppenheim loan of 1873 came to a head in the early part of 1876. Up to this time Ismail Pasha had remained undisputed master of the land of Egypt. The suspension of his payments on the Treasury bills, hateful though this course of action was to him, did not cause him undue apprehension. He was confident, and not without reason, that he could ride the storm without difficulty. His action was not without precedent; as has been noted, the Imperial Ottoman Government had in the previous October defaulted upon their payments, but the jealousies and mutual suspicions of the Powers had prevented any united action to enforce payment. Ismail Pasha was confident that he could in like fashion play off the Powers against each other. In this forecast however he miscalculated.

There is no reason for supposing that he intended to repudiate his debts – the existence of the recently established Mixed Tribunals precluded that – but that he proposed to adjust the terms of repayment unilaterally, better to suit the country's ability to pay. It was clear in any case that the old system of raising new loans at ruinous rates of interest to pay old debts had to come to an end. Some rearrangement or composition had to be effected to place the finances and debts on a firmer footing before a complete débâcle overwhelmed the country. This was the burden of Mr Cave's report. It is useless to speculate whether Ismail Pasha would have been able to effect a satisfactory compromise with the bondholders, if he had attempted to negotiate with them. At any rate he took the matter into his own hands and on 2 May he signed a decree instituting a Commission of the Public Debt, followed five days later by a further decree consolidating all the debts of Egypt and of himself into one Public Debt amounting to £91 million. Under the terms of these decrees the Commissioners of the Debt were to be nationals of the powers interested nominated by their respective governments and to act as servants of and responsible to the Egyptian Government. Their principal duties would be to receive from the Government the funds necessary for the interest and sinking fund of the debt and to pay the money to the bondholders. Apart from this they would have no other powers and could be dismissed from their posts by the Khedive at will.

Under normal circumstances such an arrangement would have been greeted with approval by all concerned, but in this case the consolidation of all the various debts into one public debt by no means satisfied many of the creditors. For one thing, the interest was to be seven per cent, including one per cent sinking fund, the whole redeemable in sixty-five years. Some of the loans had been contracted on much more favourable terms to the creditors and were moreover secured on certain revenues of the state, e.g. the Daira Sanieh, the railways, the port of Alexandria and the customs and certain provinces. The English who held most of these stocks objected to the holders of the floating debt, who were mostly French, being placed on the same footing as themselves.

In consequence, when Ismail issued invitations to Britain, France, Austria and Italy to nominate their Commissioners of the Debt, the three latter countries responded with alacrity, but Lord Derby, the British Foreign Secretary, refused to make a nomination on the ground that the financial arrangements proposed did not commend themselves to the British Government. This was undoubtedly only an ostensible reason, for it was in fact part of the tradition of British foreign policy that Britons who invested their capital in foreign ventures did so at their own risk and could not expect the British Government to come to their aid when these ventures miscarried. The British Government were therefore reluctant to interfere in any way in the Khedive's relations with his creditors. Undaunted by this refusal, the Khedive made his own nomination for Britain, and selected Major Evelyn Baring. The representatives of France, Austria and Italy were M. de Blignières, Herr von Kremer and Sr Baravelli respectively.

It is not clear how Ismail Pasha proposed to pay a seven per cent interest on a debt amounting to £91 millions. This would have required an annual payment of a figure in the region of £6,400,000 and would in fact have swallowed up the greater part of the national revenue. The only way to meet such a commitment would have been by the employment of the most rigorous methods of extortion from the *fellahin*. This might not have perturbed the bondholders unduly, but in any case they were not yet disposed to accept the financial position of Egypt on Ismail's own evaluation, nor did they feel that the Cave Mission had in the few weeks of their residence in Cairo probed to the bottom of the situation. Many believed that the Khedive could pay in full, if he were made to do so. Meetings were held in London and Paris by the bondholders who insisted that a further independent investigation should be made. It was finally agreed that two representatives, one English and one French, should go out to Egypt and make a further enquiry and effect the best bargain they could with the Egyptian Government for the bondholders.

Mr G.J. Goschen, who had been a member of the banking house of Frühling & Goschen which had negotiated the earlier loans, was elected to represent the British element, and M. Joubert, an eminent Paris financier, to represent the French. They arrived in Egypt in October 1876 and after a short series of negotiations with the Egyptian Government they succeeded in obtaining a number of modifications to the existing financial arrangements which were embodied in a decree dated 18 November 1876, as follows. While the total amount of the public debt was fixed at £91 million, the Daira loan, as a personal transaction with the Khedive, was taken out and made the subject of a special arrangement, while the loans of 1864, 1865 and 1867 would continue to draw their interest until redemption according to the terms of the original contracts. These special arrangements left the Unified Debt at a figure of £59 million, the interest and sinking fund of which were to be fixed at six and one per cent respectively which would be received and distributed by the Commissioners of the Debt. Further, a five per cent preference stock was created with a capital of £17 million. The law of the Mukabala was to be continued and its revenues applied to the service of the loans of 1864, 1865 and 1867. So much for the financial arrangements. It was estimated[1] that these charges would cost Egypt £6,565,000 a year, about £185,000 more than the charge of seven per cent on the total debt of £91 million, as fixed by the Khedive in his decree of 7 May. One further modification was extracted from a reluctant Khedive. In order to ensure that the revenues would in fact be applied to the service of the debts, as set out above, it was agreed that two European Controllers-General should be appointed to supervise the revenues of the State.

The functions and powers of the first comprise the collection of all the revenues of the State, and their payment into the several special chests to which they are allocated; and for this purpose he is invested with full authority over the tax collectors, nor can any direct tax be levied unless sanctioned by his counter-signature of the tax paper – a provision that effectually protects the peasants from the arbitrary exactions of the old régime. Similarly, the Controller-General of Audit exercises supreme check over the account keeping of the Treasury and all the public offices into which any revenue is paid; and as a security that the Budget estimates of the year shall not be exceeded, his counter-signature is necessary to all departmental cheques or orders for payment.'[2]

In addition, a mixed board of English, French and Egyptians was set up to manage the State railways and the port of Alexandria, the revenues of which were to be applied to the five per cent preference stock.

A few days before the promulgation of the decree of 18 November an extraordinary occurrence took place. The details are not entirely clear, but what is certain is that the Khedive suddenly had the Mufettish, Ismail Pasha Sadiq, arrested and put on board a Nile steamer. The fate of the old Mufettish, who had been for years the Khedive's right-hand man in all his financial manipulations, has since been shrouded in mystery; but he was never seen again alive. The Khedive put it out that the Mufettish had been detected in a conspiracy against himself, and had therefore been arrested and banished to Dongola where he died shortly afterwards. There were, however, strong suspicions current that the Khedive had been engaged in certain transactions of a fraudulent nature which were coming to light, and that by disposing of the Mufettish on a charge of conspiracy, he could declare complete ignorance of all financial operations undertaken in his name and cast all blame on the vanished minister. Perhaps the Mufettish, who for years had wrung the last piastre from the wretched *fellahin*, deserved his fate – it is believed he was murdered on board the steamer – but the confidence of all the Egyptian officials in the ability of their master to protect them in face of increasing European intervention, was rudely shattered. The Khedive thus alienated his own employees.

Messrs Goschen and Joubert, in their anxiety to extract as much as possible from Egypt for the bondholders they represented, had taken far too optimistic a view of the general financial situation. They had apparently taken no account of the variations in climatic and other conditions; they had ignored the fact that the revenues of Egypt were almost entirely dependent upon the annual Nile flood, and that this sometimes did not reach its usual level. Under the Goschen-Joubert arrangements the last piastre would be extorted from Egypt and nothing would be left to tide the country over bad times. These were not long delayed in their arrival. In fact, the arrangement was quite impossible of execution. It was based on the collection of a revenue of £10,500,000 which was a vast, almost unreal, over-estimate. Lord Cromer points out that 'twenty years later, after a long period of honest and careful administration, the Egyptian revenue was only about £11,000,000.'[3]

The struggle to meet his commitments was for Ismail Pasha a forlorn one. Even had Egypt enjoyed a period of exceptional prosperity, the outcome would have been doubtful. As it was, the Turko-Russian War which obliged the Khedive to send 30,000 troops to the Balkans in 1877, an exceptionally bad Nile and a general trade recession, fell upon Egypt at the time of her greatest financial embarrassment. Only by the employment of the most ruthless severity was the money collected from the *fellahin* during the year 1877. 'The Treasury chest is empty,' Mr Vivian reported in November 1877, 'the troops and Government employees are many months in arrears of pay, and among the latter class the greatest distress and misery prevails. The whole administration of the country is at a deadlock.'[4]

The position in 1878 was even more desperate and it was evident that total collapse could not long be delayed. Only a month before the May coupon of £2 million was due for payment a bare quarter of that sum was available. Even the Commissioners of the Debt considered that payment ought to be deferred. 'We should have preferred the financial collapse which was manifestly inevitable to come at once as a preliminary to the establishment of a better order of things.'[5] But the French bondholders were adamant and were warmly supported by their own Government. The French Government also persuaded the British Government to this view and Egypt was ordered to pay. The fact that the Congress of Berlin was about to be held in which it was considered politically necessary that there should be no separation of France and England, no doubt lent some weight to the British decision, but it must be a severe condemnation of international politics that common humanity in Egypt was sacrificed to political expediency in Europe. But the British Government allowed themselves to be associated in the most inhuman measures against the Egyptian people in order to satisfy the clamour of those who had rashly invested their money abroad. 'Two of the most iron-fisted pashas who could be found were sent into the provinces. They were accompanied by a staff of money-lenders who were prepared to buy in advance the crops of the cultivators ... In some cases,' Sir Alexander Baird wrote, 'perfectly authenticated corn was sold to the merchants for 50 piastres an *ardeb*, which was delivered in one month's time when it was worth 120 piasts an *ardeb*.' The money was however obtained. The last instalment was paid to the Commissioners of the Debt a few hours before the coupon fell due. The great diversity of currency, and the fact that many of the coins were strung together to be used as ornaments, bore testimony to the pressure which had been used in the collection of the taxes.'[6] Nothing could be more condemnatory of the bondholders and their representatives than the fact that in this, perhaps the most fertile land in the world, famine stalked the land and thousands died from starvation.

During this troubled period the Khedive himself had taken little active part in affairs; indeed there was little he could do inasmuch as everything was subordinated to the vain endeavour to find money to meet the coupons as they fell due. So far, however, his position as lord and master of Egypt was unassailed. No distinction had yet been made between the public revenues proper and his own income; one fifth of the cultivable land still lay in his and his family's possession. These two facts caused angry buzzings among the creditors, and it was believed by many that the Khedive had undisclosed sources of wealth and could easily meet his engagements if he chose to do so. Since it was clearly no longer possible to meet all future commitments under the present arrangements, there was obviously something amiss with the estimates of revenue, as had been ascertained by Messrs Goschen and Joubert. It seemed that the true, unvarnished facts were yet to be brought to light.

A clamour arose for a fresh investigation of Egypt's financial situation, this time on an international basis and completely independent. It appears that this idea of a new enquiry originally emanated from Ismail Pasha himself, who allowed it to filter through to the British bondholders. He felt himself on fairly safe ground since any further enquiry could only result in the recognition that Egypt was no longer able to bear her present charges and that some further reduction must be made. The Khedive was thus willing to agree to the appointment of a Commission of Enquiry whose duty would be to investigate the national income. The bondholders, however, were by no means satisfied with the proposal. What they wanted was a true and complete statement, not only of the national income, but of the national expenditure. It was this latter item that Ismail baulked at. Any investigation into the manner in which public money was spent was for him fraught with danger. At the best it could only result in a reduced income for himself, while at worst it might well disclose all those dubious dealings in which he had for so long been engaged.

Therefore, ignoring the sentiments of the bondholders, the Khedive issued a decree on 27 January 1878 instituting a Commission of Enquiry into the national revenue. This was greeted by an explosion of public opinion and a large section of the creditors 'expressed themselves in terms condemnatory of any enquiry as they considered that the Egyptian Government could meet all its commitments.'[7] Urgent representations were made by the Commissioners of the Debt to the Khedive to yield to the demands of the creditors to institute a complete enquiry into both revenue and expenditure. After three weeks of argument and discussion the Khedive yielded. There were two alternatives: a complete and impartial enquiry or a continuance of the present arrangements as effected by Goschen and Joubert. The latter being impossible, the enquiry became inevitable and it was accordingly decreed on 4 April 1878. Even at this stage the Khedive endeavoured to make the best of a bad situation by himself selecting the members of the Commission to conduct the enquiry. His mind immediately reverted to his European friend and admirer, Colonel Charles Gordon, whom he had appointed Governor-General of the Sudan. Gordon, as Ismail knew, was an idealist, a missionary, with an undisguised aversion for money-lenders and bondholders. So out of sympathy was he with nineteenth century commercialism that he was considered by Gladstone 'not quite right in his head'. He was, moreover, a strong partisan of the Khedive, especially as he had led the crusade against slavery in the Sudan. Ismail therefore decided to appoint him chairman of the Commission but Baring bitterly resisted this proposal, and the Khedive was finally obliged to accede. Even Gordon himself admitted that he was not suitable for this type of work and was only to be a figure-head. The final composition of the Commission of Enquiry was as follows: M. de Lesseps as President though he took no part and left Egypt the following month; Sir Rivers Wilson who had been Controller of the British National Debt Office; Riaz Pasha, the Minister of Commerce; and the four Commissioners of the Debt, i.e. Baring, de Blignières, von Kremer and Baravelli.

Under the direction of Sir Rivers Wilson the Commission of Enquiry went to work with a will. There had already been two investigations of Egypt's finances but this one, they were determined, should be the last. It was to be exhaustive and ascertain to the last penny, as far as was humanly possible, the exact state of Egypt's indebtedness and her revenues, and should form the basis of a settlement which would stand the test of time. For the next four months they ploughed through the Egyptian financial labyrinth, endeavouring to disentangle the tortuous operations of the Khedive and his former Finance Minister, the Mufettish. On 13 August 1878 they issued an interim report which revealed the complete chaos prevailing in the financial administration. Every means fair or foul had been adopted to raise money;

the Mukabala and Rouznameh operations have already been mentioned as typical. New taxes had been raised and old ones increased without reference to any law or decree. Extortion, forced labour and bribery had been rampant. The Government had seized under the pretence of borrowing the funds of the Ministry of Wakfs and of the Beit-el-Mal.[8] In spite of the tremendous and often callous efforts which had been adopted to bring in revenue to meet the coupons as they fell due, it appeared that after all the country had fallen even deeper into debt. 'Besides sums due to bankers and contractors, we found that there were numerous claims from such humble individuals as camel-drivers, barbers, donkey-boys, etc. all of which had to be included in the floating debt.'[9] Few, if any, salaries to civil servants or the army had been paid for months and these officials were hovering on the brink of starvation and destitution. In all it was discovered that a further debt of £9,244,000 had accrued to be added to the already crushing burden which was weighing Egypt down.

The actual investigation and discovery of the true state of affairs was a prodigious labour in itself, but this paled into insignificance when it came to the question of proposing an arrangement or composition to effect a permanent settlement. One fact, however, stood out above all others. The old age of arbitrary rule, of indiscriminate taxation and reckless expenditure must come to an end. All taxes must be revised and levied according to law and not to expediency, and the accounts departments must be reorganised. But all these reforms would take time and the needs of the moment were urgent. In order to stave off the handing of Egypt over to the liquidator, funds had to be raised immediately, and the *fellahin* were already bled white. There remained one asset which could be used to raise ready money, the vast estates of 916,000 *feddans* in the personal possession of the Khedive and his family which had for the most part been acquired at the public expense. Rather less than half of these lands were already mortgaged but the remainder were still unencumbered. The creditors and the Debt Commissioners both felt, and rightly felt, that the separation of the State debts and the Khedive's personal debts was fictitious, inasmuch as Ismail had freely disposed of both, and that as long as these lands remained in his possession, it was absurd for him to say he could no longer meet his liabilities.

The Khedive, sensing the results of the enquiry, had already realised that the demand for a surrender of these lands would be made, and had offered 289,000 *feddans* of the unencumbered land back to the State. The Commissioners refused to entertain the offer; they demanded that the whole property should be restored. To Ismail, whose greatest mania was the ownership of land, the demand was a severe blow, but there was no alternative. After much delay and altercation he issued a decree ceding nearly all the Khedivial properties to the State. With these as security a new loan was negotiated with Rothschilds for £8,500,000. The money was applied to meet the pressing urgencies of the moment which could not be staved off until the general finances of the country were rehabilitated and placed on a firm footing.

The Commission further recommended that the Government of Egypt should pass from the arbitrary personal rule of the Khedive into the hands of a responsible ministry. The Khedive, by way of compensation for losing his power over the finances, was to receive a civil list. Hateful as this proposal was to Ismail, who had been reared to accept personal rule as the natural order of things, there was no way of evading it. He could not afford to ignore the recommendations of a commission which he in theory had set up, especially as the bondholders were attentively watching every development.

On 23rd August 1878 Ismail declared himself in the following terms to Sir Rivers Wilson, President of the Commission of Enquiry:

Quant aux conclusions auxquelles vous etês arrivé, je les accepte; c'est tout naturel que je le fasse; c'est moi qui ai désiré ce travail pour le bien de mon pays. Il s'agit actuellement pour moi d'appliquer ces conclusions. Je suis résolu de la faire sérieusement, soyez-en convaincu. Mon pays n'est plus en Afrique; nous faisons partie de l'Europe actuellement. It est donc naturel pour nous d'abandonner les errements anciens pour adopter un système nouveau adapté à notre état social. Je crois que dans un avenir peu éloigné vous verrez des changements considérables. Ils seront amenés plus facilement qu'on ne le croit. Ce n'est au fond qu'une simple question de légalité, de respect à la loi. Il faut surtout ne pas se payer des mots, et pour moi je suis décidé à chercher la réalité des choses. Pour commencer et pour montrer à quel point je suis décidé, j'ai chargé Nubar Pacha de me former un ministère. Cette innovation peut paraître de peu d'importance; mais de cette innovation, sérieusement concue, vous verrez sortir l'indépendance ministérielle, et ce n'est pas peu; car cette innovation est le point de départ d'un changement de système, et d'après moi, la meilleure assurance que je puisse donner du sérieux de mes intentions rélativement à l'application de vos conclusions.'[10]

This was indeed a point of departure for Egypt; a responsible ministry was to be formed, the first ministry in the history of Egypt, and Nubar Pasha was to head it. Had Ismail seriously intended to observe the sentiments piously expressed in his declaration he might have lasted to the day of his death on the throne of Egypt. He knew, however, that a 'responsible ministry' would inevitably fail of itself. For one thing Egypt had for centuries known only the despotic and personal form of Government, the only method known or understood by the people at large. The terms 'responsible ministry' and 'constitution' had no connotation in the Egyptian mind. The mysterious processes of Allah had made Effendina lord and master of all he surveyed, the sole arbiter of destiny. No ministerial responsibility, however benign, could alter the conservative attitude of the *fellahin*.

No one knew this better than Ismail Pasha, although Wilson and Baring undoubtedly had some inkling of it, for they stressed the need for the Khedive to associate himself and co-operate with the ministry to be formed. But Ismail Pasha realised that the times immediately confronting Egypt were likely to be stormy and some ferment was to be expected from the people following the imposition of the reforms which were required. It would in fact suit him well to stand aside while the storms were raging. He could pass responsibility for the inevitable trouble which would ensue to the shoulders of the ministry he was forced to establish. Thus, on 28 August, the Khedive charged Nubar Pasha with the formation of a ministry.

At the same time a further innovation was to be introduced. In order to ensure that the financial administration was carried out in accordance with the existing obligations to the bondholders, European ministers were to be included in the Government. Sir Rivers Wilson, who had headed the Commission of Enquiry, was now appointed Minister of Finance to give effect to the findings of the Commission. Although France and England had in this instance united to intervene in Egypt as far as the financial question was concerned, the traditional jealousy of one for the other's influence in Egypt was just as strong as formerly, and possibly even more aggravated. Thus the appointment of an English Minister of Finance created an explosion of public opinion in France, and to soothe ruffled pride England – and the Khedive – were reluctantly compelled to agree to the appointment of M. de Blignières as Minister of Public Works.

The financial direction of the country having now in effect passed into European hands, the Controllers-General who had previously been appointed to superintend revenue and expenditure under arrangements made by Messrs Goschen and Joubert became redundant, and these posts were allowed to lapse subject to the provision that they were to revive automatically in the event of either of the European Ministers being dismissed without the consent of their governments. Thus armed, the Nubar Ministry embarked on its perilous voyage. The Khedive sat back and awaited events.

In practice, the supposed constitutional ministry was in no sense constitutional. It was an attempt to transfer to a body of ministers the power of the Khedive the exercise of which in the past was considered by Nubar to be the cause of all the evils which beset Egypt. The Ministry, though in theory appointed by and responsible to the Khedive, consisted of men who were to a great extent hostile to him and his views. They were acting largely on behalf of the bondholders, and the fact that they were appointed with the approval of the British and French Governments lent colour to the view that they were partially responsible to those governments, at least to the extent that they were not likely to adopt any policy at variance with the wishes of their own governments. Nubar Pasha himself, as an Egyptian, was interested only in the welfare of his country. He believed that nothing but ill could follow from the unfettered power of the Khedive, that the welfare of Egypt depended upon a vigorous policy of reform. He believed, moreover, that he was the man most capable of putting this policy into effect.

The situation of Egypt, when the Ministry embarked on its short career in November 1878, was as black as ever. No fresh composition had been effected with the creditors, and the passage of the months brought the ever-recurrent pressing demands upon an empty treasury. In November over a million and a quarter pounds had to be taken from the new Rothschild loan to meet the interest on the Unified Debt. No sooner had one coupon been paid than urgent attention had to be given to meeting the next. As Lord Cromer wrote: 'In fact, at this time the Egyptian Government lived from coupon to coupon.'

It was impossible in a few months to effect any reforms or improvements which would bring immediate relief to the tax-payers. The situation was even further aggravated by the effects of the low Nile of the previous year, and the revenues were slow in coming in. Progress was in fact negligible. '*Nous tournons dans un cercle vicieux. Nous ne marchons pas,*' said Nubar.

The situation would undoubtedly have been much improved, had the Ministry even tried to secure the cordial co-operation and assistance of the Khedive. For sixteen years Ismail had ruled Egypt; he knew every thread and ramification of the administrative machine. Had he been consulted and invited to participate, there is little doubt that he could have found a way out of most difficulties. But Nubar Pasha and Sir Rivers Wilson were entirely averse to allowing the Khedive any hand whatever in the government of

Egypt. He was to be treated as a mere cipher whose sole function was to register the decrees of the Ministry. Lord Vivian, who was British Consul-General at the time, favoured a much less rigorous and bureaucratic approach to the problem. He thought that

> Nubar Pasha had overrated his own strength and underrated the power of the Khedive. That power was still an important factor in the government of a country which he and his predecessors had ruled for so long and in so absolute a fashion. The Khedive was the only authority recognised and obeyed by all classes in the land. There was no middle course between deposing him or counting with his power. The only system which presented a chance of success was not to put the Khedive on one side altogether, but to invite his co-operation while at the same time the exercise of his authority would be controlled.[11]

A curious feature of this period was the attitude of the British Government which was set forth in an instruction to Lord Vivian:

> In the opinion of Her Majesty's Government a very grave responsibility will rest with His Highness the Khedive for the success or failure of the new régime, especially as regards the collection of taxes. Rumours have already reached Her Majesty's Government which . . . might cause them to apprehend that, under cover of the interference of foreign Governments, attempts will be made in high quarters to throw off all responsibility . . . [12]

Somewhat naturally the Khedive took umbrage at these declarations. He had, he said, acceded to the request of the Commission of Enquiry for a constitutional government and himself had taken up the position of a constitutional ruler. 'If he rightly understood the first principles of constitutional government, it was that Ministers and not the Chief of the State, were made responsible.'[13] His advice and experience were moreover available to the ministers, if they chose to ask for them. Such arguments are dismissed by Lord Cromer[14] as sophistry, and there might well have been some justice in this view had it not been for the fact that the two principal Ministers, Nubar and Wilson, were violently opposed to enlisting the assistance of the Khedive in the government of the country. The Khedive, therefore, wisely and rightly it would appear, refrained from forcing his opinions on the Ministry. At the same time he protested against his anomalous position in which he was to be held responsible for the good government of the country while he was precluded from taking any active part in it. There is no doubt that his position irked him considerably, and that he was only waiting for some event which would overthrow this troublesome ministry and restore the reins of power into his own hands. He had not long to wait.

To meet some of the most pressing financial necessities it was decided by the Ministry to lighten the burden of the State somewhat by discharging about 2,500 officers of the army and placing them on half-pay. These were already many months in arrears with their pay, and it was proposed to retire them without fully liquidating their arrears. 'The result was that many officers and their families were reduced to a state of complete destitution.'[15] From this it seems indisputable that the interests of the bondholders were placed before those of Egypt; it must thus be questioned whether the Ministry appointed to serve the interests of Egypt were doing their proper duty. The officers were summoned to Cairo to deposit their arms and receive a portion of their arrears. There were thus in the capital in February 1879 a large body of seething, discontented officers who attributed their unfortunate position to the presence of an Armenian Christian and a number of Europeans, representatives of the bondholders, in the seats of power to the detriment of the rightful ruler, Ismail Pasha.

On 18 February as Nubar Pasha was driving to his office he found himself surrounded by a mob of infuriated officers who stopped the carriage. Sir Rivers Wilson, who likewise happened to be passing, saw that something was amiss and jumped out and went to the assistance of Nubar. Together they were roughly handled and hustled by the mob to the Ministry of Finance where they found sanctuary. The officers remained clustered around the building and cut the telegraph wires. A message, however, was sent to the Khedive at Abdin Palace. The latter himself appeared on the scene shortly afterwards and restored order by promising the officers that their grievances would be investigated, and the crowd thereupon dispersed. In the whole incident a few people were hurt but no great damage was done.

It has been suggested by Lord Cromer and other writers that this episode was engineered, or at least encouraged, by the Khedive himself, but no evidence has been produced to support this allegation beyond the fact that it was 'likely'. On the other hand he had had no hand in the decision to retire the officers nor, as far as is known, to summon them to Cairo. It would therefore appear very doubtful whether there is any substance in the allegation.

Whether the Khedive was involved in the military *émeute* or not, it furnished him with the pretext he required to get rid of Nubar Pasha. The following day he declared that he would not be responsible for public tranquillity unless Nubar Pasha were removed and himself given some share in the government of the country, or allowed to preside at the meetings of the Council of Ministers, or appoint a President in whom he could have confidence.[16] This declaration placed Nubar in a predicament. He believed he was proceeding along the road to reform and rendering his country good service; he could also, if necessary, lean on his colleagues, Wilson and de Blignières, to keep him in office. But he was forced to realise that in the long run the Khedive was still the foremost power in the land, and could stir up unrest which he, Nubar, could not control. Yielding to necessity, Nubar resigned.

The fall of Nubar Pasha did not create undue alarm in London or Paris. It was, after all, recognised that the Khedive had the right to appoint, and therefore dismiss, his own ministers, and the Englishman and Frenchman were still entrenched in their posts and could be relied upon to ensure that Ismail Pasha lived up to his declarations of 28 August, i.e. that there would be no change in the policy of ministerial responsibility. The next problem was to find a successor for Nubar. Sir Rivers Wilson who was by character and temperament unsuited to taking a hand in the affairs of an oriental state pressed for the reinstatement of Nubar, but his counsels did not prevail. As a compromise the Khedive's son and heir, Tewfik Pasha, was nominated to the vacant post of President of the Council of Ministers. Tewfik Pasha was not a man of remarkable personality, was still a young man of twenty-seven and apart from a tour of duty as Governor of Cairo had had no experience of government. It is said that Ismail had no particular affection for his son and that the latter was overawed by his father.

It is clear, therefore, that it was intended that Tewfik should be little more than a figurehead in the Government. The European Ministers expected him to be guided by their counsels, and the Khedive could be sure that he would not endorse policies radically opposed to his own wishes. The appointment, which was made on 22 March, was the first step in the Khedive's plan to regain his lost power. The next step was already prepared.

In the earlier years of the century Mohammed Ali had had occasion to convene a Chamber of Notables who in theory would assist him with their advice in the government of the land, but whose duty in practice lay in approving the decisions the Pasha had already taken. Ismail Pasha had himself in 1866 revived this rather dormant assembly with the same objects as those of his grandfather. Their deliberations lent a fictitious parliamentary flavour to Ismail's personal rule. 'Though nominally elected by the population, these delegates were in reality the nominees of the Government, and possessed neither the powers nor the courage to act as representatives of the nation.'[17] This is not remarkable inasmuch as the Khedive disposed of all life and property at his will.

Ismail Pasha's plan was to revive the Chamber of Notables once more as a sort of parliament expressing the national will, although he had no intention of handing over his power to any sort of elected body of representatives. Yet, he thought, Europe, or rather England and France whose great love was parliamentary institutions, would smile on any oriental ruler who of his own volition established such a system in his own country.

In the meantime the work of the Commission of Enquiry had been continuing. The issue of their report in the previous August setting forth the financial condition of Egypt in detail had marked the first stage of their labours. Since then the second task, the preparation of a settlement or final composition between Egypt and her creditors, had been under way. At the same time, during which he had been excluded from any share in the government, Ismail Pasha had, secretly it can be presumed, been preparing a financial scheme of his own. The intention was clear. If he could submit a scheme which would satisfy the creditors and if he could carry it out, there would be no further need for European Ministers or European intervention in Egypt's affairs. Ismail would resume his rightful place as ruler of Egypt, and everyone would be happy.

The revival of the Chamber of Notables and the preparation of a financial scheme were the two important preliminaries to the campaign envisaged. The final report of the Commission of Enquiry which was issued on 8 April 1879, set forth the measures which should be taken to effect a settlement. The previous day, however, Ismail had dismissed his two European Ministers, Wilson and de Blignières. Dicey relates[18] that when 'they presented themselves at their offices, they found their places occupied by native ministers, and in the course of the same day they received official notice that they were no longer in His Highness' service.' The Khedive had accurately gauged the situation. No effectual protest was forthcoming from London or Paris. Cherif Pasha was thereupon charged with the formation of an entirely Egyptian Ministry.

At this time there arose considerable activity among the Notables and *Ulema* in the capital. There were many comings and goings and secret conferences between them and the Khedive or his intermediaries. It was evident that the Khedive was preparing a further coup. Before their dismissal in April the Ministers, acting in their capacity of members of the Commission of Enquiry, had recommended to the Khedive that the coupon of 1 May on the Unified Debt should be postponed in view of the exhausted state of the Treasury. Almost unaccountably the Khedive refused to sign on the ground that it would constitute an act of bankruptcy. This refusal might have appeared especially remarkable inasmuch as it was the Khedive himself who had always so bitterly complained of the excessive financial burdens thrust upon the Treasury. But now his carefully laid plans to throw off the fetters of Europe and bring Egypt back under his own control were matured. The final report of the Commission of Enquiry was now complete and it declared Egypt to be in a state of bankruptcy. Bankruptcy necessarily implied liquidation and it was certain that this would be accompanied by more European supervision and interference. Ismail Pasha could not afford bankruptcy. It was only by keeping Egypt solvent that he could regain and retain his power on the ground that as long as the bondholders were satisfied there was no necessity for European intervention.

On 9 April he assembled the diplomatic corps and declared that the actions of the European Ministry had created such unrest in the country that he felt bound to take drastic action to allay it. The country furthermore protested against the declaration of bankruptcy, he said, and was willing to make any sacrifices to avert it. Prince Tewfik, yielding to the will of the nation, had resigned and a new all-Egyptian Ministry would be formed by Cherif Pasha. Three documents were presented to the Consuls-General. The first of these purported to be an address from the now revived Chamber of Notables protesting against the declaration of bankruptcy and the proposed repeal of the law of the Mukabala, and accusing the Ministry of acting contrary to the true interests of the country. The second was a further address from various delegates to the effect that they rejected the proposed settlement of the Commission of Enquiry, and that Egypt was able to meet all her debts. The third was a plan supposedly drawn up by the Chamber of Notables for a financial settlement. The plan allowed for the re-establishment of the Financial Control which had been allowed to lapse on the formation of the European Ministry. Further, laws were to be drafted for the formation of a constitutional Chamber '*dont les modes d'élection et les droits seront réglés de façon à répondre aux exigences de la situation intérieure et aux aspirations nationales.*'

The coup of Ismail Pasha, temporarily at least, stunned the European Ministers and officials but in point of fact, apart from the financial plan, Ismail had not exceeded his powers. Both Wilson and de Blignières sent protests to their governments, but these were allowed to pass unnoticed. The Khedive had shown that he was master of the situation for the time being at any rate.

Had the financial settlement, drawn up in theory by the Chamber of

Notables but in fact by the Khedive himself, been capable of execution, possibly the Powers might have accepted Ismail's *coup d'état* and refrained from further action. The plan, though protesting against a declaration of bankruptcy, itself committed an act of bankruptcy by reducing the interest on the Unified Debt from six to five per cent. Further, its execution necessitated all the old methods of extortion from the *fellahin* in order to meet the coupons. Since it was this extortion in the past which had brought the country to such a parlous plight, it was only to be expected that a further breakdown would ensue if it were revived.

For a time, however, matters were allowed to run their course, and might have been further allowed to do so had it not been for a move from an entirely unexpected quarter. On 18 May 1879 the German and Austrian Consuls, acting on instructions from Prince von Bismarck, protested against Ismail's settlement. A few German creditors and holders of the floating debt, not having received satisfaction in the financial plan, had brought actions in the Mixed Tribunals against the Government and obtained judgment. The Egyptian executive had taken no steps to implement the judgments. Bismarck took up the cudgels on behalf of his nationals in making this protest. No doubt there were other political motives which prompted the German Chancellor to action, but these do not concern the present story. The results were instantaneous and startling.

Hitherto France and Britain alone of the European Powers had effectively intervened in Egypt's affairs; both these countries had considered their special interests sufficient motive for so doing. They had thus secured a special or privileged position in that country. The sudden appearance of Germany on the Egyptian scene caused much excitement in London and Paris which culminated in the issue of similar protests on the part of the British and French Governments against Ismail's acts.

With the principal Powers of Europe thus united against the Khedive the final denouement could not be long delayed. The Powers were determined that Egypt should accept their aid in the management of affairs and the good government of the land. Ismail Pasha had given effective proof that he regarded the proffered assistance with distaste and could be reckoned to dispense with it at the first opportunity. He had in fact done so and would resist any further attempts to have European assistance forced on him. Ismail realised that his situation was precarious but he was counting on the support of the Sultan and the Porte into whose hands he had for so long poured so much gold. But he was leaning on a broken reed. The Sultan himself would be obliged to bow to the combined will of Europe if pressed to do so.

On 19 June, through the medium of the Consul-General Sir Frank Lascelles who had replaced Lord Vivian, the British Government advised the Khedive to abdicate. Their advice was couched in such language as to constitute a threat, in case of non-compliance: 'We must not conceal from Your Highness that if you refuse to abdicate, and if you compel the Cabinets of London and Paris to address themselves directly to the Sultan, you will not be able to count either upon obtaining the civil list or upon the maintenance of the succession in favour of Prince Tewfik.'[19] The French representative was instructed to present similar advice to the Khedive.

Ismail Pasha was at first disposed to avoid the proposal by submitting it to the Porte, from whom he expected support. Had the Porte not been subjected to considerable pressure from the ambassadors of the Powers this support might have been forthcoming. But on 26 June 1879 a telegram from the Sultan was received in Cairo addressed to 'The ex-Khedive Ismail Pasha notifying him that the Khedivate had now passed to Tewfik Pasha, and inviting him to retire from public affairs.' Another telegram notified Tewfik of his accession. Upon receipt of these Ismail Pasha bowed to the inevitable. He had played out the game and lost.

The same day Ismail formally made over his power to his son Tewfik and began preparations for his departure from Egypt. On 30 June, together with his family, harem and possessions, he left Cairo by train for Alexandria where he embarked on his yacht, *Mahroussa*. 'He departed from Alexandria with all the military honours due to his rank. Salutes were fired from the batteries he had erected and from the men-of-war lying in the harbour he had created.'[20] The scenes attending the departure of Ismail Pasha were said to have been touching. There was no popular demonstration in his favour, but 'the scene was so affecting that there were few among the spectators who were able to refrain from tears.'[21] Ismail Pasha bore himself through this harrowing experience with courage and simple dignity; his courtesy and polish never deserted him although he was labouring under intense strain and leaving for ever the land which in his fashion he had loved so well and for which he had laboured so long. Whatever may be said of his conduct during his reign, his departure was worthy of a king.

It is difficult not to feel compassion for the deposed monarch. In the case of Ismail Pasha he had loved his country and had done much to advance it. His misfortune lay in the fact that in so doing he had cumbered it with a vast, an unendurable load of debt. He was born in the traditions of despotic power and personal government. In the struggle to preserve what was to him the divine right of kings he met his defeat at the hands of Europe. He was conscious of having done no wrong but only that he had suffered defeat and deposition by greater powers than him. Perhaps this was to him the greatest tragedy.

From the day Ismail Pasha sailed out from Alexandria into exile he ceased to be a figure in Egyptian history. He spent the remaining years of his life in Italy and various other cities of Europe until 1887 when he was invited by the Sultan to come to Constantinople where he died on 8 March 1895. His mortal remains, however, were brought for their final repose to Egypt, the land of his love.

CHAPTER 13

Arabi Pasha

With the passing of Ismail Pasha there was ground for hope that the Egyptian ship of state might be steered into calmer waters. The most urgent necessity was a period of peace during which a stable government might be formed and the country given a breathing space to prepare to meet the pressing commitments it had to face.

The new Khedive, Tewfik Pasha, was a young man of twenty-seven with no experience of government having hitherto been completely overshadowed by his father. He is described by Dicey[1] as

> spare of figure, with a plain but not unkindly face, gifted with good intentions, but with narrow views; a devout believer in Islam; a Turk of the Turks, imbued with all the prejudices of his race and caste against the Giaour and against Christian civilization; a good husband; a man, according to Oriental ideas, of moral domestic life; a frugal administrator.

De Freycinet[2] speaks of him as 'honest, well-intentioned, of perfect manners, frugal but weak, lacking in prestige and of narrow outlook, tossed about by opposing influences and incapable of dominating a difficult situation.' Such was the man called upon to guide the destinies of Egypt through the perilous times ahead.

The accession of a new Khedive was always the subject of an imperial firman from Constantinople. In this instance the Sultan attempted to tighten Turkish control over Egypt by cancelling the firman of 1873 which, it will be remembered, had granted various substantial privileges to the Khedive. But both England and France took exception to the Sultan's attempts to modify the firmans governing the relations of Egypt with the Empire, and their ambassadors at Constantinople were instructed to inform the Porte that no

189

modification could be allowed without the concurrence of their governments, and that 'in their endeavour to tighten their hold on Egypt, they ran a risk that the country would escape from their grasp altogether.'[3] Once again the Sultan was obliged to bow to the power of the mighty, and on 7 August the imperial firman of accession was finally promulgated, in substance the same as that of 1873 except that the army in time of peace was to be limited to 18,000 men and the power to raise loans was withdrawn. As Egypt was already staggering under a colossal load of debt the last provision seems almost redundant.

The most important problem to be faced was, what form was the government of Egypt to take and to what extent was Europe to take a hand in it? The experiment of employing Europeans as ministers of the Egyptian Government had already been tried and found wanting. Their presence in the Ministry had only served to aggravate prejudice and arouse discontent. It was decided that only a wholly Egyptian Ministry would suffice to allay suspicion, and in September 1879 Riaz Pasha who had previously held ministerial office was invited to form a government. The Khedive however reserved the right to preside at the meetings of the Council whenever he thought fit. European control of Egyptian affairs, upon which both France and England were determined, was therefore to be more indirect but none the less effective.

The first step was the revival of the Financial Control which had originally been established in May 1876 transferring the supervision of the national receipts and expenditure to English and French hands. This Control had lapsed when the Europeans had been included in the Nubar Ministry and was now to be restored. The two posts were offered to, and accepted by, Major Evelyn Baring and M. de Blignières. The decree re-establishing the Control was issued by the Khedive on 4 September 1879, and a further decree of 15 September defined its duties. Under the latter the Controllers were granted extensive powers of investigation, and were given the right to attend and speak at the meetings of the Council of Ministers, but without a vote. To this extent the financial, and therefore the supreme, control of the country was once again vested in English and French hands.

The second step to be taken was the preparation of a final settlement of the Egyptian Debt problem. Any settlement effected would theoretically have to be agreed by every creditor, but to effect a composition which could actually be carried out and which would satisfy every bondholder would in fact have been quite impossible. It was therefore necessary to persuade the Powers to agree to the appointment of a body charged with the preparation of a settlement which would be binding on the Powers and, more important still, upon the Mixed Tribunals. Long negotiations were therefore instituted by the Controllers, and on 31 March 1880 the representatives of the five principal Powers, France, Britain, Germany, Austria and Italy, signed a convention in Cairo which was made the subject of a Khedival decree on the same day. Under this the conclusions reached by the Commission of Liquidation were to be recognised by the Mixed Tribunals as binding on them. The remaining Powers who had agreed to the establishment of the Mixed Tribunals were invited to adhere to this proposal. In April 1880 the Commission of Liquidation was appointed to prepare the settlement; it consisted of the four Commissioners of the Public Debt, an additional Frenchman and a German, with Sir Rivers Wilson as its President. The most difficult hurdle was thus surmounted.

During the next three months the Commission of Liquidation devoted its attention to effecting a final permanent settlement between Egypt and her creditors. With such a mixed composition of members it was inevitable that agreement was not easily reached, some of the members taking too optimistic a view of the revenue, while others were perhaps a little more realistic. The result which was presented to the Khedive on 17 July was largely a compromise. It is unnecessary to dwell in detail on the provisions of the settlement; a summary of the principal items will suffice to indicate its general character. The law of the Mukabala was repealed and the benefits promised to those who had paid it were lost. Interest on the Unified Debt, about £57 million, was fixed at 4% plus 1% sinking fund. A further issue of £5,600,000 Preference Stock was made to pay off the Floating Debt and this was added to the Privileged Debt (bringing it to £22,530,000) which carried a 5% interest and was secured on the revenues of the railways, harbours and telegraphs, and if necessary of four provinces. 'The holders of the floating debt were divided into various categories, of whom some received their money in full, and others had to submit to a reduction of their claims of varying extent.'[4]

This settlement became in effect the financial charter of Egypt for years to come and on the whole it stood the test of time reasonably well. The most significant aspect of it was the great reduction in the rate of interest to a figure which was both reasonable and more adapted to the country's ability to pay. Even so two-thirds of the revenue were to be applied to the service of the debt for years to come. Clearly the administration of the country would have to be run with the most stringent economy. It is melancholy to reflect on how much Egypt paid in the end for the benefit of the loans so rashly incurred by Ismail Pasha and so rapidly spent. If an exact tally were made of the whole affair from the date of the first loan to the repayment of the last instalment, it would probably be discovered that for every pound borrowed several were repaid.

To ensure that no further difficulties or controversies arose over this final settlement the Controllers exercised a rigid control over the Government. Much remained to be done to bring some degree of stability to the country. Reform, especially in regard to taxation, was urgent and some measures were indeed taken to abolish the most flagrant abuses. Lord Cromer[5] gives a summary of these among which are the following. A more equitable rate of taxation was instituted as between Ushuri and Karadji lands; poll-tax was abolished, as was the professional tax on agricultural workers. 'Twenty-four petty taxes of a vexatious nature were abolished by a stroke of the pen.'[6] Salt-tax was cancelled and the commodity made a government monopoly. Land taxes were in future to be payable only in money, and the dates of collection to be regulated to suit the convenience of the tax-payers, and a proper register of tax-payers and the amounts due from them was made. Each landowner was informed of the amount due from him and when it would be payable. Some of these reforms were undoubtedly effected on paper only. Mr Villiers Stuart, MP, who made a tour of Egypt in 1883, a few months after the battle of Tel-el-Kebir, records conversations with villagers and peasant workers which indicate that many of the 'vexatious taxes' which were supposed to have been abolished two or three years earlier were still in fact levied.[7]

In June 1880 Major Baring was appointed Financial Member of the Governor's Council in India and his place as Controller was taken by Sir Auckland Colvin of the Indian Civil Service. The institution of reform in Egypt necessarily implied suitable officers to carry it out, and it was at this period that there began a substantial recruitment into important posts of Europeans, mostly French and English. Such was the jealousy and suspicion of the one Power for the other, that whenever a national of the one was given a post in Egypt, an equivalent position had to be found for a national of the other. This state of affairs was the cause of much bitterness to the Khedive and Riaz Pasha, both of whom considered that Egypt was standing in danger of being internationalised, as indeed she was. The weight of the influence of the Controllers, however, was too great to be resisted, and the steady influx of Europeans into the administration continued. The Controllers were too immersed in the financial problems to notice the political dangers that might ensue from neglecting the prejudice and damage to Egyptian *amour propre* engendered by excessive recruitment of European officials. Riaz Pasha was willing to co-operate with all his power with the Controllers in effecting the reform of Egypt, but he did not admit the necessity of employing large numbers of Europeans to carry out the work.

Tewfik Pasha for his part was continually humiliated by the knowledge that he owed his throne to the power of England and France, that he was only maintained on it by them and could, like his father, be removed by them if he failed to acquiesce in their wishes. He was conscious that he was little more than a puppet in the hands of his European mentors and that he had no power to alter his position. To a man of his character and outlook, a true Turk, this never failed to be the source of keenest resentment. Under the circumstances, although the government of Riaz Pasha enjoyed a comparatively peaceful two years of office, there existed in fact no real harmony between the principal actors on the Egyptian stage. Riaz resented European supervision, and the Khedive suspected his principal Minister of being too closely in collusion with his European mentors. The Controllers, supported by their respective consuls, were intent only on the efficient financial administration and reform of the country primarily in the interests of the bondholders. Had there been any degree of cohesion or identity of outlook among the principals, the cataclysm which was shortly to engulf the country might have been detected in time and averted. As it was, the storm-clouds gathered unnoticed on the horizon.

When in 1879 Ismail Pasha had summoned the Chamber of Notables and announced his intention of granting the country liberal institutions, he had acted thus only for temporary expedience. His purpose had simply been to call the Chamber together to express his own will, as though in the name of the people, and then to dismiss them. The majority of the Notables well understood that their master for reasons of his own desired them to express certain opinions and knew that it was in their own interests to do so. Even so this germ of constitutionalism sown by the ex-Khedive fell in a few fertile places. There were men of intelligence and education who had begun to take note of the constitutional procedures current in some of the Western countries. The doctrine of democracy, of the right of the people to manage their own affairs, had begun to filter into Egypt. Ismail Pasha himself had even had some difficulty in dismissing his Chamber:

> The chamber of deputies . . . is no longer to be despised. They have shown various signs of life and independence, and the last has not been the least . . . Riaz Pasha, the Minister of Finance, went the other day formally to close the

session. He made the representatives a polite and graceful speech as regards their services, while he intimated that their duties were fully and finally discharged . . . The Assembly refused to dissolve, and found a spokesman in a notable, who declined to accept the valedictory compliments. On the contrary, he declared on behalf of the Parliament that they had as yet done nothing, and had much to do in the way of supervision of the Ministry, and that therefore they refused to separate . . . The Egyptian Parliament consequently continues its sittings, and now contends that all Ministers, whether foreign or native, shall be dependent on its will and responsible to it for their conduct of affairs . . .'[8]

From this it is clear that the idea of democracy, although somewhat rudimentary, was gaining ground in Egypt even in the reign of Ismail Pasha. From this time forward a Nationalist Party began to be formed centred largely upon the University of El Azhar, having for their aim the transfer of power from the Khedive to an assembly representative of and elected by the people.

There is, however, no truth in the proposition which has been advanced that the Egypt of that time was a land of patriots and democrats struggling to be free. To the vast majority of the people, the *fellahin*, the theory of democracy would have been incomprehensible. The only system of government that they had ever known or could understand was that of personal government by and submission to 'Effendina', the Khedive. The *fellahin* had no interest in politics or forms of government. All they wanted was to be left alone to till their fields in peace and to be relieved from oppression by the tax-gatherer. At the other end of the social scale the traditional ruling class of Turks and Circassians likewise had little conception of, and certainly no love for, the theory of democracy. To them it was ordained that they should rule and grow fat on the province of Egypt. The idea that Egyptians should have any part in their own government was to them absurd. Thus the seeds of democracy fell only upon a small class of intelligent and educated natives who clustered round the Moslem University.

Of all the various elements that constituted the population of Egypt at this time the most thoroughly discontented was the army. Already it had suffered great reductions in the time of Ismail which had caused the outburst of 18 February 1879. In this disturbance the officers found, much to their surprise, that they held in their own hands the power to compel the Government to listen to their demands. Though the trouble had been tided over at the time, the causes of discontent still remained. With the accession of Tewfik the army had to be reduced to 18,000 men. On grounds of economy it was in fact reduced to a much smaller figure. This was generally a cause for rejoicing among the troops who were mostly *fellahin* forced into the army by the usual press-gang methods, but among the officers it was a source of great dissatisfaction. Many were dismissed on half or no pay and consequently lost their careers and means of life. These hardships fell particularly on the native Egyptian element, while the Turkish-Circassian officers escaped. Preferment in the army, as in most other departments, was largely a matter of favour by the Khedive. In earlier days Said Pasha had leaned much towards the native elements and had made singular promotions. But both Ismail and Tewfik despised the native officers and rarely promoted them above the rank of captain; the higher ranks were reserved for the Turks and Circassians.

The discontent which prevailed among the Egyptian element of the army first made itself felt in May 1880, when a group of native officers submitted a petition to the Ministry setting forth a number of complaints regarding the employment of troops on *corvée* work, such as digging canals and agricultural work on the Khedive's estates and on questions of pay. Again on 15 January 1881 a further petition was submitted to Riaz Pasha complaining that the Egyptian officers had been unjustly treated in the matter of promotions and requesting that the Minister of War, Osman Rifki Pasha, should be dismissed and that an investigation should be made into recent promotions. The leaders concerned in these petitions were Ali Bey Fehmi, Ahmed Bey Arabi[9] and Abdel-Aal Bey Helmi, colonels of the 1st, 4th and Black Regiments respectively. The submission of these petitions was an act which required some degree of courage on the part of the officers concerned, especially as they belonged to the despised native element and were without influence at Court or in the Ministry. That their petition was based on legitimate grievances did not alter the fact that by their action the colonels stood in danger of incurring the displeasure of the Khedive and the War Minister. The latter, Osman Rifki Pasha, was 'an extreme representative of the class which for centuries had looked upon Egypt as their property and the *fellahin* as their slaves and servants.'[10]

Riaz Pasha was more or less impartial in this matter and attempted to conciliate the disaffected officers, but the latter insisted that their petition should stand, with the result that on 30 January it was finally brought before the Council of Ministers presided over by the Khedive himself. The Controllers were excluded from this meeting, presumably on the ground that this was an entirely domestic matter. If the origins of the military revolt which was shortly to engulf Egypt and nearly to topple the Khedive off his throne are to be sought, they will be found in the action decided upon by this meeting of the Ministers. With the Khedive himself presiding, it was inevitable that his own views should carry the day, and to that extent the Khedive was personally responsible for the disasters which followed.

A full enquiry into the complaint mentioned in the petition might have revealed that it was substantially justified, and this would have reflected invidiously on Osman Rifki and on the Khedive himself. On the other hand, serving soldiers, even though they were colonels, had no right to demand the removal of a minister, which is the prerogative of the ruler himself. The obvious procedure would have been to take notice of the complaint and investigate it, and at the same time to reprimand the officers concerned for making demands which were beyond their competence. The Council of Ministers, however, decided on neither of these courses. Instead they determined to prepare a trap for the officers. It was arranged that the three colonels concerned should be ordered to attend a meeting at the Ministry of War to discuss the ceremonial arrangements in connection with the forthcoming marriage of the Princess Jamila. On their arrival they were to be arrested and tried summarily by Osman Pasha. It is not difficult to imagine what would have been the outcome of this trial, had the plot succeeded.

As it turned out, however, the plot miscarried. The colonels were fore-warned of what was intended and they arranged with the officers and men of their own regiments that if, when they went to the Ministry, they did not reappear within two hours, the units were to come in strength and forcibly to deliver them.

The plans of the colonels were better laid than those of the Khedive. The following passage from Lord Cromer's *Modern Egypt* aptly summarises the events of 1 February 1881:

> The Colonels were summoned to the Ministry of War . . . They obeyed the summons. On their arrival at the Ministry of War, they were arrested and placed on their trial. Whilst the trial was proceeding, the officers and men of their regiments arrived, and broke into the room where the court was sitting. They treated the Minister of War roughly, destroyed the furniture and delivered the Colonels, who marched with their troops to the Khedive's palace, and demanded the dismissal of the Minister of War.[11]

Thus instead of ridding himself of some troublesome native officers the

Khedive found himself at the mercy of a mutinous army. Having no force immediately at his disposal upon which he could call for assistance in quelling the mutiny, he had no alternative but to give way. Osman Pasha Rifki was dismissed and Mahmud Pasha Sami el Baroudi, a nominee of the colonels, was appointed in his place. The colonels were allowed to retain command of their regiments, and they renewed their submission to the Khedive. Thus occurred the second act of mutiny in the Egyptian Army.[12]

Mutiny is generally held to be an unforgivable sin in an armed force. There are however occasions when the circumstances are extenuating, and this was one of those occasions. If the Khedive and Council of Ministers had dealt with the petition and complaint in a reasonable manner instead of by treachery, the mutiny might never have occurred. If any blame can justly be laid on the colonels, it can only be for demanding the removal of a minister. Apart from that it is difficult to see what else they could have done. To have walked consciously into the trap would have been to court disgrace and dismissal at best, or exile and death at worst. To refuse to obey the summons to the Ministry of War would have been in itself an act of mutiny, and it is beyond human nature that men should knowingly place themselves in danger without taking some precautions to extricate themselves, and this is what the colonels did. In so doing they discovered that with their troops behind them they were the masters of the situation. The only cause for wonder is that the troops of the regiments willingly associated themselves with their commanding officers in a mutiny against the Khedive, the ruler of Egypt.

In these events the lead had been taken by the colonel of the 4th Regiment, Ahmed Bey Arabi. Since he was to take a prominent part in Egyptian affairs during the two following years, a thumbnail sketch of his antecedents may not be out of place. Of *fellah* origin, he was born at Horiyeh near Zagazig in 1840, the son of a local sheikh and farmer. After a period of two years at El Azhar University he was taken into the army by Said Pasha who, it will be remembered, had conceived the plan of conscripting the sons of village sheikhs and making them do something useful. It is illustrative of the efficiency of Said Pasha's army that Arabi became a lieutenant at seventeen, a captain at eighteen, a major at nineteen and a lieutenant-colonel at twenty! This rapid promotion can only be ascribed to Said Pasha's preference for native Egyptians as against Turks and Circassians. On the accession of Ismail Pasha, the favour Arabi had hitherto enjoyed ceased abruptly, and he was relegated to minor duties in the transport services and semi-civilian posts.[13] From this time onward he appears to have joined the ranks of the discontented in the army, and to have engaged in various intrigues against the Khedive Ismail which however came to nothing.

As a matter of interest, when Arabi's own previous career is considered, it becomes apparent that he had little cause for complaint regarding the system of promotion current in the Egyptian army. It was surely only favouritism that elevated him to the rank of lieutenant-colonel at the early age of twenty. Thus, in complaining 'that the Egyptian officers had been treated unjustly,' he was in fact only criticising the system which had led to his own promotion. The fact that the boot was now on the other foot made no difference. However, allowance must be made for human nature.

To return to the events of 1 February 1881, although the colonels had obtained their demands and won the day, they had little cause for elation. They realised that they had not only flouted the authority of the Khedive but had humiliated him as well. If the traditions of the Orient were any guide, it was only to be expected that the Khedive, though having ostensibly pardoned their misconduct, would never rest until he had avenged himself upon them. The Khedive was still the ruler, the head of the state and could pull many strings and exert his influence covertly against the rebels. Even if the Khedive be credited with magnanimity in having forgiven the colonels and forgotten the incident, the latter were not to know this – at least they could never be sure. Henceforth they must be continually on their guard, anticipating and averting any attempt the Khedive might make against them. Fear of reprisal and treachery became a dominant emotion. The Khedive was, in fact, unlikely to forgive the insults and humiliations he had suffered at the hands of a group of officers he most despised. Tewfik likewise understood oriental psychology. He realised what must be the attitude of the officers, and he too was in consequence haunted by the fear that they would take further action in an attempt to get rid of him before he got rid of them. There could thus be no peace of mind for either party as long as they both remained on the scene. It had become impossible to maintain the status quo for an indefinite period.

As long as the colonels remained with their regiments in Cairo, the Khedive regarded their united strength as a weapon which might be turned against him at any moment. The obvious solution was to order them to separate stations in the provinces. But this very order might well precipitate the crisis, and for some months the Khedive hesitated. In August Tewfik finally plucked up courage to instruct the new Minister of War to move the regiments. But Mahmud Pasha Sami was sympathetic to the colonels and demurred against the instruction, whereupon the Khedive dismissed him on the spot and appointed his own brother-in-law, Daoud Pasha Yeghen, to the vacant post. The order to move was issued to the regiments of Arabi and

Abdel-Aal forthwith.

The two colonels reacted immediately. On 8 September they announced that they intended the following day to march with their regiments to Abdin Palace in Cairo, there to make a demonstration and present the following demands to the Khedive: the dismissal of the Ministry; the convocation of a national assembly; and the raising of the army to its full strength of 18,000 men. A consideration of these demands shows a marked difference in the new attitude and policy of the colonels. Up to the incident of 1 February they had been simply native officers full of resentment against what they considered unjust treatment in the army, and had used the muskets and bayonets of their troops to obtain redress. But here was a clear departure. The demands to be presented showed little connection with military grievances. Arabi and his colleagues were now entering the arena of politics, not even as supplicants but as arbiters of the nation. Clearly in the interval between February and September some profound influence had been exercised over them. The nationalist party, looking for some means of fulfilling their ambitions, had seen in the mutinous army a suitable instrument and had begun to instil the doctrines of democracy and self-determination into the *fellah* colonel, Arabi. The seed fell on fertile ground, for the idea of native Egyptians having some control over their own destinies agreed well with his own detestation of Turkish traditional supremacy and favouritism. A national assembly with powers to overthrow Turkish supremacy, and incidentally the European Control with all its trappings, made an instant appeal to Arabi Bey, and it must be admitted that there was some right on his side. On the other hand, the right can never be conceded to serving officers to use the military power they command to dictate the policy of the nation, to overthrow ministries and take a hand in the government themselves. In that direction lies rebellion.

Not so easy to understand is the demand to raise the strength of the army to 18,000 men. It cannot be said that Egypt at this time was menaced from without, unless it was thought possible that the European Controllers might persuade their own governments to military intervention, in which case no army Egypt could raise could resist a concerted invasion by either England or France. There might, of course, be a possibility of military action by the Sultan who had no love for democratic constitutions, but perhaps the true motive for demanding an increase in the strength of the army lay in the fact that it would give employment to many half-pay officers and would thus strengthen the military party.

On the following day, 9 September, the demonstration duly took place. There was nothing secret or sudden about it; the Khedive had previously been informed. Calling Sir Auckland Colvin to his side, he set out on a tour of the other regiments in Cairo to ascertain the strength of their loyalty; but without obtaining much satisfaction. By the time he returned to Abdin Palace, he found the mutinous regiments drawn up in the square facing the palace with Arabi at their head. On the appearance of the Khedive in the square, Arabi rode forward and addressed his demands. Tewfik did not agree immediately, on the ground that it was not fitting to negotiate with army officers on matters affecting the whole state, and therefore retired himself into the palace leaving Colvin and Sir Charles Cookson, acting British Consul-General, to negotiate with the military. The outcome was an almost complete capitulation by the Khedive. He agreed to dismiss the Ministry of Riaz Pasha and to invite Cherif Pasha to form a new one. The other questions were to be temporarily left in abeyance, but only in theory, since Cherif Pasha was a constitutionalist and favoured the establishment of a national assembly. He was not, however, immediately willing to take office upon the instigation of a group of rebellious officers and was only persuaded to do so provided the officers agreed to obey orders to disperse to the stations allotted to them. This they agreed to do. Mahmud Sami was reinstated as Minister of War.

The victory of the military party was thus complete. By force of arms they had imposed their will on the Khedive and obliged him to dismiss one ministry and appoint another which would adopt a policy more in keeping with the view of the military and nationalist parties. The suggestion has been put forward that the whole episode was the outcome of a pre-arranged intrigue between Arabi and the Khedive, both of whom were anxious to get rid of Riaz Pasha. This is the view put forward by Wilfred S. Blunt in his *Secret History of the English Occupation of Egypt*. The principal events which started in February 1881 and culminated in the battle of Tel-el-Kebir in September 1882 are not in dispute, but there is some doubt about the true causes and motives which brought them about. The country was plagued with factions, parties and conflicting interests, viz., the Khedive and his Turko-Circassion palace group; the Financial Control with their bond-holding interests; Riaz Pasha and his ministry; the foreign Consuls with their tremendous powers of influence; the military party led by the 'three colonels', and the nationalists. It is impossible to state with any degree of accuracy to what extent collusion and intrigue existed between the various combinations enumerated above, for intrigue is by its very nature secret and leaves little record for the historian, but it is unlikely that in the incident of 9 September there was any collaboration between Arabi and the Khedive merely to dismiss the Riaz Ministry. It is beyond belief that the proud Turk would publicly humiliate himself merely to rid himself of an obnoxious Minister when other more discreet ways were open to him. The explanation given by Lord Cromer,[14] that the mutiny was inspired by fear of retribution, seems more probable.

Some word of explanation is here necessary of the activities of Mr Wilfred Scawen Blunt mentioned above, who took an active part behind the scenes of the Arabi Rebellion. Mr Blunt was an Englishman, a dilettante of some wealth and connection, who took it upon himself to espouse the cause of Moslem liberation from the Turkish yoke in general, and of Egyptian nationalism in particular. Mr Blunt became a fanatic on the Egyptian question, and in this state of mind it was not difficult for him to be persuaded by the nationalist and military parties to their cause. He was undoubtedly an idealist imbued with lofty sentiments, but like most idealists he was incapable of seeing anybody else's point of view. He and Sir William Gregory, a man of similar but less rigid sentiments, became the self-appointed mentors of a rather ignorant, but well-meaning, native Egyptian army colonel. Edward Dicey effectively describes their influence in the following words:

> . . . it was through their instrumentality that he (Arabi) was led to present himself before the British public in the guise of a reformer anxious to redress the grievances of his fellow countrymen, of a champion of Egyptian nationality, and of a patriot desirous to establish the independence of his country and to free her from foreign rule. I should doubt extremely how far Arabi understood the phrases his English counsellors placed in his mouth, or whether he ever read the letters composed for him, which bore the signature of 'Achmed the Egyptian'.[15]

At any rate Blunt became not only a persuasive influence behind the scenes in Egypt, but also a vociferous champion of Arabi in England and a voluminous correspondent on the subject.

The dominant question that now loomed up was, what was the attitude of the powers, England and France in particular, likely to be in the face of recent events? By taking the initiative in deposing Ismail Pasha and setting up Tewfik in his place, they had assumed a certain responsibility for the tranquillity and good government of Egypt. As long as the Khedive working in co-operation with a benevolent ministry remained in control, the two powers had every reason to suppose that Egypt would proceed more or less smoothly along the path of reform mapped out for her by the Dual Control and the other Europeans associated in the government, and that the obligations imposed by the Law of Liquidation would be honoured. But the incidents of February and September had unmistakably proved that the effective control of Egypt had passed out of the hands of the Khedive and his Council of Ministers into those of an oligarchy of army officers. Already these were beginning to talk publicly of liberating Egypt from the European bondholders and of establishing a native parliament which would formulate policy and direct the destinies of the land. Under such circumstances there could be no guarantee that the pledges and obligations would be honoured. The Consuls-General, Sir Edward Malet and M. Sienkiewicz, in reporting these events to their respective governments, dwelt in detail on the critical situation.

Not only was there apprehension for the future of Egypt on the part of the powers, but a considerable element of doubt and mistrust existed among the Egyptians regarding the intentions of the powers. Only recently, on the flimsiest pretext, France had torn the province of Tunis from the flank of the Ottoman Empire, an action which gave ground for the suspicion that France at any rate, and possibly England, was intent on empire-building and fears among the Egyptians that their own country might be next on the list were not entirely unfounded.

But the mutual suspicions and jealousies of both countries automatically precluded anything in the nature of intervention or annexation by one to the exclusion of the other. England still clung to the belief that as long as Egypt remained within the Turkish Empire she could not belong to any European power and therefore be under any influence hostile to England. France on the other hand regarded the nominal Turkish suzerainty over Egypt as a deterrent to the expansion of her own influence and as something to be diminished as much as possible. It was not, however, worth risking a war with England on this count. Both powers had thus arrived at the conclusion that the best, or perhaps least dangerous, *modus operandi* lay in concerting with each other in matters affecting Egypt. Their policy may perhaps concisely be summed up in the three words: 'Neither or both.'

But events were hastening forward some form of intervention from outside. From the English and French point of view, it was becoming evident that something must be done to re-establish the authority of the Khedive and his government before the country fell into the grip of a military dictatorship. Although the Khedive still remained on his throne and the Ministry of Cherif Pasha in theory governed the country, in practice Egypt had already fallen to the military dictatorship. Everywhere Arabi was talked of as '*El Wahid*', the One, i.e. the Leader, the holder of power and the saviour of the nation from foreign domination. He was waited on by delegations and 'people were flocking from all sides to Cairo to lay their grievances before him.'[16] The Consuls had been instructed to give all support to the Khedive and were doing their best, but this availed him little when faced with the threats of direct action by army officers with their regiments behind them. It was a fact not clearly recognised in London and Paris at the time that armed force could only be met by armed force, and in Egypt there was no such force in existence capable of subduing Arabi.

The danger of anarchy in Egypt became the subject of many diplomatic exchanges between Whitehall and the Quai d'Orsay. Both governments agreed that action of some sort should be taken to combat the danger; both agreed that they should concert together in this matter. The only point of divergence between the two governments, but the most important point of all, was the nature of the action to be taken. Lord Granville, the British Foreign Secretary, viewed a combined Anglo-French military intervention with much distaste. Firstly he had no wish to see British troops in Egypt at all, still less French troops alone, and least of all both together. In this he was undoubtedly right. It is certain that Anglo-French amity would have foundered on the Egyptian rock sooner or later. The only alternative to direct European action in one form or another which occurred to Lord Granville was the intervention of the Sultan as suzerain of Egypt – with safeguards. The Sultan was in fact only too anxious to reassert himself in Egypt. For the past forty years Egypt had held a position of almost complete independence ratified by the firmans of 1841 and more recently confirmed by that of 1879. Sultan Abdul Hamid would have given much to bring Egypt back into the Turkish fold, and here indeed was a golden opportunity. Even at the time of the September incident preparations were going on in Constantinople to send a force to occupy Egypt.

True to traditional policy, in French eyes any solution to the Egyptian problem was better than that offered by Turkish intervention; France regarded this cure as worse than the disease. It is difficult to understand the obstinacy with which France adhered to this turkophobe policy in Egyptian affairs. Perhaps the true motive may be found in the fact that the French Government, ever at the mercy of financial interests, were considerably influenced by the Egyptian bondholders. A Turkish intervention would not have been to their advantage. The only action which would have satisfied this group would have been an intervention which included French forces. As this could only be effected with English support and assistance, the solution which commended itself to the French Government was an Anglo-French military intervention. This was the policy towards which French diplomacy was working and against which Lord Granville was feebly struggling. The policy succeeded at any rate to the extent of persuading Lord Granville to instruct the British Ambassador at Constantinople to unite with his French counterpart in urging the Sultan not to send troops to Egypt. These persuasions proved successful and no Turkish force was sent. But the Sultan, in order to give some positive evidence of his nominal authority, instead dispatched two commissioners, Ali Fuad Bey and Ali Nizami Pasha. They arrived in Egypt on 6 October. The precise object of their mission is not entirely clear; indeed, it may well be doubted whether the commissioners themselves had any idea beyond endeavouring to remind the parties concerned that they were all subjects of His Imperial Majesty and that the Khedive was his deputy. Shortly afterwards a British warship, HMS *Invincible*, arrived at Alexandria, ostensibly to provide a sanctuary for the European element in the event of hostile native demonstrations. There was some argument as to which should be the first to quit Egypt, the British warship or the Turkish commissioners. A compromise was effected by arranging both their departures for the same day. The Turkish visit at least achieved one result of note: it persuaded Arabi quietly and obediently to move his regiment to Suez.

On 4 October 1881 the Khedive issued a decree convoking the Chamber of Notables, to be elected under a law of 1866, and to meet on 23 December following.[17] Thus during the next two months the Notables began to assemble in Cairo for their deliberations and the Government, as also the British and French representatives, began to look for some indications of future probabilities.

Arabi and his following let it be known to Cherif Pasha that they now expected, nay required, the army to be brought up to its full strength of 18,000 men. This of course was almost entirely a financial question, and its fulfilment in the first instance must necessarily depend upon the state of the Treasury. No demands upon the national income could be considered without the consent of the Controllers-General. In this case Sir Auckland Colvin was not blind to the necessity of re-establishing equilibrium even though this might entail conceding something to the military party. But the sum required to give effect to the proposal amounted to £268,000, a figure far in excess of what could be found from the country's straitened resources. Cherif Pasha however managed to steer a middle course by inducing the military to accept an increase of £168,000 and leaving it to them to stretch it as far as possible. For the moment the outlook seemed rather brighter. The Notables, though not having yet officially assembled, looked as if they were going to be cautious and reasonable in their deliberations. The Chamber was formally opened by His Highness on 26 December. A few weeks before, on 14 November, the French Ministry of Jules Ferry had fallen and the Presidency of the Council taken by M. Gambetta who also took the portfolio for foreign affairs. M. Gambetta was a man of extremely forceful character and furthermore knew exactly what he wanted. In matters affecting Egypt he was completely unyielding and he was determined that either the existing status quo must be maintained in its entirety or that it should be replaced by a direct Anglo-French intervention. He undoubtedly sensed that any resistance to French demands in Egypt would have similar repercussions in France's newly-acquired 'province' of Tunis.

Immediately on his entry into office, M. Gambetta put himself into communication with Lord Granville at the British Foreign Office and impressed upon him the necessity of the two powers concerting together and acting identically in all matters affecting Egypt. Lord Granville was disposed to agree with this general principle but he had no clear idea of what the operation of this principle was likely to involve, or exactly what should be done. M. Gambetta, however, was by no means devoid of ideas. In view of the fact that the Chamber of Notables was about to meet in Cairo, he suggested taking this opportunity of sending a message from the two powers 'to convey collectively to Tewfik Pasha assurances of the sympathy and support of France and England, and to encourage His Highness to maintain and assert his proper authority.'[18] Lord Granville sent this proposal to Sir Edward Malet for his opinion. On the surface it looked harmless enough, especially if construed to mean that the Khedive was to be encouraged not to capitulate to the military party in their demands, but to support the Chamber of Notables in their legitimate and reasonable aspirations. In fact, Sir Edward Malet replied on 27 December, 'I see no objection to M. Gambetta's proposal. The support that the Khedive is most likely to require is towards the maintenance of the independence of the Chamber against the jealousies and suspicions of the Porte.'[19]

Lord Granville thereupon allowed himself to be persuaded to this proposal, and M. Gambetta promised to prepare the text of the note himself. It was sent to both the Consuls-General on 6 January 1882 with instructions to deliver it to His Highness. The wording of this joint note was as follows:

Sir, You have already been instructed on several occasions to inform the Khedive and his Government of the determination of France and England to afford them support against the difficulties of various kinds which might interfere with the course of public affairs in Egypt. The two Powers are entirely agreed on this subject and recent circumstances, especially the meeting of the Chamber of Notables convoked by the Khedive, have given them the opportunity for a further exchange of views. I have accordingly to instruct you to declare to Tewfik Pasha, after having come to an arrangement with M. Sienkiewicz, who is instructed to make an identic and simultaneous communication, that the English and French governments consider the maintenance of His Highness on the throne, on the terms laid down by the Sultan's Firmans, and officially recognised by the two Governments, as alone able to guarantee, for the present and future, the good order and the development of general prosperity in Egypt, in which France and England are equally interested. The two Governments, being closely associated in the resolve to guard by their united efforts against all cause of complications, internal or external, which might menace the order of things established in Egypt, do not doubt that the assurance publicly given of their formal intentions in this respect will tend to avert the dangers to which the Government of the Khedive might be exposed, and which would certainly find France and England united to oppose them. They are convinced that His Highness will draw from this assurance the confidence and strength which he requires to direct the destinies of Egypt and its people.

If this Note was intended to allay suspicion of aggressive intentions by England or France, and to show that the two Governments viewed benevolently the orderly development of a Chamber expressing popular views and aspirations, it failed lamentably. Its effect was exactly the reverse. Up to the time of its presentation the influence and popularity of Arabi and the military party had tended to wane a little, and there had been every reason to expect that Cherif Pasha would be able to guide and direct the proceedings of the Chamber of Notables, his own creation, along pacific and progressive lines. There had already been some suggestion that the Chamber should be empowered to discuss and vote on that part of the Budget which was not devoted to the service of the national debt. This proposal had, of course, been contested by Sir Auckland Colvin, and Cherif Pasha had persuaded the Chamber not to press this point, at least during the present session. This concession is adequate evidence that the Chamber was amenable to the influence and wishes of the Government.

The joint Note destroyed almost everything that had been built up. Its effects were summed up by John Morley in the *Fortnightly Review*:

At Cairo, the Note fell like a bombshell. Nobody had expected such a declaration, and nobody there was aware of any reason why it should have been launched. What was felt was that so serious a step on such delicate ground could not have been taken without deliberate calculation nor without some grave intention. The Note was, therefore, taken to mean that the Sultan was to be thrust still further in the background; that the Khedive was to become more plainly the puppet of England and France; and that Egypt would, sooner or later, in some shape or other, be made to share the disastrous fate of Tunis. The general effect was, therefore, mischievous in the highest degree. The Khedive was encouraged in his opposition to the sentiments of the Chamber. The military, national or popular party was alarmed. The Sultan was irritated. The other European powers were made uneasy. Every element of disturbance was roused into activity.[20]

Whatever M. Gambetta may have hoped to achieve by the presentation of this note, it resulted in the instant destruction of the generally good accord which the British Consul General had built up between his country and Egypt. Sir Edward Malet had made a favourable impression upon the various parties in Egypt, and they looked to him for support in developing those liberal and democratic institutions so dear to the hearts of Englishmen. But England's co-operation in the Joint Note shattered the illusion, if illusion it was. It now appeared that she was scheming in conjunction with France to take over Egypt completely. 'I come to be looked upon as an arch-traitor who has lured them on to obtain an excuse for intervention,' wrote Sir Edward Malet.[21] The net result was that the national and military parties fused together completely in face of what appeared to be a common peril. Lord Granville realised immediately that he had made a mistake, that the Note was, in fact, far from expressing the true sentiments of England, and he endeavoured to persuade M. Gambetta to join in sending a further note explanatory of the first. M. Gambetta refused point blank, and Lord Granville was thus obliged to abide by his declaration.

In Egypt the Note resulted in an immediate hardening of the attitude of the Chamber. The question of the Budget was immediately revived, the Notables insisting on the right to vote that part of the Budget not devoted to the national debt or the Tribute. In truth, this was a reasonable proposal. The powers were only interested in the repayments to the bondholders and that the order established to secure these should not be disturbed. The Notables had no intention of infringing these rights, but considered that they were entitled to discuss and vote on the apportionment of the remaining revenues.

If the Chamber was not allowed any power in this direction, it is difficult to say precisely what purpose it was intended to serve. Lord Granville was disposed to concede the point, but at every juncture the rigid obstruction of M. Gambetta was interposed. Every approach tended to show that France at any rate was determined to interfere in every detail of Egyptian internal affairs. Lord Granville allowed himself to be dragged along the same path by the masterful Frenchman.

The Khedive himself was the greatest victim of the fatal note, for it was thought that he himself had requested from the powers a declaration of the purport contained therein, and was thus attempting to ally himself with the powers against his own people. From this point onwards he was regarded with suspicion and contempt by his own subjects and by the nationalist-military party in particular. The unfortunate Cherif Pasha was tossed about between the irate Chamber and the Consuls General, asserting the views of their respective governments, and by the end of January 1882 the deadlock was complete, the Chamber insisting upon its rights to vote the Budget and Cherif Pasha enforced by the powers to refuse it.

On 2 February 1882 a deputation of the Chamber waited on the Khedive and insisted on a change of ministry. 'His Highness asked on what law of the Chamber they founded their right to make the request. This they could not answer, but insisted on the change.'[22] The Khedive was obliged to accede because, he said, he had no force to resist. At the instance of the Chamber Mahmud Sami Pasha was appointed President of the Council and Arabi Bey Minister of War. The direction of the country thus passed completely into the hands of the military party.

CHAPTER 14

The British Occupation

Although Mahmud Pasha Sami became President of the Council of Ministers, it was well recognised by all that the real power was vested in Arabi, for it was he who had led the revolts of February and September, he who commanded the support of the regiments and he to whom people brought their grievances and looked for redress. Arabi thus became the supreme power in the land of Egypt. In consideration of his ministerial rank, he was made a *pasha*.

One of the first acts of the new Ministry was the introduction of a *Leyha*, or Organic Law, granting a constitution to the country. This was to provide for an elected chamber endowed with the widest powers in framing laws and supervising the Ministry. We are told that the new Ministry contemplated a number of practical reforms 'which have since been included in the list of benefits conferred on the country under British occupation and which Lord Cromer has adopted on his own.'[1] It requires no great administrative capacity to contemplate such reforms; it does, however, require some degree of energy and ability to carry them out. Arabi Pasha was not, however, specially notable for administrative ability, and these reforms remained during his ministry only in the stages of contemplation. But he did initiate an enormous programme of promotion in the army, and on 11 April Sir Edward Malet reported that five hundred officers had been advanced in rank. 'The Controllers-General are unacquainted with the manner in which the increase of pay is provided for, but it is supposed that the augmentation of the army has been more or less left aside, and that the money intended for this service is being used to pay the officers.'[2] It will be recalled that the first revolt of Arabi had been based on the discrimination against native Egyptian officers in the matter of promotions.

In the new promotions the Circassian element was entirely ignored, and

209

the discontent which had animated Arabi and his colleagues to revolt a year before now filled the neglected Circassians. The Khedive reminded Arabi of his own law which required the previous examinations of officers under the rank of colonel, but Arabi answered that the officers 'were of such well-known capacity that examination was unnecessary. Moreover . . . they refused to be examined, and were supported in their refusal by the rest of the army.'[3]

This question of promotion has been dwelt on in some detail because it was to have important repercussions and it also brings out three significant points: that the administrative acts and interests of the Arabi Ministry seem to have been confined to satisfying the army; that the army had lost all discipline; and that Arabi failed, or refused, to realise that the discriminatory policy of promotion was arousing dangerous discontent in the neglected element. During the first two months of the Ministry, February and March, relative peace reigned in Egypt, but the general standard of administration of the provinces began to deteriorate. The civil authorities, the *mudirs* and *mamurs*, tended to lose their authority, while the army did whatever it pleased. The European residents, regarded by the army as an instrument of Egyptian subservience, became nervous for their property and lives.

At the same time events in Europe were tending towards some form of intervention. A few days before the dismissal of Cherif Pasha and the accession of Arabi to power, the Ministry of M. Gambetta in France was defeated in the Chamber of Deputies on an internal issue and resigned. Gambetta was succeeded on 30 January 1882 by M. Charles de Freycinet. In spite of the brevity of M. Gambetta's tenure of office, a matter of two and a half months, his effect on Egyptian history was of a much more enduring nature. He was the driving force behind the policy of foreign, i.e. Anglo-French, intervention; he was the author of the Joint Note, and the prime cause of the union of the nationalist and military parties and of the entry of Arabi Pasha to power. As Lord Cromer states, 'Lord Granville, M. de Freycinet and others might do their best to put back the hands of the clock, but it was impossible that they should ever restore the *status quo ante* Gambetta.'[4] However much his successor might dislike the policy set forth in the Joint Note, he was bound to adhere to it. In fact, M. de Freycinet viewed the policy of French military intervention with some distaste. It was not so long ago since France had suffered so disastrously at the hands of Germany, and the fears of a further rupture in the relations of the two countries were ever present with him. A military expedition to Egypt necessarily implied a diminution of France's ability to defend herself. M. de

Freycinet wanted his soldiers at home, not across the seas in Egypt. Neither did he want an English intervention and, true to French tradition, he was likewise averse to Turkish action. He was therefore much more amenable to some form of compromise than his predecessor had been. In a series of negotiations which Lord Granville opened with de Freycinet early in February the latter was persuaded to agree to the principle that any action taken in Egypt should be of a European character, if necessary in concert with the Porte, rather than confined to the two powers England and France. Thus on 11 February 1882 a circular was addressed to all the principal European Powers proposing an exchange of views on the Egyptian question and mentioning that the Sultan 'should be a party to any proceeding or discussion that might ensue.'[5] It was pointed out however that as yet no situation had arisen to justify any action in Egypt, but that should any such situation arise, it was hoped that any action taken should represent a united Europe.

Nothing occurred to cause ground for anxiety until the middle of April when it was announced that sixteen Circassian officers had been arrested on a charge of conspiracy to murder Arabi Pasha and the leaders of the military and nationalist parties. By 22 April the number of arrests had increased to nearly fifty. There is some doubt whether there was in fact any such conspiracy. It was certainly not beyond the bounds of possibility, but what is certain is that there did exist a body of extremely discontented officers who had been passed over in promotion and who could see no hope for the future as long as the country was controlled by Arabi and his party. There may have been loud recriminations and threats among the Circassians, but whether their discontent actually crystallised into planned conspiracy against the lives of the military leaders is not clear. At any rate, the idea became firmly implanted in Arabi's mind that his life was in danger, and the arrests were made. Unrest immediately became prevalent throughout the land. The accused were placed on their trial by court-martial, the composition of which gave much doubt as to the impartiality of the proceedings. The trial was held in secret, the accused were allowed no counsel to defend them, and, furthermore, three officers whose lives were alleged to have been threatened in the conspiracy sat on the bench. On 2 May it was announced that 'forty officers, among whom is Osman Rifki, ex-Minister of War, have been condemned to exile for life to the furthest limits of the Soudan.'[6] The sentence would of course be subject to confirmation by the Khedive. Tewfik Pasha was either not convinced of the justice of the proceedings and sentence, of which the latter was equivalent to a sentence of death, or felt that in confirming the sentence he would be alienating from himself the only group, the Circassian element of the army, on which he could place any reliance. A fresh struggle thus flared up between the Khedive and his ministers. Osman Pasha Rifki bore the rank of *ferik*, or General, which had been conferred on him by the Sultan. The Khedive used this fact as a pretext for referring the whole matter to the Porte. This incensed the Ministers considerably, and, rather than incur the interference of the Porte, the ministers on 6 May proposed to the Khedive that he should commute the sentence to one of simple banishment. The Khedive however now replied that the matter was in the hands of the Porte.[7] But without waiting for a reply from Constantinople he requested the advice of the Consuls who were of the opinion that he should 'simply exercise his prerogative and decree a commutation of the sentences pronounced.'[8] Tewfik adopted this course and on 9 May the decree commuting the sentences to one of simple exile from Egypt was issued; the officers concerned were to retain their ranks, privileges and pay. But such lavish concessions were regarded by the ministers as a deliberate flouting of their will by the Khedive, and the breach between them now widened to such a point that reconciliation became well-nigh impossible. It became a trial of strength, the Khedive relying largely upon the moral support of the Consuls and the Powers they represented, while Arabi Pasha and the Ministry believed, with some cause, that France would never permit a Turkish intervention nor would she now intervene herself. Provided they could carry the country with them there was no obstacle, they thought, to deposing the Khedive and appointing one of their own choice. To this end Mahmud Pasha Sami took the step of convoking the Chamber of Notables to lay the dispute before them.

Section 9 of the Organic Law had laid down that 'in case of necessity the Chamber will be convoked in Extraordinary Session by the Khedive.' The Ministry had thus no proper authority for bringing the Chamber together without the Khedive's consent but this did not deter them from so doing. The unfolding of these events had been watched with some concern in London and Paris. Both governments had hitherto hoped that the moral support afforded by their respective representatives in Cairo to the Khedive would be sufficient to deter the Arabi Ministry and the military party from a further clash. These hopes had proved vain. In order to anticipate and thus prevent any Turkish move, M. de Freycinet took the initiative on 12 May by sending a note to Lord Granville proposing that the two Powers should each send a squadron of six warships to Alexandria, that the Sultan should be invited for the moment to refrain from action in Egypt, and that the other four great Powers should be notified of this intention and invited to request their own ambassadors at Constantinople to make similar representations to the Porte. The note went on to say that while France was still opposed to Turkish intervention, she would not regard as such the employment of Turkish troops operating under English and French control for a specific purpose and under defined conditions. Finally the Consuls-General were to be instructed not to recognise any authority other than the Khedive's and not to enter into any negotiations with any other government except for the purposes of securing the safety of their nationals.[9]

The move proposed by de Freycinet was welcomed by Lord Granville, and instructions were issued that a naval squadron should be sent to Alexandria. It was considered that such a demonstration of material support would be sufficient to bring about the submission of the Ministry to the Khedive. The announcement that the ships were coming certainly had some effect at Cairo. Hitherto the Chamber of Notables which included a considerable moderate element had been virtually terrorised by the military party into acceding to its demands, but some were personally inclined to support the Khedive, feeling no doubt that the course pursued by the military would only lead finally to intervention from outside. They were also tired of the military rule to which the country had been subjected during recent months and the continuous struggle between the ruler and his Ministry. The news of the coming of the fleets strengthened this attitude. Thus, when the Notables assembled in Cairo they were by no means disposed to support Arabi's proposal to depose the Khedive. They preferred to see some reconciliation between the two parties, and on 13 May Sultan Pasha, the President of the Chamber, approached Tewfik with a request of this purport. The latter refused; he would not, he said, be reconciled to a ministry which had openly defied him, threatened his family and himself and violated the law.

As the Khedive was adamant, the only alternative that would offer a solution was the retirement of the Ministry and the appointment of another. Sultan Pasha therefore proposed that the Khedive should accept the resignation of Mahmud Pasha Sami, the President of the Council. But the chief difficulty lay in finding someone to take his place. An offer was made to Mustafa Pasha Fehmi, the Minister of Foreign Affairs and Justice, a man of moderate views, but he refused to entertain it. It was in fact impossible to find any one willing to assume the responsibility as long as Arabi Pasha remained in Egypt, since he controlled the army, the only force in Egypt capable of asserting itself. Likewise Arabi Pasha refused to be moved from office unless the Chamber of Notables desired it, and while the latter were not disposed to go to the extreme of deposing the Khedive they were nonetheless sufficiently inspired with fear at the consequences which would ensue from requesting the Ministry to resign. The deadlock was thus complete.

Neither the military party nor the Chamber of Notables was prepared to admit the right of England and France to interfere in the internal affairs of Egypt as long as the country's contractual obligation, i.e. to the creditors, was honoured. In the present dispute between Khedive and Ministry both parties looked to the Sultan as the ultimate authority. The Sultan was annoyed at the dispatch of the warships to Alexandria on the ground that it was an encroachment on his authority. It was unfortunate that the full co-operation of the Sultan was not secured in the action to be taken in Egypt, but de Freycinet, though he privately concurred with Lord Granville in the principle of utilising Turkish forces if necessary, was most reluctant that this policy should be published, as it might cause an explosion of public opinion in France. He was therefore exerting every effort to prevent any Turkish action in Egypt in the hope that the problem could be solved without it. The result was that the Sultan was never fully taken into the confidence of the Powers and it was believed, and rightly believed, in Cairo that he would not countenance any foreign interference. This tended to strengthen Arabi Pasha in his stand against the Khedive.

On 25 May the initiative was taken by Sir Edward Malet and M. Sienkiewicz to break the deadlock. They presented a note to Sami Pasha, President of the Council, in the following terms:

The undersigned . . . considering that His Excellency Sultan Pacha, President of the Chamber of Delegates . . . has proposed to Mahmoud Pacha Sami, President of the Council, as the only means of putting an end to the disturbed state of the country, the following conditions:

(1) The temporary retirement from Egypt of His Excellency Arabi Pacha with the maintenance of his rank and pay;

(2) The retirement into the interior of Egypt of Ali Fehmi Pacha and Abdoullah Pacha who will also retain their rank and pay;

(3) The resignation of the present Ministry.

Considering that these conditions . . . may prevent the misfortunes which threaten Egypt . . . the Undersigned recommend these conditions to the most serious attention of the President of the Council and his colleagues, and, if necessary, will insist on their fulfilment. The Governments of England and

France, in intervening in the affairs of Egypt, have no other object than to maintain the status quo and consequently to restore to the Khedive the authority which belongs to him, and without which the status quo is continually in danger. The intervention of the two Powers being divested of all character of vengeance or reprisal, they will use their good offices to obtain from the Khedive a general amnesty, and will watch over its strict observance.[10]

On being acquainted with the contents of this note the Ministry forthwith presented their resignation to the Khedive, charging him at the same time with betraying the interests of the country to the Europeans by accepting the conditions of the Note. The army, however, refused to accept the resignation of Arabi Pasha and declared they would allow the Khedive twelve hours to reinstate him. The army had now taken the bit between its teeth and was willing to sweep away the Khedive, the Europeans and any other elements which threatened to oppose it. The Khedive was actually in danger of his life and unrest was rife throughout the country. Tewfik Pasha appealed to the Consuls for advice regarding his intolerable situation, but they were unable to give any.

He is in an extremely painful position. Menaced with death, prevented by England and France, while yet there was time, and not permitted to appeal for assistance to the only quarter from which it can effectually come [i.e. the Sultan], His Highness must bitterly feel the present apparent result of following our counsel and relying on our support.[11]

On 28 May all the sheikhs, *ulema* and Notables waited on the Khedive and begged him to reinstate Arabi Pasha. 'He refused, but they besought him, saying that, though he might be ready to sacrifice his own life, he ought not to sacrifice theirs, and that Arabi had threatened them all with death if they did not obtain his consent.'[12] The Khedive finally yielded but only to preserve public tranquillity. The next day Tewfik Pasha made application to the Sultan for the despatch of a Turkish Commissioner to Egypt to adjudicate and restore order. In response, Dervish Pasha, a Turkish general, left Constantinople on 4 June and arrived at Alexandria on the 7th. Instead of declaring boldly to the mutineers that he had come to restore order and that if his commands were not obeyed a Turkish army would be landed forthwith to restore order by force of arms, Dervish Pasha attempted to negotiate between the various parties for a settlement. Arabi Pasha had been intriguing for some time with Constantinople, affirming that he was only acting on behalf of His Majesty by frustrating the efforts of France and England to get control of Egypt. The Sultan had from time to time sent encouraging responses. Dervish Pasha was thus in a dilemma. On the one hand it was his duty to support the Sultan's legitimate viceroy, while at the same time he wanted to avoid as far as possible giving offence to the Sultan's self-styled adherent, Arabi Pasha. But compromise and negotiation were impossible. Arabi Pasha and the army had gone too far to turn back and they showed no disposition to listen to Dervish Pasha's pleadings.

Within a few days of his arrival, on 11 June a riot broke out in Alexandria. A fanatical mob surged through the streets shouting, 'Death to the Christians!' 'Some fifty Europeans were slaughtered in cold blood under circumstances of the utmost brutality. Many others, amongst whom was Sir Charles Cookson the British Consul, were severely wounded and narrowly escaped with their lives.'[13] No blame for this outburst can be attached specifically to any individual. It was undoubtedly the result of the political unrest which prevailed throughout the land. For years the infidel Europeans had been battening on Egypt, and there was barely a peasant cultivator in the Delta who was not heavily in debt to the European usurer or who had not been dispossessed of his holding by foreclosure, while the age-old régime of the capitulations protected the European from all Egyptian jurisdiction. It is probable that the Alexandria riots were simply the expression of the pent-up resentment of years against the privileged *giaour*. The civil authorities appear to have done little to check this disturbance which went on until the following day when Arabi Pasha sent troops into the town to restore order.

The consuls of the Powers went in a body to Dervish Pasha demanding measures for the security of their countrymen, but the Commissioner had to confess that he was powerless and must therefore decline responsibility, and it was left to Arabi Pasha himself to guarantee good order. It was thus shown that Dervish Pasha had been unable to exert any influence on the military party; his mission had failed and Arabi remained supreme. He had the solid backing of the army behind him, and there was no means of overthrowing him except by the employment of a superior army. The presence of the Anglo-French naval squadrons in the harbour of Alexandria made little impression, particularly as the admirals had no authority to land forces against the army. In any case only about three hundred men were available.

If the European position in Egypt was ever to be restored, now was the time to act. The European nationals in a panic for their lives were leaving the country in their thousands, and with their departure the army became more and more arrogant. The *fellahin*, seeing in the departure of the Europeans hope of release from their burdensome debts, likewise took a brighter view of the future and encouraged the army. Henceforth, they thought, Egypt would be for the Egyptians. But England and France were by no means willing to abandon their position. Their countrymen, such as were left in Egypt, were clamouring to their consuls for some measure of protection; the bondholders were becoming worried about their dividends.

Already Lord Granville and M. de Freycinet had agreed upon the necessity of calling a conference of the Powers to consider what action should be taken in Egypt. It was suggested that this should be held in Constantinople and should consist of the ambassadors of the Powers and the Turkish Foreign Minister. This course was agreed upon and the conference opened on 23 June. The Sultan, however, was unwilling to take part in it, especially as he came to understand that he was to be expected to provide an armed force to quell the mutiny, but acting under European control and for certain defined objects. In fact Turkish action was to be hedged around with so many restrictions that the Sultan refused to be a party to a proposal so little consonant with his dignity and prerogatives. M. de Freycinet insisted that whatever was decided at the conference, the following conditions must be observed:

(a)   the maintenance of the respective rights of the Khedive, as also of existing international arrangements and engagements;

(b)   respect for the liberties guaranteed by the firmans;

(c)   the prudent development of Egyptian institutions.[14]

When it became known that the Sultan was unwilling to enter the conference, the other powers showed reluctance to commit themselves to any course of action, no doubt considering that the Sultan was the rightful party to take action in Egypt. In consequence the conference dragged on in Constantinople without making any headway. Finally, on 6 July, the conference got as far as issuing a note inviting the Sultan to send a force to Egypt, '*suffisantes pour rétablir l'ordre, abattre la faction usurpatrice, mettre fin à l'anarchie qui désole ce pays et a amené l'effusion du sang, la ruine et la fuite de milliers de familles européennes et musulmanes et compromis les intérêts nationaux et étrangers.*'[15]

In Egypt the machinery of government had come virtually to a standstill, but on the representations of the German and Austrian consuls the Khedive, now at Alexandria, appointed Ragheb Pasha President of the Council in order to get the machinery in motion again. Arabi Pasha remained Minister of War. Arabi well realised that there was now imminent danger of intervention either by the Powers or by the Sultan acting with their consent and co-operation. He had no intention of allowing himself to be overthrown by any such combination and during June and July 1882 he proceeded to put the country into an active state of defence. Levies were called up from among the *fellahin* on the promise that all debts and mortgages would be cancelled and that the infidels would be finally driven from the country. The *fellahin* had indeed some justification for rallying around Arabi Pasha. One of the measures concerted was the reinforcement of the batteries commanding the harbour of Alexandria, including the repair and strengthening of the earthworks and the emplacement of additional heavy guns. Sir Beauchamp Seymour, commanding the British naval squadron, regarded these works as a direct menace to his squadron in the harbour and sent a message to the commander of the garrison on 6 July requiring him immediately to discontinue the work. There was a momentary pause but three days later the work was recommenced, Arabi Pasha informing the Khedive that it was part of the normal repairs and renovations of the garrison. On 10 July Seymour, having previously obtained the sanction of his government, issued an ultimatum to the effect that 'unless the forts on the isthmus and those commanding the entrance to the harbour were surrendered', he would open fire.[16]

In acquiescing in this action the British Government notified the Powers of their intention and proposed to France that she should give similar authority to Admiral Conrad commanding the French squadron at Alexandria. M. de Freycinet declined. The reasons he gives are not entirely convincing. He states:

> D'une part, ne serait-ce pas manquer aux engagements pris au sein de la conférence, d'après lesquels était exclue toute action isolée, à moins que la vie des nationaux se trouvât en danger? Or ici rien ne les menaçait encore, et loin de les garantir, on risquait de les exposer en surexcitant le fanatisme musulman par une aggression injustifiée. D'autre part, la prudence la plus élémentaire voulait, si l'on se lançait dans une telle aventure, qu'on fût pourvu de troupes de débarquement afin de réprimer les excès que la soldatesque égyptienne ou les Bedouins seraient tentés de commettre.'[17]

The argument has much the appearance of *ex post facto* reasoning, since it could not have been anticipated that an action between the squadrons and the shore batteries would be followed by 'excesses' in the town. In searching for reasons for the withdrawal of the French fleet one is forced to the conclusion that the French Government were apprehensive for the safety of their ships in a duel with the shore batteries, and considered discretion the better part of valour. The English admiral had no such fears about the Egyptian prowess in artillery. Moreover, having once insisted on the discontinuance of the fortifications it was impossible to retreat. Had both squadrons sailed out of Alexandria under the guns of the garrison, the Egyptians would have been fortified in their belief that only a show of force was necessary to scatter the ships of England and France. On 10 July the French squadron sailed out of the harbour for Port Said leaving the English squadron to make good their ultimatum. The following day, no answer having been received at 11 a.m., Seymour ordered a general attack on the shore batteries. The first round was answered by the Egyptian guns and action was joined. The fact that even by 5 p.m. not all the shore guns had been silenced is evidence of the tenacity with which the Egyptian detachments stood to their guns, but the outcome was never in doubt. The freshly recruited *fellahin* were no match for the seasoned veteran gunners of the British navy and by 5.30 p.m. the action was over. The British ships suffered no serious casualties, but the Egyptian garrison, terrified and demoralised by the outcome of the encounter, took to flight.

In the ensuing panic Alexandria was set on fire, pillaged and plundered. It has never been satisfactorily established who was responsible for the burning of Alexandria, it being variously alleged that shells from the British fleet, the retreating Egyptian garrison and plundering Bedouin started it. At any rate the British Admiral, having no authority to occupy the town, was obliged to keep his troops on board from which they witnessed the destruction of the town. It was not until 15 July that a force was disembarked to restore order. The person of the Khedive was taken under the protection of the British guards, so that after many harassing months his life was removed from danger.

Whether or not the bombardment of Alexandria was an unjustified or unjustifiable act of aggression against the independence of Egypt, it could not be regarded as anything other than an act of war. It was greeted with a considerable diversity of feeling at Constantinople where the ambassadors were still in laborious conference as to what was to be done about Egypt. In truth, it seemed rather futile to debate the question further when England had taken it upon herself to solve the problem. For England had now committed herself beyond redemption. An act of war had been committed; the Khedive was under English protection, and from Kafr ed Dawar, where Arabi had gathered his forces and entrenched himself, he issued a proclamation that 'irreconcilable war existed between Egyptians and the English and all those who proved traitors to their country would not only be subjected to the severest punishment in accordance with martial law, but would be for ever accursed in the future world.'[18] There was no going back.

None of the Powers represented at the Constantinople conference in practice approved of the British action taken at Alexandria; on the other hand, none felt disposed to disavow it except the Sultan who protested vigorously. Mr Gladstone and Lord Granville, realising that their action had produced a somewhat frigid atmosphere at the conference, were nevertheless anxious to associate all Europe in any further intervention in Egypt, but none of the Powers now felt disposed to intervene actively themselves. They still clung to the principle previously arrived at that any intervention should be effected by the Sultan as the legitimate suzerain over Egypt. The Sultan had already been invited to co-operate and send his Foreign Minister to take part in the conference; he had also been notified of the decision of the Powers that he should be invited to send a force to restore order. The invitation had, however, been hedged around with so many conditions and restrictions that he had delayed accepting it, no doubt believing that his aid was indispensable and that by procrastinating he could secure more liberty of action. As a matter of fact, his aid was by no means indispensable, and Mr Gladstone in a speech to the House of Commons on 22 July let it be known that with or without co-operation from other powers England was ready to go forward in restoring order in Egypt. Realising that he might be excluded from all action in Egypt the Sultan finally decided to send his representative to the conference. This was taken by England to imply that further lengthy delays and evasions would follow, and this she was not prepared to endure. As M. de Freycinet writes: '*Pour qui connaît la diplomatié orientale il était visible que ce coup de théâtre préludait à de nouveaux atermoiements.*'[19] Had the Sultan there and then despatched a force to Egypt all would have been content; even France would have been forced to acquiesce. But the moment was allowed to slip by, and active preparations in England were put in hand to bring a conclusion to the interminable Egyptian question.

In Egypt, following the bombardment of Alexandria, Arabi Pasha had retreated to Kafr ed Dawar which stands on the neck of land separating Lake Mariotis from Lake Edku. This neck along which runs the railway formed the only link between Alexandria and the Delta. Arabi's position there thus blocked the advance of the enemy forces into the Delta. There was, however, another line of approach into the interior open to the invader, down the Suez Canal by ship to Ismailia. Arabi and his staff recognised this potential threat but neglected immediately to take steps to block it. But a force was sent to Tel el Kebir on the railway and Sweetwater canal between Zagazig and Ismailia to throw up defensive earthworks. The reasons for Arabi's failure to seize and block the Suez Canal are of interest. The Canal was a neutral waterway guaranteed free and open to all the ships of the world at all times. Its neutrality was guaranteed by the Egyptian Government, and Arabi hesitated to set this guarantee at nought. He referred the matter to de Lesseps who had recently arrived in Egypt. The old man, full of bombast and convinced in his conceit that none would dare to infringe the rights of his precious canal, replied to Arabi: '*Ne faites aucune tentative pour intercepter mon [sic!] canal. Je suis là. Ne craignez rien de ce côté. Il ne se débarquera pas un seul soldat anglais sans être accompagné d'un soldat français. Je réponds de tout.*'[20] Trusting these assurances, Arabi allowed himself to be persuaded that there was no danger from the Suez Canal.

The importance of the Canal as a means of approach was not lost on the British and French Governments. The reaction in Paris was that Arabi would take immediate steps to block or destroy it. For reasons which will be set forth presently, France was now unwilling to take part in the intervention in Egypt, but de Freycinet was anxious about the security of the Suez Canal, the masterpiece of French engineering and visible evidence of French influence in Egypt. He urged upon the Chamber of Deputies the necessity for strong measures for the protection of the Canal.

But in Europe France was experiencing a strong sense of isolation. The general view of the deputies, an echo of de Freycinet's own sentiments, was in direct contrast to the policy of Gambetta. They were disinclined to countenance any intervention in Egypt, not so much because such intervention was distasteful, but because it would involve the despatch of French forces to a distant theatre. The uneasiness felt by France about the breakdown of the European Concert was reflected in the deliberations of the Chamber. M. de Freycinet had no difficulty in persuading the Chamber to sanction expenditure on strengthening the Mediterranean Fleet and in preparing transports to take on board French fugitives from Egypt. But when, two weeks later on 24 July, he approached the Chamber again for a modest sum to provide forces for the protection of the Suez Canal, the sentiments of the Deputies on the whole Egyptian question were crystallised. The Chamber refused to sanction the expenditure. While on the one hand they were willing to consider expenditure simply for the protection of the Canal the majority felt that such protection would involve landing a force along its banks which might, and probably would, lead to a clash of arms with the Egyptian army, and thus involve France in a full scale war in Egypt. '*Pouvez-vous nous donner la certitude que l'occupation du canal ne vous entraînera pas plus loin? que les puissances n'entreront pas en ligne? que vous ne serez pas pris dans un engrenage irrésistible?*'[21] The majority opinion was that

> L'intérêt de la France était de ne pas intervenir en Égypte et de ne point immobiliser dans une expédition lointaine une partie de nos forces militaires. Sans méconnaître que la politique de non-intervention avait ses périls, ils ont exposé que la politique d'intervention leur paraissait plus dangereuse encore dans la situation actuelle de l'Europe.[22]

On the defeat of the motion the de Freycinet Cabinet resigned, and their successors, the government of M. Duclerc, considered themselves bound to this policy, and France in consequence declined to co-operate with England in defending the Canal or in restoring the situation in Egypt.

On France's refusal to take any part, the British Government addressed themselves to Italy who had previously shown a disposition to be consulted in matters relating to Egypt. The approach was apparently sufficient to satisfy Italy's *amour propre*, for though she declined the invitation, she expressed her thanks 'to the British cabinet for having entertained the idea that the friendship of Italy for England might take the form of an active co-operation.'[23] England was thus left to take the field alone. In conclusion it may be said that the true wishes and interests of the Powers were largely frustrated by circumstances. England had no desire to go to Egypt, but preferred a Turkish intervention. The Sultan had no wish for English or any European action, but had procrastinated too long.[24] France had succeeded in avoiding a Turkish intervention but had acquiesced in something which eventually proved more distasteful, a British one.

The story of the campaign that ensued may be briefly outlined. The British force under the command of Sir Garnet Wolseley arrived at Alexandria on 13 August. The speed with which this force was assembled and ferried to the theatre of operations is clear evidence that the plans and preparations had long been made, and only the signal was required to put them into operation.[25] A few days later the force sailed for Port Said, seized the Canal in spite of the protests and threats of de Lesseps, and landed at Ismailia on 21 August. The English advance on Ismailia appears to have taken Arabi Pasha by surprise, and the bulk of the Egyptian troops had to be switched hurriedly to Tel el Kebir where the earthworks were by no means completed. This period marked the defection of several senior officers who realised the futility of opposing with their poorly trained and equipped troops a well disciplined British army. The Egyptians are estimated to have numbered about 20,000 troops including a large proportion of *fellahin* pressed into service. During the end of August and the first half of September a number of skirmishes took place in the vicinity of the Canal and between Ismailia and Tel el Kebir. The night of 12 September 1882 found the main body of the Egyptian Army behind the entrenchments at Tel el Kebir, with Arabi Pasha at his headquarters a mile to the rear. A secret night march by the English enabled them to deliver a surprise attack on the Egyptian position at dawn on 13 September. In the short and sharp battle which lasted about an hour the British troops stormed the entrenchments and over-ran the Egyptian position. This battle virtually marked the end of the military operations in Egypt. From the English point of view, the whole campaign was little more than a military promenade. The troops were supplied with all necessary equipment, they were well trained and keen to get at grips with the enemy. Every step in the campaign was planned carefully beforehand and prosecuted vigorously. On the other side the Egyptian troops were for the most part untrained and hurriedly recruited *fellahin*. 'Stone Pasha, the American, after the war stated it freely as his opinion that not one of the whole number had ever as yet fired a ball cartridge, and this was probably true.'[26] Even so, many of the Egyptian soldiers stuck stubbornly and bravely to their posts in the face of fierce attack fighting hand to hand with their adversaries. The greatest defect of the Egyptian army in the campaign was the quality of command. Arabi Pasha himself appears to have remained almost totally inert during the whole war. Many of his senior commanders were, like himself, incompetent and unworthy of the troops they commanded. Others deserted to the enemy or slipped away. Had the Egyptian troops been commanded by an able and resolute body of officers with a certain amount of dash and initiative, the war would have been a much lengthier and more costly affair. The outcome in any case would not have been different.

When it became known at Egyptian headquarters that the day was lost, Arabi Pasha escaped to Bilbeis whence he took a train to Cairo. Blunt states that he 'seems to have had hopes of continuing the patriotic struggle by defending the city.'[27] But news had already filtered through that the Sultan had issued a proclamation declaring Arabi Pasha a rebel and that he had lent his countenance to the British expedition in Egypt. The Egyptians still looked upon His Imperial Majesty as the ultimate authority and in consequence they were no longer prepared to support Arabi in the face of the Sultan's declaration. On 14 September the city surrendered to a small British force which had raced there from Tel el Kebir. The rebellion and the war in Egypt were over.

Almost immediately upon the disembarkation of the British troops in Egypt the Khedive, acting under the guidance of Sir Edward Malet, dismissed the Ministry of Ragheb Pasha who had been completely subservient to Arabi, and appointed Cherif Pasha President of the Council with a Ministry loyal to himself. An arrangement was made between Wolseley and Cherif Pasha that all Egyptians taken prisoner of war should be handed over to His Highness' Government, but only on the understanding that none should be put to death without the consent of Her Majesty's Government. In fact the opening of the campaign marked the period when Egypt became completely subservient to England. The Ministry found itself unable to take any action beyond that of mere routine without first consulting and securing the approval of the British Consul General who likewise received his instructions from London.

On the cessation of hostilities the question that immediately posed itself was, what was to be done with the rebels? There is little doubt that if the Khedive and Egyptian Government had been allowed to decide this question, the rebels would have been arraigned on a court-martial, tried in summary fashion, convicted and immediately executed. This procedure was indeed what was expected by the populace at large; to them it was inconceivable that the Khedive should adopt any other course of action. But the undertaking had been extracted from a reluctant Egyptian Government that there should be no executions without English consent. As a result of Mr Blunt's clamourings and propaganda for the Nationalists and for Arabi Pasha in particular, there sprang up in England a party of sympathisers who were not without influence. Under the circumstances it was impossible for Mr Gladstone and Lord Granville to sanction the rough and ready justice which would have been meted out to Arabi Pasha and his confederates by a free Egyptian Government. Moreover, there was a strong body of public opinion in England which did not consider political offences such as rebellion sufficiently heinous to warrant a capital penalty. Thus it was in effect decided in London long before any trial took place that Arabi Pasha and his friends should be tried, convicted and sentenced to exile. The trial was in reality to be not much more than a formality to legalise the proceedings.

But Mr Blunt and his following were not to be content with such a solution. They bombarded the Foreign Office with demands that the prisoners should be allowed a public trial, British counsel to defend them and permitted to call whatever witnesses they pleased. The proceedings thus threatened to be protracted interminably, and the court to become an arena for political propaganda. Cherif Pasha was profoundly perturbed by the prospect. He pointed out:

> that the prestige of the Khedive and the authority of his Government will be again compromised in the eyes of the population if the Egyptian authorities appear, in the face of a revolt without example, powerless and subordinate to an intervention which manifests itself in appearance as being to the advantage of the recognised chief of the rebels, guilty of crime towards the person of the Sovereign, responsible, even admitting the absence of all effective co-operation, for all the disasters and all the ills which, during the past year, have been heaped upon Egypt.[28]

These forebodings were amply justified. September passed, October and November dragged through their course without any trial or sentence, and the Khedive began to lose the newly-acquired respect of the people which had accompanied his re-accession to power. They thought that both he and the English still feared Arabi and dared not punish him. Fresh unrest broke out in the provinces, and once again Europeans were subjected to insults and threats of violence by the natives. If the authority of the Khedive was to be maintained and tranquillity restored, the question of Arabi's disposal had to be settled quickly. At the end of November a compromise was agreed upon between the Government and Arabi's counsel. He would plead guilty to rebellion and be sentenced to death, the sentence to be commuted to one of perpetual exile from Egypt. Thus it happened. The court-martial assembled on 3 December, the prisoner pleaded guilty to a charge of rebellion and was sentenced to death. The same day the Khedive commuted the sentence to one of exile. Mahmud Sami, Ali Fehmi, Abdel Aal and Toulba, Arabi's original friends and confederates in the revolt from the beginning, were dealt with in the same way. On 26 December these officers were placed on board ship at Suez and sent to Ceylon where they spent their exile. Tribunals were set up in various parts of the country to deal with cases of robbery, violence and other offences against people and property, and although some were convicted, a few even sentenced to death, the courts in general acted with considerable leniency. A general amnesty for all political offences was decreed on 1 January 1883, and the matter finally resolved. It may be mentioned that Arabi Pasha lived to see his native country again. He was allowed to return in 1901.

Before we leave this unhappy period of Egypt's fortunes, one or two aspects are worthy of comment. The Arabi Rebellion has gone down in history as a purely military revolt. This is not entirely the case. It started, it will be remembered, with the protests of a small group of officers against injustice in the army. If the Khedive had dealt fairly with the matter on this occasion, instead of resorting to a stupid and treacherous trick, events might have followed a different, more peaceable, course. As it was, a discontented and fearful army united itself with the incipient nationalist movement which was inspired by genuine ideals. The Nationalists simply wished to overthrow the centuries-old arbitrary rule of the Turkish *pasha*, as represented by the Khedive and his dynasty, and to see the transfer of power to the chosen representatives of the Egyptian people. Such an evolution, carried out gradually, would have constituted an important step in the political progress of Egypt. But political progress, if it is to be laid on firm foundations, must be slow, almost imperceptible. There can be no sudden transfer of power from a personal ruler to a parliament of representatives who have had no experience of government. The transfer to be durable must be effected little by little. Unfortunately Arabi Pasha and the Nationalists fell under the spell of the Utopian ideals of Mr Blunt and Sir William Gregory. These painted the rosy picture of Egypt for the Egyptians, the overthrow of the Turks, the expulsion of the Europeans and a fine parliament expressing the desires of the people. They encouraged Arabi and his party in open rebellion, assuring them that they had nothing to fear from foreign intervention, that they only had to hold on to the army to emerge victorious, the leaders of a new Egypt. Mr Blunt was a man of education, culture and some influence; he was also impractical. Arabi Pasha on the other hand was a simple, rather mediocre soldier with no education beyond a smattering of religious lore acquired at El Azhar. His principal asset was a certain simple eloquence and sincerity which appealed strongly to the native Egyptian and which gave him an ascendancy even over Mahmud Sami, a much more able and intelligent man. It is not surprising that the adulation poured on him by Blunt with his wealth and connection should have gone to his head, and made him believe that he was 'El Wahid', the One, chosen to lead Egypt from bondage into liberty. Arabi Pasha was far more a victim of circumstance than a schemer intriguing his way to power. From February 1881 when his troops liberated him from the Ministry of War he lived in constant fear of retribution from a vengeful ruler. To save himself, he was compelled to go forward continually until the time came when a direct struggle for power was fought between the Khedive and himself. The nature of oriental society and conduct precluded any real or sincere reconciliation between them. The struggle had to be fought out to its logical conclusion. In the end the Powers, or rather England stepped in to restore the established order which Arabi threatened to topple over. In so doing they fulfilled the half-century-old prophecy of Kinglake. 'The Englishman, straining far over to hold his loved India, will plant a firm foot on the banks of the Nile and sit in the seats of the faithful.'[29]

CHAPTER 15

Egypt's Empire - the Sudan

At the end of the war some effort was needed to gather up the debris of Egypt and reassemble the shattered structure into some semblance of stability. For the time being, at any rate, Lord Granville made it clear that the Egyptian Government would have to follow the instructions, or more diplomatically perhaps accept the advice, of Her Majesty's Government. He sent to Egypt one of his most experienced diplomats and administrators, Lord Dufferin, British Ambassador to the Sublime Porte, to conduct negotiations with the Egyptian Government on all matters affecting the resettlement of the country. Lord Dufferin arrived in Cairo on 7 November 1882 and for the moment superseded Sir Edward Malet, the British Consul General.

The state of Egypt was deplorable. A revealing picture is painted of the conditions prevailing in the provinces by Mr Villiers Stuart, MP in his book, *Egypt after the War*, written following a tour of the country shortly after the cessation of hostilities. Mr Stuart's book is for the most part a catalogue of the miseries and abuses suffered by the unfortunate *fellahin*. Even when allowance is made for the *fellah*'s tendency to answer questions in the sense he believes most acceptable to his foreign interrogator, it is clear that the condition of the *fellahin* was as bad as it could be. Arabi Pasha had requisitioned their cattle, camels and crops for the prosecution of the war with a promise that they would be returned or paid for after victory and, even more important, that the bonds and mortgages of the Greek and Syrian usurer would be torn up. He had also press-ganged the *fellahin* into military service, and many families were left without the means of support. But Arabi Pasha had failed; the Europeans remained and the pack of Levantine money-lenders continued to batten on the helpless peasants. Taxes had still to be paid and their crops had been taken away. They were compelled by sheer necessity to borrow from the usurers on terms which would have made Shylock feel a profound sense of inferiority. The average rate of interest was four or five per cent per month! In many cases the land had in fact passed completely into the hands of the creditors.

Mr Villiers Stuart found during his tour that many vexatious taxes which Lord Cromer mentions as having been 'abolished by a stroke of the pen' in 1879 were still in operation and exacted mercilessly. For example, sheep were taxed, young and old, to such an extent that very few were reared, the natural wealth of the country being thus considerably diminished. Likewise a tax was levied on every date palm, even those that did not bear fruit. In the Said (Upper Egypt), where only one crop could be grown a year, the land tax varied scarcely from that levied in the Delta where two or even three crops were grown. These and a score of similar onerous impositions were strangling the economic life of the country.

The British Government had sent a force to quell a rebellion, to restore order and re-establish the authority of the ruler, the Khedive. These objects having now been achieved, what was to be done to ensure that good order and authority were maintained in the future? The need for real reform was urgent, but who was to carry it out? If the forces which had restored order were now to depart, what was to prevent a resurgence of disorder? The principal object of Lord Dufferin's visit to Egypt was to 'report upon the measures which were necessary in order that the administration of affairs should be reconstructed on a basis which would afford satisfactory guarantees for the maintenance of peace, order and prosperity in Egypt, for the stability of the Khedive's authority, for the judicious development of self-government, and for the fulfilment of obligations towards the Powers.'[1] At the same time it was understood and assumed that the British occupation force would be withdrawn in the immediate future. Although he did not expressly state it, Lord Dufferin suggested in his report that the two conditions were mutually exclusive. For if the guarantees mentioned above were to be given, if peace, order and prosperity were to be evolved and self-government judiciously developed, Lord Dufferin indicated that Europeans would be necessary to carry out the work, and that moreover these Europeans would require some external influence to support them – in fact the British army of occupation. If the British power were withdrawn, there could be no such guarantees of peace, order and prosperity. For the moment, therefore, the question of the withdrawal of the occupation force was left in abeyance pending the establishment of some *modus operandi*. In the meantime, rumblings of further trouble and disorder had begun to make themselves heard from another, more distant quarter, the Sudan.

In order to fit the Sudan into its proper place in the Egyptian puzzle, it is necessary to go back to the early years of the Great Pasha, Mohammed Ali, in whose time the story of the Sudan, in so far as it affects the history of Egypt, commences. The Sudan exercised a special attraction for the Great Pasha; it was a vast tract of land unexplored and unknown. There were, however, rumours that gold and precious stones could be mined there, but, more important, it possessed an abundant supply of manpower which Mohammed Ali hoped to utilise in building his armies. In 1819 his troops consisted mainly of Albanian mercenaries, bold and courageous fighters but turbulent and untrustworthy. Perhaps the Sudanese would be more amenable to discipline. A further attraction of the Sudan was the fact that it belonged to no one, or rather that none of the Powers had any interest in it, and there was nothing to prevent him from occupying it.

In 1820 Mohammed Ali's son Ismail led an expedition of some 4,000 troops south of Wadi Halfa into the virgin territory. His advance up the Nile met with little resistance, the petty chiefs and sheikhs freely offering their submission to him as emissary of the Sultan and Khalif. On reaching the junction of the Blue and White Niles he pressed on up the former and penetrated as far as Sennar which was likewise brought under Egyptian sovereignty. At about the same time another force, under the command of Mohammed Ali's son-in-law, Mohammed Bey, penetrated into Kordofan and Darfur on the west bank of the White Nile. In all the campaign offered no serious difficulties.

On returning in 1822 towards Egypt Ismail began to collect money and slaves for his father. Arriving at Shendy, he made demands for these upon the local chief who pleaded his inability to provide, whereupon the Pasha ordered him to be flogged. This harsh treatment occasioned a conspiracy among the local chiefs against Ismail's life. One account states that he was stabbed to death, while another has it that he was trapped in a house which was set on fire and he was burnt alive. When the news reached Mohammed Bey in Kordofan, he swooped down on Metemma and Shendy, burnt the villages to the ground and butchered the inhabitants. Thirty thousand people are said to have been massacred in this reprisal.

The whole of the northern Sudan was thus conquered and brought under Egyptian control during the reign of Mohammed Ali. Khartoum was founded and a civil administration under a governor was established. But service in the Sudan was never popular among the Turkish *pashas* and Egyptian troops sent to administer it. A tour in the Sudan was virtually equivalent to a sentence of exile. But it had one compensation in that it possessed a potential wealth in the form of slaves and ivory, and the officials sent to govern the country were not slow to take advantage of the opportunity to feather their nests. Khartoum became the centre of the slave trade which poured its produce down the Nile into Egypt. Large tracts were farmed out to so-called 'traders' and the government received about two-fifths of the profit. A system of wholesale extortion and oppression settled on the Sudan which continued almost uninterrupted during the reigns of Mohammed Ali and Abbas.

On his accession in 1854 Said Pasha paid a visit to the Sudan and was very disturbed by the misery and evil conditions he saw there. He ordered a reduction in taxation and the abolition of slavery, but the orders were not obeyed. The slave trade continued to flourish. Again in 1863, when Ismail succeeded to the Viceregal throne, he decided to take measures to ameliorate the conditions in the Sudan and also to extend his domains in a southerly direction, and in so doing to strike a blow at the notorious traffic in human lives. Most of the slaves were taken in the equatorial regions of the Nile and brought downstream to Khartoum for sale. Ismail Pasha thought that if he could establish a series of military posts on the equatorial Nile with strict orders to suppress slave raiding, the trade would substantially diminish. It was moreover well recognised that the only way to suppress the slave trade was to open up the territories to civilising influences and normal trade. As an earnest of his sincerity Ismail Pasha appointed an Englishman of some reputation, Sir Samuel Baker, to lead an expedition into the equatorial Nile regions and establish Egyptian authority over the southern Sudan. Baker's instructions were:

> To subdue to our authority the countries situated to the South of Gondokoro; to suppress the slave trade; to introduce a system of regular commerce; to open to navigation the great lakes of the equator, and to establish a chain of military stations and commercial depots, distant at intervals of three days' march, throughout Central Africa, accepting Gondokoro as the base of operations.[2]

The story of Baker's adventures in the southern Sudan is well told in his book *Ismailia*. He cut a navigable channel up the Bahr el Zeraf, a tributary of the White Nile, through the *sudd*, and established his chain of posts from Gondokoro which he renamed Ismailia in honour of his master. He certainly succeeded in reducing the volume of the slave trade down the main stream, but he could not entirely eliminate it; the influence of Khartoum and Cairo was too strong.

Baker spent four years in the southern Sudan and was succeeded by another prominent Englishman, Colonel Charles Gordon, 'Chinese Gordon' as he was known for his achievements in the Far East. Gordon had much of the spirit of the missionary; he was intensely, almost fanatically, religious, altruistic and, like most idealists, out of touch with ordinary mundane interests and affairs. In most respects however his appointment was a happy one, for it was a man of his temperament, sincerity and doggedness that was most needed to bring about peace and stability to the newly acquired domains of the Khedive. Characteristically he refused the generous salary of £10,000 per annum and contented himself with a modest £2,000.

His tour of duty which lasted from February 1874 to December 1876 was almost a replica of Sir Samuel Baker's. Most of his time was occupied in suppressing the slave traders or nullifying their efforts. But where these could not use the main stream to transport their prisoners, there were other routes overland of infinitely greater hardship and misery for the wretched captives. Gordon occupied much of his time in exploration and traced the great river to its source in Lake Victoria. In so doing he was compelled to abandon his ambition of setting the Khedive's steamers on the inland waters of Africa. The last section of the Nile between Dufile and Victoria Nyanza he discovered to be a series of rapids and falls impassable to navigation. He sent a party to circumnavigate the mysterious Lake Albert and dispelled the myth that it was the northern end of Lake Tanganyika.

An interesting diversion grew out of Gordon's governorship of Equatoria. One of his greatest problems was obtaining supplies from his base in Cairo. Khartoum was always the bottleneck, and it often happened that supplies which were sent to him from Egypt were diverted at Khartoum by the Governor-General. It occurred to Gordon that a shorter, more reliable route might be opened overland to the east coast of Africa. He wrote to the Khedive suggesting that an Egyptian naval force should be sent to occupy a part of the coast near Formosa Bay, a suggestion which Ismail Pasha adopted with alacrity. McKillop Pasha, an English naval lieutenant in the service of the Khedive, was sent with a small force. But this territory belonged nominally to the Sultan of Zanzibar and, on the representations of the British Consul, Kirk, the expedition had to be withdrawn.

In December 1876 Gordon returned to Egypt with the intention of resigning his post. But Ismail Pasha, exerting all his personal charm and powers of persuasion which were considerable, induced him to accept another tour, not as Governor of Equatoria, but of the whole Sudan. He returned to Khartoum at the beginning of 1877. During the following two years he toured nearly every part of his command and covered 8,000 miles by camel, thereby earning the admiration and love of the Arabs for his prowess as a camel rider. One of his most noteworthy acts was the issue of a proclamation forbidding all Europeans from holding slaves. All others were to be registered and freed after a period of twelve years. Unhappily, the melancholy events which were shortly to befall the Sudan prevented the fulfilment of this ambition.

Gordon had a sincere admiration for his master the Khedive and held in contempt the European bondholders and all their machinations. It was undoubtedly his lack of sympathy for these which created an antipathy between himself and Major Baring. On the fall of Ismail Pasha, Gordon refused to serve under Tewfik and resigned his appointment, determined never to return to the Sudan. He left in June 1879.

One episode which took place during his tour as Governor of Equatoria is worthy of mention because it was to have important repercussions at a later date. In the Bahr el Ghazal area an Arab, one Zobeir Rahama, who claimed descent from the Koreish tribe of the Prophet, had established himself as a slave trader and over the course of the years had built up a large personal army of black troops. In consideration of his influence and prowess he was given the rank of Pasha and made Governor of the Bahr el Ghazal. This promotion created some jealousy and mistrust in the heart of the Governor-General, Ismail Pasha Ayoub, and a quarrel broke out between them. Zobeir wrote a letter of protest to the Khedive and offered to go to Cairo to state his case. The Khedive accepted this suggestion and Zobeir departed for Cairo. Gordon comments: 'He went; and is not coming back again if I can help it.' Zobeir was in fact detained in Cairo, the Khedive not permitting him to return, but he had left his son Suleiman in the Bahr el Ghazal, who soon raised the local tribes in revolt. Gordon had him captured and shot.

On the resignation of Gordon the post of Governor-General fell to Rauf Pasha who by his cunning had raised himself from obscurity to a position of authority and influence. During Baker's tour in Equatoria Rauf had commanded his small detachment of troops, but had readily connived with the principal slavers in their wretched commerce. Since then he had held a number of positions in the Sudan, but had only distinguished himself by his lack of responsibility, and his cruelty and venality. It is difficult to understand how this man now came to be appointed to the highest post in the Sudan, but no doubt trading interests in Cairo had some influence on the promotion.

The general condition of the Sudan was even more lamentable than that of Egypt during the first years of Tewfik's reign. Gordon had done his utmost to stamp out the extortion, oppression and peculation that pervaded every department, but he had been one man among many and his influence was too temporary to have any tangible effect. The administration of a primitive country of about a million square miles cannot be reformed by one man in two years. The appointment of Rauf Pasha marked the reappearance of all the traditional Turkish methods of government. In a word, the Egyptians were cordially detested by the Sudanese in every province of the land. Nothing was wanting but the spark to ignite the flame of rebellion against the ancient tyranny. In 1881 the spark was supplied.

At that time there dwelt on the island of Abba on the White Nile about 150 miles south of Khartoum a holy man who during the past few years had acquired the reverence of the people as an ascetic and one well versed in the scriptures. This man, Mohammed Ahmed, was a native of Dongola and had in his youth been apprenticed to his uncle as a boat-builder at Khartoum. His interests, however, lay more towards religious studies and he was sent to a number of religious schools. He finally took up his abode in a cave on Abba island and began his life as a religious mystic. He was at first regarded as another of the multitude of *fakirs* who abound in the East, but by the time he had reached the age of forty he had established a great reputation for piety and holiness, and he was treated with reverence by all who came into contact with him. Rauf Pasha even gave orders that the Nile steamboats should refrain from requisitioning food and fuel at Abba island out of respect for the holy man.[3]

In August 1881 Mohammed Ahmed proclaimed himself as the long awaited Mahdi of Islam, upon whose coming the world would be converted to the Mohammedan religion.[4] His proclamation was couched in the following terms:

In the name of the gracious and merciful God, praise to the noble master and blessing upon our Lord Mohammed and upon his race. This is sent forth from the servant of his Lord Mohammed, the Mahdi, son of Seid Abd Allah, to his beloved friends in God and to all those who follow him, and give their help towards the restoration and victory of the faith . . . Know that God has called me to be a Caliph, and that the Prophet, Lord of life, whom God bless, has proclaimed that I am the expected Mahdi. And he has told me that whosoever doubts my mission does not believe in God, or in His prophets, that whosoever is at enmity with me is an unbeliever and that whosoever fights against me will

234

be forsaken and unconsoled in both worlds (in heaven as well as on earth) and that his goods and children are a prey for the believers.[5]

The proclamation was not regarded very seriously by the Government at Khartoum until the sheikhs and tribes to whom it was sent began to flock to the *fakir*'s standard. In common with the majority of insurgences this particular movement had gathered a certain amount of momentum before official notice was taken of it. Rauf Pasha sent a demand to Mohammed Ahmed that he should present himself at Khartoum. The Mahdi (for so he will be called from this point onwards) declined to obey the governor's order, whereupon a force of about three hundred troops was despatched to bring him in. When the troops disembarked at Abba island the Mahdi's disciples and followers fell on them and annihilated them almost to a man. With this act of resistance to established authority, what had up to the present been little more than a religious movement assumed the character of open rebellion.

This act of revolt was the spark which ignited the whole Sudan. At last a leader had been found to unite the tribes in a crusade to drive out the hated administration, a leader, moreover, inspired with a religious fervour calculated to have the greatest appeal to the simple but fanatical minds of the Sudanese Moslems. The tribes flocked to his standard in their thousands. There is little doubt that Mohammed Ahmed was sincere in his belief that he was the true Mahdi inspired to go forth into the world and lead the faithful in a crusade against the heretics, infidels and defilers of the true faith. He was not by any means a vague dreamer; he was evidently a practical man and he realised that he was now the official enemy of the Government. While, therefore, Rauf was considering what steps to take next, the Mahdi with his adherents left his abode on Abba island and struck off south to the Gebel Gedir in the fastnesses of the Dar Nuba district where, legend has it, the Prophet himself had once rested. Here he proceeded to organise his following into military formations and plan his campaigns. His followers were given the uniform of the *jibbah*, or patched cloak, a sign of poverty, and they became known in consequence as dervishes or poor men. Command of his armies was given to the chief of the fierce Baggara tribe, Abdullah the Khalifa. His plans in brief were firstly the conquest of the Sudan and the overthrow of the Egyptian authority, followed by an invasion of Egypt itself, the cleansing of the country of all infidels and then a march on Mecca and Constantinople; an ambitious programme but not by any means incapable of execution, for support could be expected from all true believers at every stage of the advance.

It is evident that Rauf Pasha did not appreciate the gravity of the new situation, for he sent the Mudir of Fashoda with four hundred troops, a mere handful in comparison with the Mahdi's forces, to the Mahdi's camp at Gebel Gedir. This expedition was likewise annihilated. News of the revolt had now filtered through to the Government in Cairo, itself still in the grip of the Arabi movement. At all events it appears to have been appreciated that Rauf Pasha was incapable of controlling the Sudan, and he was recalled and replaced by Abdul Kader Pasha, a man of sterling qualities, a brave and capable soldier and administrator. But in the interval between the departure of the one and the arrival of the other the governorship of the Sudan devolved temporarily upon Gieger Pasha, a German engineer. He it was who witnessed the first spread of the rebellion throughout the provinces. Sennar suddenly responded to the Mahdi's call and for a time the situation in that town was critical and it was only held by the Egyptians at great cost in human life.

In 1882, his preparations now complete, the Mahdi emerged with his armies from his stronghold at Gebel Gedir and commenced his programme of conquest in the Sudan. His immediate objective was El Obeid in Kordofan province. He came up under the walls of the town in September 1882 (i.e. at the same time as the battle of Tel el Kebir) with an army of about 150,000 dervishes. The garrison was commanded by one Mohammed Pasha Said who put up a singularly vigorous defence and beat off the attackers with great slaughter. So great were his losses that the Mahdi abandoned his attempt to take the town by storm and laid siege to it. This lasted four and a half months, the defence being brilliantly conducted by its commander; but eventually the extremes of hunger and privation brought about the capitulation of El Obeid. This was the Mahdi's first great success, but it is noteworthy that Egyptian troops (who were labelled by the British as 'utterly worthless') could give an excellent account of themselves when led by able and courageous officers.

These early successes awakened the Cairo Government to the realisation that something very serious was happening in the Sudan. This was no petty sheikh or tribal chief raising a local revolt which could be suppressed by the Egyptian forces on the spot. The Mahdi's rebellion bore every resemblance to a snowball rolling down a hill, gathering mass and momentum. Its tremendous force could be witnessed in the fanaticism of its adherents who, armed only with sticks and spears, were overwhelming organised forces with rifles and guns, and throwing their lives away in an ecstasy of religious fervour, strong in the belief fostered by the Mahdi that death on the battlefield against the Turks and infidels was the passport to Paradise. It became clear at Cairo that unless something was done quickly to combat the insurgent movement, it would sweep like a flame across the Sudan and Egypt's empire would disintegrate overnight. The outcome of the various encounters and skirmishes which had so far taken place between the Government troops and the rebels indicated that the revolt had now assumed proportions too large for the local garrisons to deal with alone. It was thus vital to put in the field an army adequate to deal with the situation. But the Egyptian army in Khartoum was in no condition to fight; in 1883 it was still riddled with Arabist sympathies; its discipline was shattered and its loyalty doubtful. As to their military training, a British officer, Colonel Stewart reported:

> The troops in garrison here (at Khartoum) are working at elementary drill and tactics, and are making some progress. It is, however, very uphill work; the officers are so ignorant and so incapable of grasping the meaning of the simplest movement. Quite one third of the troops are also ignorant of the use of the rifle, and they would be more formidable as adversaries were they simply armed with sticks.[6]

Such was the material available for a campaign against an army imbued with fanaticism and hatred.

But the effort had to be made. A motley force was assembled at Khartoum under the command of General Hicks, a retired British army officer who had taken service with the Egyptian army in the Sudan early in 1883.[7] So important was the projected expedition in the eyes of the Egyptian Government that somehow a sum of £147,000 was scraped together from Egypt's scanty resources to finance it.

The story of General Hicks' expedition may be briefly told. He left Khartoum on 8 September 1883; his objective was El Obeid, now the headquarters of the Mahdi. On leaving the Nile and penetrating into Kordofan he was betrayed by his guides, secret agents of the Mahdi, who led him into waterless scrub and forest where they slipped away leaving him hopelessly lost, his army maddened with thirst and crippled by disease. At Kashgil, a few miles from El Obeid, the dervishes suddenly fell on the demoralised Egyptians and annihilated them almost to a man. News of this disaster which took place on 5 November 1883 did not reach Cairo until 22 November.

Some months before the dismal events related above, trouble began to manifest itself in another quarter. From his base at El Obeid the Mahdi had sent out a proclamation to the Arabs of the Eastern Sudan, enjoining them to rise and throw off the Egyptian and Turkish yoke. Osman Digna, an Arab slave dealer, answered the call and raised the Hadendowa and other tribes into insurrection, and proceeded to beleaguer the various garrison towns of the province. In August 1883 he arrived under the walls of Sinkat, about fifty miles inland from Suakin, and demanded its surrender. Tewfik Bey, the garrison commander, refused and drove off the dervishes with considerable loss. The latter thereupon laid siege to the town and also to Tokar further south. Two expeditions were sent from Suakin to effect the relief of these towns, but both were intercepted by Osman Digna and almost exterminated. Here again it became apparent to the Government in Cairo that outside assistance was necessary to combat these new threats. The army in Egypt had been completely shattered by the Arabi rebellion; it was now in process of being reformed and retrained by English officers recruited for the purpose. It was certainly not yet in a condition to take the field against the resolute and fanatical hordes of the Mahdi. The only other available organised body of men was the Gendarmerie, Egypt's national guard, a motley collection of Turks and Egyptians under the command of Sir Valentine Baker.[8] The Khedive enquired of Baker whether he would be willing to undertake an expedition to Suakin and relieve the beleaguered garrisons of Sinkat and Tokar. Sir Valentine, who had been obliged to leave the British army under a cloud, readily accepted this commission, hoping no doubt to redeem his tarnished reputation, and in December 1883 he and his force left Egypt for Suakin. Baker had small prospect of success. Most of his troops were of poor quality; some even refused to go and could not be compelled as they were not subject to military law. However, a proposal was brought up that Zobeir Pasha, the former slave trader who, in spite of his long detention in Cairo, was reckoned to have great influence over the Sudanese Arabs, should be sent to Suakin to help Baker relieve the garrisons. This proposal was put forward by the Egyptian Government, and had it been allowed there might have been a fair prospect of success. Zobeir was a great name in the Sudan; he had had a magnificent personal army, and he above all understood the Sudanese mode of fighting and how to get the best from his troops. But the Egyptian Government was tied hand and foot to England, and one of the most militant movements in England at the time was the Anti-Slavery Society. Zobeir Pasha had been the most notorious slave trader of his time, and no government in England would have had the courage to advocate the employment of one of such antecedents as Zobeir, no matter what the military or political necessity might be. The proposal to send Zobeir to

Suakin was therefore allowed to drop and Baker was left to do what he could alone.

By the time Baker left Egypt news of the Hicks disaster had already arrived. Every hope was therefore centred upon this last remaining force that Egypt could muster. The fact that it was the last ounce of Egypt's strength made it all the more important that it should be preserved. Baker in fact received explicit instructions to act with the utmost prudence:

> The enforced submission of the men who have been holding out at these two places [i.e. Sinkat and Tokar] would be very painful to His Highness the Khedive, but even such a sacrifice is better, in his opinion, than that you and your troops should attempt a task which you cannot fairly reckon to be within your power.[9]

Baker and his force arrived at Suakin on 27 December 1883. At the beginning of February he advanced south with the intention of relieving Tokar. On the 5th his force, comprising some 3,500 men, met up with Osman Digna's dervishes near the wells of El Teb. In the conflict which ensued the Egyptians were utterly routed and about two thousand of them killed. Thus in her struggle to quell the great rebellion in the Sudan, Egypt had put forth her last ounce of fighting strength and lost.

With the failure of Baker's expedition hope of relief died in the two beleaguered garrison towns of Sinkat and Tokar. A week later Tewfik Bey, the commander of the former, who had so long and so heroically kept the besiegers at bay, sallied forth to fight his way through the dervish lines. He and his gallant force perished in this attempt. A few days later, on 24 February, Tokar capitulated to the enemy. The only territory remaining to Egypt in the Eastern Sudan was Suakin itself which daily threatened likewise to fall to the victorious dervishes. It was held for the moment by Admiral Hewett and his British soldiers.

Some mention must here be interposed of the attitude and actions of England in regard to the Sudan. It will be recalled that in August and September 1882 England had been driven more or less by force of circumstance into a limited intervention in Egypt for the purpose of putting down the rebellion of Arabi Pasha and restoring the authority of the Khedive. This intervention was regarded as distasteful, even though necessary, by all concerned, not least by England herself. No sooner had she placed her feet on the banks of the Nile than she struggled to withdraw them. But in intruding by force into the affairs of Egypt England found herself in a position from which she could not readily extricate herself. The necessity for re-establishing peace and good government made it highly desirable that she should retain her soldiers on Egyptian territory until these objectives were achieved. The Egyptian Government were made to understand that every action they desired to take must first be submitted via the British Consul-General to the British Government for approval and, furthermore, that any advice offered by England must be accepted. Within a few months of the British occupation the Sudan flamed into revolt. It is not surprising therefore that the Egyptian Government turned for advice to England on what action she should take. The British Government headed by Mr Gladstone viewed these new developments with horror. At the same time as they were casting about for some means of withdrawing their troops from Egypt and leaving the country to look after itself as of yore, new events were thrusting them deeper and deeper, not merely into Egypt but even into the Sudan. British intervention into the Sudan was the last thing Mr Gladstone would countenance, and every effort must be made to prevent responsibility for the Sudan devolving on the British Government. One of the first actions taken by the Cabinet to this end was to instruct Sir Edward Malet in August 1883 (when the Hicks expedition was being prepared) that Her Majesty's Government assumed no responsibility whatever in regard to the conduct of affairs in the Sudan, and that General Hicks should understand that it was their policy to abstain as much as possible from interference in the action of the Egyptian Government in that quarter.[10]

What Mr Gladstone and Lord Granville failed to understand was that a mere declaration of this nature did not in fact absolve them from responsibility; responsibility is not so easily thrown off. The Sudan was a sort of sub-empire of Egypt governed by officials appointed by the Khedive. Egypt herself lay in the grip of the British army of occupation; the word of the British Consul-General was, in practice, law. The link between the British Government in London and the Sudan was direct and obvious, yet the Cabinet failed to see it. They failed to see it because they did not want to see it. Such self-inflicted blindness is generally the forerunner of disaster.

In the earlier phases of the Mahdi rebellion there was undoubtedly some justification for British inaction. The true nature and extent of the rebellion was not appreciated either in Khartoum or in Cairo. It is not unnatural therefore that it was not understood in London either. In the later stages after the Hicks and Baker disasters there was much less justification for failing to appreciate the nature of the rebellion.

On 11 September 1883, i.e. three days after Hicks had set out from

Khartoum, Sir Edward Malet left Egypt to take up another appointment in Brussels, and his place as British Consul-General was taken by Sir Evelyn Baring who was no stranger to Egypt. He realised the gravity of the situation in the Sudan immediately, and he lost no time in communicating his views and apprehensions to the Foreign Office. If, he reported on 19 November, General Hicks was unsuccessful, it was probable that Egypt would lose the whole of the Sudan and she might be obliged to abandon it unless some outside assistance was received. This forecast was, in fact, substantially correct. The defeat of General Hicks at Kashgil in November 1883, followed shortly afterwards by the defeat of Baker at El Teb in February 1884, completely drained Egypt's military strength. Even had Egypt at the time possessed an efficient army, her treasury was exhausted and no further funds could have been found to launch an expedition of reconquest.

At the time Egypt derived little advantage from the Sudan, apart from a certain amount of prestige which she gained as conqueror and overlord of a vast tract of Africa. Up to this time the Sudan had never brought in any revenue to the Egyptian Treasury; on the contrary, the revenue did not even cover the cost of administration, and in consequence the Sudan required a substantial subsidy from Egypt annually to provide the expenses of government. When therefore Baring hinted that the Sudan might have to be abandoned, this was not a particular cause for concern to London, but rather the contrary. If the Sudan was going to be a financial and military millstone round Egypt's neck, better to throw it off. If, on the other hand, Egypt for reasons of her own was anxious to retain possession of the Sudan, there was no objection to her doing so provided that she had the means. But she must be made to understand that there was no prospect of any British military assistance.

The Egyptian Government headed by Cherif Pasha entertained the strongest objections to any policy of abandonment. As soon as the news of the defeat of General Hicks reached Cairo at the end of November 1883, it became clear that the road lay open to the Mahdi to Khartoum itself, and that the capital stood in great danger of falling to the dervishes. Lord Cromer mentions that 'daily discussions took place in Cairo about the policy which was to be pursued.'[11] In these deliberations it became apparent to the Egyptian Government that they had not the means themselves to hold the Sudan. Outside assistance must therefore be found and the only possible source was the Sultan as suzerain of Egypt and the Sudan. On 12 December 1883, Cherif Pasha called upon Baring and informed him that the Egyptian Government 'had resolved to place themselves absolutely in the hands of

Her Majesty's Government. They wished the British Government to arrange the conditions under which Turkish aid would be afforded, the principal of these conditions being that the Sultan's troops should leave the country when their presence was no longer required.'[12] The British Government offered no objection to this proposal provided that the Turkish troops were paid by the Porte and that they entered the Sudan through Suakin; there was clearly no intention of allowing Turkish troops in Egypt itself. But the British Government's best advice to Egypt was to abandon all the Sudan south of Wadi Halfa.

There is no record that the British Government did in fact open negotiations with the Porte on the question of sending Turkish troops to the Sudan. The attempt might well have been made, even though it would undoubtedly have been a waste of time. It is certain that the Porte would never have agreed to lay out money and men to recover the Sudan under the conditions that were to be imposed, but it would have been a gesture of good faith at least to have made the effort. The policy recommended by Baring was the abandonment of the Sudan, and this was the policy the British Government was disposed to pursue. On 4 January 1884 Lord Granville sent the following telegram to Baring:

> It is essential that in important questions affecting the administration and safety of Egypt, the advice of Her Majesty's Government should be followed, as long as the provisional occupation continues. Ministers and Governors must carry out this advice or forfeit their offices . . .'[13]

On being informed of the substance of this telegram Cherif Pasha resigned.

It was feared that there might be some difficulty in finding someone to form a new ministry but the Khedive, accepting the inevitable, agreed to the policy of evacuation and called upon Nubar Pasha who, since his dismissal in 1879, had been in the political wilderness, to form a new government. It now remained to implement the policy of evacuation.

CHAPTER 16

The Fall of Khartoum

The events of the year 1884 form possibly the most controversial period of the history of modern Egypt. Even after the passage of the years there is still a certain element of doubt as to what actually did happen, and who was right and who wrong. The principal actors in the drama which was to unfold were General Charles Gordon who conducted the epic defence of Khartoum and Sir Evelyn Baring (later Lord Cromer) who, in his capacity as British Consul General in Egypt, acted as intermediary between Gordon in Khartoum and the British Government in London. The Khedive and his Government were relegated to the status of bystanders while the great tragedy was played out. Thus, whatever may be said about the responsibility for the disaster, at any rate no blame can attach to the Egyptian Government.

General Gordon went to Khartoum in 1884 and never came back. He was therefore precluded from speaking for himself. His journals, which were subsequently recovered, contained writings which were frequently the jottings of a man filled with despair and the sense of having been betrayed and deserted by his own countrymen. Lord Cromer, on the other hand, lived for many years and was able to vindicate himself as far as possible from the blame for the tragedy which befell Egypt and the Sudan in January 1885. Thus one of the principal authorities for the events of this period is Lord Cromer's *apologia pro sua vita, Modern Egypt*, which dwells in some considerable detail on the Mahdi rebellion and the subsequent fall of Khartoum. Anyone reading this book diligently cannot help being struck by the impression that the author must have combed the writings of Gordon himself to find material proving that he was too unstable and inconsistent by nature to be entrusted with the execution of a most difficult task. The burden of Lord Cromer's report in fact was that if blame was to attach to anyone for the fall of Khartoum and its attendant loss of life, it should attach to General

Gordon himself for failure to carry out the policy with which he was entrusted. An entirely different picture is painted in Mr Bernard Allen's account, *Gordon and the Soudan*, a painstaking and detailed investigation of the chain of events which culminated in Gordon's death, and a careful analysis of the letters, telegrams and other correspondence relating to Gordon's appointment, his orders and his conduct of affairs at Khartoum. Probably the prime cause of the disaster was the fact that shortly after Gordon's arrival in Khartoum, the telegraph line was cut and thereafter communication between Khartoum and Cairo became so chaotic that it was impossible for either of the principals to know what was in the other's mind or what was happening at the other end of the line. Under the circumstances it seems that it should have been the duty of the British Government to make every effort to re-open the lines of communication, so as to obtain a clear picture of what was the situation in Khartoum in those critical days. No action was taken, however, until it was too late.

Dotted about the Sudan in the villages, military posts and settlements, there were many thousands of Egyptian garrison troops, government officials and Egyptian nationals, with their families. In London and Cairo the policy of evacuation had been decided upon. The question that followed from this decision was, how was this evacuation to be effected; how were all these troops and officials and their families to be withdrawn to a place of safety, so that the Sudan could be abandoned to her own devices? One of the principal difficulties was that any substantial signs of evacuation from the Sudan would only lead to the tribes, who were either still loyal or were hovering, going straight over to the Mahdi. The evacuation would thus be rendered much more difficult and even impossible, if the towns and garrisons were surrounded by hordes of fanatical rebels. What was required was someone who by his influence and prestige could keep the country tranquil while the evacuation was being effected.

Even before the policy of evacuation had been forced on the Egyptian Government, Baring had already made up his mind what was wanted and had sent a telegram to Lord Granville on 22 December 1883, advising the evacuation and adding that 'it would be necessary to send an English officer of high authority to Khartoum with full powers to withdraw all garrisons in the Soudan and make the best arrangements possible for the future government of the country.'[1] After a further exchange of telegrams, Lord Granville stated that General Gordon would be willing to go back to Khartoum to evacuate the garrisons. Baring concurred in this proposal in a telegram stating: 'Gordon would be the best man if he will pledge himself to carry out the policy of withdrawing from the Soudan as quickly as is possible consistently with saving life.'²

It may be added that in his book Lord Cromer goes to some considerable length to suggest that he was not in favour of sending an English officer at all to Khartoum, least of all General Gordon. He even misquotes his own telegram, cited above, by omitting the word 'English' from the phrase, 'it would be necessary to send an English officer of high authority . . .' When he sent this telegram, he must inevitably have had General Gordon in mind. No Englishman had spent so long in the Sudan in such high position; certainly no Englishman had the same prestige and authority as Gordon. It is difficult in fact to conceive that Baring could have had anyone else in mind. There had been a proposal at the time that Abdul Kader Pasha should go, but this idea came to nothing. There was no other person who had the least chance of executing the policy determined upon.

There appears to have been some mishandling in the actual appointment of General Gordon and the issue of instructions to him. What happened was that he was summoned to a Cabinet meeting at the War Office and asked formally if he would go back to the Sudan. Gordon replied that he would. When he left the meeting he went away under the impression that he had been instructed to go and effect the withdrawal of the garrisons. Yet the Ministers, Northbrook, Dilke, Granville and Hartington, record that he was going for the mere purpose of reporting on the situation and on the best method of withdrawal, quite a different thing. Although Gordon's written orders, later issued by the Cabinet and supplemented by the Khedive, instructed him to effect the evacuation, this first misunderstanding engendered in the mind of Mr Gladstone, the Prime Minister, a suspicion that General Gordon had altered his instructions and usurped authority to which he was not entitled. It may be that this suspicion was the cause of Mr Gladstone's subsequent inertia or reluctance to take action whenever the situation in Khartoum was later discussed.

General Gordon realised that his own presence in the Sudan would not be sufficient to keep the tribes in check while the evacuation proceeded. In this he was undoubtedly right. It was inconceivable that the rebels would stand idly by while the Egyptian soldiers and their families quietly trooped out. What was urgently required was some form of settled government which would at least have sufficient power and influence to maintain tranquillity while the withdrawal was being carried out. Gordon hit on the idea of setting up in the principal towns the families of the sheikhs and petty sultans who had ruled there in the days before Mohammed Ali's conquest of the Sudan.

He appreciated that there would be some difficulty about Khartoum and Kassala which had sprung up since that time. During his voyage to Egypt Gordon drew up some proposals embodying this idea and suggesting also that he should be reappointed Governor-General of the Sudan.

On his arrival in Egypt Gordon had an interview with Baring and the Egyptian Government at which his final instructions were drafted. Two points are worthy of emphasis because they were later used by Baring to attempt to show that Gordon had not carried out his instructions. Gordon was told: 1. 'You will bear in mind that the main end to be pursued is the evacuation of the Soudan,' and 2. 'I understand, also, that you entirely concur in the desirability of adopting this policy, and that you think it should on no account be changed.'[3]

At the same time the Khedive decreed the appointment of General Gordon as Governor-General and issued him with two proclamations which he could use at his own discretion. The one notified the people that Gordon was reappointed Governor-General, the other that independence of Egypt was to be granted to the families of the former rulers of the Sudan: in other words, that Egypt was proposing to abandon the country.

During the two days spent at Cairo, Gordon met by chance his old adversary, Zobeir Pasha. This fortuitous encounter made a tremendous impression on him, for here, he realised, was the very man to assume the reigns of government in the Sudan during and after the evacuation. If by a promise of moral support and a small subsidy for the first year or so Zobeir could be persuaded to forget past grievances and co-operate in the evacuation operation, there was an excellent prospect that not only a strong and settled government would be left at Khartoum, but also a new power of no mean proportions would be erected as a counterpoise to that of the Mahdi.

Gordon therefore requested that a formal interview should be arranged between himself and Zobeir Pasha. This was agreed and the meeting took place on 26 January, just prior to Gordon's departure for Khartoum. 'The scene was dramatic and interesting. Both General Gordon and Zobeir Pasha were labouring under great excitement and spoke with vehemence.'[4] Zobeir

refused to shake hands with Gordon and evidently cherished a feeling of indignation against him. He reproached him fiercely for the death of his son and the confiscation of his property. Gordon maintained with passionate insistence that Suleiman had been justly put to death, as he was guilty of the cold-blooded murder of 200 Egyptian soldiers, and also that Zebehr himself had been equally justly condemned by a court-martial because he had incited his son to rebellion. Zebehr contended that the letter he had been accused of writing was a forgery and claimed that it should be produced . . . (it could not be found) . . . In the end Zebehr seemed to be somewhat pacified when Gordon admitted that, if Zebehr had not written the letter, he had been unjustly condemned.[5]

Following the interview, the merits and demerits of the proposal that Zobeir should accompany Gordon to Khartoum were discussed. Baring disapproved and placed his veto on it. There were many arguments both for and against. It must be stressed, however, that General Gordon had been commissioned by Her Majesty's Government to carry out a task of exceptional danger and difficulty. He was given a free hand in theory to execute it in any way he thought fit and by any means at his disposal. It is therefore reasonable to suppose that the Government reposed confidence in his discretion, judgement and ability. In the case of Zobeir, Gordon had, for want of a better word, an intuition that he would be the key to the problem. Gordon realised that there would be a certain element of danger in taking Zobeir to Khartoum and investing him with considerable power, but he balanced this risk against the tremendous advantages that would accrue if he could win Zobeir's confidence and co-operation. Having placed their confidence in Gordon the British Government should have shown it by acceding to his request. Unfortunately they did not do so and Zobeir was not allowed to go. Looking back over what happened, it cannot but be felt that the Government made a great blunder for, even if Zobeir had gone with Gordon, events could not have turned out any worse than they actually did, and there is reason for supposing that they might have turned out much better. It is, of course, easy to be wise after the event.

That night, 26 January 1884, accompanied by Colonel Stewart, Gordon left Cairo on his last long journey south. On arriving at Berber on 11 February he showed his secret decree, i.e. that which announced the abandonment of the Sudan, to the local Governor, Hussein Pasha Khalifa. Hitherto the Egyptian Government had made no announcement of their intentions, and it was commonly thought that the Government would fight the Mahdi and hold the Sudan. There had, of course, been a crop of rumours to the contrary, but these had not been believed. General Gordon had now publicly disclosed the Government's intention to evacuate the Sudan. His own view was that the sooner the local authorities knew of this intention, the more would they be encouraged to organise themselves to take over the administration of their localities as completely independent units. This would be in accordance with his plans of setting up a stable government prior to withdrawal. On the other hand the publication of the policy of abandonment might equally mean that the Egyptian Government were too weak to deal with the rebellion, as indeed they were. This interpretation would be all that was necessary to drive into the arms of the Mahdi the tribes which for some time had either been neutral or were hovering on the brink of rebellion. Under the circumstances the wisdom of making this announcement was debatable. On balance it would probably have been more prudent for Gordon to wait until he had arrived in Khartoum and gained an accurate picture of the general situation in the Sudan. At any rate it now became well known that Egypt proposed to abandon the Sudan and that General Gordon was being sent to carry out the evacuation.

On 18 February Gordon and Stewart arrived at Khartoum, and the inhabitants turned out in full strength to give them a tremendous welcome. Undoubtedly Gordon's presence did much to allay the fears and tremblings of the population and his first actions there did even more.

> The Government books, recording from time immemorial the outstanding debts of the overtaxed people, were publicly burnt in front of the Palace. The *kourbashes*, whips and other instruments for administering the *bastinado* from Government House were all placed on the burning pile. The evidence of debts and the emblems of oppression perished together.[6]

The policy of evacuation was initiated immediately. Gordon separated the Egyptian from the Sudanese troops, and organised the feeding and transport of the first consignment of evacuees. These measures occasioned uneasiness in the minds of the civil population who regarded the presence of these troops as a guarantee of their own protection and safety. Gordon took no notice and hurried on with his preparations.

It will be recalled that at about the same time as Gordon was making his journey from Cairo to Khartoum, i.e. the end of January and the first half of February, Sir Valentine Baker was arriving with his gendarmerie at Suakin. His defeat at El Teb at the hands of Osman Digna and his dervishes took place on 5 February. By this time considerable interest in the Sudan question had been roused among the public in England and sympathy felt for the unfortunate Egyptian garrisons besieged in their towns, and the British Government themselves began to be pressed by public opinion to take some action in their defence. When Baker was defeated at El Teb, there was great danger that the dervishes would forthwith march on Suakin itself and storm the town. Although far outside the borders of Egypt proper, Suakin was regarded as being an integral part of Egypt itself. It was an acquisition made for Egypt by the Khedive Ismail who had virtually bought it from the Sultan. At any rate, a threat to Suakin was regarded as a threat to Egypt, and the British Government, by virtue of their military occupation, felt a strong sense of responsibility for the protection of the country. With the defeat of Baker the Government felt disposed to take action not only to defend Suakin against attack but also, if possible, to effect the relief of the two garrisons of Sinkat and Tokar which were still holding out. Thus during the end of February a force of about 4,000 British troops under General Graham was sent to Trinkitat, the nearest seaport to Tokar. But by the time they arrived Tokar had capitulated to the dervishes (24 February) and to that extent this British expedition had failed in its objective even before it arrived.

The Government found themselves somewhat embarrassed by these developments. The expedition had gone to the eastern Sudan expecting a fight; even more important, the public at home expected a fight. Were these four thousand fighting British troops to be held merely as a garrison for Suakin against a possible attack? Baring urged on the Cabinet that a few should be left in Suakin and the bulk withdrawn to Egypt. The Government, however, were unable to resist the public clamour for an attack on Osman Digna, and Graham was authorised to seek him out and attack him. The ostensible reason was to disperse the enemy which might now attack Suakin, but actually both the army on the spot and the public at home were spoiling for a good fight. 'On . . . February 29th, Sir Gerald Graham advanced with his entire available force. He found the Dervishes entrenched at El Teb; they were attacked and driven from their position with heavy loss. The British loss amounted to 189 of all ranks, killed and wounded.'[7] On 7 March a further blow was struck at the dervishes at Tamai, a few miles from Suakin, when a force of about twelve thousand dervishes was attacked and routed with heavy loss. With the successful outcome of these actions the British Government's appetite for battle was more or less satisfied. It was moreover felt that the threat to Suakin was now dissipated. This sentiment was by no means shared by General Graham and his troops. By this time Gordon was at Khartoum and the desirability of reopening the Suakin-Berber road was obvious, as this route would provide an important and probably the only line of retreat for the outcoming garrisons. In Cairo Baring likewise urged this necessity upon the Government in London in a telegram dated 16 March: ' . . . It has now become of the utmost importance not only to open the Berber-Suakin route, but to come to terms with the tribes between Berber and Khartoum. If we fail in the latter point, the question will very likely arise of sending an expeditionary force to Khartoum to bring Gordon away.'[8] This telegram, embodying the views of the commanders on the spot and of Baring himself, was in fact a forthright invitation to the Cabinet to engage in a deep penetration of the Sudan. But from this policy Gladstone shrank in horror and thus contributed substantially to the great tragedy that was to ensue. Gladstone's greatest phobia was foreign entanglements. Unwittingly he had allowed Britain to become involved in the affairs of Egypt, and while he was casting about for means to extract his country from these, new developments were thrusting her deeper and deeper, this time into the heart of the Sudan. Yielding to public clamour, he had authorised an expedition to the eastern Sudan in a vain attempt to relieve the beleaguered garrisons of Sinkat and Tokar, but it had arrived too late. To satisfy the public at home and the army on the spot he had permitted the troops to seek out the enemy and deal them a blow. It was now proposed that the troops should embark on a campaign into the heart of the country. This, Mr Gladstone feared, would be followed by proposals to subdue and reconquer the whole of the Sudan. At this point Mr Gladstone jibbed. No further expeditions were to be undertaken in the eastern Sudan; no evidence had been produced that General Gordon was in any danger at Khartoum; there was therefore no need, for the present at any rate, to send him any relief. This decision to withdraw the British force was to have the most unfortunate repercussions.

The tasks entrusted to Gordon and Stewart were twofold; firstly to effect the evacuation of all the Egyptian garrisons in the Sudan; and secondly to establish some form of stable government prior to the Egyptian withdrawal. In fact the two tasks were almost inseparable, the first being largely contingent on the second. For though it would have been feasible to remove the Khartoum garrison, there remained nearly fifty others in various parts of the country whose safety had also to be secured. Nothing could be done about these unless some tranquillity reigned in the interior, and this could only be ensured by setting up an interim government.

Almost immediately after his arrival at Khartoum, Gordon came to the conclusion that his mission was incapable of realisation under the present conditions and limitations imposed on him. His original idea of re-establishing the descendants of the petty sultans who had reigned in the Sudan prior to Mohammed Ali's conquest had to be abandoned for the reason that too great an interval of time had elapsed for the descendants to have any influence over the tribes. His mind reverted to the need for a strong man to take over from him and keep the country peaceful. Zobeir Pasha was the only man who would have any prospect of success in this task, and both Baring and Colonel Stewart, who had discouraged this proposal in January, were now compelled to admit the wisdom of it in March. From Cairo Baring exerted himself to the utmost in urging this view on the British Government in London, but all to no avail. The Government refused to be moved in the matter of Zobeir Pasha. The principal objection to his employment was the fact that he had been a notorious slave-trader; it was feared that his employment in the Sudan would only lead to a revival of his former activities; it might even appear that the British Government, which for years had been besieged by the Anti-Slavery Society for action, were lending their countenance to it. Baring himself pointed out that the policy of abandonment automatically implied the acceptance of a revival of the slave trade since there would be no power to prevent it, and that therefore the sending of Zobeir would not affect the question one way or the other. But Gladstone shrank from this course of action and his weakness, or rather his failure to look the facts in the face, resulted in disaster. The final result was that the proposal to send Zobeir Pasha to Khartoum was vetoed. When this decision was made known to Gordon on 23 February, he replied immediately in the following terms:

Telegram of the 23rd February received respecting Zobeir. That settles question for me. I cannot suggest any other. Mahdi's agents active in all directions. No chance of Mahdi's advance personally from Obeid. You must remember that when evacuation is carried out, Mahdi will come down here, and, by agents, will not let Egypt be quiet. Of course, my duty is evacuation and the best I can for establishing a quiet government. The first I hope to accomplish. The second is a more difficult task, and concerns Egypt more than me. If Egypt is to be quiet, Mahdi must be smashed up. Mahdi is most unpopular, and with care and time could be smashed. Remember that once Khartoum belongs to Mahdi, the task will be far more difficult; yet you will, for safety of Egypt, execute it . . . [9]

The sending of this telegram is singled out as 'the turning point of General Gordon's Mission' in his book *Modern Egypt* by Lord Cromer who accuses him of marking out for himself 'no less than five different lines of policy, some of which were wholly conflicting one with another.[10] These five different lines are summarised as follows: 1. In London Gordon was merely to report on the situation; 2. on his journey out, he wished to be named Governor-General with full executive powers; 3. on 8 February from Abu Hamed he advocated evacuation but not abandonment; 4. on 18 February he advocated that the British Government, and not the Egyptian, should take control of the Sudan administration; 5. on 26 February he proposed that the Mahdi should be smashed up. 'In thirty-nine days therefore, General Gordon had drifted by successive stages from a proposal that he should report on the affairs of the Soudan, to advocating the policy of "smashing up" the Mahdi.'[11]

An unbiased examination of the facts, however, does not confirm the view expressed that Gordon drifted by successive stages from one policy to another wholly conflicting. On the contrary, he saw with admirable clarity the turn that events would take under existing conditions; his prophecy in fact was fulfilled to the letter. The Mahdi came to Khartoum; by agents he did not let Egypt be quiet; the British Government finally did execute the policy of smashing up the Mahdi (actually his successor). There can be no doubt that Gordon kept firmly before his mind the tasks which had been entrusted to him: the evacuation of the garrisons and the setting up of a stable government in one form or another. The important point was that as he became more conversant with the actual situation in the Sudan, he saw that the methods by which his tasks were to be executed would have to undergo modification, and these modifications formed the subject of the various proposals summarised above. As time went by, it became no longer simply a matter of collecting the various garrisons together and sending them down the Nile or to Suakin, for the simple reason that the Mahdi's followers were preventing them from going. Gordon recognised that it was impossible to extricate the garrisons without first 'smashing up' the Mahdi. His conclusions were amply justified by events. On 12 March 1884, twenty-three days after his arrival at Khartoum, the dervishes occupied the banks of the Nile north of the town, cut the telegraph cable and closed all access to the north. The siege of Khartoum had begun.

Gordon's position in Khartoum was one of exceptional difficulty even before the communications were cut. For one thing, he had been sent to carry out his tasks fortified only by his own prestige and reputation. Apart from the garrison troops he had no force to use as a persuasive influence on the hovering tribes; his mission was to be a purely peaceful one. Yet at the same time the guns and bayonets of General Graham's force at Suakin were dealing out death and destruction among the tribes of the eastern Sudan. It was incomprehensible to the Sudanese that the British Government should send one man to Khartoum bearing the olive branch and another to Suakin on a war-making expedition. It was not unnatural that Gordon was regarded in Khartoum with something akin to suspicion. General Graham's expedition had a further unfortunate repercussion. Some discussion took place regarding the desirability of the troops advancing to Berber to re-open the road, and Gordon was cognisant of these proposals. In fact, he confidently expected the British troops to make an appearance at Berber some time during the end of March or in April. While he was under this impression the telegraph line was cut between Khartoum and Berber. In order therefore to reassure the inhabitants of Khartoum he announced that British troops were on their way to Berber. What Gordon did not know was that Gladstone had suddenly taken fright and ordered the withdrawal of General Graham's force from Suakin. As the weeks went by and there was no sign of any British advance, Gordon began to be discredited in the eyes of the people of Khartoum.

Undoubtedly there would have been great difficulties about sending a British force, large or small, from Suakin to Berber. Opinion in Cairo among the generals was divided as to the possibility, and even those who considered it feasible recognised its hazardous nature. The principal obstacles were the unbearable climate at that time of the year and the absence of water over a large tract of the route. Even so, if in face of these it had been decided simply to postpone the expedition to Berber until the autumn when the climate would be more seasonable, and to notify Gordon to that effect, all might have turned out well. In face of the difficulties it was decided to do nothing at all, at any rate until some definite signs of danger to Gordon became apparent. It must appear strange, however, that even the cutting of the telegraph cable and the surrounding of Khartoum by the rebels sounded no warning note in Mr Gladstone's ears, who contented himself with sending a message to Gordon to the effect that he could stay at Khartoum as long as he wished or thought necessary, or retreat to the south. This proposal was characteristic of Gladstone's refusal to face the facts: on the one hand it completely ignored Gordon's own character in that he would have been the last man in the world to retreat from Khartoum without taking the garrison with him and anyone else who wished to come; on the other hand, it was quite impossible to evacuate Khartoum in any direction without coming to blows with the rebels.

As a final effort Gordon made a further proposal that the Turks should be invited to come down and take over the Sudan, at the same time crushing the rebellion, that if necessary they should receive a subsidy from the British Government to enable them to do so. This message, which eventually arrived at Cairo, tended to fix in the minds of Baring and the British Government the impression that Gordon was far more intent on 'smashing up' the Mahdi than extricating the garrisons. 'The proposal to hand over the Soudan to the Sultan and to utilise Turkish troops to crush the revolt of the

Mahdi was, however, opposed both to the spirit of his instructions, and to the views which he had persistently advocated up to that time.'[12] On the other hand it does not seem to have been realised that Gordon was still intent on carrying out his instructions, i.e. to extricate the garrisons, but that it was now no longer possible to do this without some form of military intervention and that the various proposals Gordon made were simply designed to assist in carrying out this policy. It is clear that it never even entered his mind that he might slip away and leave the garrisons to their fate, nor did it occur to him until too late that the British Government would abandon the garrisons themselves. When in April he was informed that no immediate assistance would be forthcoming he wrote to Baring:

> You state your intention of not sending any relief up here or to Berber, and you refuse me Zobeir. I consider myself free to act according to circumstances. I shall hold out here as long as I can, and if I can suppress the rebellion, I shall do so. If I cannot, I shall retire to the Equator, and leave you the indelible disgrace of abandoning the garrisons of Sennar, Kassala, Berber and Dongola, with the certainty that you will eventually be forced to smash up the Mahdi under great difficulties if you would retain peace in Egypt.[13]

It can well be imagined that Gordon now felt that he had been sent by his government into a trap from which there was no way out, and that he was to be abandoned to his fate. It is not therefore surprising that he spoke of the 'indelible disgrace' that would attach to England for so doing.

In Cairo Baring, though apparently not overmuch concerned with the fate of the Egyptians in Khartoum and elsewhere in the Sudan, recognised that Gordon and Colonel Stewart were now in great danger. Perhaps with some justice he felt that the Egyptians themselves were to blame for their own plight, but the British Government had sent two officers into danger and it therefore behoved them to extricate them. As the danger was growing more and more imminent, not a moment was to be lost. Clearly a military expedition was needed to effect the relief of General Gordon and Colonel Stewart beleaguered in Khartoum. It was known that Gordon had sufficient provisions to hold out in Khartoum for six months, and it was beyond question that he could hold the town against any attack the dervishes might attempt. On the other hand the despatch of a relief expedition would be an operation of the greatest complexity and would have to be very carefully planned, and would take some time. For climatic reasons it was considered most undesirable to attempt the relief in the summer months; the autumn was the only reasonable suitable period for military operations in the Sudan.

On 14 April Baring wrote to Lord Granville stressing the plight of General Gordon and the necessity of initiating operations without delay:

> I wish again to draw Your Lordship's attention to General Gordon's position at Khartoum . . . I have no sort of wish to urge that an expedition should be sent to relieve General Gordon, unless, after very full consideration, it would appear that no other alternative can be adopted . . . Lord Hartington had declared in the House of Commons that Her Majesty's Government feel that 'they are greatly responsible for General Gordon's safety,' and even if no such declaration had been made, the fact is, in itself, sufficiently obvious . . . All the authorities whom I have consulted say that, if any operations are to be undertaken along the valley of the Nile, which is by some considered the best route, no time should be lost in making preparations, so as to be ready to move directly the water rises . . .'[14]

It must be explained that although the telegraphic communications were cut in the middle of March, a few of the messages sent were delivered somewhat erratically to their destinations for some time afterwards. But after the end of March communication became so chaotic that messages which eventually filtered through seemed more to confuse the recipients than to inform them. Even so, by the middle of April two facts became evident beyond all question: that Khartoum was surrounded and cut off from the north; and that unless an expedition was sent quickly to its relief, the town would fall to the rebels. It would therefore seem that there were grounds for urgent action. Baring pressed for it, but Gladstone refused to see the facts. He refused to believe that Gordon was in any danger until he had word from Gordon that this was so. How he expected to receive messages from Khartoum which was now in the grip of a siege, is not however very clear. As late as August Lord Granville telegraphed to Cairo, 'Inform General Gordon of the preparations for his relief in case of need; refer him to former messages, with directions from Her Majesty's Government to conform to them, and ask the causes of our not having received any reply.'[15] Had it not been for the gravity of the situation there might have been an element of humour in the last clause of this telegram.

The British Government, though warned of the danger in April, refused to take any immediate action. Such was the inertia in ministerial circles that the Queen herself was obliged to intervene and appeal to the War Minister for action to save General Gordon.[16] Even this failed to budge Mr Gladstone;

let us wait and see how the situation develops, he proposed, and if no improvement takes place, we will act in the autumn when the climate is more suited to English troops. Clearly the subject of Gordon and the Sudan was unpalatable to Mr Gladstone. 'Mr Gladstone was slow to recognise facts when they ran counter to his wishes. The natural result ensued. The facts asserted themselves.'[17] What Mr Gladstone failed to realise was that if operations turned out to be necessary in the autumn, preparations would have to be initiated immediately, i.e. in April or May. As it was, the vital summer months were allowed to slip by with nothing done. By August it was recognised that the expedition would have to be sent, and a credit of £300,000 was voted 'for preliminary measures with a view of moving troops south of Wadi Halfa.' Four months were thus wasted as a result of which a heroic garrison and a great leader lost their lives. For by this time it was impossible to get the troops to Khartoum 'in the autumn'. The autumn was almost come, yet not even the preliminary plans had been drawn up. No decision had even been made on the route to be followed, and long discussions took place regarding the respective merits of the Suakin-Berber route and the Nile. The latter was finally decided upon. Even then no element of urgency was displayed; the commander-in-chief, Lord Wolseley, did not arrive in Cairo until 10 September, nor did he receive his orders until 8 October. The whole operation took on the semblance of a great but leisurely military exercise with every precaution taken, every detail planned, nothing overlooked – except one factor: that every day that passed was one day nearer the exhaustion of the Khartoum garrison and its eventual fall. The one element most vital to the success of the operation was lacking, the sense of urgency. Admittedly, the operation was difficult. It involved moving a self-contained force over vast distances through enemy-occupied territory where provisions were non-existent. Every item of food and equipment required for the force would have to be carried with it. Even so, with time such a critical factor, some element of dash, some risk might have been taken to reach Khartoum in time.

When the dervishes swarmed down to the Nile on 12 March and cut the communications between Khartoum and the north, the possibility of extricating the garrisons peaceably disappeared. The siege of Khartoum had begun, and General Gordon lost no time in putting the capital in a state of defence. He had in the town supplies enough to last five or six months, but he initiated a series of sallies against the besieging enemy and sent foraging expeditions along the river collecting food and provisions. So successful were these that he was able to supplement his stores with enough supplies for a further four months. His principal assets in the epic defence were his small fleet of 'penny-steamers' which could ply up and down the river almost unscathed. In fact they provided the only contact between Khartoum and the outside world. On 26 May the strategic centre of Berber fell to the dervishes, a bitter blow to Gordon who saw in its capture the disappearance of all hope of escape from Khartoum, and the enforced abandonment of all evacuation plans. Clearly there was no prospect of any escape from Khartoum unless Berber was recaptured. Even this event did not serve to arouse the British Government to a sense of peril.

As the summer months rolled by without any sign of assistance materialising from the outside world, Gordon decided to make a final attempt to make the position of Khartoum known abroad. Following a series of successful expeditions against the dervishes stationed along the nearby reaches of the Nile, on 9 September he sent Colonel Stewart and Mr Power, the *Times* correspondent, down the river on the little steamer *Abbas*, which he had fitted out with every care and attention to detail to ensure a safe passage. The two Englishmen nearly achieved success. Running the gauntlet of rifle fire from both banks of the river they passed Abu Hamed on the great bend, but as the little ship neared the fourth cataract it fouled a submerged rock and stuck fast. Stewart and Power were enticed ashore by some treacherous Arabs and murdered. Unfortunately Stewart carried with him the cipher key and other important papers which were captured, and Gordon, now alone in Khartoum, was thereafter unable to read any of the messages which subsequently filtered through except those written in clear or carried by word of mouth.

On 20 September a slip of paper was smuggled into the besieged fortress bearing a message from Major Kitchener who had been sent as an advance party to Dongola: '. . . The relief expedition is evidently coming up this way, but whether they will go by Berber, or attempt the direct road from here I do not know.'[18] At last there was concrete news that a relief expedition was on its way; the news was received with great rejoicing at Khartoum, and inspired the gallant defenders to renew their efforts. It also served to allay the tremblings of the population and prevent further desertions to the Mahdi's camp. The stubborn resistance of Khartoum over the long months created considerable uneasiness in the mind of the Mahdi. He sent repeated messages to Gordon urging him to surrender and become a dervish. Such invitations were of course rejected with contempt. The Mahdi thus finally decided to leave his retreat at El Obeid and bring the whole strength of his army against Khartoum. The march occupied many weeks, and it was not until the autumn that it came up under the walls of the great Arab town of Omdurman on the left bank of the Nile opposite Khartoum. The siege of Omdurman commenced on 23 October. Every attack of the dervishes was thrown back with heavy loss by its gallant commander, at the same time withstanding a perpetual and heavy artillery bombardment; its garrison, like Gordon, hoping for and expecting every day some sign of the relief expedition which was known to be on the way. But in the end, driven to the extremes of privation and hunger, on 15 January 1885 Omdurman opened its gates and capitulated to the Mahdi.

During the siege of Omdurman the enemy had brought up a quantity of heavy artillery which gave Gordon in Khartoum great anxiety. Hitherto he had been able to use his little fleet of steamers to make raids, collect provisions and maintain contact with Omdurman across the river. Specially fitted by Gordon with armour plate, they could withstand rifle fire, but they became increasingly at the mercy of the enemy guns deployed along the river banks. One shell could easily send a steamer to the bottom and Gordon was therefore obliged to restrict their use.

Daily his situation was becoming more and more critical; even the forces of nature began to operate to his disadvantage. During the autumn the Nile was in flood and overflowed its banks, thus forming a great lake to the west and south-west of Khartoum which, combined with numerous minefields which Gordon laid down, prevented any attack from that quarter. When the floods receded, the ramparts protecting the southern perimeter of the fortress were destroyed, and the Mahdi was informed of this breach in the defences by a traitor who slipped across and gave him the secret.

In the meantime the relief expedition from Cairo was moving slowly forward. Since it was now realised that time was a vital factor, it was decided to move up the Nile as far as Korti where the river begins its great detour to the north-east, and cross the loop by forced marches to Metemmah. Even in his extremity, Gordon had been mindful of the welfare of the relieving force. He got a message through warning Wolseley not to bypass Berber and leave it untaken in his rear.

By the end of December, Lord Wolseley was ready to move from Korti across the desert to Metemmah. News had been received that supplies were running short at Khartoum, and it was clear that if General Gordon was to be saved not a day would have to be lost in establishing communications with him. It was resolved to divide the British force into two portions. One division under Sir Herbert Stewart was to take the desert route. The other under General Earle was to follow the course of the Nile with a view ultimately to the capture of Berber which General Gordon had warned Lord Wolseley 'not to leave in his rear.'

On December 30th, the day on which Sir Herbert Stewart left Korti, a messenger arrived with a piece of paper the size of a postage stamp, on which was written, 'Khartoum all right. 14.12.84. C.G. Gordon.' This was in General Gordon's handwriting and his seal was affixed to the back of the document. The letter was accompanied by a verbal message from General Gordon which showed the straits to which he was reduced, 'Our troops' he said 'at Khartoum are suffering from lack of provisions. The food we still have is little, some grain and biscuit. We want you to come quickly . . . In Khartoum there is no butter, no dates, little meat. All food is very dear.'[19]

On 30 December Sir Herbert Stewart pushed on with his force across the desert, but so difficult was the supply position that he was compelled to halt at Jakdul, dump his stores there and return to Korti for another trip. On 8 January 1885 he left Korti for the second time and pressed on across the desert. On approaching the Nile near Metemmah he found himself faced with a dervish army at Abu Klea. A desperate battle took place in which the dervishes suffered heavy losses, but the battle caused some delay to Stewart's advance. During the final approach to the Nile both Sir Herbert Stewart and Colonel Burnaby, his second in command, were sniped and fatally wounded. This was a great calamity, for the direction of operations fell upon Sir Charles Wilson who had had no previous experience of commanding a field force. On arriving at the Nile at Metemmah the force met up with Gordon's steamers which he had sent down to meet them. They also carried six volumes of his journals,[20] and his last heroic message, 'Khartoum is all right. Could hold out for years. C.G.Gordon, 29.12.84.' For some incomprehensible reason Wilson delayed setting forth upstream for three days. Mr Theobald, in his book *The Mahdiya,* states:

He could have left on the afternoon of 21st January, but he did not actually start till the morning of the 24th. It appears that his naval colleague was suffering from boils. Anxious not to miss such an historic adventure, Beresford made the most of rumours of approaching Mahdists, and induced Wilson to waste time in making reconnaissances to the south and to the north on the 21st and 22nd.[21]

If such be the true reason for this fatal delay, it must for ever remain a blot on the name of Sir Charles Wilson, for this futile delay and hesitancy cost

General Gordon and his heroic garrison their lives. Thus on 24 January Wilson set out in the steamers for Khartoum, a distance of something over a hundred miles. Progress was difficult and slow, but four days later, on 28 January, the steamers, having run the gauntlet of rifle fire from both banks of the river, hove in sight of the fortress of Khartoum. But Khartoum had fallen. The gallant town and its indomitable defenders had succumbed to the combined assault of the dervish hordes. The relieving force had arrived two days too late.

Gordon had detected the weakness in his defences as the level of the Nile gradually dropped, and had endeavoured to strengthen them, but the exhaustion of his troops and the intense artillery fire from across the river had prevented the work from being completed. At this time, the traitor Omar Ibrahim slipped across and told the Mahdi of the gap in the defences. News of the approach of the relief expedition had already reached the Mahdi and anxious consultations took place whether the siege should be abandoned or the fortress attacked in force. The Mahdi himself is said to have favoured abandonment.[22] After three days, on 25 January, it was decided to assault the town immediately. A moving account of the fall of Khartoum is given by Mr Bernard Allen in his book *Gordon and the Soudan*, and is reproduced here:

That night the moon shone out over the expectant Dervishes in their tents and the wearied watchman behind the ramparts of Khartoum. Midnight passed. Two hours more and the moon had sunk below the horizon. Another hour passed . . . The hour of sacrifice had come.

Slowly through the darkness the Dervishes crept up to the spot where the Nile had opened a way through the defences. As they advanced upon the town, a fierce bombardment burst out from the Mahdi's guns, directed against every part of the lines. Under cover of this the advancing troops rushed forward, and breaking through the fire from the three protecting barges on the Nile and from the ramparts on the right, overpowered the line of enfeebled troops that tried to cover the gap, and within a few minutes were inside Khartoum. Then sweeping to the right and taking the defenders of the ramparts in the rear, they forced their way along the lines and by sheer weight of numbers bore down all resistance. By four o'clock they had gained possession of the town.

A number of those who poured in through the opening dashed off towards the palace three miles away on the banks of the Blue Nile. Swarming in at the garden entrance at the back, they despatched the few troops and attendants who were there and rushed up the staircase that led to Gordon's room.

Gordon came out to meet them at the top of the stairs, and as he stood facing them, a Dervish plunged his spear in his breast.

A few hours later, Slatin (a captive of the Mahdi) who had listened from his tent in the Mahdi's camp to the sounds of the night assault, saw a group of Dervishes advance towards him, carrying something in a cloth. When they came up to him, they undid the cloth, and he saw before him the head of Gordon.

'The blood rushed to my head and my heart seemed to stop beating' he writes, 'but with a tremendous effort of self-control I gazed silently at this ghastly spectacle. His blue eyes were half open; the mouth was perfectly natural; the hair of his head, and his short whiskers, were almost quite white.

"Is not this the head of your uncle, the unbeliever?" said Shatta holding the head up before me.

"What of it?" I said quietly: "A brave soldier who fell at his post; happy is he to have fallen; his sufferings are over."

That night the stars looked down upon a city of anguish, stained with the blood of ten thousand victims – men and women whom Gordon went out to save.

Another night of anguish and then as the sun rose, two vessels came into view, pressing on over the last few miles that lay between them and Khartoum. As they passed along Tuti Island, the *Bordein* and her sister ship were met by a furious cannonade from the banks. Still they struggled forward under a withering fire till they came to the point where the two Niles meet. There as they looked upstream, the Englishmen on board caught sight of the houses of Khartoum and of Gordon's palace. But Gordon's flag had gone. They were two days too late.[23]

A wail of sorrow went up from the British people when they heard the news of the death of their gallant countryman; the Queen herself was deeply moved. Sorrow soon gave place to indignation and a demand for revenge for Gordon's death and the humiliation of the British army. Although it was well realised that the relief expedition had failed in its objectives and that its *raison d'être* had ceased to exist, the Cabinet of Mr Gladstone, trimming their sails to the parliamentary breezes, allowed themselves to be swept along on the crest of public opinion and re-echoed the cry for revenge. In a packed House the Government only narrowly escaped a vote of censure by fourteen votes in a debate on the events in the Sudan. For the moment it became the policy of the Government to 'smash up' the Mahdi, retake Khartoum and establish a settled government in the Sudan. This policy was, somewhat naturally, supported by Wolseley and his humiliated army which was remustered at Korti. Orders were issued to Wolseley to capture Berber as a preliminary to Khartoum, and General Graham was instructed to return to Suakin and destroy the power of Osman Digna in the eastern Sudan. It is almost comical to consider the Government of Mr Gladstone, after obstinately refusing for so long to take any action in the Sudan, after ridiculing Gordon's prophecy that the Mahdi would have to be smashed up, now issuing orders in all directions for the destruction of the Mahdi's power and for the recapture of the lost garrison towns. These panic-stricken directives were not productive of anything useful, they merely resulted in the needless outlay of expenditure and some loss of life. In March General Graham arrived in Suakin and proceeded to seek out Osman Digna, but apart from some short and sharp skirmishes, he was unsuccessful, for Osman Digna's dervishes vanished into the hills. Operations were even started for the construction of a railway from Suakin to Berber.

Early in March 1885 General Wolseley drew the attention of the Government to the fact that his expedition had been planned and was only sufficient for the original task of relieving Khartoum, and that the operation now envisaged, i.e. the reconquest of Khartoum and the overthrow of the Mahdi's power, were of quite a different order, and that his force would therefore require substantial re-equipment and reinforcement. This pronouncement had a very sobering effect on the Cabinet. They suddenly realised that they were now in 1885 hurrying along the path which they had sedulously avoided the previous year; they were in effect on the point of undertaking large scale military operations against a people who were in Mr Gladstone's words, 'rightly struggling to be free'. The public clamour for revenge had now subsided and the Government, profiting by this, revised the orders they had given in the heat of the moment; the Khartoum expedition was to be abandoned and the British troops withdrawn from the Sudan.

Thus disintegrated the vast empire carved out sixty years previously by Mohammed Ali and enlarged by the Khedive Ismail. While it is probably true that the empire was built on rotten foundations, insufficient credit is generally accorded to Egypt for her own unaided efforts to save it. With the Hicks and Baker expeditions she put forth her last ounce of military strength. It is often stated that these expeditions were doomed to failure, even before they set out, because the Egyptian Government failed to recognise the true nature and extent of the rebellion. In fairness, it must also be pointed out that the British Government likewise failed in this respect. In truth, Britain played a sorry part in the whole affair. Although in military occupation of

Egypt, the British Government thought to throw off all responsibility for Egyptian affairs in the Sudan by a simple declaration to that effect. Driven to the necessity shortly afterwards of accepting some measure of responsibility, they sent a noble and gallant soldier to Khartoum and abandoned him to his fate until too late. Thousands of Egyptians, many of whom conducted themselves nobly, likewise perished. Every statement and prophecy made by General Gordon was substantially proved, yet the Government refused to follow any of his recommendations. Had even a small detachment of British troops been sent to Khartoum in 1884, the town and its garrison would certainly have been saved, and the Mahdi rebellion might easily have collapsed. But instead of adopting a bold policy, the Government dithered and hesitated until disaster finally overtook them. Further, instead of the relatively small force which would have sufficed to save the Sudan in 1884, a large scale operation had to be launched twelve years later to effect its reconquest.

The events of 1884 and 1885 in the Sudan make a lamentable catalogue of blunders on the part of the British Government. The brunt of these fell largely upon Sir Evelyn Baring in Cairo to whom fell the unpleasant task of explaining and justifying British policy to an anxious and helpless Egyptian Government. The responsibility and the odium of the final disaster might easily have been thrown on his shoulders, had he not more than once risked his career by stating the plain facts to a Government which did not wish to hear them and urging immediate action. The fact that his pleas were ignored was certainly not due to his lack of insistence, but to the wilful blindness of his masters in London. The conduct of affairs during these first years were certainly no good augury of the British administration of Egypt which the next two decades were to witness. Fortunately, largely as a result of the patience and ability and resolution of Sir Evelyn Baring, England did much to redeem her tarnished reputation.

CHAPTER 17

The Years of Lord Cromer

Since 1882 attempts have frequently been made by Britain's detractors to make out a case proving that the British occupation of Egypt was the final outcome of a carefully laid and sinister plot to annex Egypt and incorporate it in the British Empire. The facts however do not support such a contention, unless it can be conceived that the public utterances of British ministers were simply intended to throw dust in the eyes of the world. To any impartial student of the events which culminated in the British military intervention in 1882 it must be evident that Britain drifted into a situation which was distasteful to her, even though she considered it necessary in the best interests of all concerned. If Britain erred in her policy as regards Egypt it was not in 1882 but in 1876 when she allowed herself to be involved in the financial difficulties of the Khedive Ismail. A policy more in keeping with British tradition would have been to refuse to shoulder the cause of the bondholders and, more important, to insist that France likewise refrained from doing so. In that event the bondholders might, and probably would, have lost their money, but Britain would have saved herself much of the trouble and embarrassment which her peculiar position in Egypt subsequently brought her. Having however embarked on the policy of interference Britain found herself pushed step by step into the situation logically dictated by the course of events, a military occupation of Egypt.

By one of those strange twists of fate, misfortune had consistently dogged the steps of France in respect of Egypt. Ever since Bonaparte's invasion in 1798 France had in one form or another adopted an aggressive policy in Egypt. For eighty years she had sought by every means open to her to secure a dominant position in the land of the Nile, but at every trick of the game she found herself worsted by Britain who paradoxically had no particular interest in Egypt beyond that of maintaining her in the status quo as part of the

264

Ottoman Empire. Indeed, much of French policy was based on bluff and it fell to Britain from time to time to call it. But in 1882 France had every opportunity of joining Britain in the military intervention in Egypt. She had been the principal exponent of intervention; M. Gambetta had done everything in his power to force it. But under his successor in power, M. de Freycinet, France had at the last moment drawn back, leaving Britain to go in alone. It is difficult to understand why France suddenly panicked at the prospect of military intervention. The reason advanced by M. de Freycinet was that France was experiencing a sense of isolation in Europe, that she was nervous for her own security and loath to send abroad any part of her military strength. On the other hand, he makes it clear that the policy of intervention in Egypt was not of itself distasteful to France. While this may have been the major cause for hesitation, there is also the possibility that France vastly overestimated the military strength of Arabi Pasha. M. de Freycinet was undoubtedly under the influence of old de Lesseps who thought that the defeat of Arabi would be a very exhausting and difficult task. In fact the reason for France's refusal to take any steps to protect her beloved Suez Canal was the possibility that her troops might find themselves embroiled with Arabi's forces.

At all events France was surprised, even shocked, at the ease and rapidity with which the British forces dealt with Arabi Pasha. '*On a expliqué de diverses manières cet étrange combat. La raison généralement admise c'est qu'il s'était établi une sorte d'entente entre le commandant anglais et Arabi.*'[1] There is of course no truth in this reason 'generally admitted'. The simple facts which France could not bring herself to believe were that Arabi and his hurriedly conscripted army were no match for the well trained and disciplined British troops. Almost immediately it dawned on the French Chamber what a grievous blunder they had committed. For so long they had sought a legitimate pretext for intrusion in Egypt's affairs; for so long they had played the game of 'neither or both' with Britain. In 1882 the golden opportunity presented itself. Had France seized it she might easily have persuaded the British Government that as France was primarily a military and Britain a naval power, France should provide the soldiers while the British provided the ships. Such an arrangement might eventually have left France in control of Egypt. But the golden opportunity had been allowed to slip by with the result that Britain was now in complete military control of Egypt, while France was left to play the sorry part of envious spectator. Her cup of humiliation overflowed; her national pride was wounded to the core; French nationals in Egypt could not see a British soldier in the streets of

Cairo or Alexandria without experiencing a pang of mortification. Now that the British were in Egypt the most urgent necessity was to get them out at the earliest possible opportunity; *'l'évacuation de l'Egypte'* became *'le grand but à atteindre.'*[2] At every opportunity that offered the French Government made approaches to Britain with this object in view. These negotiations will be touched on later, but it will not perhaps be anticipating this narrative too much to state that they failed. For twenty-two years France kept up the unequal struggle, and it was not until 1904 that she accepted the inevitable and concluded the Anglo-French Agreement binding herself to recognise the freedom of Britain in Egypt.

In August 1882 a British army landed in Egypt. It was sent for the specific purpose of putting down the rebellion of Arabi Pasha and reinstating the Khedive Tewfik in his rightful position as ruler and head of state. Within a few weeks both these objectives had been attained. There was therefore no apparent reason for the British army to remain in Egypt. On 3 January 1883, that is to say only one month after Arabi Pasha had been tried and exiled, Lord Granville sent a note to the Powers in the following terms:

> Although for the present a British force remains in Egypt for the preservation of public tranquillity, Her Majesty's Government are desirous of withdrawing it as soon as the state of the country and the organisation of proper means for the maintenance of the Khedive's authority will admit of it. In the meantime the position in which Her Majesty's Government are placed towards His Highness imposes upon them the duty of giving advice with the object of securing that the order of things to be established shall be of a satisfactory character, and possess the elements of stability and progress.[3]

The policy expressed in this note was eminently reasonable. Considerable sums of money had been spent and some life lost in the expedition. Clearly it would be folly to pack up and march off again without taking any precautions against a resurgence of rebellion or further unrest in the country. Arabi Pasha and his friends might be safely out of harm's way, but that was no guarantee that others would not step into their shoes as soon as the British army had turned their backs. Obviously not only was it necessary to remove the turbulent elements, but also to seek out and remove the causes of their turbulence. The Khedive was now back on the throne, the head of the state, but it was well understood by all that he had been reinstated by British bayonets, and was maintained by this same agency.

Hitherto Egypt had been governed by a personal ruler, the Pasha, Viceroy or Khedive, in whom was vested virtually supreme authority and control over life and property. The very name of '*Effendina*' was sufficient to inspire dread in the breasts of high and low. None had ever dreamt of questioning his right or authority to direct the destinies of Egypt and its peoples. As long as this tradition of unquestioning obedience to the Khedive continued, so long did his personal power remain. But the Khedive was only a man, and once anybody of influence began to question his right and shake the props of his position, his power fell from him like a cloak. Arabi Pasha had not only shaken the props, he had hurled the whole edifice of personal rule by the Khedive to the ground. He had brought to the humble people of Egypt the realisation that there was no divine right of kings or *khedives*, but that power was vested only in him who could seize it and hold it. Thus, if the Khedive was to continue as head of the state, he must at least be supported by the goodwill of the people or, if this was lacking, by some agency more powerful. During and immediately after the rebellion, Tewfik Pasha had no support from the people; he was regarded as one of the oppressive and hated class of Turkish *pasha*-dom and as a puppet in the hands of the European bondholders. These impressions were for the most part erroneous, but they nonetheless existed. If therefore he was to be maintained on his throne, it must be by another agency. It was the realisation of this that underlay the phrase in Lord Granville's note regarding 'the state of the country and the organisation of proper means for the maintenance of the Khedive's authority'. The British Government thereby implied that they were taking upon themselves the task of organising the means which would secure the Khedive on his throne, and that until this was done, the British army would have to remain.

The British Government had only a vague idea of the task they were assuming. All that was necessary, they considered, was to establish a stable government, effect a few necessary reforms and build up a stable Egyptian army loyal to the Khedive and his government, and Egypt could then be left to look after herself. In the meantime the Khedive and Government were left in no doubt that as long as the British army remained in Egypt, they would be expected to accept any advice which they received from the British representative. But in general the presence of the army was cordially welcomed by most sections of the population; the Khedive and Ministry owed their position and authority to it; the *fellahin* in the fields and the townsfolk in the cities felt the necessity for peace and good order; the Europeans owed their lives and property to it. In April 1883 the latter even presented a petition to Lord Dufferin, then temporarily in the country, praying that the British occupation might be permanent. One indubitable benefit at least was conferred on Egypt by the presence of the troops; peace and stability were restored. The great problem was to devise some means of ensuring the continuance of these necessities without the British army.

Almost immediately two further factors arose which tended to complicate the situation and render the withdrawal of the army inadvisable. As has been narrated in the two previous chapters, the Sudan flamed into revolt and was finally lost to Egypt. Not only this, but out of the loss grew the danger that Egypt herself might be attacked by hordes of fanatical dervishes swarming down the Nile. Egypt had no army to defend herself; it had been disbanded by the Khedive six days after the battle of Tel el Kebir. Until the army could be re-formed the British troops were the only organised body of men in Egypt capable of offering any resistance to an invasion from the south.

The other factor was financial. The Law of Liquidation pressed with exceptional severity upon the Egyptian Treasury. The disturbances of the previous two years had resulted in the exhaustion of the national coffers, and there was imminent danger that the country would default in her obligations to the creditors. Such a catastrophe might have resulted in the handing over of the country and its resources to the bondholders or to a complete international control acting on their behalf. Only the power and influence of a great nation, taking up the cudgels for the stricken country, could prevent this. For the Law of Liquidation was supported by and binding on the Mixed Tribunals which in turn were supported by fourteen foreign countries. A default would have rendered the Government liable to actions in the courts, and government property might well have been attached in satisfaction of the debts. Thus easily could the country have been sold up, and would have been sold up without the support of Britain.

In the eyes of the British Government the principal defect of Egypt was that while in commerce, wealth and civilisation the country had made truly remarkable progress in the preceding half-century, the government and administrative system had remained almost mediaeval; the only limited advance made in this respect was the principle of ministerial responsibility, and even this had been extorted from a reluctant Khedive under strong foreign pressure. Even so, the ancient methods of government still remained. The only effective tool of administration was the *courbash*; the most potent influence in matters of justice was King *Bakshish*, public works were still carried out by the wasteful employment of the *corvée*. If the country was to possess 'the elements of stability and progress' mentioned by Lord Granville, it was clear that these archaic and arbitrary methods of government must be swept away and replaced by others more adapted to the new status of the country.

In theory, an archaic practice or institution could be abolished by a stroke of the pen, but it was no use abolishing it without substituting something in its place. Egypt was above all conservative and traditional and her people did not take easily to change, even though the change might be to their advantage. Tact, patience and tenacity were necessary, not only to effect a reform, but to get it accepted by the people. The truth of this was well illustrated by the action of Lord Dufferin when he came to Egypt in 1882 as Special Commissioner. He was outraged at the use of the *courbash* as the normal instrument of government. He insisted that it should be abolished and the decree, signed by the Minister of the Interior, went forth into the provinces. The immediate result was that the *mudirs* and *mamurs* were deprived of the only method of government they knew. The natural result ensued; crime and disorder increased because the criminals knew that they could not be *courbash*ed into confessing or witnesses into giving evidence.

In September 1883 Sir Edward Malet, Her Majesty's representative in Egypt, was posted to Brussels and his place taken by Sir Evelyn Baring who, as a former Commissioner of the Debt and one of the Controllers-General, was no stranger to the affairs of Egypt. To a careerist in the British Diplomatic Service the post of Consul-General in Egypt, a mere province of the Ottoman Empire, could only be regarded as a stepping-stone to something better. Possibly Baring returned to Egypt with this thought in his mind. But he was destined to remain for the rest of his career in the land of the Nile and to be rewarded for his great services with an earldom. He held the post of British Consul-General for nearly twenty-four years. Strictly speaking the British Consul-General was a diplomatic representative in the same way as, and with no more influence or precedence than, the representatives of the other Powers; certainly he was not invested with any more authority in respect of the internal affairs of Egypt. But from 1883 onwards, although in theory his position remained unaltered, he was possessed of powers and influence far exceeding those of any of the other diplomatic representatives, in that he was the envoy of the country whose troops were now in military occupation of Egypt, of the country moreover which had arrogated to itself the right of giving advice to the Government of His Highness and which expected the advice thus tendered to be accepted. In this way Her Majesty's Consul-General in Egypt became in effect almost a personal ruler, in much the same way as the Khedive Ismail had been. Sir Evelyn Baring from the time of his appointment in September 1883 to his resignation in May 1907 was virtually the uncrowned king of Egypt.

This nebulous, undefined position of Britain in Egypt was anathema to France to whom the '*situation nette*' is so dear. It was the bitterest humiliation to her that Britain could always counter her charges of interference in Egypt's affairs by pointing out that she was merely giving advice to the Government of Egypt which that Government generally saw fit to accept, when all the time it was known on both sides that the Egyptian Government was given no option about accepting or declining it. The position of Britain in Egypt became virtually one of a veiled protectorate, veiled because it was never openly declared as such, but a protectorate in sum and substance nonetheless. The Consul-General assumed the functions, if not the title, of Resident. In this guise Sir Evelyn Baring set himself the task of reforming the government of Egypt.

It is not intended here to do more than mention briefly the reforms that were effected in the ensuing years; in more than four hundred closely packed pages Lord Milner has given some account of those which were effected up to 1904 in his book, *England in Egypt*. After the military occupation England was in a position, had she thought it desirable, to take over in theory as well as in practice the direct government of Egypt by simply appointing a Cabinet composed of Englishmen. Yet a number of factors made this potentially dangerous and unwise, especially as it would have exacerbated the prejudices of France and the other powers, and militated against the policy of teaching Egypt eventually to rule herself. A solution was found, no doubt the product of Baring's fertile mind, which while being fairly effective in its ultimate results, was not likely to endear itself either to the Egyptians or to the foreign minorities. The Government was to remain in the hands of the Khedive and his Council of native Ministers, but to every ministry was attached an English 'adviser' and his staff whose functions in theory once again were to advise and assist the Minister in administering the departments of government under his control. In rank and position these English advisers were subordinate to the Egyptian Ministers, were simply employees of the Government and could be appointed and dismissed by the Khedive. In practice however their position was vastly different. The advisers knew they were employed to effect necessary measures of reform, and to get their views adopted and put into practice whether the Ministers liked it or not. In time of difficulty or opposition they turned to the British Consul General for support, with the result that his powerful influence was exerted on their behalf on not infrequent occasions. Through the years this anomalous situation became the cause of bitter resentment and humiliation to the

Government of Egypt. For one thing the Ministers were expected to affix their signatures to decrees and support policies which they might not, and frequently did not, approve. The Minister was supposedly the executive authority; in fact however he was the servant of his subordinate. It was not unnatural that he should feel the invidiousness of his position deeply. Lord Milner in *England in Egypt* illustrates in an imaginary conversation the sentiments of the Egyptian Minister:

> I am an Oriental and I want to be a master or to have a master. I am prepared to be your humble, obedient servant, or I am prepared, quite prepared, to do without you. But I don't understand divided responsibility·or limited freedom of action. Your kind consideration in letting me have my own way at times – just when it happens to suit you – does not make me feel a bit more free, but only a great deal more uncomfortable.[4]

With such an unstable structure was the reform of Egypt undertaken. The structure however rested on one great pillar of strength, that is, the principle that the advice offered must be accepted, that Ministers who refused it must forfeit their offices.

Before dealing with the period of reform some mention must be made of the sequence of events which took place in the political and international field subsequent to 1882. The Arabi rebellion, the destruction by fire of Alexandria and the Sudan rebellion had shattered the fabric of finance so delicately adjusted by the Law of Liquidation. All the progress made in 1880 and 1881 was now lost and the country was swamped in a fresh load of debt which she had no prospect of meeting unless some modification of the Law of Liquidation was effected. Alone she could never have struggled through the morass of international diplomacy. Any modification of the Law would require the consent of all the Powers, and it is certain that, left to her own devices, she could never have secured agreement among them all. It is indeed regrettable that on hardly any occasion during the next two decades was any Egyptian question or problem considered by the Powers simply on its own merits. A number of such questions arose on which Britain had to consult the Powers, and almost invariably acceptance of her proposals was conditional upon Britain agreeing to some other proposition which had nothing whatever to do with the original problem. In fact the Powers, especially France, used Britain's policy of reform and amelioration in Egypt as a lever or bargaining counter for extorting some other totally unrelated concession. In all these diplomatic wrangles Egypt was the victim. Thus it was in the financial crisis of 1884.

The first move was made by Lord Granville in approaching the French Government with a view to securing some reduction in Egypt's commitments. M. Ferry, President of the Council, welcomed these overtures, hoping thereby to force the British Government to name a date for the evacuation of the troops from Egypt. In this he was successful to the extent that the British Government engaged themselves to withdraw the troops in 1888, provided her present proposals were accepted and that the Powers considered that peace and good order in Egypt would not be endangered thereby. The price of this promise was to be a reduction of one half per cent in the interest on the Debt. The French Chamber of Deputies, anxious as they were to get the British troops out of Egypt, froze at the prospect of demanding any 'sacrifices' from the creditors. The negotiations thus came to nothing.

Undaunted, in 1884 the British Government made a further attempt to get the Law of Liquidation modified, and in March 1885 agreement was finally reached at the Convention of London. The critical factor which persuaded the Powers, and even France, to concur in the Convention was the Alexandria Indemnities. 'Great Britain was in a perfectly inexpugnable position in refusing to settle those claims unless all other outstanding liabilities of the Egyptian Government were provided for at the same time.'[5] In other words unless the Powers agreed to reduce the liabilities of Egypt, none of their nationals would receive any compensation for the losses they had suffered in the Alexandria fire.

The concessions secured at the Convention of London are of interest. A new loan of £9,000,000, guaranteed by the Powers and bearing interest at the rate of 3%, was authorised.

> To obtain nine millions in cash for an annual payment of £315,000 was something quite unheard of in the history of Egyptian finance. No fairy godmother ever produced a richer or more unexpected gift. The sum in question not only paid the Alexandria Indemnities and wiped out the deficits of the years 1882-85, but provided a round million for new works of irrigation.[6]

In addition a slight temporary reduction in the rate of interest on the National Debt was authorised. Certain other modifications were also secured which had the effect of easing the country's immediate financial position, but which proved to be more in the nature of an impediment at a later date when Egypt became more prosperous. An example of this was the fixing of the 'authorised expenditure'. Under this arrangement the expenditure of every department of the Government was assessed, and all these amounts were added together to make up the total of £5,237,000. This sum became the limit of expenditure which the Government was authorised to use for the normal administration and improvement of the country. If the revenues assigned to the Government fell short of this amount, application could be made to the *Caisse* to make up the difference from any surpluses it held. Conversely but with a vast difference, if the Government wished to exceed its 'authorised expenditure' it could do so from any surpluses in its own revenues, but for every pound it spent above the authorised limit, it had to pay a pound to the *Caisse*. This peculiar condition operated with much unfairness on the Government, for if, for example, they required £10,000 for some particular work of improvement which did not fall within the authorised expenditure, they had to raise no less than £20,000, one half of which went to the *Caisse*. It thus frequently happened that an improvement which was well worth the expenditure it required itself, had to be rejected because it was not worth double the sum. However, the odd million pounds made available by the Guaranteed Loan made possible the drastic reorganisation and improvement of the irrigation system. This single million out of all that had been borrowed during the previous twenty years proved the saving of Egypt. It resulted in such an increase in agriculture and consequent revenue that Egypt was thereafter able to meet all her obligations, and although stringent economy had to be exercised for some years to come, the financial question never again assumed serious proportions.

It will be observed that in the earlier negotiations of 1884, as an inducement to France to concur in the financial proposals they were laying before her, the British Government had signified their willingness to name a date for the evacuation of Egypt. This evacuation in French eyes was '*le grand but à atteindre,*' and in 1884 France was given the opportunity of realising this aim simply by accepting a slight reduction of interest to the bondholders. It can only be deduced that she was prompted to decline purely by avarice. In 1885 further proposals, i.e. those mentioned above, were submitted to the Powers which were accepted, but this time no mention was made of evacuation, the incentive on this occasion being the settlement of the Alexandria Indemnities. Britain thus retained her liberty of action in Egypt and once again French financial interests triumphed at the expense of French political aims, an event bitterly lamented by M. de Freycinet: '*Ce fut une faute de notre part. Il eût mieux valu consentir à la réduction d'intérêt, à la condition qu'elle n'avait son effet qu'à partir du jour de l'évacuation.*'[7]

Even after three years the British Government was still groping, somewhat blindly perhaps, for some solution which would guarantee the two desired requirements: the preservation of good order in Egypt coupled with judicious development, and the withdrawal of the British troops. In spite of the failure of the proposals of 1884 a further attempt to find a solution was made in 1885. In truth, the British handling of the 'Egyptian Question' had not so far been notable for brilliance or success. In the circumstances, immediate and effective results were impossible of execution, although this was not generally appreciated. There was no magic wand which could be waved over Egypt to produce instantaneously order from disorder, peace and stability from anarchy. These could only be achieved by years of steady and patient labour, a fact which does not appear to have been fully realised. One criticism however is fully justified. Never on any question connected with Egypt had the government of Mr Gladstone displayed any quality approaching determination or a true appreciation of the position. Under the direction of Mr Gladstone, Britain had drifted haphazardly and allowed herself to be tossed about on the political storms of the moment. This lack of policy had resulted finally in an unwanted military occupation of Egypt from which Britain found it difficult to extricate herself. She was still adhering to the belief that the creation of a strong and loyal Egyptian army and the initiation of a few elementary reforms were all that was necessary to enable her to withdraw. Only those on the spot, the British Consul-General and the British officials associated in the administration, appreciated that these works would, in the face of international obstruction as evidenced by the capitulations and the bondholding interest, occupy a period of several years.

In June 1885 the Government of Mr Gladstone gave place to that of Lord Salisbury who set himself immediately to grapple with 'the Egyptian Question', and to find a means of withdrawing the troops. The continued occupation was becoming a source of considerable embarrassment to Britain. It was regarded with some suspicion by Europe generally; it was a constant source of irritation to the Sultan whose sovereign rights were being infringed; a substantial element of the Egyptian population was beginning to find it irksome; it was the only rift in the general harmony which reigned between Britain and France, and French resentment was settling down into intransigent obstruction and even hostility. These foreign sentiments were grave disadvantages to offset the possible benefits of an Egyptian occupation. As the Sultan was the nominal sovereign of Egypt, Lord Salisbury took the view that the settlement of Egypt must be effected by direct negotiation with him and his government. In August 1885 he appointed Sir Henry Drummond Wolff Envoy Extraordinary and Minister Plenipotentiary to the Sultan, and charged him with the task of negotiating a settlement of the Egyptian question.

> He was given a sort of general commission to examine into Egyptian affairs. He was to invite the co-operation of the Sultan in the settlement of the Egyptian question; more especially it was thought that it was 'in His Majesty's power to contribute materially to the establishment of settled order and good government' in the Soudan.[8]

Sir Henry Drummond Wolff's first task was to go to Constantinople and settle with the Turkish Government the nature of the questions which they were to discuss. On 24 October he signed a preliminary convention with the Porte by which a British and a Turkish Commissioner were to be sent to Egypt to investigate the state of affairs, preparatory to their submitting reports to their respective governments which would form the basis of a formal agreement between the two powers. Wolff himself assumed the role of British Commissioner, the Porte nominating Ghazi Mukhtar Pasha, an eminent Turkish soldier. Arrived in Egypt at the end of 1885 they set themselves to examine the situation.

One of the subjects of discussion was the reorganisation of the Khedive's army. It appears that Wolff had little confidence in the native Egyptian as effective fighting material and urged that Turkish troops and officers should be recruited. On this particular point, fortunately as it turned out, the Sultan refused to concur, and the army was thus left to be remodelled by British officers. Another point of interest was the proposal that the Sudan should in some way be pacified. Lord Salisbury apparently laboured under the delusion that the dervishes, being Moslems, would willingly listen to the Sultan in his capacity as Khalif and bow to his will. Sir Henry

> spoke of negotiations being undertaken between the Khalif and those who recognised his authority. Moukhtar Pasha and other Turks were naturally slow to believe that any Mohammedans refused to recognise the authority of the Sultan as Khalif. But everyone in Egypt knew that the Mahdi confounded Christians and Turks alike in one common anathema, and that the idea of conjuring with the Sultan's name in the Soudan was a delusion.[9]

These negotiations thus fell to the ground. An examination of the internal state and administration of Egypt itself revealed that everything that could be done was being done by the Consul-General and the British advisers in association with the Government. In other words, the mission of Wolff and Mukhtar Pasha was barren of result except in one particular. This was the Convention finally drawn up between Wolff and the Turkish Government in May 1887; this was designed to pave the way for the withdrawal of the British troops.

Under the terms of Clause 5 of the Convention, the British forces were to be withdrawn within three years from the date of the Convention provided that no external or internal danger arose which might necessitate the postponement of the withdrawal. In this case the troops would remain until the danger had passed. In the event of subsequent danger to peace arising, only Turkey and Britain would have the right to send troops to Egypt, and the two powers would act in concert and would both withdraw their troops as soon as the danger had passed.

The Convention was to be ratified by the two governments within one month of its signature by the plenipotentiaries, failing which it would become inoperative. Britain thus pledged herself to a definite date for evacuation which was for France a most urgent necessity. Yet paradoxically both France and Russia strongly opposed the Convention on the ground that it was creating a political condominium over Egypt on the part of Britain and Turkey in place of the former financial condominium exercised by France and Britain. The French Ambassador at Constantinople was instructed to urge upon the Sultan that he was thereby abdicating his sovereign rights over Egypt by sharing them with Britain. The Sultan 'was told that if he ratified the Convention, France and Russia would thereby be given the right to occupy provinces of the Empire, and to leave only after a similar Convention had been concluded. France might do so in Syria and Russia in Armenia.'[10] By these diplomatic manoeuvres France undoubtedly expected to procure a modification of the Convention which had been the outcome of two arduous years of negotiation and investigation. But the British Government called the bluff and was not to be moved. The Sultan was perplexed; under pressure from France and Russia he appealed to Sir Henry Drummond Wolff for advice. The latter had none to offer; he had, he said, exhausted his terms of reference; the Convention must either stand in its present form or fall to the ground. By the end of the month no move had been made at Constantinople to ratify the agreements, and it became a dead letter. Thus ended the last negotiation, having for its object the withdrawal of the British troops from Egypt, until after the First World War.

Once again a golden opportunity had been presented to France of realising her great ambition, the evacuation of British forces from Egypt and the restoration of French influence in that country, at least on a parity with that of Britain. Once again she had thrown it away. The Convention had envisaged evacuation at the end of three years unless some danger to Egypt arose during that period. Yet it was almost inconceivable that any danger would or could arise as long as the British troops remained. It follows therefore that evacuation would have been a virtual certainty. Thereafter, although some trouble might conceivably have arisen to warrant a fresh intervention, its occurrence would have been highly improbable, and the possibility of Britain renewing her foothold in Egypt would have been remote. The ambitions of France would thus have been easily realised. But France strained at the gnat; she could not stomach the idea of Britain having any political rights in Egypt, even though it was in the highest degree improbable that she would ever have the opportunity of exercising them. She thought to compel Britain to abandon those rights, and in so doing she defeated her own objects and Britain stayed in Egypt. Not only this but she placed Britain in an impregnable position, for henceforth the British Government could with justice declare that they had offered to evacuate Egypt, nay, had even drawn up a Convention with the Sultan to that end, only to have her efforts frustrated by France. If at any time the Sultan liked to re-open negotiations on the same basis as the Convention, Britain would be willing to listen. But no further approaches were made, and the evacuation of Egypt was postponed *sine die*.

When the British army landed in Egypt in 1882 it was well understood that not only was the mutinous rabble of Arabi Pasha to be put down, but also that new conditions should be created which would render any further resurgence improbable. The first object of Britain's reforming intentions was therefore the Egyptian army. Only a few days after Tel el Kebir it was disbanded under a Khedivial decree. The wisdom of this measure was indisputable. While an army for a number of reasons was indispensable, it was hopeless to attempt to remodel the existing rabble of discomfited and demoralised troops that constituted Arabi's following into an organised and disciplined force. Far better was it to demolish the rickety structure completely and to replace it with another built on more durable foundations. It was current opinion among the uninformed that the Egyptian native was useless as a soldier, an impression fostered no doubt by the performance of some of Arabi's troops during the war. During the Drummond Wolff negotiations of 1885-7 a proposal was put forward that troops and officers should be recruited from Turkey to lend strength to the new Egyptian army. Fortunately these proposals came to nothing. There is a sufficient body of evidence to show that the Egyptian *fellah* makes a very good soldier provided he is commanded by capable and determined officers. Under the leadership of Mohammed Ali and especially Ibrahim Pasha the *fellah* army had conquered the Sudan, seized Syria, routed the fierce and fanatical Wahabis in Arabia, and even threatened the Sultan's capital, while in more recent times they had offered heroic resistance to the dervish hordes in the Sudan under General Gordon and other courageous Egyptian officers in the beleaguered garrisons. It was only on occasions when the command was cowardly, incompetent and corrupt that the Egyptian army showed itself in such a sorry light, but this would undoubtedly apply in other countries under similar conditions. The *fellah* soldier may not have been conspicuous for his dash and initiative, but he possessed sterling qualities which under favourable conditions could make him a formidable adversary: physical toughness and endurance; a good physique and in general good health; an infinite capacity for hard work; docility of character; and amenability to discipline and training.

The task of creating a new Egyptian army was entrusted to Sir Evelyn Wood and a small body of selected British officers. Funds for the purpose were very limited, but on the other hand this of all the various departments of government was saved from the bane of international interference and bickering, and the British officers were able to proceed with their labours undisturbed. In the new army the accent was to be on quality rather than quantity, and a modest establishment of six thousand was selected as a first effort. The newly enlisted troops

> found themselves properly fed, clothed, housed. Discipline was strict, but as long as they conducted themselves well they were absolutely safe from oppression. Their pay was reasonable in amount and it was never stopped except for misconduct. They were looked after when ill . . . A very great impression was likewise made by the fact that the conscripts were now not only entitled to leave, but regularly allowed to take it. The reappearance of the *fellah* soldier in his native village, after an absence of a year in barracks – not crawling back, mutilated or smitten by some fatal disease, but simply walking in as a visitor, healthy, well-dressed and with some money in his pocket – was like a vision of a man risen from the dead.[11]

In fact the new order established in the army was based on justice, humanity and the recognition that the soldier was entitled to consideration. The British officers quickly fell in love with their troops, and this affection was reciprocated by the native troops in the form of loyalty and respect. Of all the reforms effected during the period of the British occupation the army was one of the most successful, and the work undertaken was destined to reap a lavish harvest when the Sudan later came to be brought back to the Egyptian fold.

Britain's most significant and enduring triumph in Egypt was in the field of irrigation. It has often been said with truth that Egypt is the Nile and the Nile Egypt. The spreading of the waters of the mighty river over the fields is indeed a matter of life and death. Although in former years many new canals had been dug in the Delta, the method of irrigation had remained in principle the same as it had been for centuries, i.e. the basin system which depended upon the Nile flood spreading over the fields and draining off as it fell. Even the construction of the great Nile Barrage in earlier days had not substantially modified this system. But the annual rise and fall of the river was by no means constant and the frequent variations resulted in greater or less disaster for the inhabitants of the Nile Valley, a low Nile inevitably bringing famine, while a high Nile could, and frequently did, destroy the crops it normally nurtured. As long as the traditional basin system was in operation, there was necessarily a limit to the area of land which could be watered and cultivated, and therefore to the economic prosperity of the people. So delicate was the financial position of Egypt that a bad harvest could easily mean economic ruin; there were no reserves to tide the country over a bad period. Clearly irrigation was outstandingly the most important question. Fortunately Britain, the occupying power, had at her disposal an expert body of hydraulic engineers who had gained their experience in fighting the irrigation battle in India. A number of these were brought to Egypt to improve and rebuild the derelict system, and this small body of men set themselves to pit their skill and knowledge against the vagaries of the river, and to harness its life-giving properties to the service of man. The surplus million pounds from the loan of 1885 mentioned above proved the saving of Egypt. Armed with this sum the engineers repaired the Nile Barrage, dug new canals, cleared old ones and instituted an efficient drainage system. The engineers took no interest in politics; their sole concern was the river and the bringing of its waters to the fields. Whatever the *fellah* might think about the British occupation of his country, the one thing he understood was water, the liquid gold which meant life or death to him, and once he realised that this small band of British engineers had no other object than to help him, he welcomed him as a friend and co-operated in the irrigation work with all the means in his power. The only disgruntled section of the population was the large landowning class who found themselves expropriated of their former privileges of taking the lion's share of the water to the detriment of the peasant smallholder. The policy was now changed to 'fair shares for all'. The land immediately responded to the expert touch of the engineers. Year by year the yields increased; more land was brought under cultivation; the revenues were augmented; and Egypt was enabled to meet her obligations, grievous though they were. So successful was the work of the engineers that a further sum of £800,000 was somehow scraped together in 1890 to carry on with their development work. The crowning achievement of the Irrigation Service was the building of the great Aswan Dam, begun in 1898 and completed in 1902. From that time onward complete control of the Nile waters became possible and thereafter nearly all Egypt was converted to the perennial system of irrigation by which the supply of water was made available in adequate quantities all the year round by regulating the output at Aswan. Instead of the former single annual crop of Middle and Upper Egypt, two and three crops became possible. Praise for the engineer friends of Egypt was universal; Lord Milner in his book, *England in Egypt* reports the following incident:

> I remember once discussing our position in Egypt with a native statesman, honest but narrow-minded, who avowed himself bitterly opposed to our presence and to our policy. I could not help asking him how he thought the country would get on without the British engineers, He promptly answered, 'You do not suppose that if Great Britain were to retire from Egypt we should let the engineers go. I myself should be the first to do everything I could to retain them.' I merely mention the incident as a proof of the way in which, even among the most anti-English natives, the work of these officers is appreciated.[12]

During this period the problems of reform were attacked in nearly all the other departments of Government: police, prisons, health, public works and justice, to mention but a few. The degree of improvement somewhat naturally varied according to the special circumstances surrounding each branch of administration. The reform of the judicial system, for example, presented difficulties of the highest order, inasmuch as it came on the one hand within the orbit of the religious law or *Sheria*, which could not be tampered with by Christian hands, and on the other within the province of the Mixed Tribunals, set up by the capitulatory powers without whose consent no modification could be effected. Once again, impartiality and efficiency could not be suddenly achieved in the courts by the wave of a magic wand. The improvements had to be gradual and public opinion had to be persuaded to recognise the benefits of the new methods, a slow process in conservative Egypt.

Britain has been roundly accused by her antagonists of neglecting the education of the Egyptian masses in favour of those reforms which would bring in more money, and of deliberately keeping the Egyptians ignorant to keep them submissive. Whether or not these accusations be true, it must be admitted that the progress in the field of education lagged behind that made in other departments of the administration. But the reform of the educational system posed problems of exceptional complexity. In the first place, there was practically no money, and even when a few extra thousand could be scraped together, the limitations imposed on exceeding the 'authorised expenditure' often prohibited the use of the money. Secondly, as with justice, education was inextricably interwoven with the religious life of the country, the bulk of the native schools, such as they were, being part of the mosques and devoted only to ramming a few verses of the Koran into the minds of the children. Any trespass on religious ground by foreign Christians would have met with the bitterest opposition by the *ulema*, and the only solution was to establish separate Government schools. Thirdly, competent teachers could not be created suddenly or manufactured like a locomotive in a short space of time. The building up of a capable teacher is, as has been found in other countries, a process extending over many years. This combination of circumstances resulted in only a modest advance in the educational system during the last two decades of the nineteenth century, but even so some progress was made. In 1877, i.e. in the bitter years of Ismail Pasha, only £29,000 was allocated to education, whereas in 1908 this sum had risen to £450,000. By this time the fetters on authorised expenditure had been thrown off and the Government were able to devote a much more substantial part of their revenues to this important department.

Some mention has already been made of the delicate financial position of Egypt subsequent to the British occupation. Although the Convention of London secured a respite sufficient to tide the country over her most critical period and provided the vital loan of £9,000,000, nevertheless for some years to come the budget was only balanced by resort to desperate expedients. On one occasion equilibrium was only achieved by deferring the payment of civil service salaries due on 31 December by one day, thus bringing this item into the next year's expenditure. During the most critical years up to 1889 the finances of Egypt were directed by Sir Edgar Vincent who, though very youthful in years, was old in the manipulation of finances and singularly fertile in devising ways through the financial labyrinth of Egypt. By 1890

Egypt was sailing in calmer waters and as the years went by her financial strength increased so substantially that Egyptian stock became much sought after. So sound were these investments that the bondholders attempted to resist any conversion of the loans which aimed at reducing the interest.

It will be recalled that during the time of Arabi Pasha and even earlier in the reign of Ismail Pasha the seeds of popular government had been sown in the guise of the Chamber of Notables, and fostered by the Organic Law of 1882 which had been introduced by Arabi. With the rebellion and the subsequent British military occupation these had been swept away and the government was once more vested in the hands of His Highness the Khedive. Such a return to the system of personal government was not, however, consonant with Britain's attachment to parliamentary forms, and in consequence when Lord Dufferin was sent to Egypt in 1882 to survey the various problems, it was expected he would make recommendations regarding the judicious development of popular institutions. Lord Dufferin's conclusions on this difficult problem were embodied in a new Organic Law which was promulgated on 1 May 1883. Under this law provincial councils were established under the presidency of the *mudirs* which were granted power to deal with minor local matters. Further, a so-called Legislative Council was created, partly by the nomination of the Government, partly by election from the provincial councils, but it possessed no executive power. Its functions were little more than consultative and advisory, and the Government was under no obligation to accept its views. A further creation of the Organic Law was the Legislative Assembly which was in fact the Legislative Council writ large by the inclusion of the six Ministers and forty-six delegates elected by the population.[13] Again the Assembly had no executive power save in a negative sense; no new direct tax could be levied without its consent. Although these may seem somewhat phantom institutions, as indeed they were, they were not entirely without their uses and, more importantly, they provided an avenue for the representatives to voice their views on current questions, and they also served as a training ground for future Egyptian politicians and administrators. While these various institutions were sufficient to satisfy the parliamentary leanings of the British, they were, as has been stated, little more than consultative, and the executive power continued to lie in the hands of the Government of His Highness who in turn was saddled with a number of British advisers and officials whose advice he was expected to accept. In time of difficulty these officials tended to turn to the Consul General, Lord Cromer, who on occasion was obliged to exert diplomatic pressure on the Egyptian Government to ensure that the advice offered was in fact accepted and put into effect.

It is not surprising under the circumstances that the British administration, though actuated by the best of motives, the improvement of the lot of the common people of Egypt, was not by any means popular. In general the British official was selected with great care. In addition to his technical qualifications he had to be

> a man of high character. He must have sufficient elasticity of mind to be able to apply under circumstances which are strange to him the knowledge which he has acquired elsewhere. He must be possessed of a sound judgment in order to enable him to distinguish between abuses which should be at once reformed, and those it will be wise to tolerate, at all events for a time. He must be versatile, and quick to adapt any local feature of the administration to suit his own reforming purposes. He must be well mannered and conciliatory, and yet not allow his conciliation to degenerate into weakness, etc.[14]

Even so, mistakes in selecting these officers were occasionally made, and these, few though they were, did much to damage Britain's reputation in Egypt. Mr Clifford Lloyd, for example, created a furore in the Department of the Interior and finally insisted that either he or the Minister must be replaced. Mr Lloyd was relieved of his post.

The process of reform was slow, inevitably so; time had to elapse before the reforms bore their first fruit. The native Egyptians not appreciating this, were dissatisfied and saw little benefit accruing from the British administration. The Pasha class, irritated by the curbs placed upon their former privileges, were equally hostile, while some of the foreigners, particularly the French element, did all in their power to heap opprobrium upon the British administration. The French press, the *Bosphore Egyptien* in particular, protected from Government interference by the capitulations, poured forth a stream of invective against the British officials and the Egyptian Government. Nubar Pasha the Prime Minister was, in this case, finally obliged to ignore the capitulatory rights by suppressing the seditious paper, an act which involved him in much trouble with an outraged France. The Ministers themselves were not unnaturally continually incensed at having to bow to the will of their nominal subordinates. Even though they may have agreed with their policies, it was a source of humiliation to them that they had no discretion in the control of their own departments. Nubar Pasha who held office as President of the Council of Ministers was himself a great reformer, a diplomat of considerable ability and imbued with the highest ideals, but he never admitted the necessity for large scale recruitment of Britons into the Egyptian Civil Service. He believed that Britain should confine herself to maintaining peace and good order in Egypt and allow his Government to embark on the programme of reform. The partnership of Lord Cromer and Nubar Pasha was not therefore a particularly happy one. 'The prestige which had grown around him [Nubar] in former years, the influence he had acquired in the country, his long connexion with public life, combined with his personal characteristics, unsuited him to enter into any partnership in Egyptian administration in which he was not the dominant figure.'[15] After a long unequal struggle Nubar finally resigned in 1888 and was succeeded by Riaz Pasha. Although he made a brief reappearance in public life in 1895, this was Nubar's last substantial performance on the Egyptian stage. He was probably the greatest of Egypt's politicians, for his devotion to his country and her interests was unquestionable. He never hesitated to answer the call when none other dared to incur the responsibility; as an Armenian and a Christian he worked under a cloud of suspicion and veiled hostility, yet his charm, powers of persuasion and his diplomatic and political ability generally carried him through to success. Nubar's monument was undoubtedly the creation of the Mixed Tribunals which survived until after the Second World War.

The Khedive Tewfik, though disliking the British military occupation and interference in the government of his country, yet realised the necessity for them and saw that Egypt would eventually profit thereby, Tewfik Pasha therefore did his best to co-operate in the new order, and in general the relations between him and the British were cordial. He will never be remembered as a great man, but he possessed certain qualities and virtues which were wholly praiseworthy. His courage in adversity, though of a passive nature, was great, for he bore himself nobly in the face of great personal danger during the Arabi Rebellion, and in the remaining years of his reign, a period of exceptional difficulty for any ruler in such an invidious position, his conduct was steadfast and dignified, and he regained his lost respect among his own people by his sterling qualities. He died suddenly at Helwan in January 1892. Consternation and sorrow were universal. Never was a good and useful life cut off at a more inopportune moment.'[16]

Tewfik Pasha was succeeded by his son Abbas Hilmi who became known as Abbas II. Far different in character and outlook was the new Khedive from his father. Tewfik had come to the throne at a time when Egypt was entangled in the international web; he had been baptised in the fire of the Arabi Rebellion and had learned in the school of adversity. These hardships had helped to purge him of the traditional Turkish *hauteur* and arrogance, and he had thus finally emerged as a serious, well-intentioned man, anxious only to secure the well-being of his subjects. For various reasons Tewfik had refrained from sending his son Abbas to France or England to be educated and had finally decided upon Austria. The choice of this country was not particularly happy for the son of a ruler who was obliged to bow to foreign dominion. For Austria was the land of militarism, autocracy and imperialism, and in Vienna the head of the young Abbas was filled with ideas of the untrammelled rights and powers of rulers. During his period abroad he fell under the influence of the critics of Britain who sowed in his mind the anglophobe ideas which he was subsequently to manifest on his accession. Abbas suffered no such ordeals as his father had; during the eight years preceding his accession the country had enjoyed a period of peace and recuperation. These and various other factors combined to instil in his mind the belief that he could flout the British administration and occupation with impunity.

The sentiments of the new Khedive made themselves felt immediately upon his accession. The considerable anglophobe elements were encouraged tacitly to exert themselves, while those who had either agreed with or acquiesced in the British occupation were placed in a difficult position. This arose from the fact that Britain had never made any formal declaration of her intentions. While she showed as yet no disposition to evacuate Egypt, there was no assurance that some political occurrence might not prompt her to do so. In this case, those who had co-operated with the British would have been left to face the displeasure of an autocratic and anglophobe Khedive. These elements thus found themselves in a quandary as to what attitude they should adopt, the only solution being as far as possible to run with the hare and hunt with the hounds.

So keen was the feeling of unrest that the British garrison was reinforced. It was a good occasion for the malcontent foreign element in Egypt, and we may be sure that the most was made of it. The English classes in the Government schools were gradually deserted, and the scholars crowded the benches of the French instructors.[17]

In January 1894 an opportunity arose for the Khedive to engage in a test of strength with his British co-adjutors and to test his authority. He made a tour of Upper Egypt and visited Wadi Halfa where a review of the garrison was to be held in his honour. Since 1882 the army had been reborn and trained under the direction of British officers, and the Sirdar or Commander in Chief at this time was General Sir Herbert Kitchener. During the review at Wadi Halfa the Khedive expressed his dissatisfaction with the way in which the manoeuvres had been performed, and so biting was his criticism of the army that it was clear that he was attacking the British officers. 'To show the sense of the slight upon his troops, the Sirdar sent in his resignation on the spot.'[18] When the news of this incident reached Lord Cromer in Cairo, he informed Riaz Pasha

> that the censure passed on the British officers of the Egyptian army must be withdrawn, and that the Sirdar must be induced to retract his resignation. Riaz Pasha conveyed this communication to the Khedive and . . . did not hesitate to express his opinion that if His Highness did not give way, the consequences might be serious.[19]

The Khedive was obliged to climb down and to reaffirm his confidence in the command of the army, and the *contretemps* was thus smoothed over, but his humiliation was undoubtedly galling to the autocratic young Khedive and did not help to improve his relations with his British masters. Thereafter the Khedive's antagonism became less overt but by no means diminished.

During the decade following the occupation, Egypt continued to remain, nominally at any rate, part of the Empire of the Sultans, as defined in the firmans of 1841 and those subsequently promulgated. Yet it was evident to the world that the imperial authority over the province was nothing but a shadow, and that it was Britain who held the reins. As head of an empire which, if not actually in the process of disintegration, was steadily losing influence and authority, the Sultan could afford to neglect no opportunity which offered of reasserting himself. During this period such occasions only arose on the death of one Khedive and the accession of another, it being understood that accession to the Khedivate was by virtue of an imperial firman. On the occasion of Abbas Hilmi's accession the Sultan made a further, if abortive, attempt to assert his waning authority by defining the north-eastern boundary of Egypt as a line running from El Arish to Suez, thus excluding the whole of the Sinai peninsula from the domains of the Khedive. This unwarranted contraction of Egypt's territory the British Government were unwilling to tolerate, especially as it would have the effect of bringing the Sultan's soldiers almost to the banks of the Suez Canal. Diplomatic pressure was brought to bear upon the Porte to modify the firman to the extent of re-establishing the former frontiers of Egypt.

From September 1883 to May 1907 Lord Cromer held the post of British Consul General in Egypt. For nearly a quarter of a century, fortified by the presence of the British troops, he moulded and remodelled the entire administration and economy of the country. Egypt finally emerged from the feudalism which had dominated her since the dawn of history into a modern progressive state. The centuries-old system which recognised the Khedive or Pasha as the sole arbiter of fate and the inhabitants as his chattels to dispose of as he wished was swept away; it was replaced by a system which recognised the inhabitant, both high and low, as a human being endowed with human rights and entitled to freedom, justice and equality in the eyes of the law.

In the normal course of events the duties of a diplomatic agent were confined to protecting the interests of his countrymen and carrying out the policy of his government, but so unusual was the position of the British Consul General, Lord Cromer, and so weighty his influence, that he found himself called upon to perform a very varied and even bizarre range of tasks. In his book, *Modern Egypt*, he devotes some pages to listing a few of the peculiar questions with which he was called upon to deal.

> If a young British officer was cheated at cards, I had to get him out of his difficulties. If a slave girl wanted to marry, I had to bring moral pressure on her master or mistress to give their consent. If a Jewish sect wished for official recognition from the Egyptian Government, I was expected to obtain it . . . If the inhabitants of some remote village in Upper Egypt were discontented with their Sheikh, they appealed to me . . . I have been asked to interfere to get a German missionary, who had been guilty of embezzlement, out of prison; in order to get a place for the French and Italian Catholics to bury their dead; in order to get a dead Mohammedan of great sanctity exhumed; in order to prevent a female member of the Khedivial family from striking her husband over the mouth with a slipper; and in order to arrange a marriage between two members of the same family whom hard-hearted relatives kept apart, etc.'[20]

Such incidents, petty though they were, are illustrative of the ascendancy which Lord Cromer exercised over all elements, both native and foreign, which dwelt in the Nile Valley, and much of this ascendancy may be attributed to his own high moral character, his great ability as a diplomat and administrator and perhaps above all to his good sense and knowledge of human nature.

Before he left Egypt in 1907 Lord Cromer was able to see the realisation of his greatest ambition, the liberation of Egypt from the most baneful of the international shackles which had for so long fettered her and impeded her progress and development. Chiefly responsible for these shackles was France who, in her humiliation at having been excluded from taking a hand in the administration of Egypt, had cast every obstacle in the way of the British in their efforts of reform, although during later years there had been some grudging recognition in France that the peace and tranquillity resulting from the British occupation was beneficial to French interests in Egypt. By 1904 the shadow of the German Kaiser was beginning to spread over Europe, and Britain and France tended to draw closer together. At the same time France was beginning to interest herself in Morocco, acquisition of which would give her control over the whole north-west African littoral. The time was thus ripe for a settlement of all outstanding differences between the two great Western powers. On 8 April 1904 an Anglo-French Agreement was concluded which brought to an end all French obstruction and opposition to Britain in Egypt in return for which Britain recognised the freedom of France in Morocco. As far as Egypt was concerned the Agreement had significant consequences. In brief, all restrictions imposed upon the Egyptian Government by the Law of Liquidation and the London Convention of 1885 were swept away; the *Caisse* or Commission of the Public Debt was henceforth debarred from any interference in the Government provided that the amounts requisite to pay the bondholders were forthcoming. The railways, telegraphs, ports and customs whose revenues had hitherto been pledged to the service of the public debt and had therefore been managed by international boards were released from all charges, the general land-tax of the whole country being substituted as security. Henceforth all revenues received by the Government over and above the Tribute and the Debt charges were to be at the entire disposal of the Government. In addition, certain arrangements were made for the conversion and liquidation of some of the debts.

The attitude of France to the new agreement is not without interest. Certainly it was tinged with regret at the final abandonment of the policy of interference in Egypt. Characteristically, even while grudgingly accepting her defeat, France struggled to secure the last piastre for the bondholders. The Egyptian Debt which in 1876 had been scarcely worth the paper the bonds were written on, had during the past twenty years of careful financial administration become so gilt-edged that the French bondholders were loath even to see the debts finally paid off and liquidated. The truth was that the French did not want to give up their bonds; they preferred to hold on to them as long as they could, not only because they were drawing a good dividend, but because they provided them with a pretext, albeit flimsy, for intruding in the affairs of Egypt. Commenting on the Agreement M. de Freycinet writes:

> Le décret khédivial visé dans l'article Ier (of the Agreement) . . . fixe les délais de remboursement facultatif ou de conversion des diverses espèces de dettes. Pour les unes, les dattes fixés par les lois d'émission sont maintenues ou reculées, ce qui est à l'avantage des créanciers, peu desireux, dans l'état actuel du crédit, de se voir remboursés . . . Mais il ne faut pas perdre de vue que le remboursement, s'il effectue dans certaines conditions, peut avoir pour conséquence de faire disparaître prématurément la Caisse de la Dette laquelle est, avec les tribunaux mixtes et les capitulations, le témoin le plus important des droits de l'Europe dans les affaires d'Égypte. Ceci évidemment entraînerait une diminution pour nous.

Surely a sorry admission!

Except in regard to the capitulations and the Mixed Tribunals Egypt was liberated from all other foreign interference than that of Britain whose dominant position in Egypt was now perforce recognised and reluctantly accepted by France. Necessarily the concurrence of the other powers, notably Italy, Austria and Russia, to the proposals had to be secured, but since their financial and political interests in Egypt were negligible in comparison with those of Britain and France, no difficulty was to be expected.

One further development occurred during the stewardship of Lord Cromer of great political importance. The Sudan, which had been abandoned to the power of the Mahdi in 1885, was brought back into the Egyptian fold. This event forms the subject of the following chapter.

CHAPTER 18

Omdurman

It is not the purpose of this work to give any detailed account of Sudan history except in so far as it impinges upon the affairs of Egypt. As has already been related, this great tract of the African continent which had been conquered by Mohammed Ali earlier in the century had been lost to Egypt in 1885, and with the fall of Khartoum the Mahdi had been left the sole arbiter of its destinies. Not content with his great conquests the Mahdi made haste to execute the second stage of his design, the conquest of Egypt. In May 1885 orders were issued for an expedition down the Nile. However, on 20 June the Mahdi suddenly died and this event delayed the forward movement of the dervishes until December. On the 30th of that month a combined British and Egyptian force under the command of Sir Frederick Stephenson met the advancing dervishes at Ginnis about midway between Dongola and Wadi Halfa on the right bank of the Nile. In this encounter the dervishes suffered a bloody defeat and heavy losses. The projected conquest of Egypt was therefore abandoned for the time being; the dervishes retired south, while the Anglo-Egyptian forces moved back to Wadi Halfa, at which point it was decided to hold and defend the frontiers of Egypt.

On the death of the Mahdi command of the dervishes devolved upon his lieutenant, Abdullahi ibn el-Saiyid Mohammed, more generally known as the Khalifa. It was impossible for him completely to replace the Mahdi as he could lay no claim to the religious adoration of his followers, except in so far as he proposed to continue the Mahdi's work. Religious fervour was somewhat dampened and additionally, rivalries tended to spring up between the tribal chiefs and the Khalifa. In consequence the latter was obliged to settle the internal affairs of the Sudan and consolidate his power. In this he was largely successful but in the process some minor portions of the Sudan were allowed to escape from his grasp. European powers snapped up the districts bordering the Red Sea and Indian Ocean, Eritrea and Kassala falling to the Italians, while parts of Somaliland were divided among the British, French and Italians; the Equatorial Province was left almost undisturbed.

Apart from a certain amount of skirmishing and desultory fighting between Osman Digna and the Anglo-Egyptian forces in the neighbourhood of Suakin, which was still held by Egypt, contact was broken for a period of some years after the encounter at Ginnis. During the next four years the Khalifa was busy pacifying his provinces and organising his administration; even so, he never lost sight of the ultimate aim of Mahdism, the conquest of Egypt and the expulsion of the Turks and infidel Europeans. In the middle of the year 1889 the project was once again essayed, and on 1 July the dervishes crossed the Egyptian frontier at Wadi Halfa. Command of the expedition was entrusted to the most courageous of all the dervish emirs, Wad el Nejumi, who burnt his house at Omdurman and vowed that he would never return until he had conquered Egypt. The Egyptian army under the Sirdar, Sir F.W. Grenfell, was ready. By skilful tactics the Sirdar kept the dervish army away from the banks of the Nile as it advanced northward into Egypt, thus preventing the enemy from getting food and water. Although his troops were feeling the fierce pangs of hunger and thirst, Wad el Nejumi continued to press on into Egypt and by 3 August had reached the village of Toski, about eighty miles north of Wadi Halfa. Here on a broad flat plain the dervishes were forced to give battle with the Egyptian troops. As in every encounter with their enemies, the dervishes displayed unparalleled bravery and dash, counting their lives as nothing in the fight for Mahdism. But their courage was not enough to offset the training and discipline of the new Egyptian army. Their charges disintegrated before the wall of fire and steel, and the invasion of Egypt was utterly broken on the field of Toski. Wad el Nejumi perished on the field and even his bodyguard died to a man in defending the body of their chief. Thus ended the last attempt of the dervishes to carry their flag into the land of Egypt. During the ensuing years the Egyptians at Wadi Halfa and the dervishes to the south continued to glare at each other, but neither made any further hostile move.

It is not clear precisely when the idea of reconquering the Sudan was first mooted. It is stated by some that Egypt had never relinquished her claim on the Sudan and had never recognised its independence. The suggestion is therefore that Egypt considered she had withdrawn temporarily but that her rights over the Sudan continued unimpaired, and that as soon as a favourable moment presented itself, she would reoccupy the country and resume the administration. This hypothesis is however difficult to reconcile with the declarations made in 1884 by the Khedive and Nubar Pasha 'who entirely concurred in the wisdom of abandoning the Soudan, retaining possession of Suakin.'[1] Whether any residual rights remained to Egypt over the Sudan would therefore turn on the precise connotation given to the word 'abandon'. In general it must necessarily follow that if a power abandons territory and withdraws in the face of an enemy it is unable to overcome, it automatically abandons any rights to that territory. Rights in any case can only be held by a power which can exercise them physically and effectively. In the case of Egypt and the Sudan during the years following the fall of Khartoum, no matter how loudly the Khedive, or the British Consul General for that matter, might have raised their voices, they would have fallen on deaf ears in the camp of the dervishes at Omdurman. Under the circumstances, to suggest that any rights over the Sudan remained to Egypt would be little more than playing with words. Egypt's claim to the Sudan had rested on the right of conquest, a title which was indisputable and well recognised. But the Sudan had been wrested from her grip by the armies of the Mahdi who now exercised the rights of conquest which were inherited by the Khalifa on his death.

There is however a point of sufficient importance to merit restatement. The Sudan was abandoned by Egypt, not of her own volition, but at the express order of the British Government. It was one of the arguments on the Egyptian side in subsequent disputes that she was forced by Britain to abandon the Sudan, that otherwise she would have continued to hold it. The argument thus enters the realms of hypothesis and must there remain. The question is, could Egypt have held on to the Sudan after the Hicks disaster in 1883, could she have raised another army of sufficient strength and adequate finances to defeat the Mahdi and quell the rebellion? It was the considered opinion of Baring and the British Government that Egypt was not in a position to do so, and that to attempt to do so would only be throwing good money after bad, and that it was in Egypt's own interests that she should be forced to face these facts. It will not perhaps be anticipating this narrative too much to state that the Sudan was eventually reconquered, but it is as well to note that it took two years and the combined resources of Egypt, with a newly trained and equipped army and a healthy exchequer, and of Britain, to defeat an enemy which was less formidable that the fanatical and exultant hordes of the Mahdi had been in 1883 and 1884. It is not therefore unreasonable to draw the conclusion that it was well beyond the powers of Egypt in those years to defeat the Mahdi and hold the Sudan, and that the

British Government was right in insisting on abandonment.

Once the Sudan had been given up Egypt accepted the situation with resignation. In the ensuing years the initiative passed almost entirely to the British Government who, as has been related, assumed the administration of Egypt. It does not appear that any practical proposals emanated from the Egyptian Government that operations should be undertaken with a view to the reconquest of the Sudan and smashing the power of the Mahdi until 1895. There were however thoughts in this direction current in Britain who, though the furore had died down, still smarted at the recollection of her humiliation at the hands of the Mahdi and remembered that the death of her gallant son, General Gordon, remained yet unavenged. During these years stories began to filter out of the Sudan of the oppression and barbarous conduct of the Khalifa's administration and of the terrible depopulation which resulted. Even so the British Government entertained no thoughts of reconquest, for the present at any rate. Lord Cromer reports[2] that in October 1895 the financial situation had been sufficiently restored in Egypt to permit of her either building a dam and creating a reservoir at Aswan or of opening operations for the reconquest of the Sudan. On being approached on this matter the British Government informed Lord Cromer in November that 'there was not any present prospect of the Government consenting to the dispatch of a military expedition into the Soudan, etc.'[3] About four months later, on 12 March 1896, a secret and most urgent telegram was received by Sir Herbert Kitchener, Sirdar of the Egyptian army, at Wadi Halfa direct from the British Government in London, requiring him to advance south and reoccupy Dongola without an hour's delay. Not even the Khedive Abbas was informed of this order issued by the British Government to his army.

Such an extraordinary *volte-face* merits a word of comment. Lord Cromer, in his explanation of this sudden move, is unconvincing and evasive, no doubt intentionally so. The Italians who had previously occupied Massawah, Kassala and Adowa were being pressed by King Menelik of Abyssinia and the Mahdists who were said to be co-operating in driving the Italians from these territories. On the defeat of the Italian forces at Adowa, the Italian Ambassador in London appealed to the British Government to create a diversion, presumably with the intention of drawing off some of the pressure of the enemy. This explanation is hardly acceptable for how could an advance on Dongola have any appreciable effect on operations which were going on at Kassala four hundred miles away, or at Adowa nearly twice that distance? The reasons for the sudden decision to advance into the Sudan must be sought elsewhere.

The scramble for Africa was in full swing. Those areas of the still dark continent which had not yet been snapped up were the subject of fierce rivalries among the colonial powers of Europe. In East Africa Germany was busy converting Tanganika into a colony, while the British were penetrating from Mombasa towards Lake Victoria and Uganda; the Italian penetration into certain areas of the eastern Sudan has already been noted; France occupied a great tract west of the Sudan and in equatorial Africa, and the Belgians were in the Congo. Thus with a few exceptions the whole of the great continent was either directly under the control of the European powers or recognised as within their respective 'spheres of influence'. But the Sudan, where the Khalifa and his native tribal chiefs still held sway, remained inviolate. So intense was the scramble for Africa that it was even deemed advisable on occasion to make more or less formal agreements defining their spheres of influence. In 1890 a convention was framed between Britain and Germany to regulate their zones in eastern Africa. In this convention the Upper Nile Basin was placed within the British sphere as far as the boundaries of Egypt, and again in 1894 a further agreement was made between Britain and the Belgians of the Congo Free State with similar objectives. Under this latter agreement a certain area on the Equatorial Nile known as the Lado Enclave was leased out to the Congo Free State.

To both these agreements France took the strongest exception. For the first time in a century France started talking about the rights of the Sultan, for did not these arrangements dispose of areas of the Sudan, and was not that country part of the Ottoman Empire? The simple facts were that the Sudan had been a sort of sub-empire of Egypt which was in turn a nominal province of the Ottoman domains. To that extent the Sultan had been theoretically entitled to regard the Sudan as within his domains, but it was recognised the world over that the Sultan's authority in respect of the Sudan had been so tenuous as to be negligible; certainly no Turkish soldier ever set foot on the banks of the Upper Nile as the emissary of His Imperial Majesty, and no governor held his commission direct from Constantinople. Prior to 1885 the Sudan had been the private reserve of the Khedive of Egypt. The Khedive had now willy-nilly evacuated it and with the evacuation the Sultan's rights over the Sudan had become even more shadowy than ever.

However, in this instance it suited France to make the best use of whatever pretexts were available, flimsy though they were. Since such protests as France was able to put forward were barren of result, she shifted her ground somewhat in 1895. M. Hanotaux the French Foreign Minister stated:

294

Les régions dont il s'agit sont sous la haute souveraineté du Sultan. Elles ont un maître légitime, c'est le Khédive. Quand l'heure sera venue de fixer les destinées définitives de ces contrées lointaines, je suis de ceux qui pensent qu'en assurant le respect des droits du Sultan et du Khédive, en réservant à chacun ce qui lui appartiendra selon ses oeuvres, deux grands nations sauront trouver les formules propres à concilier leurs intérêts et à satisfaire leurs communes aspirations vers la civilisation et le progrès.[4]

From this declaration of policy it may be gathered that France did not now consider herself precluded from occupying territories over which the Sultan and Khedive were recognised to possess rights, and that the first comer had the right of occupation. Nor was this a mere academic statement for in 1896 Major Marchand was commissioned to lead a small 'exploratory' expedition from French Equatorial Africa across the continent to Fashoda on the Upper Nile. He arrived at Loango on the Atlantic coast in July and pressed forward with his mission without delay.

The intentions of France could not remain hidden from the British Government. As long as the Sudan lay in the declining power of the dervishes there was no urgent need for any forward action. Britain's primary interest was in Egypt, and as long as the Sudan was held by a primitive and barbaric people who had been proved to be incapable of disturbing their northern neighbour, there was no cause for alarm. Sooner or later a convenient opportunity would offer itself of picking up the Sudan cheaply and restoring it to the Egyptian fold. But the occupation of the Sudan by another European power, especially France, would radically alter the situation, for it was well recognised that whoever occupied the Upper Nile Valley could exercise a stranglehold on Egypt. The life blood of Egypt, the Nile, flowed from the Sudan, but the precious waters could be dammed, diverted or played with in any way by a power possessing sufficient technical skill. France who had for the past thirteen years done everything in her power to obstruct and frustrate the British in Egypt could well be expected to prove a most fertile source of embarrassment if she obtained control of the waters of the Upper Nile. The only possible way of circumventing a French occupation was to occupy the territory first. The reasons behind the sudden and secret telegram to Kitchener thus become clear. Britain and Egypt must make a forward move into the Sudan and establish that first right of occupancy which figured in French declarations of policy. Clear too become the reasons why the apparent discourtesy was committed of not consulting the Khedive about the projected advance beforehand. Had any mention been made of the proposal in Cairo, beyond doubt the news would have leaked out immediately and been flashed to Paris.

That the move was considered of the greatest urgency is amply supported by the fact that little, if any, consideration was given in the British Cabinet's councils to the financial aspect of the operation beyond the presumption that the expenses would, and should, be borne by the Egyptian Government. There must even have been an element of panic in the sudden decision, since a moment's reflection would have reminded the British Government that even though Egypt's finances were at last flourishing, they were bound by international shackles, and not a piastre could be spent upon any 'unauthorised' account without the concurrence of the *Caisse* of the Debt. As was to be expected France was secretly mortified at having been once again outmanoeuvred, but she had a powerful lever in the presence of her own representative on the *Caisse* which she did not hesitate to use. As soon as the expedition under Kitchener moved forward from Wadi Halfa, an application was made by the Egyptian Government for the release of £500,000 from the General Reserve for the prosecution of the war. The voting was four to two in favour of authorising the release, the two dissidents being characteristically France and Russia. It was decided by the Commissioners that the majority decision should prevail and the money was accordingly paid over to the Egyptian Government. Immediately the dissident Commissioners brought an action in the Mixed Tribunals demanding repayment of the money to the *Caisse* on the ground that the unanimous consent of the Commissioners was necessary for the authorisation of the release.

The findings of the Court delivered on 8 June 1896 upheld the plaintiffs and required the Government to repay the money. But the delays in legal process for once came to the assistance of the Egyptian Government; an appeal was lodged which was not heard until December. Although the Court of Appeal upheld the lower court's judgment, by this time the damage had been done and the Egyptians were in possession of Dongola. The French scheme to prevent the campaign into the Sudan thus proved a total failure or achieved at most a Pyrrhic victory. However the Court had directed that the money should be repaid to the *Caisse*; the Egyptian Government had not now got the money; it had been spent on the campaign. The Government were placed in a difficult position but were happily rescued by the British Consul General, Lord Cromer, who, having anticipated the decision of the Court of Appeal, had made arrangements with the British Government for a loan of £800,000 to Egypt at 2¾%.[5] This enabled Egypt to repay the *Caisse*.

It may be added that the French Government, hearing of the proposed loan from Britain, did their best to prevent the transaction but without success. Too late they realised that they had unwittingly once again strengthened the position of Britain in Egypt.

Malgré les méritoires efforts de notre diplomatie, il ne tourna pas, sous le rapport pratique, à notre avantage. L'expédition militaire à laquelle nous nous étions opposés pour des raisons non seulement financières mais politiques, s'était faite malgré nous . . . et notre succès devant les tribunaux mixtes n'eut d'autre resultat que de faire verser les sommes par Angleterre elle-même et de lui mettre un titre de plus entre les mains.[6]

It is particularly noteworthy that although the decision to penetrate the Sudan was taken in London, it was expressly intended that the operation should be undertaken by the Egyptian army in the name of the Khedive and that the expenses should be defrayed from Egyptian funds. There was not the slightest suggestion that Britain should participate in any way whatever; on the other hand it was clearly intended that Egypt should herself act with the object of regaining the territory she had lost to the Mahdi eleven years previously.

From a technical point of view the reconquest of the Nile Valley as far as Dongola was not particularly noteworthy, but the campaign was remarkable to the extent that it illustrated the great importance of adequate supply and transport arrangements. The operation was successful largely because the commander of the force was a martinet for detail, especially in regard to supply and transport. Sir Herbert Kitchener, the Sirdar, an engineer by training and possessed of unrivalled knowledge of the requirements of operations in the Nile Valley, paid painstaking attention to every detail and as far as was humanly possible left nothing to chance. The railway was extended from Saras southward as the army advanced. As it approached Akasha a large force of dervishes was waiting at Firket a few miles further south. Battle was given on 7 June in which the dervishes were utterly defeated. Marching along the right bank of the Nile the Egyptian force pressed on and finally occupied Dongola on 23 September. Kitchener had now fulfilled his instructions and the campaign was over. Battle casualties had been almost negligible although cholera and other hardships had taken some toll. Expenses amounted to about £700,000, a modest sum for the re-acquisition of Dongola and 450 miles of the river.

At last a blow had been struck at the dervishes and much territory regained, but the power of the Khalifa was by no means overthrown. Only his outposts had been assaulted and it was reckoned that no long period would elapse before he would retaliate. The Egyptian forces at Dongola stood at the end of a line of communications over a thousand miles long and could only be supplied and reinforced with some difficulty. Moreover, the presence of the Egyptians at Dongola would have no political or military significance if the French expedition across central Africa reached the Upper Nile and claimed the territory it could occupy. There was every reason for pressing on and carrying the war into the Khalifa's camp at Omdurman. The time had now come for a concerted effort to overthrow the Khalifa and restore the Sudan to Egypt. Kitchener therefore returned to Egypt to press these views on the British Government.[7] His listeners were sympathetic; the war had so far been cheap, profitable and popular; the projected campaign looked equally easy. In December 1896 Kitchener returned to the Sudan to put in hand the new campaign.

The operation offered obstacles of no mean order. Before him stretched the winding course of the great waterway broken by shallows, rapids and cataracts which could only be passed during flood time, and great expanses of desert, rock and mountain. Throughout the hundreds of miles that lay between the Egyptians at Dongola and the Khalifa at Omdurman the dervishes could be expected to offer bitter opposition to their advance, and no reliance could be placed on finding any food or provisions on the way. Finally, at Omdurman itself, the whole weight of the Khalifa's fearless army would be awaiting any force that penetrated so far. Clearly this was going to be an operation of the first magnitude, calling for the most careful planning and preparation. Kitchener decided that it should be no mad dash through unknown dangers to Omdurman, as had been the relief expedition twelve years earlier, but a deliberate and consolidating advance, the route and lines of communication to be systematically built up as the advance proceeded. The S-shaped course of the river offered a number of alternative routes each with its own advantages and disadvantages, and Kitchener finally decided to cross the great loop between Wadi Halfa and Abu Hamed by bridging this gap with a railway, and then follow the river to Omdurman.

The building of the railway thus became the essential preliminary to the new campaign, but some months elapsed before it could be taken in hand. It was started in May 1897 and during the next four months the permanent way was laid down at a rapid pace. Before it could be completed the village of Abu Hamed had to be cleared of the enemy and it was taken with comparative ease in August. In this campaign, as in the days of Gordon's heroic defence, the key to Khartoum and the Sudan was Berber which, though insignificant in itself, stood astride the only approach from the north and also the main road to Suakin in the east. Yet for some unexplained reason the Khalifa neglected to garrison this vital junction effectively. In fact, the commander of the garrison, Zaki Osman, evacuated the town and fell back to the Atbara even before the Egyptians could arrive, and the town was occupied unopposed by forty Ababda camelmen on 31 August.[8]

Throughout the campaign so far the Khalifa appears to have remained inert, relying on the defences of the various garrisons to beat off the invading Egyptians. Yet golden opportunities must have abounded for swift and bold raiding parties, well mounted and lightly armed, of descending upon the extended line, cutting communications, killing stragglers, destroying or capturing stores, or harassing the relatively small Egyptian force. Yet the Khalifa took no notice of these opportunities, perhaps pinning his faith to the belief that the invaders would be annihilated on the field of Omdurman.

After the capture of Berber some considerable pause was necessary to enable Kitchener to consolidate his gains and bring up reinforcements. As yet the railway had not reached Abu Hamed and his hold on the captured villages was weak. Even a small force of dervishes could have ejected the Egyptians without much difficulty, and it is incomprehensible that they did not make the attempt. The railway finally reached Abu Hamed on the last day of October, and during the following months the sleepy village became a bustling forward supply depot and concentration area. So far, the new Egyptian army had exceeded all expectations in its performance in the field. The soldiers had performed prodigious feats in building the railway, sometimes laying as much as a mile a day, and they had shown themselves steadfast and resolute in the face of the enemy. But the total strength of the Egyptian army was small, comprising only a few battalions, and it was manifest that unaided it would not be able to vanquish the hordes of dervishes who awaited them upstream at Atbara and Omdurman; reinforcement would be essential. Lord Cromer had already informed Kitchener that he could count on the assistance of British battalions for the final assault on the dervish fortress, and accordingly, on 1 January 1898, the Sirdar submitted a request for a British brigade, a regiment of cavalry and a battery of guns.

His forecast of the force which would be necessary was wonderfully accurate. The force which eventually advanced on Khartoum was precisely identical with that which Sir Herbert Kitchener specified early in January 1898. To have advanced with a smaller force would have been dangerous. A larger force would have been unwieldy, and its employment would have increased the difficulties of supply and transport.[9]

In the early months of the new year the bulk of the army moved forward to Berber preparatory to the final push up the Nile to Omdurman.

In the meantime a large force of dervishes under the emir Mahmud had begun to move forward down the left bank of the river. Arrived at Metemmeh it crossed over to Shendy and after a further advance downstream to Aliab it struck off inland to the Atbara where it crossed over to the north bank at Nakheila and pitched camp. On receipt of information regarding the dervish advance Kitchener brought his forces out of Berber and up to the Atbara to meet them. After a few days reconnaissance Kitchener decided to attack the enemy who had by now entrenched themselves behind a strong stockade. The battle of the Atbara took place on 8 June 1898. While it lasted the battle was fierce and bitterly contested and casualties on both sides were heavy, but the Anglo-Egyptian army was victorious. 'Mahmud himself was captured, 3000 of his army were killed, and the remainder dissolved in rout.'[10]

After a further three months of consolidation and reinforcement Kitchener began the final advance on the dervish stronghold at Omdurman. On 1 September he arrived on the plain between the Kerreri Hills and Omdurman about six miles north of the fortress where the full strength of the Khalifa's armies stood poised for battle. The epic struggle which took place on the following day, 2 September, has been too often narrated to warrant repetition in detail. The dervishes outnumbered the Anglo-Egyptian forces by about three to one, but they were armed mostly with spears, swords and sticks; such guns and rifles as they possessed were obsolete and unserviceable. On several occasions on that historic day the Allies were in difficulties and the situation approached the critical, but the discipline and valour of the troops and their tactical handling by the commander got them out of difficulties. The great battle started at dawn and finished before midday. By that time the dervishes were completely defeated and put to flight; the Khalifa himself was a refugee in the tangled bush.

'The honour of the fight . . . must still go with the men who died. Our men were perfect, but the Dervishes were superb – beyond perfection. It was their largest, best and bravest army that ever fought against us for Mahdiism, and it died worthily of the huge empire that Mahdiism won and kept so long. Their riflemen, mangled by every kind of death and torment that man can devise, clung round the black flag and the green, emptying their poor rotten home-made cartridges dauntlessly. Their spearmen charged death at every minute hopelessly . . . A dusky line got up and stormed forward; it bent, broke up, fell apart and disappeared. Before the smoke had cleared, another line was bending and storming forward in the same track.'[11]

Where the dervish casualties amounted to nearly 30,000 in killed and wounded on that day of carnage, the British and Egyptian losses did not amount to one hundredth part of this terrible total.

Within a few days of the battle of Omdurman, news reached Kitchener, conveyed by a Mahdist steamer from the south, that a foreign expedition commanded by white officers was encamped on the banks of the Nile at Fashoda, about 470 miles south of Khartoum. Kitchener realised that this was probably Major Marchand's expedition which was known to have set out from the west coast of the continent two years before. Here was a situation fraught with the gravest dangers not only for the Sudan, but for the peace of Europe. Kitchener resolved to go himself and interview the strangers. On 18 September he was sufficiently close to Fashoda to send a message forward announcing his arrival – a prudent move designed to prevent any outburst or exchange of fire between the two parties. The following day Kitchener and Marchand met. Both commanders were struck with the vital necessity for discretion; both were soldiers acting under the instructions of their respective governments and were bound to carry them out to the best of their ability. The *pourparlers* that took place on Kitchener's steamer were therefore marked with a great show of courtesy and amity on both sides, Kitchener complimenting Marchand on his spectacular feat in trekking across the African continent, the Frenchman likewise offering his congratulations on Kitchener's victory at Omdurman. They explained to each other their instructions, which were substantially identical, i.e. Marchand to plant the French flag over Fashoda and the Bahr el Ghazal, and Kitchener to hoist the Egyptian flag over the whole of the Nile Valley. Both commanders were wise enough to agree to allow their respective governments to decide the issue, and for the time being both French and Egyptian flags were flown within a short distance of each other.

During the next two months the dispute was argued back and forth between London and Paris, and public opinion on both sides became inflamed. The possession of a few wretched villages in the desolate fastnesses of Africa became a point of minor importance in comparison with the national honour and prestige that were involved; all the pent-up bitterness of France against Britain for having bested her in Egypt and the Sudan, and British irritation at France's policy of obstruction in Egypt found vent. For a moment the situation became tense and in France there was even talk of war. The British Government viewed these threats with composure. Her armies stood in strength on the White Nile and could eject the handful of French troops without difficulty. Furthermore they knew that however much French public opinion might rave against the insult to her national honour, France was in no position to go to war over such a minor issue. Her position in Europe was far too precarious and isolated for her to risk a clash of arms with the country she might need for an ally. Thus, after allowing sufficient time for public clamour to cool, France yielded and abandoned all claim to territory lying within the Valley of the Nile. As has already been related the long-standing rivalry between the two nations was finally brought to a happy conclusion in the Anglo-French Agreement of 1904.

With the battle of Omdurman, Mahdism in the Sudan crumbled in the dust. The Khalifa himself, at the head of the remnants of his followers, escaped capture for over a year in the fastnesses of Kordofan until on 24 November 1899 he was brought to battle not far from Abba Island, from which the Mahdi had launched his great crusade twenty years earlier, and perished. Thus ended the régime of Mahdism in the Sudan; the remainder of the great territory was quickly and easily pacified and the whole country was once more brought back within the Egyptian fold, but with modifications.

The circumstances surrounding the campaign of reconquest produced problems of some complexity when the time came to consider precisely what was to be done with the Sudan now that it had been regained. The first campaign to Dongola had been ordered by the British Government, but it had been carried out entirely by the Egyptian army in the name of the Khedive and at Egyptian expense. The action of the British Government in authorising the campaign was consistent with the role which they had assumed of 'offering advice' to the Egyptian Government. In giving the word to advance, the British Government had had no intention of acting on their own account or of obtaining any position of authority in the Sudan in excess of that which they already exercised in Egypt. Although evacuation was still as shadowy as ever there is no doubt that, had such evacuation taken place then, the gains which Egypt had made as far as Dongola would have been left to the Egyptian Government.

The decision to continue the advance as far as Khartoum and to annihilate the power of the dervishes somewhat altered the position in detail, but not in principle. The new campaign was still to be an essentially Egyptian operation with Egyptian troops and Egyptian piastres. Yet it seemed probable that with her present resources Egypt would be unable to find the means to complete the campaign. Her army, though it had proved itself beyond all expectation, was still too small numerically to overcome the dervishes; financially Egypt would have been well able to meet the expense but for the fact that nearly all her reserves were in the jealous and miserly hands of the Commissioners of the Debt. To ensure the success of the operation Lord Cromer had offered the Sirdar the assistance of British troops and these were employed in the final assaults on the dervishes. The British Treasury likewise advanced £800,000 of the £2,354,000 which was the cost of the campaign. A point worthy of consideration is the fact that no formal agreement had ever been suggested that the Sudan campaign should be a joint venture of Egypt and Britain, each providing equal forces and equal finances. It was clearly the intention of the British Government that it should be an entirely Egyptian venture to which Britain would afford assistance, if necessary. Lord Cromer confirms this view in stating:

> The conditions under which the campaign was conducted were, in fact, very peculiar. In official circles it was dubbed 'a Foreign Office War.' For a variety of reasons . . . the Sirdar was, from the commencement of the operations, placed exclusively under my orders in all matters. The War Office assumed no responsibility and issued no orders.[12]

It is unlikely that the future administration of the Sudan after a successful conclusion to the campaign had received adequate consideration. The precipitation with which the venture was undertaken supports the view that the general policy was to reconquer the country before any other European nation entrenched itself on the Upper Nile, and to worry about the details of administration afterwards, but it was generally understood that the intention was to restore to the Khedive the domains he had been forced to abandon thirteen years earlier.

Sooner or later some thought had to be given to this important question, and with his usual political foresight Lord Cromer had determined his line of action even before the campaign was brought to a successful conclusion. The simple solution which would have been in keeping with the intentions of the British Government would have been to hand back the Sudan to the Khedive while at the same time providing certain safeguards against mis-government and a resurgence of rebellion. In the opinion of Lord Cromer however this policy was open to a number of objections which could not be ignored. 'If,' he points out, 'the political status of the Soudan were to be assimilated in all respects to that of Egypt, the necessary consequence would be that the administration of the country would be burthened by the introduction of the Capitulations and, in fact, by all the cumbersome paraphernalia of internationalism which had done so much to retard Egyptian progress.'[13] On this ground the simple solution was held to be unsatisfactory. A more important point which led to its rejection was the fact that it in no way gave recognition to the substantial part which Britain had played in regaining the Sudan. A true imperialist, Lord Cromer could not endure the thought that Britain should receive no reward for her outlay of men and material in the campaign. He was determined that not only should Britain have some say in the future of the Sudan, but also that she should have the chief say. It cannot be denied that these sentiments, patriotic though they were, tended to sway the great Consul's reasoning.

> It is true that the Egyptian Treasury had borne the greater proportion of the cost and that Egyptian troops, officered however by Englishmen, had taken a very honourable part in the campaign. But alike during the period of the preparation and of the execution of the policy the guiding hand had been that of England. It is absurd to suppose that without British assistance in the form of men, money and general guidance, the Egyptian Government could have conquered the Soudan. From this point of view therefore the annexation of the reconquered territories by England would have been partially justifiable. There were, however, some weighty arguments against the adoption of this course. In the first place, although in the Anglo-Egyptian partnership England was unquestionably the senior partner, at the same time Egypt had played a very useful, albeit auxiliary part in the joint undertaking, etc.[14]

These arguments were tantamount to damning with faint praise Egypt's part in the war. True it was that the officers were Englishmen, but they were in the service of the Khedive and received their pay from the Egyptian Government; their loyalties and duties lay to the government they served. In this particular instance England had not really been the guiding hand, for as Lord Cromer points out, 'the War Office assumed no responsibility and issued no orders.' The guiding hand in this case was Lord Cromer himself and Sir Herbert Kitchener, Sirdar of the Egyptian Army and servant of the Egyptian Government. While it may be said that Lord Cromer was himself a servant of the British Government, he was in Egypt for the special purpose of guiding the Egyptian Government and promoting and protecting the interests of the Egyptian people. It is scant praise and hardly in accordance with the facts to state that 'Egypt had played a very useful and honourable, albeit auxiliary part in the joint undertaking'. Egypt in fact provided two-thirds of the money and men and was in action throughout the campaign, while the British contingent took no active part until the battle of the Atbara in March 1898. The presence of the British troops was only required to strengthen the Egyptian forces and ensure success of the campaign. The argument may most fairly be settled by stating that in the long run both elements were necessary for success. At any rate an outright annexation of the Sudan by Britain could not have been under any circumstances even partially justifiable. This would have been an act of vandalism and a grievous breach of good faith which would have shocked the world and shattered all belief in the minds of Egyptians about the good intentions of the British towards them.

Thus, while unable entirely to repress his imperialistic bent, Lord Cromer wisely refrained from outright annexation. Instead he set himself to frame a political status for the Sudan which, while it gave an apparent recognition and authority to the Khedive, vested the entire executive power in the British Government. In the creation of the Condominium Agreement Lord Cromer displayed a skill and dexterity which has rarely been surpassed. The text of this Agreement is reproduced in the Appendix. Its clauses regulated the status of the Sudan from the time of its signature on 19 January 1899 until 1953. The essence of an agreement is that it is entered into freely and willingly by the parties concerned, but it is more than doubtful whether the Egyptian Government felt well disposed towards the agreement which was placed before them for signature. There was no negotiation, no discussion regarding its clauses. Lord Cromer informs us that it was prepared under his instructions by Sir Malcolm McIlwraith the Judicial Adviser.[15] It was then merely placed before the Egyptian Government for signature. Inasmuch as they and their country were still in the grip of the occupying power the Egyptian Government had little alternative. A refusal to accept the terms of the Agreement would probably have resulted in the outright annexation of the Sudan to Britain, and Egypt excluded entirely from any participation. The Agreement as it stood, although it left Egypt shorn of any executive power, at least recognised to a certain extent the suzerainty of the Khedive. In short it left Egypt with a footing which might possibly be strengthened in years to come. At the same time the glory of victory glossed over the lack of equity, but a dispassionate appraisal of the Agreement must condemn it as a discreditable move on the part of the British.

It will be seen from the clauses of the Agreement that the jurisdiction of the Mixed Tribunals was not to be recognised in the Sudan (Article 8), and that no foreign consular officials would be allowed to reside there without the consent of the British Government (Article 10). It was Cromer's justification for the Condominium Agreement that it prevented the capitulations and 'all the cumbersome paraphernalia of internationalism which had done so much to retard Egyptian progress' from taking root in the reconquered country. Yet it would have been quite easy to prevent these diseases spreading into the Sudan by a simple declaration to that effect. Certain it is that none of the capitulatory powers would have objected. They were much puzzled by the hybrid Condominium, a system of government and a political status hitherto unknown, but they accepted it nonetheless. Much more easily would they have accepted an uncomplicated sovereignty of the Khedive tempered by British guidance, and a total prohibition of all foreign influence and foreign rights in the Sudan. None of them were in any position to make any claims in a land which had just been reclaimed from barbarism by the arms of Britain and Egypt, and none would have done so. However, although the Condominium was founded on a breach of faith, it was beneficial to the Sudanese people. Its practical results were that they were brought under the guidance of a nation which was well fitted to promote their interests and welfare, to evolve order out of chaos and to replace anarchy with peace, justice and good government.

CHAPTER 19

The New Nationalism

The years immediately subsequent to the occupation were devoted to the grim struggle against bankruptcy and to general rehabilitation after the hard years of Ismail Pasha, the exhaustions of the Arabi Rebellion and the Revolt in the Sudan. At this time the necessity for making the annual payments and wringing the means of life, however scanty, from the soil dominated every activity and thought of the Egyptian people and left them little time or inclination to reflect on the political condition of their country. To the native cultivator and smallholder the domination of the British masters was undoubtedly welcome, for at least he knew where he stood with them; he knew that once his taxes were paid he would not be asked for them again, that he would receive his proper share of the precious waters of the Nile and, perhaps most important of all, he would not be arbitrarily seized and dragged away from his fields for service with the hated army.

The *pasha* class recognised the firm hand of the British Agent and the power of his supporting arm, the British army of occupation. While they chafed somewhat at the restraints placed upon them from following their traditional calling, the spoliation of the poor, at the same time they also recognised the advantages of not being despoiled themselves by avaricious *khedives* or rebellious troops. By about 1890 the corner was finally turned and the threat of national bankruptcy began to recede further and further into the distance; memories of the former years of turmoil, strife and exaction began to grow dim; the *courbash* was a thing of the past; the *corvée* had disappeared; the luxuriant soil of the Nile Valley, responding to peace and loving care, was once again yielding its abundance. A sense of relief and recuperation pervaded the land and it was now possible for men to turn their minds for a moment from the grim necessities of daily toil and take stock of their position.

An inevitable and perhaps beneficial concomitant of the national revival was an increase in political consciousness. In the early years the British occupation was accepted with the traditional resignation of the Orient, especially as the repeated declarations of the British Government and eminent politicians stressed its provisional and temporary character, but with the passage of the years it became increasingly evident that there was not, nor likely to be, any sign of its termination. As long as Tewfik Pasha sat on the throne the rumblings of discontent were subdued, but the advent of the anglophobe Abbas II gave a strong impetus to the incipient revolt against British domination. The new Khedive's trial of strength with Lord Cromer has already been noted, and the humiliation he experienced on that occasion continued to rankle in his breast. Consequently, although he proceeded more circumspectly thereafter, he refrained from using his influence to restrain the anti-British movement which was born in the latter years of the century.

From 1882 until 1904 the foreign press in Egypt, the French particularly, protected from interference by the capitulations, poured forth a stream of abuse on the British occupying power and upon any Egyptian Government or dignitary who showed any sign of co-operating. The native Egyptian press, taking due note, began to do likewise, at first cautiously and then more openly when they perceived that the occupying power did not intend to retaliate. It was one of the anomalies of the British occupation that the British, while insisting on the Egyptian Government deferring to their advice and not hesitating to remove anyone who refused, placed no check on the native press which was capable of inflaming public opinion against them. Undoubtedly it was the long tradition of the freedom of the press, an article of faith in British life, which prevented the occupying power from taking any action. Consequently the occupation became more and more unpopular as time passed. A number of factors contributed to this growing sentiment. The British, according to their own declarations, had come to teach the Egyptians how to govern themselves, yet after twenty years they had shown no inclination to relax their tutelage and hand over the reins of government to those whom they professed to teach. On the contrary, the tendency lay in the opposite direction. In the early years of the occupation a mere handful of carefully selected British officials had been recruited to assist in the reorganisation of Egypt, but during the latter years of Lord Cromer's tenure of office and after his resignation the number of British officials increased considerably, and in a number of cases it appears that quality was sacrificed to quantity. The Egyptian Civil Service was rapidly becoming a pleasant and even luxurious harbour for many young men from the English public schools, who became as much addicted to the social attractions and pleasures of the big cities as to the work of promoting the welfare of the people of Egypt. This decline in the quality of the British official accelerated rapidly during the years between Lord Cromer's departure in 1907 and the outbreak of war in 1914.

At the same time a new generation of Egyptians was rising, better able to take a part in the administration of their country. Lord Cromer himself wrote, 'As to the governing capacity of the Egyptian Ministers and their subordinates, a steady improvement has been going on for a quarter of a century. A very fair standard of honesty and capacity prevailed. The future was bright with the hope of further progress in this direction.' But the new generation of Egyptians found all promotion to the senior grades of the civil service blocked by the presence of an increasing number of young Britons whose sole qualification for their posts was the fact that they had been to a good public school. Moreover, the pay of the average native civil servant was wretchedly inadequate, and it was no wonder that some of them occasionally resorted to peculation to augment their salaries, a practice which was seized on by the British officials as evidence that the Egyptians were as yet unfit to govern themselves.

In former years the small band of Britons had worked in close co-operation with their Egyptian counterparts and had in most cases become on terms of cordial friendship with them. The majority made a serious effort to learn the intricate Arabic language and were thus able to communicate freely and easily with the people. The new swarm of young men from England were less conscientious and began to live in the little British enclave on the Gezireh and thus lost the valuable contacts so carefully built up by their predecessors. The Egyptians, a quick-witted and highly sensitive people, were quick to note this rapid change in British officialdom and felt, and no doubt rightly felt, that the spirit of the disinterestedness which had motivated England in early years was now fast disappearing.

This combination of circumstances gave birth to a new spirit of nationalism, a sentiment nurtured in the hearts of the people by the falling-off of their British mentors. A patient and docile people generally, the Egyptians had accepted the situation with resignation as long as the occupation was declared to be only temporary, but the 1904 Anglo-French Agreement made it abundantly plain that its temporary character was likely to continue into the remote future. Certain it was that Britain would never of her own volition lay down her charge; some form of coercion would be necessary.

Egyptian nationalism in the early years of the century tended to develop along two lines and found expression in the birth of two political parties. The Hisb-el-Umma or Party of the Nation contained what may be called the moderate element, those who looked forward to the emancipation of Egypt from foreign tutelage, but who considered that the road to freedom lay to a great extent in co-operation with the British administration and in the gradual transfer of power from British to Egyptian hands. The policy of the Party was not therefore in conflict with the declared aim of the British Government, reaffirmed on several occasions during the previous two decades, of leading the Egyptians to self-government. It was not unnatural therefore that Lord Cromer smiled benevolently on the Hisb-el-Umma and took an interest in its activities. Prominent among the leading spirits was Saad Zaghlul Pasha, a man of *fellah* origin who by his abilities and character had commended himself to the great Consul. Lord Cromer had selected him for the post of Minister in the newly reconstructed Ministry of Education, and in his farewell speech on leaving Egypt in 1907 had predicted a great future for him.

> Unless I am much mistaken, a career of great usefulness lies before the present Minister of Education, Saad Zaghlul Pasha. He possesses all the qualities necessary to serve his country. He is honest; he is capable; he has the courage of his convictions; he has been abused by many of the less worthy of his countrymen. These are high qualifications. He should go far.[1]

Lord Cromer, not usually prone to political predictions, was singularly accurate in this particular case. Zaghlul Pasha became well connected politically by his marriage to the daughter of Mustafa Fehmi Pasha who had for some years been Prime Minister and close collaborator of Lord Cromer.

The other nationalist element was represented by the Hisb-el-Watan or Patriotic Party, undisguisedly hostile to the British occupation and British tutelage 'due to a mixture of causes ranging from sincere fanatical patriotism, through all the degrees of political grievance, to an unashamed ambition to return to the *status quo ante*.'[2] Through the medium of its newspaper *El Lewa* its leaders Mustafa Kamel and Sheikh Shawish conducted a continuous crusade against the British occupation and called for the creation of a constitution and popular representation. The principal aim of the Hisb-el-Watan was the overthrow of the traditional rule of the Turkish *pasha*, i.e. the Khedive and his Ministers, and the substitution of a popularly elected parliament expressing the will of the nation. To that extent the Party was the legitimate successor of the movement created and led by Arabi Pasha.

Still the most influential power in Egyptian politics was His Highness the

Khedive Abbas, and the attitude he adopted was typical of the traditional Turkish *pasha*. Abbas believed in the divine right of kings and *khedives*; he resented any curbs placed on his autocratic powers; he looked, not to the example of his father, but to that of his grandfather Ismail; he schemed and intrigued to divest himself of the yoke placed upon him by Lord Cromer; he hated the Egyptian Ministers who collaborated with the British in the administration of the country. His antipathy fell largely on the Prime Minister, Mustafa Fehmi Pasha and his son-in-law Zaghlul Pasha. The only element which openly expressed hatred for the British was the Patriotic Party of Mustafa Kamel, and it was to this that the Khedive offered his tacit support. Thus, by one of those paradoxes which pervaded the land of the Nile, the Khedive, who was working for the restoration of his own untrammelled power, lent his support and influence to the party which had for its principal aim the sweeping away of all autocratic powers and personal rule as typified by the Khedive. But Abbas was by no means devoid of political acumen. He believed, probably with some justification, that once he could divest himself of British supervision, he could without difficulty sweep away all nationalism and constitutionalism and bring the whole country under his personal sway. The Nationalist Party was simply a tool, a means to an end, to be discarded as soon as that end was achieved.

Mustafa Kamel and his followers gathered under their banner many of the discontented and genuinely patriotic elements in the country; but they could make little impression on the vast mass of the population, the *fellahin* who on the whole were fairly well content with the existing order of things. The majority of these, when they thought about it at all, recognised that it was the British irrigation officers and others they had to thank for the fair and plenteous distribution of the Nile waters and for the curb placed upon rapacious tax-gatherers. What the Patriotic Party most needed was some means of whipping up prejudice among the *fellahin* against the British administration. In 1906 the British obligingly furnished them with the weapon they had so ardently sought.

The Denshawi Incident occurred in June 1906 when Lord Cromer was absent in England on holiday. A party of British officers went out one day shooting near the village of Denshawi. It appears that during the sport the officers shot some pigeons which were the property of the villagers. This led to a heated altercation between the officers and the villagers which was aggravated by the fact that the officers were unable to understand or make themselves understood to the peasants.[3] A scuffle ensued in which two British officers were badly wounded and one subsequently died. The incident

in itself was quite insignificant; it was clearly the outcome of a misunderstanding which would probably have been avoided had the officers been
able to speak Arabic. But the British administration, lacerated by the repeated
attacks of the native press, chose to see in it a demonstration of political
aversion and a symptom of rebellion. They determined to take strong
measures, presumably with some idea of strengthening British prestige and
authority, and a special court was convened under the presidency of Boutros
Ghali Pasha, and undoubtedly the authorities let it be understood that they
required severe retribution. As a result some of the peasants were executed
and others flogged. The sentences were maliciously vindictive, and Lord
Cromer himself, though called upon to take responsibility and justify them,
considered them unduly severe. All commentators have since condemned
them as being brutal and in contradiction to the principles on which British
justice is founded.

> No Englishman can read the story of the wretched men's execution without a
> qualm of compunction. Trivial grievances, often of a personal character, help
> to explain the increasing jealousy of British ascendancy in the newly-educated
> classes and especially amongst Egyptian officials, but it is Denshawi that
> rankles in the memory of the fellaheen.[4]

This outburst of malice on the part of the British administration provided
the Nationalists not only with ammunition for their campaign, but also with
fuel to inflame the *fellahin* who were now in large measure brought to
regard the British with fear and distrust.

The Denshawi Incident was an unfortunate end to Lord Cromer's lengthy
sojourn in Egypt. For twenty-three years he had guided the destinies of the
country with a firm but beneficent hand; he had brought her from ruin to
security, if not to unprecedented prosperity. But in 1907 he decided to retire.
Apart from the fact that his health was deteriorating he himself was the first
to recognise that Egypt was in a period of transition requiring some departure
from the old methods and policy, and that these should be carried out by
younger men with a newer and fresher outlook. He left Egypt on 6 May
1907 and was succeeded by Sir Eldon Gorst as British Agent and Consul-
General.

Gorst had already served in Egypt in high office in the Ministry of the
Interior and as Financial Adviser, and had then returned to the Foreign
Office in London. He was thus no stranger to the affairs of Egypt, but it was
his unfortunate lot to be called upon to succeed a man who by his exceptional

powers of administration, tact and diplomatic skill had built up a reputation rarely to be surpassed. Stepping into the shoes of such a one is no easy task. It is probable that Gorst received certain directions from the Foreign Office as to the policy he was to pursue in Egypt. At any rate he went to Egypt with the intention of implementing a gradual and limited transfer of power from British to Egyptian hands. The legitimate ruler of Egypt was the Khedive in whom theoretically all power was vested and without whose decree no act or statute was valid. In pursuance of the new policy of allowing the Egyptian Government greater freedom Gorst considered that this should be manifested by a relaxation of the restraints on the Khedive's personal power. The danger of vesting too much freedom of action in a prince who had amply demonstrated his marked autocratic proclivities were not lost on Gorst, but against this he balanced the possible change of attitude on the part of the Khedive which might be expected from according him more freedom and enhancing his prestige. Gorst's courtship of Abbas, thus begun, was to have strong repercussions among the political parties.

The Popular Party of the Prime Minister Mustafa Fehmi Pasha and his colleagues who had given their full support to the British Agent during the previous decade and had therefore incurred the hostility of the Khedive, now saw the new Agent courting the Khedive, humouring his fancies and indulging his whims. Feeling insecure and even abandoned by those he had helped so long, Mustafa Fehmi resigned the office of Prime Minister which he had held for thirteen years. Similarly the Patriotic Party, seeing in Gorst's policy the revival and increase of the Khedive's personal power, viewed events with alarm and distrust, especially as it became more evident that Abbas' benevolence towards themselves had only been a mask to conceal his aspirations. Gorst's new policy thus had the effect of bringing a rapprochement between the two parties, a rapprochement which was to grow with the passage of the years and to solidify at the end of the First World War.

In the formation of the new Government, Abbas played his cards well by willingly agreeing to the British suggestion of Boutros Ghali Pasha as Prime Minister, recognising that his cordial relationship with the British was more than compensated by the odium in which he stood with many Egyptians. For Boutros Pasha was a Copt and a Christian, always suspect in Moslem Egypt; he it was who had signed the Sudan Condominium Agreement which was already being regarded as a betrayal of Egypt's rights, and he who had been the President of the Court which had tried the Denshawi defendants. By character he was honest, capable and guileless. All these were serious disabilities for a Prime Minister which the Khedive reckoned to be able to turn to good account. In 1908, in pursuance of the new policy, Sir Eldon Gorst introduced proposals for enlarging the scope and functions of the Provincial Councils. It is unnecessary to enumerate these in detail; it is sufficient to state that the advances proposed were limited and did little, if anything, to satisfy the demands of the Nationalists whose main political plank was the transfer of power from the ruler to representative institutions. The Nationalists regarded Gorst's proposals as merely scratching the surface and refused to be palmed off with the spurious for the genuine article. The measure did little to pacify the discontented or to render the British occupation any more acceptable.

In 1909 the matter of the Suez Canal once more appeared on the political stage. This great venture had shown a loss up to 1875 but thereafter a profit had been made which increased substantially and regularly year by year, and by this time it was regarded as a veritable gold mine by the shareholders. Even more important, there was every likelihood of the dividends going from strength to strength in the years to come. The concession had been granted for a term of ninety-nine years from the date of opening which was in 1869 and forty years of this precious concession had already lapsed; the prospect of handing over the enterprise to Egypt in the not too distant future filled the Company with horror. The Company therefore made an approach to the Egyptian Government for an extension of the Concession for a further forty years after 1968 in return for which they offered the following: a cash payment of £4 million; a share in the profits of the Company ranging from 4% in 1922 to 12% in 1961; after 1968 half the profits where these exceeded 100 million francs, or the surplus over 50 million if they did not reach the 100 million mark. At the same time however, the Egyptian Government would be required to assume the payment of pensions to the Canal staff and certain other financial responsibilities.

By and large the offer had a certain superficial attraction, but it was by no means comparable with the benefits which Egypt could expect to enjoy as sole proprietor of the Canal after 1968. There is some ground for believing that the Company exerted a certain amount of pressure on the Government to accept the offer by threatening to reduce the transit dues so drastically prior to 1968 that the Government would be unable to operate it at a profit. At any rate the Government were disposed to accept the offer and the British Financial Adviser recommended acceptance.[5] The news of the negotiations soon became public property, and the Nationalist element denounced it as a betrayal of the national interest. So insistent became the clamour that the Government decided to refer the matter to the General Assembly, even though that body had no competence to deal with the question, the Government undoubtedly holding the view that on a matter which concerned the future of the country so intimately, they should at least receive the approval of the nation as represented by the Assembly for the action they proposed.

Hitherto it had been the function of the Assembly to listen, not to dictate, and Boutros Pasha did not anticipate any difficulty in the present issue. The proposal was introduced on 9 February 1910, and the tenor of the debate indicated to an astonished Ministry that the measure was not going to be tamely accepted. The Government were in fact clearly very much out of touch with public sentiment. Egypt had given much of toil and treasure to the Canal, but the twist of circumstance had deprived her of enjoyment in its benefits, and she was obliged to stand aside and watch the proceeds disappear into the pockets of foreign shareholders. But one day the time would come, distant though it may be, when they would inherit the enterprise they had contributed so much to create, and the proposal to delay that time by another forty years seemed a flagrant act of treachery. They were not to be deprived of their rights by an offer of £4 million and an inadequate share of the profits. The generation of 1910 were willing to forego these small advantages so that their children might inherit their birthright.

The attitude of Boutros Pasha was upright and honest; he believed sincerely that he was doing the best for his country in accepting the offer, especially as the Financial Adviser had urged it. But the Assembly was eminently reasonable too, and showed a keen sense of legitimate patriotism in protesting. Unfortunately, a wanton act of barbarity was to cast a shadow over the nationalist sentiment. On 10 February 1910 Boutros Pasha was assassinated as he was standing on the pavement about to enter his carriage by a young nationalist fanatic, Ibrahim Nassif el Wardani. Boutros Pasha was an earnest and sincere man, intent only on the advancement and prosperity of his country; he did not deserve the assassin's blow. His error lay in failing to gauge accurately the strength of national sentiment and of the undisciplined forces of the Patriotic Party.

In a further debate on the Canal question the battle between the Government and the Assembly was resumed. Though Zaghlul Pasha, speaking for the Government, exerted his full powers of persuasion, his words fell unheeded and the proposal was rejected unanimously. Although the Government was not legally bound by this decision, it dared not fly in the face of national opinion so unequivocally expressed, and the proposal was tacitly allowed to drop. As the matter then stood, the Canal Concession would remain due to expire in 1968 when the Government would be entitled to enter into full possession of the Suez Canal.

Sir Eldon Gorst was soon forced to the conclusion that his policy had failed. He had tried to foster the growth of liberal institutions and at the same time to relax the restraints on the Khedive. The two policies were impossible of execution because they were mutually exclusive under the conditions which prevailed at the time. There could be no advance in democracy as long as Abbas II was the chief political power on the Egyptian stage; a necessary preliminary to political advance was the almost complete suppression of the Khedive. Gorst had however proceeded in the opposite direction by giving him a freer hand. In attempting to please all he had pleased none, for even the British officials viewed his policy with disfavour, especially as it tended towards the diminution of their own authority and the increase of that of the Egyptian Ministers. But Gorst's tenure of office was short; he died in England on 10 July 1911 while on leave. It is worthy of mention that Abbas had no personal antipathy for Gorst himself, for he made a secret journey to England to see him on his deathbed.

It has been said that the principal disability of Sir Eldon Gorst was the fact that he could not command the loyalty and support of those whom he was expected to lead. There may be some justice in this view, but undoubtedly the bottom fact of his failure was due to his attempt to carry out policies which were impossible of execution. Had he confined himself to restoring and strengthening the position of the Khedive, all might have been well, for the moment at any rate, for Egyptians were well accustomed to looking up to one man as ruler and arbiter of destiny. Alternatively he could have disregarded the Khedive completely and concentrated his attention on fostering the democratic movement.

Gorst's successor as British Agent and Consul-General was the victor of Omdurman, Sir Herbert Kitchener. He had spent many years in Egypt and had made his reputation there. As Sirdar of the Egyptian army he was well known to the humbler classes from whom the troops were drawn and in whom he showed great interest and sympathy. But Kitchener was a soldier not a diplomatist; he had been accustomed to issuing his orders and knowing that they would be obeyed. He was now called on to quit the military sphere and to shelve his reliance on military discipline; he was required to steer his way through the political labyrinth with only his prestige and powers of persuasion to rely on. Kitchener had many admirable qualities, but he had neither the breadth of view nor the political detachment of Lord Cromer. He was interested in certain things and these he was prepared to do his utmost to further; matters which bored him received the minimum of attention. As far as the Khedive was concerned he was prepared to forgive and forget the unfortunate accident of 1894 at Wadi Halfa, and he treated him with studied courtesy, but he was not prepared to follow Gorst's policy of giving him a free hand.

The outbreak of war between Turkey and Italy, who had recently annexed the province of Tripoli, placed Kitchener in a delicate position. Naturally enough the Egyptians, as Moslems, looked up to the Sultan as Khalif and were the partisans of Turkey, but for reasons which do not concern us here Britain had no wish to offend Italy by allowing Egypt to go to the assistance of Turkey. The Foreign Office therefore ruled that Egypt should observe a strict neutrality, and it is a tribute to Kitchener that he steered Egypt through this delicate period without giving offence to either side.

Kitchener fell into the same trap as his predecessor, but in a slightly different way. He set himself to promote the growth of parliamentary institutions and at the same time to shake Egypt free of the time-honoured abuses, the capitulations. Any revision or limitation of the capitulatory rights of the foreigners could only be effected by the agreement of the powers concerned, and the condition precedent upon such agreement was an assurance that the Government of Egypt should not fall into hands which would disregard the rights and privileges of foreigners, but would guarantee to uphold them and resist any attempt at anti-foreign discrimination. Had Britain annexed Egypt outright or even declared a permanent protectorate, there would have been little difficulty in sweeping away the whole paraphernalia of the capitulations, Mixed Tribunals and other foreign obstacles. But Britain had never gone beyond declaring her occupation to be temporary. In the circumstances there could be no assurance that the foreigners would be fairly treated if the capitulations were abolished, especially if the British occupation were finally terminated and a parliamentary régime established. On the contrary, it could reasonably be expected that the foreign minorities would immediately become a prey to the nationalists, if such an eventuality occurred. The Powers therefore refused to abandon the capitulations.

Although he failed in this matter, Kitchener made an important contribution to the advancement of Egyptian representation. The old Legislative Council and General Assembly, the creations of Lord Dufferin in 1883, were now merged into one Legislative Assembly under the Organic Law of 1913. 'It was composed of seventeen nominated members, and sixty-six elected

317

members all of them returned by indirect suffrage in the second degree.'[6] As with the previous institutions, the new Assembly was largely consultative or advisory and had no executive power except in a negative sense. 'It had power to veto proposals for the increase of direct taxation . . . Its proceedings were to be public; it could delay legislation; compel Ministers to justify their proposals at length, interrogate them and call for information.'[7] Although the new Assembly did not even begin to satisfy the extreme nationalists, at least it constituted a considerable advance, for the country was provided with an instrument through which it could voice its opinions on current questions, opinions to which the Ministry were bound in their own interests to give the greatest heed. Even more important, it gave Zaghlul Pasha, the future nationalist leader of Egypt, the vantage point from which he could exercise the *métier* which best suited him, out of office and in opposition. He was elected Vice-President of the Assembly.

With the customary eye of the soldier to possible military necessities, Kitchener gave much attention to the question of transport, and to him Egypt owes many of her fine roads. But his chief interest was in the welfare of the *fellahin*. Even the steady growth over the last quarter of a century had not greatly altered the condition of the peasant cultivator; the increase in productiveness had been attended with the normal result, an increase in population, and the smallholder was still as much in debt to the Greek and Syrian usurer as ever. Kitchener saw that the whole economy of the country rested on the peasant smallholder, and that it was contrary to the public interest that he should be dispossessed of his land by foreclosure. To prevent any further tendency in this direction he evolved the Five Feddan Law under the terms of which the land of farmers who did not own more than five feddans could not be seized for debt. By this measure the *fellahin* were saved to a great extent from their own folly and improvidence, and the power of the usurer over them was drastically curtailed. In every sense the measure was beneficial; the *fellah* not now being able to pledge his last bit of land as security was coaxed towards a certain degree of thrift and his future was better assured.

Kitchener paid little attention to the Khedive Abbas and allowed him to proceed in his own way so long as this did not conflict with his own policies. In 1913 however he had a clash with His Highness over the question of the Mariut Railway. This was a line privately owned by the Khedive on his estates lying to the west of Alexandria. It appears that Abbas had been privately negotiating with the Italian Banco di Roma for the sale of this railway, and had even given the Italians an option over it. When Kitchener heard about it, he intervened and forbade the sale. In the same year a further collision took place over the administration of the *Wakfs* or religious trusts and endowments. By tradition the administration of the *Wakfs* had been under the control of the Khedive, but the sharp practices and malversation of funds became such a matter for scandal that Kitchener was compelled to remove them from the Khedive's control and create a separate Ministry. By the time Kitchener went to England on leave in 1914 he was resigned to the prospect of having to remove Abbas from his position, recognising at last that there could never be any rapprochement between him and the British occupying power.

But before Kitchener could return, the great conflagration which was to engulf nearly the whole world was ignited and Kitchener never came back to Egypt.

The dominant characteristic of Egypt during the years between the resignation of Lord Cromer and the outbreak of the First World War was nationalism, a force which the occupying power found itself singularly ill-fitted to contend with. The defect of the British administration was that it was founded on a paradox. Its status was ill-defined; in fact it was never defined at all. It pursued a sort of nebulous policy involving two principal aims which directly conflicted with each other. On the one hand it was endeavouring to promote the prosperity of the country and to introduce modern European methods of administration; at the same time it declared its intention of teaching the Egyptians to govern themselves. It encouraged and spread the growth of the democratic idea, but it refused to transfer the executive power to the people. To the British administrative officer it was clear that a sudden or rapid transfer of power could only spell disaster because it could well be anticipated that it would be used for selfish ends. But at the same time it was well-nigh impossible to make the nationalists appreciate this maxim, and perhaps somewhat naturally so, for it is almost inconceivable that any nation would willingly admit its inability to rule itself. All indications pointed towards the creation of a deadlock. Nationalism had succeeded to the extent of obtaining a majority support in the new Legislative Assembly from which it could render the task of the Ministry almost impossible. The British were still trying to carry on the administration through a native Ministry which was beginning to find itself between the hammer of British pressure and the anvil of nationalist obstruction. But for better or for worse a moratorium was created by the outbreak of the First World War.

CHAPTER 20

Egypt and the First World War

The advent of war in August 1914 threw the continent of Europe into a state of turmoil and anxiety; Egypt it left calm and indifferent. Apart from the possible repercussions which the war might have on Egyptian trade, there was no reason why it should affect her at all. It was no concern of hers and a judicious neutrality was the obvious course to pursue. Yet Egypt was not destined to escape unscathed, and from a long term point of view it eventually operated to her advantage in some ways, for during the next four years Egypt was turned into a vast armed camp and military base for the Allies, and her contribution to the war effort was substantial. This contribution provided Egypt with her most valuable weapon in the struggle for freedom during the years following the war, and it is certain that the war hastened her independence, the prize she most coveted. The war years witnessed a marked falling-off of British diplomacy especially in Egypt; promises were broken, misunderstandings created, and hardships inflicted on that section of the population which Britain had especially undertaken to foster and protect; even the *fellahin* became estranged, with the result that Egyptian nationalism was welded into a solid block. Britain soon found herself deep in the desperate struggle for survival and clutched at every available straw to help her emerge triumphant from the ordeal, and it would be unreasonable to censure her overmuch for taking advantage of every resource at her disposal, even though this might entail the sacrifice of ideals. But the Egyptians had been taught that Britain kept her promises and expected her to do so.

When the war broke out Egypt was slumbering peacefully through the summer months, as was her wont. The British Agent, Lord Kitchener, was in England; the Khedive Abbas was taking his summer holiday in Constantinople; the Legislative Assembly was adjourned; and the Prime

Minister, Hussein Rushdi Pasha, was acting as Regent. Upon him and the Council of Ministers fell the task of deciding what attitude Egypt should adopt in regard to the war. They had little time to reflect on the problem. Mr Milne Cheetham, the Acting British Agent, lost no time in pressing Rushdi Pasha to pronounce in favour of Great Britain, and the latter had little or no option. The most convincing argument was the presence of the British army of occupation which was capable of overthrowing the Government and annexing Egypt outright to the British Empire. At the time no one would have lifted a finger to prevent it, and the safest course that Egypt could pursue under the circumstances was to go along with Britain and let events take their course. On 5 August the Government issued a declaration to the effect that the presence of the army of occupation rendered Egypt liable to attack and that therefore certain measures would be taken to put the country in a state of defence. These required that no commerce should be held with the enemy, no Egyptian ships were to enter enemy ports, British armed forces were to be allowed the use of Egyptian ports, facilities and installations, and the people were urged to give every assistance to the British. In this declaration, issued on the second day of the war, Egypt promised her support to her guide and preceptor, and during all the stormy and uncertain years of war she never wavered or flinched in pursuing this policy. Even if not a comrade in arms, Egypt was one of Britain's staunchest allies and supporters. The new situation required certain measures to be put into effect to assure the welfare of the people and the defence of the country. For one thing, the great demand for Egyptian cotton abroad in recent years had led to a change in agricultural practice in the Delta. Land which had formerly been cultivated for food crops was now sown with cotton, and Egypt was to a certain extent dependent upon imports for her food supplies which were carried in foreign ships, Egypt having few of her own. But now the demands made upon shipping by the belligerents reduced the import of food, and to augment the supplies of home-grown food-stuffs the Egyptian Government issued instructions that only one third of the cultivable land should be given up to cotton. Regulations were also made to stabilise the currency.

While the population accepted the defence precautions calmly and without complaint, it did not necessarily follow that these and other actions of the Government met with their approval. Rushdi Pasha and his colleagues were prepared to carry out the behests of the British Agent so long as they met with no opposition from their compatriots, but the Legislative Assembly was due to sit again shortly and would no doubt hold an inquest on the Government's stewardship during the recess. Bitter criticism from the

Nationalists could well be expected in the form of debates, press reports and public clamour, a cause of some apprehension to the Prime Minister. As a stop-gap measure and with the consent of the British Agent the next session of the Legislative Assembly, which was to have taken place in November, was postponed for two months under a decree of 18 October. But there was nothing to prevent members of the Assembly from meeting in private and discussing matters of national interest, and such meetings would receive just as much publicity as an official session and the results would have been much the same. To circumvent this possibility a law was enacted on 20 October declaring any assembly of five or more persons unlawful unless previously authorised.[1] These precautions surmounted the immediate difficulty, but were only to be regarded as a temporary expedient. Rushdi Pasha had gained a breathing space, but the two months' postponement of the Assembly's sittings would soon slip by, and he would then be faced with a barrage of questions and criticisms. Britain found a very useful friend and ally in the Egyptian Prime Minister and were anxious to retain him in power. He was an able and courageous man, of moderate views, and he believed that the road to independence for Egypt lay in co-operating with Britain and giving her the utmost support.

It was becoming increasingly evident during the first three months of the war that no long period would elapse before Turkey entered the conflict on the side of Germany. In the event of an Allied victory Egypt would have a good case for independence, but if German arms triumphed there could be no doubt that Egypt would once again be saddled with the Turkish yoke, the last thing any Egyptian wanted. Rushdi Pasha realised this, but there were strong elements in Egypt who judged the Government only on their attitude to Britain, and any well-disposed minister was certain to bear the brunt of their hostility and abuse. Rushdi Pasha was therefore inclined to resign office before the storm could burst about his ears, but the British Government in their anxiety to keep him in office were prepared to assume the burden of responsibility by declaring martial law on 2 November. The effect of this action was that whenever the Government was required to pass legislation likely to be unpopular to the people of Egypt, the blame could be fastened on British shoulders and the Government could disclaim all responsibility. There was, however, no intention of replacing the civil administration with a British military government. However imperfect the former might be it was as efficient as the times required, while the British Government shrank from the task of finding competent administrators from their own people. The arrangement affected by the declaration to martial law was generally satisfactory. The Egyptian civil administration carried on the day-to-day routine of government with the British military power behind it to enact measures necessitated by the war. The only accusation that could be aimed at Rushdi Pasha was that he consented to remain in office under the British, but this he felt he could bear with fortitude. As will be mentioned later, martial law came to be used on occasion for the advantage of Egypt when the civil administration was powerless to act.

The proclamation of martial law vested military control of the country in Lieutenant-General Sir John Maxwell, who immediately followed this declaration with another intended to allay Egyptian fears. As has already been explained, the civil administration would remain, compensation would be paid for requisitioned property and no civilian would be subjected to interference provided that he conformed to the orders of the military authority.[2]

Three days later, Turkey declared war on Great Britain. This event was not unexpected; indeed, it had been obvious for some time that Turkey was only awaiting a convenient opportunity to take the plunge, and she had been utilising her short period of neutrality to marshal her forces which were now concentrated in Syria. The reasons which motivated Turkey to go to war with Britain form no part of this story, but her entry immediately switched attention to Egypt, for it was certain that she would attack the British forces in the Delta. The state of war with Turkey was made known in a proclamation by General Maxwell in which he outlined the breaches of neutrality which Turkey had committed, instancing her concentration of troops in Syria and her violation of Egyptian territory by invading the Sinai peninsula. Britain would therefore fight to protect Egypt from invasion and accepted sole responsibility for the defence of Egypt. All commentators have been unanimous in condemning this last clause. The British Government probably thought they were acting reasonably in undertaking sole responsibility, but it was just such a mistake as this as was calculated to wound Egyptian national sensibility. Why should Egypt not assist in defending her own land? Here indeed was an opportunity of uniting the two countries in the brotherhood of arms, and as Lord Lloyd so justly states, 'the Egyptian army was ridiculous if it did not exist to fight, and what better ground could it have for fighting than the defence of the country from invasion?' In these early days of the war it was folly to assume that the situation would never arise when the British would be obliged to call upon Egypt for assistance. Who could tell in what direction the fortunes of war would proceed? Shortly after this categorical assurance was given, Egyptian units were called upon to assist in the defence of the Canal, and during the years of the war ever-increasing demands were made upon Egyptian resources and manpower for the prosecution of military operations.

Turkey's entry into the war created a situation which even Britain, though well accustomed to political anomalies, could not stomach. For in spite of the British occupation and administration of the country, Egypt was still theoretically an integral part of the Ottoman Empire. Egyptians were Ottoman subjects; the Khedive was appointed by the Sultan; and tribute was paid to Constantinople. Egyptians therefore should be following their overlord into war against the country which was her occupier, Britain. The facts of course were perfectly clear to everybody. In reality, Egypt had long since ceased to be in practice a part of the Ottoman Empire; she was rather a part of the British Empire, although this fact had been concealed in a fiction. At any rate the British Government considered that the time had now come to cut the knot by adjusting the international status of Egypt. Purely by force of arms or right of conquest, ancient and easy to understand, Britain might have considered herself legitimately entitled to annex the country outright. No better opportunity for this course of action could have presented itself. The Khedive Abbas Hilmi, ever hostile to Britain, was absent in the camp of the enemy at Constantinople, the Council of Ministers had declared in favour of Britain in August, and the country was now under British military control. From here to outright annexation was but a short step, and one which would not have been obstructed by the other Powers. This course had already been decided on by the British Foreign Secretary, Sir Edward Grey, and the concurrence of France obtained. But Mr Cheetham, the Acting British Agent, was opposed to the course. It would involve setting up a new administration; it would completely reverse all of Britain's assertions that the occupation was only temporary; and her promises would be shown to be worthless. For years the British Government had led Egypt to believe that she was being gently guided to self-government and political independence. Annexation would make a mockery of these promises and declarations, and would certainly not encourage Egypt to give her assistance and support in the present conflict. The principal ambition of Egypt was independence and she could be reckoned to give her support to any country which promised it to her. Mr Cheetham's view was that as long as the government of Egypt lay in Egyptian hands, there were excuses for administrative shortcomings, but these would disappear with annexation and Britain would be responsible for every failure and difficulty which might arise.[3] The policy of annexation was therefore reluctantly abandoned.

Instead Britain, always partial to nebulous international relationships the conditions of which could be easily interpreted to suit the circumstances, compromised on a protectorate which was declared on 18 December 1914. Precisely what a protectorate signified was not clear to any class of Egyptian. The British Government had already undertaken to protect Egypt from aggression, but the situation was somewhat clarified the following day when the Foreign Secretary announced that Turkey's suzerainty over Egypt was terminated, that the Khedive Abbas Hilmi II was deposed and that Prince Hussein Kamil would succeed him with the title of Sultan of Egypt. The disappearance of Abbas from the Egyptian scene excited little regret as he had been unpopular with all classes. Prince Hussein was an excellent choice. As a son of Ismail Pasha he was in the direct line of descent in the dynasty of Mohammed Ali; he was a man of high character, an experienced farmer and a wise and kindly employer. No one could object to the succession of such a popular and sterling character.

The new conditions Egypt accepted calmly; to the bulk of the population they made little difference. As the war progressed Egyptian cotton became more and more sought after, and prices rose to a figure hitherto undreamed of. The mustering of large forces of British and Imperial troops, avid for the pleasures that Egypt could offer and with their pockets bulging with money, brought a new prosperity to the small trader. At least any disadvantages entailed by martial law and the influx of foreign troops in the towns of the Delta were amply compensated for by the affluence which attended them.

It is not proposed to trace in detail the sequence of military operations in the Egyptian theatre in this narrative; this belongs more to the realms of British military history. A few notes will suffice to explain their relationship to Egyptian affairs during this critical period. As has been remarked, the Turkish forces were already concentrated in Syria and along Egypt's north-east frontier when war was declared. Djemal Pasha the Turkish commander cherished dreams of invading Egypt, vanquishing the small British garrison and making his triumphal entry into Cairo as Egypt's deliverer from the oppression of the foreign infidel. Egyptians did not share his ambitions; they had no delusions about what deliverance from the British by the Turks would imply. They wished their co-religionists well – but from afar. British occupation, hateful though it was to the politically conscious classes, had certain advantages and compensations which could not be ignored. No one could dispute that the country was prospering, that it had successfully emerged from the load of debt which had been Ismail Pasha's legacy to his subjects. Development projects and public services had made steady progress under Britain's guiding hands and, though reluctant publicly to admit it, Egyptians were fully conscious of it. Such benefits were not likely to continue if the country fell once more into the hands of the Turks. If these unpleasant considerations were known to Djemal Pasha, he preferred to ignore them. At any rate his general plan was to get into Egypt and drive the British out.

But this policy was not shared by his Chief of Staff, the German von Kressenstein, who was under no delusions about the political situation. What he did realise was that Britain attached much importance to the security of the Suez Canal and was prepared to go to any lengths to protect it. The Suez Canal was a hundred miles long, a wide front to hold and defend for a few battalions of half-trained troops. In such situations the attacker has the advantage. He has the initiative, he can select any objective he likes, he can concentrate his strength at any point for the attack, he has the advantage of surprise. The defence however must inevitably to some extent spread its strength and suffer the demoralising effects of being compelled to wait and speculate with uncertainty where the attack will fall. It was clear to von Kressenstein that even if the Turks failed to capture or block the Canal, their presence as a potential threat would certainly draw off a large body of Allied troops which might usefully be serving elsewhere. To that extent at any rate his strategy was successful; both British and Empire troops were detailed to defend the waterway. The attack was delivered on the Canal on 3 February 1915 in the central sector south of Ismailia. The Turkish force succeeded in reaching the banks and a number managed to cross on pontoons. But the defence was ready and, aided by a violent sand-storm which suddenly blew up, repulsed the attackers. Realising that nothing was to be gained by a fresh assault, the Turkish commander withdrew and retreated in good order to his base at Bir Sheba.

During this period, which might have been a critical one, Egyptians remained calm and carried on their daily business. Any fears that the British authorities might have entertained that the people would covertly support and assist their co-religionists in the Ottoman armies were shown to be unfounded. Egypt remained loyal and faithful to her pledges of August 1914. At the same time it cannot be said that the imposition of martial law or the great influx of Imperial troops bore heavily on the native population during the first year or so of the war. On the contrary, martial law was employed from time to time as an assaulting weapon on the obstinate defences of the capitulations. For some time foreigners had been importing into an abstemious Moslem Egypt the European addiction to alcohol, and European drink-sellers had no difficulty in obtaining licences to carry on their alcoholic businesses, and many abused their privilege by selling drink of very inferior quality. Entrenched behind the capitulations they were immune from action or prosecution by the Government. The influx of British and Empire troops into Egypt with their unquenchable thirst stimulated the drink-sellers into intense activity. Bars and public houses were opened on nearly every street corner of the garrison towns such as Port Said, Alexandria and Ismailia, and any foul concoction which even remotely resembled alcohol was easily sold. Penalties for selling adulterated liquor were absurdly low and were willingly paid by those convicted. Business was booming, and what were a few pounds in fines compared with the enormous profits? With a stroke of the pen General Maxwell defied the capitulations by issuing a decree under martial law authorising the Egyptian police, without consular permission, to enter any bar and seize spirits believed to be contaminated, and imposing heavy fines and long terms of imprisonment on those convicted. Absinthe, a particularly vicious poison, was strictly prohibited. Martial law also came to the aid of the Egyptian Government on the question of the Ghaffir Tax which was levied on native Egyptians for the maintenance of a force of watchmen to patrol residential and business premises during the night. The foreigners possessing capitulatory rights were not compelled to pay this tax, although they as much as any other section of the community profited by the service which it provided. In September 1915 General Maxwell intervened to remedy this injustice by issuing an order requiring all inhabitants to contribute to this particular tax, a measure which was greeted with considerable applause and satisfaction by the native population, who had long resented the injustice of having to pay for guards to protect other people's property.

During 1915 certain dislocations of ordinary civil life began to manifest themselves, particularly with regard to food supplies. The decree of 1914 limiting the area of land to be planted with cotton had had the required effect, and the food crops of maize, wheat, barley and beans had shown a marked upward trend, and there was an adequate supply for local needs. But at the same time the demand for Egyptian cotton which had temporarily slumped during 1914 was now reviving rapidly, and Britain in particular wanted Egyptian cotton. Under pressure from the land-owners the Government revoked the restrictions on agriculture, and even permitted the export of food crops which were similarly fetching good prices abroad. The inevitable consequence was that food fell in short supply again and hoarding began with the object of securing the highest price, and it required a further proclamation under martial law forbidding the hoarding or illegal export of food supplies.

It was during 1915 that the disastrous attempt was made to force a landing on the Turkish mainland at Gallipoli. As is well known, the attempt was unsuccessful and the British forces were compelled to retire. They naturally fell back on Egypt which became an important base and reception area. The situation was much complicated by the fact that the Imperial forces in the Delta were split up into different commands – the Force in Egypt, the Egyptian Expeditionary Force, and the Levant Base. Among these, conflicting orders were sometimes given which caused a good deal of puzzlement and irritation to the Egyptians. General Maxwell, who had up to this time conducted military affairs with tact and skill and had managed to maintain cordial relations between the army and the civil population, now found himself very much overshadowed and to a great extent superseded by General Sir Archibald Murray, commander of the Expeditionary Force, a keen and forceful soldier who kept his attention focused on the enemy and refused to let sundry matters of internal administration and policy divert him from his military operations. At all events General Maxwell relinquished his post and left Egypt in March 1916.

From this time forward relations between Britain and Egypt deteriorated and continued to do so during the remaining course of the war. During his term of office General Maxwell had kept the balance; he had secured the general goodwill and co-operation of the Egyptian Government; he had also exerted himself for the welfare of the country; and the partnership of British General and Egyptian Government had been a reasonably happy one. Maxwell had used his powers under martial law with discretion, and it was not until December 1915 that he had used his powers of requisition when he authorised the compulsory acquisition of land to build a second railway track from Zagazig to Ismailia to facilitate the movement of troops and supplies to and from the Canal Zone. Thereafter martial law was used solely as an instrument for the prosecution of the war, and the demands on Egypt, her manpower and resources became more frequent, pressing and exacting. It must be remembered that as early as November 1914 the British Government, in announcing the imposition of martial law, had declared that Britain assumed sole responsibility for the defence of Egypt and the prosecution of the war. No suggestion had been made that Egypt should be invited to associate herself actively in the war, nor had she been given the opportunity of making such an offer. Yet right at the beginning of the war in August 1914 Egypt had declared herself on the side of the Allies, and the attitude she adopted then was quite consistent with the idea that she might freely volunteer her resources and assistance, even her army, if she were invited to do so. But the British Government at the time were confident of winning the war without any assistance from Egypt. All they wanted Egypt to do was to stand aside and let the British get on with the job. By 1916, gone were the prospects of a six-months war and a quick victory, gone were the illusions of Allied superiority and German weakness. The grim struggle in France showed no sign of abating, nor was there any immediate hope of victory and peace. The war was now clearly a struggle for existence, and every resource available had to be grasped and put to good use. Even so it was not too late for the British Government to revise their attitude and formally approach the Egyptian Government and seek their aid, not as a subject race, but as an ally who could afford valuable assistance in this critical hour. Had Egypt been invited to assist in the prosecution of the war, it is reasonable to suppose that she would have demanded her independence as the reward for her efforts. But what actually happened was that she gave her assistance nonetheless, because it was requisitioned under martial law and with no promise of reward. Egypt provided labour, land, food and even her precious camels, but the basis of all the demands she met was not allied or friendly co-operation, but military power and force of arms.

The trouble started with the virtual conscription of Egyptian labour for various purposes. In every army formation there are a large number of routine labours of an unskilled nature to be done, and it had hitherto been usual for the army to provide this labour from its own strength. But in time of war, when every soldier who could handle a rifle was urgently needed for offensive and defensive purposes, this drain on the army's fighting strength was considerable. During the Gallipoli campaign a small force of Egyptian labour had been recruited which not only released fighting men for the front, but did their work with conspicuous success. Long inured to heavy manual labour in the fields the Egyptian *fellah* dug, carried and hauled far more efficiently and with less effort than his British counterpart, and Egyptian labour thus became much sought after in the army. No complaint could be raised as long as the *fellah* enlisted voluntarily into the Egyptian Labour Corps. Pay was good, food and clothing adequate; he was well looked after and he received justice. Moreover, contracts were for relatively short periods and the work was well within his capacity.

But the Egyptian *fellah* is difficult to entice away from his village, family and fields, no matter what the inducements. During the war, probably for the first time in history, the *fellahin* were prospering. The demand for their agricultural produce, food and cotton was booming as never before and prices were rising to unprecedented heights. Many an Egyptian smallholder, for years smothered by crushing debts and mortgages, was now able to pay off his debts and still have money in his pockets. Little wonder is it that the response to the call of the Egyptian Labour Corps was unsatisfactory. But Egyptian labour became the fashion in the army and the demand for it was far outstripping the supply. This demand was further strengthened by a change of strategy along the Canal Zone. For the defences of the vital waterway had up to this time been laid along its banks, and the Canal used as a natural obstacle to an enemy advance. This defensive plan might have been justified had the defence of Egypt been the principal objective, but it was manifestly inadequate to defend the Canal itself. In short, the lines of defence had to be pushed out in front of the Canal into the desert of Sinai. This involved the construction of a new railway line to supply the troops as they moved forward, and a considerable increase in the supply of labour and camel transport. Not only that, but the demand for labour was keenly felt on the battle fronts of Europe, and a considerable part of the Egyptian Labour Corps had been packed off to France. Not by the greatest stretch of the imagination can it be supposed that service in France was assisting in the defence of Egypt.

The British troops, looking round themselves in Egypt, could not fail to note the tide of prosperity which the war had brought to the country. In ignorance of the true facts it is not surprising that they felt resentment that they were shedding their blood and expending their treasure in the defence of a country which was taking no part in the war and which moreover was waxing rich and fat on it. But the blame for the existence of this situation lay at the door of the British Government who had laid down the policy in clear and definite terms at the very outset; Egypt was precluded from participation in the war. But the British military authorities had no difficulty in persuading themselves that Egypt was profiting and prospering by the war and that her contribution was inadequate. The army wanted labour and camels, and these they must have. The Egyptian Government responded to the pressure in the belief that every assistance offered to the Allies would be compensated after the war. While refusing officially to countenance conscription of labour, the Government made it clear to the *mudirs* of the provinces that they were expected to produce the necessary quota of men for the Labour Corps, and that they would incur official displeasure if their contributions were insufficient. The provincial authorities lost no time in getting to work. All the old traditional methods of the *corvée* and the press-gang magically reappeared. The *fellahin* were seized and bundled off to the nearest recruiting depot and enrolled in the Labour Corps. Unfortunate it is that the British officials of the Administration were so engrossed in the furtherance of the war and out of touch with affairs in the provinces that not a word of protest escaped their lips. In this way the British lost the only friends they had in Egypt, the *fellahin*, who had been wont to look on the British as their protectors from the oppression of the *pashas* and usurers. The British, they felt, were turning away from their responsibilities and betraying their trust and were no better than the Turks. This resentment was in due course inflamed to fury when the requisitioning of their beasts of burden took place. The army's need for camel transport increased in proportion as the Expeditionary Force advanced into Palestine. The Purchasing Commission was quite prepared to pay for the animals, but payment could in no way compensate the *fellah* for the loss of his most cherished possession and his only form of transport. The camel was his one and only means of conveying his produce to market, and was thus one of his most vital tools of production and means of livelihood. But the army was inexorable. The camels were requisitioned and all those in fit condition disappeared into military service. The *fellah*'s cup of bitterness was filled to overflowing when even the female camels were taken.

Nor were these the only demands on Egypt. The army, now enormously swollen in 1917, required food for the troops and fodder for the animals. These too had to be found in large quantities and although a close control was exercised over the supply and distribution of food, the inevitable happened; the poorest classes could not get enough for themselves. In all these measures it was the poor, the *fellahin* and the white-collar town workers who suffered most. They gave their food, their labour, their animals and frequently their lives to the British army; the wealthy classes, the *beys*, the *pashas*, landowners and merchants escaped these sacrifices. Thus unhappily almost every section of the Egyptian population were united in their detestation of the British – the *pasha* class who resented the curbs placed on them, the foreigner who resented the paramount position of the British in the land and the measures which assailed their capitulatory privileges, and the *fellah* who lost so much of his worldly goods. The Government sat tight hoping that when the war was over, all would be forgotten and forgiven when the reckoning came to be paid and Egypt was given her independence.

During 1917 the health of Sultan Hussein declined and it was recognised that he might not have long to live. The possibilities of his early death once again reawakened fresh consideration of the future of Egypt and her relationship with Britain. For a moment the policy of annexation to the British Empire was revived, especially as the ailing Sultan himself was known to favour it in the best interests of the country and also because his son, Prince Kemal-ed-Din who was at first thought to be a likely successor, was unwilling to undertake the duties of head of the state and voluntarily renounced his rights of succession. In the end annexation was abandoned as a practical solution of the Egyptian problem. Sultan Hussein died on 9 October 1917, and his brother Prince Ahmed Fuad was selected to be his heir to the Sultanate. Prince Fuad was a worthy son of Ismail Pasha and inherited much of his character, notably his ambition and his adhesion to the age-old system of personal government; he was by nature an autocrat. He had spent much of his early life in Italy to which his father had gone in exile, spoke Italian better than Arabic,[4] and was perhaps too westernised to commend him warmly to oriental Egypt. Nevertheless he was well known in the country and took an active part in public affairs. He had done valuable work in reviving the moribund Red Crescent Society, the Moslem counterpart of the Red Cross, during the war and was a keen patron of science and the arts. He was destined to play a prominent part in Egyptian affairs after the end of the war.

CHAPTER 21

The Struggle for Independence

In the previous chapter little reference has been made to the functions and activities of the British civil authorities during the war period, for the reason that they were almost entirely overshadowed by the armed forces functioning under military law. On the declaration of the protectorate in December 1914 the British Agent and Consul General was elevated to the status of High Commissioner. As had been previously noted, Kitchener was destined never to return to Egypt and his post was held temporarily by Mr Milne Cheetham as *locum tenens* until the appointment of Sir Henry MacMahon who, however, played an insignificant role in the affairs of Egypt, for he concerned himself more in negotiating with the leaders of Arabia and promoting the Arab Revolt from Turkish rule. His term of office was short; at the end of 1916 he was succeeded by Sir Reginald Wingate who had previously been Governor-General of the Sudan and was well acquainted with the affairs of Egypt. Even so his influence carried little weight and the Foreign Office showed no disposition to treat his advice with the consideration it deserved, especially as this advice did not particularly tend to accord with the views generally held in Whitehall.

The British Government, somewhat understandably perhaps, focused their whole attention on the winning of the war to the exclusion of all other considerations. In Egypt they found ready to hand an extremely useful base for operations in the eastern Mediterranean and an abundant source of supply for labour, food and transport and other necessities. Loyal to their declarations of 1914, the Egyptians, though precluded from any active participation in the war, did their best to supply every want of their British protectors for which they expected, and were entitled to expect, their just reward. During the war years the politically-conscious classes refrained from any overt activity or agitation, but this did not imply any diminution of political feeling. On the contrary, nationalism was on the increase and received a considerable impetus from the ill-considered demands made upon the *fellahin* by the military authorities. Even so, the nationalists were content to relax their propaganda during wartime which was not opportune for pressing for constitutional changes, while the moderates hoped that when the war was over a grateful Britain would bestow on Egypt the gift she most desired, freedom and independence.

But the British misjudged the situation entirely, largely because their officials in Egypt, preoccupied with the prosecution of the war, had lost touch with popular sentiment. All they saw was a country apparently peaceful and prosperous and therefore contented with the existing order of things. They forgot that the British occupation was supposed to be temporary and that the declared intention was to lead Egypt to self-government. After thirty-six years the stage had been reached when the British regarded themselves in occupation and control of Egypt as of right and Egypt to dispose of as they thought fit. The temporary nature of the occupation was now forgotten and this was regarded as one of the permanent features of life. Egypt had now after four centuries been completely severed from the Ottoman Empire and a British protectorate declared over her. British control was thus formally asserted and hardly an Englishman gave a thought to the future of Egypt except as a protectorate subject to British control for an indefinite period or even as part of the Empire. Indeed, the idea of outright annexation was again seriously considered in 1917, but was eventually abandoned with some reluctance.

Although the British were so much out of touch with Egyptian public opinion during the war years, the reverse was by no means the case. The Egyptians, highly sensitive to any fluctuations in the political breezes, were in no doubt about the British attitude and the nationalists, led now by Zaghlul Pasha who had joined forces with the most ardent group, recognised that after the war a grateful Britain was not going to present Egypt with the gift of independence. There was going to be a struggle and Zaghlul Pasha prepared himself for it. Quietly he gathered the nationalist forces around him and accumulated whatever material he could that might prove useful in the ensuing struggle. In this he was much assisted by the idealist utterances of the Allied leaders, especially President Woodrow Wilson who proclaimed the principle of self-determination. Where prior to the war Egypt might have been reasonably satisfied with a substantial measure of self-government she had now advanced considerably in her aspirations; complete independence was her goal.

Thus when the Armistice Day came in November 1918 the Allies leaned back with a sigh of relief. All they wanted for the moment was breathing space and a brief opportunity to rejoice at their deliverance; the only immediate object they had in view was the settlement of the peace treaty; no thought at all was given to petty foreign policies, least of all to Egypt. Zaghlul realised this only too well and he knew that if any concessions were to be wrung out of Britain, the campaign must be launched before the Allied statesmen sat down at the peace table to decide the destinies of the world. Two days after the Armistice, Zaghlul Pasha presented himself at the British Residency at the head of a delegation, and in an interview with Sir Reginald Wingate made a formal demand for the independence of Egypt. This sudden demand caught the High Commissioner off balance and he was obliged to reply that he was not acquainted with the intentions of the British Government with regard to the future of Egypt. It is probable that in making this somewhat evasive reply the High Commissioner was playing for time, at least sufficient time to notify the British Government of the trend of events in Egypt and to warn them what to expect. At any rate the reply was undoubtedly what Zaghlul expected and two days later he requested permission to proceed to London with his delegation to present their case to the Government.

It was at this point that the British Government made the first of a series of blunders which was to precipitate open rebellion. Zaghlul's request was brusquely brushed aside. In the meantime the Egyptian Prime Minister, Rushdi Pasha, who had carried the burden of office and cooperated loyally with Britain throughout the war, realised that the ground was being cut from under his feet and his position undermined by Zaghlul Pasha who was claiming leadership of the nation. Theoretically the Prime Minister was the official representative of the country, but in fact of course, as he had been placed in office by the ruler on the recommendation of the British Agent, there is no reason for supposing that he was the real nominee of the Egyptian masses who had had no voice in his appointment. It would appear that Rushdi Pasha was himself out of touch with what was going on behind the scenes, otherwise he would have known of Zaghlul's intentions. As it was he allowed himself to be anticipated. Somewhat belatedly therefore he followed Zaghlul's suit by making a formal request to the High Commissioner for permission to go to London to open up negotiations with regard to Egypt's future. This request was likewise refused on the ground that at that particular moment all the ministers were busy preparing for the peace conference, and that the time was not opportune for discussing the affairs of Egypt.

In refusing these requests the British Government erred grievously. If Zaghlul Pasha had been permitted to go to England, he would not have had an easy passage at the Foreign Office. Indeed, as he had no official standing in Egypt he would have had difficulty in substantiating his claim and title to leadership of the Egyptian people and he might, and probably would, have come away empty-handed and been discredited in the eyes of his followers. There might have been some justification for refusing to discuss the affairs of Egypt with Zaghlul who was only a private citizen, but there was no excuse for refusing Rushdi Pasha, the Prime Minister. Egypt had taken a substantial part in the war and had every right to be heard. By rejecting Rushdi's request the British Government indicated that they had no intention of modifying the status of Egypt and thus opened the floodgates of rebellion. Had the British Government invited Rushdi Pasha to the Peace Conference, had they been prepared to discuss the future of Egypt with him and make a few generous concessions to legitimate national aspirations, had they even formally acknowledged the great assistance they had received from Egypt during the war, Rushdi would have returned with his prestige enhanced in the eyes of the people, and the demands for independence might have been modified or at least postponed to a more opportune time. But the British Government was silent on all these points.

Zaghlul now embarked on a furious campaign to rally all elements of the country openly to his cause. What goaded the Egyptians into action even more than the cavalier treatment they had received during the latter phases of the war and the lack of recognition for their services, was the fact that the Arabs and Syrians were to be represented at the Peace Conference where they were to receive their independence, while the Egyptians, a far more progressive and civilised people, were to be kept in subservience. If the dismembered provinces of the defunct Ottoman Empire were to be granted their autonomy, surely Egypt by virtue of her importance, wealth and progress was the most deserving of the provinces to receive this benefit. But because she was under the thumb of the British army the idea of independence for Egypt appears not even to have occurred to the British Government in London or their representatives in Cairo. The Egyptian leaders Zaghlul and Rushdi had both offered negotiations and discussion as a way to a solution; both had been repulsed, the former somewhat brusquely. What alternatives were there of realising what the Egyptian nationalists considered a legitimate and proper aspiration, the freedom and independence of their country from foreign control? Peaceful negotiation having been rejected by the British, the only remaining alternative was active agitation, and Zaghlul threw himself into the campaign. 'Local committees were formed, public meetings were organised throughout Egypt, and signatures were collected wholesale for a mandate investing Zaghlul and his associates with authority to act on behalf of the Egyptian nation.'[1] As the campaign gathered momentum, the Prime Minister realised that he no longer commanded the confidence of his people and resigned in February 1919.

The British Government, now forced to the conclusion that they had been too hasty in rejecting the overtures of Rushdi Pasha, hurried to make amends by inviting him to London for discussions. But they had waited too long; in the space of two months the situation had radically altered. Zaghlul's campaign had borne fruit and the whole country acknowledged him as their leader and the champion of the national aspirations. Rushdi Pasha no longer commanded their confidence, and he was sufficiently well versed in the psychology of his people to recognise that any negotiations he undertook with the British Government would be given scant attention by the masses who looked only to Zaghlul. If there were to be any negotiations or discussion Zaghlul Pasha must certainly figure in them, otherwise it would be a waste of time, and Rushdi's answer therefore was that if he was to accept the invitation Zaghlul must come too. This view was also supported by the High Commissioner, Sir Reginald Wingate. The Foreign Office was clearly still very much out of touch with the Egyptian situation, for the proposal to bring Zaghlul Pasha to the talks was rejected. Wingate was called home to explain the situation.

For three months the campaign of agitation had been building up and by the beginning of March 1919 Egyptian public opinion was at boiling point; the British officials realised somewhat belatedly that public tranquillity and good order were in serious jeopardy. Zaghlul Pasha and his principal colleagues were therefore summoned to the presence of the General Officer Commanding, General Watson, and ordered to desist from any further agitation. But the die had been cast; there could be no drawing back now without losing all face and prestige in the eyes of the people. The warning was ignored and two days later the principals, Zaghlul, Ismail Sidky, Hamid el Bassal and Mohammed Mahmud were arrested and forthwith deported to Malta. This rash and hasty action was the spark which ignited the whole of Egypt. Within a few days the flame of rebellion swept the land from the Mediterranean to Wadi Halfa. It is unnecessary to dwell in detail on the riots and acts of violence perpetrated by the inflamed populace; suffice it to say that many Englishmen were savagely attacked and some brutally murdered.[2] Railway lines were torn up, telegraph and telephone lines were cut, and by

17 March Cairo was completely isolated from the rest of the world. It was finally realised in London that something was seriously amiss in the land of the Nile, that a sudden rebellion had broken out which could only be quelled by the employment of physical force. General Bulfin and the British troops were called in to take vigorous action, and by the middle of April the disorders had been quelled and the situation somewhat restored.

Much has been said and written about the fury and brutality of the Egyptian mob towards helpless Britons who fell victim to the rebellion during the riotous days of March 1919. It cannot be denied that many people died, that millions of pounds worth of damage was done, that for a period the inflamed populace became mad and ran amok, and that those who had stirred the people to rebellion either would not or could not restrain the forces they had unleashed. Nevertheless it must be remembered that the political leaders of Egypt had been forced by the obstinacy and intransigence of the British Government to adopt the only alternative open to them of drawing attention to their grievances, and of persuading the British authorities that they were no longer prepared to be fobbed off with empty and specious promises.

The Government in London were astounded and shocked by the fury of the rebellion in Egypt. The uprising had certainly produced the effect it was intended to produce; it had brought recognition that a new and unexpected situation existed in Egypt which demanded urgent attention. In Paris the eye of the British Prime Minister, Lloyd George, looking round anxiously for a capable and resolute man to deal with the emergency in Egypt, alighted on the soldierly figure of General Allenby, the victor of Palestine who had been summoned to the Peace Conference as Commander-in-Chief, Syria and Palestine. Allenby was forthwith appointed Special High Commissioner in Egypt with instructions

> to exercise supreme authority in all matters military and civil, to take all such measures as he considers necessary and expedient to restore law and order, and to administer in all matters as required by the necessity of maintaining the King's Protectorate over Egypt on a secure and equitable basis.

The General was bundled off without a moment's delay on his new commission and arrived in Egypt on 25 March when the rebellion was beginning to exhaust itself.

General Allenby was given a task of exceptional difficulty and complexity to perform. Although a capable soldier, commander and administrator, he had had no training in or experience of diplomacy or of the manifold political ramifications of a complex oriental society. He was being packed off without a moment's delay to a strange country which was boiling with revolt, a country which had no government and in which no native ministers could be found to take office. His first task was to bring the disturbances to an end, and it appeared logical to him that if the causes of the disturbance were removed, the latter would disappear. His first enquiries into the situation in Egypt led him to the conclusion that the immediate root of the trouble had been the arrest and deportation of the nationalist leaders, Zaghlul Pasha and his colleagues. He therefore advised that they should be released from custody and allowed to proceed where they would.

> This recommendation came as a shock to the British Government; they had sent a strong man to reduce a recalcitrant people, and his first proposal was to make a concession they had already twice refused . . . But the Government could hardly disregard the advice of the man to whom they had given full powers . . .; they agreed somewhat reluctantly to his proposals.[3]

The Egyptian leaders were accordingly enlarged on 7 April.

Allenby's action was at the time, and has since been, bitterly criticised on the ground that he yielded to the forces of disorder and gave the Egyptians ground for believing that they had only to resort to violence to gain their ends. 'A Foreign Office spokesman concluded a contemporary résumé of the events with the words, "Thus a fortnight of violence has achieved what four months of persuasion failed to accomplish. The object lesson will not be lost in Egypt and throughout the East." '[4]

A more searching probe of the situation would have revealed much deeper causes of the unrest in Egypt. The bottom fact was that during recent years the policy of Britain in Egypt had undergone substantial modification. If we look back to the origins of the occupation, it will be recalled that the sole justification for the presence of the British in Egypt was the declaration of Lord Granville made in January 1883: 'The position in which Her Majesty's Government are placed . . . imposes upon them the duty of giving advice with the object of securing that the order of things to be established shall be of a satisfactory character and possess the elements of stability and progress.' The intention of the British Government in those days had been to establish a stable and progressive régime for the benefit of the Egyptian people, and to retain the army of occupation while this régime was being achieved. There was never any suggestion that British interests were involved, apart from ensuring the regular payment of the coupons, or that Britain was defending any position she may have had in the country. At that time she had no interests in Egypt, no position to defend and her actions in Egypt may therefore be regarded as disinterested. But in 1919 the position was completely changed. The British Government had asserted a protectorate, and had begun to talk of 'British interests in Egypt'. In a word, accent on the peaceful development, stability and prosperity of Egypt had been conveniently forgotten and had given place to less disinterested consideration, i.e. the benefits afforded by British control of the country to Britain and the Empire.

The events of the recent war had brought home to the British Government the fact that Egypt lay astride the most vital link in her imperial communications, the Suez Canal, and that this link was peculiarly susceptible to attack, as had been illustrated by the Turkish offensive of 1915 which very nearly succeeded. It was thus discovered that Britain had substantial interests in Egypt, interests which had not been fully appreciated prior to the war, but were well appreciated now. The twist of fate had fortuitously thrown Egypt into Britain's lap thirty-seven years previously when she had taken upon herself the task of supervising the government of the country and promoting peace and prosperity and making way for stable self-government. But in 1919 it was realised that self-government was inextricably bound up with abandonment of the occupation and of the British control. It was realised that the army of occupation which for nearly four decades had been stationed in Egypt for the purpose of supporting the British-controlled Government, likewise served the purpose of garrisoning Egypt against foreign aggression and of defending the Suez Canal. It was now apparent that the interests which Britain discovered she had in Egypt would be placed in jeopardy by any modification of the political status of the country which tended to relax British control.

For an entirely different reason and more as a stop-gap measure Britain had declared a protectorate over Egypt on the outbreak of war which was assumed to be temporary only, for the duration of the war. Whether this assumption was valid for the British Foreign Office is not very clear, but it was most certainly so in Egyptian eyes, and all in Egypt had been looking forward eagerly to the time when it could be abolished and Egypt left to look after herself. But the protectorate strengthened and formalised Britain's control and afforded better guarantees for the maintenance and defence of her interests. Thus it was that Allenby's instructions included 'the necessity of maintaining the King's Protectorate over Egypt on a secure and equitable basis'. But Britain had already placed herself in an impossible position by her repeated declarations in the past regarding the temporary character of the occupation, by her war-time declarations that the war was being fought for the freedom of the small nations and by her adhesion to the principle of self-determination. The Egyptians had never been consulted about the imposition of the protectorate nor had they accepted it. They had raised no protest because they had not been allowed to, and in any case they only regarded it as a temporary measure occasioned by the war. But Allenby's instructions left no room for doubt about the intentions of the British Government. Allenby had come to maintain the protectorate, not to abolish it, and if Egypt was to achieve her independence it was no use looking towards Britain for it. There was some reason for hope that the other world powers might afford support for Egypt's demands for freedom. Zaghlul Pasha, now released from Malta, therefore hastened to Paris where the representatives of the powers were assembled to settle the future of the world.

In Egypt, the release of the nationalist leaders was heralded with demonstrations of joy and for the moment it seemed as if the country would return to peace and good order. At any rate, sufficient tranquillity prevailed for the moment to persuade Rushdi Pasha to take office again on 9 April and form a new Ministry. But the release of the nationalist leaders did not produce any relaxation of political agitation; on the contrary it was intensified, the campaign being conducted from afar by Zaghlul Pasha now in Paris. The results are well summarised by Lord Lloyd:

> Their demands at once hardened and their activities increased. On April 9th the military were again in collision with the crowds, and between that day and the 11th there was a sinister crop of murderous assaults upon isolated Europeans. The campaign of violence had proceeded to the inevitable next step. Strikes were organised everywhere; strike-breakers were violently attacked and intimidated; a National Police Force, so called, was set up which endeavoured to usurp the authority of the Government forces, and there was a sudden outpouring of pamphlets and broadsheets containing fierce attacks upon the traitors who dared to hold moderate views or refused to take orders from the Nationalists.[5]

The Government of Rushdi Pasha, after a few days of abortive effort to induce the Government officials to return to work and to restore normal conditions, resigned on 21 April only twelve days after taking office. Not only was the country once more left without a government, but most of the officials were on strike. Allenby was finally obliged to issue a warning that any officials who were absent from their posts the following day would be regarded as having resigned and that anyone found endeavouring to intimidate them would be prosecuted by a military court. The next day found most of the officials back at their work and a period of relative calm ensued.

By this time the British Government had concluded that the recent unrest in Egypt was not simply an isolated incident which could be dealt with by a strong man, but a genuinely national movement carrying the support of almost the entire population of the country. It was therefore decided to resort to that favourite device of British Governments for deferring any immediate decision while at the same time giving the appearance of action, a Commission of Enquiry. Thus one more entry was to be made in the catalogue of missions which had been sent out during the past fifty years to solve the riddle of Egypt.

The story of the Commission of Enquiry may be briefly told. It was headed by Lord Alfred Milner who had seen much distinguished service in Egypt and was the chronicler of British achievements in his book, *England in Egypt*. He was now a Cabinet Minister and the Commission thus became known as the Milner Mission. The despatch of such a mission had first been suggested by Allenby in April 1919 and it is possible that if his suggestion had been acted upon immediately, it might have produced a solution acceptable to both Britain and Egypt. But the sense of urgency did not sufficiently impress itself on the Cabinet with the result that the Mission did not arrive until the following December. Eight months were allowed to elapse which gave Zaghlul Pasha, still in Paris, time to decide what attitude should be adopted towards the Mission and to formulate his plans accordingly. Thus when the terms of reference were published and the Mission arrived, plans were ready laid. The terms of reference were

> to enquire into the causes of the late disorders in Egypt and to report on the existing situation in the country and the form of a constitution which, under the Protectorate, will be best calculated to promote its peace and prosperity, the progressive development of self-governing institutions, and the protection of foreign interests.

The nationalists took the strongest objection to two conditions in these terms. One was the implication that the protectorate was to continue, with its corollary that British influence was to remain paramount; the second was the proposal that the Mission, a body of Englishmen, was to suggest 'the form of constitution'. The nationalists felt that if Egypt was to have a constitution her own leaders could frame it without any assistance from Britain. Zaghlul therefore decided that the Mission should be completely boycotted, and all arrangements to this end were well made with the result that the Mission had a most difficult and unsatisfactory sojourn in Egypt. Almost their only contacts were with the Sultan Fuad and a few officials, although in fact a few secret interviews were arranged. To conciliate Egyptian opinion, the Mission put out a statement that they had been sent 'to reconcile the aspirations of the Egyptian people with the special interests which Great Britain had in Egypt, and with the maintenance of the legitimate rights of all foreign residents in the country.'[6] This declaration was a considerable concession to Egyptian opinion, for it made no mention of the protectorate and has been strongly criticised by Lord Lloyd on the ground that 'the Mission tore up its own terms of reference and committed the British Parliament to the abandonment of the Protectorate which until that moment had been solemnly declared to be a cardinal point of British policy.'[7]

But on the other hand the members of the Mission would have been failing in their duty if they had refused to see the situation as it actually was, and had bound themselves to terms of reference which, they saw, were clearly impossible of execution. They saw that the protectorate was objectionable to the majority of Egyptians, that its continuance could only be effected by the employment of force and that to that extent it was incompatible with 'progressive development of self-governing institutions'. The Mission also put forward the view that Egypt was not and never had been a part of the British Empire. Lord Lloyd strongly contests this opinion and asserts that by virtue of the protectorate Egypt was *de facto* and *de jure* a part of the Empire and quotes Lord Cromer in support. It is however more than doubtful whether the unilateral declaration of the protectorate constituted an act of incorporation within the Empire, for it will be recalled that at the time the question arose in December 1914, there was considerable discussion whether Egypt should be annexed outright or not. Annexation would of course have meant incorporation in the Empire, but this policy was abandoned. It must therefore be concluded that Egypt, although under British protection, was not a part of the Empire and that the Mission was right in so stating.

The Mission remained in Egypt for three months and returned to England in March 1920 to draw up their report. They had early decided that the maintenance of the protectorate, one of the principal clauses in their terms of reference, was unworkable and incompatible with harmonious Anglo-Egyptian relations, and that they should recommend the Government to

343

cancel it and replace it with a freely negotiated treaty. But so far they had had no contact with the nationalist leaders who were still in Paris. As these would undoubtedly take a prominent part in any negotiations for a treaty, it was necessary at least to sound them and discover their views before making any formal recommendations to the Government. Adly Yeghen Pasha, a prominent Liberal and moderate 'who commands the universal respect of his countrymen and whose advice has been of the greatest value to us in Egypt, paid a visit to Paris and at once put himself into communication with Zaghlul Pasha with the object of bringing about a meeting between him and the Mission.' Zaghlul Pasha was beginning to be somewhat concerned about the partial deterioration of his standing with the Egyptian masses. In Paris he had been singularly unsuccessful in gaining the ears of the delegates to the Peace Conference; President Wilson had even recorded the adherence of the United States to Britain's protectorate over Egypt. At the same time, so far from home, Zaghlul was unable to bring his magnetic personality and heady oratory to bear on his inflammable compatriots, who were beginning to pay attention to the more sober counsels of the moderates such as Adly Yeghen. Zaghlul recognised that if he was to retain his ascendancy, it behoved him to keep in the limelight by returning to the political arena. The invitation to go to London afforded him an excellent opportunity.

The Mission's intentions in inviting Zaghlul to London were merely to conduct some exploratory conversations with him with the object of getting an accurate picture of his views and some idea of the minimum concessions which nationalist Egypt would require for a freely negotiated treaty. But in its dealings with Zaghlul Pasha in London the Mission allowed itself to be diverted from this course, and the ensuing discussions became tantamount to active negotiations for the proposed treaty. No doubt the anxiety of the members to produce a satisfactory solution was largely responsible for this peculiar conduct, for the Mission had of course no authority to enter into negotiations with Zaghlul or anybody else. Realising the dangerous position they were placing themselves in, the members had to stress that they had no authority to conclude a formal treaty, but this pronouncement was rightly discounted in Egypt, for Milner himself was a member of the Cabinet and whatever concessions he agreed to in discussion with Zaghlul were regarded as binding on the British Government. However, after long argument and discussion, a number of proposals were finally drawn up which it was thought would serve as a basis for the negotiation of a treaty, although these fell short to some extent of the main planks on which the Egyptian Nationalist cause had been erected. In brief the proposals envisaged:

344

1. The independence of Egypt,
2. The abolition of the capitulatory rights of foreigners,
3. Britain to guarantee the defence of Egypt and Egypt to render all necessary assistance in case of war,
4. Egypt to be represented in foreign capitals by ambassadors, but not to adopt any attitude inconsistent with the treaty of alliance with Britain,
5. Egypt to grant Britain the right to maintain military forces on Egyptian soil for the protection of her imperial communications,
6. Egypt to appoint, in concurrence with the British Government, Financial and Judicial Advisers,
7. Egypt to recognise the right of the British representative to intervene to prevent the application of any law which would under present circumstances require foreign consent, but Britain would only exercise this right if such laws operated inequitably against foreigners,
8. The British representative to be accorded an exceptional position with precedence over all other foreign representatives,
9. The appointment of British and foreign officials of the Egyptian Government could be terminated within two years; compensation terms to be determined by the Treaty.

Such were the principal agreements reached between Zaghlul and the Milner Mission, but although they embodied the very limit of concession which the mission was prepared to recommend to the British Government, they fell short to some extent of the oft-declared aspirations of the Egyptian Nationalists. Even so, they constituted a substantial advance which, given the right lead, Egypt might be expected to embrace gladly.

Zaghlul of course had no authority to commit his country any more than the Milner Mission. The proposals were merely intended as a basis for negotiation, and they would have first to be considered by Egypt. But someone was required to take the initiative and give a lead to the country, someone laying claim to the confidence of the people to stand forth and urge that these proposals were advantageous to Egypt and the best that could be secured. Clearly the one man who could have undertaken this role was Zaghlul himself. But 'Zaghlul was afraid of public opinion and did not have the courage to give it a lead.'[8] He feared lest he might be accused of bartering away Egypt's rights by accepting the limitations on Egypt's independence implicit in certain of the proposals. No word of encouragement or approval emanated from Zaghlul, and his Nationalist compatriots were quick to take due note. In informal conversations the Milner Mission had made substantial concessions to Egyptian aspirations; certainly, they thought, Britain could be squeezed for more in formal treaty negotiations. In fact the conduct of the Milner Mission had virtually pledged the British Government to a series of agreements which represented the extreme limit of concession, while on the other hand Egypt had pledged herself to nothing; Britain had placed all her cards on the table while Egypt kept her hand hidden.

The report of the Milner Mission was submitted in January 1921 and published the following month, nearly two years after the Mission had first been suggested by Lord Allenby. Whatever the outcome of its deliberations, the Mission had at least served the purpose of providing a moratorium, but this had brought no substantial change in the situation. Acting on the recommendations of the report, the British Government forwarded a request to Sultan Fuad for the despatch of an official delegation to negotiate the proposed treaty. But by this time the intricate political situation in Egypt made even the formation of a delegation difficult. In March 1921 Adly Yeghen Pasha, the Liberal, became Prime Minister and, as the official head of the Government, he expected to lead the delegation to London. But Zaghlul Pasha had done all the preliminary spade-work in getting the negotiations advanced so far and he considered that he was entitled to take the leading part in the next stage. He hurried back at last to his native country, arriving at Alexandria on 4 April, and was greeted with tremendous demonstrations of national rejoicing; his journey to Cairo resembled a Roman triumph. While openly declaring his support of Adly Pasha, he made it clear that he expected to lead the delegation himself and that members of his party should comprise the majority. It must be admitted that he had every justification for making this claim, but of course Adly Pasha, in his official capacity as Prime Minister, refused to concede the leadership to his rival, and the final composition did not include Zaghlul or his followers.

> The answer of the mob was 'Long live Saad. No president of the negotiations but Saad. Saad has our confidence. Down with the Government,' and riots in Cairo and Alexandria. Out of a total population of about 14,000,000 over 17,500,000 signatures purporting to be those of adult males were affixed to a declaration of lack of confidence in the Ministry.[9]

Thus, while Adly Pasha was in London negotiating with Lord Curzon, the Foreign Secretary, Zaghlul back in Egypt was stoking up the fires against the absent Prime Minister; in the circumstances Adly's mission was doomed to certain failure. Adly Pasha knew that he could not return to Egypt with a treaty which did not meet the demands of the Nationalists in every particular, and Zaghlul took care to ensure that these demands were far in excess of any concessions the British Government could be expected to make. After several months of protracted negotiation – the main point of difference being the maintenance of British troops on Egyptian soil – Adly Pasha returned empty-handed and resigned the Premiership on 9 December. Lord Curzon was very annoyed at the failure of the discussions which had consumed so much time and effort. He instructed Lord Allenby, the High Commissioner, to present a note to Sultan Fuad which was not calculated to ease the tension between the two countries. The note contained a résumé of events from the British occupation to the present time, and specifically mentioned the points on which the Egyptian gratitude should have been forthcoming; it also contained a number of unpleasant home truths well calculated to touch the *amour propre* of nationalist Egypt. The note in fact gave every indication of being the outraged expression of disappointment at the failure of the treaty talks. Perhaps from the British point of view it might have been more profitable simply to state that as no agreement had been reached, the status quo would be maintained firmly and vigorously in the future.

Lord Allenby had no faith in the protectorate as an instrument for maintaining British interests in Egypt. As has been noted, British policy had undergone considerable modification and now centred upon the security of the imperial communications. With the eye of a soldier Allenby saw that these interests did not depend upon the protectorate, but upon the army of occupation and British naval supremacy in the Mediterranean. As long as these forces were present, it mattered little whether Egypt was a protectorate or an independent state. Since nearly the entire Egyptian population was clamouring for independence, it was desirable, in Lord Allenby's view, to satisfy these aspirations in so far as they did not conflict with British and other foreign interests. Although Allenby had been sent out to maintain the King's protectorate, he early came to the conclusion that it was not in the best interests of either Egypt or Britain, a conclusion which the Milner Mission likewise reached independently.

The situation had thus been reached when no Egyptian could be found to form a ministry without some substantial concession from Britain who had now in effect committed itself. During the absence of Adly Pasha in London the Minister of the Interior, Sarwat Pasha, had acted as Prime Minister and had shown his capacity for firmness, and it was to him that Allenby now looked to form a new government. But Sarwat Pasha was unwilling to take office on the status quo, feeling, probably very justifiably, that he could make no progress in face of the national unrest and the political activity of Zaghlul Pasha and his adherents.

> On the 11th [December] he submitted a programme which ignored the treaty negotiations so far as they related to British claims, but accepted them so far as they related to British concessions. If the protectorate was terminated, the sovereign independence of Egypt recognised, and the Egyptian Ministry of Foreign Affairs reconstituted, Sarwat Pasha would be prepared to take office and to prove to Great Britain that her obligations and interests could safely be entrusted to the care of Egypt.[10]

The British Government finally accepted these proposals, but even then Sarwat found himself unable to form a ministry largely owing to the renewed agitation of Zaghlul. As a result of this fresh disorders broke out, and Zaghlul was again warned to cease all political activity. On his refusal he and a number of colleagues were arrested on 22 December and deported, first to Aden and finally to the Seychelles Islands. At the same time Allenby put out his full naval and military strength to patrol the towns and ports, and good order was maintained. But still no ministry could be formed and considerable, and at times acrimonious, correspondence followed between Allenby in Cairo and Lord Curzon in London.

> Put as briefly and as simply as possible, the difference between Allenby's standpoint and that taken up hitherto by His Majesty's Government was as follows: the Government was prepared, subject to the approval of Parliament, to abolish the Protectorate and recognise the independence of Egypt, provided the Egyptians would first bind themselves to conditions regarding certain British interests and rights, of which the chief were the safeguarding of our Imperial communications, the protection of the foreigners in Egypt, and our position in the Sudan. This the Egyptians refused to do. Allenby proposed that the Government should abolish the Protectorate and grant independence forthwith, but should announce at the same time that Britain retained liberty of action . . . in certain matters, afterwards known as 'the reserved subjects, until such time as an amicable agreement on these matters could be reached.[11]

It is unnecessary to dwell on the long dispute between Allenby and the Cabinet on this difference of opinion. Allenby threatened to resign if his proposals were not accepted – for which he was accused of holding a pistol at the Government's head – and he was called hurriedly to London to confer with the Prime Minister, Lloyd George. The Government finally yielded and Allenby won his point. On 28 February 1922 he returned to Egypt bearing a unilateral declaration granting independence to Egypt. The declaration, though of far-reaching importance, was brief and to the point:

Whereas His Majesty's Government, in accordance with their declared intentions, desire forthwith to recognise Egypt as an independent sovereign state; and whereas the relations between His Majesty's Government and Egypt are of vital interest to the British Empire; the following principles are hereby declared:

1. The British Protectorate over Egypt is terminated, and Egypt is declared to be an independent sovereign state.
2. So soon as the Government of His Highness shall pass an Act of Indemnity with application to all inhabitants of Egypt, Martial Law as proclaimed on 2nd November 1914 shall be withdrawn.
3. The following matters are absolutely reserved to His Majesty's Government until such time as it may be possible by free discussion and friendly accommodation on both sides to conclude agreements in regard thereto between His Majesty's Government and the Government of Egypt;
   (a)   The security of the communications of the British Empire in Egypt.
   (b)   The defence of Egypt against all foreign aggression or interference direct or indirect.
   (c)   The protection of foreign interests in Egypt and the protection of minorities.
   (d)   The Sudan.

Pending the conclusion of such agreements the status quo in all these matters shall remain intact.

This date, 28 February 1922, was a memorable day in the history of Egypt. After many centuries of domination by a succession of foreign nations, Egypt was recognised by the world as free and independent. The only limitations on her liberty as a sovereign state were those embodied in the four 'reserved points' enumerated above. Memorable though this occasion was, it produced no joyous reaction or even acclamation from the Egyptians. For indeed, while the Declaration of 28 February 1922 constituted the most substantial advance in the political history of Egypt to date, it still fell far short of the deepest aspirations of the nationalists who felt that they had only won the husk, but had been robbed of the real fruits of victory. The four reserved points imposed severe restrictions on the freedom of the country both in internal and external affairs; these therefore merit attention. The first and second points signified that there would be no modification of the British military occupation, for the British Government now regarded the presence of the troops as a guarantee of the security of the Suez Canal and as a deterrent to any aggression from abroad. Britain, in assuming responsibility for the defence of Egypt, also insisted upon paramount influence in Egyptian military and foreign policy; the Sirdar of the Egyptian army, for example, would continue to be a British officer. The third point meant that Britain reserved to herself the right of safeguarding the interests of the foreign minorities resident in Egypt and would therefore insist on the continued employment of British officials in the main departments of the administration, particularly the Ministries of the Interior, Finance and Justice. The fourth point implied that the 1899 Condominium Agreement would remain in force unimpaired, i.e. that the Sudan would remain under British control. The Declaration thus imposed severe restrictions on the freedom of action of the Egyptian Government, but left the way open for securing agreement on these points 'by free discussion and friendly accommodation on both sides'.

At any rate the concessions now granted were sufficient to permit a Ministry to be formed under the leadership of Sarwat Pasha on 1 March. But as a nominee of the High Commissioner Sarwat of course commanded no following among the people and was almost universally disliked. The sole function of the new Government was to act as a caretaker until such time as a Constitution could be framed and an election held. At this point the shadowy figure of the Sultan Ahmed Fuad who had remained in the background during the months of turmoil, now began to emerge and make its presence felt. On 15 March 1922 he assumed the title of King Fuad I of Egypt. A true disciple of his father Ismail Pasha, he had no belief in parliamentary democracy as an instrument of government for his country, nor any relish for the role of constitutional monarch under such a system; the tradition of personal rule was as strongly engrained in him as it had been in his father. His first act therefore was to attempt to interfere in the framing of the constitution with the object of securing substantial powers for the monarchy. When Sarwat Pasha, under whose aegis the constitution was being drafted, resisted these attempts, the King was not slow to use his versatile flair for intrigue to remove his Prime Minister from office. The precise relationship of the Sudan with Egypt furnished him with the necessary pretext. The Commission set up to draft the Constitution defined the Sudan as a part of Egypt, and this produced a sharp reaction from the British Government who reminded the Commission that the Sudan, being specifically one of the 'reserved subjects', was outside their province. As was only to be expected, this produced a storm of protest and abuse in the Nationalist press, and the King's open support of the Nationalist claim sufficiently conveyed to Sarwat Pasha the desirability of relinquishing his office. He resigned in November, and the King immediately replaced him with a man more amenable to his wishes, Tewfik Nessim Pasha.

All through the year the Nationalists had been active in discrediting the Sarwat Government, denouncing the February Declaration as being unilateral and therefore not binding on Egypt, and provoking unrest. Hostility to the British remained undiminished and a series of attacks on British officials and murders continued regularly during the year. Allenby was slow to intervene on this account. He took the view that if the Egyptians were henceforth to govern themselves, they must learn to face their problems alone and unaided. The foreign minorities, outraged at the steady succession of atrocities against themselves, bitterly condemned the High Commissioner for making no attempt to stop them. At the end of the year, therefore, all signs of stability and progress were singularly lacking.

The British Government who had hoped much from the Declaration, a return to peace and good order, a constitution and a parliamentary régime, were becoming impatient with the impasse but no progress could be made as long as King Fuad persisted in his claims to sovereignty over the Sudan, and in the end Allenby was obliged to address a strong warning to His Majesty that unless he desisted in his claim the British Government would 'review at once and radically their recent declarations of Egyptian policy.'[12] Fuad had to bow to this ultimatum, and on 15 March Tewfik Nessim was replaced as Prime Minister by a relatively unknown man of no party affiliations, Yehia Pasha Ibrahim, upon whom fell the burden of framing the Constitution. No doubt King Fuad expected to exercise as much influence over the new Prime Minister as the old, but Yehia Pasha was not to be deflected from producing a Constitution which truly reflected the democratic spirit, and in this he was well supported by Lord Allenby whose intervention from time to time placed a check on the astute monarch. After several months of impasse it seemed that at last some of the difficulties were being surmounted and progress made towards the establishment of a democratic régime. It is therefore a cause of some puzzlement that this particular time was selected for the enlargement of Britain's most formidable opponent and Egypt's most active political leader. Zaghlul Pasha had been confined in the Seychelles Islands but, his health suffering, he had been transferred to Gibraltar. On 24 March it was announced that he was to be released. But Zaghlul did not return to Egypt until the following September, and in the interval much was done to clear the way for an election. On 19 April 1923 the Constitution was promulgated, and since this was to be the political charter somewhat intermittently for the next few years, its main provisions are worthy of note:

1. Egypt was declared a sovereign independent state under a hereditary monarchy and with representative government.
2. All power emanated from the nation. The King exercised legislative powers with the Senate and Chamber of Deputies. Each house had the right to initiate laws, but the King and Chamber of Deputies could alone deal with taxes. No measure could become law unless voted by Parliament and sanctioned by the King.
3. The Throne was to be hereditary in the house of Mohammed Ali and succession in accordance with existing rescript.
4. The King could dissolve the Chamber of Deputies to which Ministers were responsible.
5. Power could only be exercised by Ministers. No non-Egyptian national, nor any member of the reigning house, could hold office.
6. Ministers were to be appointed and dismissed by the King.
7. Parliament was to consist of a Senate and a Chamber of Deputies. Of the Senate two-fifths were to be nominated by the King and three-fifths elected each for a period of ten years, one senator to every 180,000 inhabitants.
8. Deputies were to be elected by universal suffrage, one to every 60,000 inhabitants for a period of five years.
9. Taxes could only be imposed or modified by law; no loans, concessions or monopolies could be allowed without the consent of Parliament. Existing financial or international obligations could not be modified.
10. The Constitution was applicable to Egypt without prejudice to the rights which Egypt had in the Sudan.[13]

The Electoral Law promulgated on 29 April 1923 made voting indirect. Every adult male of twenty-one years or more had the suffrage, and each group of thirty electors could nominate one delegate to participate in the election. Candidates for the Chamber of Deputies must be at least thirty years of age and for the Senate forty years. All voting was to be secret.[14]

Before any arrangements could be made for an election martial law which had ruled the country for the past nine years had to be abolished, and a preparatory step to this was an act of indemnity. Both these measures were put into effect peacefully and with little comment in July, and the way lay open to Egypt to govern herself on democratic lines. One further matter which had to be settled was the position of the British officials in the service of the Egyptian Government. The Milner Mission had somewhat optimistically put forward the view that 'the idea of any Egyptian Government, however free to do so, attempting to make a clean sweep of its foreign officials is a chimera.' The trend of events, however, was affording ample evidence that this pious hope was entirely unfounded and that the Egyptians were only too anxious to divest themselves of all foreign encumbrances. The officials concerned were therefore much perturbed about their future, and there was clearly need for some definite agreement between them and the Egyptian Government regarding their continuing in their offices, or for compensation should their services be dispensed with. Hitherto the Government, ever with an eye to public opinion, had been evasive on this question, but Yehia Pasha courageously tackled it and produced a reasonably satisfactory compromise.

Zaghlul Pasha returned to Egypt in September in time for the election nominations, and was greeted with enthusiastic demonstrations from the populace. He put himself at the head of the Nationalist Party, now known as the Wafd or Delegation, and proceeded to organise the campaign. His principal opponents were the Liberal Constitutional Party of Adly Pasha. The Wafd had a programme based on complete freedom and independence, with phrases and catchwords well calculated to appeal to the populace, and the party was moreover highly organised. When the election took place in January 1924 the Wafd completely swept the board, gaining 190 seats out of a total of 214, and on 27 January Zaghlul Pasha was invited by the King to form the first democratic government in the history of Egypt.

This was a memorable day in the story of modern Egypt, the day on which for the first time a representative government took over the reins with the idol of the people at its head. Complete independence was not yet achieved; it was restricted by the four 'reserved points' of the 1922 Declaration, but the British Government had indicated its willingness to negotiate agreements on these matters. The prospect for the future was particularly bright; the Treasury was full and the new Government had every opportunity of strengthening its position and reputation by initiating a policy of internal reform for the welfare of the masses, by carrying out new public works and improving education, health and other social services. The new Government could have no stronger weapon in any future negotiations over the reserved points than a record of solid honest administration, stable government and social improvement. But this was not the course to be chosen by Zaghlul Pasha. He had risen to the crest of the wave by a campaign of inflammatory oratory and hostility to Britain; the only way he knew of riding the wave was by the continuance of this hostility. Careful administration and social reform were not the subjects to hit the headlines and would arouse little acclamation among the masses; reform and social improvement could only be effected by cutting at traditional privilege and incurring the enmity of powerful groups. Zaghlul had no desire to lose any part of his popularity. The 1922 Declaration provided him with plenty of fuel to keep the fires of hate burning, and the Zaghlul Government of 1924 devoted most of their energies to stoking the fires.

At the same time as Zaghlul Pasha and the Wafd took office in Egypt, the first Labour Government came to power in Britain under the leadership of Ramsay Macdonald. During the preceding years of unrest various Labour leaders, Macdonald included, had expressed sympathy for Egypt in her national aspirations, and it now appeared that with the new Labour Government in power there could be no better opportunity for extracting the maximum concessions from Britain in respect of the four reserved points. The recent events in Egypt would have warned any experienced government in Britain that the best way they could serve their interests in Egypt was to take a firm stand on the 1922 Declaration and to show no inclination to open negotiations for its modification, but to wait for Egypt to make the first approaches. But the Government of Ramsay Macdonald, politically inexperienced and anxious to prove their theory that all problems could be settled at the conference table, lost no time in making the first overtures. Thus, when the Egyptian Parliament opened on 15 March, Macdonald sent a congratulatory telegram affirming his belief in the bonds of friendship between Britain and Egypt and stating his willingness 'now and at any time to negotiate with the Egyptian Government'. Such manifest anxiety to come to terms gave the impression that Britain was dissatisfied with the present relationship between the two countries, when in fact she had every reason to be content with them. Where Macdonald's message was wide and general in its expression, Zaghlul's response, as indicated in King Fuad's speech from the throne, was much more specific:

My Government is ready to enter into negotiations, free of all restrictions, with the British Government so as to realise our national aspirations with regard to Egypt and the Sudan.

Had Zaghlul played his cards well by a studied programme of conciliation, there is good reason for supposing that he would have obtained handsome concessions from the new Labour Government, but he seemed unable to curb his traditional hostility. One of his first acts was to inform Lord Allenby that he proposed to modify the law enacted the previous year by Yehia Pasha regulating the indemnities of the British officials. 'From telegrams of expansive benevolence Mr Macdonald was at once compelled to turn to grave warnings, the effect of which was of course weakened by his previous attitude.'[15] This proposal was typical of the irresponsibility of the Wafd leader and was not calculated to impress the world with his good faith and stability. It is the essential feature of any agreement between a government and its officials that it is permanent and binding and not to be tossed about the political forum. The arguments of the supporters of Zaghlul are excellent examples of sophistry:

> . . . while compensation was due to many who had taken their positions on the assumption of their being permanent, it was hardly a guarantee given by Egypt and in any case not by Nationalist Egypt. Nor perhaps, was it necessary to set the standard of this compensation so high that British officials were in many cases eager to take the cash and let the office go. It is certainly the duty of a head of a government to see that there is no unnecessary extravagance, especially when such extravagance means taxing his own people for the benefit of foreigners.[16]

It cannot be regarded as coincidence that as soon as Zaghlul Pasha took office political agitation and unrest made an appearance in the Sudan, and particularly in the Egyptian army units stationed there, which resulted in riots in Omdurman in June 1924, demonstrations by the cadets of the Military School at Khartoum and a mutiny of the Egyptian Railway Battalion at Atbara.

Mr Macdonald was soon to find the cordial offer of negotiation that he had made a source of embarrassment for, although during the following months Zaghlul Pasha's declarations were such as to preclude even the remotest possibility of agreement, the offer having once been made could not be withdrawn. The farce was accordingly played out. Zaghlul was again invited to London to negotiate a treaty. He left Egypt on 25 July but proceeded first to Paris and did not arrive in England until late September. There was in fact no negotiation. Zaghlul simply stated his demands, viz., 'the withdrawal of the British army from Egypt, and of the Financial and Judicial Advisers; disappearance of every vestige of British control, and that His Majesty's Government should drop their claim to protect foreigners, minorities and the Suez Canal.'[17] That was the end of the negotiation. This and subsequent attempts to reach a settlement lend strength to the view that the Wafd was never anxious to conclude any settlement, but preferred to keep the pot boiling so that they would always have a whipping post to fall back on in case of need. The one notable exception, the 1936 Treaty as will be later narrated, was forced on the Wafd by external forces. In the negotiations of 1924, had Zaghlul concluded a treaty with Britain, he would have deprived himself of his mainstay in Egyptian politics, hostility to Britain, and left himself only that honest and progressive administration for which he had neither taste nor talent. Mr Macdonald was left little time to reflect on the failure of his round-table efforts; his Government fell in October 1924, and the Foreign Office under the new Conservative Government was taken over by Mr Austen Chamberlain.

Nor indeed was Zaghlul Pasha himself to remain long in office. His incessant campaign of hostility to Britain and the agitations and intrigues of his followers soon bore fruit. On 19 November 1924 Sir Lee Stack, Governor General of the Sudan and Sirdar of the Egyptian army, was assassinated in broad daylight near the Ministry of Education. Through all the long months of tension and disturbance Lord Allenby, the British High Commissioner, had, as far as was humanly possible, refrained from intervention, but this latest atrocity spurred him to action. In Allenby's opinion this murder was the direct and logical result of Zaghlul's campaign of hate and on him should be placed the prime responsibility. There was the danger that Zaghlul would resign office within a matter of hours in order to escape having to face the wrath of Britain as the official head of the government whose conduct had led to the outrage. Allenby did not therefore wait to consult with his Government in London, but on his own initiative presented the following note to Zaghlul Pasha:

> The Governor-General of the Sudan and Sirdar of the Egyptian Army who was also a distinguished officer of the British Army has been brutally murdered in Cairo. His Majesty's Government considers that this murder, which holds up Egypt as at present governed to the contempt of civilised peoples, is the natural

outcome of a campaign of hostility to British rights and British subjects in Egypt and Sudan, founded on a heedless ingratitude for benefits conferred by Great Britain, not discouraged by Your Excellency's Government and fomented by organisations in close contact with that Government. Your Excellency was warned little more than a month ago of the consequences of failing to stop this campaign more particularly as it concerned the Sudan. It has not been stopped. The Egyptian Government have now allowed the Governor General of the Sudan to be murdered and have proved that they are incapable or unwilling to protect foreign lives. His Majesty's Government therefore require that the Egyptian Government shall:

(1) Present ample apology for the crime.

(2) Prosecute enquiry into the authorship of the crime with the utmost energy and without respect of persons, and bring the criminals, whoever they are, and whatever their age, to condign punishment.

(3) Henceforth forbid and vigorously suppress all popular political demonstrations.

(4) Pay forthwith to His Majesty's Government a fine of £500,000.

(5) Order within 24 hours the withdrawal from the Sudan of all Egyptian officers and the purely Egyptian units of the Sudan Army with such resulting changes as shall be hereafter specified.

(6) Notify the competent Department that the Sudan Government will increase the area to be irrigated at Gezira from 300,000 feddans to an unlimited figure as need may arise.

(7) Withdraw all opposition in the respects hereafter specified to the wishes of His Majesty's Government concerning the protection of foreign interests in Egypt.

Failing compliance with these demands, His Majesty's Government will at once take appropriate action to safeguard their interests in Egypt and the Sudan.

A certain amount of criticism has since been levelled at Lord Allenby's ultimatum to the Egyptian Government. It is stated, for example, and with some truth that the increased irrigation of the Sudan Gezira had no connection with the murder of the Sirdar and should not have figured in the ultimatum. Yet it was clearly Allenby's intention to indicate, by including this demand, that the same irresponsibility which had led to the crime was present in the internal administration of affairs and that 'the Gezira irrigation demand was

. . . intended to impress on Egypt the power we could wield if necessary by our control of the Sudan.'[18]

The Zaghlul Government would only agree to the payment of the indemnity and in consequence Allenby took the matter into his own hands and ordered the withdrawal of the Egyptian units from the Sudan and the seizure of the customs house at Alexandria by the British army of occupation. Zaghlul thereupon resigned his premiership on 24 November having held it for only ten months. Although he was never to hold office again he yet remained the most powerful political personality in Egypt. This first Ministry of democratic Egypt was one of the most barren of her political, social and economic development. The most ardent supporter of Zaghlul would have the greatest difficulty in pointing to any single achievement of his which contributed to the welfare of the country. The apologists of Zaghlul suggest that he should never have taken office on the ground that 'to take office without authority is a dangerous and possibly a disastrous policy'.[19] If it is suggested that the support of 190 out of 214 Deputies is not having authority, it is difficult to understand the precise connotation of the word 'authority'. It is certainly true that it is easy and popular to stand aside and criticise the government, but there can be little sympathy or respect for one who refuses to take responsibility when urged to do so by the whole nation for fear of losing popularity.

However the irresponsible policy of hatred pursued by Zaghlul during his Ministry, instead of strengthening the position of his country, struck it a cruel blow, for it drove Britain to declare and exercise her power to intervene and served only to weaken Egypt's links with the Sudan. When the Egyptian troops were withdrawn, the remaining Sudanese were removed from the Egyptian army and incorporated into a new Sudan Defence Force which owed allegiance, not to King Fuad, but to the Governor-General of the Sudan alone.

A man of moderate opinion, Ahmed Ziwar Pasha was now called to form a government. He recognised that the only path for Egypt lay in co-operating with Britain, and accordingly the demands of Allenby's ultimatum were either met or modified by mutual agreement. One development resulted from the murder of Sir Lee Stack. Hitherto the offices of Sirdar and Governor-General of the Sudan had been combined in one person, invariably a nominee of the British Government. The two offices were now separated and although no new Sirdar was appointed by Egypt, at least she threw off a further shackle, i.e. a British officer in command of the Egyptian army.

The murder of the Sirdar which led to the resignation of Zaghlul struck a heavy blow at the Wafd who for a time lost many of their adherents. Nevertheless the Chamber remained predominantly Wafd, a situation which Ziwar Pasha found embarrassing to his government. He prevailed upon the King to dissolve the Chamber, a move which His Majesty accepted with alacrity. King Fuad had not during recent months been idle. He had brought into existence a new party, the Ittehad or Party of Union, which so strongly voiced the views of the monarch that it became known as the Palace Party. New elections were held in February 1925 which had the appearance of producing a non-Wafd majority, but when it came to electing a President of the Chamber the Deputies repented their desertion and elected their old leader Zaghlul. Ziwar Pasha thereupon offered his resignation to the King, but was persuaded to retract it on condition that the Chamber was again dissolved. The result was substantially a temporary return to the *status quo ante* the Constitution, a Ministry appointed by the King and leaning on the British High Commissioner for advice and support. It is illustrative of the demoralisation of the Wafd Party that they accepted this suspension of constitutional government for nearly a year without demur. At least for the time being the forces of disorder were quelled, largely as a result of the strong measures of the Minister of the Interior, Ismail Sidky Pasha, a man of forceful character, courage and administrative ability.

In the ensuing months of relative calm Lord Allenby resigned his post of High Commissioner. For six arduous years he had calmly and resolutely managed affairs and helped to shape the future of Egypt. To Allenby Egypt owed her independence, the policy which he had steadfastly, even obstinately, fought for against the strongest opposition of his own Government even to the point of resignation. Likewise Egypt owed much to him for his policy of restraint and forbearance during the difficult transition to constitutional government, and the remarkable tributes of esteem paid to him by Egyptians on his departure are ample evidence of the respect in which he had been held.

Lord Allenby was succeeded by Lord Lloyd who arrived in Egypt in October 1925. Lord Lloyd had already had a distinguished career in India; 'he had been a soldier, a governor and a politician in turn, and achieved credit in each. His confident air and agreeable manner left a happy impression, and Egyptians talked of the coming of another Cromer.'[20] In face of the fluid situation and the continuous variations of the political breezes Lord Lloyd cast about for some rock on which to anchor his policy. This he found in the 1922 Declaration. 'And when I undertook the office of High Commissioner it was with the determination to make the policy of 1922 a real policy – to leave no doubt in any minds that whilst the measure of independence granted under the Declaration must be real, the reservations and Egypt's respect for them must be equally real and our intention to see them respected made evident.'[21] In looking back over the events of the past few years Lord Lloyd was struck with the fact that Britain had successively taken up a number of stands and then proceeded immediately to recede from them, with the result that British prestige and authority had undergone a progressive deterioration, that disorder had reigned and all the elements of stability had been lacking; in Lord Lloyd's own words, a policy of erosion and *grignotage* had been encouraged.[22] He was determined that as long as he was High Commissioner this process of erosion would be checked and the rights which Britain had reserved to herself would be fully maintained and respected.

Inasmuch as Egypt had embarked on a constitutional régime, the Government of Ziwar Pasha could not expect to exist indefinitely without a Chamber. Yet any election held under the existing electoral laws could only have one result, a further sweeping majority for the Wafd, and a return to the confusion which existed prior to the murder of the Sirdar. Ziwar was therefore working on a reform of the electoral laws which would have the effect of disenfranchising a large section of the population which invariably voted on the Nationalist ticket. This and a number of other somewhat arbitrary measures by the Government were having the effect of uniting the political parties, Liberal and Wafd, into a solid block of opposition, as they feared that a continuance of the present régime would ultimately lead to the return of autocratic government under the influence of the King. In short there was a danger of fresh disorder which Lord Lloyd felt it his duty to allay. Pressure was brought to bear on Ziwar Pasha to withdraw the new electoral law and to hold new elections under a modified law of 1924.

As was only to be expected, the election which took place on 22 May 1926 once again resulted in an overwhelming victory for the Wafd who secured 144 seats out of 201. This result posed a problem of some complexity for the new High Commissioner. The British Government had fostered the growth of popular democratic government and under the 1922 Declaration had paved the way for its institution. Under this system the leader of the party with the majority vote was entitled to be invited to form a government. Thus in 1926 the position arose in which the legitimate successor to power was once again Saad Zaghlul Pasha under whose régime in 1924 unrest and political clamour had been fomented to an extent which finally resulted in the assassination of the Sirdar, and who had in reality been driven from office by British intervention. Were the British Government now going to stand aside and allow the man who above all others had shown himself to be the inveterate enemy of Britain to assume power in accordance with the democratic principle, or were they going to intervene to prevent him from taking office again? The policy decided upon by the British Government was that Zaghlul could not be allowed in office again. Fortunately they were not in the event called upon to implement this decision because in the end the Deputies of the Chamber virtually decided the matter themselves in that sense. The Wafd Deputies had fought the election and were eager to enjoy the fruits of office; they knew that the further accession to power of Zaghlul would inevitably lead to another suspension of the Constitution and the consequent loss of their own privileges and emoluments. Thus when Zaghlul offered to let the Deputies decide for him whether or not he should accept office, the latter gracefully but unmistakably threw their leader overboard. Adly Pasha, the most able politician available, was invited to form a new government. It must be said that Zaghlul, who was elected President of the Chamber by way of recompense, handsomely offered Adly Pasha his support and that of his followers. From this it was obvious that Zaghlul Pasha had at least learned that it was dangerous to twist the lion's tail too much and that he was now prepared to moderate his attitude.

That the progress of affairs during the next few months was relatively peaceful can be largely attributed to the policy steadfastly pursued by the British High Commissioner. As has already been stated, this was based on the Declaration of 1922, not because he had any particular affection for it, but because a rigid adherence to the principles contained therein was the only way of showing Egypt that Britain intended to be fair but firm. Looking back on the events of the previous years Lord Lloyd came to certain conclusions. The 1922 Declaration having been only a unilateral pronouncement on the part of Britain, was not binding on Egypt and had never been formally accepted by Egypt. At the time it was made, it was the best that Britain felt she could do to satisfy Egyptian aspirations and safeguard her own interests, but at the same time it was a makeshift device to be replaced by something more durable and more binding on both sides. In consequence Britain had been anxious to negotiate a formal treaty with Egypt which would supersede the 1922 Declaration and place Anglo-Egyptian relations on a more satisfactory basis. The attempts of the Milner Mission, Lord Curzon and Ramsay Macdonald to effect a settlement were ample evidence of Britain's desire to secure a treaty, but this very anxiety had so far been Britain's principal disability, for Egypt, or rather Zaghlul, had used it to attempt to force more concessions out of Britain than she had been prepared to make. In all these cases negotiations had broken down, and Lord Lloyd took the view, and undoubtedly the right view, that any further negotiations would likewise break down as long as Britain continued to evince such eagerness for a treaty. In brief Lord Lloyd's view was as follows: We shall only get a treaty acceptable to us when Egypt desires a treaty as much as, if not more than we. If we are going to have a strong bargaining position in any future negotiations the first approaches must come from Egypt. We have a policy to follow, the 1922 Declaration. We may not like it very much, but it will serve for the time being, and not only that, if we make it quite clear to Egypt that we intend to follow it firmly and unequivocally, that is, to leave Egypt to her own devices except on matters touching the four reserved points, Egypt will in time come to the conclusion that the old game of twisting the lion's tail is unprofitable and decide that it will be more in her interests to negotiate a final settlement rather than have her sovereignty restricted indefinitely by the reserved points. 'My objective was to impress upon Egypt that we were firmly determined to maintain the status quo established by the 1922 Declaration, and that nothing was to be gained by attempts to infringe it, and that her own interests could best be served by realising this and acting accordingly.'[23] If we pursue a policy of masterly inactivity except in regard to the reserved points, sooner or later Egypt will be demanding a treaty more than Britain.

Thus Lord Lloyd stood aside from the domestic affairs of Egypt, but kept a vigilant eye for any activities which might affect the reservations of the Declaration. On occasion he was obliged to intervene in this sense, once regarding the continued employment of Europeans in the Ministries which most closely affected the interests of the foreign minorities and the defence of the country, and again in regard to an army crisis which came to a head early in 1927. This crisis arose from a long sustained process of infiltration into the Egyptian army by the extremist section of the Wafd which aimed at securing control of the army and using it to overthrow the monarchy. Inasmuch as this process of erosion seriously affected the protection of Egypt and the foreign minorities, it necessarily became a matter of concern to the High Commissioner who was obliged to intervene and require the Egyptian Government to take certain measures designed to bring the army under more effective control. At one stage the situation became extremely tense, but the firm stand taken by Lord Lloyd eventually induced the Egyptian Government to give way and the crisis was averted. It was during the course of this crisis that Adly Pasha resigned, and once again Sarwat Pasha, as acceptable to the Wafdist majority of the Chamber, was invited to head the

Government.

It would perhaps be unjust to criticise in too harsh terms the first Egyptian attempts at democracy and constitutional government, for the sudden transition from subjection to independence, from tutelage to responsibility, created a certain vacuum which could only be filled with the passage of time. It is undoubtedly true that Zaghlul Pasha had no particular flair for the ordinary humdrum routine of administration, but more particularly is it true that when he headed the first democratic government of Egypt he found his former hostility and attitude of intransigence something of an embarrassment. The main plank which had brought him to power was the policy of the elimination of Britain from Egypt and the abolition of the army of occupation. When he came to power he found himself unable to go back on his previous declarations without laying himself open to charges of betraying his country. He had no alternative but to go on, even though he may have had an inkling that he was marching inevitably towards his own destruction. After his fall from power he appears to have learnt that the outright struggle against Britain was too unequal to pursue with any hope of profit, and that the complete emancipation of Egypt from British influence could only be effected by a more moderate and conciliatory attitude.

CHAPTER 22

Treaty Negotiations

Lord Lloyd's policy of taking a firm, even intransigent, stand on the 1922 Declaration appears to have been largely successful. At any rate the more turbulent elements among the Wafd found no encouragement in this uncompromising attitude, and there emerged at last a tendency for the Chamber to stop troubling the waters and to begin to pay attention to the welfare of the people. The situation in Egypt was thus relatively peaceful when in the middle of 1927 King Fuad and Sarwat Pasha paid a state visit to Britain.

From the purely British point of view there was every reason for pursuing the policy of masterly inactivity and waiting for Egypt to make the first advances for settling the problems outstanding between the two countries. But the age-old riddle of Egypt seems to have exercised a fatal fascination for British politicians. None seems to have been able to resist the temptation to try and solve it. The Milner Mission, Lord Curzon and Ramsay Macdonald had all pitted their wits in this problem and all had failed, and although in 1927 there was nothing to suggest that any further attempts would be more successful, Sir Austen Chamberlain, now Foreign Secretary, was likewise unable to resist the temptation. At the first opportunity during the Royal visit he brought Sarwat Pasha to the Foreign Office and re-opened 'conversations'. In a memorandum of these events prepared afterwards by Sir Austen Chamberlain he stated: 'I did not suggest that we should carry on any negotiations during his visit to London, but might we not prepare the way for conversations between himself [i.e. Sarwat Pasha] and Lord Lloyd when they had both returned to Egypt.'[1] But the Foreign Secretary was unable to overcome his enthusiasm, for 'the very next day permanent officials of the Foreign Office began negotiations with Sarwat, suggesting there and then that a treaty of alliance should be concluded.'[2] The unhappy Egyptian who in the interview with Chamberlain had only expressed an opinion that there must be friendly collaboration and that the aid of Great Britain was necessary to Egypt,[3] now found himself being hurried along the road to negotiation for a treaty. He had no mandate from the Chamber of Deputies to negotiate nor had he any advisers to help him resist the onslaught of the Foreign Office. Perhaps the most surprising feature of the whole affair was the fact that Lord Lloyd was himself in London at the time and had no inkling that any sort of negotiation was taking place, and furthermore that he had been assured by the Foreign Office 'that if at any time negotiations should appear to be possible, they would be conducted in Egypt and not in London'.[4]

It has been suggested[5] that it was Sarwat who opened the question of fresh negotiations, and first submitted an Egyptian draft for a treaty to the Foreign Office. But the wording of this draft makes it sufficiently clear that it had originally been drafted by British hands and revised to present the Egyptian view. It is probable that the draft had been given to Sarwat Pasha to study when he first went to the Foreign Office. This point is of some importance because, as the negotiations eventually came to nothing, Chamberlain was anxious to disclaim responsibility for starting them, and tried to convey the impression that it was not he, but Sarwat Pasha who had first raised the question. The evidence tends to point the other way.

Mistakes were made on both sides which finally led to the discomfiture of one and the damnation of the other. By raising the treaty question at all the Foreign Office dashed to the ground the whole structure of Anglo-Egyptian relationships which Lord Lloyd had so laboriously built up. By betraying their impatience for a treaty, they had once again seriously weakened Britain's bargaining position and thrown away their best counters. The mistake which Sarwat Pasha made was in consenting even to consider negotiating a treaty, and even more in drafting an Egyptian version. Once he had done this he found himself so deeply committed that he could not withdraw. The British officials were willing to discuss or modify every point of difference and go to the farthest limits to meet the Egyptian point of view, while at the same time the heaviest guns and the most persuasive tongues of the Foreign Office were brought to bear on him to make him see and agree to the basic essentials of British requirements. What the Foreign Office failed to understand was that however much Sarwat Pasha might agree with them personally, he in no way represented the views of his countrymen, least of all of the Wafd, and that any treaty which did not commend itself to that party was automatically doomed to failure.

It is unnecessary to dwell on the terms of the draft provisionally agreed between Chamberlain and Sarwat Pasha. It covered modification of the capitulations, Egypt's entry into the League of Nations, the appointment of Judicial and Financial Advisers, training of the Egyptian army and a number of other points which were not in dispute. No mention was made of the Sudan, as the difficulties of finding an agreed solution of this question were considered so great that it was thought better to leave it for separate negotiation at a later date. The critical clause of the proposed draft was the maintenance of British forces in Egypt for the protection of the imperial communications. Sarwat agreed to this principle although it was specified that 'the presence of these forces shall not constitute in any manner an occupation and will in no way prejudice the sovereign rights of Egypt.'

The great difficulty was going to be getting Egypt to accept the draft, but Sarwat Pasha was not without hope at first that he might succeed. Paradoxically, he was relying on the changed attitude of the national leader, Zaghlul Pasha. Ever since 1924, when the Stack murder had ejected him from power, Zaghlul had been studiously moderate in his attitude. He had promised the Ministry his support and as President of the Chamber he had kept his supporters in order and quashed any attempt on their part to introduce matters of a controversial nature. There was therefore just a possibility that Zaghlul could be persuaded to give the proposed treaty his support which would of course be followed by the nation. Unfortunately on 23 August 1927 the veteran leader, who had long been ailing in health, died. Saad Zaghlul well deserved his sobriquet 'Father of the Nation' for indeed he was the first man to unite Egypt into a democratic country. He it was who had clamoured, toiled and suffered for Egyptian freedom, he who had shaken loose the bonds of British rule and, against every opposition internal and external, had achieved the great ambition, the independence of his country for the first time since the epoch of the Pharaohs, and introduced the democratic system of government. On Gezireh Island in the centre of the road stands a great statue looking along the Nile Bridge towards Cairo. The statue bears no name; none is required for the *fellah* founder of democratic Egypt.

The mantle of Zaghlul as leader of the Wafd now descended upon his lieutenant, Mustafa el Nahas Pasha, whose antipathy for Britain was well known, and all possibility of Egypt accepting the proposed treaty was thus dissipated. However, although this was partially realised in London, the British Government, having once initiated the negotiation, were committed to see it through. Sarwat Pasha for his part knew that the death of Zaghlul heralded his own political annihilation, for sooner or later he must present the terms of the draft treaty to Egypt for her opinion and approval. Back in Egypt he resorted to every device to delay presenting the draft to his compatriots, to stave off the ruin which was bound eventually to encompass him. Thus from October 1927 to February of the following year every point of possible doubt or ambiguity in the draft was raised by him with Sir Austen Chamberlain for elucidation or interpretation. As this continuous stream of queries poured into the Foreign Office from Cairo, Chamberlain's attitude changed from one of expansive benevolence towards Sarwat Pasha to suspicion and anxiety. Questions were beginning to be asked in the House of Commons about the outcome of the negotiations with Egypt, and Chamberlain, who had hoped to lay that most coveted prize, an Anglo-Egyptian treaty, before the House, was becoming much embarrassed by the procrastination of Sarwat Pasha in acquainting Egypt with the terms of the draft. On 5 February 1928 the Foreign Secretary wrote to Lord Lloyd requesting him to urge upon Sarwat the necessity of placing the draft treaty before his colleagues without delay and proceeding to its signature at the earliest moment.

On receipt of this message Sarwat recognised the uselessness of trying to postpone the inevitable any further. He showed the draft to his colleagues in the Government who, following the lead given by Nahas Pasha, rejected it. On 4 March Sarwat notified Lord Lloyd to this effect and offered his resignation to the King. Once again the treaty negotiations had come to nothing. This latest effort, as has already been noted, resulted only in the political damnation of an Egyptian Prime Minister and the discomfiture of a British Foreign Secretary. Furthermore, relations between the two countries which in the previous two years had become more stabilised were now further embittered. The draft treaty had gone to the extreme limit of British concession to meet Egypt's aspirations, had granted almost complete freedom in every respect to the Egyptian Government, but under Article 7 had insisted on the presence of British forces on Egyptian territory 'in order to facilitate and secure . . . the protection of the lines of communication of the British Empire.' It was on this clause that the treaty foundered, for Nahas Pasha 'confined himself to asserting with a damnable iteration that it was quite useless to discuss this or any other treaty which did not provide for the complete evacuation of Egyptian territory by the British Army.'[6]

With the death of Zaghlul the hand of restraint was removed from the Wafd Party who began to plan a campaign designed to overthrow the monarchy and give the Wafd untrammelled power. Having a substantial majority both in the Chamber and the Senate they had, even before the resignation of Sarwat Pasha, introduced a new Assemblies Bill which was specifically framed to deny the Executive authority to limit or restrain public demonstration or meetings. The provisions of the Bill were such as to reduce the penalties which could be inflicted for disorder to nominal amounts, but to increase the punishments which could be imposed on the Police for interfering in public demonstrations for insufficient reason. The measure was clearly designed to surrender political power to the mobs in the streets who were strong supporters of the Wafd, and was in fact a carte-blanche invitation to anarchy and rebellion. The passage of this Bill to the statute book would be an obvious threat to public security and to the lives and property of the foreign minorities. As long as the treaty negotiations had been in progress the British Government had contented themselves with keeping a vigilant eye on these happenings, but had refrained from active intervention. But as soon as the negotiations broke down it became clear that some action was necessary. By the time Nahas Pasha came to power on 15 March the Bill had passed nearly all its stages and little remained to be done to place it on the statute book. Lord Lloyd made repeated verbal representations to the Prime Minister to dissuade him from proceeding with the Bill, and it must have been obvious to Nahas Pasha that he was treading on dangerous ground, but the possibility of incurring the displeasure of the British Government apparently weighed less with him than the odium he would incur from his own party, if he gave way. His refusal to withdraw the Bill finally led on 29 April to a direct ultimatum from Lord Lloyd requiring him 'as head of the Egyptian Government, immediately to take the necessary steps to prevent the Bill regulating public meetings and demonstrations from becoming law.'[7] If the Egyptian Government failed to give assurances to this effect by 2 May, the British Government would hold themselves free to take such action as the situation might require.

The reply to this ultimatum was cunningly contrived. Egypt, said Nahas, did not recognise the right of Britain to intervene in Egyptian affairs, but as an earnest of goodwill the Government would postpone consideration of this Bill until the next session of the Chamber. This was not as much as the British Government had demanded, but it was well recognised that Nahas' reply was only a face-saving gesture and that the bill would be tacitly dropped. It was thus deemed expedient to let the matter lie. In consequence Nahas remained in office, but only for a few weeks.

Many years previously, in 1898, the great-grandson of the celebrated Ibrahim Pasha, Prince Ahmed Seif ed Din, had attempted to murder Prince Fuad. He was afterwards pronounced insane and confined to an English institution. His estates and personal fortune which were considerable were confiscated and vested in the Crown. For years the Prince's mother had been fighting for the restoration of this great fortune, but without success. Thus it happened that a bombshell exploded on 19 June 1928 when a copy of an agreement purporting to be between the Prince's mother and Nahas Pasha and two other lawyers was published in the press. According to the contract, Nahas Pasha agreed to secure the restoration of the Prince's fortune for a fee of £130,000. From this it was obvious that Nahas was willing to use his political power to sway the judgement of the courts. Such a public scandal could not be passed over, and the King, who cordially detested and feared the Wafd, eagerly seized the opportunity presented by this development and summarily dismissed Nahas Pasha from office.

At the same time Mohammed Mahmud Pasha, a prominent and able Liberal, was invited to form a new Government, an offer which Mahmud Pasha accepted on the understanding that the Chamber which was overwhelmingly Wafd should be dissolved. The King willingly agreed and on 19 July issued a rescript dissolving the Chamber for three years during which period Egypt would be governed by his own Cabinet d'Affaires. The suspension of the Constitution was the first open sign of the secret struggle which had been going on between the King and the Wafd, both of whom were seeking supreme, even dictatorial, power in the land. Under the modified Constitution which gave the direct vote to every adult male, most of them illiterate, ignorant and a prey to inflammatory nationalist propaganda, the Wafd could always count on an overwhelming majority at the polls. The King therefore, if he was not to be deprived entirely of any say in the affairs of the nation, was driven to battle not only with the Wafd, but with the constitutional régime which maintained them in power. Once more the Constitution which sat so uneasily on Egypt's shoulders had broken down, but at least a period of relative tranquillity ensued in which the Mahmud Ministry was able to devote itself to some solid, honest administration. Notable among the achievements effected by the new Government was the signature of an agreement with Britain on the control and allocation of the Nile waters, thus securing to Egypt by formal agreement her historic and natural rights to her share thereof. The successful conclusion of these negotiations well illustrated that when a moderate government was not hampered by all the political clamour and strife of the constitutional system, solid progress could be made and measures of far-reaching importance to the welfare of the nation affected.

The fact that for about a year there was very little of significance to report is indicative of the tranquillity which reigned in Egypt under the Mahmud Government. Party politics were at a low ebb while the Wafd was licking its wounds and living down the disgrace of the previous year. This situation was not however to endure for long. In June 1929 the second Labour Government of Ramsay Macdonald took office in Britain with Mr Arthur Henderson at the Foreign Office. Like all his predecessors, Mr Henderson was hypnotised by the riddle of Egypt and dazzled by the prospect of carrying off the great prize, a solution of the problem and an Anglo-Egyptian treaty. Some mention has already been made in this and the preceding chapter of Lord Lloyd's policy of standing firm on the Declaration of 1922 and waiting for Egypt to make the first approaches. Mr Henderson saw in the continued presence of Lord Lloyd as High Commissioner in Egypt the greatest obstacle to his ambitions, and determined to get rid of him at all costs and at the earliest opportunity. If Lord Lloyd's own account of the affair is to be believed – and this is fairly well authenticated – the means employed by Mr Henderson to achieve his object were, to say the least, not very creditable. Lord Lloyd was virtually turned out of office and resigned on 24 July 1929. The way was thus cleared for Mr Henderson to try his hand at the great riddle. Mahmud Pasha paid a visit to England on 18 June 1929 and Mr Henderson, either ignorant or heedless of the examples and failures of his predecessors, plunged straight into negotiation.

There is, as in the previous case, some conflict of opinion as to who was in fact the prime mover in the ensuing negotiations. On 23 December Mr Henderson stated in the House that he did not initiate the conversations. On the other hand Mahmud Pasha is reported to have come to England 'with the intention of discussing with the British Government the reform of the capitulations in Egypt and of exploring the ground for the admission of Egypt to the League of Nations, and not with the expectation of negotiating on larger political issues.'[8] It is probable that the latter version is more strictly correct and that Mahmud Pasha, having broached to the Foreign Office the subjects which formed the purpose of his visit, was steered into conversations on the wider issues. In any event it seems unlikely that Mahmud Pasha, with the fate of Sarwat fresh in his mind, would have voluntarily raised the treaty question. He was not prepared to accept the role of plenipotentiary, but only to act as intermediary. He adopted the well-tried formula that any treaty between Britain and Egypt must be submitted to the Egyptian people for their approval. However, as the Chamber had been dissolved for three years by royal rescript, it was not clear precisely how the treaty could be considered in an authoritative manner. In any case the approval of the party leaders would have to be secured, and on his return to Egypt in August 1929 Mahmud Pasha was able to obtain the general concurrence of the Liberal and Ittehad parties, but the Wafd, who were beginning to recover from their wounds, saw in the new development an excellent opportunity of regaining their lost power. Nahas Pasha refused even to look at the treaty until a new election had been held and the Chamber reinstated, well knowing that an election would result in another overwhelming victory for the Wafd. Mr Henderson was thus obliged to curb his impatience until this problem was settled, but no doubt his anxiety was to some extent instrumental in persuading King Fuad to reverse his decree and agree to a new election. Mahmud Pasha resigned on 2 October, to make way for an interim government which would handle the elections. For this purpose Adly Pasha temporarily took office and the elections were duly held on 21 December. As had been predicted the Wafd gained an overwhelming victory and the King had no alternative but to invite his enemy Nahas Pasha as leader of the Wafd to return to power.

Now that a new Parliament had been elected which could be reckoned to voice the views of the Egyptian people, the way lay open for a resumption of the treaty negotiations. The position of Nahas Pasha was somewhat complicated. On the one hand he could not expect a real victory in Egypt unless he could make a settlement with Britain which was a substantial advance on the proposals agreed between Mahmud Pasha and Mr Henderson. He would thus be obliged to wring from the British Government concessions which went beyond the limits which Mr Henderson had agreed the previous year. On the other hand, Nahas had already learnt to his cost that the power of the monarch Fuad was great enough to unseat him even despite the popularity of the Wafd with the masses. What he required to combat the intrigues of the Palace was a further counterpoise, and this might well be found in the support and benevolence of the British Government which he might reasonably expect as a reward for a satisfactory agreement. Thus when he went to London in March 1930 he had on this occasion a powerful motive for burying the hatchet and establishing cordial relations.

The negotiations between Nahas and Henderson proceeded smoothly over thirteen of the sixteen clauses. Even the garrisoning of the Canal Zone by British troops was conceded – this in spite of Nahas Pasha's earlier avowals that 'it was quite useless to discuss any treaty which did not provide for the complete evacuation of Egypt by the British Army'. The Sudan had always been a knotty problem in previous discussions, and in the present case it proved to be the stumbling block on which the whole negotiation foundered. The British negotiators were anxious to include a clause in the Treaty: 'While reserving liberty to conclude new conventions in future modifying the conventions of 1899, the High Contracting Parties agree that without prejudice to Egypt's rights and material interests the status of the Sudan shall be that resulting from the said conventions.'[9] This was unacceptable to the Egyptian representatives who wanted a definite agreement that further negotiations should take place on the Sudan within one year of ratification of the treaty. As the treaty envisaged the entry of Egypt into the League of Nations, acceptance of the Egyptian proposals would have given Egypt the right to raise the whole question of the Sudan before the General Council. The British were therefore unable to accept the Egyptian amendment. Proposal and counter-proposal followed without agreement until 17 April when it was finally announced by the British Government that unless Egypt accepted the latest British draft, there could be no treaty. Nahas Pasha stood firm on this point and the negotiations were broken off. Both sides however took care to put it out that in spite of this fresh breakdown relations between the two Governments remained excellent, and that although they had failed to obtain a treaty, they had cemented the friendship between the two countries.

Indeed, Nahas Pasha felt the need for the support and friendship of Britain, for he was aware that he was returning to a fresh crisis and struggle in Egypt. Ever since the Wafd victory at the elections of the previous December, King Fuad by the devious means open to him had been pursuing a policy of solid obstruction to the Government, and it was clear that a crisis could not be long delayed. Nahas Pasha feared that the King might repeat his manoeuvres of 1928 by dismissing him from office, dissolving the Chamber and ruling by decree. Nahas intended to forestall this possibility by himself introducing legislation ensuring the continuance of the parliamentary system, by providing for the severe punishment of any 'ministers who should be guilty thereafter of violating the Egyptian constitution'.[10] These bills were in fact a direct attack on the prerogatives of the King, and Fuad therefore naturally refused to initial them. Within a few days the business of government threatened to come to a standstill and on 17 June Nahas Pasha decided to resign. Precisely why is not very clear unless he expected that his resignation would be followed by a popular outburst. If so, he was disappointed for the King responded with alacrity, accepted his resignation and called upon Ismail Sidky Pasha. Sidky was an ardent nationalist but also an autocrat by nature; he had no faith in the parliamentary system as at present constituted in Egypt and believed in government by a strong hand. These ideas marched well with King Fuad's own sentiments and a mutually satisfactory partnership was formed.

On 21 June, one day after Sidky's accession to power, parliament was prorogued, and on 12 July the session was closed by Royal Decree.[11] Thus the condition of Egypt shifted rapidly from a Wafd-dominated parliamentary régime to a virtual dictatorship by Sidky Pasha acting on behalf of and in conjunction with his Majesty. Egypt had slipped back to her traditional form of government. These changes led to a certain amount of incipient unrest during July 1930 to an extent which prompted Ramsay Macdonald, the British Prime Minister, to address a warning to Sidky Pasha regarding the protection of foreign minorities, and to send warships into Egyptian waters. But Sidky replied accepting responsibility for the safety of foreigners and he was strong enough to carry out his promises. The unrest was ruthlessly quelled and Sidky and the King were left in command of the situation. Even so, as the constitutional régime was in theory the political charter of Egypt, there were difficulties and embarrassments in the method of governing by decree. The holding of new elections under the 1923 Constitution could only have one result, another victory for the Wafd, and this the King was determined to circumvent. The obvious solution would be the abrogation of the old Constitution and the establishment of a new one which would guarantee a Chamber fully supporting the system of Palace government.

On 22 October 1930 Fuad issued a rescript promulgating a new constitution and electoral law, the latter reinstating the two-degree method of election. 'All the changes were in the direction of reducing the powers of the electorate and increasing those of the Ministry and the Crown.'[12] The new measures not only separated the Wafd further from the Palace, but also created a rift in the Liberal Party, Mohammed Mahmud its leader taking his stand on the old constitution, while Sidky drew off a section of the Party which he reconstructed into a new group called the Shaab or People's party. The elections which took place under the new law were undoubtedly 'managed' and resulted in a convincing majority for Sidky's new party which, together with the substantial backing of the Ittehad, the Palace Party, dominated the Chamber. All was thus set for a legalised continuation of Palace government.

Whatever may have been the ethical position of the constitution, at any rate a marked degree of political stability was achieved, and for the next two years peace reigned and Egypt faded almost completely from the news. Sidky and Fuad between them ruled the country for thirty-nine months until 21 September 1933 when the Prime Minister, exhausted and ailing in health, was obliged to resign. Fuad continued to maintain his ascendancy by appointing as Prime Minister a man subservient to his will, Abdul Fattah

Yehia Pasha, and peaceful conditions continued for another year and might well have continued to do so, had it not been this time for a breakdown in the King's own health. All this time there had been no further mention of a treaty; indeed it appeared that the British Government had finally taken to heart the lesson which Lord Lloyd had so earnestly tried to teach, that there was nothing to be gained by displaying undue anxiety for a treaty. Likewise in Egypt it was well recognised by the King that a treaty was out of the question, as a *sine qua non* was its ratification by the nation, which would imply new elections and return of the Wafd to power. Thus during these years Anglo-Egyptian relations continued to be governed by the 1922 Declaration, the old horse which, although it had in the past been almost flogged to death, still continued to give good service.

It appears that during the King's dictatorship he had succeeded to a great extent in restoring the traditional prestige and respect for the throne in the eyes of the people, and there had therefore been a general acquiescence in the return to autocratic government. But when the King fell ill and the power fortuitously slipped into the hands of a Palace official, Zaki Pasha el Ibrashi, murmurs of discontent began to arise from the people and the parties. The Prime Minister, Yehia Pasha, was not the man to dominate a situation of this sort. To yield to Ibrashi would be courting the condemnation of the country; to resist him would be risking the displeasure of the monarch. He anxiously sought a way out of this invidious situation, and approached the acting British High Commissioner, Mr Peterson, for his advice. The advice received was not to the liking of the Prime Minister who very disingenuously launched a press campaign accusing the Residency of interfering in the internal politics of Egypt. On this ground he resigned from office on 6 November 1934 and the King was left to look for a suitable successor. But there was no one who was willing to take over the role of puppet of the King in the government of the country, no one at any rate who could command the respect of the people at the same time. The game of Palace government had been played with considerable success by Fuad and Sidky, both strong and competent men, but now with the withdrawal of the one and the ailing health of the other the game was played out. Egypt was ripe for a change and a return to the parliamentary régime. After a fruitless search for a minister the King was obliged to yield and finally called on one of the elder statesmen, Tewfik Nessim Pasha, to form a government. But Nessim Pasha was unwilling to take over on the existing basis, and he extorted considerable concessions from the King including the abrogation of the 1930 Constitution. In making this concession it is probable that the King realised that with the decline of

374

his health he was a waning force, and perhaps even that his days were numbered. Thus the return to the old constitution was the only possible bequest he could leave to his people.

At the same time as these changes were going on in Egypt, pressure from an entirely external force was moving her forward to a return to the constitutional régime. Signor Mussolini, the Italian Duce, was busy carving out his new Roman Empire in north-east Africa and was in process of adding Egypt's and the Sudan's neighbouring state, Abyssinia, to the Italian bag. Egypt was thus likely to be surrounded on many sides by this new empire, and who could say when Mussolini might try to fill the gap separating the western parts from the eastern? Indeed, Egypt had every reason for being nervous of the present developments on her borders; not only that, there were other aspects to consider. Her relationship with Britain was still governed by the 1922 Declaration and the four 'reserved points' under which Britain reserved to herself the security of the communications of the British Empire and the defence of Egypt. The Italian aggression in Abyssinia had resulted in a state of tension between Britain and Italy to an extent where the possibility of war could not be ruled out. In such an eventuality it was beyond doubt that the principal scene of operations would be the Valley of the Nile. There was no understanding or agreement of any sort in existence defining precisely what Britain could or could not do in operations for the defence of Egypt, but it was certain that she would regard herself as having a free hand in the country and the Sudan. There was thus even the danger that the independence which Egypt had wrested after so many centuries of servitude might once again disappear in the melting-pot of war. What was now wanted, and particularly in Egypt, was an agreement clearly defining the rights and limits of Britain in Egypt in any eventuality. In fact the time which Lord Lloyd had so strongly stipulated as offering the only possibility of a treaty was now in sight. But no treaty could be signed and ratified without the endorsement of the nation, and this could only be expressed by a freely elected and representative assembly of the people.

Likewise in Britain the desire for a formal treaty on Anglo-Egyptian relationships was re-awakened by the trend of events in north-eastern Africa. As is well stated in the Survey of International Affairs:

the stand which Great Britain was taking against an Italian act of aggression upon a backward African state might be weakened morally by the spectacle of Great Britain preparing to vindicate the principles of the Covenant by strengthening her forces in a much more civilised African country which she herself had been holding without any legal title for more than half a century by means of a military occupation which had originally been established by force of arms.[13]

The general desire in Egypt for a formal settlement – and this was stimulated by certain military and naval movements by the British in the Delta – led to at least a temporary coalition of the parties in a United Front, but the question of the Constitution remained to be resolved. In November 1935 a statement by the British Foreign Secretary, Sir Samuel Hoare, that 'when, however, we have been consulted we have advised against the re-enactment of the Constitutions of 1923 and 1930, since the one proved unworkable and the other universally unpopular' provoked a storm of protest from all sides in Egypt, on the ground that this constituted an unwarrantable intrusion in her private affairs. It appears also that when Nessim Pasha received this advice, he had regarded it as a simple veto by Britain on both constitutions. Further speeches by Sir Samuel Hoare, intended to allay the suspicions of Egypt, only reacted the other way, although the wording and tenor of these speeches were clearly conciliatory. The result of these declarations was the exertion of intense pressure by the parties on Nessim Pasha who had during his tenure of office been co-operating to a certain extent with Britain in the military measures which had recently been taken. As a result of the interpretation of the British expressions of opinion, viz., that Britain would veto both the 1923 and 1930 Constitutions, Nessim Pasha decided to resign, but before he could do so the British High Commissioner, Sir Miles Lampson, intervened by explaining personally to Nessim Pasha that Britain had no intention of interfering in the promulgation of any Constitution and that Egypt was free to do as she pleased in this matter. This advice was sufficient to induce Nessim Pasha to stay in office and also to demand of the King the re-establishment of the old 1923 Constitution. Thus was the way cleared for the resumption of parliamentary government and, perhaps more important still, negotiations for a treaty which was now ardently desired on all sides in Egypt. On this occasion the time factor was of some importance, for it was recognised that if British action in Egypt was to be defined and limited, the treaty must be agreed before the tension between Britain and Italy gave way to an open passage of arms. Thus, even before the new elections which eventually took place in May 1936, a delegation was formed under the leadership of Nahas Pasha – it being apparently well recognised that the forthcoming elections would bring him back to power – for the purposes of conducting the preliminary conversations.

Nessim Pasha resigned on 21 January 1936 to make way for a caretaker government under Ali Maher Pasha who had been Chief of King Fuad's Royal Cabinet. The elections which took place in May produced the inevitable result, another overwhelming victory for the Wafd, but this time King Fuad was not destined to see his inveterate enemy in power for the third time. The ailing monarch, now sixty years old, died on 28 April and was thus spared that humiliation. The King's only son Faruk was still a minor at Sandhurst in England, but the constitutional difficulty was overcome by the formation of a Regency Council composed of members of the Royal Family. Nahas Pasha became Prime Minister on 10 May and immediately formed an all-Wafd government.

Even before this steps had been taken to initiate the treaty negotiations. In February 1936 Mr Anthony Eden, the new British Foreign Secretary, authorised Sir Miles Lampson to commence conversations with the Egyptian delegation in Cairo, and for this purpose senior officers of the British armed forces were sent to advise the High Commissioner on the military aspects. It had been hoped on the Egyptian side that Britain would respect the promises made by the Labour Foreign Secretary, Mr Henderson, five years previously that Britain would not regard as voided those clauses which had been agreed in the negotiations of 1930, and that the new conversations could therefore commence at the point at which they had previously been broken off.

But as a result of the new military situation occasioned by Mussolini's incursions into North Africa and the rapid technical advances in methods of warfare, the British military advisers insisted on going over this ground again. In the 1930 negotiations agreement had been reached that Britain should be empowered to maintain forces in certain defined localities in Egypt to facilitate and secure the protection of the Suez Canal. But this time the activities of Italy on Egypt's western frontier made it appear to the British advisers that this previously agreed clause was now insufficient to provide for the effective defence of Egypt, and consequently far-reaching demands were made on the Egyptian delegation for more freedom of action for the British forces. These concessions the Egyptian delegation were unwilling to grant and by the month of June the whole negotiation threatened to come to a new deadlock, this in spite of the evident and sincere desire of both sides to reach an agreement. It was perhaps natural that the advisers should do their utmost to obtain 'perfect military security, watertight for all time and circumstances,'[14] but nothing was to be gained by insistence on this if it was going to lead to a new breakdown in the negotiations. Like Allenby in 1922 Sir Miles Lampson exerted himself to break the deadlock by flying to London and arguing the Egyptian case with the British Government. Again, like Allenby, he won his point and on his return to Egypt on 30 June talks were again officially resumed which this time led to agreement on both sides. The draft was initialled by Nahas Pasha and Sir Miles Lampson, and all that remained to be done was the formal signing of the Treaty. In August the Egyptian delegation left for London, arriving on the 23rd. Three days later the Treaty was duly signed at the Foreign Office by Nahas Pasha and Mr Eden.

Thus after fourteen years of endeavour and frustration the objective so ardently sought, particularly by Britain, was finally achieved. The 1922 Declaration, that uneasy document, was now consigned to the limbo of the past and Britain, instead of having to justify herself in the eyes of the world by an instrument which was in effect simply a demonstration of superior force by one country over another, could now declare with truth and justice that her interests in this vital link in her empire communications were maintained and protected by her own troops with the full concurrence of the country in whose territory they were stationed.

There was likewise ample room for satisfaction in Egypt. By the enactment of a formal defensive alliance Italy was warned that any incursions into Egypt or the Sudan would be met with the full weight of Britain and Egypt together. Mussolini at any rate was left in no doubt about the consequences of any such aggression, and it soon became clear that he was not prepared to ignore the omen. Even more important, the powers and rights of British troops to range freely over Egyptian territory were abolished. All such movements could henceforth be made only with the permission of the Egyptian Government. The price Egypt was paying was small, the grant of a right to the British to station a few troops in the deserts bordering the Suez Canal out of sight of the Egyptian people and no longer a constant affront to the national dignity. They could now look forward to the time when the British uniform would no longer be seen in Egyptian towns and cities.

Two further benefits accrued to Egypt. The capitulations, the centuries-old outmoded relics of the Ottoman Empire which survived in Egypt alone, would shortly be swept away and Egypt would finally have the power to regulate and control all who had made Egypt their home irrespective of race or nationality. In the Sudan her prestige which had suffered so grievously in 1924 after the murder of the Sirdar, would be restored and her influence would be much enhanced by the freedom of immigration bestowed by the new treaty. All in all Egypt had good cause to be well satisfied with the efforts and persistence of Nahas Pasha and his colleagues. Finally it must be reiterated that Lord Lloyd's premise had been amply justified by the result; the Treaty had only been possible when Egypt herself actively wanted it.

CHAPTER 23

Egypt and the Second World War

The acclamations which greeted the signature of the Treaty and the return of the delegates to Egypt were amply indicative of the general relief felt by all sections of the population, and for the time being it was forgotten or glossed over that the Wafd which from the time of its foundation to 1930 had obstinately adhered to the principle of the complete evacuation of Egypt by the British army, had now not only substantially receded from this stand, but had formally authorised the continued maintenance of British forces on Egyptian soil. At the time no doubt the general relief tended to obscure this retrogression, but as the tension between Britain and Italy eased and the prospect of a clash of arms receded, the significance of the terms of the Treaty became more apparent, and it began to be questioned whether in fact the Wafd had driven such a good bargain after all.

However, these doubts were for the moment thrust into the background by the imminent prospect of casting off a further shackle on Egypt's independence. Under Article 13 of the Treaty it had been agreed that 'the capitulatory régime existing in Egypt was no longer in accordance with the spirit of the times and with the present state of Egypt,' and that steps should speedily be taken to abolish it. As a result a conference was called at Montreux on 12 April 1937 attended by representatives of all the powers possessing capitulatory rights in Egypt, and for the next four weeks negotiations for the abolition of the ancient privileges took place, during which every aspect of the position and rights of foreigners in Egypt was thrashed out. In brief, the Convention which was signed on 8 May 1937 finally abolished this traditional fetter on Egypt's liberty to control and regulate foreigners residing within her frontiers, and made arrangements for the transfer of the judicial powers of the Mixed Courts, which had since 1875 adjudicated in cases involving foreigners, to the Egyptian national tribunals. The transfer was to be spread over a transition period dating from 15 October 1937 to 14 October 1949 on which date the Mixed Courts would cease to exist. Egyptian courts would thereafter assume jurisdiction in all cases. With the disappearance of the capitulations the last vestiges of the now defunct Ottoman Empire disappeared from Egypt, and another landmark in her independence was made. A few days later, on 26 May, Egypt was formally elected a full member of the League of Nations in accordance with Article 3 of the Treaty thus setting the seal on her status as a free and sovereign state.

These various developments during 1936 and 1937 served to maintain the already enhanced popularity and prestige of Nahas Pasha and the Wafd, both of whom enjoyed the limelight of public applause. But during these two years there was rapidly emerging another contender for the title of popular idol, the young King Faruk. The antipathy of the Wafd for the Palace and vice versa was traditional and sustained. In spite of the relatively indifferent appeal which the late King Fuad had enjoyed with the masses, he had always managed to outmanoeuvre the Wafd, and if his son, who was now showing every sign of winning the affection of the people, intended to follow his father's autocratic footsteps, a clash would sooner or later be inevitable. It was the intention of Nahas Pasha to bring the young monarch under his tutelage and to thrust him in the background as much as possible, but although only sixteen years of age, King Faruk was to prove himself unpliable material in this respect. In spite of his youth and inexperience he was determined to continue his father's struggle and to use all the natural advantages available to him to this end. To his youth, his good looks and his personal charm he added an aspect of extreme piety to Islam, and his regular Friday attendances at the mosques among the people and his benefactions to El Azhar and to needy students all assisted him in his campaign to win the affection of the masses. Within a short space of time the race for popularity between Nahas and Faruk increased in intensity, and the latter soon began to overhaul his rival. This process was much facilitated by the attitudes of the non-Wafd parties. With the signing of the Treaty the United Front had lost its *raison d'être* and had disintegrated, and the anti-Wafd parties, delighted at finding such a splendid rallying point, clustered round the Palace.

As the threat to his supremacy increased, Nahas Pasha became more and more autocratic in his attempts to drive a wedge between the King and the people. Indirect attacks were made on the *ulema*, in particular the Rector of El Azhar, and attempts were made to reduce their traditional authority in the educational system. Likewise the dictatorial attitude adopted by Nahas Pasha, his tendency towards nepotism and the interference of his wife in the Government to the advantage of her family[1] all combined to create dissatisfaction, not only among the parties, but in the Wafd itself. The rumblings of discontent became even more pronounced when the important Ministries of Finance and Foreign Affairs were given to two Copts, respectively Makram Ebeid Pasha and Butros Ghali Pasha. These appointments were regarded as an attack on the Moslem character of the country.

By December 1937, instead of having quelled all opposition to his leadership and annihilated his political enemies, Nahas Pasha had succeeded in effecting the reverse. Attempting to take a leaf out of Hitler's book (he had already started a para-military organisation known as the Blue Shirts) he summoned a meeting of the Wafd deputies and demanded that they take an oath to support him alone as Prime Minister.[2] Even this failed to strengthen his position, for a further rift in the lute took place when a dispute arose between the Finance Minister, Makram Ebeid, and the Minister of Communications, Nokrashy. Nahas Pasha's support of the Copt cleft the Wafd in twain and resulted in the formation of a new splinter party called the Saadists, after Saad Zaghlul, under the leadership of Nokrashy and Ahmed Maher. Taking advantage of this low ebb in the fortunes of the Wafd, on 30 December 1937 King Faruk suddenly dismissed Nahas from office, appointed in his stead Mohammed Mahmud and called for new elections. These took place in March 1938 and, although it is not known to what extent they were 'managed', the results sufficiently reflected the general dissatisfaction of the country with the previous administration. For the first time in the history of constitutional Egypt the Wafd, i.e. that section of it led by Nahas Pasha, suffered a crushing defeat, gaining only twelve seats. The new splinter party, the Saadists, took eighty-four, while the Liberals and their allies gained a majority with ninety-nine seats and thus confirmed Mahmud Pasha in power.

For about eighteen months a period of relative peace descended on the country, but in the distance the storm clouds were gathering. Egypt, which three years previously had gladly entered into a treaty with Britain to protect herself from the Italian peril, now became increasingly anxious lest this same treaty should embroil her in the war which was threatening to burst over Western Europe. If war came between Britain and Germany, what attitude was Egypt going to adopt? According to the terms of the Treaty she was bound to afford certain assistance to her ally, and this she already recognised, but on the other hand a subtle and insidious stream of propaganda had for some time been focused on Egypt and other countries of the Near East which had not failed to make an impression. Arab sympathies in regard to the incipient struggle in Palestine tended to awaken some response to the Nazi policy of anti-Semitism. Mussolini too had skilfully managed to allay Egyptian fears of Italian aggression by declaring himself the friend and protector of Islam, while underlying all political sentiment in Egypt was the increasing resentment engendered by the thought that in spite of the so-called bilateral treaty Egypt had allowed herself to be trapped in the negotiations, and was still in fact a client state of Great Britain, with British troops still stationed on her soil. Memories were short, and now that the danger which had made the treaty possible three years previously had receded into the distance, the acclamations which had greeted its signature were conveniently forgotten. In the eyes of many Britain was still the bogey, and it was feared that she was going to drag Egypt into a new war which was no concern of Egypt's and use her as a mere tool.

A few weeks before the outbreak of war in September 1939 between Nazi Germany and the British and French allies, Mahmud Pasha had resigned from office on the grounds or pretext of ill-health, and the young King, now firmly in the saddle of public affairs, filled the breach with his own guide, mentor and Chief of his Royal Cabinet, Ali Maher Pasha. By this step the hold of the Palace on the affairs of state was substantially tightened, and the subsequent actions of the Government well reflected the sentiments and attitude of the Palace which were unreservedly hostile to the British connection. Now that the war had come, what was Egypt to do? None could foresee the eventual outcome, but the general feeling in Egyptian political circles was that it would be stupid to give umbrage to the side which was going to win. She had no alternative but to play the part allotted to her by the treaty, but – in case the Axis powers should ultimately prevail – there was no reason why she should go one inch beyond the terms of the treaty in affording her aid to Britain. Thus the degree of cordiality towards Britain tended to oscillate as the tide of war ebbed and flowed during the early indecisive months of the war.

Immediately on the outbreak of hostilities the British Ambassador interviewed Ali Maher Pasha and requested him to implement the relevant clauses of the treaty. Accordingly, a state of siege was proclaimed, a censorship imposed, and the ports, installations and transport system were placed at the disposal of the British armed forces; diplomatic relations with Germany were broken off. Even so the spirit of close and cordial collaboration which the British Government had hoped for from Egypt – that same spirit of amity and identity of interests which had prevailed at the signing of the treaty – was singularly lacking. Such assistance as was compulsory was grudgingly given, and indeed there were not a few influential people, Sidky Pasha included, whose advocacy of the fascist ideology was almost blatant, and there was even some suggestion in Cairo political circles that Egypt should take advantage of the difficulties in which Britain now found herself to extort substantial modifications in the treaty as a price for the aid which she was legally and morally bound to give.

But the British Ambassador, Sir Miles Lampson, was in no mood to be trifled with. On occasion he was obliged to exert pressure on a reluctant Egyptian Government to give effect to necessary measures affecting security, control of espionage and other matters, and although the public utterances of the Government were full of patriotism and avowals of good faith, the relations between Britain and Egypt became increasingly strained. Indeed the tension was the automatic result of the clear divergence of outlook of the two treaty-bound countries, the British expecting and requiring the close collaboration and support of her ally in the struggle against tyranny, and Egypt wishing to dissociate herself as much as was humanly possible from a war which she felt, and no doubt rightly felt, was no concern of hers. Not only this but King Faruk, the power behind the scenes, made no pretence of disguising his antipathy for Britain, the country whose troops were still on Egyptian soil. During the pseudo-war which had lasted until the German onslaught in May 1940 these differences of opinion were largely concealed from the public eye, but with the surrender of France and the rout and evacuation of the British army at Dunkirk, Britain's prospects of winning the war, in the unbiased opinion of the world, diminished substantially, and in Egypt there seemed even more reason for separating herself from her failing ally. The greatest apprehension also reigned regarding the intentions of Mussolini's Italy now firmly welded to Hitler's Germany. Italy was known to have large armies stationed in Libya and Abyssinia, much exceeding the modest British force in the Delta. In spite of the blandishments and assurances of Count Mazzolini, the Italian Ambassador at Cairo, that Italy had no aggressive designs on Egypt, a lively apprehension was awakened by the possibilities of Italy's entry into the war at the side of Nazi Germany. Whether or not Mazzolini's protestations were sincere, it was certain that in such an event Italy would engage the British forces in the Delta, and it therefore appeared inevitable that Egypt would become a battlefield for two foreign powers in a war from which she had nothing to gain.

On 10 June 1940 Mussolini declared war on the Allies, and on the representations of the British Ambassador Egypt formally severed diplomatic relations. Two days later, at a secret meeting of the Council of Ministers, the policy of Egypt in face of the new development was formulated; Egypt would not enter the war unless her territory or towns or military objectives in Egypt were attacked and bombed. The apprehensions aroused by Italian participation in the war and the doubts entertained about the possibility of a British victory were well reflected by the evident reluctance of the Egyptian authorities to take security measures with regard to the large Italian population resident in the country. This was a further cause for dissension between the British and Egyptian Governments, and rumours became current, undoubtedly at the instigation of the Prime Minister Ali Maher, that Britain was demanding the formal entry of Egypt into the war at her side. On this pretext Ali Maher chose to resign on 26 June, but there is little doubt that he was so unconvinced of an ultimate British victory that he preferred to withdraw from office rather than be compelled to give the nation's aid and support to the loser. A coalition government under a man of no party affiliations, Hassan Sabri Pasha, followed and renewed protestations of loyalty to the treaty and its spirit were sufficient to allay British anxieties about their reluctant allies.

Egypt's declarations of June that she would fight if attacked were shortly afterwards to be put to the test when in September Graziani's columns breached the frontier and advanced on Sidi Barrani. Now, more than ever before, the vacillating Government found themselves on the horns of a dilemma. Egyptian territory had been violated by a foreign aggressor, and there could be no better justification for boldly taking up arms and summoning every ounce of strength to hurl the invader back. She did not stand alone. Great Britain and the full weight of the Empire stood at her side. Here indeed was an opportunity to range herself actively against aggression at the side of her ally, not only in the rearward areas as required by the treaty, but on the battlefield in the defence of her own soil. Such direct participation in the war would give her every right to a seat and full voice at the peace conference.

But fears and apprehensions gnawed at the hearts of Egypt's leaders. Supposing Britain lost the war – and the events of the first half of 1940 gave plenty of substance to that possibility – what would be the terrible price that the triumphant Fascists and Nazis would exact from a wretched collaborator of the British? The least Egypt could expect would be incorporation into the Italian Empire and a return to subservience to a foreign power and the annihilation of her democratic régime. This was the awful problem on which the hesitant Hassan Sabri and his Government were called upon to make a decision. Characteristically they drew back from the course which would plunge the country actively into hostilities and make her a legitimate spoil of war. But this decision split the Government asunder, for Ahmed Maher Pasha (brother of Ali Maher) stated that unless Egypt declared war and defended her own territory, he would withdraw the powerful support of the Saadist Party, and in consequence the four Saadist Ministers resigned. On this occasion the veteran party leader, Ismail Sidky Pasha, in urging Egypt to remain neutral, once again displayed his marked proclivities for the dictator states.

No doubt the weight of responsibility which he was called upon to bear in this complicated situation was contributory to the sudden and spectacular death of Hassan Sabri the Prime Minister. While reading the Speech from the Throne to the Chamber of Deputies on 11 November 1940 he was seized by an apoplectic stroke and succumbed immediately. He was succeeded by a new government of Liberals and Independents under the leadership of Hussein Sirry Pasha, a man of much experience in the affairs of state, having at various times occupied important posts in the Irrigation, Survey, Public Works and other Ministries; he was also closely connected by marriage with the Royal Family. His tenure of office for a period of fourteen uneasy months and his good relations with the British allies testify to his firmness and strength of character.

During the remainder of 1940 and the whole of 1941 the tide of war ebbed and surged round the frontiers of Egypt bringing with it fears and reliefs to the Egyptian people. The Italian attack on Greece and the heroic resistance and successes of that tiny nation; the Syrian affair; the Rashid Ali rebellion in Iraq; disorder in Persia; and the campaigns in the Western Desert all produced minor ripples in the currents of popular opinion, but the vigorous conduct of the war by the British forces which held the enemy at bay and kept Egypt safe re-established a sense of confidence and relative security. Thus during the year 1941 little of note took place in Egypt. The country did not escape the inevitable consequences of the war. In normal times the fertile Nile Valley was so devoted to the cultivation of cotton that Egypt could not even supply her own requirements of foodstuffs, the deficiency being met by foreign imports, particularly of cereals. The great demands on foreign shipping occasioned by the war substantially reduced the imports into Egypt, and the immediate reaction was a rise in the price of these commodities. High prices and shortages exacerbated by hoarding brought hardship to the populace, and at the same time the difficulties of marketing and exporting the cotton crop, the economic life-blood of the country, increased. This problem was solved in 1940 by the British Government agreeing to buy the whole crop.

Thus the Government of Hussein Sirry Pasha was primarily concerned with problems of internal administration and with carrying out in cordial spirit the terms of the treaty. Party politics at this time were at a low ebb and the few incidents which did occur served to underline and reinforce the Anglo-Egyptian *entente*. During May 1941 the Egyptian Chief of Staff, Aziz el Misri Pasha, whose loyalty to the treaty had long been suspect, was detected trying to escape by air to Syria, and was forced to land on Egyptian soil and arrested. At about the same time Ali Maher Pasha who, as confidant of the King and Prime Minister during the first months of the war, had shown such marked hostility to the British connection, was ordered to desist from all political activity and retire to the country. Two stumbling blocks to harmony were thus eliminated.

By the turn of the year 1942 the surge of new events disturbed the equilibrium and precipitated a crisis. To improve the food situation the Government ordered the area devoted to cotton cultivation to be reduced and allocated to food crops – a measure well calculated to disaffect the wealthy land-owners who derived much more profit from cotton than from cereals. On 2 January Hussein Sirry Pasha enhanced his power by adding to his portfolios of Prime Minister and Minister of the Interior, that of Minister of Finance, a measure which was greeted without enthusiasm by a jealous Chamber of Deputies. For some months previously the relations between the Vichy Government of Marshal Petain and Nazi Germany had been the subject of some anxiety to the British Government, and it was finally decided to bring pressure on the Egyptian Government to suspend, if not to sever, diplomatic relations with Vichy France. Hussein Sirry Pasha's submission to this demand provoked a storm of protest about his ears. The social, economic, cultural and political ties between France and Egypt were of long standing; the Vichy Minister in Cairo, M. Pozzi, was popular, and as far as Egypt was concerned relations between the two countries had been both correct and cordial. This move was regarded, and no doubt rightly regarded, as clear proof that the so-called equality of the two treaty-bound countries was a sham and that Egypt was subservient to, rather than allied with, Britain and that she even had no freedom in her diplomatic relationships. Chief among the critics of the Government was Ismail Sidky Pasha who pointed out that the treaty contained no clause requiring Egypt to sever relationships with a state which was not at war with her ally, Britain. This was undoubtedly true in theory, but Vichy France was so much under Hitler's thumb as to warrant her being regarded as hostile. On the other hand it was questionable whether the advantages afforded to Britain by compelling Egypt to sever her relations with Vichy were sufficient to outweigh the resentment aroused in Egypt against Britain at having to accede to the demand.

In the military sphere the situation deteriorated dangerously. After all their successful actions and campaigns of 1940 and 1941 in the Western Desert, in January and February 1942 the British were suddenly driven back to the Egyptian frontier by the German Desert Fox, General Rommel. The great German advance excited into feverish activity all the fifth-column elements and Axis sympathisers in the Delta, of whom there were many, and crowds openly went about the streets chanting, 'We are Rommel's soldiers.' This combination of new difficulties shook the power and reputation of the Government, and it was clear that a crisis could not be long delayed. This was precipitated on 2 February by the King himself.

At the time the relations with Vichy had been suspended the King had been absent from the capital and, declaring that he had been insufficiently consulted on this step, demanded the resignation of the Foreign Minister, Salib Samy Pasha, whereupon the Prime Minister and the whole Cabinet offered their resignations which were accepted by the King. The British Ambassador

> sought to smooth the matter over; but it became evident that political forces inspired by Ali Maher were at work in the Palace to bring in a government less committed to support of the British, so that a policy of reinsurance might be initiated to meet the possibility of an Axis victory which seemed not improbable at this time.[3]

Theoretically of course the British Government had no right to interfere in any way in regard to the structure and composition of the Egyptian Government, but at this critical stage of the war they felt they could not stand aside and allow power to fall into the hands of those who were or might be hostile to British interests, or who might even attempt to treat with the enemy. What the British Government wanted was a man in power who could be relied upon to adhere faithfully and wholeheartedly to the terms of the treaty, who could at the same time carry the country with him, and who had the strength of character to be ruthless in enforcing his will if necessary. The only man who filled this specification, in the opinion of the British

Ambassador, was the dictatorial leader of the Wafd, Nahas Pasha, who, as Egypt's principal signatory to the Treaty, was bound to uphold it to his utmost. Thus, by one of those paradoxes for which Egypt was famous, here was the British Ambassador urging upon the King the appointment to power of a man who was not only the King's mortal enemy, but who also had for the best part of his political career been unceasingly hostile to the British connection. The King's refusal to accede to this request heightened the tension. Faruk called a meeting of all the principal political leaders with a view to forming a national Government, but it was currently believed that he intended to reintroduce Britain's old adversary, Ali Maher Pasha, to power. It is reported[4] that on 4 February all the leaders were agreeable to the formation of a national government, even under the leadership of Nahas Pasha, but the latter, who had his eye on the main chance, refused to take part in any other than an entirely Wafd Government.

While these discussions were going on, the British Ambassador's requests were transformed into outright demands, and the King was informed that unless the British authorities were notified by 6 p.m. that evening of 4 February that Nahas Pasha had been invited to form a government, His Majesty must expect the consequences. At 9 p.m. that evening British tanks and Bren carriers were thrown round Abdin Palace, and Sir Miles Lampson, accompanied by General Stone, entered and saw the King. As a result of this interview Nahas Pasha was called to power. It is safe to assume that thereafter the King never forgave the British for this humiliation.

The British intervention was dictated by political expedience and designed to yield an immediate profit, but could only lead to future embarrassment. But the profit immediately anticipated was considered to be well worth the risk, for by this time Rommel's Africa Corps was sweeping all resistance from its path on the road to Egypt, and the presence of a loyal support holding the reins of power behind their backs was regarded by the British as a vital necessity in this critical moment. Whatever the price which might ultimately have to be paid, this had to be accepted in advance. Indeed although for most of his political life Nahas Pasha had been the inveterate opponent of Britain, since the outbreak of war his attitude had sensibly changed. This is not to suggest that the lion had become the lamb or that he was willing to forget the past and all the outstanding questions between Britain and himself, but rather that as the principal signatory of the Treaty he was bound to honour it. It may be that Nahas Pasha had sufficient acumen to foresee that an Axis victory could only mean the annihilation of Egypt as a free and independent state and that Egypt had therefore everything to gain and nothing to lose by a British victory. Egypt thus had the best reasons for giving the fullest support and assistance to Britain in her struggle to win the war. At the same time he did not lose sight of the possibility of extracting further concessions from Britain in return for Egypt's co-operation after the war.

Immediately on his assumption of power he addressed a letter to the British Ambassador requesting recognition of the principle that neither the treaty nor the situation in Egypt gave Britain the right to interfere in Egypt's internal affairs and particularly in the formation and resignations of ministries. Sir Miles Lampson, having now gained his objective of securing a government acceptable to Britain, was well content to concede this principle.

The immediate future was fraught with difficulty for Nahas Pasha. Not only was there danger of a German advance into the Delta, but the humiliated King's hatred for himself was intensified, and furthermore he had laid himself open to the charge, freely expressed by his rivals, that he had allowed himself to be hoisted into power by British bayonets, for although a curtain of secrecy had been thrown over the events of 4 February, the story quickly spread that the King had been threatened with deposition by the British unless Nahas Pasha was summoned to power. Nevertheless, with the full weight of the British authorities at his back he threw himself relentlessly into the task of mastering the situation heedless of the sneers and criticism of his compatriots. He dealt ruthlessly with the instigators of political discord, the stormy petrel Ali Maher Pasha being arrested and many active partisans of the Axis cause deprived of their liberty; the deterioration of public security received a salutary check. Vigorous measures were taken to relieve the economic situation including the imposition of penalties for hoarding food, increasing agricultural wages and improving food distribution. Undoubtedly a strong hand at the helm of state was asserting itself at this critical time.

On 24 March 1942 Nahas Pasha was reinforced in his position by the results of new elections in which the Wafd Party won 234 out of 264 seats. Unquestionably the elections were 'managed' to the extent that Nahas placed a ban on all reference to recent events leading to the change of government, to the King and to Great Britain in the election campaign.[5] The Liberal and Saadist Parties therefore boycotted the election and left a clear field for the Wafd.

During the dangerous months of 1942 the British Army at el Alamein and the Wafd Government in Cairo held firm until October when General

Montgomery's Eighth Army turned on the enemy and rolled them ever backwards into the desert until the final surrender and humiliation of the Axis forces in Tunis in May 1943. With this historic event war finally disappeared from Africa and the countries of the Near East. The passing of all danger became the signal for the renewed and frenzied political activity in Cairo.

But long before this, difficulties, some of his own making, began to beset Nahas Pasha in power. Only two months after the election a serious split developed between the Prime Minister and his influential Finance Minister, Makram Ebeid Pasha. The precise nature of the difference is not known, but it was almost certainly the outcome of Nahas Pasha's despotic conduct of affairs. Although he had for years posed as the champion of democracy, he was by nature an autocrat in the grand old tradition. Reinforced by the state of emergency, by the censorship and the powerful backing of the British, he regarded the Chamber as little more than a rubber stamp to register his decrees, and he expected the same implicit obedience from his Ministry. It seems however that Makram Ebeid Pasha was by no means willing to act the compliant subordinate, and after only three months of office the Government was split asunder, and in the subsequent reconstruction of the Ministry Makram Pasha was excluded. He immediately passed into opposition, taking fifteen Deputies with him, and was formally expelled from the Wafd Party. This was a foolish mistake on the part of Nahas Pasha. His opponent had for years been Secretary-General of the Wafd and knew all its secrets, its machinery and ramifications and moreover its weaknesses. This together with his solid reputation for integrity made him a formidable potential enemy. Without delay he formed a new splinter party of his followers, el Kutla el Mustakilla or Independent Wafdist Group, and embarked on a campaign to haul his rival from the pedestal of power.

This commenced with the clandestine publication of a pamphlet under the title of *The Black Book* alleging corruption in the Government and abuse of power. Indeed there was unquestionably much substance in the accusations, for whenever he was in office Nahas Pasha seemed unable to resist the temptation to use his power for his own and his family's advantage. In this case *The Black Book* alleged that prominent members of the Wafd and the Wakil family, to which Nahas Pasha's wife belonged, were enriching themselves by illegal and black market transactions. Attempts were made in the Chamber to force the Prime Minister to arraign Makram Ebeid Pasha before the courts for libel, but Nahas, fearing lest such a process might confirm the charges against him, refused to be drawn. He declared that this was a political question for the Chamber, not a legal question for the courts. This supine but inescapable attitude did much to damage his reputation, and other factors contributed substantially. An epidemic of malignant malaria broke out and raged in Upper Egypt from 1942 to 1944 which the Government preferred to ignore rather than admit their incompetence to deal with it by accepting British and American offers of medical assistance to combat the disease, and many thousands died. An absurd suggestion was made in the Senate that the epidemic had been brought by British aeroplanes, just as the present Government had been imported by British tanks. But it was in this fact that Nahas Pasha was most vulnerable, the common knowledge that the British had put him in power and kept him there in direct opposition to the King and the other parties. Although in May 1943 there were general acclamations of joy and relief when the German armies in Africa were finally broken at Cape Bon in Tunisia, these were quickly forgotten, and the British in their role of main prop to a dictator government became less and less the protectors of Egypt from Nazi tyranny and more and more the subject for vituperation as imperialists and tyrants themselves.

By February 1944 a supplement to *The Black Book* was published making further allegations against the Wafd Government and accusing Nahas Pasha of subordinating the country's sovereign rights to Britain. A National Front was formed of all opposition parties and a manifesto secretly distributed against British imperialism. '*L'Indépendence d'Egypte, y était-il dit, est bafouée, les libertés menacées, la presse étauffée; les innocents arrêtés; les moralités vendues; les habitants souffrent; la faim se propage.*'[6] In fact Britain and Nahas Pasha were now lumped together by the opposition as the common enemy. King Faruk added all his support to this bitter campaign. It must be admitted that the British military authorities did nothing to counter the renewed campaign of hostility. Indeed the British army had always displayed a peculiar reluctance to evacuate places occupied, even when the original reason for its presence had disappeared. During the first three years of the war an enormous base with vast establishments had been built up in the Delta with Cairo the site of GHQ Middle-East. The battle of el Alamein took place in October 1942; by May 1943 the war in North Africa and the Middle East was finished, and the entire body of the fighting forces was now well over a thousand miles from its base. Yet the British Army showed no disposition to pick up its tail and take it with them to Europe. On the contrary there was even a tendency to dig in deeper in the comfortable, even luxurious surroundings of Cairo. Thus, though the war had disappeared into the distance, even across the sea into Europe, the bases and staffs with all their attendant retinues flocked the streets, cinemas and hotels of Cairo. What they were doing it is difficult to say. Quite understandably, the suspicion grew in Egypt that the old days of the occupation had returned and that the country was slipping back into the British clutches once more. Was not the unpopular and corrupt Government of the Wafd put in office and kept there by British bayonets? Was not Egypt once again subservient to a foreign power? Had there been the slightest indication that the British planned to evacuate their surplus forces from Egypt, to withdraw their garrison to their allotted places in the Canal Zone as stipulated by the Treaty, these fears might have been somewhat assuaged, but no such signs were forthcoming.

Nahas Pasha himself was not blind to the trend of public sentiment, nor had he in fact ever ceased to campaign for substantial rights and concessions from Britain as compensation or payment for Egypt's share in the war effort. In November 1943 he had succeeded in obtaining a guarantee from the British Ambassador that after the war Egypt should enjoy equal representation in negotiations on any matter which affected her directly and that no question touching Egypt would be discussed without consultation with the Egyptian Government. Even so, by the middle of 1944 the campaign of intimidation and vituperation by the opposition and the Palace had so successfully undermined the prestige of Nahas and the Wafd that by way of reinsurance the latter were themselves obliged to join in the common attack on Britain. Now that the military dangers had long since passed the British Ambassador felt no further obligation to maintain his support of the Wafd Government, and the King, who had been waiting impatiently for the first opportunity of ridding himself of his obnoxious Minister, dismissed him from office on 8 October 1944.

The fall of Nahas Pasha and the Wafd was accepted without demur and even relief by the people. Indeed, there had been a steady deterioration in the Party's prestige ever since its glorious birth in the time of Zaghlul, and its administration during the critical war years had done nothing to enhance its reputation in the eyes of the people. Its original claim to be the sole voice and representative of the nation was now no longer valid; it had lost many of its original and powerful supporters who had refused to bow to the arbitrary and dictatorial conduct of Nahas and had broken away and formed new parties of their own. But the greatest damage to the Wafd's prestige was due to the fact, now commonly known, that it had been hustled into power by the British. After the dangers of the war had receded, it was held rightly or wrongly by all the parties in Egypt that there must be a drastic modification in the relations between Egypt and Britain, in short that after the war the

British must quit entirely and hand over the Sudan. Everyone anticipated a struggle and Britain was going to be the adversary; and the charge of being bolstered up by the British was difficult to refute and live down. Even so the Wafd was not without weapons. It had an elaborate organisation throughout the country and a tight hold on its supporters, and a certain element of party discipline which made it powerful in opposition. It refused moreover to form coalitions or otherwise co-operate with any other party, and thus preserved a distinct identity.

A new Ministry was formed by Ahmed Maher Pasha, leader of the Saadist group, and included Makram Ebeid Pasha as Finance Minister, and for the next four months the course of affairs proceeded smoothly. The principal activities of the new Government consisted of reversing all the decisions of the previous administration and of blackening its reputation, which was not difficult. They demanded of Nahas Pasha the return of £170,000 which had been collected for the benefit of the victims of the malaria epidemic, but which had somehow found its way into Nahas Pasha's bank account instead of into the Treasury.[7]

In February 1945 the question arose whether Egypt should formally declare war on Germany and Japan so as to secure a seat at the Peace Conference and become one of the founder members of the United Nations. As the war was clearly in its closing stages an Egyptian declaration of war would involve her in no real obligations, and the Prime Minister considered that such a step would be to Egypt's advantage. There was a certain amount of resistance to this proposal which Ahmed Maher brushed aside. On 24 February he announced his intention to the Chamber of Deputies, but as he was leaving the building he was shot dead by a young fanatic. The Foreign Minister, Nokrashy Pasha, took his place and the Cabinet remained substantially unchanged. Two months later, on 8 May, the war in Europe was over, and Egypt once more girded herself to resume the struggle with her traditional opponent, Great Britain.

CHAPTER 24

After the Second World War

There is an astonishing resemblance between the sequence of events which took place immediately after the Second World War and that which followed the First. In many respects the situation was identical. In both cases Egypt had been at the beck and call of Britain; in both cases she was struggling for the removal of the power which Britain exercised over her, struggling to be rid once and for all of the British connection. In the First War she had been a protectorate of Britain, in the Second a treaty-bound ally; in both cases the results had been in practice the same. It made no difference in Egyptian eyes that her connection in the Second World War had been the outcome of a treaty which she had freely and willingly negotiated. She felt she had paid her debts and now wanted to be released from further obligation. By the end of the War most Egyptians had hypnotised themselves into believing that the 1936 Treaty had been negotiated for the specific purpose of rendering Britain aid in the coming great war, in recompense for which Britain would gratefully hand over the Sudan and evacuate all her troops from Egypt – a remarkable example of *ex post facto* reasoning and self-delusion. The fact that during certain critical periods of the war Egypt had been a most unwilling ally and that she had on occasions only given her assistance under duress, was conveniently forgotten. The dangers of the war were now past and she wanted to stand alone, independent and free to make her own way in the world untrammelled by interference of any sort, in particular from Britain who had for so long bound Egypt to her apron strings.

The British view was that the war was an episode which had occurred during the life of the Treaty, but which in no way affected the validity of the Treaty. This was a logical attitude to adopt. In return for certain concessions, notably the right to station her forces in the Canal Zone and to require from Egypt certain assistance in time of war, she had engaged herself to render

Egypt all assistance in case of war and in effect to defend Egypt from foreign aggression. This was the essence of the Treaty. Britain had played her part, as was evident from the fact that Egypt was free from any foreign invader and free to do as she pleased, and Britain expected her ally to continue to honour her side of the bargain. But Egypt could not see it in this light; she could only see that in spite of all her efforts, her assistance and co-operation, British troops still trod the soil of Egypt and that it was Britain who was denying her what she considered to be her rights in the Sudan. Was there never to be an end? She had done her part in the war and the accounts were therefore all square. No matter how political shades of opinion might vary among the parties, this stand was common ground to all.

Had the death-struggle in which Britain had been locked for six calamitous years against the forces of tyranny and aggression finally resulted in the annihilation of those forces, so that the world could breathe freely once more, there would have been a good chance of Britain giving sympathetic consideration to what were largely legitimate national aspirations. But out of the debris of the war, even from among the victors, there arose a potential force of aggression even more fearful than Hitler's Germany had ever been. Communist Russia, arrogant from her victories and merciless in her ideologies, was now stretching out her claws to seize the world. By the end of the war half of Europe lay helpless in her grip, large areas of Asia were beginning to succumb, and the Russian net was being cast further afield. Were the free nations of the world who had poured out their life-blood against one tyranny to fall to another? These sinister developments checked the natural flow of events which might have taken place in a world finally at peace. Defensive strongholds and strategic points which Britain might willingly have abandoned in such a world now assumed an importance as great as in the time of fascism and nazism. Guarantees and assurances became more vital than mere good neighbourliness. With Egypt Britain had a treaty, a treaty which afforded such guarantees. She could not throw these so lightly away. It was against this background that the problem of Anglo-Egyptian relationships was to be revived after the war.

Just as twenty-seven years previously Zaghlul Pasha had greeted the end of the First World War with an approach to the High Commissioner for negotiations, so now did his successor, Nahas Pasha, on 30 July 1945 present a memorandum to the British Ambassador setting forth the claims and aspirations of Egypt. Clearly, in spite of the long interval, there had been very little change in the political climate. That the government of Nokrashy Pasha was thinking along similar lines – indeed no party whether in or out of office could do otherwise – was demonstrated by the announcement of Makram Ebeid Pasha the Finance Minister that the Government did not intend to make any provision for building the barracks for the British army in the Canal Zone, as required by the terms of the Treaty. Instead the Government would ask for the complete evacuation of the troops from Egypt.[1] During the latter half of the year the increasing pressure of public opinion and clamour in the press, together with the accession to power of a Labour Government in Britain – always a source of encouragement to nationalist Egypt – induced Nokrashy Pasha on 20 December to address a request to the British Government for the opening of negotiations for a revision of the Treaty on the general ground that the circumstances had changed. But by this time public opinion, particularly in the political hotbeds of the universities, had advanced a stage further. No longer was a revision demanded but an outright denunciation, and on 9 February 1946 a demonstration of thousands of Egyptian youths surged through the main streets of the capital demanding the dismissal of the Government which they thought was not forceful enough in its stand against Britain, shouting anti-British slogans and roughly handling any British troops they met on the way. In truth, as has been remarked in the previous chapter, even at this late date, over three years after the battle of Alamein, the cities were still full of British troops, a perpetual offence to Egyptian pride. Had they all by this time been evacuated to their proper stations on the Canal, the situation might have been somewhat easier.

On 14 February 1946, feeling that they no longer enjoyed the confidence of the nation, or perhaps more probably torn between the necessity of maintaining public order and the fear of courting the animosity of the mob by enforcing public order, the government of Nokrashy Pasha resigned, and the elder statesman Ismail Sidky Pasha, friend of the Palace and enemy of the Wafd, formed a new government. A few days later, on 21 February, more demonstrations took place which resulted in several deaths and much damage to foreign property, the attentions of the mob this time not being confined only to British persons and property.

It was in this atmosphere charged with violence and disorder that Sidky Pasha attempted to form an all-party delegation to negotiate. The intransigent and arrogant Wafd, true to its traditions, refused to take part unless it led and formed the majority of the delegation, and it is tempting to wonder whether this line was adopted to ensure their exclusion from the delegation on the presumption that the mission was unlikely to succeed in its efforts. At any rate Sidky Pasha formed his group without the Wafd and preliminary conversations opened in Cairo on 15 April 1946. The British delegation led by Lord Stansgate, Secretary of State for Air, was first met by the uncompromising statement; 'You can have no agreement with Egypt except on the basis of evacuation.'[2] The British were eventually persuaded to the principle of evacuation but only on the understanding that some effective means of ensuring Middle East security could be worked out and agreed upon. It is to be observed that, as in the case after the First World War, British policy and interest in Egypt had undergone some modification. During the inter-war years Britain's main preoccupation had been the security of the Suez Canal, the vital artery linking the empire with the mother-country. This special interest appears to have been subordinated now to much wider considerations affecting the defence of the Middle East region as a whole from Soviet aggression or communist-inspired revolutions. What Britain now required was not just an assured means of safeguarding the Canal, but a base from which operations could be launched in any part of the Middle East, should the situation at any time require it. Both delegations were in a delicate position; both had to take into account the weight of public opinion in their own countries. In Britain powerful Conservative opinion was against any abandonment of the British position in Egypt, and even the Labour Government required guarantees of some sort against the growing Soviet menace. In Egypt ardent nationalism was demanding total rejection of any concession whatever to Britain. No Egyptian negotiator could afford to ignore these sentiments.

Although no agreed formula was reached during these conversations in Cairo, Sidky Pasha believed that sufficient advance had been made to justify his proceeding to formal negotiation in London with Ernest Bevin the British Foreign Secretary. He arrived with his Foreign Minister in London in October and between 17th and 25th direct conversations took place as a result of which a draft agreement was finally initialled. As in all cases of negotiations between Egypt and Britain the Egyptian delegates had no authority to proceed there and then with the signature of a treaty on behalf of their country. The draft must first be laid before the Chamber for approval and ratification. The proposed agreement constituted a substantial advance on anything that had ever been suggested before. The existing 1936 Treaty would be cancelled immediately upon the entry into force of the new. The evacuation of the Delta and its cities would be completed by 31 March 1947 and of the rest of Egypt, including the Canal Zone, by 1 September 1949. In order to meet Britain's demand for security in the Middle East, Egypt agreed that in the event of her becoming the object of armed aggression, or in the event of the United Kingdom becoming involved in war as a result of armed aggression against countries adjacent to Egypt, they would take, in close consultation and as a result of consultation, such action as might be recognised as necessary until the Security Council had taken the necessary measures for the re-establishment of peace. For this purpose the two Governments would set up a Joint Board of Defence to study and make recommendations on the measures of co-operation that would be necessary in such cases.

The Sudan as usual provided a knotty problem, as is demonstrated by the wording of the relevant clauses:

> The policy which the High Contracting Parties undertake to follow in the Sudan within the framework of the unity between the Sudan and Egypt under the common crown of Egypt will have for its essential objectives to assure the well-being of the Sudanese, the development of their interests and their active preparation for self-government and consequently the exercise of the right to choose the future status of the Sudan. Until the High Contracting Parties can in full common agreement realise this latter objective after consultation with the Sudanese, the Agreement of 1899 will continue and Article 11 of the Treaty of 1936, together with its annex and paragraphs 14 to 16 of the Agreed Minute annexed to the same Treaty will remain in force notwithstanding the first Article of the present Treaty.

This was, to say the least, a peculiarly phrased clause open to the charge of obscurity or lack of precision, and is clearly the result of an attempt to reconcile two conflicting attitudes. Egypt wanted to have recognised formally the union of the Sudan with Egypt under the Egyptian Crown while the British Government, having repeatedly in the past declared their policy to be to lead the Sudan to self-government with the right of self-determination, could not on any account subscribe to a policy which might clash with these declarations. It appears therefore that the above protocol must mean in substance that Britain was prepared to recognise 'a symbolic dynastic union between Egypt and the Sudan', but that this must in no way involve any change in the present system of administration or prejudice the Sudan's right to self-government and self-determination.

When Sidky Pasha returned to Egypt with the draft in his pocket the story got about, which was not contradicted by him, that Britain had conceded the unity of the Sudan with Egypt, and indeed the Prime Minister was credited with saying that it had 'been definitely decided to achieve unity between

Egypt and the Sudan under the Egyptian Crown.'³ Although of course there was some slight substance in this assertion, it was by no means a complete statement of the facts. But it was at any rate sufficient to inflame the politically conscious elements in the Sudan who immediately accused the British Government of 'breaking their pledge and of selling them to Egypt.'⁴ Sir Hubert Huddleston, the Governor-General, was hard put to it to maintain order in the Sudan during this critical time.

When a closer inspection of the terms of the draft was made in Egypt, it was greeted with a singular lack of enthusiasm which soon changed to active hostility, the Sudan clause being the target of most of the abuse, while even those relating to the evacuation did not escape criticism. Nevertheless, on the whole the proposed treaty dealt very fairly with Egypt and granted that for which she had clamoured for so long, the complete and final evacuation of the British forces from her territory. It was to leave her entirely free and independent, complete mistress of her own destinies. But this was not enough for Egypt. The rights of self-government and self-determination which she had demanded so insistently for herself she was not prepared to concede to the Sudanese. The incessant propaganda over the previous twenty years and more had succeeded in hypnotising the Egyptian people into believing absolutely in their rights to the Sudan and made them impervious to any logic or argument to the contrary. Nevertheless every party leader and politician in Egypt, particularly those who had had any dealings with the British Government, knew full well that Sidky had pushed the British Government to the extreme limit, that he had extracted concessions which Britain had never before been even willing to consider. Yet, instead of thanking and congratulating Sidky for his fine achievement, in their cupidity for power and eagerness to haul down their rival they seized on the draft as a weapon of attack against the ailing old man. New campaigns and violent demonstrations were launched through the streets accusing the Government of violating the Constitution, flouting the national will and persecuting patriots. These charges were the result of certain security measures which the Prime Minister was obliged to take to maintain public order in face of the violent agitation which was inflaming the masses. Indeed the activities of the extremist parties, particularly the Wafd and the Moslem Brotherhood, a fanatical religious organisation, produced unrest throughout the country. In face of this the universities, ever the hotbeds of sedition and disorder, were closed; armed police patrolled the streets; many agitators were arrested; Nahas Pasha was refused access to Tantah where he was organising a political demonstration. Still, although it was known that seven of the twelve members of the delegation (only two had gone to London) were against acceptance of the treaty, Sidky Pasha still commanded a strong following in the Chamber, and on 26 December obtained a vote of confidence from 159 of the 264 Deputies, and it seemed that the way was clear for ratifying the Treaty.

But a few days later Sir Hubert Huddleston, the Governor-General of the Sudan, having returned from consultations in London, made an announcement intended to allay the suspicions and anxieties of the Sudanese about the Sudan protocol of the Treaty. He stated that the British Government were determined that nothing should be permitted to deflect the Sudan Government, whose constitution and powers remained unaltered by the recent conversations, from the task to which the Government had committed themselves – the preparation of the Sudanese for self-government and for the task of choosing freely what their future status was to be.[5] This uncompromising announcement which apparently directly contradicted the claims that Sidky Pasha had made, persuaded him to abandon his attempt to reconcile the inflamed opinion of Egypt with the stand taken up by the British. Attempts had been made by both Sidky Pasha and Mr Bevin to get agreed interpretations of the Sudan protocol but without success. Sidky Pasha resigned from office on 9 December 1946 and the proposal to ratify the Treaty was dropped. This was a bitter blow for Bevin who had tried his utmost to meet the Egyptian view and at the same time preserve Britain's vital interests.

One cannot help wondering why Egypt refused the proposed revision of the Treaty. Mr Bevin had suggested that the Sudan question could be separated from the evacuation and defence question and made the subject of later negotiations. If Egypt had accepted this proposal she would not only have lost nothing, but would have gained the point which was of most immediate concern to her, the evacuation of the British forces from Egyptian soil. Once this had been achieved she could have returned to the attack on the Sudan question. What was it then which prompted her to reject these proposals? The answer can probably be found in the social conditions of the country. For centuries Egypt had been conservative and traditional. The development of constitutional life had made little impression on the social and economic system; Egypt was still the land of enormous wealth and abysmal poverty. Up to this time the peasant *fellah* in the field and the labourer in the factory had regarded it as part of the natural order of things that he should exist on the brink of starvation and destitution, while the *pasha* and landowner lived in luxury. But with the advent of the war the order of things showed signs of changing. The ideologies of socialism and even of communism had at last begun to seep into the country; by 1945 groups and parties had started to spring up decrying the social injustices of the times and demanding better conditions for the peasant and the working classes. For a quarter of a century the Wafd had preached and taught the doctrine of government by demonstration, riot, mob law and disorder. These had been the principal weapons of the Wafd in their struggle for power and the Egyptian people were now well versed in the arts of violence. To this training was now being added an indoctrination of socialism. The two together could easily spell revolution. In all the multiplicity of parties political and religious there was none which truly reflected the working class point of view. In spite of their rivalries and differences all represented the governing and wealthy classes; all had a vested interest in maintaining the existing social order. But it was becoming more and more difficult to divert the interests and attentions of the masses from social and economic injustices. The only way the parties knew of doing this was by focusing their attentions and animosities elsewhere, and what more suitable target could there be than Britain and the old Anglo-Egyptian question? As long as these controversial issues could be kept at boiling point there was a chance that internal problems could be glossed over. But if these questions came to be finally settled, the masses would sooner or later begin to look at their own condition, and the inevitable clamour would arise for social amelioration and economic reform. There was good reason in fact for refusing a settlement with Britain, even though advantageous in every respect.

But there could be no halt in the anti-British campaign; it was essential to keep the people's minds firmly fixed on it, and the newly created United Nations Organisation provided the means. After the resignation of Sidky Pasha in December 1946 Nokrashy Pasha formed a new Government with a Liberal and Saadist following. After a few weeks of uncertainty as to the best course to pursue Nokrashy Pasha announced his Government's intention of taking the whole question of Egypt and the Sudan to the United Nations. This declaration was sufficient to keep the country at peace, but tensely expectant, until the dispute was heard. It was publicly debated before the Security Council in July 1947 between Nokrashy Pasha on behalf of Egypt and Sir Alexander Cadogan for Britain. The arguments produced by Nokrashy were typical of the sophistry which had for so long passed for reasoning in Egypt. His historical survey of the Anglo-Egyptian connection was little more than a travesty of the facts. 'Egyptian rule,' he stated, 'opened the Sudan to modern civilization. The chaos and anarchy which had existed were replaced by order and prosperity . . . Such was the picture when the United Kingdom directed its covetous gaze to the valley of the Nile.'[6] Again, 'No one can seriously claim that the restrictions on Egyptian sovereignty were intended to continue after the war. The war was the implicit term to these restrictions, and the 1936 Treaty has now outlived its purpose.'[7] If this latter argument is to be accepted as valid, it must be supposed that the Egyptian delegates who negotiated the treaty were visionaries who foresaw the advent of the war three years later, but were careless enough to omit any mention of it in the Treaty.

Sir Alexander Cadogan had no difficulty in disposing of the flimsy edifice of Nokrashy's case. He refuted the right of any party to a treaty to break it at their convenience, and quoted evidence of the welcome with which the Treaty had been greeted in Egypt in 1936. The British Government had agreed to negotiate a new treaty and had in fact done so, but this had been unacceptable to Egypt and the original agreement must therefore stand.

The Security Council, animated by the doctrine of freedom and self-determination of the small nations, were at least disposed to listen to Egypt's case on the evacuation question although reluctant to commit themselves to an expression of opinion which, by recognising the right of a country to repudiate a formally and freely agreed treaty, would strike at the foundations of international law and practice. Nokrashy's case was on much weaker ground in regard to the Sudan. After pointing out that Mohammed Ali had conquered the country in 1821 he went on to try to build up a picture of the natural unity of the Nile Valley and of the common interests, aspirations, cultures, language, religion and race of its people. After having previously dwelt in detail on the rights of Egypt to independence and self-determination, he was in the awkward position of having to demand that these same rights should be denied to the Sudanese. Indeed the weakness of the Egyptian case was patent to all. Cadogan was on unassailable ground when he set forth the British policy of leading the Sudanese to choose freely their future status, complete independence or unity with Egypt. If there was in fact such an identity of race, culture and interest between the Egyptians and the Sudanese, Egypt had nothing for fear, for obviously the Sudanese would choose unity. In the discussion which followed in the Council the Chinese delegate pointed out, 'I cannot see how this Council can be a party to any arrangement which would deprive the Sudanese of this right of self-determination which is the foundation of the Charter of the United Nations.' In spite of the political rivalries of the cold war which tended to govern all voting in the United

Nations none of the delegates could openly disavow this view, and finally no decision was reached or judgement given. On 10 September 1947 the Council adjourned, leaving the Egyptian question on its agenda. It is almost comical to consider Egypt in all these arguments and discussions trying to condemn British imperialism in Egypt and at the same time to defend Egyptian imperialism in the Sudan. It is perhaps surprising that Egypt never attempted to utilise the one argument which gave a solid foundation to her claims on the Sudan – the right of conquest.

It may be that in the councils of the post-war world there would have been some reluctance to recognise claims based on forceful conquest, but on the other hand it was a right which had been acknowledged since the dawn of mankind and still conditioned the political status of large areas of the world. Between 1820 and 1875 Egypt had occupied the vast tract of Africa known as the Sudan and brought it under Egyptian sovereignty. She had subsequently lost it all in the Mahdi Rebellion and regained it in the campaigns of 1896-8. Although the conduct of the war of reconquest had been largely in the hands of Lord Cromer and Sir Herbert Kitchener, it had been fought with the object of restoring the Sudan to the Egyptian fold, and the bulk of the troops and the money had been Egyptian. The British forces which assisted in the final stages of the campaign had been loaned to ensure success. It is clear from a study of this episode that Britain had no intention of acquiring for herself any special rights in the Sudan when the 1896 campaign was launched, and that the idea of a Condominium in which Britain would assume the dominant role was an *arrière pensée*. The logical conclusion therefore is that Lord Cromer's insistence on the Condominium was a breach of faith towards Egypt, and that a fairer course of action at the time would have been to recognise the major role which Egypt had played in the reconquest by regarding the Sudan as part of Egypt. This is the one valid argument which Egypt could have used to support her claims on the Sudan, but the arguments which she consistently used were baseless. There was no more truth in the unity of the Nile Valley than there is in the unity of the valleys of the Danube or the Rhine. Even on the question of water rights it must be pointed out that most of the water on which Egypt depends comes not from the Sudan but from Ethiopia, Uganda and even Lake Victoria, but there has never been any suggestion that these territories should be united with Egypt on the ground that they form part of the Nile Valley. Similarly, except in the northern areas of the Sudan, there is no identity of race, culture, language or religion. This is so obvious that it barely needs stating, and it is safe to suppose that by adopting these consistently poor contentions Egypt materially weakened rather than strengthened her claims to her southern neighbour.

Nor was Britain free from fault in this dispute. It had been forcibly impressed on the British Government times without number during the past half-century that in the eyes of Egypt the presence of a foreign army on her soil was a national insult which could only be wiped out by evacuation, that this constituted the major cause of stress and disaffection between the two countries. It is difficult to understand what profit or advantage was to be gained by the maintenance of thousands of troops in a land which was becoming so hostile to their presence that a time was not far distant when the troops would be compelled to protect themselves from their unwilling hosts. The strategic value of the base in the Canal Zone was not constituted by the presence of these troops alone; an essential element was the abundant and willing supply of labour and provisions afforded by the Egyptian people. Without these the base was worthless and could even prove an embarrassment and incumbrance. Yet there was no one in the British Government with the breadth of vision to realise that British interests, the security of the communications and defence of the Middle East, depended far more on a spirit of mutual interest and co-operation with a friendly Egypt than barren insistence on the terms of a treaty which had, as the Egyptians urged, been negotiated under entirely different conditions.

In the Sidky-Bevin negotiations of 1946 Britain had agreed to withdraw her troops by September 1949, but merely because these negotiations had not given birth to a treaty the offer was withdrawn. If it had been concluded in 1946 that Britain could safely withdraw in 1949, it is difficult to see why this policy was not implemented. It can hardly be thought that Britain would have been seriously prejudiced by lack of formal agreement on the projected Joint Board of Defence and mutual consultation in the event of armed aggression in the adjacent areas, for such consultation would not have amounted to guarantees of joint military action. Thus Britain failed to make the gesture which would not have seriously embarrassed her, but which would have gone far to healing the rift between the two countries. She failed to realise that an unwilling ally is no ally at all.

The failure of Nokrashy Pasha's pleas to the United Nations stunned the Egyptian people. So convinced by the incessant drumming of nationalist propaganda in their ears were they that they could scarcely believe that the nations of the world did not support their claims, and threats were even launched at the embassies and legations of countries which had made alternative proposals in the United Nations debate. But for the moment there seemed no alternative course to pursue except to keep a vigilant eye on British activities in the Sudan. For already in that country in 1944 tentative steps had been taken by the British-controlled government towards the establishment of representative institutions in the setting up of an Advisory Council for the Northern Sudan. This was the seed from which were to spring proposals for a legislative council in 1948. It was realised in Egypt that unless some effort was made to participate actively in the condominium, the Sudan would shortly have advanced so far on the road to self-government that Egyptian claims over the country would have become stripped of all but academic interest. Consequently when in May 1948 they were invited by the British Government to consult on constitutional changes in the Sudan, the Egyptian Government readily responded. In the ensuing negotiations between Khashaba Pasha the Foreign Minister and the British Ambassador, Egyptian representation in the projected executive council and joint supervision in the forthcoming Sudanese elections were secured. But the Egyptian Foreign Affairs Committee refused to ratify Khashaba's arrangements, and the British Government was left to proceed to implement the contemplated changes on her own. Egypt proceeded to boycott the elections in the Sudan, and in the result the Umma Party which advocated independence ousted the Ashigga, or Egyptian Unionist Party. In Egyptian eyes the whole operation was a British plot to separate further the Sudan from Egypt and to reinforce British control over the country. In justification it was incomprehensible to Egypt that Britain which for over half a century had insisted on imperialism in Egypt through the medium of the army of occupation could be believed to be sincerely taking the Sudan along the road to independence. Whether the boycott of the elections was induced by a lack of conviction in the validity of Egyptian claims, i.e. that the majority of Sudanese ardently desired union with Egypt, or whether they could not trust an election which they did not exclusively manage themselves, is uncertain, but at any rate the result was that Egypt stood by inactive and permitted another step to be taken to divorce her from the Sudan.

In the meantime developments elsewhere were to make their mark on the course of Egyptian history, this time in Palestine. The story of Jewish settlement and the creation of 'a national home for the Jews' in Palestine form no part of this narrative. Suffice it to say that it had originated in a letter written by Lord Balfour in November 1917 which stated:

His Majesty's Government view with favour the establishment in Palestine of a National Home for the Jewish people . . . it being clearly understood that nothing shall be done which may prejudice the civil and religious rights of existing non-Jewish communities in Palestine, etc.

The immigration of Jews into Palestine once commenced received an irresistible impetus after the Second World War which released the remnants of the Jewish people in Central Europe from their years of bondage, torment and humiliation. The eyes of all were turned towards the land which offered them hope of a refuge and place of their own to live in, and Britain who since the Treaty of Versailles had held the mandate for Palestine after the break-up of the Ottoman Empire, found herself in the embarrassing position of having to repel the flood of Jewish immigration which she had 'viewed with favour' thirty years earlier. The furious and treacherous attacks of Jewish terrorist gangs on the British administration and army, and on the native Arab population, placed the British Government in such a predicament that 'the Palestine problem' was referred to the United Nations Special Committee. This in September 1947 recommended the partition of the country and the creation of a separate Jewish state. Such a proposal was clearly prejudicial to the 'non-Jewish communities in Palestine', but by this time it was too late to turn back the clock. A substantial population of Jews had by this time consolidated themselves in the Arab lands of Palestine and, far from being satisfied with the mere concept of 'a Jewish national home', were far advanced in their plans for an independent sovereign Jewish state. By 1947 the irreconcilable policies of the British Government in relation to Palestine and the Jews, and the promises they had made at various times to both Arabs and Jews, had placed them in an impossible position to which the only solution was abandonment and evacuation. Left to themselves the British Government might conceivably have evolved a compromise which, if not entirely lacking in prejudice to the Arabs, would have secured a certain amount of protection and guarantee for their interests. But the inexorable pressure of the United States with its vast Jewish-controlled interests operated to prevent the feeble Labour Government of Attlee from honouring Britain's promises to the Arabs.

The introduction of the Palestine problem to the United Nations and the partition plan of the Special Committee in September 1947 gave the British Government the opportunity they anxiously sought of extricating themselves. They declared that they would on 15 May 1948 terminate their mandate and evacuate the country, leaving it to the United Nations or to its own devices. The contemplated removal of the British army and police opened the way for the Arab states, under the aegis of the Arab League which had been formed in 1944, and the Jews of Palestine to settle their differences in their own way, that is, by fighting it out. The objectives were clear. The Arab states naturally espoused the cause of their brethren who had lost their lands and rights to the immigrant Jews and proposed to concert together to expel the invaders. The Jews on the other hand with powerful organisations in Europe and America at their back intended not only to hold what they had already secured, but to enlarge their domains at the expense of the neighbouring Arab territories. On 15 May 1948 when the last British soldiers embarked, the stage was set for the conflict. Egypt and the Arab states plunged into war with the Jews of Palestine.

Sympathy for their brother Arabs was not, however, the sole motive which drove Egypt into the war. By 1948 the country was seething with unrest and was hovering on the brink of chaos. The climate of war was, as it were, in the air and a campaign in Palestine would be a safety-valve and a release from internal tension. Since February 1942 when Faruk had weakly submitted to the threat of British tanks and guns, his popularity with the masses had been reduced to open contempt. His surrender to the British had been regarded as a betrayal of the nation and had heaped insult on insult. He had since fallen into the hands of debased and unscrupulous advisers who willingly fed his appetite for depravity. In the space of a few years the handsome and slim young man, the idol of the people, had degenerated into a sack of debauch.

Clandestine movements and organisations were stirring in the country imbued with yearnings for social change and revolution to which the effete monarchy and its constitutional trappings were only hindrances to progress. Of these the most menacing was the Moslem Brotherhood or Ikhwan el Muslimin, the creation in 1929 of Sheikh Hassan el Banna at Ismailia. This, like the Wahabi movement of the previous century, had for its aims the return to the 'way' as laid down by the Koran, the purification of religious practice and the cleansing of the country from impious foreign influences. This movement with its predominant appeal to religious fervour and the crusading spirit of its founder exercised a profound influence not only over the simple *fellahin*, but more particularly over the youth and intelligentsia of the towns and the students of the universities. At first a religious organisation, it had within the space of ten years developed into an instrument with immense political potential, as the indefatigable Sheikh, or Supreme Guide as he called himself, travelled the land forming branches and cells and recruiting fanatics and terrorists to his flag. At the time of the Second World War a formidable organisation with tentacles stretching throughout the country lay at his command and further strengthened itself by the caches of arms and substantial financial resources.

The same period which witnessed the rise of the Brotherhood saw the decline of the Wafd. Internal dissension, corruption and lust for power among its principals had resulted in splinter groups breaking away with a consequent weakening of the core. Further, its wartime collaboration with the British had still to be lived down and forgotten. In post-war Egypt the Wafd was still the leading, but no longer the dominating, party; much of the allegiance it had commanded was now transferred to the Moslem Brotherhood. This canker of fanaticism which fastened on the usually tolerant body of Egypt in the early post-war years constituted a standing menace to public order, the monarchy and constitution, and it is not improbable that if the Sheikh had raised the banner of revolt, he might without difficulty have overthrown the government and seized power. Yet, remarkable in his power over the emotions of the masses and his capacity for organisation, Sheikh Hassan lacked the courage to screw himself up to the point of rebellion. He merely contented himself with exhortation, criticism of the Government, intrigue and isolated acts of terrorism. Though the menace of the Brotherhood hung heavy over the Government, it lacked the legal power in time of peace to suppress it. But in a state of war with the Jews of Palestine the Government could take special powers under martial law and deal in more effective fashion with the potential threat.

At the same time an as yet undetected revolutionary movement was spreading through the army. In its origins it closely resembled the movement conceived and nurtured by Arabi half a century before. It was the despised native Egyptian officers, sons of the *fellahin* and petty officials who were the principal exponents of nationalism and independence and who felt most keenly the humiliations of the British occupation. Of all the events of the decade the capitulation of Faruk and the acceptance of office by Nahas Pasha and the Wafd under the protection of the British power were to them the greatest betrayal. During and immediately after the war occasions arose to tempt the more headstrong and emotional officers to some symbolic coup or act of violence against the British, which would only have served to expose the movement without useful result. But a somewhat forbidding and thoughtful young officer, Gamal Abdul Nasser, who was the driving force behind the conspiracy, was able to restrain his colleagues from open foolishness and to keep his organisation intact and undetected until the propitious moment arrived. During this time a certain amount of contact and collaboration took place between the secret movement, the Society of Free

409

Officers, and the Moslem Brotherhood, the astute Supreme Guide realising how useful an adjunct a military corps would be to his organisation. But Nasser recognised that the essential aims and objectives of the two movements were different and refused to let himself be drawn and submerged in the fanaticism of the Brotherhood.

The conduct of the Palestinian war was theoretically under the aegis of the Arab League which had been formed with the blessing of the British in 1944 to foster unity and co-operation among the Arab states. Egypt, by virtue of her great predominance of population, wealth, culture and civilisation, expected to assume the ascendant role, and an Egyptian, Abdul Rahman Azzam Pasha, had become Secretary General. Indeed, although the relations of the member states of the League were generally far from cordial and tinged with mutual suspicion and jealousy, they had sufficient common interest to unite in the campaign against the Jews, for they all feared that if the Jews once established themselves as an independent sovereign state in Palestine, they would not long be content with their restricted frontiers and would seek further expansion at the expense of their Arab neighbours. This fear was undoubtedly justified. But in their conduct of the campaign the Arabs were labouring under the delusion that a mere show of force would scatter the immigrants to the winds, and expected little more than a military promenade. For although in recent years Jewish immigration into Palestine had been heavy, the total population of Jews was infinitesimal compared with the swarming millions of Arabs, and it was inconceivable that this handful would offer more than a token resistance to a concerted attack from all sides. But large numbers of Jews had fought in the World War; there had been a Jewish Brigade in Italy and they were hardened and experienced in the art of war and had been nourished with substantial supplies of modern armament. Above all, there burnt in the heart of every Jew in Palestine an irrevocable determination to die in his tracks rather than yield an inch of the ground he occupied. At last, after two thousand years of wandering as strangers and foreigners on the face of the earth, they stood on the threshold of a land they could call their own. There was to be no retreat or surrender.

On 15 May 1948, while the last British troops assembled at Haifa to embark, the Arab forces descended from all sides on Palestine. But there was neither plan nor collaboration in the attack; it consisted of unco-ordinated advances from Syria and Lebanon in the north, Jordan and Iraq in the east and Egypt in the south. Only the Egyptians made progress, reaching Gaza and Beersheba; the remainder were halted and thrown back by a handful of Jews. Jewish tenacity and resistance dumbfounded the politicians in Egypt. They sought to hide the truth by publishing glowing accounts of spectacular victories and successes against the Jews, and the people were therefore discomfited to learn that only after one month of campaigning a truce arranged by the United Nations had been accepted. The fact gradually emerged that there had been no spectacular victories.

Fighting was resumed a month later, but the Jews had taken full advantage of the short respite to mobilise their power, and when a further truce was arranged in July 1948 they had considerably improved their position. In October they resumed the offensive and wrested Beersheba from the Egyptians who were reluctantly compelled to realise that they were no match for the Jews. On 24 February 1949 an armistice was signed by Egypt and Israel at Rhodes, and in March the Jews occupied the Gulf of Aqaba. This was the sorry end of the campaign to evict Jews from the Arab lands.

The whole campaign had been a completed disaster for Egypt. It was the first occasion since the Battle of Omdurman in 1898 that the Egyptian army had operated on its own initiative, and its result was humiliation. It was subsequently claimed, and undoubtedly with justification, that the arms supplied to the army were obsolete and defective, the result of shady deals at the Palace by unscrupulous politicians who had made handsome profits out of them. But this was subsidiary to the real cause of defeat, the fact that in its higher command, staff work and supply echelons the Egyptian army was entirely unequal to the task of conducting a campaign beyond its own frontiers against a hardened, resolute and fanatical enemy. The troops at the front gave a good account of themselves, and among those who were distinguished for courage and resistance were General Mohamed Neguib and Colonel Gamal Abdel Nasser whose stand at Faluja was one of the few redeeming features of the campaign. But the army, and the Society of Free Officers in particular, were convinced that they had been betrayed by their own Government and sacrificed to the greed of corrupt politicians.

CHAPTER 25

Revolution

The disaster in Palestine was the forerunner of the breakdown of the established order in Egypt. No one could disguise the defeat and humiliation that had been suffered. The army was finally and completely alienated from the Palace, the Moslem Brotherhood was preaching sedition and revolution in barely concealed terms; public security deteriorated; depression and unemployment were rife; and the government of Nokrashy Pasha had no policy. But in face of the threat to public order Nokrashy eventually in November 1948 ordered the suppression of the Brotherhood. This challenge was forthwith answered by his own assassination in December in the lift of the Ministry of the Interior by thugs disguised as policemen.

The government was then taken over by Ibrahim Abdel Hadi Pasha, Chief of the Royal Cabinet and a King's man who immediately tackled the menace to public safety by seeking out, arresting and detaining thousands of members of the Brotherhood. In this process the Supreme Guide, Sheikh Hassan el Banna, himself met his death on 13 February 1949 in the open street. It is thought that the assassins were the secret police and that 'this was a state murder, the deliberate removal of a man it was otherwise difficult to dispose of.'[1] It is indeed extraordinary that the Brotherhood with its cadres of gunmen, its organisation of cells throughout the country and its popular appeal allowed itself to be decapitated and broken without lifting a finger to protect itself, but the inability of Sheikh Hassan to take a decision at the moment of crisis and advantage seems to account for this. At any rate the deterioration of security received a check under Hadi Pasha, and it is possible that had he been given sufficient time, he might have effected some improvement in the social and economic condition of the country. But never since the unique combination of King Fuad and Sidky Pasha in the early 1930s had it been possible for an oligarchy to govern in an atmosphere of stability. It was not so much that autocratic and authoritative government was unpopular with the masses, but that the political parties, ever avid for power, maintained a persistent clamour against it and did all in their power to decry it. As an election was due in 1950 Hadi Pasha's term of office was necessarily short, but even so he was able to conclude beneficial arrangements with Britain on a development plan for the Nile and for participation in the Owen Falls project in Uganda, and also with the Suez Canal Company 'which brought tangible benefits to Egypt but mitigated some of the rigours of the Egyptian law dictating the proportion of Egyptians who must be employed, etc.'[2] In fact, since the Palestine war there was a noticeable relaxation in the campaign against Britain the hereditary enemy and the British occupation. By this time the British army had withdrawn from its havens of luxury in Cairo and Alexandria and had taken up its quarters along the Canal. To some extent out of sight meant out of mind, except to the large number of workmen in the cities who had lost their employment with the British and the traders who lamented their departure. The disaster in Palestine had cast some doubt upon Egypt's ability to defend herself and the Canal, and no doubt the presence of a screen of British troops between Israel and the Delta afforded a certain sense of security. Sidky Pasha even advocated Egypt's closer association with the Atlantic powers.[3]

Hadi Pasha viewed with great disfavour the conduct and excesses of the dissolute Faruk which were bringing the monarchy into open contempt, and further made known his intentions of investigating the shady arms deals of the Palace clique. He thus became the enemy of the King who cast about for means of replacing him. This led to another of those curious paradoxes which beset the land of Egypt. By this time the Wafd had managed to live down to a certain extent the slurs on its reputation, and although it had lost the glamour of being the champion of Egypt's freedom and independence, it had remained the party with the most effective propaganda organisation and with the largest following in the country. The Wafd

> stands for the freedom of the press, questions in the House, student gatherings, congresses and back-slappings. It is . . . the lower bourgeoisie greedy for freedom and power; the landed Third Estate gradually being urbanised through the University; the legal and administrative professions, and those of the big land-owners who chose to cut their losses by financing the 'popular' party after electing it, and thus keeping their hold on it. It is also a form of liberalism, a typically Egyptian tolerance in the approach to religious and racial problems.[4]

413

Up to this time under the leadership of Nahas Pasha it had also been the inveterate enemy of the King. But now it was avid for power and the King needed an ally. They formed an alliance, a typical horse-treader's deal. Faruk dismissed Hadi Pasha in February 1949, and invited Hussein Sirry Pasha to lead a caretaker government to supervise the forthcoming elections which took place in January 1950. The Wafd was returned to power with a massive majority of 228 out of 319 seats.

This was the seventh occasion since 1924 that the Wafd had been called to power, and the fifth time Nahas was to lead it. Out of office the Wafd had had a splendid record of opposition and popularity with the masses; in office it had always been a dismal and humiliating failure and had sometimes been kicked out for discreditable reasons. What then were the prospects for this latest accession to office? Had the Wafd learnt the lessons of the past, that patient, stable and honest administration were the real rewards, that incessant propaganda against the British was profitless and comfortless? Would it have the courage to resist corruption and alienate the powerful *pasha* class by sincere efforts at social reform? No long period was to elapse before these questions were answered.

In its election campaign the Wafd had addressed itself to a measure of social reform, but in office its efforts were little more than superficial. It was easy to win the popularity of the townsfolk by granting cost of living increases, but as this only resulted in higher prices and inflation, it failed to achieve any easement of the economy. The Minister for Social Affairs, Ahmed Hussein, planned a social security scheme but it remained largely in the stages of contemplation. 'The distribution of government and royal land to needy peasants was pilloried in the anti-Wafdist press on the grounds that the so-called needy were relatives of Madame Nahas and other prominent Wafdists.'[5]

But in order to live down and consign to oblivion that unfortunate period of collaboration with the British during the War and to keep Egyptian minds off their own humble problems, it was essential to revert to the old methods and practices of Wafdist rule. The scapegoat, the British connection, was to be revived with full force. In the Speech from the Throne delivered in November 1950 it was declared that total evacuation of the British army would be demanded and the unity of the Nile Valley proclaimed, precisely the same claims that had been made a quarter of a century earlier.

By this time British policy in Egypt had undergone a further shift. No longer was it merely the security of imperial communications that exercised the British Government; it was the security of whole regions that was being planned by the West. NATO and SEATO had been born, and it was now proposed to complete the chain of Western defence by the formation of a Middle East Defence Organisation in which a solid bloc of Middle East states supported by Britain, France and the United States, would face the threat of communist expansion from the north and secure the vital oil pipelines from Iraq to the Mediterranean and the sea-lanes from Abadan and Arabia. In this optimistic scheme it was hoped that the Arab states would sink their differences with Israel and unite in a common scheme of defence. No scheme ever devised took less account of popular susceptibilities. For close on seventy years Egypt had suffered an abhorrent connection with the British. Of all things, release from this connection was what she wanted most. It is thus almost inconceivable that such a scheme of collaboration could even have been contemplated, let alone broached to the Egyptian Government, and it can only be assumed that the British Foreign Office which could not have been entirely blind was pushed to it by an ingenuous United States Government. At any rate, when it was put to the Egyptian Government that evacuation of the Canal Zone would be conditional upon Egypt's participation in the defence organisation, that was enough to kill the scheme. Egypt would have nothing to do with it. Under no circumstances would she participate in any scheme which had any colour of further subordinating her to the policies and defences of Britain and the Western bloc. To clinch the matter, on 8 October 1951 Nahas Pasha announced the unilateral abrogation of the Treaty of 1936 with Britain and proclaimed Faruk King of the Sudan.

These declarations heralded a transition from mere verbal protest and argument with the British to unofficial but active hostility. Although the Government took no part officially and did not even break off diplomatic relations with Britain, it connived in the formation of a 'liberation army' of all groups to menace and disrupt the British position in the Canal Zone. For this purpose hundreds of Moslem Brothers who had been detained by Hadi Pasha were released to take part in the guerrilla campaign and all ardent nationalists were similarly encouraged. The army secretly provided arms and ammunition for the campaign. All British officials in the public service were dismissed summarily. A boycott was placed on British goods. The supply of fresh food to the British army was stopped and, even more serious, the entire Egyptian labour force was withdrawn.

The advantage to the Egyptians of the guerrilla campaign was that it made every movement in the Canal Zone extremely costly . . . In the final analysis it was the need to expand the base to accommodate the coloured forces brought in as labourers, and Egyptian attacks on the water supplies of the base which forced an extension of military action by Britain and precipitated the final crisis.

In fact the British army was compelled to drop the role of mere passive and neutral occupation and put itself into an active state of defence. In this it was hampered by the fact that it was precluded by the Treaty from undertaking operations outside the Canal Zone itself and could not therefore seek out the nests of partisans who conducted their guerrilla operations from the safe bases of Zagazig. They were limited to defensive tactics. The principal towns in the Zone, Port Said, Ismailia and Suez, were brought under British military control.

By January 1952 an unofficial and sporadic state of war existed between the Egyptian Liberation Army and the British. On the 12th a substantial foray was launched against the great base at Tel el Kebir and General Erskine, the British commander, resolved on retaliation. On 25 January he delivered an ultimatum to the Buluq Nizam, or auxiliary police garrison, at Ismailia requiring them to surrender their arms within two hours, and British tanks were thrown around the police barracks. Colonel Raif, commanding the auxiliary police at Ismailia, immediately telephoned for instructions to Fuad Serag ed Din, the Wafd Secretary General and Minister of the Interior. He, realising the great advantages which this ill-considered action by Erskine had conferred on the Egyptian cause, ordered the garrison commander to resist. The British troops attacked the police depot and before the morning was out about fifty Egyptians were dead and a hundred wounded. Another Denshawi incident was conveniently provided by the British to give substance to the Wafd claims of British imperialism and oppression, but the very forces which the Wafd and Palace had unleashed to feed the flames of nationalism and anglophobia within a few days became beyond control and encompassed the destruction of their authors.

When the news of the Ismailia massacre, for as such it was regarded, reached the capital, the Government was faced with the demand for a great demonstration against the British. This was precisely what the Wafd which for thirty years had preached and taught the doctrine of mob violence wanted. The only condition exacted by Serag ed Din was that there should be no demonstration against the King. 'An extraordinary Council of Ministers, meeting during the night, took decisions of the utmost gravity, to break off diplomatic relations with Britain, appeal to the Security Council, and arrest as hostages some eighty people belonging to the British colony in Cairo.'⁶

On the morning of Saturday 26 January 1952 all the elements of disorder, the Wafd youth, the Moslem Brotherhood, communists, university students and the riff-raff of the streets were out, and they were joined by the auxiliary police in Cairo who went on strike in protest against the murder of their colleagues at Ismailia. With the barriers of restraint thus thrown off the mobs surged into the streets of the city.

The demonstrations started early in the Saturday morning when processions moved from various districts in the city and were harangued by politicians and demagogues of various colours of opinion, but all united in their condemnation and vilification of the British. Although the police and security forces took little part in controlling the demonstrations, the crowds were comparatively well-behaved until nearly midday when disorder suddenly erupted at the Badia Casino in the Midan Ezbekia. This seems to have been the signal to a secret but monstrous conspiracy of arson. The casino was invaded by the mobs and set on fire. The fire brigade raced to the scene and did their best to extinguish the blaze until their hoses were slashed by the conspirators. Like a flash arson raced through the streets of Cairo. Everything had been well planned by the incendiaries; torches and bottles of petrol were all ready for use. Under the cloak of the mobs in the streets the fire-raisers raced from one establishment to another leaving each in flames. It is clear that all had been selected with care and deliberation: the cinemas, the bars, the banks, the Turf Club and some of the fashionable shops; even Shepheard's Hotel, the pillar and symbol of Europe in Egypt, went up in flames at the hands of the fire-raisers, aided and abetted by the now frenzied and uncontrollable mobs. 'The streets were littered with charred motorcars lying on their sides. Everywhere were the same blackened faces, streaming with sweat, disfigured by hatred and hysteria. Towards four o'clock two new phenomena were to be seen. The crowd which since the burning of Badia had been little more than a bewildered witness or an accomplice made drunk by such strange sights, now began to plunder. The fire-raisers turned them away from the British or European firms and directed them to Jewish shops and in some cases synagogues.'⁷

Against this madness and frenzy the Government and the forces of law and order took no action. The auxiliary police had themselves joined the rioters, the army was in its barracks at Abbassieh and its officers were being banqueted by King Faruk at Abdin Palace, together with principal Ministers and officials of the state. If the account published by Serag ed Din Pasha is to be believed, he was already making urgent calls to the Palace by 1.30

p.m. demanding the assistance of the army to clear the streets and restore order, but it was not until four hours later that any troops appeared. By this time the fire-raisers' work had been done. Four hundred buildings were ablaze and Cairo was enveloped in smoke and flames. How many people died in the disaster is not accurately known, but material losses amounted to about £23 million.[8] Throughout the day the Government and Palace remained palsied and paralysed. The Wafd Government, which for so long had preached the doctrines of violence and gutter rule, perished in the catastrophe it had created. Even while the fires were raging round the city Nahas Pasha offered his resignation to the King, and the following day Ali Maher Pasha formed a new government.

Who then was the author of this abominable crime? Even now no one seems to know, or at least no one has ever been brought to justice. Even speculation offers little reward, for the possibilities are legion. All that can be asserted with any degree of assurance is that the great fire of Cairo on Black Saturday was no accident; it was the outcome of a deliberate conspiracy. If the nature and quality of the places destroyed are any guide, the finger of suspicion must be pointed at the Moslem Brotherhood, for it was the cinemas, the bars and the haunts of the Europeans which bore the brunt of the attack. But perhaps the burning of the City was 'an explosion of vengeful spite on the part of a people whose unendurable poverty was flouted by the luxury of the Court and the foreigner.'[9]

The riots and destruction that took place on 26 January had a sobering effect on all sides. A momentary glimpse was vouchsafed to the government of the imminence of anarchy and chaos unless steps were taken to prevent it. Ali Maher affirmed his determination to pursue the principles adopted by his predecessors, evacuation and the unity of the Nile Valley – no leader could do otherwise – but at the same time the tacit policy of guerrilla war against the British in the Canal Zone was called off, and tension was somewhat eased. There was even recognition that further negotiation with Britain might be the best course. British public opinion was likewise shocked by the violence of these days, and some heart-searchings took place as to Britain's own responsibility for the deterioration in Anglo-Egyptian relations. The tone of the British press was often apologetic and couched in terms of self-justification.

Thus the curious result of the Cairo riots which had their origins in anti-British resentment was a partial rapprochement between the two countries. Ali Maher's plan to form a national front including the Wafd was disappointed, but there was nevertheless hope that, if a little urgency and understanding were displayed, Anglo-Egyptian differences might be patched up, and provision even made for the projected Middle East Defence Organisation. Amr Pasha, the Egyptian Ambassador in London, had a number of informal talks with Eden, the British Foreign Secretary, in February 1952, and arrangements were made to open negotiations in Cairo on 1 March.

Unfortunately on that date an internal dispute on whether Parliament should be suspended for a month led Ali Maher to resign, and the expected talks did not take place. He was succeeded by Neguib el Hilaly Pasha, a former professor of law, who announced his intention of continuing the policies mapped out by his predecessor in the forthcoming negotiations and also of pursuing a more vigorous enquiry into the Cairo riots and promising to root out the corruption which permeated the government machine. These were ominous words for the Wafd which immediately withdrew its support from Hilaly and embarked on a virulent campaign of abuse and obstruction. Hilaly retaliated in March by ordering Serag ed Din Pasha, Secretary General of the Wafd, and Abdul Fattah Hassan Pasha, a militant Wafd nationalist, to their homes. At the same time the British made a gesture of goodwill by restoring control of Ismailia to the Egyptian administration, and informal exchanges were re-opened between Hilaly and Stevenson on the possibility of further negotiations. Feeling no doubt that a successful conclusion to these would be impossible so long as the Wafd dominated the Chamber of Deputies Hilaly procured from the King a dissolution of the Chamber with further elections to take place in May. In the interval it was hoped to amend the electoral legislation which always enabled the Wafd to secure a majority of seats in the Chamber on a minority vote, and that a coalition of Saadist and Liberal parties would wrest control from the Wafd and obtain the nation's approval for any negotiations with the British. Martial law, which had been imposed by the Wafd during the January riots, was maintained as a means of keeping disorderly elements in check, much to the disgust of the Wafd its originator.

In the meantime informal exchanges continued between Egypt and Britain, both sides seeking a formula for a preliminary statement of the objects of the negotiations. While Britain was willing to recognise the principle of evacuation, Egypt for her part was prepared to concede the necessity of maintaining the Canal base in a state of readiness. The perennial difficulty was the Sudan. Probably the Egyptian Government recognised that eventual self-determination could not be avoided, but having proclaimed Faruk King of the Sudan, they were the prisoners of their own declarations and the problem was 'to find a formula for recognition of the King's title that could not be regarded as prejudicing the eventual status of the Sudan.'[10]

It was at this stage that Britain committed one of her habitual gaucheries in Egyptian affairs by allowing the British-controlled Sudan to announce a new constitution which represented 'the last stage in the country's advance towards self-determination'. Nothing could have been more calculated to arouse Egyptian suspicions of Britain's good faith. Indeed it seemed futile to cast about for a suitable formula on the Sudan while Britain was hurrying the country along the road to independence. The release of a further £10 million of sterling balances did little to lessen the suspicion, although it considerably eased the country's financial difficulties which had arisen from a fall in cotton prices. In its leading article of 8 April 1952 *The Times* defined the problem. After pointing out that 'Egypt had mainly herself to thank for her exclusion from any share in guiding the changes [in the Sudan]', it goes on to declare that

> the zeal of the British officials in the Sudan . . . must also bear some share of the responsibility for Egypt's unco-operative attitude. The condominium still exists, unaffected by Egypt's unilateral denunciation . . . Egypt cannot be excluded, and the British task is to seek some way of reconciling the pledges given by this country to the Sudanese people with the legitimate interest of Egypt in a close understanding with her southern neighbour. To do this may be formidably difficult, but it certainly cannot be done unless British policy towards the Sudan and British policy towards Egypt are pursued, not in isolation as at present, but as related parts of a single whole. Only a serious failure of co-ordination between them can explain the tabling of the new Sudan constitution at a moment when it nearly wrecked the Anglo-Egyptian conversations in Cairo.[11]

The result was that by the middle of April no substantial progress had been made in the negotiations, and nomination day for the forthcoming Egyptian elections in Egypt was imminent. The promised purges and investigations into corruption had not been completed, nor had the electoral system which gave such weight to the Wafd been amended. The elections could have no other result than to sweep the Wafd back into power and bring the country once again to the verge of anarchy on which it had hovered in January. Hilaly therefore postponed the elections.

The Anglo-Egyptian discussions – they never advanced to the stage of formal negotiations – dragged on throughout April and May, at first in Cairo between Hassouna Pasha the Egyptian Foreign Minister and Stevenson the

British Ambassador, then in London between Eden and Amr Pasha, and again back in Cairo. The question of evacuation which to the impartial observer might have been regarded as the principal subject of negotiation was thrust into the background by the interminable and obstinate problem of the Sudan. By this time both countries had taken up positions from which it was impossible to withdraw and which were impossible to reconcile by any formula. By the unilateral declaration of October 1951 Egypt had declared Faruk to be King of the Sudan and was now committed beyond redemption to securing formal acknowledgment of Egyptian sovereignty over the Sudan by Britain. If only this acknowledgment could be secured, the Egyptian Government would have been prepared to recognise the Sudan's right to self-government and future self-determination and to limit sovereignty to the merest shadow, but acknowledgment was the indispensable preliminary to any further agreement. Britain for her part had been fostering the principle of self-determination in the Sudan, and although there was in the Sudan a party, the Ashigga, who favoured union with Egypt, the main trend of opinion was in the direction of complete freedom to decide her own future, and further, the British Government had given an undertaking not to alter the constitutional position without the consent of the Sudanese. The most that Britain was prepared to concede was recognition of Faruk's sovereignty provided the Sudanese leaders themselves agreed and accepted it.

In a last attempt to break the deadlock, Hilaly Pasha invited Sir Abdel Rahman el Mahdi Pasha, the foremost political leader in the Sudan, to send a delegation to Cairo to discuss this delicate question and sound out the feeling in the Sudan. The delegation headed by Abdullah el Fadil duly arrived in Alexandria to which the Government had moved for the summer months at the end of May, and ten days of consultation took place. While Hilaly pressed the delegation to accept at least the symbolic sovereignty of King Faruk on the analogy of Britain and Canada, the Sudanese preferred to hear concrete proposals on how this would benefit the Sudan. At any rate the delegation returned to Khartoum at the beginning of June 1952 after undertaking to convey Egypt's views to el Mahdi Pasha. The position now was that the whole future of the Middle East defence rested on the reaction of the Sudanese leader to the proposal that the Sudan should accept some sort of Egyptian sovereignty over her. Both Britain and Egypt anxiously awaited a reply from Khartoum, but were met only with silence.

During this time forces were at work in Egypt to undermine Hilaly's position. His promises to investigate corruption and purge the administration, as witnessed by an Origin of Fortunes Bill designed to give the Government power to investigate the acquisition of fortunes by holders of official appointments, and his probings into the arms scandal with which the Palace was intimately concerned, raised a solid block of opposition to him in influential circles. He was moreover powerless to provide remedies for the mounting economic crisis, a legacy from the Wafd Government which had been tampering with the cotton market. These difficulties, coupled with the inordinate delay in securing a settlement with Britain, drove Hilaly to resign at the end of June.

It was clear that by this time the constitutional and party political system was rapidly breaking down. It was days before anyone could be found to form a new government, but finally Hussein Sirry Pasha succeeded on 3 July. It was to be a non-party government, but the presence as Minister of State of one Karim Thabet Pasha who had been the King's press counsellor and was said to exercise enormous influence over him, indicated how much the new government was to be the tool of the Palace. In the meantime martial law was to continue and the elections to be indefinitely postponed, and the pressure which Hilaly had exerted on the Wafd was to be eased. Fuad Serag ed Din was released from detention.

But on 20 July Hussein Sirry Pasha too offered his resignation. A crisis had arisen over the selection of a Minister of War, the King refusing to accept General Mohamed Neguib, the nominee of the Prime Minister, for, as will shortly be recounted, General Neguib was thought to be connected with a dissident group of officers in the army which was openly hostile to the monarchy, and above all Faruk could not tolerate anyone with such affiliations in control of the military machine of the state. It was essential to have his own man in this key post. Faruk was cornered and he was compelled to do a deal with Hilaly Pasha. Hilaly agreed to return to office but only on condition that he was given a free hand to resume his investigations into corruption; at the same time Faruk forced on him his own brother-in-law, Ismail Sherin, as Minister of War. This took place on 21 July. The next day the military revolution which was to sweep away the old order and the dynasty of Mohammed Ali moved into action.

In order to appreciate the events which took place subsequently it is necessary to turn back the pages of history and look more particularly at the military movement, the Society of Free Officers, which has already been mentioned in preceding pages. As with all successful revolutionary movements a certain aura of romance hangs over its origins. This movement started with genuine ideals among a handful of young Egyptian officers in 1939, the authors being Gamal Abdul Nasser, Abdul Hakim Amer and

Anwar el Sadat. 'We must fight imperialism, monarchy and feudalism,' wrote Anwar el Sadat, 'because we are opposed to injustice, oppression and slavery. Every patriot wants to establish a strong and free democracy. This aim will be achieved, by force of arms if need be. The task is urgent because the country has fallen into chaos. Freedom is our natural right. The way lies before us – revolution.'[12] These words were probably written after the revolution and wear the aspect of *ex post facto* reasoning. They do however embody the main doctrines of the revolutionary movement which grew up in the army before the war. As with all patriots the continuing British occupation was the source of the deepest humiliation and was to be eradicated at the first opportunity. In the eyes of the revolutionary spirits the serfdom and feudalism of the social order were the direct outcome of the monarchy which had a vested interest in preserving them; and the monarchy, it seemed to them, was sustained by the British. The outbreak of war scattered the group of conspirators and brought the full weight of British control and coercion over Egypt, and the revolutionaries were powerless to further their ambitions. But through these long years the flame was kept burning by this small nucleus of officers, but they were compelled to bide their time. Throughout the War they remained hostile to the British connection, ever resentful of the auxiliary but collaborative role which Britain forced their country to play. To them Britain was the main enemy and some sought to collaborate with the Germans and Italians. What treatment Egypt would have received at the hands of a victorious fascist Axis must remain a matter of speculation, but the fact remains that sympathy with Hitler and Mussolini was the natural corollary of antipathy to Britain, and this was strengthened beyond all measure by King Faruk's abject surrender to British demands in February 1942.

When after the War the British finally quitted the Delta and moved to the Canal Zone in 1947 one of the obstacles to the military movement was cleared out of the way. At least the possibility of British support for the monarchy seemed reduced, and the movement gathered momentum. Its leader Gamal Abdul Nasser had devoted himself for years to the study of the technique of revolution. He succeeded in concealing his identity as leader of the movement; he organised it into cells and branches throughout the corps of officers; he refused to compromise it by coalition or absorption into the Moslem Brotherhood of Hassan el Banna; he kept his eye fixed on the main objective and restrained his eager colleagues from precipitate and foolhardy escapades; he counselled patience throughout the long and difficult years and yet held the organisation together; withal he remained in the background

423

and almost unknown. Few there were who suspected that this aloof and reticent young officer was the driving force behind the flood of revolution which swept across Egypt in July 1952. For weeks after the revolution no mention was made of his name in the press.

Although the identity of the leaders remained unknown the existence of the movement eventually became common knowledge. Both the King and the secret police knew of it, but seem to have discounted it as mere disaffection or discontent which could always be quelled by administrative action. However in December 1951 the King experienced his first challenge from the officers. The presidency of the Officers' Club was a position of some importance and influence, and it was a matter of prestige to the King that his own nominee should be elected to it. In this instance the Free Officers were instrumental in securing the election of General Neguib against the wishes and to the humiliation of the King. Not that General Neguib was a leading light in the revolutionary movement; on the contrary he had no part in it. But Colonel Nasser and his colleagues had recognised that if their projected *coup d'état* was to be successful, it must at least have an acceptable figurehead, and they had already included General Neguib, a popular soldier with an unblemished reputation, in their list of suitable persons. His election to the Presidency of the Officers Club was the first overt sign of resistance to the King. But it was Black Saturday on 26 January 1952 when anarchy was let loose and Cairo went up in flames that decided the conspirators that their time had come. The Executive Committee of the Society held a meeting on 10 February at which it was decided that the revolution should be launched in March. It is clear that the success of the coup would depend on the loyalty of the troops to their officers and their willingness to execute without question their orders to haul down the lawfully constituted authority of the King and the constitutional monarchy. The unanimous resolution of the officers themselves was an even more vital element and any defection at the last moment could spell disaster and death. When it became apparent that one of the leading spirits, Colonel Mehanna, an artillery officer, was wavering and had in fact procured his own posting to El Arish in order to be well away from the scene of operations, the revolutionary committee postponed their plans until the beginning of August. In the meantime the secret police of Ibrahim Iman had been probing the movement and no long period could be expected to pass before wholesale arrests of the leading conspirators were made. Time was running out. When therefore the report reached the officers on 20 July that Hussein Sirry Pasha was resigning and that the King intended to impose his own creature on the next government as Minister of War, and that the leaders of the movement would be immediately arrested, it became merely a question which could act first, the Government or the Officers.

Gamal Abdul Nasser reacted at once and ordered the revolution to be brought forward to the night of 22 July. The Army Command had somehow got wind of the plot, for on the night of the 22 July a meeting was held at General Headquarters at which orders were issued for the immediate arrest of the Free Officers who were assembling at Manshiyat el Bakri. But the captain who was sent to make the arrests merely joined the conspirators himself, and the troops with Abdul Hakim Amer at their head returned to GHQ, forced an entry into the building and took the General Staff prisoner in one swoop.

At about 11 o'clock that night the troops under the command of the Free Officers moved into action in Cairo.

> Khaled Muhi ud Din's armoured cars surrounded the military area containing Abbasieh, Koubbeh, Manshiyat el Bakri and Heliopolis. Hussein el Shafi's tanks entered the city where they occupied strategic points, especially the broadcasting buildings, the telephone exchange, the airports and the station. Apart from a short struggle outside the GHQ where two soldiers were killed – the only victims of the coup d'état – the army and the city passed from Faruk's hands into those of the Free Officers.[13]

By three o'clock in the morning Neguib who only the previous day had been acquainted with the intention to launch a revolution was invited by the rebels to assume the post of Commander-in-Chief and was installed in his new office. The British and American embassies were notified of what had happened and warned not to interfere. The only apprehension of the plotters was that the British might intervene to uphold the constitutional order and keep Faruk on his tottering throne, and a mixed force was sent out to take up positions on the Suez road with orders at all costs to prevent any British advance on the city from the Canal Zone. But on being assured that the army would be responsible for the safety of foreign nationals, the British made no move to save the King.

At 7 a.m. on 23 July Abdul Hakim Amer broadcast to the nation. He announced that the army had been taken over by patriots, that the former army chiefs were now under arrest, and that the army would be responsible for law and order. 'I particularly wish to reassure our friends, the foreign nationals in Egypt, that the Army considers itself entirely responsible for the protection of their persons and property.' This news was received in Cairo that bright sunny morning with calm, with relief and even with joyfulness. The first stage of the revolution was over; the capital city was in the hands of the officers. But the King and Government were still at Alexandria; these remained to be dealt with.

Whatever happened after July 1952 it is evident that initially officers had no thought or intention of themselves taking over the adminstration of the state. They still looked to the democratic and constitutional system to provide the machinery of government, but they were resolved that the King must go and that the corruption which permeated the country must be rooted out. They themselves would merely be the bayonets to support the civil power in the execution of these objectives. Thus, when questioned that morning of 23 July as to his intentions, General Neguib replied that he proposed to respect the constitution, reform the army and the state, recall the parliament and bring in Ali Maher Pasha to form a new government. Ali Maher was dug out of bed that morning and offered the Presidency of the Council by Anwar el Sadat, the emissary of the officers. After some hesitation he agreed to accept the invitation, provided that the summons to form a new government came from the King himself. The King was still unaware of the imminence of his fall. He believed that the army was simply cleaning up its own ranks, and that afterwards things would go back to normal.

But the decision to dethrone Faruk had already been taken by Colonel Nasser, although it is not clear that General Neguib had been informed of it, and the scene of the revolution shifted to the shores of the Mediterranean. Ali Maher Pasha went to Alexandria on 24 July and interviewed the King. He placed before him the first demands of the army, the dismissal of Haidar Pasha, the detested Commander-in-Chief of the army and creature of the Palace, and of the Palace entourage who had brought the monarchy into such contempt: Karim Thabet the King's evil genius; Elias Andraos his economic adviser and author of many dubious financial transactions; Pulli his secretary; and Yussuf Rashad his physician. Ali Maher demanded in the name of the army a new government with himself at its head. Faruk had no alternative but to yield; he probably felt that his life was in danger and was prepared to concede anything. At the same time in Cairo the heads of the secret police and the political bureau were rounded up, thus frustrating in advance any measures the King might attempt to defeat the revolution.

It was vital that Faruk should be removed immediately before he could rally any support to himself. There was always a possibility that he would call on the British in the last resort, and it was thought by some that there had been a secret clause inserted in the 1936 Anglo-Egyptian Treaty by which Britain guaranteed to maintain Faruk on his throne. Colonel Nasser had decided that the King must leave the country within forty-eight hours. On 25 July General Neguib, accompanied by other officers of the revolution, went to Alexandria. Their welcome was 'overwhelming. The "saviour of the country" was engulfed in a happy roaring tide of humanity, madly exhilarated.'[14] Thus assured of the support of the army and the nation, Neguib presented an ultimatum for Ali Maher to deliver to the King:

Whereas the total anarchy in which the country has of recent months been thrown and which has spread to all domains, is a result of your bad administration, your violations of the Constitution, and your disregard of the will of the people, to a point where no citizen could feel secure in his life, dignity and property:

Whereas your persistence in this course has compromised the name of Egypt among the nations, and treacherous and corrupt persons have, under your protection, continued to amass shameful fortunes and to squander public funds while the people remain a prey to hunger and poverty:

Whereas these facts have been brought to light by the war in Palestine, the traffic in defective arms and ammunition, to which it gave rise, and the judgements pronounced by the Courts on those responsible revealed your intervention – intervention which distorted truth, shook confidence in justice, encouraged traitors in their crimes, enriched some and corrupted others:

Therefore the Army representing the power of the people, has authorised me to demand that Your Majesty abdicate the Throne in favour of the Heir Apparent, His Highness Prince Ahmed Fuad on this day, Saturday July 26th 1952, and that you leave the country before 6 p.m. of this same day. The Army holds Your Majesty responsible for any consequences which may result from your refusal to conform to the will of the people.

Commander in Chief of the Armed Forces,

Mohamed Neguib

Tanks and troops were thrown round the palaces of Ras el Tin and Montaza, as Ali Maher presented the ultimatum to Faruk. The net had closed round the degenerate monarch whose only course was to capitulate.

He accepted the demand and requested that he should be permitted to leave on the royal yacht *Mahroussa* – it was a yacht of that name which had borne the Khedive Ismail into exile in June 1879. The request was granted, and the Admiralty was instructed that the *Mahroussa* should be authorised to sail for any port of the King's choice. At the same time the instrument of abdication was being drafted by two eminent lawyers, Abdel Razek Sanhoury and Soliman Hefez.

Whereas we have always sought the happiness and welfare of Our People, and sincerely wish to spare them the difficulties which have arisen in this critical time, We therefore conform to the will of the People. We have decided to abdicate the Throne in favour of Our Heir, Prince Ahmed Fuad, and in the present Rescript do give Our orders to this end to His Excellency Aly Maher, Prime Minister, that he may act accordingly.

It is reported that the King had some difficulty in signing the instrument in his agitation, and finally signed it twice. The *Mahroussa* lying at Alexandria was made ready and at about 6 p.m. that evening ex-King Faruk, resplendent in the white uniform of an Admiral of the Fleet, descended to the quay of Ras el Tin and went on board, accompanied by Queen Narriman and his infant son, the new King. General Neguib, Ahmed Shawki, Hussein el Shafi and Gamal Salim, all principal actors in the revolution, went out to the *Mahroussa* to take formal leave of the deposed King. As the yacht sailed out of Alexandria, a destroyer fired a salute of twenty-one guns. The scene enacted by his grandfather Ismail Pasha, seventy-three years earlier, was re-enacted in almost identical detail by King Faruk, the only difference being that where Ismail had been deposed by the powers of Europe, Faruk was driven out by his own people.

CHAPTER 26

The Birth of a Republic

The events of July 1952 have been described in the preceding pages as a revolution and such in fact they were. Yet an examination of the resulting position shows that the juristic framework of the established constitution had been left undisturbed. A king had abdicated but the monarchy was continued in the person of the infant king Fuad; the Chamber of Deputies although still suspended as it had been prior to the coup remained a constitutional organ; executive power was exercised by a Prime Minister or President of the Council of Ministers in the person of Ali Maher duly and lawfully appointed by the King. The political parties and their organisations continued to flourish, at least for the present. All that was lacking was a Regency Council to exercise the functions of the infant King and this was a matter which received early attention.

If this then was the resultant position, in what sense can it be asserted that a revolution had swept the land of the Nile? The truth was that the legal framework of the constitution had been retained, but there had been a radical shift in the seat and source of power. Ali Maher Pasha nominally exercised all the powers of a prime minister, but it was recognised immediately and by all that he was no more than the agent and instrument of General Mohamed Neguib, Commander in Chief of the Armed Forces, and that he in his turn derived his authority from the bayonets, guns and tanks of the army. It came to be known that there was in the background a supreme committee or junta of army officers who made it their business to formulate policy, and it was first commonly thought that Neguib was the guiding spirit of this committee. Few there were who suspected that this was not the true position, that this bluff, hearty, pipe-smoking countryman in khaki was himself only the spokesman of a committee which took its lead from the tall, brooding young Colonel Gamal Abdul Nasser who was, for the time being at any rate, content to let the shadow of power rest on others while the substance remained in his own hands.

Ali Maher and Mohamed Neguib were the only names that appeared in the local and world press for weeks after the revolution as embodying the power of the state, and it was not until September that some glimmer of the actual position began to emerge. In an article on Egypt on 10 September *The Times* mentioned Nasser as being the most influential of the group of politically minded officers, and added that he was in charge of the Commander-in-Chief's office. The nominal cabinet of Ali Maher consisted of independents little known inside Egypt and not at all outside and merit no further mention. But the all-powerful 'Committee of Nine' forming the military junta are worthy of attention. These were: Gamal Abdul Nasser, President of the Committee, Abdul Hakim Amer, the principal figure in the military sphere and subsequently Minister of War and Commander-in-Chief; Abdul Latif Boghdadi, an original member of the Society of Free Officers; Salah Salim who later became known as 'the Dancing Major'; Khaled Muhieddin, a man of strong left wing affiliations; Hassan Ibrahim; Anwar el Sadat, an early colleague of Nasser, a virulent anglophobe with a record of political terrorism and association with the Germans during the war; Kamal ed Din Hussein; and Gamal Salim. These were the effective rulers of Egypt after July 1952.

All the rival factions and political groups welcomed the coup of the young officers, and hastened to shower their congratulations on them. Certainly it seemed to each that the army had cleared the way for their own reappearance on the political stage and accession to power. Each spoke as if the army had been the instrument of their own policies and designs. Nahas Pasha and Serag ed Din who were holidaying in Europe hurried back to proclaim the alliance of the Wafd with the army and to assure the officers that they could now safely leave the regeneration of Egypt to their well-experienced and trusted hands, and to persuade the army that it was now its duty to hand over its power to the one and only national party. 'The revolution was a national movement and the Wafd was the nation,' declared Nahas. Sheikh Hassan el Hodeiby, the successor of Sheikh Hassan al Banna, declared, 'The Koran is our only constitution' and demanded six ministries for the Moslem Brotherhood.[1] The extreme left saw in the fall of Faruk and his advisers an open path to communism. All were eager to jump on the army's band-waggon.

But the military committee had other ideas. Though still wedded to the ideals of democratic government they wanted to see the reform and regeneration of the country and the strengthening of the army with up-to-date equipment. They were resolved that a radical programme of reform should be instituted and pushed through to fulfilment, not the mere shuffling of a few names and personalities, but otherwise business as usual. Within a few weeks of the revolution the Government announced that if the political parties wished to take any further part in the affairs of the state, they must first purge themselves of all elements of jobbery and corruption. This demand was mainly directed at, and most keenly felt by, the Wafd which had a shameful record of corrupt practice while in office. Nahas Pasha and Serag ed Din probably did not take this demand seriously and thought that it could be glossed over, but as the month of August wore on and General Neguib continued to make frequent reference to the necessity of the parties cleaning themselves up, and pointing out that no elections would take place until they did so, it became clear that the army was by no means disposed to hand over all its hard-won gains to the Wafd, and the patronising geniality of Nahas and his colleagues to the new régime rapidly changed to anger and hostility. It was announced on 11 August that elections would take place the following February, by which time it was presumed that the parties would have reorganised themselves on democratic lines and dismissed the dishonest.

An even more serious shock to the Wafd with its great following among the land-owning interests was the announcement of the policy of agrarian reform. Measures were to be worked out to break up the great estates and limit individual ownership of land to two hundred feddans. The basic principle of this proposal was sound for, apart from the great appeal it would have among the landless *fellahin*, up to this time land and buildings were practically the sole avenue for the investment of capital. Few capitalists were prepared to venture their money in commerce and industry as long as land could be bought, with the result that industry was starved of money for development and land was over-valued. The restriction of land-ownership to a relatively small area would eventually compel capital to seek out other forms of investment to the advantage of industrial development. Land-owners were of course violently opposed to the proposal.

In order to regularise the constitutional position a Regency Council was appointed consisting of Prince Abdul Moneim, a well respected member of the royal family and son of the Khedive Abbas, Bahieddin Barakat and Colonel Rashad Mehanna, that same officer who had been suspected of defection from the revolutionary cause, but who commanded too much influence both inside and outside the army to be lightly disposed of. He was given the nominal portfolio of Minister of Communications as qualification

431

for appointment to the Regency Council. It is reported that he began to give himself the airs of a monarch and was shortly to overreach himself. But an omen of the approaching doom of the monarchy was manifested by the abolition of the titles of *Pasha* and *Bey* which had been in the gift of the King.

Within three weeks of taking over power the army junta was faced with a serious crisis. On 13 August a riot broke out at the Misr Spinning Mills at Kafr ed Dawar near Alexandria following an unsatisfied demand for more pay by the labourers and complaints against the management. The police were stoned by the rioters, some deaths occurred and many were injured. Troops had to be sent to quell the disorders. Labour demonstrations of this nature were almost unknown in Egypt, and the government, feeling that this incident could easily herald a further lapse into anarchy by the country unless the strongest possible measures were taken to check it, and to demonstrate the determination of the army to maintain order, resolved on the sternest retribution. Hundreds of employees were arrested, and the following day a military tribunal was set up to try the leaders of the disturbances. Three days later a workman, one Mustafa el Khamis, was sentenced to death. The sentence was undoubtedly a difficult decision to reach, for it seemed to the world that the first victim of a revolution whose main aim was the redress of social injustice was to be a simple workman, a member of the class to whom the revolution should have the greatest appeal. The government however was convinced that the riot had been instigated by subversive elements, with the finger of suspicion pointing mainly at the Wafd, and General Neguib is reported to have offered Khamis his life if he would divulge the identity of the instigators. The man went to his death with his lips sealed. This was the signal to the extreme left wing who had had hopes that the military coup could be moulded on communist principles to denounce Neguib and the junta as a fascist dictatorship.

At the other end of the scale the British and Americans were anxiously awaiting some indications of the complexion of the new régime. Their main interests lay in settling the Anglo-Egyptian dispute and in erecting the Middle East Defence Organisation with Egypt as an integral part of it. Now that the country was governed by soldiers it was hoped that they would realise the more readily the necessity of a scheme of mutual defence than the politicians had done. At the time of the revolution the position had been that Britain was waiting for a pronouncement from the Sudan on whether Faruk's sovereignty would be recognised. If so, the way would be open for all other questions in dispute to be settled. But in the event Neguib was not prepared to pursue the negotiations until Egypt had put her own house in order. He had no interest in fanning anti-British hostility to disguise the shortcomings of the government, the traditional policy of the Wafd, and furthermore the message eventually arrived from el Mahdi Pasha at Khartoum that the Sudan would not recognise Egyptian sovereignty. In the circumstances there was no prospect of concluding immediately an agreement with Egypt, and the British Government began to canvas the idea of Cyprus as a suitable base for the defence organisation.

In order to sustain the impetus and popular support for the revolution the military committee were anxious that the land reform should be implemented without delay and the necessary legislation enacted. Ali Maher, although probably realising the need for reform of some sort, preferred to proceed a little more cautiously. The break-up of the well organised and well managed large estates which were responsible for most of the revenue and foreign trade, might well have serious effects on the economy of the country. This difference of view led Ali Maher to resign on 7 September and General Neguib himself took over the Government. At the same time wholesale arrests of political leaders took place including Serag ed Din, Hilaly and Ibrahim Abdul Hadi. The army was making it clear that it would tolerate no further delaying tactics to its plans nor opposition from the parties. Egypt was now moving openly towards direct military government.

Even so, Nahas Pasha was by no means intimidated. Still in command of the Wafd with its powerful interests and nation-wide organisation, he continued to challenge and bait the military group. The Wafd could not hope to survive the threatened purge which would eliminate all its prominent personalities, and was exerting itself to the utmost through its own press to discredit the officers and resist the proposed land reforms. They hoped to whip up enough opposition to topple the junta from the seat of power. An open struggle thus developed. The Government continued to exert pressure on the party to cast its leader, Nahas, overboard, and all through September the party anxiously deliberated whether to take the line of least resistance and remain in existence by casting Nahas aside, or to defy the government at the risk of compulsory dissolution and confiscation of its funds. By 28 September it seemed that the party had resolved to refuse to comply with the government's demand to present a declaration relative to its reorganisation, but two days before the deadline, on 8 October, the party took second thoughts and capitulated, sacrificing the aged Nahas to its own continued existence.

At about the same time a further step was taken towards strengthening the army's hold on the country when nearly five hundred officers of all ranks were weeded out and cashiered or retired. These were the elements who had not supported or had taken no part in the revolution and whose loyalty was suspect. The introduction of army personnel into the ministries and administration of the country was a further omen of things to come, but Colonel Mehanna was abruptly dismissed from the Regency Council. All remnants of opposition, actual or potential, to the army régime were being cleared out of the way.

The status and future of the Sudan was the first major external issue which had to be faced by the new government. It was hoped by the British to implement the constitution announced in May by November, and long consultations took place between General Neguib and the Sudanese leaders in October. For thirty years Egypt had followed an undeviating policy of agitation for the unity of the Nile Valley under the Egyptian crown. Neguib however adopted a different line. He realised that the prospects of securing political unification were by no means certain, but he saw that at any rate it could not be achieved as long as the British were present and in control of the Sudan. It would only become a possibility once they had left, and he therefore offered no resistance to the proposed new constitution which was to grant internal self-government to the Sudan immediately and self-determination within three years. Egypt, he thought, could use those three years in strengthening the pro-unionist parties in the Sudan and increasing their influence.

The key to the agreement between Egypt and the Sudan independence parties was General Neguib's acceptance of the principle that sovereignty over the Sudan rests with the Sudanese pending self-determination. In so doing, the General courageously reversed the policy of previous governments which had asserted Egyptian sovereignty, though conceding to the Sudanese the right to secede. His policy of working with the independence movement promises to restore Egypt to a position of influence in the Sudan, which the Wafd government threw away by abrogating the condominium agreements. By recognising the Sudan's right to independence General Neguib advances Egypt's aim of securing evacuation of the British from the Nile Valley, and has established relations with the Sudanese which should be a valuable insurance policy for Egypt's vital interests in the Nile Waters.[2]

The way was thus opened for the conclusion of an agreement on 12 February 1953 between Britain and Egypt on the political future of the Sudan. It is unnecessary to elaborate the detailed provisions of the agreement, but broadly they provided for elections to be held under the auspices of an international commission, a parliament of elected representatives and internal self-government for a transitional period of three years at the end of which the Sudan would have the option to choose complete independence or some form of union with Egypt. In the meantime the Governor-General would be assisted by another international commission in exercising his constitutional powers. The inclusion of these bodies in the arrangements suggest that although Britain and Egypt had agreed as to the future of the Sudan, neither was prepared to trust the other very far. Indeed, acrimonious disputes soon arose. The Egyptians, haunted by the fear that the Sudan would eventually choose complete independence, endeavoured to improve their position and influence on the Governor-General's commission and in the local parties, and at the same time to buy popularity by criticising the mainly British administration and bring it into disrepute in the eyes of the Sudanese. No incident, however trivial, was ignored if it could be used as ammunition in the campaign. The British on the other hand, now committed irrevocably to Sudanese self-government and independence, shrugged off these pinpricks and hurried on with the task. They were prepared to concede Egyptian demands if thereby the elections could be accelerated and the Sudanese given a reasonable opportunity of expressing their wishes at the ballot boxes.

It will be recalled that the settlement of the Sudanese question was the condition precedent to the solution of the remaining major problem in foreign affairs, the evacuation of the British army from Egyptian soil. Negotiations on this question were destined to be spread over a considerable interval of time during which developments were taking place in Egypt. At the end of 1952 the military junta under the ostensible leadership of General Neguib was still intent on consolidating its power and legalising its position. In November it procured from the Council of State, the supreme constitutional organ, a decree declaring valid and lawful all acts of General Neguib and the revolutionary government, a sort of act of indemnity and immunity, and in December it released from detention the majority of politicians and palace favourites who had been arrested as being no longer a threat to the régime.

But the government's greatest difficulty was financial. The nation expected the revolutionary régime to ease its economic plight, but this Neguib could not do. He had inherited the disastrous effects of the Wafd's manipulations of the cotton market, and it was at this critical juncture that the textile industry of Lancashire, Egypt's best customer for her cotton, experienced a trade recession and reduced its purchases of the raw material. The Egyptian cotton market was flooded and twelve million qantars of cotton remained unsold which the Egyptian Government was compelled to buy itself, a severe inflationary measure. In the Egyptian press Britain was characteristically accused of withholding her purchases to embarrass Egypt, and as an earnest of good intentions Britain released a further £10 million of sterling balances in addition to the £5 million released in October, to relieve the plight of the Government. But there was little leeway and certain measures were taken to reduce the cost of living. Strikes were made illegal, compulsory arbitration by industrial tribunals being substituted as the remedy for labour disputes, and rents and prices of certain commodities were reduced.

Notwithstanding the authoritarian measures which the junta had taken to secure its position, it contained as late as the end of 1952 elements which were still attracted to the ideal of democratic and constitutional government. But by this time the old constitution of 1923 was unworkable and must be revised in such a way as to prevent the return of all the abuses which had bedevilled the country for the past thirty years. In December it was announced that the constitution had been repealed and that a new one would shortly be promulgated and there would be a three-year transitional period to prepare for a return to parliamentary government.[3]

The political parties were dissolved and their funds confiscated, and a 'Liberation Rally', a civilian counterpart to the Society of Free Officers, was formed to give an ostensible national aspect to an oligarchical form of government. Disaffected groups attempted to retaliate by sowing discord and sedition in the army, but the régime, having trodden the path of conspiracy and revolution itself, was continually on the alert lest others might be tempted to follow the same path. Indeed the policy of agrarian reform was well calculated to arouse the bitterest opposition among the aristocracy. No long interval was to pass before such a conspiracy was revealed, largely instigated by the officers' erstwhile comrade, Colonel Rashad Mehanna. He was arrested and secretly tried by a military tribunal in March 1953 and sentenced to life imprisonment; other conspirators were given varying terms of imprisonment or cashiered. This was followed on 18 June by the abolition of the monarchy and the proclamation of a republic. Thus passed unwept, unhonoured and unsung the dynasty of the great Pasha, Mohammed Ali, which had reigned over Egypt for a century and a half.

What was however noticed was the emergence from obscurity of Gamal Abdul Nasser who dictated the republican oath to the masses assembled in Abdin Square.

Many of us felt that evening that it was not the change of regime that mattered so much as the 'introduction to the people' and the open accession to power, as Deputy Prime Minister and Minister for the Interior, of this tall bikbashi with the greenish complexion, the overlong nose and reserved yet burning eyes . . . The man speaking in such passionate tones was not the same as the decent Neguib. He was obviously a changer of history, a revolutionary. He was not liked. They felt misgivings as they saw him grow in stature, or rather come out from behind the curtain behind which he had hidden his influence. Egyptian good nature was not much in evidence in this taciturn individual who got rid of Farouk.[4]

Under the Republic Neguib was both President and Prime Minister, but the key Ministry of the Interior was in the hands of Nasser and gave him command of the police and security forces, while his intimate friend and collaborator, Abdul Hakim Amer, was Commander-in-Chief of the army. Almost the entire power of the state was thus concentrated in these two men. Already a breach was beginning to open between Neguib and Nasser, and the trial of strength was not to be long delayed. In launching the revolution the colonels had needed a personality of stature and influence to be a figurehead, to lend respectability to the *coup d'état*, and General Neguib had amply and successfully fulfilled the role assigned to him. But the officers, Colonel Nasser especially, had never intended him to become the effective leader of the régime and formulate policy. This was the function of the junta or Revolutionary Command Council, as it came to be called. But Neguib having been hoisted into the highest office of the state came to believe and to persuade himself that he was the real leader, and he was by no means willing to be merely the spokesman of a group of officers he regarded as his juniors and subordinates, and to be told by them what he was to do. In this attitude he was much encouraged by the spontaneous acclamation of the masses in his tours round the country. The unity and harmony which thus appeared to exist among the architects of the revolution in its opening phases was shortly to deteriorate into a secret struggle between Nasser the prime mover and Neguib his nominee. So evenly balanced were the forces at the disposal of the contestants that it was touch and go who was to emerge triumphant. The game was played out behind the scenes during the latter half of 1953 and culminated in the defeat of Neguib and the supremacy of Nasser in March 1954.

There was too great a difference in fundamental respects between the General and the Colonel for the association to continue indefinitely. Nasser and his friends of the Command Council were revolutionaries of long standing and by conviction, they had been the founders, the architects and mainsprings of the revolution. They were the young visionaries who saw an independent, confident and sturdy Egypt rising from the servitude, corruption and oppression of centuries. Neguib on the other hand was a bluff, hearty simple soldier of conservative principles, leaning more to the old established order than the radical policies of his colleagues, yet he was dazzled by the acclamation and fervour which greeted him on all sides as the leader of the revolution. Not without reason he saw himself as the legitimate ruler and began to claim for himself the rights of his position as chief policy-maker and director of the nation's destiny. This became a source of friction in the Council. Rumours of the rift soon leaked out.

It was the Moslem Brotherhood which brought the crisis to a head. For some time Nasser had been at loggerheads with the movement, having in September 1952 rejected the Supreme Guide's demand that all legislation should be submitted for approval to a committee of the Brotherhood, and a state of enmity had arisen between him and Hassan el Hodeiby the Supreme Guide. Even so, when the political parties were dissolved and their funds confiscated, the Brotherhood had been allowed to continue in existence as a purely religious movement on giving an undertaking not to indulge in political activities. The Brotherhood had given scant heed to this undertaking and had been infiltrating and sowing disaffection in the ranks of the army. Nasser had warned it to desist.

On 12 January 1954 a 'martyr's day' rally was held in Cairo to commemorate those who had died in previous demonstrations and events, during the course of which the adherents of the Brotherhood demonstrated and shouted slogans against the Government. The Council of the Revolution reacted immediately and surrounded the headquarters of the Brotherhood and arrested seventy-eight leading members. This action was taken without consulting or securing the assent of General Neguib who had in fact some sympathy for the Brotherhood and derived no little personal support from it, and in a bitter dispute with the Council he claimed what amounted to dictatorial powers. This claim the Council rejected and on 24 February the General offered his resignation. In explanation of the Council's attitude to this demand Major Salah Salim declared that army officers had threatened to shoot Neguib and even members of the Council if they had yielded to his demand for autocratic powers. It was officially suggested, and perhaps with justification, that Neguib had intended by his resignation to arouse public opinion in his favour and compel the Council to reinstate him with the full powers he demanded. He was more than justified in his expectations.

Reaction among the public was strongly in his favour whilst the National Unionist Party in the Sudan, Neguib's own creation, sent a flying delegation to Cairo to protest at his dismissal. But the decisive factor was the support which he drew from the cavalry colonel, Khaled Muhieddin who, although one of the officers of the revolution, had strong left wing affiliations, and the motorised Cavalry Corps of the army at Abbassieh. At a protest meeting on 26 February they declared in favour of Neguib and parliamentary government which he had led them to expect would be introduced. So strong was the support given to Neguib that Nasser was obliged to go down to the meeting and attempt to explain what had happened, but he received a hostile reception and was unable to explain that it was Neguib who was demanding dictatorial powers, that he intended to abandon the revolution and ultimately to call back the corrupt régimes of the past to power. At this meeting Nasser was defeated and he finally agreed that the Council would recall Neguib and he himself would stand down. Early on the morning of 27 February Cairo learnt that Neguib had been reinstated as President of the Republic and it appeared that all differences had been patched up. The excitement in the streets led to some violence, but there could be no doubt that even if Nasser still retained his grip on the Free Officers and the Council, Neguib was supreme in the streets. On 28 February Neguib addressed the crowd at Abdin Palace and promised a return to parliamentary government at the end of a transitional period. This was greeted with applause particularly from the cohorts of the Moslem Brotherhood which was prominent in the mob and who thought that the way was being opened for their accession to power. Neguib was in fact, perhaps unconsciously, drawing to himself as a rallying point all the elements which were disaffected and hostile to the revolutionary régime.

In the belief that he had mastered the crisis and established himself invincibly in power, Neguib flew off to Khartoum on 1 March to attend the celebrations marking the opening of the Sudan Parliament, but was greeted on arrival with violent demonstrations and clashes between the pro-Egyptian Unionists and the Umma Party of Sir Abdul Rahman el Mahdi demanding complete independence. Thirty people were killed in the riots and Neguib was obliged to take a hurried departure on 3 March. His visit, intended to strengthen the links between Egypt and the Sudan, proved a dismal failure.

In spite of Neguib's public exhortations for unity, the rift between Nasser and himself had of course not been healed. It was not merely a struggle between personalities for power; it was a fundamental difference of ideology.

The apparent surrender of the revolutionary council to popular clamour and their acceptance of his reinstatement with enhanced authority fed Neguib's belief that he was in truth the leader of the nation and the supreme arbiter of her destiny, that he could impose his wishes on the council. He contemplated an early return to a democratic régime and a civilian government with himself as President and Head of State. Put simply, he expected a resumption of the old system with himself in the shoes of Faruk.

Colonel Nasser and the Council however had radically opposed views. Having striven and plotted for years to oust the old régime which in their eyes had been responsible for the misery and servitude of their country, and having successfully toppled it, they had no intention of allowing it to return. Their country willy-nilly was going to be pushed along the road to reform and resurrection, freed from the British occupation and the graft and corruption which had permeated every department; the agrarian reform was to be implemented and the army strengthened and re-equipped. They would brook no interference with these plans. By this time they had come to realise that this programme was incompatible with a resumption of democratic government. It was clear that either Neguib or Nasser must go. Nasser learnt his lesson from the defeat of 26 February.

He recognised that unity must be maintained in the army, for it was the defection of the Cavalry officers which had enforced Neguib's reinstatement, and steps were immediately taken to put them and Khaled Muhieddin under supervision. Secondly, in order to oust his rival he must have command of the streets, for in February it had been the Moslem Brotherhood, the communists and Wafd adherents which, by their clamour for Neguib, had sought to provide a national backing for the demand for a parliamentary régime. Thirdly, Nasser recognised that given enough rope Neguib would hang himself. He laid his plans accordingly.

On 7 March it was announced that in accordance with popular demand there would be a return to parliamentary government and an elected constituent assembly before the end of June, that the revolution should be considered as having completed its mission, and that the army would stand down and return to its barracks. Censorship of the press was lifted and numerous political figures were released from detention. The Moslem Brotherhood and the old leaders of the Wafd licked their lips in anticipation. These actions wore the aspect of political suicide for the régime; they made it appear that they now intended to surrender their powers to the civilians, trusting that there would be no retaliation for the rough handling of influential personalities and that their programme of reform would be carried through by a new and unknown Government. The next day Nasser resigned his post of Prime Minister to Neguib and also his chairmanship of the Council and reverted to Deputy Prime Minister. In all it seemed that Neguib was heaping triumph on triumph. The restraints of censorship now lifted, the press broke out into a tirade of criticism of the revolutionary régime; the Wafd, the Moslem Brotherhood and the communists congratulated themselves that these irritating soldiers would soon be back in their barracks and they themselves would scramble back into power. For all these blessings they had General Neguib to thank, the national leader who set his face against a permanent military dictatorship and insisted on a return to democracy. Nasser and his colleagues let it be known that they had reluctantly been compelled to accept these demands and were only following Neguib to maintain the appearance of national unity.

It is possible that Neguib belatedly realised that he was being hurried into a trap of his own making, but having opened the floodgates of popular clamour he was powerless to resist the consequences. What he had done was to make himself the rallying point of all the old political cliques, the parties which had battened and fattened on disorder, division and unrest and the enemies of the revolution while he had completely alienated that one group on which he depended to maintain him in power, the Society of Free Officers and the army. The army and its leaders foresaw that the outcome of these recent developments would be their own subordination and return to obscurity, with reprisals for what they had done, the abandonment of the revolution and all they had striven for and accomplished, a recrudescence of all the old humiliations and miseries and a revival of the Wafd and the Moslem Brotherhood, their bitterest enemies. For all this they had one man to thank, General Mohammed Neguib, the man they themselves had hoisted into power. It was he, they thought, who was leading them to perdition.

Not content with arousing these apprehensions among the ranks of the army, Nasser turned his attention to the trade unions. To them he painted the picture of an Egypt returned to the old days, with the peasants and workers again the tools and slaves of the landowners, the abandonment of the agrarian reform, the resurrection of the great estates and the depression of the national economy. The unions were not slow to realise that a resumption of democracy under the 1923 constitution promised no advantage to them.

At the end of March Nasser began to hurry Neguib along the road to perdition. The renewed rift between the President and the officers of the Council again became public knowledge and was commented on by the press. On 25 March, in pursuit of Neguib's declared policy, it was announced that the political parties would be allowed to reform themselves, but that the Council of the Revolution would not itself form a party to take part in the elections so that the arena would apparently be an exclusive tilting ground for the Wafdists, the Saadists and the socialists and any new parties that might be formed under official auspices.[5] Reports had already begun to spread that the officers were not prepared to accept their supersession lying down, for on 26 March the *Times* correspondent commented:

> There is an element of idealism as well as concern for their personal future in the attitude of the younger officers. They had never envisaged handing back the government of Egypt to those elements which misgoverned the country under the monarchy. In spite of today's announcement, it would perhaps be well not to take it for granted that they have finally given up the fight,

a singularly accurate and perceptive forecast.

The next day the army was in a ferment at their betrayal by the man whom they had raised from relative obscurity and placed in power as head of the state. Outbreaks of unrest occurred among the working classes in the Shoubra district of Cairo who shouted slogans in support of Nasser and demonstrated against the abandonment of the revolution. By 28 March the major industries and public utilities were on strike. Nasser now had both the streets and the army at his command, while his friend, Major Salah Salim, the Minister of National Guidance and controller of the state propaganda machine, was urging the need for unity behind the Council of the Revolution and undermining General Neguib. Nasser, he said, had been the first to make plans for the restoration of democratic government, but the process must be gradual, and it was for the people to decide whether they wanted to be ruled by dishonest politicians or by men who had given Egypt her first honest government in two thousand years.[6] By the end of the month the struggle was over. With the mobs surging through the streets and attacking the offices of the Council of State and chanting Nasser slogans, with the unions on strike and the life of the nation paralysed, the Council revoked its decision to dissolve itself and give way to a parliamentary government. It resolved to stay in power and carry on the work of the revolution. For the sake of appearances, Neguib was to stay in office as President and Prime Minister, but shorn of power and subject to the Council and the army now finally under Nasser's control. Neguib, as author of the movement for the return of the old system of government, was irrevocably discredited; henceforth he was to be pushed more and more into the background until his final arrest and detention, and his disappearance from the political scene. Gamal Abdul Nasser and his colleagues of the Council of the Revolution were the sole and acknowledged masters of Egypt.

The systematic destruction of General Neguib was one of the most remarkable incidents in the history of Modern Egypt, and the handling of the manoeuvre a masterpiece of political strategy on Nasser's part, illustrating his genius for understanding the psychology of his people and moulding situations to his will. At the end of February Neguib was the idol of the people, but he failed to understand that there could be no return for the revolutionary, no abdication with safety in favour of those he had ousted from power. Dazzled by the acclamation of the masses he saw himself as the genial and benevolent constitutional head of a state ruled by a parliamentary government. He was to be the benefactor who not only wiped away the corrupt old régime, but was to take the lead in restoring it. Within the space of one month Nasser had hurled him down from his pinnacle and exposed him to the resentment and contempt of his own colleagues. It is indeed extraordinary that Neguib took no cognisance of the wishes or interests of his friends in the army, that he was unable to understand that a return to democracy meant the return of Nahas, Serag ed Din and the Wafd with all its record of mismanagement, that the army would be suppressed and its officers victimised for their part in the revolution. But Nasser saw it all, and he was the first to realise that the army would not tolerate such developments. If then Neguib was inflexible in his views, he could best be disposed of by hurrying him along his own chosen path. Nasser did no more than organise and concentrate the forces which were opposed to Neguib and enable them to administer to him the *coup de grâce* with the least disruption to the life of the nation. At the same time, as he had always done, he strengthened and revitalised that corpus or nucleus of revolutionary power in the Council and the Society of Free Officers, and instilled into them the thesis of Benjamin Franklin that revolutionaries, if they do not hang together, are likely to hang separately.

443

CHAPTER 27

The Evacuation of the British Army from Egypt

When the military party came to power in July 1952 the two burning issues were the Sudan and the British occupation. By February 1953 the Sudan issue had been largely disposed of, and it was thought both in Britain and Egypt that the outstanding problem would be quickly and easily solved. At the time of the 1936 Treaty the British had insisted that the *raison d'être* of the British army in Egypt was the necessity of defending the imperial communications between east and west. But during the Second World War Egypt had become a vast military base for the British forces, with elaborate installations, airfields and huge concentrations of stores. By 1953 the Canal Zone had become a pivot from which operations could be launched in any direction in the inflammable Middle East. The policy of securing the imperial communications had largely given way to a new western bloc policy of securing the defence of the whole region from communist infiltration or aggression from the north. Egypt had in fact become a vital link in a chain of defences stretching from the Atlantic to the China Sea. British policy in Egypt had thus undergone a further and successive shift from the time when General Wolseley's army had first landed in 1882. The new philosophy of independence and self-determination which had received such an impetus during and after the world wars compelled the British Government to recognise that the continued presence of their troops on the soil of a foreign state was no longer compatible with modern political creeds. But having poured so much wealth and labour into the Canal base and having based their system of defence on its continued existence, it was essential to retain sufficient control of it to enable any threat to be countered without hindrance or delay.

In Egyptian eyes the question was simple and unchanging. For seventy years a foreign army had been stationed in Egyptian territory against the will of the people. For the past thirty years negotiations had been directed to the removal of this running sore, all to end in bitterness, frustration and

444

humiliation. Nothing but the eradication of the last vestige of foreign influence and control would suffice to satisfy Egyptian claims and aspirations. It was against this background that cautious exchanges were resumed after the Sudan agreement of February 1953. Even so Britain was slow to take the initiative until General Neguib in the days of his ascendancy toured the country whipping up national feeling with the formula 'Evacuation or death', thus drawing British attention to the urgency of the question.

Colonel Nasser was to become the principal Egyptian negotiator and in the preliminary exchanges which took place in March 1953 the main outlines of the British proposals were communicated to Egypt. Evacuation of the British forces was to be accepted in principle, but it was essential that the base should be kept in a state of readiness and capable of being brought into commission immediately in an emergency. For this purpose it was proposed that it should be staffed by British technicians appointed by and directly responsible to the British Government. It was clear to the Egyptian side that the British were merely attempting to maintain their hold over Egyptian territory in a different guise and at the same time to link evacuation with Egyptian participation in a Middle East defence scheme. All indications to date had been that Egypt would refuse to tie the two questions together. Evacuation must first be accepted unconditionally; Egypt would then, but without necessarily committing herself in advance, be willing to consider participation in a defence scheme.

This was the position up to 12 April 1953 when Colonel Nasser made a statement of policy. The Government, he declared, desired 'to make arrangements by which, with the assistance of British technical staff, the military base could be efficiently maintained after the British troops had been withdrawn.' The régime, he said, would be discredited if it allowed the national right to evacuation to be made conditional on acceptance of a Middle East defence organisation and he put his finger on the weakness of the British position by pointing out that although Egypt could not defeat the British army, she could make their position intolerable and render the base valueless to Britain and her allies. 'We do not want this to happen. It will ruin our internal plans. What we really want is amicable relations with Britain so that Egypt can look forward to a period of progress free for ever from the running sore of its dispute with Britain.'[1]

This was a courageous attitude to adopt, for it implied a willingness now to compromise on a question on which Egypt had hitherto been obdurate. Nasser was undoubtedly running serious risk of endangering his own position in offering such a concession, but he was anxious to clear the British problem out of the way, so that serious steps could be taken towards the regeneration and internal development of the country. This declaration was the signal for renewed activity. The British Government immediately appointed its negotiators, Sir Ralph Stevenson, British Ambassador to Egypt, and General Sir Brian Robertson, up to that time Commander in Chief of the Middle East Land Forces, but now relieved of this post to enable him to take part in the discussions. Neguib and Nasser led the Egyptian delegation.

The talks opened in Cairo on 27 April, but within two weeks reached a deadlock. The British wanted to hurry the Egyptians into discussion of all the technical details and arrangements for the maintenance of the Canal base, no doubt with the object of convincing the Egyptians that they alone had not the necessary personnel and resources, and that these must therefore be provided by Britain. But the Egyptians refused to be deflected from the principle of unconditional evacuation of the British army first and the removal of every vestige of British military control from Egyptian territory. They accepted that the base was an important factor in Middle East defence, they recognised the necessity of maintaining its installations, and they conceded that they had not the necessary resources themselves. But they utterly refused to concede that Britain should have the right to employ technicians under British military control and answerable to the British Government. Reduced to its simplest terms, the British were attempting to continue the occupation under a different guise, while the Egyptians were adamant that the occupation must come to an end. It is indeed extraordinary that the British should even attempt to beguile Egypt with such a transparent device. Eden was at the Foreign Office and he it was who should have best known and understood the nature of Egyptian aspirations and how little prospect there was of moving them in this matter. Not even offers of substantial military assistance could induce Egypt to give way.

Both sides began to glower at each other in their frustration. The advantage was slightly on the side of Egypt, for although they could not drive the British out by force they knew – and the British knew as well – that by withholding supplies and labour and by reverting to the policy of sabotage and guerrilla warfare, they could make the maintenance of the base more costly than it was worth. There were already between 70,000 and 80,000 troops in the base, many times the number authorised by the 1936 Treaty and maintained at immense cost to the British Government. General Neguib hoped to enlist the sympathy of Mr Dulles, the new United States Secretary of State, who was to visit Egypt on a fact-finding mission. Mr Dulles did indeed listen to the Egyptian pleas, but he was far more interested in the efficient maintenance of the base as a bastion of the defence scheme, and Egypt got little encouragement from him during his visit. His statement that the Canal base was a matter for legitimate and grave concern for other countries than Egypt was coldly received.

The breakdown of the talks in May was not followed, as in 1951, by a campaign of violence or sabotage against the British. Nasser calculated – and events were to prove him correct – that time was on the side of Egypt, that Britain would eventually have to give way to Egyptian demands. He therefore held his people in check and prevented any resurgence of violence. In July and August a few isolated incidents took place including the abduction of two airmen and some shooting at Port Said, but these were not apparently Government inspired, although they served to remind both countries that the situation was potentially explosive. At the end of July informal exchanges and confidential discussions were resumed between the delegations which, if they did not lead to an early agreement, at least enabled a considerable exploration of the problem to be carried out. Reactivation of the base, the conditions under which Britain and her allies would be allowed to re-enter, and the number of technicians required to maintain it, were the subjects of detailed studies.

By the middle of September 1953 speculation was rife as to the possibility of Egypt accepting an agreement with Britain on the Canal base on the best terms she could get. This was given credence by the fact that the Government suddenly arrested several hundred communists and notified the press that censorship would be continued until the press had purged itself. It appeared that the Government was giving advance notice to all those who might oppose or attempt to sabotage any Anglo-Egyptian agreement that might be concluded, that it was not prepared to tolerate any opposition to the régime or its acts. The arrest of a number of prominent Wafdists took place, and Ibrahim Abdul Hadi, the former Prime Minister, was seized and placed on trial for high treason and for complicity in the murder of Sheikh Hassan el Banna, the Supreme Guide of the Moslem Brotherhood. These lent substance to the belief that an elaborate plot was on foot to destroy and replace the revolutionary régime. Abdul Hadi was condemned to death, but a few days later the sentence was commuted to life imprisonment.

The informal meetings and discussions on the Canal question continued to drag on through September 1953, but at the beginning of October there was some indication that both sides were close to an agreement. However, by the end of the month it was clear that this was an illusion, that in spite of apparently accepting the principle of evacuation Britain was determined to

447

maintain the occupation in one form or another. It is otherwise impossible to explain why they insisted that the technicians to maintain the base should be in uniform. It cannot by any stretch of imagination be maintained that in order to do their job the technicians had to wear uniform. It was the very presence of foreign military uniforms in their country which so much insulted Egyptian sensibilities. It can only be concluded that in spite of all her years of association with Egypt and of the long days spent in discussion, the British were completely out of touch with Egyptian sentiment. Of all the points of difference which had come out of the negotiations this was the one which Britain could most easily have conceded without weakening her position, yet it was the one in which she showed herself most obstinate.

Another more serious question was the conditions under which Britain would have the right to re-enter and reactivate the base. Egypt was prepared to permit re-entry in the event of aggression against her Arab neighbours and the members of the Arab Collective Security Pact, but Britain wanted the right extended in the event of aggression against Pakistan, Iran and Turkey. She eventually abandoned the claim in respect of the first two countries, but was anxious to retain the condition in the case of Turkey, a claim which Egypt, separated from her former overlords by several hundred miles, found difficult to understand. The Egyptians were moreover anxious not to retreat from the stand they had first taken up that evacuation must be unconditional and not tied to a security pact. It is evident that they had come to concede a certain amount of ground on this point, provided that it could be clothed in words which did not blazon the fact before the world. Provision in the case of aggression against one of their Arab allies could easily be justified to the people of Egypt, but how to explain and justify the concession in the case of an attack on Turkey or more distant countries? This would have been an open admission that they had allowed themselves to be manoeuvred into the very position they had declared they would resist.

Although no official announcement was made by the end of October it was clear that negotiations had again reached deadlock, and the restraints which the Egyptian Government had exercised over its spokesmen and the press were relaxed. Accusations were launched against Britain for interfering in Sudan affairs, difficulties were made for British subjects in Egypt and some were arrested on various charges or pretexts. General Neguib in a visit to Nubia spoke of the coming struggle with the British who were led to understand that Egypt's patience was exhausted and it was up to them to come forward with acceptable proposals. At a press conference on

30 November Neguib said that the Egyptians had gone as far as they could to meet the British, but there was a limit and it remained for Britain to close the gap. The points of difference were the questions whether the maintenance staff should wear uniform and whether, as Britain wanted, an attack on Turkey should provide grounds for re-entry into the base.

For some months after the end of October no exchanges, formal or informal, took place between the Governments, the Egyptians biding their time and waiting for renewed approaches from the British, the latter regarding with some uneasiness the turn that events were taking in Egypt. In January 1954 acts of violence and terrorism were renewed against individual troops and vehicles in the Canal Zone. Whether or not these were instigated by the Government in Cairo, the latter took no action to repress the campaign which increased as time went on. During February and March Nasser was preoccupied with his struggle against Neguib and beyond ensuring that the campaign of violence against the British did not exceed all bounds of restraint, he was content to remain inactive and allow the British to relearn the lesson that the Canal base was an encumbrance as long as they held it against the wishes of the nation. British accusations that Egypt was permitting a recrudescence of lawlessness in the Canal Zone were answered by accusations of oppression and aggression against Egyptian subjects. By the middle of that month the spate of incidents had caused such a deterioration in relations that Eden at the Foreign Office announced that further negotiations with Egypt were impossible in the present conditions. Neguib had himself about the same time stated publicly that Egypt was not anxious for a settlement unless she could have it on her own terms.

When Nasser succeeded in wresting power from Neguib in March 1954, he was anxious to conclude an agreement with Britain over the Canal and finally dispose of this problem, so that the Government could turn its full attention to the internal problems of reform which urgently awaited solution. He allowed the sporadic warfare to continue and even develop in April in order to create an atmosphere of relief and inclination to treat when the campaign was finally called off. But it was also necessary to condition his own compatriots to accept a settlement with Britain. His long and frequent discussions with the British in recent months had led him to realise that Egypt would not succeed in obtaining total and unconditional evacuation; she would have to concede something, if only the presence of British maintenance staff and a right of re-entry in certain circumstances. But it had always been concessions of this sort in the past which had enabled a hostile press and politicians in opposition to prevent ratification of any draft treaty, and Nasser was not prepared to have any agreement he might reach with the British sabotaged by his opponents. From April to June 1954 he set himself to stifle all opposition. The press was the major objective and victim. A purge of all elements in the press which had corruptly taken bribes was announced, and the Aboul Fath brothers, the proprietors and publishers of *Al Misri*, the Wafd daily, were charged with corrupt practices and sentenced to imprisonment. The paper was closed down and the Wafd deprived of its principal instrument of criticism of the régime. The cavalry officers and a number of civilians who had collaborated with Khaled Muhieddin in supporting General Neguib in February were arrested and tried by military tribunals for fomenting insurrection in the army and imprisoned or cashiered. Leading members of the old political parties including Nahas, Serag ed Din, Salah ed Din of the Wafd, and Neguib el Hilaly of the Saadists, and the eminent lawyer, Abdul Razzak el Sanhoury, were deprived of their political rights for ten years. Having muzzled the principal sources of opposition, the Egyptian Government let it be known that they were willing to resume talks on the Canal question, and the campaign of violence in the Canal Zone was substantially abated.

The ground having thus been prepared, on 7 July 1954 *The Times* in a leading article urged the need for a final settlement under the heading 'Urgent business' stressing the difficulties confronting Britain as a result of the withdrawal of Egyptian labour and the necessity of maintaining large British forces in their place. Negotiations were immediately opened between the two countries in Cairo. To help create an amicable atmosphere Britain released a further £10 million sterling to Egypt and Egypt relaxed her restrictions on sterling imports. Even so fresh suspicions of British good faith were aroused when the latter sought to reopen and secure further concessions on a number of points which had already been agreed and settled in the previous negotiations. Mr Anthony Head, Secretary of State for War, was dispatched to Cairo to resolve the difficulties, and on 27 July heads of agreement were signed on both sides. The principal terms of the draft agreement were:

1. The agreement was to last for a period of seven years from the date of signature.
2. All British military forces were to be withdrawn from Egyptian territory within twenty months, and the Egyptian Government would give all necessary assistance in the movement of men and material.
3. During the seven year period the Canal base would be kept in

operational order and capable of immediate use in the event of any armed attack by an outside power upon any country of the Arab League states or upon Turkey. In this case Egypt would permit Britain to re-enter the base and put it on a war footing.

4. Egypt would afford overflying, staging and servicing facilities to Royal Air Force aircraft.

5. After withdrawal of the British forces the British Government would employ firms of contractors for the maintenance of the base and its installations. The contractors would have the right to engage Egyptian labour and British technicians not exceeding a certain number to be agreed.

6. The British Government would be given facilities for inspecting the base and its installations.

7. During the last year of the agreement the two governments would consult on future arrangements.

These were the main features of the agreement and represented a substantial compromise on both sides. Britain finally recognised that the time had come for her army to quit Egypt entirely and that she must put her faith in the goodwill of Egypt for the protection of the Canal and its installations. They also abandoned the demands that the technicians should wear uniform and be directly answerable to the British Government, and that the base should be reoccupied in the event of foreign aggression against Iran. On her part Egypt accepted that an attack on Turkey should be a cause of re-entry and also the continued presence of British technicians, but won her point that these should be civilians and not soldiers in disguise. A compromise was also reached on the period required for evacuation. As by this time Britain had about 80,000 troops in the Zone it had become physically impossible to move them out in much less than twenty months. The fact that a definite date had at last been fixed for evacuation, although more distant than the Egyptians had hoped, was sufficient inducement to accept the additional delay.

The formal agreement was signed in Cairo on 19 October 1954 by Anthony Nutting, Minister of State for Britain, and Prime Minister Gamal Abdul Nasser for Egypt. In concluding the agreement both governments faced a certain amount of criticism by elements in their respective countries for having bartered away their rights. Indeed, in Britain there was a militant group of about forty Conservative MPs known as the Suez Group who were actively hostile to the evacuation of British military power, but the

Government could expect substantial Labour support in this transaction. In Egypt acceptance of the continued presence of British personnel in the base for at least another seven years could be construed as having the appearance of an extension of the occupation. But in contrast with all previous occasions when Anglo-Egyptian agreements appeared to be concluded, on this occasion Colonel Nasser had all potential critics effectively silenced and no Chamber of Wafd deputies to encounter.

Nasser therefore had good reason to be satisfied with his achievements. The intractable and interminable problem that had eroded Anglo-Egyptian relations for half a century had finally been disposed of, or so it seemed, in October 1954. He could now take in hand that other, even more intractable, problem that confronted his country, the raising of the masses from the poverty, disease, ignorance and serfdom which had chained them for thousands of years. Both countries seemed content with the agreement to which the United States Government gave its blessing. In Israel, however, fears were aroused that the evacuation of the British would remove the thin red line along the Canal which gave her a certain sense of security, and open the way to the revival of aggression from Egypt and the Arab states. It looked too as if the blockade which Egypt had imposed on Israel in 1949 and the embargo of Israeli-bound ships through the Canal would be intensified. But both Egypt and Britain entertained hopes that the settlement would herald a new era of cordial relations between them – hopes which were destined shortly to be shattered by the thunder of cannon.

CHAPTER 28

Prelude to Suez

At the end of 1954 the sole remaining organised opposition to the military régime was the Moslem Brotherhood which, because of its wide following among all sections of the population, had been allowed to remain in existence as a religious movement. But the Government and the Brotherhood were bitterly hostile to each other, and the latter was conspiring with the communists to overthrow the Government by spreading subversion in the army. The signing of the Anglo-Egyptian agreement on evacuation furnished these fanatics with a stick to beat the Government which they openly accused of concluding a treasonable agreement with the British. At the same time a plot was on foot to assassinate Gamal Abdul Nasser. On 26th October while he was addressing a huge crowd in Liberation Square at Alexandria, a member of the Brotherhood, one Mahmud Abdul Latif, a tinsmith from Cairo, fired a number of shots at him. Although shaken by this murderous attack Nasser was unhurt and, quickly rallying, he turned the incident to good account, declaring, '. . . If Gamal Abdul Nasser dies or is killed, every one of you is another Gamal Abdul Nasser. Egypt has now obtained her independence and regained her dignity, and if I am killed Egypt will go on and must live.' He was greeted with a tumult of cheering.

Within hours the police were out hunting down the Brotherhood and by the next day hundreds had been arrested. Within a few days all the leaders were in custody, Hassan el Hodeiby the Supreme Guide, Sheikh Mohamed Farghaly, Abdul Kader Awda the General Secretary and others. They were put on trial immediately and sentenced to death together with the attempted assassin. Hodeiby's sentence was commuted to life imprisonment, but on 7 December six of the principals went to the gallows, an event which occasioned fierce rumblings in the neighbouring Arab countries who still thought of the Brotherhood as a purely religious rather than a political movement. In the meantime the police and security forces ruthlessly rooted out and destroyed the organisation and in the process seized large caches of arms and explosives, ample testimony to the terrorist character of the movement. The Brotherhood was then proscribed and finally broken.

At the same time the Council of the Revolution decided to jettison the remaining encumbrance to their régime. Ever since March the discredited President, General Neguib, had lingered on in the twilight of affairs, rebuffed, ignored and silent. It had got about that he was critical of the Anglo-Egyptian agreement and moreover that he enjoyed the support of the Moslem Brotherhood who regarded him as a rallying point in their resistance to Nasser. The attempted assassination and the systematic destruction of the Brotherhood afforded the Council a convenient opportunity of removing Neguib. On 14 November he was formally deprived of the office of President and placed under house arrest at Marg in a suburb of Cairo. His dismissal was no more than had been expected by the populace for a long time and passed with little comment. He had played the part allotted to him in the initial stages of the revolution, but he had never been a true revolutionary or a member of the inner circle, and had now outlived his usefulness. He was thrust back into the obscurity in which he thereafter remained.

Having eliminated all opposition Nasser was faced with the problem of constructing a policy, particularly in the field of foreign affairs. When the Arab League was originally projected in 1944, it had been hoped and intended that it would create a spirit of unity and common purpose among the Arab states, but within a short time it developed into a struggle for hegemony between Egypt, by far the most advanced and civilised but the least Arab of the members, and Iraq which for years had been steered by the adroit, pro-Western Nuri es Said Pasha. Both Jordan, an impoverished state, and Iraq, which was deriving substantial revenues from the oil concessionaires, were in treaty relations with Britain on lines similar to those of Egypt, and provided bases for the British armed forces. The new Anglo-Egyptian agreement prompted both these states to consider revising their own relations in the same way, but with this important difference. Egypt, situated on the continent of Africa, entertained none of the fears of aggression and infiltration which haunted the northern tier of the Middle East, Turkey, Iraq and Iran, and turned instinctively to the neutralist policy propounded by Nehru in India and Tito in Yugoslavia. In Iraq on the other hand not only was Nuri es Said the product of Western civilisation, but also the position of his country next to the Soviet Union and its vulnerability to attack dictated a close alignment with the powers which could offer some measure of protection, i.e. the Western block. Jordan too, although moved by different considerations, was in a similar position. Her problems were mainly financial, for it was the annual contributions and subsidies from Britain which propped up her economy and enabled her to maintain the Arab Legion, a vital force in face of the expansionist proclivities of Israel. Neither Iraq nor Jordan were in a position to part company with Britain, but they both desired some modification of their relations to minimise the appearance of being mere client states of their Western ally.

On 13 December 1954 the Iraqi Foreign Minister, Musa el Shabander, announced in Cairo that his country would conclude an agreement with Britain similar to that of Egypt, by which British troops would be permitted to re-enter Iraq in the event, *inter alia*, of an attack on Iran. This declaration immediately aroused suspicion in Egypt for the reason that an attack on Iran was one of the eventualities which she had refused to accept as a cause of re-entry in the Canal Zone. Iraq and Egypt were both members of the Arab League collective security pact, and it followed from Iraq's declared intention that an attack on Iran might be followed by one on Iraq. This would give the British the right of re-entry. It suggested that Britain, having been foiled at Cairo, was now accomplishing her objective in Baghdad. Further, indications put out by Iraq that she was contemplating aligning herself with Turkey in a defensive treaty cut right across Egypt's contention that the Arab states should look only to their own collective security pact for their mutual defence, and that there should be no alignments by any of the member states with outside power blocs.

> Egypt's defence policy as defined by Major Salim is to convert the Arab League security pact, which was directed against Israel, into an exclusive instrument for the defence of Egypt and the Arab world against aggression from outside the Middle East. That conflicts with the idea put forward by the Prime Minister of Iraq that a regional pact should be negotiated based on Middle East countries including Turkey and Egypt, and linked to the Western powers.[1]

One of the inducements held out to Iraq for following this policy was the prospect of receiving military supplies and assistance from the West. Egypt, said Major Salah Salim on 28 December, could have all the arms she wanted from the United States if she had been prepared to tie herself to the Western scheme of defence, but she had resolutely refused to commit herself to such an alignment.

These exhortations failed to deflect Nuri es Said Pasha from his course. On 12 January 1955, after a visit to Baghdad by Mr Menderes, Prime Minister of Turkey, it was announced that a treaty of mutual defence would be signed between Iraq and Turkey. Not only this, but Menderes announced that this was not to be simply a bilateral agreement, but was to achieve the co-operation of the entire Middle East region, in other words the first steps in implementing the British and American policy of a Middle East defence organisation linked to the Western powers. Nasser's reaction was immediate and he hastened to urge the other members of the Arab League that any treaty which directly involved one of the Arab states in obligations to outside blocs was at any rate premature and that such a step should not be taken without the agreement of the others. He summoned a meeting of the League members in Cairo. It has been suggested, and there may be some ground for the view, that Egypt's opposition to the Baghdad Pact sprang primarily, not from the involvement of the Arab states with outside powers, but from resentment at being forestalled by Iraq as architect of Middle East policy, for Egypt's Foreign Minister, Dr Ibrahim Fawzi, hastened to say that Egypt's opposition to the treaty did not connote hostility between the Arab world and the Western powers, but that Arab opinion would first need to be conditioned to the idea of co-operation with the West, and that their military and economic strength should first be built up so that they could enter such an alliance as full partners rather than as poor relations.

Egypt was however unable to dissuade Iraq from concluding the proposed treaty with Turkey and to carry the other Arab states with her; her only immediate supporter was Saudi Arabia which had a dynastic feud with the Iraqi monarchy. Nasser's failure to prevent the conclusion of the Turko-Iraqi treaty was the first substantial setback of his career. He had failed to carry the Arab League with him and he had failed to reassert Egypt's leadership of the Arab world. In his eyes, not the least responsible for this rebuff were the machinations of Britain who had welcomed the treaty as being the first step in setting up the Middle East defence system. As Turkey was already an adherent of the North Atlantic Treaty Organisation Iraq was thereby drawn within its orbit. To that extent Nasser's policy of neutrality and self-sufficiency for the Arab world was already eroded. Eden's visit to Cairo on 20 February 1955 did nothing to remove the newly formed suspicions of Western 'imperialist' manoeuvres, and the first rift was opened in the harmony which had reigned between Britain and Egypt since the conclusion of the agreement of October four months earlier. When the pact was ratified in Baghdad Nuri es Said said he hoped that Britain and the

United States would adhere to it and that Pakistan and Iran would also be welcomed. It is clear that it was at this period that Nasser decided to haul down Nuri es Said from his pre-eminence in Iraq, for as early as February 1955 it was observed that 'Egyptian diplomacy, press and radio were being used to bring about the downfall of the distinguished Iraqi statesman, on whom more than any other the stability of his country depends.'[2]

It was at this critical juncture that Israel launched a fierce and unprovoked attack on the Egyptian frontier post at Gaza. Thirty-eight Egyptian troops were killed and others wounded. What prompted this outburst is uncertain, but it was probably the cumulative effect of a series of minor incidents. Two Jews had recently been executed in Egypt for espionage; Ben Gurion, a militant hater of the Arabs, had recently returned to power in Israel; and the continued reiteration by the Arab states of their hostility to Israel during the Baghdad treaty crisis, all contributed to the growing nervousness of the Jews which was reflected by the Gaza attack of 28 February. There was no substantial military retaliation by Egypt, for she was probably not in a position to reply with force, but the incident led to important developments. This recent outburst of aggressiveness by Israel drew together the three states contiguous to her, Egypt, Syria and Saudi Arabia. Jordan, Israel's other neighbour, was still too closely involved with Britain to pursue any independent policy of her own and to associate with the grouping which Egypt was attempting to form in competition with the Baghdad Pact. But Syria was for some time a doubtful and uncertain ally and attempted to compromise and conciliate between Egypt and Iraq. Her adherence to the one or the other was enough to swing the balance in the struggle for leadership of the Arab world, and Nasser's failure to bring her over squarely to his side, led him temporarily to abandon his vendetta with Iraq. Arab unity in the face of the common enemy, it was declared, was essential.

A further development was the clamour for modern arms by Egypt, for her existing equipment was largely obsolete and of poor quality. With all her past associations and affiliations with Europe she naturally looked there and to America to supply her needs. But the Western powers, in their anxiety to keep the peace between Israel and her Arab neighbours and to keep on good terms with both, had been reluctant to supply weapons of offence unless the Arab states participated in the Middle East defence organisation in which they would be subjected to a certain amount of military supervision. The supply of arms to Egypt had therefore so far been small and limited largely to those necessary merely for defence. This was the source of humiliation and frustration to an independent Egypt which was intensified by the Israeli attack of 28 February, and the Egyptian Government became all the more determined to acquire armaments on a massive scale. Nevertheless the United States persisted in their policy of enforcing the peace by starving the Arabs of arms, and in March declared that they had not and would not grant military aid to any country of the area which was likely to use such aid in an aggressive manner, and would only extend military assistance for collective defence. Neither the Jews nor the Arabs, now fiercely engaged in an arms race, welcomed the declaration.

At the anniversary of the Revolution on 24 July 1955 Colonel Nasser announced that Egypt would establish her own factories for the manufacture of heavy and medium weapons, and the foundation stone was laid for a steel factory at Helwan a few miles south of Cairo. But it was clear that Egypt could not make herself self-sufficient in all the complicated and technical equipment that comprised the sinews of modern warfare. If she was to re-arm, she had no alternative to looking outside her own borders. Indeed she had negotiated the purchase of two destroyers from the British Government, a transaction which occasioned considerable adverse comment in the House of Commons as a result of an incident in which a British ship had been fired on in the Gulf of Akaba, a further sign of disharmony between Egypt and Britain. This was further aggravated by events in the Sudan. The agreement of February 1953 had contemplated that the Sudan would after a suitable period elect for complete independence or some form of unity with Egypt. After thirty years of incessant propaganda by Egypt that she and the Sudan were one nation and that it was only the machinations of the British imperialists that had kept them apart, it was of vital importance for the prestige of Egypt that when the time came for the Sudan to make her election, she should choose unity with Egypt. But as the time drew near, fear haunted the Egyptian Government that the Sudan would choose the other alternative, especially as Ismail Azhari the Sudanese Prime Minister made it known that this was what he favoured. The supersession of General Neguib, himself of Sudanese origin, had dealt a sharp blow to relations between the two countries, a squabble over the allocation of the Nile waters had dealt another, and Egypt's frenzied efforts to buy support in the Southern Sudan which culminated in a mutiny in August 1955, led to a further deterioration. Nurtured for years to the idea of Egyptian-Sudanese unity it was incomprehensible to the Egyptians that the Sudanese should choose independence. To them the only explanation was that the British had succeeded in seducing them from their natural allegiance; the old imperialist game of divide and rule was still being played and Ismail el Azhari was castigated in the Egyptian press for being a stooge of the imperialists in Whitehall. There was of course no foundation or substance in these accusations, and the British were considerably irritated by these wild charges. The simple fact was that the Sudan wanted to be free from both countries, and when the time came she made her choice accordingly. Major Salah Salim, Minister for National Guidance and personally responsible for Sudan affairs, was removed from office.

In September 1955 it became known that Egypt had received an offer of arms from Soviet Russia. This set the cat among the pigeons in the West, but it was the natural, inevitable and foreseeable outcome of the policy which the Western powers had deliberately pursued. Up to recent times Russia had taken little interest in the southern areas of the Middle East, but now in the climate of world politics any area had become grist to her mill, and the Western-sponsored project of a Middle East defence organisation which was aimed solely at containing the communist bloc, led the Kremlin to extend the area of its activities. Egypt which was now largely severing its links with Britain as a result of the 1954 agreement became a fertile field of endeavour. In September 1953 Russia sent Mr Daniel Solod to be her ambassador in Egypt. During the early months of his tour he played the game of masterly inactivity and stood aside from Egyptian affairs, for he realised that now that Egypt was finally shaking herself free from foreign shackles, her suspicions would immediately be aroused by direct approaches from elsewhere, particularly from Russia. He carefully avoided the tactics of America which, like a bull in a china shop, rushed in as soon as the British showed signs of retreat, with offers of military and economic assistance, subject of course to certain objectionable conditions, and thereby suffered a rebuff. Solod's policy of studied indifference paid handsome dividends, for Egyptian apprehensions that Russia might be trying to get her foot in the Egyptian door were allayed. Solod offered no alliances or alignments, no loans or free gifts, nor did he protest when Nasser's Government continued to throw Egyptian communists into gaol. Russia, having previously had no standing in Egypt, had nothing to lose. Any diminution of Western strength in the region was a gain for Russia. The West, he saw, had foolishly committed itself to a policy of supporting two blocs which were mortal enemies, Israel and the Arab states, and was trying to keep them at arms length by starving them both of armaments. Both blocs chafed at the restraints placed on them by the West. The year 1955 was a period of skirmishes and tension in the Gaza Strip; all that the West would provide was arms for defence only. When therefore in May 1955 Solod enquired of Nasser if he would like to buy arms from the Soviet Union a new vista of opportunity appeared to open. An attractive aspect of the offer was that it was unaccompanied by any objectionable conditions, that it was to be a straightforward purchase and could be paid for in cotton. As Britain's purchases of Egyptian cotton had fallen substantially, the opening of a new market for Egypt's principal commodity was extremely welcome. Nevertheless the Egyptian Government was aware of the dangers of becoming too closely linked to the communist bloc. Such a move would be antagonistic to the agreement with Britain which was based on mutual recognition of the necessity of keeping Russian influence out of the Middle East.

But the Russian offer strengthened Egypt's bargaining powers for arms from the West. News of the possibilities of an arms deal with Russia was allowed to leak out in September 1955 and created considerable alarm in London and Washington. It seems that the two Western powers were unable to decide whether to treat this possibility as real or a mere bluff. They were moreover committed to the policy of maintaining parity in strength between Arabs and Jews. If they yielded to Egyptian pressure and supplied their demands, it seemed that they would be preparing the way for a new outbreak of war in the area, and would be laying themselves open to charges of treachery from the Jews in Israel. It seems that they finally came to the conclusion that the threat was only bluff and that Egypt would not dare to flout the West by bartering with the East on such a crucial matter. If so, they were to be bitterly disappointed. On 27 September at an Army Fair Colonel Nasser announced that he had concluded an agreement for the supply of arms from Russia and Czechoslovakia. No details of the purchase were given, but it was reckoned that it would at least include heavy weapons of attack and Russian MIG fighter planes.

Britain and America were dumbfounded by the news. The whole structure so laboriously built up by the West in the Middle East seemed to collapse overnight.

It will not only increase the dangers of a new Palestine conflict, . . . it will probably deepen the rift between Egypt and that other dynamic force in the Muslim world, Iraq which is now . . . more deeply involved in the policies of the west and is a staunch opponent of all things communist . . . It may well put fire into the efforts of those extremists in Israel who believe that forceful action is now the only insurance against nemesis. No less important, acceptance of Russian arms may be the thin end of the wedge leading to increased Russian influence among the Arabs.[3]

Eden, who had encountered substantial opposition from the 'Suez Group' of his own party to the evacuation agreement, had staked his reputation on the expectation that close and cordial relations would be maintained with Egypt, and that Egypt would offer no obstruction to Western defence policy in the Middle East. Nasser's opposition to the Baghdad Pact had already given him a rude and worrying shock, but this latest development exposed him to the ridicule that he had surrendered Britain's defences for nothing, and that in consequence the Russians were hurrying down to the banks of the Nile. Eden's resentment against Nasser, which was shortly to develop into active hatred, dates from this time. To him Gamal Abdul Nasser had become the greatest menace to world peace and Western diplomacy.

Israel too was put in a fever of apprehension at the prospect of unlimited supplies of armaments pouring into the camp of her southern enemy. To all this criticism Nasser replied that he had bought arms from the East because the West would not supply them, that Israel herself had been receiving massive quantities of arms, and that what he had bought was only to maintain parity, 'to enable him to sleep safe at night', and that he had no intention of allowing communism to infiltrate into Egypt as a result of the purchase. Indeed, Britain and America were hard put to it to refute these arguments, but they distrusted Egypt's ability to keep the communists out, and could not be sure that Egypt did not intend to reopen a full-scale war on Israel. Nasser was henceforth to be treated as an object of the deepest suspicion by Eden and the British Government, and at least as a slippery customer by the United States. But the Arab states generally hailed his arms deal with Russia as a victory over the Western powers and their 'imperialist machinations' in the Middle East, and acknowledged Egypt as the leader of the Arab League. Nasser's prestige in the Arab world rose enormously.

The result was that Syria which a few months back had been wavering whether to support Egypt in her proposed counter-alliance against the Baghdad Pact, now came over solidly on her side and signed a military alliance. Saudi Arabia immediately adhered to it as well. In the meantime Iran and Pakistan had joined the Baghdad Pact, thus creating a continuous northern tier across the Middle East which became split into two competing factions, the one encouraged by Soviet Russia which offered military assistance to the states of the Egyptian group, the other leaning on the Atlantic Treaty powers. Between the hammer and the anvil lay Israel, detested by the Egyptian group and disliked by the Baghdad powers. She could only look to America and the West for safety. It is perhaps paradoxical that Britain gave her sympathy to the country which owed its origin to

461

British interest and repaid her by a vicious campaign of murder and terror against British troops in the years 1946 to 1948, and at the same time alienated the Arab states which had been her friends for many decades.

A further result was a rapid expansion of Soviet influence in the Middle East. With the conclusion of the arms deal Russia now wore the mantle of a sincere friend of Egypt and her allies. The Russians, adept in the art of establishing social relationships, as compared with the aloof and stiff-necked British, easily penetrated Egyptian society, and cultural missions, literature, the theatre and other forms of propaganda began to flow into the country from the communist world. The seal of goodwill was set when the possibilities were mentioned of financial and technical assistance to build the High Dam at Aswan.

Of all the plans evolved and nurtured by the Council of the Revolution for the promotion of prosperity in Egypt the High Dam at Aswan was the most important, for its completion promised a further two million *feddans* of agricultural land and unlimited electric power. But the cost of such a feat of engineering was far beyond Egypt's own resources. In 1955 it was estimated that over £200 million would be required, 45% of which must be in foreign currencies. Only assistance on a large scale from abroad could bring this project to reality. The financing of the Dam was first considered by the World Bank, and negotiations were put in hand for the necessary loan. It was contemplated that the Bank would advance the money, provided Britain and America agreed to contribute $70 million between them and provided that Egypt secured consent of the other riparian states of the Nile, notably the Sudan which would be vitally affected by the Dam. But by October 1955 these negotiations had not proceeded to finality, for it was in that month that Russia, on the crest of popularity in Egypt, expressed her willingness to provide financial and technical assistance for this and other projects in the Middle East. Once again it looked as if the West was going to be forestalled by Russia. The financing of the Dam and its construction by Russia would complete the process of annihilating Western influence in the Middle East, and it was considered by the West better to swallow the insult of the arms deal and attempt to restore the position by giving assistance for the Aswan Dam than stand aside and watch the Russians take over entirely. Nor did Colonel Nasser relish the prospect of tying himself too completely to the communist block. It was too dangerous. It was one thing to buy their arms, another to give them unrestricted access to his country with all their powers of subversion. He was well aware of the need for a long spoon when supping with the Devil. But the offer was a valuable lever in coercing the

West to give him the money he needed for the Dam, and he was not defeated in his expectations. In December Britain and America promised an initial loan of 70 million dollars between them, thus fulfilling the first condition of the World Bank loan.

In January 1956 Mr Eugene Black, President of the World Bank, hurried to Cairo for discussions on financing the Dam, and on 9 February it was announced that agreement had been reached for a loan of 200 million dollars to finance the initial stages of construction. The loan was contingent on Egypt not incurring any other foreign loans without the consent of the Bank, for the advance to be made by the Bank was estimated to stretch Egypt's credit-worthiness to the limit, and also upon Britain and America making a grant of 70 million dollars between them. It seemed therefore that the West had saved the day and prevented any further Russian penetration into Egypt.

All this time the British had been honouring the evacuation agreement to the letter by withdrawing their troops from the Canal Zone, and it seemed that a rapprochement might be possible between the two countries whose relations had been so seriously deteriorating. But at bottom of all the differences was the Baghdad Pact. Although it had not been the actual creation of Britain, she had welcomed it and had consistently supported it as a prop to the defence of the Middle East. Egypt had unswervingly opposed it and had succeeded in the space of a year in rallying a large area of the Arab world to her view. This was the fundamental cause of suspicion and dissension between Britain and Egypt. Nor did Western attitudes to the Arab-Israeli dispute improve matters. At the end of March 1956 Selwyn Lloyd, British Foreign Secretary, paid a visit to Cairo with the object of explaining British policy to Colonel Nasser and of healing the breach between the two countries. It was, however, an unfortunate coincidence that on that very day King Hussein of Jordan dismissed Glubb Pasha and other British officers from command of the Arab Legion. Jordan's Arab Legion was very dear to the hearts of the British, and the presence of British officers in command was regarded as an insurance and guarantee of the loyalty of Jordan to the British connection and of restraint in regard to the Arab-Israel dispute. Ever since the signing of the Baghdad Pact Egypt had been exerting her influence in the neighbouring states to rally them to her policy of non-alignment and neutrality, and a constant stream of propaganda had been directed from Cairo to Amman charging the Jordan Government and monarchy with subservience to foreign imperialism and exhorting her to throw off the British connection. Only two months earlier active consideration had been given by the Jordan

Government to joining the Baghdad Pact, but this had caused riots in the capital and brought about the downfall of the Government. Egypt, Syria and Saudi Arabia had offered financial assistance if Jordan would forego the subsidies she received from Britain.

The news of Glubb's dismissal was published while Selwyn Lloyd was in Cairo. One more prop of the British position in the Middle East was undermined, and it seemed to Lloyd that this was the direct result of the machinations of the smiling young man whom he was talking to and trying to persuade of the good intentions of the British in the Middle East. He departed for India in a huff. The dismissal of Glubb was viewed as a major set-back for Western policy in Washington, London and Paris. In the House of Commons Eden's policy of evacuation from Egypt was vigorously criticised and he was confronted with a demand for an emphatic reassertion of British interests in the Middle East. America too was shocked at the loss of British prestige and influence, and for the first time the wisdom of the Baghdad Pact began to be questioned, for instead of strengthening the Western position in the Middle East, it seemed to be having completely the reverse effect. It also began to be doubted whether the United States had been wise in urging the British to evacuate the Suez Canal. Mollet, the French Premier, was particularly critical of American policy which, he declared, was wandering along in isolation in efforts to protect its oil interests. Western policy, he said, was setting fire to the whole area and if it continued in this way, the West would lose the game.

France was moreover becoming increasingly irritated by the physical and moral support which Egypt was openly giving to the rebel movement in Algeria. At the same time Egypt was directing a stream of virulent radio propaganda towards Kenya where Britain was heavily engaged in subduing the Mau Mau rebellion. Both Britain and France had problems of exceptional complexity to deal with in their respective overseas territories, and these were considerably exacerbated by the nationalist and anti-colonial slogans which poured from Cairo radio station. In all Colonel Nasser was making himself cordially disliked by every partner in the Western alliance. By the end of March 1956 it was freely admitted by the British Foreign Office that relations with Egypt were poor and that there was little prospect of improving them as long as Egypt continued her present line of conduct.

After the announcement of the arms deal with Czechoslovakia tension on the Israeli-Egyptian frontier had been at breaking point, and clashes and forays, major and minor, were frequent. Powerful elements in Israel were urging a 'preventive' war against Egypt before her new access of strength in arms from the East gave her the advantage. Mr Hammerskjold and General Burns, the United Nations Chief of Staff in the area, were constantly occupied with keeping the snarling opponents from each other's throats. This situation as much as any other factor was causing the Western powers the gravest apprehension, for it seemed that at any moment a major war might flare up to engulf the whole Middle East with unforeseeable consequences to the world. However, following some strictures from the Kremlin from which it appeared that Russia too was opposed to an outbreak of hostilities in the area, a truce was again patched up between Israel and Egypt on 19 April. Nevertheless it marked no real change of attitude; it was no more than an armistice to be broken at the first opportunity. At the same time Egypt added Yemen to her company of allies in opposition to the Baghdad Pact.

In May and June a certain tranquillity marked the Egyptian scene, and the country's recent campaign of hostility to Britain and the West substantially abated. For one thing Russia was becoming a little nervous about the trend of events and let it be known that she was not prepared to take sides in the Arab-Israeli question, and the enthusiasm which had greeted Russia's appearance as the champion of Arab interests was somewhat dampened. Colonel Nasser too, although unswerving on the policy of Arab neutralism and resistance to involvement in power blocs, nevertheless felt that the time had come to tone down the campaign of abuse of the West, for he could not afford to cut himself off entirely from a quarter to which he might have to apply for financial assistance, particularly for the financing of the Aswan Dam. The British evacuation of the Canal Zone had been proceeding smoothly and efficiently and was well ahead of schedule, so that by April barely a handful of troops remained. The evacuation was completed on 13 June, thus bringing to an end a military occupation which had lasted in one form or another for nearly seventy-four years. The occasion was marked by celebrations in Cairo a few days later at which at least expressions of friendship and goodwill were exchanged between the two countries. Thus the dream of many decades in Egypt had at last been brought to reality, a triumph for Nasser and the Revolution. A notable guest at the celebrations was the Soviet Foreign Minister, M. Shepilov, who had the satisfaction of seeing Russian tanks in a great military parade through the streets of Cairo. As Britain stepped out of Egypt, Russia had stepped in.

These celebrations were capped by the translation of Gamal Abdul Nasser to the office of President of the Egyptian Republic by means of a plebiscite at which voting was compulsory. As only one candidate was nominated for the office, and the voters were only required to say whether or not they approved the candidature of Colonel Nasser, it was not perhaps surprising that 98% of the electorate voted for him. The Revolutionary Council was replaced by a cabinet and a constitution on the Napoleonic pattern inaugurated. Theoretically military government was at an end.

It was rumoured during M. Shepilov's visit that the subject of Russian financial assistance for the completion of the High Dam had been broached. By this time estimates had set the total cost of building it at $1,300 million of which the World Bank had offered to lend $200 million provided that Britain and America made a grant of $70 million. This they had indicated they would do. But Shepilov made no offer apparently, for in July the Egyptian Ambassador in Washington announced that his government had decided to seek assistance from the West, thereby indicating that Egypt now wished to enter formal negotiations for the $70 million promised and make arrangements for the remaining sums required. At this juncture the United States and Britain committed, not only a serious breach of faith, but a political blunder which was shortly to precipitate a world crisis. On 19 July 1956 the State Department announced that the United States had concluded that it was not feasible in present circumstances to participate in financing the Aswan Dam project.

CHAPTER 29

Suez

Since only a few months earlier America and Britain had promised financial assistance for the High Dam, some comment is necessary to account for the extraordinary volte-face of July 1956. The ostensible reason put out was that since the offer had first been made doubts had been growing as to the capacity of the Egyptian economy to stand its share of the cost, it being understood that Egypt had committed herself to paying much greater sums than had first been estimated for her supply of arms from Czechoslovakia, and had mortgaged the greater part of her cotton crop, her main source of foreign exchange. But even if true, this was no ground for repudiating a promise so recently made. If there had been such doubts about Egypt's financial stability, it would have been more appropriate to voice them through the medium of the World Bank. The motive was political rather than financial.

The State Department had been considerably embarrassed and vexed by the course of events in the Middle East and the penetration of the communist bloc into that area, particularly by Nasser's opposition to the Baghdad Pact and his courtship with Russia culminating in the Czech arms deal. Dulles was bitterly disillusioned, and there were influential sections in the Senate who regarded Nasser as a military dictator who had gone over to the communist camp. Any proposal to give financial assistance to Egypt was clearly going to encounter substantial resistance in Congress. On the other hand, the position had by no means been reached where Egypt must be regarded as irrevocably lost to the communist bloc. The agreement with the World Bank had been prompted by the desire to restore the position, and Egypt's announcement that she intended to secure further financial assistance from the West was clear indication that she was not turning her back on that quarter. There is no doubt, however, that Nasser had been playing America and Russia off against each other, for there had been much publicity recently given to the possibility of Russia providing Egypt with the funds to build the High Dam on terms more generous than those expected from the West. But some sections of public opinion in America regarded the repudiation of her promises with considerable uneasiness and feared that it would only drive Egypt further into the communist camp. This was part of the 'calculated risk' which Dulles admitted he had taken. He was not prepared to allow Russia to bask in the glory of having promised to supply the money, while America actually footed the bill. He reckoned that by withdrawing the American offer, he would compel Russia to honour the half-promises she had made or retire discredited and humiliated from the Egyptian scene. Nasser himself would suffer in reputation from such a result and he would be compelled to adopt a less uncompromising attitude to the West. It is probable that Dulles already knew that Russia would not in fact be willing to finance the scheme alone, and this lent encouragement to the action he decided on. Still, the decision to repudiate a promise of assistance must have been a hard one to take, for it was contrary to American morality to welsh on a promise, and the fact that the American announcement was immediately followed by one almost identical from the British Foreign Office suggests that the decision was taken after joint consultation, not independently, and it is possible that the impetus came in the first place from Eden.

Eden could justifiably attribute to Gamal Abdul Nasser the frustration of his entire policy in the Middle East and his own humiliation in the eyes of the British people and the rest of the world, and it may be inferred that resentment towards Nasser and the desire to humiliate and pull him down exerted a powerful influence on the British Prime Minister. So far Nasser had achieved nearly every Egyptian and Arab aspiration, save only the unification of the Sudan with Egypt, and had enhanced his prestige as the champion of Arab and Egyptian nationalism with every step. Far from over-reaching himself, he was constantly consolidating his position, and it was becoming increasingly difficult to devise a means of his departure. But he had staked his reputation at home on the regeneration of Egypt by means of the High Dam. If the money he had promised to get was no longer forthcoming from either East or West, he in turn would be humiliated and perhaps cast out by his own people who, though they respected him, had yet to learn to love him. Herein, it seems, lay the motive for denying Egypt at the last moment the aid which had been promised. To the extent that the scheme depended upon Russia failing to deliver the goods, the British and American prognostications proved correct, for only three days after the British and American withdrawal of their offers Shepilov announced that Russia did not intend to assist in financing the Dam.

The American and British announcements came as a deadly affront to Nasser and Egypt, and on 24 July the President publicly denounced the shamelessness of Washington for welshing on its engagements and attempting to dominate the Egyptian economy. He declared that Egypt would nevertheless go forward with her plans for industrialisation, and promised a reply to the American action for the following Thursday. During the next few days further addresses were made to Russia for financial assistance, and it was put out that this had been promised. But these reports conflicted with those emanating from Russian official sources which stated that Russia was prepared to assist with other industrial development projects but not with the High Dam at Aswan. Nasser was forced to the realisation that he could not, in the immediate future at any rate, count on external assistance for this prime objective, and was driven to the one expedient which had not figured in Dulles' calculated risk. On 26 July at a mass rally at Alexandria he announced his intentions. Egypt, he declared, had decided to nationalise the Suez Canal. 'We shall build the High Dam by restoring our rights in the Suez Canal. We shall take the income, 100 million dollars a year and build the High Dam. The Company would be transferred to the State with all its assets and liabilities.' The decree which had already been passed by himself was being published in the *Gazette* and Government agents were at that very moment taking over the Company. The crowd roared with delight. The Suez Canal, dug by the hands and over the bodies of thousands of Egyptians a hundred years before, was at last to revert to its makers. Apprehensive though some of the more sober-minded Egyptians were, none could deny the acclaim which was due to Nasser for realising this achievement or fail to admire his audacity.

Britain, France and America were stunned by Nasser's coup, but even more by his audacity. The last remaining symbol of European power, prestige and influence in Egypt was being torn from their grasp. In Whitehall it seemed beyond belief that this Egyptian upstart, this insolent thief, should dare to seize and take control of the vital waterway through which passed Europe's major oil supply and other essential materials. It was intolerable, the last straw.

Daring and defiant as this step was, an impartial examination reveals that in the eye of the law it was a perfectly valid and legal act, and indeed Britain, having nationalised all her own public utilities, was in the worst position to complain of a like action elsewhere. The terms of the concession which had been granted to de Lesseps have been mentioned in an earlier chapter and it will be recalled that these included a provision that the company should be Egyptian and subject to local jurisdiction. Even this was not essential to the validity of the nationalisation act, for it is a principle of law that every government has full jurisdiction over immovable or real property within its territory. The fact that the shares of the Suez Canal company were held largely by foreign hands made no difference to the legal position. Legally speaking therefore it is indisputable that Egypt was entitled to nationalise the Suez Canal. But the British Government, the largest shareholder, and the French people who between them held the majority of the shares, had come to regard the Canal as entirely their own preserve, subject to interference by no other.

The two governments immediately consulted together on what should be done to recover control of the Canal and get rid of Colonel Nasser. They seem to have realised that they could not attack the validity of the take-over on strictly legal grounds, and no suggestion was apparently made that the dispute should be taken to the International Court of Justice at the Hague. They based their claim on the ground that the Canal had by this time become an international waterway, that its control could not be left to the whims and politics of Egypt, that in any case Egypt could not operate the Canal alone, and that therefore some form of international control must be established. There was, of course, no ground for supposing that Egypt would restrict or interfere with the passage of shipping through the Canal; on the contrary she had every reason for actively promoting it. The nationalisation measure, while also serving the cause of Egyptian nationalism and independence, had as its prime objective the raising of money from the Canal dues, and thus depended entirely upon the freedom of navigation in the Canal. Further, the Government relied on this freedom of passage of world shipping to secure the acquiescence of the nations in the nationalisation, and was at pains to assure the world that Egypt would maintain the passage of ships through the Canal unimpaired.

But whatever the force of these arguments, they were swept aside by Britain and France who were determined to wrest control of the Canal from Egyptian hands by one means or another. The story of the three months following the seizure is the development of this theme.

Britain and France stood together, while America was in a more equivocal position. The reasons for British hostility towards Egypt in general and Nasser in particular have already been set out, but the motives of France merit a word of explanation. As has been recounted in previous pages,

French attitudes towards Egypt had largely been dominated by financial interest, and her holdings and investments in the country were considerable. But the outstanding symbol of France in Egypt had been the Suez Canal of which the concession had been made to de Lesseps, a Frenchman and the capital largely subscribed in France. The income to France was therefore substantial. The seizure of the Canal was regarded as an affront to French prestige, a subject on which post-war France was particularly sensitive. But it was the active support and material assistance which Egypt was giving to the rebel movement in Algeria that so inflamed the French nation against her. To Egyptian interference and to her harbouring of Algerian rebels France attributed the continuation of the guerrilla warfare in her most important overseas territory and the intolerable burden thrust on her in fighting the Algerian war. Every assistance given by Egypt to the rebels was regarded as an affront and provocation to France, and her indignation was even more aggravated than that of Eden the British Prime Minister.

As regards the attitude of America, Dulles realised that his action in withdrawing the offer of financial assistance to Egypt had been the prime cause of the nationalisation act, and he was conscious of a sense of responsibility for the crisis which had suddenly precipitated in the Middle East. He was bound therefore by the ties of the Atlantic Alliance to give as much support as he reasonably could to his Allies, and indeed M. Pineau the French Foreign Minister let it be known that failure to affirm the solidarity of the three states would create a very grave situation, a warning to Dulles that no back-sliding by the United States would be tolerated.

Nasser had expected his move to encounter some resistance and protest from Britain and France, but he was startled by the fury and indignation that had been aroused, and it became necessary to attempt some form of conciliation. Egypt, he said, would honour all her international obligations, uphold the 1888 Suez Canal Convention, maintain freedom of navigation, pay compensation to the shareholders based on the prices quoted as at 26 July, and would accept payment of dues in London or Paris, notwithstanding that her accounts and funds had already been blocked.

But it was too late; the decision to wrest the Canal from Egyptian control had already been taken. Naval and military preparations were ordered by the British Government 'to strengthen our position in the eastern Mediterranean and our general ability to deal with any situation that may arise.' The campaign of intimidation and pressure against Nasser and Egypt was thus launched. Left to themselves it is possible that Britain and France would have ordered an immediate invasion of Egypt, but having demanded unity of purpose from the United States it was essential to carry that country with them in any plan of action. But angered and embarrassed as Dulles was, he was far from prepared to sanction the use of force against Egypt, certainly not before all other avenues of settlement had been explored. But, having sole control over the Panama Canal and a firm intention to maintain it, the United States were reluctant to allow the unilateral seizure and nationalisation of another canal to pass unnoticed. The precedent and example were too dangerous and might encourage similar action in Panama. Yet the use of force to restore the position was repugnant to Dulles, and he was therefore disposed to support an Anglo-French proposal that an international conference should be called to work out means of establishing international control over the Suez Canal. It was therefore announced that a conference of the nations would be held in London on 16 August to consider the establishment of an international agency to ensure that the freedom and security of passage through the Canal should be preserved, and that the dues should be kept stable and equitable. Egypt replied that under no circumstances would she permit the Canal to be subject to international control.

Within a few days the furore had begun to cool as the nations saw that ships were still passing through the Canal as usual and that the take-over was not so world-shattering after all. Some of the countries invited to the conference began to question the principle of internationalisation, and made it clear that acceptance of the invitation to attend by no means implied acceptance in advance of the principle. Eden, fearing that world opinion was beginning to turn sour on him, attempted to rally public opinion by a broadcast to the nation on 8 August in which he betrayed his personal animosity towards Nasser. 'Look at his record. Our quarrel is not with Egypt, still less with the Arab world. It is with Colonel Nasser . . . We all know it is how Fascist governments behave and we all remember only too well what the cost can be in giving in to fascism.' He then went on to propound a strange policy. 'Meanwhile we have too much at risk not to take precautions. We have done so. That is the meaning of the movements by land, sea and air of which you have heard in the last few days. We do not seek a solution by force, but the broadest possible international agreement. That is why we have called the conference.' It is difficult to understand why it should have been necessary to order movements by land, sea and air, if it was the intention to settle the dispute round a conference table. It is difficult also to understand the reference to Fascism when the Western powers had been so preoccupied with the spread of communism in the Middle East, unless both terms are regarded as having the same meaning. At any rate, the threat of force was immediately recognised in Egypt where the formation of a national liberation army was put in hand.

By the time the twenty-two delegations had assembled in London on 16 August most of the nations had already decided the stands they would take. The view expressed by Britain and France was that international control and operation of the Canal should be imposed by whatever means were found to be necessary; nothing short of this would be satisfactory. That advocated by Russia and her satellites was that Egypt should retain control of the Canal, but should guarantee fair treatment for users with a right of appeal to the United Nations. A third view taken by India and the neutral states amounted to a middle course, that there should be some form of international authority to watch over, but not to control, the operation of the Canal. The American view expressed by Mr. Dulles was closer to the Anglo-French proposal, and was embodied in a four-point plan: 1. the operation of the Canal should be in the hands of an international board, 2. Egypt should have a fair return from the Canal dues, 3. fair compensation should be paid to shareholders, and 4. any dispute over compensation should be put to arbitration.

It was clear by this time that no one was prepared to contest the legal validity of the nationalisation or advocate the return of the Canal to the original company. Practically the sole question before the conference was whether Egypt should continue to have control over it with safeguards for the rest of the world, or whether she should be made to accept some form of international control. Egypt refused to recognise not only the right of any country to interfere in what she regarded as her internal affairs, but even their right to discuss them, and did not send a delegation, but contented herself with an observer.

The London Conference was a disappointment for Britain and France. Even America modified her stand as the general temper of the nations became apparent. There was no support for the proposal that Egypt must accept an international board of control, whether she liked it or not. This militant proposal was eventually watered down to one collectively made by the United States, Ethiopia, Persia, Pakistan and Turkey and known as the Five-Power Plan, to the effect that there should be some form of international board or association of users of the Canal to work in collaboration with the Egyptian authority, and that agreement for this board should be negotiated with Egypt. But this was not what the Anglo-French delegates wanted. Addressing the conference on 22 August Selwyn Lloyd said:

... there are two propositions for a solution of this problem. One method is a reaffirmation of the 1888 Convention, coupled with the establishment of an advisory body of users. That to our mind would not provide the necessary security. An advisory board would be without effective power ... The Canal would be under the effective control of one government. The second method is to have an operating organisation charged with the responsibility of managing and operating the Canal. We believe that such an agency is an essential part of any settlement, etc.

From their point of view the plan adopted by the conference not only did not provide for effective international control, but it also depended for its implementation on negotiation and agreement with Nasser. Negotiation with Nasser was the one thing they did not want, because it would wear the appearance of recognising his right to nationalise the Canal. They wanted a scheme for an international board of control to be presented to him in the form of an ultimatum.

The conference ended on 23 August on an indecisive note and without any unanimity of opinion on what should be the solution to the problem, and no statement was issued. All that was decided was that a delegation of five, headed by Mr Menzies of Australia, should go to Cairo and place the Five-Power Plan before the Egyptian Government and attempt to negotiate an agreement based on it. An Indian proposal which did little more than reaffirm the 1888 Convention would also be taken to Cairo. Thus the conference which Britain and France had hoped would adopt a threatening attitude to Egypt and demand the internationalisation of the Canal died like a damp squib. All that M. Pineau could say was that the French and British Governments had reaffirmed their solidarity during the conference.

It now remained for Menzies and his delegation to do the best they could with President Nasser, but there was little optimism about the outcome. Even before the delegation arrived in Cairo it was announced that France was sending a contingent of troops to Cyprus 'to ensure in case of need the protection of French nationals and their interests in the eastern Mediterranean', and large scale embarkations of troops and stores took place at British ports. At the same time a number of British subjects in Egypt were arrested on charges of espionage, and both countries declared certain diplomatic representatives of the other to be *personae non gratae*. It was in this strained atmosphere that the delegation went to Cairo at the beginning of September to place before the Egyptian Government the Five-Power Plan.

As was to be expected, the discussions ended in failure. Nasser refused to accept any international control board for the Suez Canal, as this would constitute a derogation of Egyptian sovereignty, but would adhere to the principles of the 1888 Convention providing for freedom of navigation in the Canal. Mr Menzies, who was obviously well aware of Anglo-French intentions in the event of failure, described the situation as 'very, very grave'. And indeed it was, for by the time he returned to London on 10 September British, French and American politicians were closeted together to consult on the next step. The rest of the world now largely regarded the nationalisation as a *fait accompli* and a dead issue, and the main current of opinion was to let sleeping dogs lie. Dulles was therefore seeking a compromise and was incurring the severest displeasure of the French for not having stood solidly with the British and themselves at the conference. At the same time Egypt addressed a note to all the nations inviting them to discuss the establishment of a negotiating body to consider freedom of navigation in the Canal, its future development and the level of dues. This invitation was dismissed by Britain and France as contributing nothing new to the solution of the problem.

All this time the question had been pending of the position of the non-Egyptian employees of the Canal company. While the London Conference and the Menzies Mission had been going on the Company had urged them to stay at their posts, no doubt in the expectation that if the international control board was brought into being, they would be secure in their persons and posts. Most of them had done so, but with the failure of the Menzies Mission the Company not only authorised them to withdraw, but announced that any who continued to work would be regarded as having broken their contracts. The object of this announcement was to coerce the employees to resign and thus bring the Canal to a standstill or to compel the Egyptian Government to restrain them from leaving. Either event would provide a pretext for military intervention.[1]

On 12 September Eden announced his bellicose intentions by stating in the House of Commons that a Suez Canal Users Association would be formed consisting of Britain, France and the United States and any other nations using the Canal who wished to join. The Association would

> employ pilots, undertake responsibility for the coordination of traffic through the Canal, and in general act as a voluntary organisation for the exercise of the rights of the Suez Canal users ... If the Egyptian Government should seek to interfere with the operation of the association or refuse to extend to it the minimum cooperation, then that Government will once more be in breach of

the Convention of 1888 . . . In that event Her Majesty's Government and others concerned will be free to take such further steps as seem to be required, either through the United Nations or by other means, for the assertion of their rights.

No one could be in doubt as to what was intended by 'other means'. Gaitskell, leading the Labour Opposition, condemned the Government's intention to use force, and warned the Prime Minister that if Britain and France were to go it alone, the whole world would be against them and the result would be disastrous. He urged that the dispute should be taken to the United Nations.

It is evident that Eden had exaggerated when he implied that America would take part in the association and be a party to asserting its rights 'by other means', for Dulles immediately made it plain that the United States had no intention of shooting its way through the Suez Canal if the Users' Association were rejected by Egypt. Although Eden secured a substantial majority on a vote of confidence, large sections of the British public viewed with the gravest concern and apprehension the warlike intentions of the Government and took refuge in the hope that it was only bluff and that the crisis would eventually blow over. But by this time Eden's resentment towards Nasser had hardened into an obsession, and nothing short of the downfall of the Egyptian President would satisfy him. The French Government too was assailed by the derision of its own people for having rattled the sabre loudly at the beginning of the crisis two months ago, but having done nothing to make good its threats.

The invention of the Suez Canal Users' Association was intended to intimidate Egypt. There was some suggestion that a convoy of ships, manned by Association pilots and with warships at each end, should present itself for passage through the Canal and challenge the Egyptian Government to let it pass. But first, having unfolded the plan for the Association, it was necessary to summon the interested parties together and ascertain how much support could be obtained for it. Another London conference was called for 19 September with the ostensible purpose of establishing a working partnership of the main users of the Canal in support of their common interests. The world was becoming rather bored with the Suez Canal question, and the second conference was even more of a disappointment for the British and French delegates than the first. Selwyn Lloyd's plea that the Canal could not be allowed to remain in the hands of one man or one government fell on deaf ears. Some of the delegates thought that the dispute should be taken to the United Nations, and in fact when the conference broke up three days later, all that had been decided was that an association should be formed 'to facilitate any steps which may lead to a final or provisional solution of the Suez Canal problem, . . . to promote safe transit through the Canal . . . and to seek the cooperation of the Egyptian authorities, etc.'

This was a humiliating result for the Anglo-French partnership. America had clearly defected; there was no suggestion of compelling Egypt to accept the control of the Association. The simple truth was that already two months had passed since the nationalisation, and in spite of the withdrawal of a large number of pilots the Canal was still open and functioning smoothly, and it was difficult to understand why Britain and France were making such a fuss. If Egypt had closed the Canal, exercised discrimination against any nation or increased the dues, the position might have been different. It had even become obvious that all the gloomy forebodings that the operation of the Canal would break down if left solely in Egyptian hands were quite unfounded, and that pilotage through the Canal was not such an esoteric art after all. Egypt was managing quite well and was doing everything possible to keep the traffic moving. Many countries tacitly sympathised with the action which Egypt had taken to recover an asset which she had largely built herself and which was situated in her own territory. In any case, the original concession was due to expire in 1968 and the Canal to revert to Egypt. What difference did it make if the transfer were effected a few years earlier?

But Britain and France refused to accept this as the last word on the question. There still remained the Security Council on which the Atlantic Alliance had a substantial majority, and the next day it was announced that the dispute would be placed before the Council. Obviously no resolution in support of the Anglo-French cause could be expected because Russia would undoubtedly use the veto, nor was there any prospect of the other members advocating the use of force against Egypt. Britain and France were becoming increasingly aware of their isolation over this question, and it began to be questioned whether they had been wise in taking up so uncompromising a stand in the first place.

Eleven days, from 4 to 14 October, were spent in interminable discussions, secret sessions and private talks in New York, but they produced only a Pyrrhic victory for the Anglo-French cause. After a secret session a compromise formula was reached which had the unanimous support of the Security Council. This was embodied in a six-point resolution, as follows:

1. There should be free and open transit through the Canal without

discrimination, overt or covert – this covered both political and technical aspects;

2. The sovereignty of Egypt should be respected;
3. The operation of the Canal should be insulated from the politics of any country;
4. The manner of fixing tolls and charges should be decided by agreement between Egypt and the users;
5. A fair proportion of the dues should be allotted to development;
6. In case of disputes, unresolved affairs between the Suez Canal Company and the Egyptian Government should be settled by arbitration with suitable terms of reference and suitable provisions for the payment of sums found to be due.

But the remainder of the resolution covering the provision for international control and the Suez Canal Users Association was lost, for Yugoslavia voted against it and the Soviet Union vetoed it. Britain and France were once again defeated in their ambitions, for the principal claim they made was the system of international control. The only method left of securing this condition was by a two-thirds majority in the General Assembly, and it was recognised that there was no possibility of achieving this.

The result was again stalemate. A long interval had passed in fruitless discussions but Britain and France were even further away from the attainment of their objectives, and they were isolated in a world of opposition or indifference. The United States had proved a broken reed, and a speaker in the French Assembly voiced the opinion of the nation when he said that France had been more humiliated at their let-down at the hands of America than by the attitude of Nasser. From this point onwards British and French diplomats in the capitals of the world began studiously to avoid any contact with their American counterparts. The two countries were forced to the conclusion that if they were to attain their ends, they would have to act alone.

Immediately after the Security Council debate, Eden and Selwyn Lloyd went to Paris to consult with Mollet and Pineau, and it is believed that it was during these discussions that the irrevocable decision to intervene by force in Egypt, whatever the consequences, was taken on 16 October. By this time there was no room for manoeuvre between Nasser on the one hand and France and Britain on the other. Both had taken up and frequently reaffirmed directly conflicting stands, and the dispute between them had become almost entirely a matter of prestige. Neither could hope to survive a retreat from their respective positions, but every day that passed was a gain for Nasser. Something had to be done quickly.

The full truth is still somewhat obscured by the part which Israel was destined to play during the next few days. Although a truce had been concluded between Egypt and Israel on 19 April 1956, there had been no true easing of tension between the two countries. On the other hand there had been no large scale clashes or incidents on the common border. But the build-up of Egyptian military power with arms supplied by the Soviet bloc in Sinai, and particularly the reinforcement of the Egyptian air force with modern aircraft, were arousing deep concern and apprehension in Israel, and for some time there had been in that country powerful elements who urged a preventive war against Egypt. Tension flared up on the Jordan border early in October and on the 10th Israeli forces blew up a Jordanian garrison post at Qalqilya. Iraq had volunteered to reinforce Jordan, and Britain and France had consented to the movement of Iraqi troops into Jordan. Britain also declared in strong terms that if Jordan were attacked by Israel, she would honour her obligations to come to her assistance. Egypt scented in the Iraqi move a plot to wean Jordan from the *entente* which had recently been developing between the two countries, and herself offered to supply reinforcements to Jordan.

It may well have seemed to Israel that these developments heralded a concerted plot on the part of her Arab neighbours to attack her on all sides, and that the prime mover was Egypt. It is probable that these suspicions were entirely unfounded and that Nasser had no intention of reopening the war with Israel, particularly at this juncture. At any rate, it is reasonably certain that Israel decided on a preventive war with Egypt during the first half of October, for it was about that time that she applied to France for military assistance. France thus found herself to possess in Israel an ally with a common purpose, and secret discussions took place on the supply of French naval and air support to Israel's projected campaign.

But France was at the same time committed to a common policy with Britain, and her difficulty was to carry Eden and Selwyn Lloyd with them at the Paris meeting of 16 October in the proposal to collaborate with Israel in her campaign. The matter was certainly discussed, but Eden, while willing and even anxious to join with France in a re-occupation of the Suez Canal by force, refused to align himself as an ally of Israel which was universally detested by the Arab states. He had, only a few days previously, warned Israel that Britain would come to the assistance of Jordan if she were attacked. Indeed, the proposed Israeli action placed the two British ministers in a dilemma whether to acquiesce in France's active collaboration with Israel or to risk a complete rupture in the Anglo-French alliance by refusing to have any part in it. They obviously concealed much of what had occurred at the Paris meeting from their colleagues in the Cabinet, because the latter were surprised by the sudden Israeli attack on Egypt and horrified when they subsequently came to be charged with collusion with Israel.

Tension abated on the Jordan border during the next few days, but by 28 October it became known that massive concentrations of troops and arms were building up in Israel, and the Government freely admitted that it was taking all necessary steps to meet any threat of aggression from the Arab states surrounding her. The next day, 29 October, Israel struck at Egypt with a deep penetration into Sinai and towards the Suez Canal, and advanced about fifty miles into Egyptian territory. The official explanation put out for the attack was that it was designed to root out and destroy the Egyptian *fedayeen* or commando bands who had their bases in the peninsula.

Under the Tripartite Convention of 1950 the United States, Britain and France had guaranteed the existing borders of Israel and her neighbours. If they intended to honour their pledge, the only course open was to demand the immediate withdrawal of the Israeli army to its own territory. The next day however Eden informed the House of Commons that Britain and France had called on Israel and Egypt to

> stop all warlike action by land, sea and air forthwith and to withdraw their military forces to a distance of 10 miles from the Suez Canal, and had asked the Egyptian Government to agree that Anglo-French forces should move temporarily into key positions at Port Said, Ismailia and Suez. If within twelve hours one or both had not undertaken to comply with these requirements British and French forces would intervene in whatever strength might be necessary to secure compliance.

It was this extraordinary statement and demand that caused the world to level accusations of conspiracy and collusion between Israel, France and Britain. To the extent that both France and Britain knew what the Israelis intended, that accusation was undoubtedly true. It would be equally true to say that whatever had passed between France and Israel, there had been no active collaboration or partnership between Britain and Israel. Only if knowledge and acquiescence amount to collusion, was Britain guilty. It is obvious of course that if the Israeli attack on Egypt had come as a complete surprise to Britain and France, they would have immediately demanded the withdrawal of Israel to her own territory, and would have secured the collaboration of the United States in insisting on Israeli compliance with this demand. Instead, however, the curious formula for restoring peace had already been carefully worked out between France and Britain in the knowledge that it would shortly be brought into force. Not only were the United States not consulted, but the demand was made of Israel and Egypt that they should withdraw their forces to a distance of ten miles from the Suez Canal.

In spite of their deep penetration into Sinai the Israelis were still a considerable distance from the Canal, and it was the most arrant hypocrisy to require them to withdraw from a place they had not even reached. The demand in fact amounted to a clear invitation to advance even further. Even more blatantly hypocritical was the demand that Egypt should take no step to defend her own territory, but abandon the entire Sinai peninsula to the Israelis and hold her forces ten miles west of the Canal, and allow the British and French to enter the corridor along the Canal. The Israelis were of course delighted. They were being given and guaranteed a free hand to take over and clear Sinai, and were promised that if the Egyptians attempted to defend their own territory, the British and French would intervene to prevent it. The latter made it clear that they were going to reoccupy the Canal in any event.

The demand was phrased in terms calculated to be unacceptable to any political leader, to say nothing to one who had risen to power on the backs of an army. Nasser rejected it contemptuously, as was probably expected and intended by Britain and France, and denounced it as an attack on the rights and dignity of Egypt and a flagrant violation of the United Nations Charter; Egypt would defend herself against any attack. The next day, the ultimatum having expired, British bombers from Cyprus attacked Egyptian airfields and commenced the systematic destruction of the Egyptian air force on the ground. The flagrance and horror of this aggression was matched only by that of Russia in Hungary which took place at the same time.

The hatred of Nasser which obsessed Eden and the French Ministers had deprived them of all sense of reality. The two countries found themselves marooned in a sea of world condemnation for their action in Egypt. The United States could scarcely believe that their two greatest allies had embarked on a hideous venture calculated to destroy every vestige of Western influence and prestige in the Middle East, to provoke a war which might easily develop into a world conflict and bring about the one event which months of discussion and negotiation had been spent to prevent, the closure of the Suez Canal. Even more scandalous was the treachery of her allies in embarking on this undertaking without a word of warning or consultation, thereby placing the United States in the impossible position of having to decide how to honour their pledge to uphold the 1950 Convention, when their own allies, the other two signatories, were collaborating with Israel to invade Egypt. Perhaps the most shocked of all were the British people who could scarcely believe that their Government had plunged them into such a shameful escapade.

In the Security Council hurriedly convened by Mr Dulles, the United States moved a resolution of censure against the Israeli aggression and called on her to withdraw her forces behind the armistice lines, and urged all members to refrain from the use of force in the area or the giving of assistance to Israel as long as she failed to comply with the resolution. For once Russia and America voted together on a major political issue; Britain and France with their backs to the wall vetoed the resolution, the first occasion on which the former exercised this power. In the General Assembly by 64 votes to 5 the Anglo-French-Israeli action was condemned in a resolution calling for an immediate cease-fire, a halt to the movement of military forces and arms in the area and a withdrawal of forces to behind the armistice lines. The only support found by the three condemned nations came from Australia and New Zealand, but the vote of sixty-four nations was the most affirmative ever registered in the Assembly.

But the censure and warning of impending disaster were ignored. The bombing of Egypt continued and by 2 November it was reported that the major part of Egypt's air force had been destroyed on the ground, a necessary preliminary to a seaborne invasion, and the Israelis captured Gaza and occupied the entire Sinai peninsula. General Hakim Amer, the Egyptian commander, withdrew the remnants of his mangled forces west of the Canal. Taken by surprise and vastly outnumbered by the Israelis, Egypt was unable to withstand the onslaught, but she could afford to lose Sinai which served only as a buffer. Much more alive to the realities of world opinion, Gamal Abdul Nasser recognised that the enemy had played right into his hands. All that was required was to hold the Delta, concentrate his forces there for its defence, do the best he could to fight off the expected invasion from the sea and air, and wait until the inexorable pressure of world condemnation compelled the invaders to withdraw. If there was any opposition in Egypt to Nasser's military régime, it was submerged in the common cause to defend the country against the enemy. Nothing could have been more calculated to unite the nation round the President than this treacherous attack from abroad. Port Said, Ismailia and Suez were put in a state of defence and the civilians armed; numerous ships were sunk across the Suez Canal. It was realised that Britain and France would ignore the United Nations resolution and would force their way ashore, and the Egyptians made ready to meet the attack.

In Britain and France the bulk of the people had been appalled by the extraordinary action taken by their governments, although they had been conditioned by months of anti-Nasser propaganda, and in Britain it was only the substantial majority of the Conservative Party that enabled Eden to survive the Labour motion of censure for leading the country into war in violation of the country's traditions, the principles of the United Nations Charter and the true wishes of the people. A substantial section of the Government's own party was horrified at what had been done, and two junior ministers resigned. But just as in Egypt the common peril had united all classes in support of Nasser, so in England the sense of isolation, the universal condemnation from abroad and the necessity to stand together in the hour of crisis, compelled the Tories to vote for Eden, even though without conviction. Such support as he secured came more from a sense of loyalty in adversity than belief in the justice of his cause. The Labour Party openly declared their intention of employing every constitutional means to haul down the Prime Minister. Never did England go to war a more unhappy and divided country.

Nor was the disastrous policy pursued by Britain and France relieved by the manner of its execution. Several days passed after the first bombing attacks on Egypt without sign of the expected landings, and the people of both countries were becoming restive at the delay which seemed to cast reflections even on their military ability. Even before the landings took place, the United Nations had accepted almost unanimously a Canadian resolution calling for the creation of an emergency international force to secure and supervise the cessation of hostilities, and another requiring all parties concerned to comply with the cease-fire resolution within twelve hours.

But on 5 November British and French airborne troops were dropped in the vicinity of Port Said, and after some vigorous fighting the town was occupied. But the invaders were now thoroughly frightened by the reactions of the world. The Canal they had come to protect was blocked from end to end, and the oil tankers on which the economy of Europe depended had ceased to pass. Disapproval and censure had now grown to violent anger in America and all the countries of Europe whose very livelihood had been so stupidly jeopardised. Unless something was done quickly Britain and France themselves would be prostrated by the economic blizzard which stared them in the face. There was no alternative to bowing to the will of the nations, and a ceasefire was ordered to take effect at midnight on 7 November.

The whole operation was a fiasco politically and militarily. It is easy to be wise after the event, but it is the duty of governments to be wise before also. Even at the time of the Suez adventure it was abundantly clear that the strategy adopted amounted to crass folly and stupidity. If the British and French Governments had not been so obsessed with malice towards Nasser, they might have realised that Israel alone would have achieved for them every objective they had set themselves to accomplish. Egypt and the Arab states had persistently refused to make peace with Israel and, notwithstanding the truce, regarded themselves as nominally at war with that country. They were not therefore in a particularly strong position to protest if hostilities flared up again. It was well known that Egypt had received massive reinforcement of her armament from Czechoslovakia which could only be directed against Israel, and the latter's anxiety at the growing peril commanded considerable sympathy and understanding in the world. When therefore this tiny nation struck at Egypt on 29 October, she might certainly expect a certain amount of censure on general principles, but not the indignation of the world which was engendered by the Anglo-French intervention. She could in any case have expected to weather whatever censure was forthcoming, provided that she also achieved her objectives.

The success of the Israelis in their first drive into Egypt and the vast quantity of prisoners and equipment seized proved beyond doubt that they could alone have annihilated the Egyptian army and driven down to the banks of the Canal. The defeat of Egypt with all its millions of people and its great strength of armament by such a tiny nation would have been beyond President Nasser's power to explain and justify to his people. His humiliation would have been complete and his downfall more than probable. Moreover, attacked by Israel alone, he would have had no ground for blocking the Suez Canal. To save his country from being overrun by the Israelis, he might have been compelled to apply to the United Nations, and even Britain, for assistance, and it is certain that this would only have been contingent on his accepting some form of international control of the Suez Canal and a permanent peace with guarantees for Israel.

But the attitude of the world was completely changed by the combined onslaught of Israel and the two major powers of Western Europe. The braggart became the helpless victim of a shameful conspiracy in the eyes of the world, and the accent of sympathy shifted entirely to the other quarter.

Britain and France thus defeated their own ends. If they had stood aside with perhaps only mild and hypocritical expressions of disapproval at the Israeli adventure, they would have achieved every objective without the loss of a life, the expenditure of a penny or loss of prestige in the eyes of the world. They would undoubtedly have been called on at some stage to restore peace in the area, and a reorientation of Egyptian policy towards the West might have been the natural outcome.

It is almost impossible to account for the British and French intervention. No doubt the plans had already been made and the operation mounted, but in the days of instant communication between governments and military commands, it could not be asserted that it was too late to countermand the orders and await the course of events. The only conclusion that can be drawn is that, whatever might be the consequences, the British and French Governments had made up their minds to tear down Colonel Nasser and his Government with their own hands, and that the Israeli attack, instead of affording them an opportunity to reflect and weigh up the position, seemed too good a pretext to neglect. The price that the two countries were destined to pay for their folly was heavy.

With the failure of the expedition Eden was compelled to shift his ground. In the House of Commons he attempted to justify the assault by declaring that it had merely been a 'police action' and had compelled the United Nations to set up an international force to police the area and bring about a final settlement. At any rate the cease-fire, the proposal to create an international force, with the Secretary-General of the United Nations assuming responsibility for negotiating a settlement of the outstanding problems, were greeted with a flood of relief in Britain and France. It seemed for a moment that they might extricate themselves from this tangle with less embarrassment than had been expected. The United Nations force would soon arrive to take over from the French and British, the Israelis were expected to withdraw, and the British Navy was hurriedly assembling vessels and equipment to lift the sunken wrecks out of the Canal. No doubt satisfactory arrangements would be worked out for the future control and management of the Canal. Eden's reputation began to revive a little at such a satisfactory prospect.

But Nasser was not prepared to let them off so lightly. Following a mission to Cairo to negotiate on the means of implementing the United Nations resolutions, Mr Hammerskjold reported on 21 November that Egypt would not permit any clearing of the Canal to commence until the British and French troops were withdrawn, and that in effect Egypt was insisting on the right to dictate the terms on which the United Nations force should enter and remain in Egypt. It thus became evident that there was no prospect of the United Nations doing what the British and French had hoped to do, viz., to sweep Colonel Nasser aside and do all things necessary for creating peace in the area and setting up an international control of the Canal. On the contrary nothing was going to be done without the licence of the Egyptian Government.

This was another source of humiliation to Britain and France, and there was a tendency for their attitude to harden. They were willing to accept a 'phased withdrawal' of their troops matching the build-up of the United Nations force, but not a precipitate scuttle. Having, according to the new line taken by Eden, done the work of the United Nations for them by preventing a conflagration from spreading in the Middle East, they were not prepared to be kicked out like interlopers. But even in the three weeks that had elapsed economic factors had begun to assert themselves. The flow of oil from the Middle East had ceased and petrol rationing was introduced with a substantial increase in price; there had been a serious flight from the pound sterling and devaluation threatened. On 23 November the United Nations General Assembly again expressed its grave concern at the continued presence of foreign troops in Egypt in defiance of their previous resolution. The Atlantic Alliance was toppling on the brink of dissolution.

By the end of November it was recognised by the two allies that they had no alternative but to withdraw unconditionally from Egypt. The whole world condemned the continued occupation of Port Said, and the United States made it clear that any assistance she might afford in easing the economic plight of the two stricken countries would be contingent on their good behaviour. The decision to withdraw was announced in the House of Commons by Selwyn Lloyd on 3 December, but he attempted to alleviate the sting by promising that the Secretary General would promote negotiations on the settlement of the Canal problem on the lines of the Security Council's proposals of 13 October. The evacuation of Port Said was completed on 23 December thus bringing to an end one of the most catastrophic episodes in British history. The repercussions and trail of disaster were to last for many months to come.

When the British and French withdrew from Egypt baffled and snarling, the Suez Canal was blocked by over forty ships sunk along its length, and Europe began to experience the worst economic blizzard since the War. Relations between America and her principal allies of the Atlantic Alliance were strained almost to the point of rupture, each blaming the other for the catastrophe which had befallen them at Suez. America found herself almost alone in the struggle against the spread of communism and Soviet domination throughout the world, and was forced to the conclusion that she could no longer rely on England and France to keep the vital oil-producing region of the Middle East safe. At the beginning of January 1957 the 'Eisenhower doctrine' was propounded, the substance of which was that America would have to assume a greater and more direct responsibility for preventing the spread of communism to an area that was 'immensely important to all freedom-loving, God-fearing people'. There was some suggestion that the United States President would seek authority from Congress to take military action in the area on his own initiative, if the situation appeared to require it.

Egypt, shaken and dazed by the events of the past few months, had however emerged from the ordeal safe and triumphant, and the former imperial powers which had dominated the country directly or indirectly for so long had been sent scuttling, frustrated and humiliated. Their combined onslaught had in fact saved Gamal Abdul Nasser, when he might well have been unseated, for they might have stood aside and forced him to incur the odium of defeat at the hands of a diminutive state like Israel.

Even after the cease-fire and the withdrawal of the British and French Israel refused to be intimidated into abandoning her positions in Sinai. As her territory bracketed the Suez Canal, with seaports in both Mediterranean and the Red Seas, it was a matter of little moment to her whether the Canal was open or not, and she was not therefore subject to the pressures exerted on France and Britain who had been made to understand that the work of clearing the Canal would not even commence until they had withdrawn their troops from Egyptian territory. Israel was determined to hold on to the positions she had seized until her major conditions were met. These were that positive guarantees should be given by Egypt that the Straits of Tiran at the mouth of the Gulf of Akaba should not be subject to blockade, that Israel-bound ships should have free access to Eilath, that Egypt should not re-enter the Gaza Strip from which the *fedayeen* raids had been launched, and that Israel should have the use of the Suez Canal.

The United Nations Assembly, irritated that Israel had so far refused to heed its resolutions, turned a deaf ear to these demands, but insisted that a complete withdrawal to the 1956 armistice lines should be made. During January and February the Assembly expressed itself in terms condemnatory of Israel's persistent defiance of its resolutions, and threatened to impose economic sanctions. For the most part Nasser sat back and let the United Nations do his work for him. In the last resort his trump card was the Suez Canal.

By the end of February most of the wrecks had been lifted out of the Canal by a United Nations salvage team, and the clearance was well advanced. But Nasser let it be known that the completion of the operation would be delayed until every yard of territory occupied by Israel had been surrendered. Having accepted the principle that the United Nations force and salvage teams were only in Egypt by the licence of the Egyptian Government, the United Nations were in no position to disregard Egyptian requirements and press on with the work, if Egypt objected. The pressure exerted on Israel to yield by the nations who were suffering from the closure of the Canal became intense, and Mr Dulles was constantly engaged in urging Israel to comply and in attempting to find suitable compromises.

It was not, however, until 1 March that Israel reluctantly yielded and agreed to withdraw from Sinai on the understanding that there would be freedom of navigation for international and Israeli shipping in the Gulf of Akaba and through the Straits of Tiran, and that the United Nations force would occupy Gaza and safeguard life and property by effective police action until a definitive agreement was reached on the Strip. This constituted a marked retreat from the stand taken by Ben Gurion on 23 January when he asserted that there would be no surrender without the guarantees demanded, and it was a bitter pill for Israel to swallow, but the world breathed a sigh of relief and looked forward eagerly to the re-opening of the Suez Canal. Mr Dulles expressed the hope that 'Egypt would not now drag her feet'.

Already suggestions had been made about the payment of the dues, and the State Department had optimistically proposed that half should be paid to Egypt and half to some international agency or the World Bank. It does not appear that any attempt was made to secure Egypt's approval for this proposal before it was published, clear indication that Dulles was far from achieving any real understanding of the Egyptian mind. Nasser was determined that the whole situation *vis-à-vis* the Canal and Sinai should revert to that which existed immediately after the nationalisation, with only this difference, that the world should recognise and accept the take-over as legal and beyond dispute, and he refused to accept any suggestion that the dues or any part of them should be paid to any other agency than the Egyptian authority. He was, however, prepared to let the United Nations force take over the Gaza Strip, for under the agreement made with the Secretary General he could require them to quit at any time, and Egyptian sovereignty was thereby unimpaired. Indeed, no sooner had the force taken possession than Nasser declared his intention of resuming its immediate administration. Mr Dulles' hopes and expectations that Nasser would follow a policy of sweet reasonableness and allow the United Nations to establish a *de facto* international régime in the area, were rapidly dissipated. It was daily becoming evident that Nasser intended to be completely intransigent and exact a full pound of flesh from the Suez disaster.

This attitude was well illustrated in the exchanges which took place over arrangements for the Suez Canal. By the end of March the Canal was largely cleared, and small and medium sized ships were able to pass, and it was anticipated that the next two weeks would see the Canal completely cleared. But no settlement of the Canal's future operation had been made, or on the payment of dues. Mr Hammerskjold accordingly went to Cairo for the purpose of securing Egypt's adhesion to the six-point resolution unanimously approved by the Security Council on 13 October 1956. But after days of private discussion he was unable to extract from Nasser a clear acceptance of the resolution. Egypt insisted on the sole and undisputed right to manage the Canal and receive all dues in full, payable moreover in advance and in currencies and to banks acceptable to her. She was, however, willing to allocate a quarter of the gross revenues to the development of the Canal and would in any case uphold the principles of the 1888 Convention, but that was as far as she would go. Nasser was not on very strong ground in taking this stand, for having insisted on the United Nations fulfilling its resolutions regarding the withdrawal of the invaders, he could hardly object to the United Nations insisting that he too complied with its resolutions.

Dulles was very perturbed about this obdurate attitude, especially as Britain, France and Israel had made it clear that they were looking to him to achieve a satisfactory settlement which would at least embody the six-point resolution, and on 24 April the United States requested a meeting of the Security Council to consider the Suez Canal question. In the debate which opened on 26 April Mr Cabot Lodge, the United States delegate, pointed to the fact that in the Egyptian plan there was no provision for the co-operation of the users of the Canal and that the plan did not come up to the requirements of the United Nations resolution, but he showed no disposition to protest in strong terms and contented himself with saying that American ships would be instructed to pay the dues to the Egyptian authority under protest, while giving the Egyptian scheme a trial. To the Anglo-French partnership this attitude appeared an abject surrender to Nasser, but there was no alternative.

Any suggestion of condemning Egypt in the Security Council would have been vetoed by Russia, and in any case after six months of shortage and hardship the nations were willing to accept almost any terms, provided they could get their ships through the Canal. Nasser had again accurately calculated that he could afford to wait. In the long run the nations must accept his terms, and so it proved. One by one the nations were forced to the conclusion that they could no longer advise their shipping interests to refrain from using the Canal. Britain and France who had been the principal users hoped to compel Egypt to come to terms by withholding their shipping from the Canal, and an interesting game of attrition thus opened, Britain and France sacrificing the economic advantages of using the short route through the Canal, and Egypt sacrificing the revenues.

Britain was the first to capitulate. She could not afford to put herself at such a disadvantage in the competition for world trade, and on 13 May 1957 the British Government announced that they could no longer advise their shipowners to refrain from using the Canal. France received this news with dismay, but declared that she would go on with the boycott, and made a further vain attempt in the Security Council to compel Egypt to implement the six-point resolution. At the end of May France too capitulated and decided to send her ships through the Canal, holding that it was futile to carry on a boycott which hurt nobody but herself, This decision gave the final victory to Egypt and vindicated Nasser's nationalisation of the Suez Canal. The entire world acknowledged, whether they liked it or not, that the Suez Canal was an Egyptian possession and that Egypt was entitled to all its revenues.

Apart from the protracted negotiations which were destined to take place on the question of compensation, the French surrender to economic necessity in May 1957 marked the end of the Suez episode, and this is an appropriate place to attempt to cast a balance sheet on the operation from the Egyptian point of view. In the first place the last vestiges of European domination and influence which had been exerted directly or indirectly since Bonaparte's invasion in 1798 were finally swept away. The Anglo-Egyptian Treaty of 1954 was of course repudiated, the great military base of Tel el Kebir and the Canal Zone was dismantled and diplomatic relations with France and Britain broken off. At the same time the Egyptian Government seized the opportunity to sequestrate and take over the major British and French commercial and financial undertakings, such as the banks and insurance companies; in fact most of their holdings, major and minor, were expropriated. The nationals of the two countries who had settled in Egypt and plied their trades and professions were forced to leave the country. In short, the British and French position in Egypt was completely liquidated. 'The Port Said invasion did the work of egyptianisation in a year that Nasser would have taken a decade or more to accomplish.'[2] For the British, who had exercised imperial power over the country for a substantial part of the past century, this was the sorry and humiliating end to a long and often amicable association. Further, Gamal Abdul Nasser and his followers were hailed as the new leaders of Arab nationalism in the Middle East.

Yet the results of the Suez operation were not all on the credit side of the account. Practically all Egypt's foreign exchange reserves were in the sterling accounts held in London which were blocked by the British Government, and Egypt was restricted to such foreign exchange as she could find from current commercial transactions. The breakdown of a substantial and long-established trade with Britain and France likewise compelled her to look for new markets which were to a great extent confined to the communist world. Nasser had always recognised the danger of tying his country too closely with countries of the communist ideology, and he did not relish the prospect of throwing off Western influences only to find himself entangled in the Eastern net. Similarly the prospects of obtaining financial aid from the West for the Aswan Dam had become more than remote. Although he now had the entire revenues of the Suez Canal at his disposal, Nasser knew that these were small compared with the country's needs. Victory at Suez was to be tempered by financial stringency throughout the country.

CHRONOLOGICAL TABLE OF EVENTS

1798	July	French invasion and occupation of Egypt under General Bonaparte.
	August	Destruction of French fleet by British squadron under Nelson at Abu Qir.
1799	July	Arrival of Turkish expeditionary force to eject the French, but defeated by Bonaparte at Abu Qir.
	August	Departure of Bonaparte from Egypt leaving General Kleber in command.
1800	January	Convention of El Arish signed, but not ratified by British Government.
	April	French victory over Turkish army at Heliopolis.
	June	Assassination of General Kleber.
1801	September	Defeat of French by combined force of Turkish and British troops, and final withdrawal of French from Egypt.
1803	March	Withdrawal of British force and commencement of internecine strife and struggle for power between the Turks, the Mameluke factions and the Albanian contingent led by Tahir Pasha and his lieutenant, Mohammed Ali.
1805	August	After various combinations the emergence of Mohammed Ali as Pasha and Viceroy of Egypt. First massacre of the Mamelukes.
1807	March	Arrival of British naval squadron off Alexandria and landing of troops at Rosetta.
	April	Defeat of British by Mohammed Ali's forces at Rosetta.
	September	Withdrawal of British from Egypt.
1811	March	Final massacre of the Mamelukes at the Citadel of Cairo.
	October	Opening of Mohammed Ali's campaign to recover possession of Mecca and Medina from the Wahabis, and conquest of Arabia, the campaign lasting until December 1819.
1814		General 'nationalisation' or expropriation of all land in Egypt by Mohammed Ali.
1821		General uprising of Christian Greeks against Turkish rule in the Morea (Peloponnese), followed by a request by the Sultan to Mohammed Ali to provide a force to subdue the rebellion.
1823	June	Assault by Egyptian force on, and subjugation of, the island of Crete.
1824	February	Landing of Egyptian army at Modon and systematic subjugation of the Morea by Ibrahim Pasha.

1825		The siege and epic defence of Missolonghi culmin-ating in the defeat of the Greek defenders.
1827	July	Treaty of London under which the European Powers sought to secure the autonomy of Greece.
	October	Unexpected clash between Turkish and Egyptian fleets and the British naval force at Navarino leading to the destruction of the Egyptian fleet.
1828	August	Mohammed Ali agrees to withdraw his forces from Greece. End of the war of Greek independence.
1831	November	Invasion of Syria by Egyptian force under Ibrahim Pasha, and outbreak of hostilities between Sultan Mahmud and Mohammed Ali.
1832	May	The storming of Acre by Ibrahim Pasha and advances into Syria with victories at Hama. Aleppo and Beilan, and penetration into the heartland of Turkey.
	December	Battle of Konia and Ibrahim's threat to the Sultan's capital at Constantinople.
1833	February	Application by Sultan Mahmud to Russia for assistance against Ibrahim Pasha. Efforts by European Powers to negotiate compromise.
	April	Temporary settlement granting to Ibrahim Pasha the *pashaliks* of Syria, Aleppo and Damascus under Convention of Kutaya.
1834		Widespread revolts in Syria against Ibrahim's harsh rule and military measures.
1839	June	New outbreak of hostilities between Sultan Mahmud and Ibrahim Pasha and defeat of Sultan's army at Nezib.
	July	Defection of Turkish fleet to Mohammed Ali at Alexandria.
		Decision by European Powers to impose a settle-ment of the 'Egyptian Question' on Mohammed Ali and the new Sultan.
1840		Serious differences between England and France on proposed settlement. Four-power convention signed. Fighting withdrawal of Ibrahim from Syria and dissolution of Egypt's sub-empire in the Levant.
1841	February	Imperial firmans promulgated conferring hereditary rights to *pashalik* of Egypt on Mohammed Ali, and effecting final settlement of the 'Egyptian Question'.
1848		Temporary assumption of power by Ibrahim Pasha until his death shortly afterwards.
1849	August	Death of Mohammed Ali and accession of Abbas, his grandson.
1854	July	Death of Abbas I, believed murdered, and accession of Mohammed Said, fourth son of Mohammed Ali.
	November	Grant of concession to construct the Suez Canal to de Lesseps, subject to ratification by the Sultan.
1859	April	Commencement of work on the Suez Canal, but without the Sultan's ratification.
1863		Death of Said Pasha and accession of Ismail, son of Ibrahim Pasha.
1864		First of the series of foreign loans contracted by Ismail Pasha, to be followed during the next nine years by further foreign loans totalling over £65 million.
	July	Revision of Suez Canal Concession and arbitration award of Napoleon III.

1866	March	Imperial firman changing order of succession in favour of Ismail Pasha's descendants by primo-geniture.
1867	June	A further firman conferring the title of Khedive on Ismail Pasha.
1869	November	Completion and opening of the Suez Canal.
1873	June	Further imperial firman consolidating and enlarging previous grants.
1874	February	Appointment of General Gordon as Governor of Equatorial Province of the Sudan.
1875		Purchase of Khedive's shareholding in the Suez Canal by the British Government.
1876	February	The Mixed Tribunals established in Egypt.
	March	The Cave Report on Egyptian finances.
	May	Establishment of the Commission of the Public Debt.
	November	The Goschen-Joubert financial arrangement.
1877		Appointment of General Gordon as Governor of the Sudan.
1878	April	Near bankruptcy of the Egyptian Government; full enquiry into both income and expenditure of the Government. First report of Commission of Enquiry.
	August	Institution of ministerial responsibility declared by Khedive. Nubar Pasha charged with formation of a ministry.
1879	February	Unrest and incipient rising of Egyptian army officers.
	March	Replacement of Nubar Pasha by Tewfik Pasha, son of the Khedive.
	April	Attempt by Khedive to impose his own financial settlement, and dismissal of the European Ministers.
	June	Deposition of Khedive Ismail by the Sultan, and his departure from Egypt. Tewfik appointed to succeed his father as Khedive.
1880	July	Promulgation of the Law of Liquidation.
1881	February and September	Unrest in and mutinies of the Egyptian Army led by Colonel Ahmed Arabi and two others. Emergence of Arabi Bey as popular leader. Growing mutual fears and distrust between the Khedive Tewfik and Arabi Bey.
1882	February	Joint Note by British and French Governments to Khedive Tewfik. Capitulation of Khedive to demands of insurgents and appointment of Sami Pasha as President of the Council of Ministers and of Arabi as Minister of War.
	June	Need for intervention in Egypt urged by France on British Government. Arrival of Turkish Commissioner in Egypt in attempt to restore order. Conference held in Constantinople to consider the situation in Egypt.
	July	Bombardment of Alexandria and fire. British Government resolution to restore order in Egypt.
	August	Landing of British military force in Egypt.
	September	Battle of Tel el Kebir and arrest of Arabi Pasha. Commencement of British military occupation of Egypt.
	December	Arabi Pasha sentenced to exile.
1883	January	Surrender of El Obeid in Kordofan province of Sudan to Mohammed Ahmed the Mahdi.

	September	Sir Evelyn Baring appointed British Consul-General in Egypt.
	November	Annihilation of Egyptian expeditionary force under General Hicks by the Mahdi's Dervishes at Kashgil.
		British Government agree to abandonment of the Sudan.
1884	January	General Gordon and Colonel Stewart leave Cairo for Khartoum.
	February	Defeat of Egyptian force under Sir Valentine Baker at El Teb. Arrival of General Gordon at Khartoum.
	March	Communications with Khartoum cut by the Dervishes and the fall of Berber. Commencement of siege of Khartoum.
	August	British Government decide to send a relief expedition to Khartoum.
	September	Lord Wolseley appointed to command expedition.
1885	January	Battle of Abu Klea. The storming of Khartoum by the Dervishes; death of General Gordon and massacre of Khartoum inhabitants. Arrival of relief expedition two days too late.
1885	March	New foreign loan of £9 million to Egypt guaranteed by the powers.
	June	Death of the Mahdi.
	October	Joint commissioners, Sir Henry Drummond Wolff and Moukhtar Pasha arrive in Egypt.
	December	Battle of Ginnis.
1887	May	Signature of Wolff Convention.
1889	August	Battle of Toski and death of Wad el Nejumi.
1892	January	Death of the Khedive Tewfik and accession of Abbas II.
1895	November	British Government declare there is no prospect of a reconquest of the Sudan.
1896	March	Urgent and secret instruction by British Government to Kitchener to advance and occupy Dongola with utmost speed.
	July	Major Marchand starts French expedition from Atlantic coast of Africa to the Sudan.
	September	Dongola occupied by Egyptian Army.
	December	British Government authorise reconquest of Sudan by Egypt.
1897	August	Abu Hamed and Berber recaptured by Egyptians.
	October	Railway completed to Abu Hamed.
1898	July	Marchand's French expedition reaches Fashoda on White Nile.
	September	Battle of Omdurman and rout of the Dervishes. Meeting of Kitchener and Marchand at Fashoda. Anglo-French dispute leading to tension.
	December	French withdraw from Fashoda.
1899	January	Signing of Sudan Condominium Agreement.
	November	Destruction of Khalifa's remaining army and death of Khalifa.
1904	April	Signature of Anglo-French Agreement (the Entente Cordiale) and French recognition of British freedom of action in Egypt.
1906	June	The Denshawi Incident.
1907	May	Lord Cromer leaves Egypt and is succeeded by Sir Eldon Gorst.

1909	February	Proposal to extend Suez Canal concession and assassination of Boutros Ghali Pasha.
1911	July	Death of Sir Eldon Gorst; Kitchener appointed his successor.
1914	August	Following outbreak of war in Europe Egypt declares in favour of Britain.
	November	Martial law declared. Declaration of war by Turkey against Britain.
	December	British protectorate declared over Egypt and Turkish sovereignty terminated. Khedive Abbas II deposed. Prince Hussein installed as Sultan of Egypt.
1915	February	Turkish attack on Suez Canal beaten off.
1917	October	Death of Sultan Hussein and accession of Prince Fuad to the Sultanate.
1918	November	End of war in Europe. Demand by Zaghlul for Egyptian independence. Similar request by Prime Minister, Rushdi Pasha. Refusal of both requests by British Government.
1919	March	Outbreak of agitation and rebellion in Egypt. Deportation of Zaghlul and others. Appointment of General Allenby as British High Commissioner.
	April	Release of Zaghlul and colleagues.
	December	Arrival of Milner Mission in Egypt.
1920	April	Discussions in London between Milner Mission and Zaghlul on proposals for a treaty.
1921	January	Report of Milner Mission and British request for an Egyptian delegation to negotiate a treaty.
	March	Visit by Adly Pasha to London and abortive treaty negotiations.
	December	Further unrest and disorders in Egypt and rearrest and deportation of Zaghlul and others.
1922	February	Unilateral declaration by Britain of independence of Egypt subject to the four 'Reserved Points'.
	March	Assumption by Fuad of title of King of Egypt and claims to sovereignty over Sudan.
1923	April	New Constitution and Electoral Law promulgated for an independent and democratic Egypt.
	July	Repeal of martial law.
	September	Creation of the Wafd Party by Zaghlul.
1924	January	First national election bringing Wafd to power with Zaghlul as Prime Minister.
	September	Further abortive Anglo-Egyptian negotiations for a treaty.
	November	Assassination of Sir Lee Stack, Governor General of the Sudan and Sirdar of the Egyptian Army in Cairo. Demand for retribution by Allenby and resignation of Zaghlul.
1925	October	Resignation of Allenby and appointment of Lord Lloyd as British High Commissioner in Egypt.
1926	May	General election in Egypt resulting in Wafd victory.
1927	August	Visit by King Fuad and Sarwat Pasha to London and unsuccessful attempts by British Government to negotiate a treaty. Death of Zaghlul Pasha and leadership of Wafd passing to Nahas Pasha.

1928	June	Dismissal of Nahas Pasha by King Fuad.
1929	July	Resignation of Lord Lloyd as High Commissioner. Further abortive negotiations for a Treaty.
	October	Commencement of 'Palace Government' by King Fuad and Sidky Pasha lasting over three years.
1933	September	Resignation of Sidky Pasha; succeeded by Yehia Pasha.
1934	November	Resignation of Yehia Pasha
1936	February	Italian empire-building in North Africa generating mutual desire for an Anglo-Egyptian treaty. Opening of negotiations.
	April	Death of King Fuad and accession of his son Faruk.
	August	Signing of Anglo-Egyptian treaty in London by Nahas Pasha and Mr Anthony Eden.
1937	May	Montreux Convention made by the Powers abolish-ing the capitulations and providing for progressive transfer of jurisdiction of the Mixed Courts to Egyptian tribunals. Egypt elected full member of League of Nations.
1938	March	Dismissal of Nahas Pasha by King Faruk.
1939	September	Outbreak of war in Europe and implementation of Treaty provisions by Egyptian Government.
1940	June	Declaration of war by Italy against the Allies. Severance of diplomatic relations by Egypt with Italy.
	September	Italian incursion into Egyptian territory at Sidi Barrani.
	November	Sudden death of Hassan Sabri Pasha in the Chamber of Deputies.
1942	January	British army driven back by German army under General Rommel in Western Desert.
	February	Ultimatum delivered by British Ambassador to King Faruk requiring him to appoint Nahas Pasha Prime Minister.
	March	New elections confirm the Wafd and Nahas Pasha in power.
	June	Split between Nahas and Makram Ebeid Pasha and formation by the latter of new splinter party.
	October	German and Italian armies driven out of Egypt by British Eighth Army.
1943	May	End of war in Africa and resurgence of anti-British feeling in Egypt.
1944	October	Dismissal of Nahas Pasha by King Faruk.
1945	February	Assassination of Ahmed Maher Pasha.
	July	Presentation by Nahas Pasha to British Ambassador of memorandum on Egyptian claims and aspirations.
	December	Request by Nokrashy Pasha to Britain for new negotiations.
1946	February	Unrest and mass demonstrations in Cairo.
	April	Opening of new negotiations with Britain in Cairo.
1946	October	Negotiations in London founder on status of the Sudan.
	December	Resignation of Ismail Sidky Pasha; new government formed by Nokrashy Pasha. Decision to take dispute with Britain to United Nations.

1947	July	Anglo-Egyptian dispute debated in Security Council.
	September	Egyptian failure to achieve favourable decision in Security Council.
1948	May	Termination of British mandate over Palestine and withdrawal of British forces. Combined assault against the Jews by Arab nations in Palestine.
	June	Palestine truce arranged.
	October	Israeli occupation of Egyptian territory at Beersheba.
	December	Assassination of Nokrashy Pasha in Cairo.
1949	February	Hassan el Banna, Supreme Guide of Moslem Brotherhood assassinated in Cairo. Mass arrests of Moslem Brotherhood.
	March	Israeli occupation of Gulf of Aqaba signalling the end of the abortive campaign to oust the Jews from Palestine.
1950	January	New elections bring the Wafd and Nahas Pasha back to power.
1951	October	Announcement by Nahas Pasha of abrogation of the 1936 Treaty and proclamation of Faruk as King of the Sudan. Formation of Liberation Army to disrupt British position in the Canal Zone.
1952	January	Unofficial state of war between Egyptian Liberation army and British forces in Canal Zone. British attack on Police Depot at Ismailia and shooting of Egyptian personnel. Mass anti-British demonstra-tions culminating in the Great Fire of Cairo.
	February	Endeavours to patch up Anglo-Egyptian differ-ences.
	April/May	Further discussions in search of new treaty. Diffi-culties over status of Sudan.
	July	Successful revolution and take-over by Society of Free Officers. General Mohamed Neguib nominally leader of revolution. Ultimatum to King Faruk requiring him to abdicate. His departure from Egypt.
	August	Riot at Kafr ed Dawar and execution of el Khamis.
	December	Repeal of 1923 Constitution and dissolution of the political parties.
1953	February	Anglo-Egyptian agreement concluded on the political future of the Sudan.
	June	Abolition of the monarchy and proclamation of a republic. Emergence of Gamal Abdul Nasser as the genuine leader of the revolution. Opening of the rift between Neguib and Nasser.
	October	Anglo-Egyptian talks on evacuation of the British Army deadlocked.
1954	January	Martyrs Day rally in Cairo followed by mass arrests of leaders and members of Moslem Brotherhood. Renewal of violence against British occupation forces in the Canal Zone.
	February	Widening of rift between Neguib and Nasser. Cavalry Corps and popular support for Neguib.
	March	Resignation of Nasser from Chairmanship of Council in favour of Neguib. Announcement by Neguib of revival of political parties and promise of new elections. National ferment at Neguib's apparent betrayal of the revolution, followed by his overthrow.
	July	Heads of agreement on evacuation of British army signed in Cairo.
	October	Formal agreement on evacuation signed by Nutting for Britain and Nasser for Egypt. Assassination attempt against Nasser at Alexandria. Mass arrests of Moslem Brotherhood.
	December	Execution of leaders, and final annihilation, of Moslem Brotherhood.
1955	February	Egyptian opposition to creation of the Baghdad Pact. Israeli attack on Egypt at Gaza.
	May	Offer by Soviet Russia to supply arms to Egypt.

	September	Announcement by Nasser of agreement to buy arms from Soviet bloc.
	December	Britain and United States promise an initial loan of $70 million to Egypt for Aswan High Dam.
1956	March	Visit to Egypt by British Foreign Secretary Selwyn Lloyd to explain British policy. Dismissal of Glubb Pasha by King Hussein of Jordan. Deterioration of relations between Egypt and Britain.
	June	Withdrawal of last British troops from Egypt and ending of the British occupation. Nasser acclaimed as President of the Republic.
	July	United States renegue on their promise to participate in financing the High Dam at Aswan, closely followed by a similar declaration by the British Government. Announcement by Nasser that Egypt has nationalised the Suez Canal.
	August	London Conference to consider establishment of control agency for Suez Canal. Britain and France dissatisfied with outcome.
	September	Abortive delegation led by Mr Menzies to Cairo to negotiate with President Nasser. Announcement by Mr Eden that a Suez Canal Users Association would be formed to exercise rights of Canal users. Further London Conference called to set up the Association.
	October	Reference of the dispute by Britain and France to United Nations Security Council. The six-point resolution. Decision by Britain and France to inter-vene militarily in Egypt. Sudden Israeli attack and penetration into Sinai followed by Anglo-French ultimatum to Israel and Egypt to withdraw from Canal area. Attack on Egyptian airfields by British bombers.
	November	British and French airborne landings at Port Said. Blockage of Suez Canal by Egypt. Ceasefire ordered on 7 November.
	December	Britain and France forced to withdraw troops from Egypt.
1957	January	United States propound the Eisenhower Doctrine.
	February	Refusal by Nasser to reopen Suez Canal until last Israeli forces have withdrawn.
	March	International pressure on Israel to withdraw from Egypt.
	May	All nations compelled to recognise Egyptian sole rights to Suez Canal. End of Suez episode. Egypt triumphant.

APPENDIX

Text of the Condominium Agreement of 19 January 1899 relating to the Sudan.

Whereas certain provinces in the Soudan which were in rebellion against the authority of His Highness the Khedive have now been reconquered by the joint military and financial efforts of Her Britannic Majesty's Government and the Government of His Highness the Khedive,

and whereas it has become necessary to decide upon a system for the administration of, and for the making of laws for, the said reconquered provinces, under which due allowance may be made for the backward and unsettled condition of large portions thereof and the varying requirements of different localities,

and whereas it is desired to give effect to the claims which have accrued to Her Britannic Majesty's Government by right of conquest to share in the present settlement and future working and development of the said system of administration and legislation.

and whereas it is conceived that for many purposes Wadi Halfa and Suakin may be most effectively administered in conjunction with the reconquered provinces to which they are respectively adjacent.

NOW IT IS HEREBY AGREED AND DECLARED by and between the undersigned duly authorised for that purpose, as follows:

Article 1. The word 'Soudan' in this Agreement means all the territories south of the 22nd parallel of latitude which:

1. have never been evacuated by Egyptian troops since the year 1882, or
2. which, having before the late rebellion in the Soudan been administered by the Government of His Highness the Khedive, were temporarily lost to Egypt, and have been reconquered by Her Britannic Majesty's Government and the Egyptian Government acting in concert, or
3. may hereafter be reconquered by the two Governments acting in concert.

Article 2. The British and Egyptian flags shall be used together both on land and water throughout the Soudan, except in the town of Suakin in which locality the Egyptian flag alone shall be used.

Article 3. The supreme civil and military command in the Soudan shall be vested in one officer, termed the 'Governor-General of the Soudan.' He shall be appointed by Khedivial Decree on the recommendation of Her Britannic Majesty's Government and shall be removed only by Khedivial Decree with the consent of Her Britannic Majesty's Government.

Article 4. Laws, as also orders and regulations with the full force of law, for the good government of the Soudan, and for regulating the holding, disposal and devolution of property of every kind therein situate, may from time to time be made, altered or abrogated by proclamation of the Governor-General. Such laws, orders and regulations may apply to the whole or any named part of the Soudan and may, either explicitly or by necessary implication, alter or abrogate any existing law or regulation. All such proclamations shall forthwith be notified to Her Britannic Majesty's Agent and Consul-General in Cairo, and to the President of the Council of Ministers and His Highness the Khedive.

Article 5. No Egyptian law, decree, Ministerial arrêté or other enactment hereafter to be made or promulgated shall apply to the Soudan or any part thereof, save in so far as the same shall be applied by Proclamation of the Governor-General in manner hereinbefore provided.

Article 6. In the definition by Proclamation of the conditions under which Europeans of whatever nationality shall be at liberty to trade with or reside in the Soudan, or to hold property within its limits, no special privileges shall be accorded to the subjects of any one or more Powers.

Article 7. Import duties on entering the Soudan shall not be payable on goods coming from Egyptian territory.

500

Such duties may however be levied on goods coming from elsewhere than Egyptian territory, but in the case of goods entering the Soudan at Suakin, or any other port on the Red Sea littoral, they shall not exceed the corresponding duties for the time being leviable on goods entering Egypt from abroad. Duties may be levied on goods leaving the Soudan at such rates as may from time to time be prescribed by Proclamation.

Article 8. The jurisdiction of the Mixed Tribunals shall not extend nor be recognised for any purpose whatever in any part of the Soudan except in the town of Suakin.

Article 9. Until and save so far as it shall be otherwise determined by Proclamation the Soudan, with the exception of the town of Suakin, shall be and remain under martial law.

Article 10. No Consuls, Vice-Consuls or Consular Agents shall be accredited in respect of nor allowed to reside in the Soudan without the previous consent of Her Britannic Majesty's Government.

Article 11. The importation of slaves into the Soudan, as also their exportation, is absolutely prohibited. Provision shall be made by Proclamation for the enforcement of this Regulation.

Article 12. It is agreed between the two Governments that special attention shall be paid to the enforcement of the Brussels Act of the 2nd July 1890 in respect of the import, sale and manufacture of firearms and their munitions, and distilled or spirituous liquors.

Done in Cairo this 19th day of January 1899.

Cromer

Boutros Ghali

NOTES

Chapter 1

1. Cameron, *Egypt in the nineteenth century*, pp.10-11
2. Fisher, *Napoleon*, p.44
3. Paton, *History of the Egyptian Revolution*, pp.109-11
4. This name has been variously transliterated as: Mehmet Ali, Mahomet Aly, Muhammed Ali, etc.
5. de Freycinet, *La Question de l'Egypte*, p.13 and Mengin, *Histoire de l'Egypte sous le gouvernement de Mohammed Ali...*Vol.I, p.4
6. Acknowledgements are made for much of the detail of this chapter to P.G. Elgood's *Bonaparte's Adventure in Egypt.*

Chapter 2

1. Murray, *A Short Memoir of Mohammed Aly*
2. ibid.
3. ibid.
4. One purse = 500 Turkish piastres
5. Mengin, Vol.I, p.364

Chapter 3

1. Dodwell, *Founder of Modern Egypt*, p.47
2. ibid.

Chapter 4

1. St. John, *Egypt and Mohammed Ali*, Vol.II, p.456
2. ibid., p.461
3. ibid., p.431
4. ibid., p.436
5. ibid., p.412
6. ibid., p.421
7. Dodwell, p.195
8. St. John, Vol.II, p.399
9. ibid., p.401
10. Dodwell, p.212
11. St. John, Vol.II, p.175
12. Dodwell, p.227
13. ibid., p.65
14. St. John, Vol II, p.45
15. Dodwell, p.225
16. ibid., p.204
17. Mengin, Vol.II, p.257

Chapter 5

1. Phillips, *War of Greek Independence*, p.183
2. ibid., p.199

3.   Dodwell, p.89
4.   ibid.
5.   Phillips, p.249
6.   Dodwell, p.91

Chapter 6
1.   St. John, Vol.II, p.486
2.   Dodwell, p.110
3.   St. John, Vol.II, p.490
4.   Dodwell, p.110
5.   ibid.
6.   Cameron, p.154
7.   Barker, Vol.II, p.188
8.   de Freycinet, p.24
9.   Cameron, p.160
10.   St. John, Vol.II, p.514
11.   *Cambridge Modern History*, Vol.X, p.554

Chapter 7
1.   Barker, Vol.II, p.204
2.   ibid., p.205
3.   *Cambridge Modern History*, Vol.X, p.559
4.   de Freycinet, p.24
5.   *Cambridge Modern History*, Vol.X, p.560
6.   Barker, Vol.II, p.237
7.   *Cambridge Modern History*, Vol.X, p.564
8.   de Freycinet, p.42
9.   ibid., p.43
10.   ibid., p.54
11.   Dodwell, p.187
12.   de Freycinet, p.84
13.   Barker, Vol.II, p.257

Chapter 8
1.   Dicey, *Story of the Khedivate*, p.19
2.   De Leon, *The Khedive's Egypt*, p.85
3.   Senior, *Conversations and Journals in Egypt and Malta*, Vol.I, p.203
4.   De Leon, p.81
5.   ibid.
6.   Senior, Vol.II, p.211
7.   De Leon, p.235
8.   Senior, Vol.I, p.31
9.   De Leon, pp.91-2
10.   ibid., p.126
11.   Russell, *Egyptian Service 1902-1944*, p.36
12.   Senior, Vol.I, p.207
13.   ibid., Vol.II, pp.55-6
14.   Cromer, *Modern Egypt*, p.614
15.   Senior, Vol.II, p.85
16.   De Leon, p.102

Chapter 9
1.   Cameron, pp.237-8
2.   ibid., p.230
3.   Dicey, p.30
4.   Morley, *Life of Gladstone*, Vol.I, p.591

5. Wilson, *The Suez Canal, its past, present and future*, p.22
6. De Leon, p.417

Chapter 10
1. De Leon, p.157
2. McCoan, *Egypt as it is*, p.89
3. ibid., p.87
4. de Freycinet, p.139
5. Crabitès, *Ismail the Maligned*, p.156
6. Dicey, p.58
7. ibid., p.63
8. ibid., p.60
9. ibid., p.61
10. *Effendina*: literally 'our Master', the name commonly used by Egyptians when referring to the Viceroy.
11. De Leon, p.197
12. ibid., p.177
13. Crabitès, *Ismail the Maligned*
14. Cromer, p.708
15. de Freycinet, p.148
16. Dicey, p.75
17. M. G. Mulhall, 'Egyptian Finance', *The Contemporary Review*, October 1882, quoted from Crabitès, *Ismail the Maligned*, p.132
18. ibid.
19 Archives, American Legation, Cairo, Vol.xv, p.2241, quoted from Crabitès, *Ismail the Maligned*, p.295

Chapter 11
1. Dicey, p.86
2. ibid., p.89
3. Cromer, pp.40-1
4. ibid.
5. ibid., p.23
6. Dicey, p.103
7. Crabitès, *Spoliation of Suez*, p.181
8. ibid., quoted from *Annuaire Statistique*, p.434
9. Rothstein, *Egypt's Ruin*, p.9
10. Crabitès, *Ismail the Maligned*, p.22
11. Dicey, p.135
12. ibid.
13. Limitations of space have precluded more than a brief survey of the Egyptian financial question, but an excellent account of the fiscal arrangements, revenues, expenditures and debts may be found in McCoan's *Egypt as it is* (see Bibliography).

Chapter 12
1. Rothstein, p.28
2. McCoan, p.145
3. Cromer, p.21
4. Egypt No.2 (1879), p.28
5. Cromer, p.28
6. ibid., p.30
7. ibid., p.34
8. ibid., p.41
9. ibid., p.42
10. Cromer, p.48
11. ibid., p.55

12.	ibid., p.52
13.	ibid.
14.	ibid.
15.	ibid., p.58
16.	ibid., p.59
17.	Rothstein, p.81
18.	Dicey, p.209
19.	Cromer, p.106
20.	Dicey, p.220
21.	Cromer, p.110

Chapter 13

1.	Dicey, p.229
2.	de Freycinet, p.179
3.	Cromer, p.122
4.	Rothstein, p.109
5.	Cromer, pp.132-5
6.	ibid., p.132
7.	Stuart, *Egypt after the War*
8.	*The Times*, 16 April 1879 quoted in Rothstein, p.83
9.	This name is properly transliterated Orabi or Ourabi, but as it is now better known as Arabi, this spelling has been followed here.
10.	Blunt, *Secret History*, p.133
11.	Cromer, p.139
12.	A slightly different version of the events leading up to the mutiny is given in Bell's *Khedives and Pashas*, pp.69-76
13.	Blunt, p.131
14.	Cromer, pp.137-151
15.	Dicey, p.261
16.	Blunt, p.169
17.	Malet, *Egypt 1879-1882*, p.201
18.	ibid., p.209
19.	ibid., p.210
20.	Quoted from Cromer, p.177
21.	Malet, p.233
22.	ibid., p.256

Chapter 14

1.	Blunt, p.210
2.	Malet, p.275
3.	Cromer, p.201
4.	ibid., p.192
5.	ibid., p.202
6.	Malet, p.292
7.	ibid., p.311
8.	ibid., p.312
9.	de Freycinet, pp.257-9
10.	Malet, pp.358-9
11.	ibid., p.368
12.	ibid., p.370
13.	Cromer, p.224
14.	de Freycinet, p.268
15.	Cromer, p.229
16.	ibid.
17.	de Freycinet, p.281
18.	Cromer, p.233

19. de Freycinet, p.287
20. Blunt, p.398
21. de Freycinet, p.307
22. ibid., p.305
23. Cromer, p.239
24. A fascinating account of the Anglo-Turkish negotiations for a military convention in August 1882 may be found in Cromer, pp.240–9.
25. Blunt, p.227, also gives some indication of this.
26. Blunt, p.420
27. ibid., p.423
28. Malet, p.471
29. Kinglake, *Eothen*

Chapter 15
1. Cromer, p.264
2. Baker, *Ismailia*, Vol.I, p.6
3. Allen, *Gordon and the Soudan*
4. Cromer, p.273
5. Allen
6. Cromer, p.274
7. After Tel el Kebir, a number of British officers were imported to reorganise the Egyptian army.
8. Brother of Sir Samuel Baker
9. Cromer, p.311
10. ibid., p.283
11. ibid., p.293
12. ibid., p.294
13. ibid., p.296

Chapter 16
1. Cromer, p.399, but variations of this telegram quoted on p.328
2. ibid., p.330
3. ibid., p.345
4. ibid., p.355
5. Allen, p.249
6. ibid., p.270
7. Cromer, p.321
8. ibid., p.418
9. ibid., p.378
10. ibid., p.379
11. ibid., p.380
12. ibid., p.430
13. ibid., p.431
14. ibid., p.432
15. ibid., p.449
16. Allen, p.304
17. Cromer, p.454
18. Allen, p.379
19. Cromer, p.464
20. Theobald, p.177
21 ibid., p.118
22. ibid., p.120
23. Allen, op.cit.

Chapter 17
1. de Freycinet, p.316
2. ibid., p.359

3. Milner, pp.26-7
4. ibid., p.33
5. ibid., p.185
6. ibid., p.186
7. de Freycinet, p.339 and in similar vein on p.436
8. Cromer, p.751
9. ibid., p.753
10. Cromer, p.756
11. Milner, p.143
12. ibid., p.254
13. Cromer, p.671
14. ibid., p.679
15. Colvin, p.190
16. Milner, p.136
17. Colvin, p.249
18. Dicey, p.464
19. ibid., p.465
20. Cromer, pp. 713-14

Chapter 18
1. Cromer, p.297
2. ibid., p.523
3. ibid.
4. de Freycinet, p.404
5. The Loan was subsequently made an outright gift to Egypt.
6. de Freycinet, p.388
7. Theobald, p.208
8. ibid., p.216
9. Cromer, p.534
10. Theobald, p.221
11. Steevens, *With Kitchener to Khartoum*, quoted in Cromer, p.540
12. Cromer, p.542
13. ibid., p.548
14. ibid., pp.547-8
15. ibid., p.550

Chapter 19
1. Chirol, *The Egyptian Problem*
2. Lloyd, *Egypt after Cromer*, Vol.I, p.69
3. ibid., p.46
4. Chirol, p.93
5. Lloyd, Vol.I, p.96
6. ibid., p.141
7. ibid.

Chapter 20
1. Elgood, p.57
2. ibid., p.85
3. Lloyd, Vol.I, p.197
4. ibid., p.259

Chapter 21
1. Lloyd, Vol.II, p.287
2. A detailed account of the rebellion may be found in Sur V. Chirol's *The Egyptian Problem*, pp.177-89
3. Wavell, *Allenby in Egypt*, p.44
4. ibid.

5.   Lloyd, Vol.I, p.310
6.   ibid., Vol.II, p.15
7.   ibid.
8.   ibid., p.25
9.   Marshall, *The Egyptian Enigma*, p.252
10.   Lloyd, Vol.II, p.53
11.   Wavell, p.70
12.   Lloyd, Vol.II, p.73
13.   Abbreviated from the version given in *Great Britain and Egypt, 1914-1951*, p.188
14.   ibid.
15.   Lloyd, Vol.II. p.84
16.   Amine Youssef, *Independent Egypt*, p.119
17.   Lloyd, Vol.II, p.92
18.   Wavell, p.114
19.   Amine Youssef, p.129
20.   Elgood, *Transit of Egypt*. p.299
21.   Lloyd, Vol.II, p.143
22.   ibid., p.142
23.   ibid., p.220

Chapter 22
1.   Egypt No.1 (1928), p.5
2.   Lloyd, Vol.II, p.228
3.   Egypt No.1 (1928), p.5
4.   Lloyd, Vol.II, p.227
5.   *Great Britain and Egypt*, p.17
6.   Lloyd, Vol.II, p.258
7.   ibid., p.272
8.   Survey of International Affairs, 1930, p.134
9.   Egypt No 1 (1930) Cmd.3575, p.21
10.   Survey of International Affairs, 1930, p.215
11.   ibid., p.216
12.   ibid., p.220
13.   Survey of International Affairs, 1936, p.672
14.   *The Times*, 10 June 1936

Chapter 23
1.   *Great Britain and Egypt*, p.48
2.   ibid., p.49
3.   ibid., p.70
4.   Lugol, *L'Egypte et la 2ᵐᵉ guerre mondiale*, footnote to p.345
5.   *Great Britain and Egypt*, p.72
6.   Lugol, op. cit.
7.   Colombe, p.227

Chapter 24
1.   *Great Britain and Egypt*, p.82
2.   ibid., p.87
3.   ibid., p.94
4.   Egypt No 2 (1947), p.7
5.   *Great Britain and Egypt p.96*
6.   ibid., p.101
7.   ibid.

Chapter 25
1.   Little, p.178

2.   *Great Britain and Egypt*, p.118
3.   ibid.
4.   Lacouture, p.240
5.   Little, p.181
6.   Lacouture, p.107
7.   ibid., pp.111-12
8.   ibid., p.116
9.   ibid., p.122
10.   *The Times*, 31 March 1952
11.   *The Times*, 8 April 1952
12.   Sadat, p.14
13.   Lacouture, p.148
14.   ibid., p.156

Chapter 26
1.   Lacouture, p.162
2.   *The Times*, 31 October 1952
3.   Little, p.204
4.   Lacouture, p.174
5.   *The Times*, 26 March 1954
6.   ibid., 29 March 1954

Chapter 27
1.   *The Times*, 13 April 1953

Chapter 28
1.   *The Times*, 29 December 1954
2.   ibid., 23 February 1955
3.   ibid., 28 September 1955

Chapter 29
1.   *The Times*, 12 September 1956
2.   Little

BIBLIOGRAPHY

Allen, Bernard, *Gordon and the Soudan* (Macmillan, 1931)
Amine, Youssef, *Independent Egypt* (Murray, 1940)
Baker, Sir Samuel, *Ismailia* (Macmillan, 1874)
Baring, Sir Evelyn, Earl of Cromer, *Modern Egypt* (Macmillan, 1911)
Bell, C.F.M., *Khedives and Pashas* (Sampson Low & Co., 1894)
Blunt, Wilfrid S., *Secret History of the English Occupation of Egypt* (Martin Secker, 1906)
Cambridge Modern History, Vol.X
Cameron, L.D.A., *Egypt in the nineteenth century* (Smith Elder & Co., 1898)
Chirol, Sir Valentine, *The Egyptian Problem* (Macmillan, 1920)
Colombe, Marcel, *L'Evolution de l'Egypte de 1924 à 1950* (Paris, 1951)
Colvin, Sir Auckland. *The Making of Modern Egypt* (Seeley, 1906)
Crabitès, *Ismail the Maligned* (Routledge, 1933)
Crabitès, *The Spoliation of Suez* (Routledge, 1940)
De Leon, *The Khedive's Egypt* (Sampson Low, 1877)
Dicey, *Story of the Khedivate* (Rivington, 1902)
Dicey, *England and Egypt* (Chapman & Hall, 1881)
Dodwell, *The Founder of Modern Egypt* (Cambridge University Press, 1931)
Egypt No.1 (1928) Cmd. 3050 (UK Foreign Office)
Egypt No 1 (1930) Cmd.3575 (UK Foreign Office)
Egypt No. 2 (1879) (UK Foreign Office)
Egypt No.2 (1947) Cmd. 7179 (UK Foreign Office)
Elgood, *Bonaparte's Adventure in Egypt* (Oxford University Press, 1936)
Fisher, H.A.L. *Napoleon* (Williams & Norgate, London, 1924)
de Freycinet, C.L., *La Question de l'Egypte* (C. Levy, Paris, 1905)
Elgood, *Egypt and the Army*, Oxford University Press, 1927
Great Britain and Egypt, 1914-1951 (Royal Institute of International Affairs)
Issawi, Charles, *Egypt, an economic and social analysis* (Oxford University Press, 1947)
Kimche, Jon, *Seven fallen pillars; the Middle East 1945-1952* (Secker & Warburg, 1953)
Kirk, George E., *A Short history of the Middle East from the rise of Islam to modern times* (Methuen, 1948)
Lacouture, Jean and Simonne, *Egypt in Transition* (Methuen, 1958)
Lloyd, Sir George, Baron of Dolobran, *Egypt since Cromer* (Macmillan, 1943) 2 vols
Low, Sidney, *Egypt in Transition* (Smith, Elder, 1914)
Lugol, Jean, *L'Egypte et la deuxième guerre mondiale* (Imprimerie E. & R. Schindler, Cairo, 1945)
McCoan, James C., *Egypt as it is* (Cassell, Petter & Galpin, New York, 1877)
Malet, Sir Edward, *Egypt 1879-1882* (Murray, 1909)
Marshall, J.E., *The Egyptian Enigma, 1879-1882* (Murray, 1909)
Mekki Abbas, *The Sudan Question* (Faber & Faber, 1952)
Mengin, Felix, *Histoire de l'Egypte sous la gouvernement de Mohammed Ali, ou Récit des évenements politiques et militaires qui ont lieu dès le départ des Français jusqu'en 1823* (Arthur Bertrand Librarie, Paris, 1823)
Milner, Alfred, Viscount, *England in Egypt* (Arnold, 1892)
Monroe, Elizabeth, *The Mediterranean in Politics* (Oxford University Press, 1938)

Bibliography

Murray, Sir Charles, *A short memoir of Mohammed Ali, founder of the Vice-royalty of Egypt* (Bernard•
  Quaritch, 1898)
Napier, Sir Charles, *The War in Syria* (John W. Parker, 1842) 2 vols
Paton, Andrew A. *History of the Egyptian Revolution* (Trubner, 1876) 2 vols
Phillips. W. Allison, *The War of Greek Independence* (Smith, Elder & Co., 1897)
Rifaat Bey, M., *The Awakening of Modern Egypt* (Longmans Green, 1947)
Rothstein, Theodore, *Egypt's ruin: a financial and administrative record* (Firfield, 1910)
Russell, *Egyptian Service 1902-1944* (Murray, 1949)
St. John, J.A., *Egypt and Mohammed Ali* (Longmans Rees, 1934)
Scott, C. Rochfort, *Rambles in Egypt and Candia* (Henry Colburn, 1837)
Senior, Nassau, *Conversations and journals in Egypt and Malta* (Sampson Low, 1882)
Siegfried, Andre, *Suez and Panama* (Cape, 1940)
Sladen, Douglas, *Egypt and the English* (Hurst and Lackett, 1908)
Stuart, Villiers, *Egypt after the War* (Murray, 1883)
Theobald, A.B., *The Mahdiya* (Longmans Green, 1951)
The Times, The War in Egypt, illust. by Richard Simkin (Routledge, 1883)
Toynbee, Arnold J., *Survey of International Affairs 1930* (Oxford University Press 1931)
Toynbee, Arnold J., *Survey of International Affairs 1936* (Oxford University Press 1937)
Wavell, Sir Archibald P., Viscount, *Allenby in Egypt* (Harrap, 1943)
Wilson, Sir Arnold, *The Suez Canal, its past, present and future* (Oxford University Press, 1933)
Young, George, *Egypt* (Ernest Benn, 1927)

The Author gratefully acknowledges the assistance of the Bodleian Library, Oxford in the compilation of this
Bibliography.